AF838693

ADVANCES IN DATA MINING KNOWLEDGE DISCOVERY AND APPLICATIONS

Edited by **Adem Karahoca**

Advances in Data Mining Knowledge Discovery and Applications
http://dx.doi.org/10.5772/3349
Edited by Adem Karahoca

Contributors
Dost Muhammad Khan, Nawaz Mohamudally, D. K. R. Babajee, Tomas Borovicka, Marcel Jirina Jr., Pavel Kordik, Marcel Jirina, Carmelo Cassisi, Placido Montalto, Marco Aliotta, Andrea Cannata, Alfredo Pulvirenti, Fadzilah Siraj, Ehab A. Omer A. Omer, Md. Rajib Hasan, Mohammad Lutfi Othman, Ishak Aris, Xingping Wen, Xiaofeng Yang, Maria Madalena Dias, Juliana Keiko Yamaguchi, Emerson Rabelo, Clélia Franco, Kohsuke Yanai, Toshihiko Yanase, Lilian Freitas, Yomara Pires, Jefferson Morais, João Costa, Aldebaro Klautau, José C. Reston Filho, Carolina de M. Affonso, Roberto Célio L. de Oliveira, Intan Azmira binti Wan Abdul Razak, Shah bin Majid, Mohd Shahrieel bin Mohd. Aras, Arfah binti Ahmad, Ghulam Mujtaba Shaikh, Tariq Mahmood, R.L.K.Venkateswarlu, R. Raviteja, R. Rajeev, Gao Jie, Dewan Md. Farid, Mohammad Zahidur Rahman, Chowdhury Mofizur Rahman, Erdem Alparslan, Adem Karahoca, Dilek Karahoca, Adela Bâra, Ion Lungu

Published by InTech
Janeza Trdine 9, 51000 Rijeka, Croatia

Copyright © 2012 InTech
All chapters are Open Access distributed under the Creative Commons Attribution 3.0 license, which allows users to download, copy and build upon published articles even for commercial purposes, as long as the author and publisher are properly credited, which ensures maximum dissemination and a wider impact of our publications. After this work has been published by InTech, authors have the right to republish it, in whole or part, in any publication of which they are the author, and to make other personal use of the work. Any republication, referencing or personal use of the work must explicitly identify the original source.

Notice
Statements and opinions expressed in the chapters are these of the individual contributors and not necessarily those of the editors or publisher. No responsibility is accepted for the accuracy of information contained in the published chapters. The publisher assumes no responsibility for any damage or injury to persons or property arising out of the use of any materials, instructions, methods or ideas contained in the book.

Publishing Process Manager Mirna Cvijic
Typesetting InTech Prepress, Novi Sad
Cover InTech Design Team

First published September, 2012
Printed in Croatia

A free online edition of this book is available at www.intechopen.com
Additional hard copies can be obtained from orders@intechopen.com

Advances in Data Mining Knowledge Discovery and Applications,
Edited by Adem Karahoca
p. cm.
ISBN 978-953-51-0748-4

We are IntechOpen, the world's leading publisher of Open Access books

Built by scientists, for scientists

4,200+
Open access books available

116,000+
International authors and editors

125M+
Downloads

151
Countries delivered to

Our authors are among the
Top 1%
most cited scientists

12.2%
Contributors from top 500 universities

WEB OF SCIENCE™

Selection of our books indexed in the Book Citation Index
in Web of Science™ Core Collection (BKCI)

Interested in publishing with us?
Contact book.department@intechopen.com

Numbers displayed above are based on latest data collected.
For more information visit www.intechopen.com

For EU product safety concerns:
IN TECH d.o.o., Prolaz Marije Krucifikse Kozulić 3, 51000 Rijeka, Croatia,
info@intechopen.com or visit our website at intechopen.com.

Meet the editor

Dr. Adem Karahoca received his B.Sc. degree in Mathematical Engineering from Istanbul Technical University, M.Sc. and Ph.D. degrees in Software Engineering from Istanbul University. His research interests and expertise include mobile telecommunication software, data mining, management information systems, bioinformatics, information systems, business intelligence, computers in education, and human computer interaction. He has written 26 IT related books and book chapters. He has supervised different variety of IT research and application projects. He is currently working on data mining applications in medicine.

Contents

Preface

Advances in Knowledge Discovery and Data Mining aims to help data miners, researchers, scholars, and PhD students who wish to apply data mining techniques. The primary contribution of this book is highlighting frontier fields and implementations of the knowledge discovery and data mining. It seems to be same things are repeated again. But in general, same approach and techniques may help us in different fields and expertise areas. This book presents knowledge discovery and data mining applications in two different sections. As known that, data mining covers areas of statistics, machine learning, data management and databases, pattern recognition, artificial intelligence, and other areas. In this book, most of the areas are covered with different data mining applications. The eighteen chapters have been classified in two parts: Knowledge Discovery and Data Mining Applications.

First part of the book consists of the first and second phases of the knowledge discovery. Second part focuses on the data mining applications from energy, electricity, speech recognition and network security.

Section 1. Knowledge Discovery

Chapter 1 presents the mathematical formulation of unified theory of data mining and multi agent system architecture. The data mining processes clustering, classification and visualization are unified by means of mathematical functions and multi agent system is developed (Khan, et al.).

Chapter 2 focuses on an overview of existing methods that deal with methods of data selection and sampling (Borovicka, et al.).

Chapter 3 provides an overview of main dimensionality reduction algorithms, together with a detailed description of the most used similarity measures in time series data mining (Cassisi, et al.).

Chapter 4 explorers the effect of different data representations on the performance of neural network and regression was investigated on different datasets that have binary or Boolean class target (Siraj, et al.).

Chapter 5 proposes employing rough set theory to obtain the knowledge about the distance protective relay under supervised learning (Othman and Aris).

Chapter 6 presents an unsupervised classification for hyperspectral remote sensing image. It can effectively extract the low reflectance object such as vegetation in shadowed region or water from hyperspectral image using spectral data mining (Wen, et al.).

Chapter 7 demonstrates that there are some parameters to be considered in the choice of visualization techniques, which are: data type, task type, data scalability, data dimension and position of the attributes in the display. Also presents the application of geometrical and iconographic techniques over results of clustering algorithm with the objective of illustrate the contribution of the guidelines (Madalena, et al.).

Chapter 8 proposes two computing frameworks for large-scale data mining via tree structured data analysis framework and parallel machine learning framework (Yanai and Yanase).

Section 2. Data Mining Applications

Chapter 9 discusses the task of modulation classification in cognitive radio. The modulation classification becomes fundamental, since this information allows the RC to adapt its transmission parameters for the spectrum to be shared efficiently, without causing interference to other users (Freitas, et al.).

Chapter 10 proposes a methodology combining ARIMA and Artificial Neural Network (ANN) for short-term energy price prediction multi-step-ahead in the Brazilian market (Filho, et al.).

Chapter 11 offers data mining application for short term electricity load forecasting to organize supply and demand fluctuations (Razak, et al.).

Chapter 12 proposes a set of five adaptive ATM interfaces, which are adapted to the behavior of an ATM customer population (Shaikh and Mahmood).

Chapter 13 benchmarks the different data mining techniques to obtain best speech recognition (Venkateswarlu, et al.).

Chapter 14 suggests remote sensing data. Elevation as a variable is considered in spatial distribution of snow, vegetation will be used as an indicator. Also chapter investigates (1) quantification of SCA (Snow-Cover Area per unit area of elevation band) – Elevation relations and NDVI-Elevation relations; (2) comparisons among Snow-Elevation-Vegetation relations, to obtain a better understanding of snow-covered area vary with elevation, and the relation to vegetation by using a quantitative method to detect the Snow-NDVI-Elevation relation (Jie).

Chapter 15 compares the perfomances of recently developed data mining algorithms for adaptive intrusion detection, which scale up the detection rates (DR) for different types of network intrusions and reduce the false positives (FP) at acceptable level in intrusion detection (Farid, et al.).

Chapter 16 reviews botnet detection, attack types caused by botnets and well-known botnet classifications and diverse types of detection techniques (Alparslan, et al.).

Chapter 17 proposes applying data mining for forecasting the wind power plants' energy production (Bâra and Lungu).

I would like to thank all the authors for their contributions, and the InTech Publishing team for their helpful assistance, and last but not least, the people who help disseminate this book. I hope that this book will inspire readers to pursue education and research in emerging field of data mining.

Assoc.Prof.Dr. Adem Karahoca
Bahcesehir University, Engineering Faculty,
Head of Software Engineering Department, Istanbul,
Turkey

Section 1

Knowledge Discovery

Chapter 1

Towards the Formulation of a Unified Data Mining Theory, Implemented by Means of Multiagent Systems (MASs)

Dost Muhammad Khan, Nawaz Mohamudally and D. K. R. Babajee

Additional information is available at the end of the chapter

http://dx.doi.org/10.5772/47984

1. Introduction

Data mining techniques and algorithms encompass a variety of datasets like medical, geographical, web logs, agricultural data and many more. For each category of data or information, one has to apply the best suited algorithm to obtain the optimal results with highest accuracy. This is still a problem for many data mining tools as no unified theory has been adopted. The scientific community is very much conscious about this problematical issue and faced multiple challenges in establishing consensus over a unified data mining theory. The researchers have attempted to model the best fit algorithm for specific domain areas, for instance, formal analysis into the fascinating question of how overfitting can happen and estimating how well an algorithm will perform on future data that is solely based on its training set error (Moore Andrew W., 2001, Grossman. Robert, Kasif. Simon, et al, 1998, Yang. Qlang, et al, 2006 & Wu. Xindong, et al 2008).

Another problem in trying to lay down some kind of formalism behind a unified theory is that the current data mining algorithms and techniques are designed to solve individual consecutive tasks, such as classification or clustering. Most of the existing data mining tools are efficient only to specific problems, thus the tool is limited to a particular set of data for a specific application. These tools depend again on the correct choice of algorithms to apply and how to analyze the output, because most of them are generic and there is no context specific logic that is attached to the application. A theoretical framework that unifies different data mining tasks including clustering, classification, interpretation and association rules will allow developer and researchers in their quest for the most efficient and effective tool commonly called a unified data mining engine (UDME), (Singh. Shivanshu K., Eranti. Vijay Kumer. & Fayad. M.E., 2010, Das. Somenath 2007 & Khan. Dost Muhammad, Mohamudally. Nawaz, 2010).

INTECH
open science | open minds

© 2012 Khan et al., licensee InTech. This is an open access chapter distributed under the terms of the Creative Commons Attribution License (http://creativecommons.org/licenses/by/3.0), which permits unrestricted use, distribution, and reproduction in any medium, provided the original work is properly cited.

A Multi Agent System (MAS) approach has proven to be useful in designing of a system where the domains require the MAS, even in those systems which are not distributed. The multiagent system speeds up the performance and operation of the system by providing a method for parallel computation i.e. a domain that is easily broken into components, several independent tasks that can be handled by separate agents, could benefit from the MAS. Furthermore, a MAS approach provides the scalability, since they are inherently modular; it is easy to add new agents in a multiagent system and robustness is another benefit of multiagent system (Peter Stone & Manuela Veloso, 1997 & Khan. Dost Muhammad, Mohamudally. Nawaz, 2010).

A first tentative to integrate different data mining algorithms using a MAS was implemented in the application of a Unified Medical Data Miner (UMDM) for prediction, classification, interpretation and visualization on medical datasets: the diabetes dataset case and the integration of K-means clustering and decision tree data mining algorithms. The study is conducted on the development and validation of a MAS coupling the K-means and C4.5 algorithms. This approach had been successful with different datasets namely Iris, a flower dataset, BreastCancer and Diabetes medical datasets (US Census Bureau., 2009). The results produced were highly satisfactory, encouraging and acceptable. The interpretation and visualization of individual clusters of a dataset and the whole partitioned clustered dataset had also been dealt with (Mohamudally. Nawaz, Khan. Dost Muhammad 2011, Khan, Dost Muhammad. & Mohamudally, Nawaz. 2011).

However, the choice of the algorithms was empirical and intuitive. Some researchers have evaluated the VC (Vapnik-Chervonenkis)-dimension of different algorithms in order to map the appropriate algorithm with a particular dataset. There have been also similar research conducted using the CV (Cross-validation), AIC (Akaike Information Criterion), BIC (Bayesian Information Criterion), (SRMVC) Structural Risk Minimize with VC dimension models. The main aim of this book chapter is to investigate into the roadmap towards using the intelligent agents in an autonomous manner to select the right model fitted for any domain or problem and subsequently conduct each task of the data mining process within the MAS architecture.

The rest of the book chapter is organized as follows; section 2 is about the problematical issues in data mining and section 3 is about Unified Data Mining Theory (UDMT). In section 4 the Mathematical Formulation of Unified Data Mining Theory is discussed, section 5 deals with the Unified Data Mining Tool (UDMTool) and finally the conclusion is drawn in section 6.

2. Problematical issues in data mining

Data mining has achieved tremendous success and many problems have been solved by using data mining techniques. But still there are some challenges in the field of data mining research which should be addressed. These problems are: Unified Data mining Processes, Scalability, Mining Unbalanced, Complex and Multiagent Data, Data mining in Distributed and Network setting and Issues of Security, Privacy and Data Integrity in data mining

(Yang. Qlang, et al, 2006). The focus of this book chapter is on unified data mining processes such as clustering, classification, visualization followed by interpretation and proposes a unified data mining theory.

2.1. Unified data mining processes

There are many data mining algorithms and techniques which are designed for individual problems, such as classification or clustering. A theoretical framework is required that unifies different data mining tasks including clustering, classification, interpretation and association rules which would help the field of data mining and provide a basis for future research (Yang. Qlang, et al, 2006 & Wu. Xindong, et al 2006).

The following two figures 1 and 2 explain the process of uniformality.

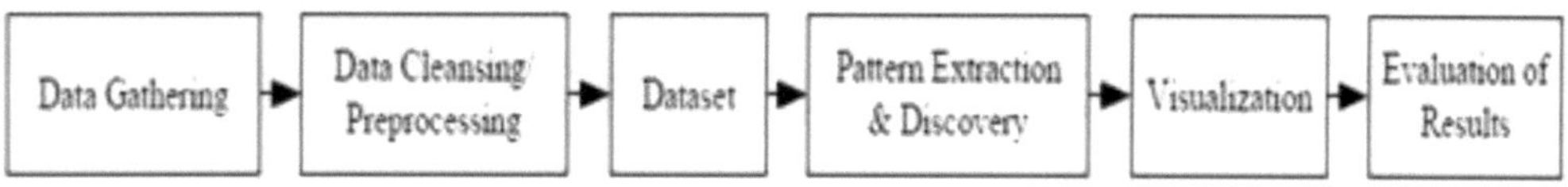

Figure 1. Conventional Life Cycle of Data Mining

Data mining is an iterative process and different stages or steps or processes are required to complete the data mining process. The figure 1 is the conventional life cycle of data mining. The first step is data gathering, then data cleansing and then preparing a dataset, the next stage is pattern extraction & discovery [The pattern extraction and discovery from large dataset is a two steps process. In the first step, the clusters of the dataset are created and the second step is to construct the 'decision rules' (if-then statements) with valid pattern pairs]. The choice of the algorithm depends on the intended use of extracted knowledge. The other stages are visualization and evaluation of results. The user has to select a data mining algorithm on each step in this life cycle, i.e. one algorithm for clustering, one for classification, one for interpretation and one for visualization. Every process is individually carried out in this life cycle.

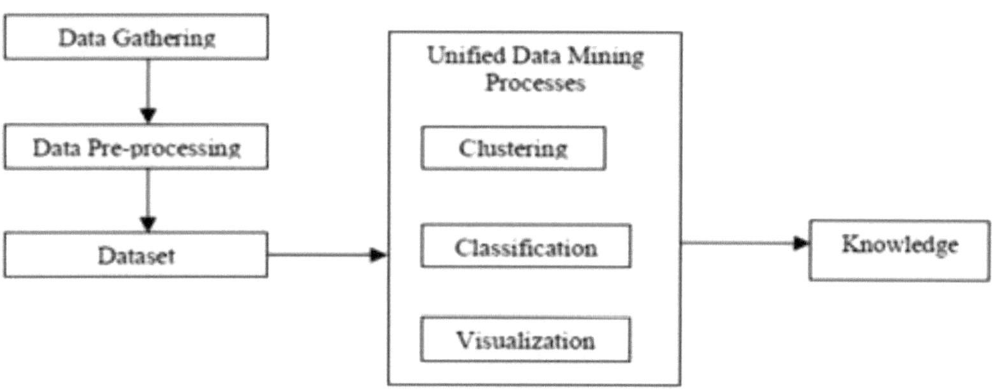

Figure 2. The Unified Data Mining Life Cycle

The figure 2 is the proposed unified data mining life cycle. The first three processes of unified data mining processes are the same as the cycle of data mining processes, i.e. data gathering, data cleansing followed by the preparing a dataset. The next process unifies the clustering, classification and visualization processes of data mining, called unified data mining processes (UDMP) followed by the output which is 'knowledge'. The user evaluates and interprets the 'knowledge' according to his business rules. The dataset is the only required input; the 'knowledge' is produced as final output from the proposed cycle of unified data mining processes. There is no need to select any data mining algorithm at any stage in the unified cycle of data mining processes. Multiagent systems (MASs) approach is used to unify clustering, classification and visualization processes of data mining.

3. Unified Data Mining Theory (UDMT)

The theories either explain little or much. Generally, science prefers those that explain much. The best theory would surely be the one that explains everything in all scientific disciplines. However, such a theory has proven hard to find. Instead the separate disciplines have been working towards unifying the sub-theories present in their respective subjects. In physics, for instance, there is an agreed upon taxonomy of the explanatory capacity of theories that illustrate strive of the unification. Physicists believe that there are four forces, or interactions, that affect matter in the universe: the strong force, the electromagnetic force, the weak force, and the gravitational force. A theory which has the set of requirements, comprehensiveness, preciseness, consistency and correctness is called a unified theory (Johnson, P., Ekstedt, M., 2007).

In 1687, Sir Isaac Newton proposed a unified theory of mechanics in order to explain and predict all earthly and heavenly motion (Newton, I., 1687). John Dalton 1803 revived a unified theory of matter, the atomic theory, explaining the nature of all physical substance (Dalton, J., 1808). In 1839, Matthias Schleiden and Theodor Schwann developed the theory of the cell, explaining the fundamental structure of living organisms (Schwann, T., 1839). In 1859, Charles Darwin proposed a unified theory of evolution by natural selection, in order to explain all variability of the living (Darwin, C., 1859). In 1869, Dmitri Ivanovich Mendeleev presented the periodic system, a unified theory explaining properties of all the chemical elements (Mendeleev, D., 1869). In mid 1800, James Clerk Maxwell, in his unified theory of electromagnetism, explained the interrelation of electric and magnetic fields. In 1884, Hertz, demonstrated that radio waves and light were both electromagnetic waves, as predicted by Maxwell's theory. In early 20th century, Albert Einstein, in general theory of relativity which deals with gravitation, became the second unified theory (Brog, Xavier., 2011) .

The term unified field theory was first coined by Einstein, while attempting to prove that electromagnetism and gravity were different manifestations of a single fundamental field and failed in this ultimate goal. When quantum theory entered the picture, the puzzle became more complex. Einstein spent much of his later life trying to develop a Unified Theory (UT) that would combine gravitation and electromagnetism. The theory resulting from the combination of the strong, weak and electromagnetic forces has been called the

Grand Unified Theory (GUT). At the end of the rainbow lies the dream of unifying all four forces. The resulting theory is often referred to as the Theory of Everything (TOE). As recently as 1990, Allen Newell proposed a unified theory of cognition in order to explain and predict all human problem-solving (Newell, A., 1990). The history of science is written in terms of its unified theories, because arguably, unified theories are the most powerful conceptual vehicles of scientific thought. Each force has a theory that explains how it works (Johnson, P., Ekstedt, M., 2007).

There is no accepted unified field theory, and thus remains an open line of research. The term was coined by Einstein, who attempted to unify the general theory of relativity with electromagnetism, hoping to recover an approximation for quantum theory. A "theory of everything" is closely related to unified field theory, but differs by not requiring the basis of nature to be fields, and also attempts to explain all physical constants of nature (Brog, Xavier., 2011, Johnson, P., Ekstedt, M., 2007, Mielikäinen, Taneli., 2004, Sarabjot S. Anand, David A. Bell, John G. Hughes, 1996).

3.1. Prerequisites for a unified theory

A good unified theory is beneficial for the discipline of data mining. In order to know whether the theory is good or not, the requirements for a unified theory need to be outlined. The important attributes of a unified theory are divided into four main categories (King, G., R. Keohane, and S. Verba, 1994, Popper K., 1980).

i. Comprehensiveness – that the theory covers all relevant phenomena
ii. Preciseness – that the theory generates applicable explanations and predictions
iii. Consistency – that the theory does not contradict itself
iv. Correctness – that the theory represents the real world (Johnson, P., Ekstedt, M., 2007).

3.1.1. Comprehensiveness

The comprehensiveness of a theory measures the scope of the theory; how much the theory can explain. All theories have delimitations, bounds outside of which they to not aspire to be applicable. Comprehensiveness is an important, not to say defining, characteristic of a unified theory. A unified theory of data mining should thus be able to express, explain and predict those issues which the users are facing nowadays (Johnson, P., Ekstedt, M., 2007).

3.1.2. Preciseness

The preciseness of a theory measures to what extent the theory is able to produce specific explanations and predictions. Theories with this capability are more useful than those that lack it, partly because precise results are generally more useful, but also because it is more or less impossible to tell whether imprecise theories are true of false. The philosopher of science Karl Popper called this property of a theory for falsifiability (Kuhn, T., 1962). A theory that is not falsifiable lacks all explanatory and predictive capacity. Ambiguous terminology ensures imprecision (Johnson, P., Ekstedt, M., 2007).

3.1.3. Consistency

A consistent theory does not contradict itself. This is a fairly obvious requirement on a theory; an inconsistent proposition is of no explanatory or predictive value. Consistency is, however, difficult to achieve. It is oftentimes difficult to once and for all verify that a theory is free of inconsistencies. However, three properties of theories greatly facilitate the identification of any self-contradictions. Firstly, small, simple, parsimonious theories are easier to grasp than large ones. It is easier to relate a small set of propositions to each other than a large set. Secondly, formalized, or structured, theories are easier to manage than poorly structured ones. Mathematically formulated theories are therefore easier to check for consistency than theories presented in natural language prose. Finally, imprecise theories may be interpreted differently. Some of these interpretations may be consistent while others are not. Precision thus also facilitates consistency checking (Johnson, P., Ekstedt, M., 2007).

3.1.4. Correctness

The arguably most important of all qualities of a theory is that it is correct, i.e. that it generates true predictions and explanations of the part of the world that it represents. It is the goal of all science to propose theories and then to test them. This is oftentimes a lengthy process, where many different aspects of a theory are tested against observations of the real world. A problem with the property of correctness is that, according to Popper, the correctness of a theory can never be demonstrated beyond doubt (unless it is a tautology), but the theory is corroborated by passing various empirical tests. Popper argues that once evidence has been discovered that falsifies a theory, it should be abandoned. Compared to established sciences such as physics, medicine and macro economics, little research effort is currently directed towards theory corroboration in data mining (Johnson, P., Ekstedt, M., 2007). According to Kuhn, this is not surprising given the scientific maturity of the discipline (Kuhn, T., 1962).

3.2. The advantages of a unified theory

A unified theory provides not only greater explanatory and predictive power, but also unifies the people involved in the discipline. Research and practice with a unified theory can become more coordinated and focused than with a set of disparate micro-theories. A unified theory provides a common vocabulary for expressing and communicating about the world, it defines common problems within that world, and it delimits the acceptable methods of reaching scientific conclusions regarding those problems. The important advantages and benefits of unified theory are, it provides better explanatory and predictive capacity, and it provides a common world view for the researchers and practitioners in the field (Johnson, P., Ekstedt, M., 2007). The following are the advantages of a unified theory:

3.2.1. Explanatory and predictive capacity

This is a question of organization of work, which also reappears as an underlying explanatory theory. Summarizing, a unified theory is liable to have greater explanatory and predictive power than a set of micro-theories (Johnson, P., Ekstedt, M., 2007).

3.2.2. Common terminologies

A unified theory of data mining implies a common terminology, by providing the facility to the users to understand each other. There are astounding numbers of definitions of many important concepts of data mining. Some of the concepts are unclear; there is no generally agreed upon definition of the term data mining (Johnson, P., Ekstedt, M., 2007).

3.2.3. Common problems

Without a unified theory of data mining the researchers will have difficulties seeing the big picture, i.e. the two disciplines at a time may have very much in common and the results of one discipline may be very fruitful for the other. Theories not only answer research questions, but they also pose new ones. They define what good research questions are. With a unified theory, researchers and practitioners in the field will see the same big picture and if the picture is the same, then the relevant problems with it are more likely to be the same (Johnson, P., Ekstedt, M., 2007).

3.2.4. Common conclusions

Without a unified theory, there is no common base from which an argument may be made for or against some proposition about the state of the world. It is equally acceptable to present an argument based on sociological research on group dynamics as one based on findings within solid state physics as one based on results in fractal geometry. This is problematic, because these scientific disciplines are not consistent with each other and may very well lead to opposing conclusions, and there is really no systematic way of drawing an aggregated conclusion (Johnson, P., Ekstedt, M., 2007).

In a good unified theory, arguments will have the same foundation. It may seem strange that truths from one discipline cannot be invoked at will in another discipline, but this is the case in all mature sciences; it is a kind of separation of concerns. In Kuhn's unified normal scientific disciplines, such as electromagnetism, there are no inter-theoretical discussions (Kuhn, T., 1962). This is of course very satisfying, because it provides a strong base for reaching the same conclusions and few discussions need to end up in stalemates (at least in principle). In pre-scientific disciplines, the debaters are at least aware of when they move from the intra-theoretical arena to the inter-theoretical one, thus maintaining a separation of concerns (Johnson, P., Ekstedt, M., 2007).

In data mining and other fragmented disciplines, the lack of unified theories makes such a separation impossible and there are no real rules for distinguishing between sound arguments and unsound ones. It is consequently quite acceptable to pick any one of the thousands of micro-theories available to support an argument and simply disregard the thousands remaining. We can thus explain and predict everything and nothing (Johnson, P., Ekstedt, M., 2007).

The advantage of a unified theory over many fragmented theories is that a unified theory often offers a more elegant explanation of data, and may point towards future areas of study as well as predict the laws of nature (Brog, Xavier., 2011, Unified Theory or Theory of Everything (TOE), 2001).

4. Mathematical formulation of a Unified Data Mining Theory (UDMT)

In this section we formulate a unified data mining theory using the mathematical functions. We start with the definition of an algorithm. An algorithm is a description of a mechanical set of steps for performing a task. The algorithms are considered a powerful tool in the field of computer science. When thinking about inputs and outputs, we can treat algorithms as functions; input a number into the algorithm, follow the prescribed steps, and get an output. A function is a relationship between an input variable and an output variable in which there is exactly one output for each input. To be a function, there are two requirements:

1. An algorithm to be consistent i.e. every time give the input, get the output.
2. Each input produces one possible output.

It is not necessary that all functions have to work on numbers and not all functions need to follow a computational algorithm (Dries. Lou van den. 2007, Lovász. L. , Pelikán. J., Vesztergombi. K. 2003 and MathWorksheetsGo, 2011). The data mining algorithms used in unified data mining processes satisfy the conditions of a function; therefore these algorithms are applied as functions.

Let S = {Set of n attributes}
A = {Set of n clusters of n attributes}
B = {Set of n rules of n clusters of n attributes}
C = {Set of n 2D graphs of n rules of n clusters of n attributes}

We can describe this in a more specific way that:

Let $S = \{s_1, s_2, ..., s_n\}$ where $s_1, s_2, ..., s_n$ are the partitions of datasets containing at least any of the two attributes and only one 'class' attribute of the original dataset.

$A = \{C_1(c_1, c_2, ..., c_n), C_2(c_1, c_2, ..., c_n), ..., C_n(c_1, c_2, ..., c_n)\}$ where $C_1(c_1, c_2, ..., c_n)$ is set of clusters of partitions 's_1', $C_2(c_1, c_2, ..., c_n)$ is set of clusters of partitions 's_2',...., and $C_n(c_1, c_2, ..., c_n)$ is set of clusters of partition 's_n'.

$B = \{R_1(r_1, r_2, ..., r_n), R_2(r_1, r_2, ..., r_n), ..., R_n(r_1, r_2, ..., r_n)\}$ where $R_1(r_1, r_2, ..., r_n)$ is set of rule of cluster 'C_1', $R_2(r_1, r_2, ..., r_n)$ is the set of rule of cluster 'C_2', ..., and $R_n(r_1, r_2, ..., r_n)$ is set of rule of cluster 'C_n'.

$C = \{V_1(v_1, v_2, ..., v_n), V_2(v_1, v_2, ..., v_n), ..., V_n(v_1, v_2, ..., v_n)\}$ where $V_1(v_1, v_2, ..., v_n)$ is set of 2D graphs of 'R_1', $V_2(v_1, v_2, ..., v_n)$ is the set of 2D graphs of 'R_2', ..., and $V_n(v_1, v_2, ..., v_n)$ is the set of 2D graphs of 'R_n'.

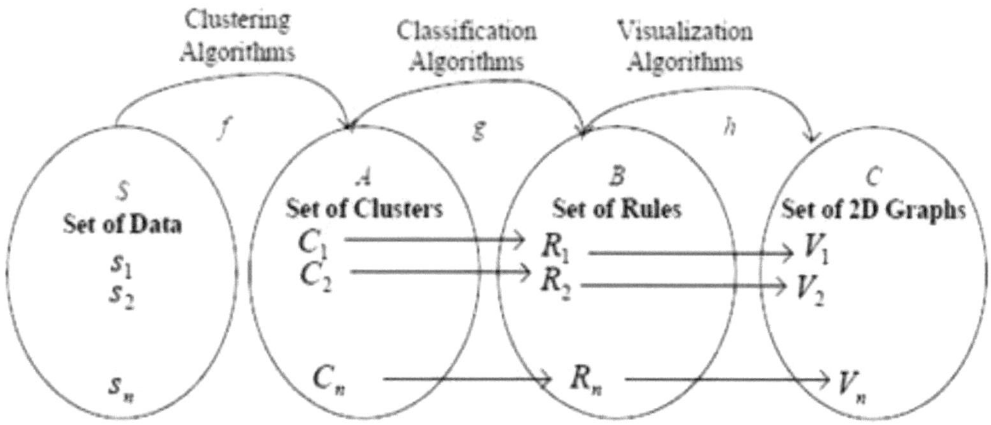

Figure 3. The Composition of the Functions

1. $f: S \rightarrow A$

$$f(s_j) = C_k, \text{ where } j,\ k = 1, 2, \ldots, n.$$

2. $g: A \rightarrow B$

$$g(C_l) = R_m, \text{ where } l,\ m = 1, 2, \ldots, n.$$

3. $h: B \rightarrow C$

$$h(R_o) = V_p, \text{ where } o,\ p = 1, 2, \ldots, n.$$

Lemma 1: *f, g & h are* functions

Proof:

1. *f* is a function

Suppose that *f* is not a function then s_1 can go to cluster 1 and cluster 2. This is impossible because clustering requires that s_1 goes to set of cluster 1. This leads to a contradiction. Therefore, *f* is a function.

2. *g* is a function

We define rule, depending on the clusters. Cluster 1 has Rule 1, Cluster 2 has Rule 2. We cannot define two rules to a cluster otherwise we would not be able to classify the attributes.

3. *h* is a function

The 2D graph will depend on the rule. A rule cannot produce two different 2D graphs.

The domain and co-domain of the functions are given by

$$dom(f) = S \qquad codom(f) = A$$

$$dom(g) = A \qquad codom(g) = B$$

$$dom(h) = B \qquad codom(h) = C$$

The function *f* is a mapping from the set of dataset to the set of clusters, the function g is a mapping from set of clusters to the set of rules and the function *h* is a mapping from set of rules to set of 2D graphs. The function *f* takes the set of data like $s_1, s_2, ..., s_n$ as input, apply clustering algorithm (K-means) and produces the clusters like $C_1(c_1, c_2, ..., c_n), C_2(c_1, c_2, ..., c_n), ..., C_n(c_1, c_2, ..., c_n)$ as the output. The function g takes the clusters like $C_1(c_1, c_2, ..., c_n), C_2(c_1, c_2, ..., c_n), ..., C_n(c_1, c_2, ..., c_n)$ as input, apply the classification algorithm (C4.5 Decision Tree) and produces the rules like $R_1(r_1, r_2, ..., r_n), R_2(r_1, r_2, ..., r_n), ..., R_n(r_1, r_2, ..., r_n)$ as the output. The function *h* takes the rules like $R_1(r_1, r_2, ..., r_n), R_2(r_1, r_2, ..., r_n), ..., R_n(r_1, r_2, ..., r_n)$ as input, apply data visualization algorithm and produces 2D graphs like $V_1(v_1, v_2, ..., v_n), V_2(v_1, v_2, ..., v_n), ..., V_n(v_1, v_2, ..., v_n)$ as the output. From the 2D graphs we can interpret and evaluate the results to get the knowledge, which is accepted or rejected by the user.

The domain and co-domain of the functions are given by

$$dom(g \circ f) = S \qquad codom(g \circ f) = B$$

$$dom(h \circ (g \circ f)) = S \qquad codom(h \circ (g \circ f)) = C$$

$g \circ f$ is a mapping from the set of data to the set of rules and $h \circ (g \circ f)$ is a mapping from the set of data to the set of 2D graphs. The knowledge is derived from the interpretation and evaluation of the 2D graphs which are obtained through the composition of the functions discussed above.

For $V_p \in C$

$\because V_p = h(R_m)$

$= h(g(C_k))$

$= h(g(f(s_j)))$

$= (h \circ g \circ f)(s_j)$ [Composition of the functions]

$$\therefore (h \circ g \circ f): S \to C \tag{1}$$

We first pass the partitions of the dataset through the composition of clustering, classification and visualization and then the results obtained are interpreted and evaluated to extract the knowledge. Therefore, we attempt to unify the processes of data mining life cycle.

The order of the functions must be the same as given in equation (1). That is, first apply the clustering algorithms, then classification algorithms, then visualization algorithms and finally the interpretation of the results of visualization. The selection of the appropriate and right result(s) will give the knowledge. This is the proof of the mathematical formulation of the unified process of data mining life cycle.

Illustration:

Let S be a dataset with two vertical partitions s_1 and s_2 , the set A is a set of clusters of each partition, the set B is the set of rules of each clusters and the set C is the set of 2D graphs of each rules. The mathematical notation of these sets is given below.

$$S = \{s_1, s_2\}$$
$$A = \{C_1(c_1, c_2), C_2(c_1, c_2)\}$$
$$B = \{R_1(r_1, r_2), R_2(r_1, r_2)\}$$
$$C = \{V_1(v_1, v_2), V_2(v_1, v_2)\}$$

Dataset S

CT	SECS	Mitoses	Class
3	2	1	Benign
5	2	1	Benign
1	2	1	Malignant
3	5	3	Malignant

s_1

CT	Mitoses	Class
3	1	Benign
5	1	Benign
1	1	Malignant
3	3	Malignant

s_2

CT	SECS	Class
3	2	Benign
5	2	Benign
1	2	Malignant
3	5	Malignant

1. $f(K - means) : S \rightarrow A$

K-means clustering algorithm takes three inputs, *'k'* number of clusters,, *'n'*, number of iteration and *'s_p'* dataset and will produce k clusters of the given dataset. The function *f* is illustrated in equation (2).

$$f(k,n,s_p) = C_k(c_k) \tag{2}$$

where k and n are positive nonzero integers.

Suppose we want to create two clusters of the datasets s_1 and s_2 and number of iteration is set to 10 i.e. $k = 2$ and $n = 10$ then the function $f(2,10,s_1) = C_1(c_1,c_2)$ is for the dataset s_1.

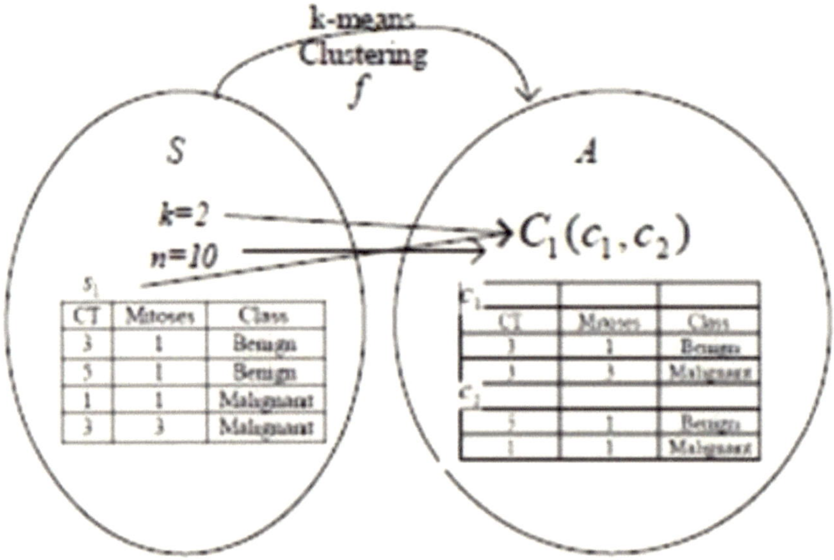

Figure 4. The mapping of function *f* for s_1

Figure 4 shows the mapping between the set *S* and the set *A* using K-means clustering algorithm as a function *f*. The values of other required parameters of this algorithm are number of clusters $k = 2$, number of iterations $n = 10$ and dataset s_1. This is m:1 (3:1) mapping because all the members of set *S* are mapped with the single member of set *A*.

Similarly, the function $f(2,10,s_2) = C_2(c_1,c_2)$ is for the dataset s_2.

Figure 5 shows the mapping between the set *S* and the set *A* using K-means clustering algorithm as a function *f*. The values of other required parameters of this algorithm are number of clusters $k = 2$, number of iterations $n = 10$ and dataset s_2. This is m:1 (3:1) mapping because all the members of the set *S* are mapped with the single member of the set *A*.

The figures 4 and 5 show that function *f* is m:1 function. Hence *f* is a function because it satisfies the conditions of the function; therefore the K-means clustering algorithm is a function. If we optimize the values of *'k'* and *'n'* then the K-means clustering algorithm will be 1:1 otherwise it is m:1. The process of creating clusters of the given dataset does not split the dataset into small datasets, the dataset remains the same and only datapoints are shifted within the dataset. For our own convenience we are illustrating different clusters of the dataset. This process does not create new datasets from the given dataset.

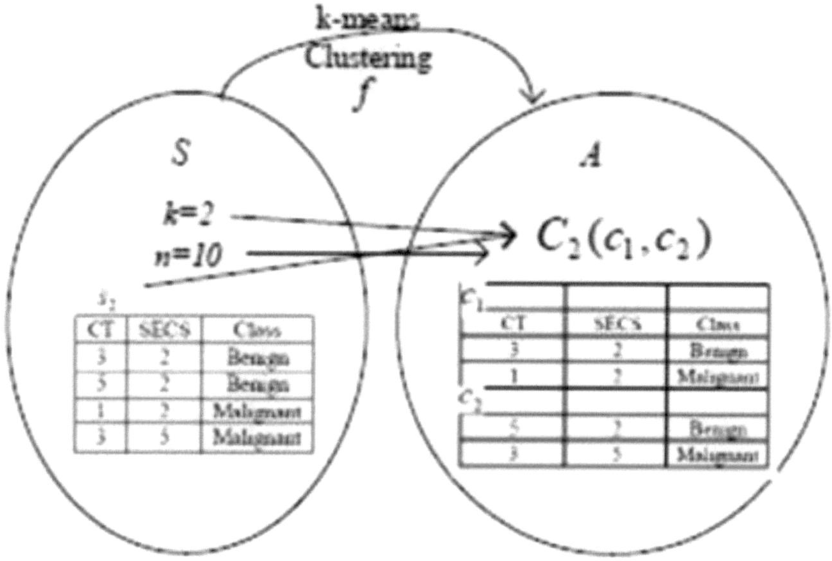

Figure 5. The mapping of function f s_2

2. $g(C4.5): A \rightarrow B$

The C4.5 algorithm takes the clusters of the dataset as input and produces the rule as output. The function g is illustrated in equation (3).

$$g(C_k) = R_k \quad (3)$$

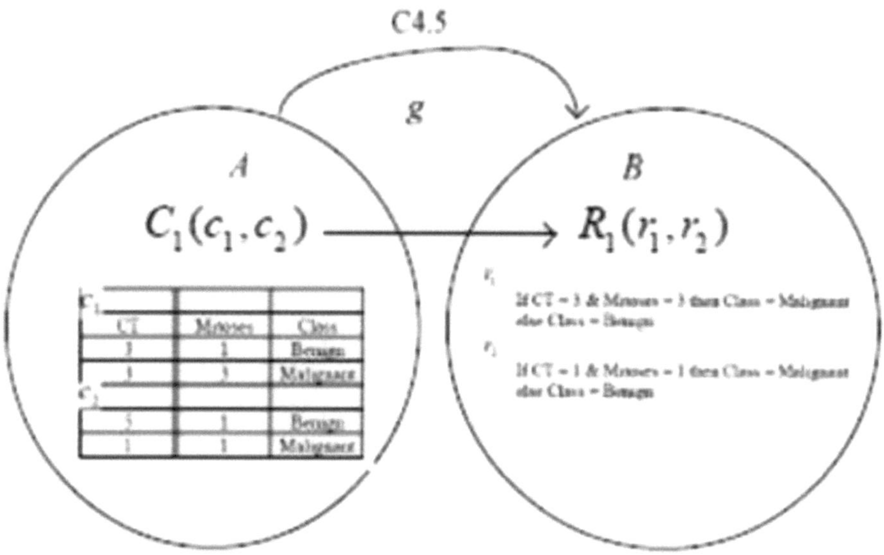

Figure 6. The mapping of function g s_1

Figure 6 shows the mapping between set *A* and set *B* using C4.5 (decision tree) algorithm as a function *g*. The algorithm takes the set of clusters $C_1(c_1,c_2)$ of dataset s_1 and produces the set of rules $R_1(r_1,r_2)$. This is 1:1 mapping because the members of the set *A* are mapped with the corresponding members of the set *B*.

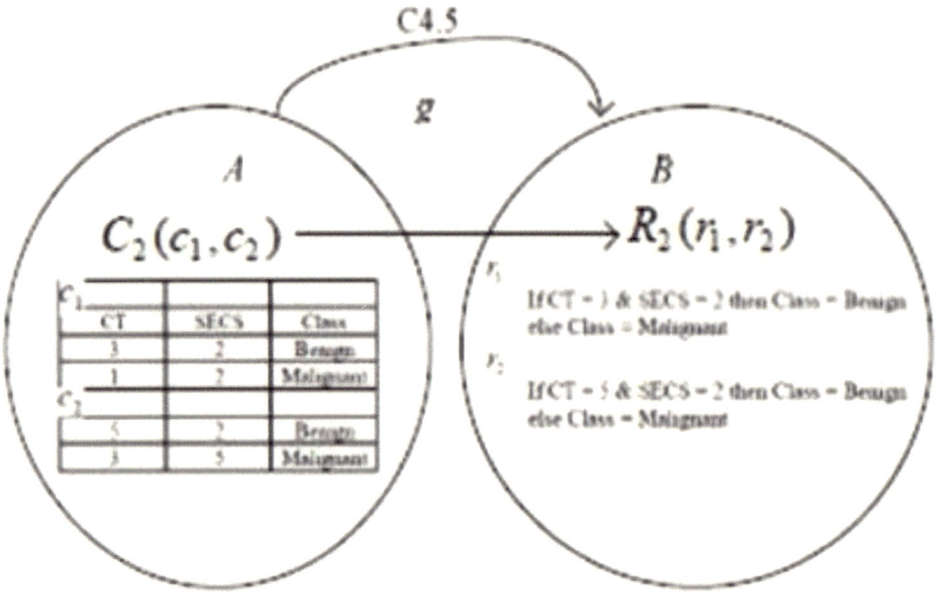

Figure 7. The mapping of function *g* s_2

Figure 7 shows the mapping between the set *A* and the set *B* using C4.5 (Decision Tree) algorithm as a function *g*. The algorithm takes the set of clusters $C_2(c_1,c_2)$ of dataset s_2 and produces the set of rules $R_2(r_1,r_2)$. This is 1:1 mapping because the members of the set *A* are mapped with the corresponding members of the set *B*.

The figures 6 and 7 show that function *g* is 1:1 function. Hence *g* is a function because it satisfies the conditions of the function; therefore C4.5 algorithm is a function. For our own convenience we are putting if-then-else in the rules created by the algorithm C4.5. The process of creating rules does not place if-then-else in any of the rules.

3. $h(DataVisualization): B \rightarrow C$

The algorithm Data Visualization takes the rules as input and produces 2D graphs as output. The function *h* is illustrated in equation (4).

$$h(R_k) = V_k \tag{4}$$

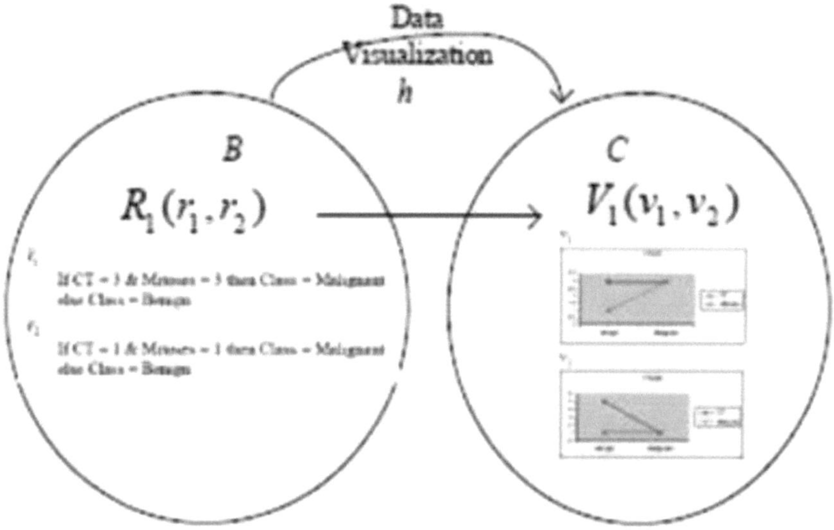

Figure 8. The mapping of function h s_1

Figure 8 shows the mapping between the set B and the set C using Data Visualization algorithm as a function h. The algorithm takes the set of rules $R_1(r_1,r_2)$ of set of cluster $C_1(c_1,c_2)$ of dataset s_1 and produces the set of 2D graphs $V_1(v_1,v_2)$. This is 1:1 mapping because the members of the set B are mapped with the corresponding members of the set C.

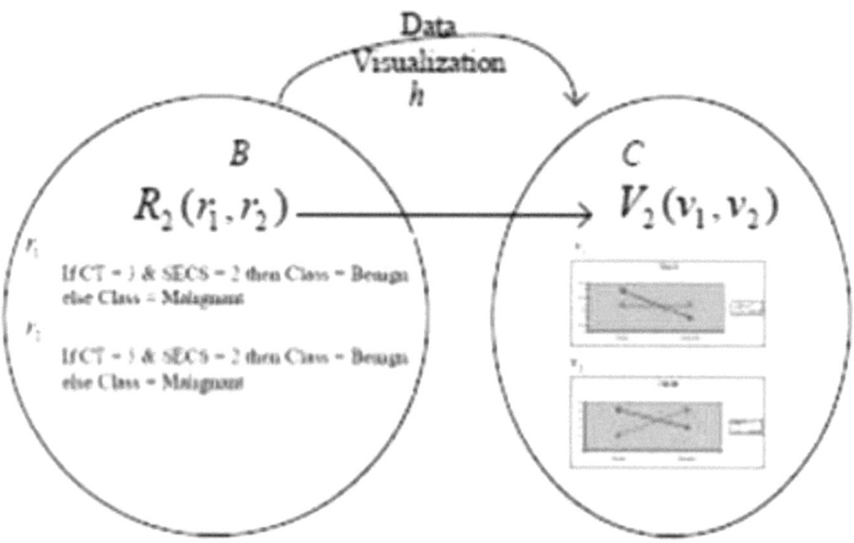

Figure 9. The mapping of function h s_2

Figure 9 shows the mapping between the set B and the set C using Data Visualization algorithm as a function h. The algorithm takes the set of rules $R_2(r_1,r_2)$ of set of cluster

$C_2(c_1, c_2)$ of dataset s_2 and produces the set of 2D graphs $V_2(v_1, v_2)$. This is 1:1 mapping because the members of the set *B* are mapped with the corresponding members of the set *C*.

The figures 8 and 9 show that function *h* is 1:1 function. Hence *h* is a function because it satisfies the conditions of the function, therefore Data Visualization (2D graphs) is a function. The purpose of 2D graph is to identify the type of relationship if any between the attributes. The graph is used when a variable exists which is being tested and in this case the attribute or variable 'class' is a test attribute. We further demonstrate the proposed unified data mining theory through the following two cases:

Case 1: BreastCancer, a medical dataset of four attributes is chosen as example to explain the theory discussed above. We create two vertical partitions, these partitions are the actual inputs of clustering algorithm and we want to create two clusters of each partition. Similarly, we will produce rules and 2D graphs of each partition and finally we will take one as output called knowledge after evaluating and interpreting all the obtained results. The whole process is discussed below:

$$S = \{s_1, s_2\}$$
$$A = \{C_1(c_1, c_2), C_2(c_1, c_2)\}$$
$$B = \{R_1(r_1, r_2), R_2(r_1, r_2)\}$$
$$C = \{V_1(v_1, v_2), V_2(v_1, v_2)\}$$

Dataset S

CT	SECS	Mitoses	Class
3	2	1	Benign
5	2	1	Benign
1	2	1	Malignant
3	5	3	Malignant

The set of data of dataset S is shown in the tables below:

CT	Mitoses	Class
3	1	Benign
5	1	Benign
1	1	Malignant
3	3	Malignant

Table 1. s_1

CT	SECS	Class
3	2	Benign
5	2	Benign
1	2	Malignant
3	5	Malignant

Table 2. s_2

The set of clusters of set of data are shown in the following tables:

CT	Mitoses	Class
3	1	Benign
3	3	Malignant

Table 3. $C_1(c_1)$

CT	Mitoses	Class
5	1	Benign
1	1	Malignant

Table 4. $C_1(c_2)$

CT	SECS	Class
3	2	Benign
1	2	Malignant

Table 5. $C_2(c_1)$

CT	SECS	Class
5	2	Benign
3	5	Malignant

Table 6. $C_2(c_2)$

The set of rules of set of clusters are described below:

$R_1(r_1)$

If CT = 3 & Mitoses = 3 then Class = Malignant
else Class = Benign

$R_1(r_2)$

If CT = 1 & Mitoses = 1 then Class = Malignant
else Class = Benign

$R_2(r_1)$

If CT = 3 & SECS = 2 then Class = Benign
else Class = Malignant

$R_2(r_2)$

If CT = 5 & SECS = 2 then Class = Benign
else Class = Malignant

The following figures show the set of 2D graphs of set of rules:

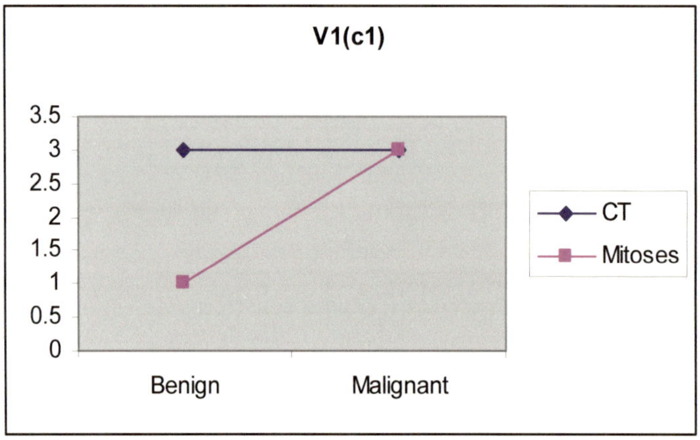

Figure 10. $V_1(v_1)$

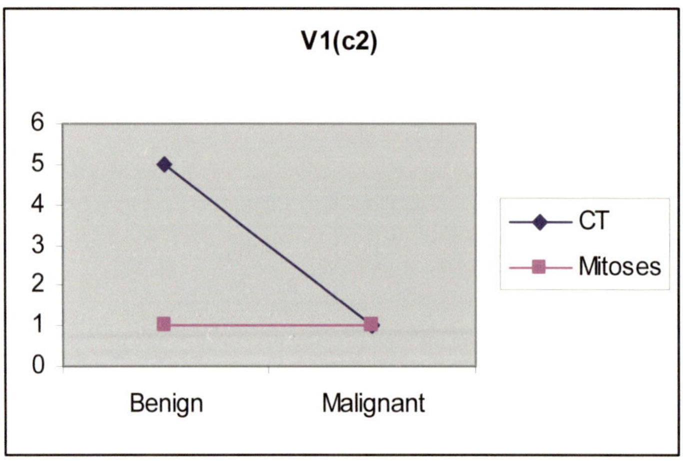

Figure 11. $V_1(v_2)$

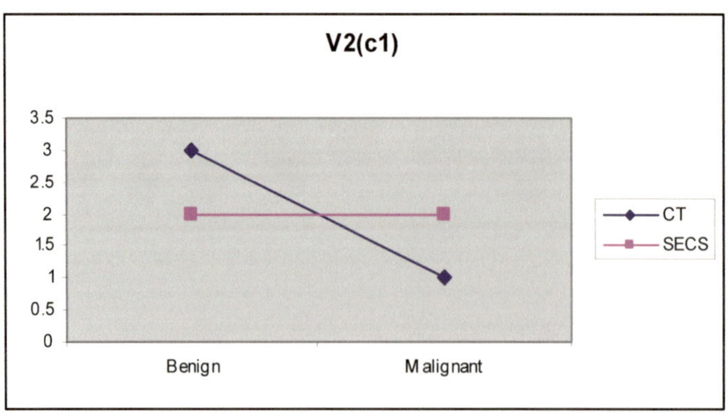

Figure 12. $V_2(v_1)$

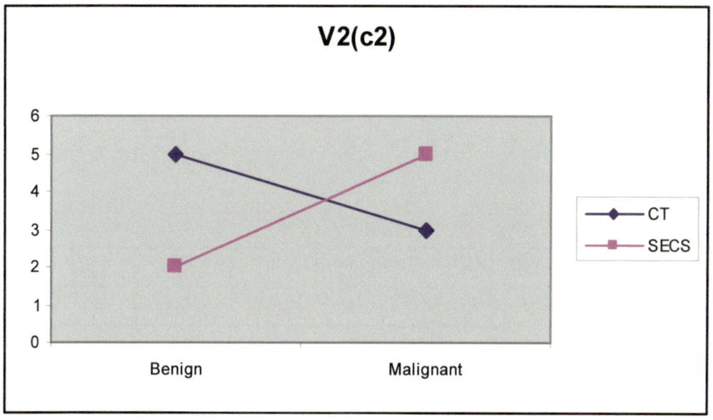

Figure 13. $V_2(v_2)$

$V_2(v_2)$ We interpret and evaluate the results obtained from the set $V_1(v_1,v_2)$. The structure of 2D graphs in figure 10 and 11 is identical. The result obtained from these graphs is that if attributes 'CT' and 'Mitoses' have the same values then the patient has 'Malignant' class of BreastCancer otherwise 'Benign' class of BreastCancer. The interpretation and evaluation of the set $V_2(v_1,v_2)$ show that the 2D graphs in figure 12 and 13 are similar. The result achieved from these graphs is if attributes 'CT' and 'SECS' have variable values then the patient has 'Benign' class of BreastCancer otherwise 'Malignant' class of Breast Cancer.

Table 7 summarizes the steps involved in the theory of unified data mining processes through the composition of functions for case 1 discussed above.

S	f	$g \circ f$	$h \circ g \circ f$
s_1	$C_1(c_1,c_2)$	$R_1(r_1,r_2)$	$V_1(v_1,v_2)$
s_2	$C_2(c_1,c_2)$	$R_2(r_1,r_2)$	$V_2(v_1,v_2)$

Table 7. Composition of the Functions

In this way the knowledge can be extracted from the given dataset S through the unified process of the composition of clustering, classification and visualization followed by interpretation and evaluation of the results which depend on the user's selection according to his business requirements.

Case 2: Diabetes, a medical dataset of nine attributes is selected. We create four vertical partitions, these partitions are actual inputs of clustering algorithm and three clusters for each partition are created. Similarly, we will produce rules and 2D graphs of each partition and finally we will select one partition as output called knowledge after evaluation and interpreting all the results. The whole process is discussed below:

$$S = \{s_1, s_2, s_3, s_4\}$$
$$A = \{C_1(c_1, c_2, c_3), C_2(c_1, c_2, c_3), C_3(c_1, c_2, c_3), C_4(c_1, c_2, c_3)\}$$
$$B = \{R_1(r_1, r_2, r_3), R_2(r_1, r_2, r_3), R_3(r_1, r_2, r_3), R_4(r_1, r_2, r_3)\}$$
$$C = \{V_1(v_1, v_2, v_3), V_2(v_1, v_2, v_3), V_3(v_1, v_2, v_3), V_4(v_1, v_2, v_3)\}$$

Dataset S

NTP	PGC	DBP	TSFT	HSI	BMI	DPF	Age	Class
4	148	72	35	0	33.6	0.627	50	Cat 1
2	85	66	29	0	26.6	0.351	31	Cat 2
2	183	64	0	0	23.3	0.672	32	Cat 1
1	89	66	23	94	28.1	0.167	21	Cat 2
2	137	40	35	168	43.1	2.288	33	Cat 2

The set of data of the dataset S is shown in tables below:

NTP	PGC	Class
4	148	Cat 1
2	85	Cat 2
2	183	Cat 1
1	89	Cat 2
2	137	Cat 2

Table 8. s_1

DBP	TSFT	Class
72	35	Cat 1
66	29	Cat 2
64	0	Cat 1
66	23	Cat 2
40	35	Cat 2

Table 9. s_2

HSI	BMI	Class
94	28.1	Cat 2
168	43.1	Cat 2
88	31	Cat 2
543	30.5	Cat 1
200	25.5	Cat 1

Table 10. s_3

DPF	Age	Class
0.627	50	Cat 1
0.351	31	Cat 2
0.672	32	Cat 1
0.167	21	Cat 2
0.2	39	Cat 1

Table 11. s_4

The set of clusters of set of data are shown in the following tables:

NTP	PGC	Class
4	148	Cat 1
2	85	Cat 2

Table 12. $C_1(c_1)$

NTP	PGC	Class
2	183	Cat 1
1	89	Cat 2

Table 13. $C_1(c_2)$

NTP	PGC	Class
2	137	Cat 2

Table 14. $C_1(c_3)$

DBP	TSFT	Class
72	35	Cat 1

Table 15. $C_2(c_1)$

DBP	TSFT	Class
66	29	Cat 2
64	0	Cat 1

Table 16. $C_2(c_2)$

DBP	TSFT	Class
66	23	Cat 2
40	35	Cat 2

Table 17. $C_2(c_3)$

HSI	BMI	Class
94	28.1	Cat 2
168	43.1	Cat 2

Table 18. $C_3(c_1)$

HSI	BMI	Class
88	31	Cat 2

Table 19. $C_3(c_2)$

HSI	BMI	Class
543	30.5	Cat 1
200	25.5	Cat 1

Table 20. $C_3(c_3)$

DPF	Age	Class
0.167	21	Cat 2
0.2	39	Cat 1

Table 21. $C_4(c_1)$

DPF	Age	Class
0.627	50	Cat 1
0.351	31	Cat 2

Table 22. $C_4(c_2)$

DPF	Age	Class
0.672	32	Cat 1

Table 23. $C_4(c_3)$

The set of rules of set of clusters are described below:

$R_1(r_1)$

If NPT = 4 and PGC = 85 then Class = Cat 2
else Class = Cat 1

$R_1(r_2)$

If NPT = 2 and PGC = 183 then Class = Cat 1
else Class = Cat 2

$R_1(r_3)$

If NPT = 2 and PGC = 137 then Class = Cat 2

$R_2(r_1)$

If DBP = 32 and TSFT =35 then Class = Cat 1

$R_2(r_2)$

If DBP = 66 and TSFT = 29 then Class = Cat 2
else Class = Cat 1

$R_2(r_3)$

If DBP = 40 and TSFT = 23 then Class = Cat 2

$R_3(r_1)$

If HSI = 94 and BMI = 23.1 then Class = Cat 2

$R_3(r_2)$

If HSI = 88 and BMI = 31 then Class = Cat 2

$R_3(r_3)$

If HSI = 200 and BMI = 30.5 then Class = Cat 1

$R_4(r_1)$

If DPF = 0.2 and Age = 21 then Class = Cat 2
else Class = Cat 1

$R_4(r_2)$

If DPF = 0.637 and Age = 50 then Class = Cat 1
else Class = Cat 2

$R_4(r_3)$

If DPF = 0.672 and Age = 32 then Class = Cat 2

The following figures show the set of 2D graphs of set of rules:

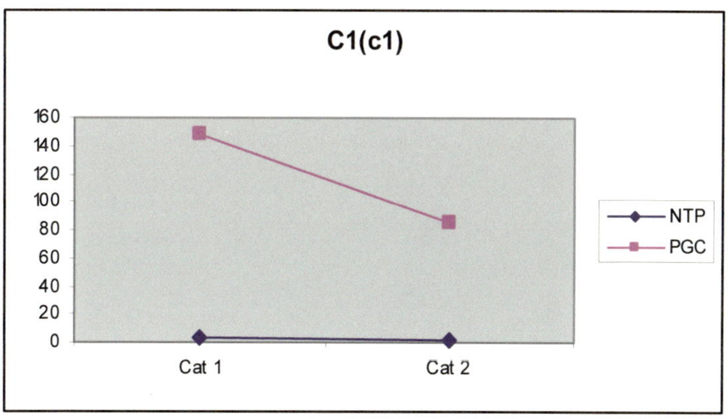

Figure 14. $V_1(v_1)$

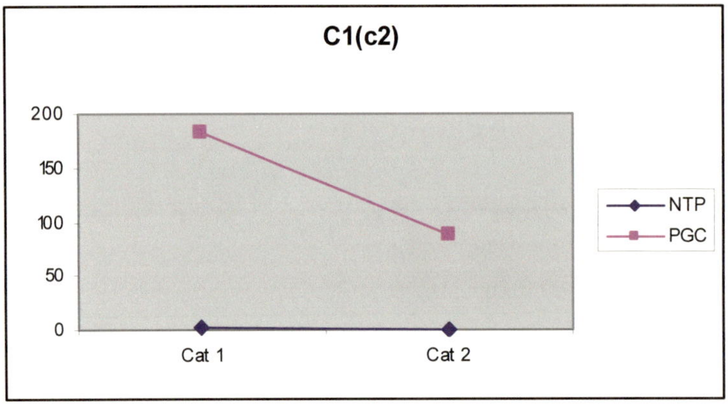

Figure 15. $V_1(v_2)$

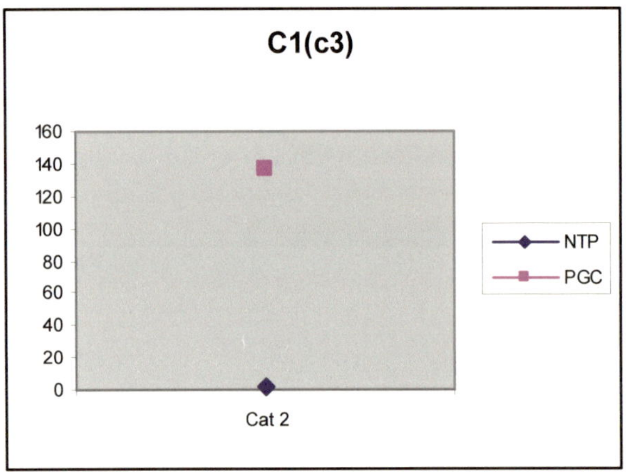

Figure 16. $V_1(v_3)$

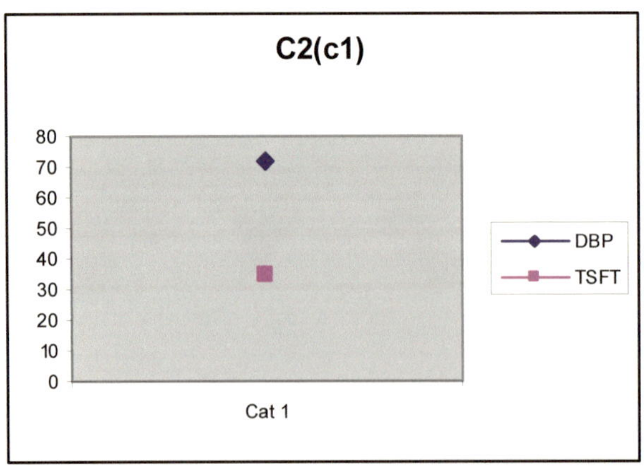

Figure 17. $V_2(v_1)$

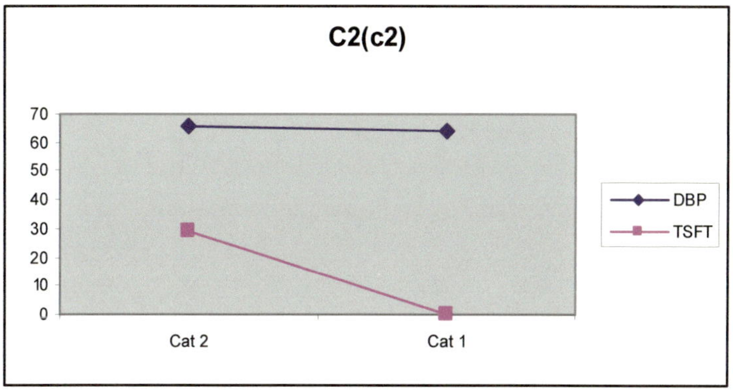

Figure 18. $V_2(v_2)$

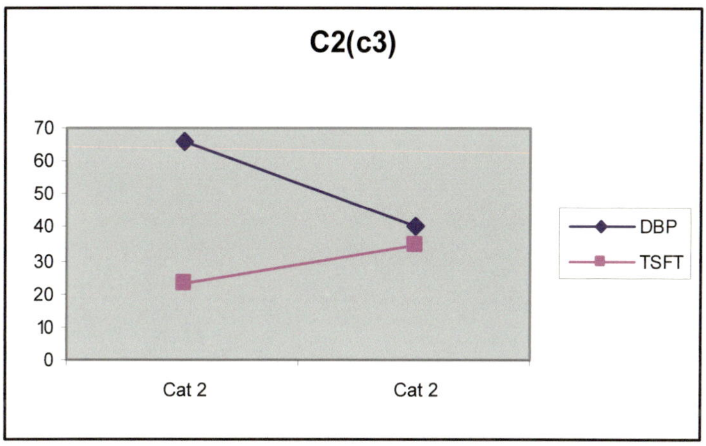

Figure 19. $V_2(v_3)$

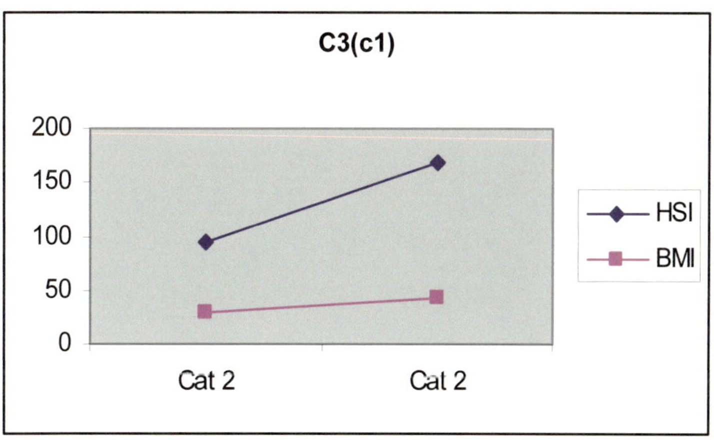

Figure 20. $V_3(v_1)$

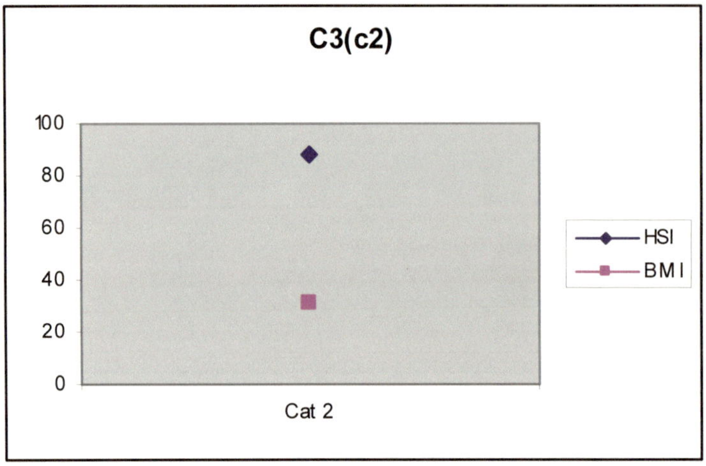

Figure 21. $V_3(v_2)$

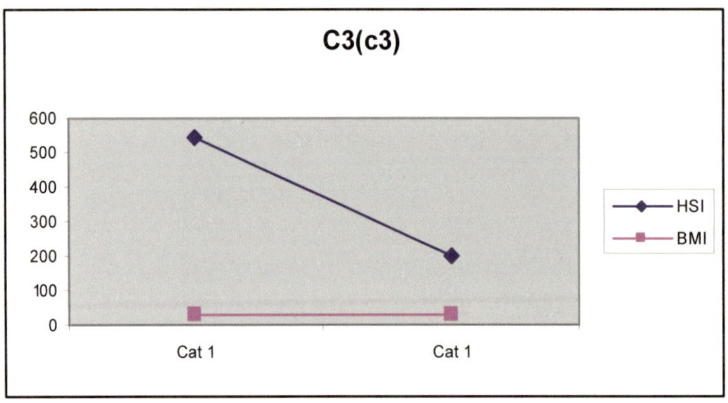

Figure 22. $V_3(v_3)$

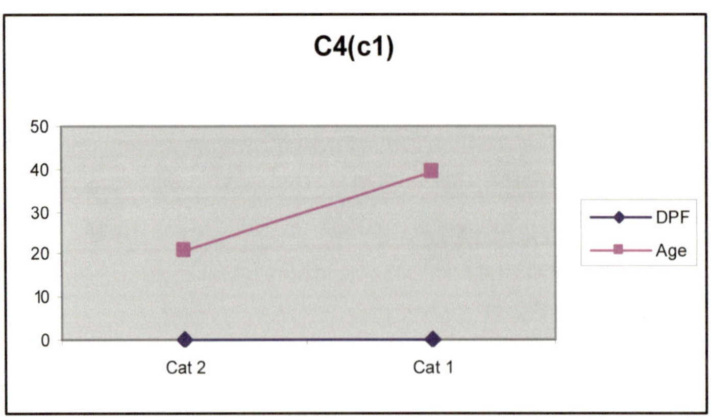

Figure 23. $V_4(v_1)$

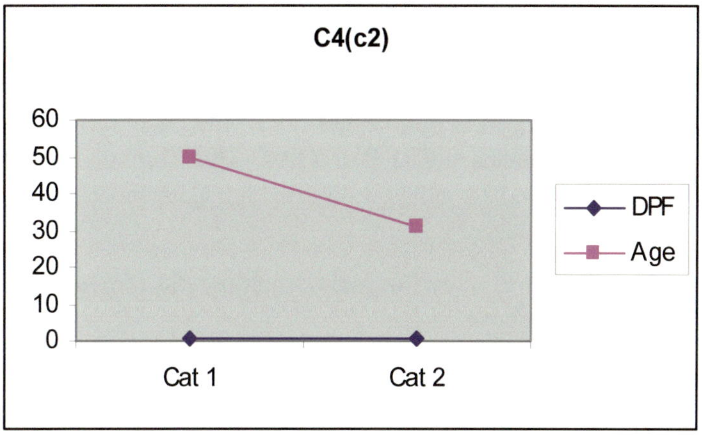

Figure 24. $V_4(v_2)$

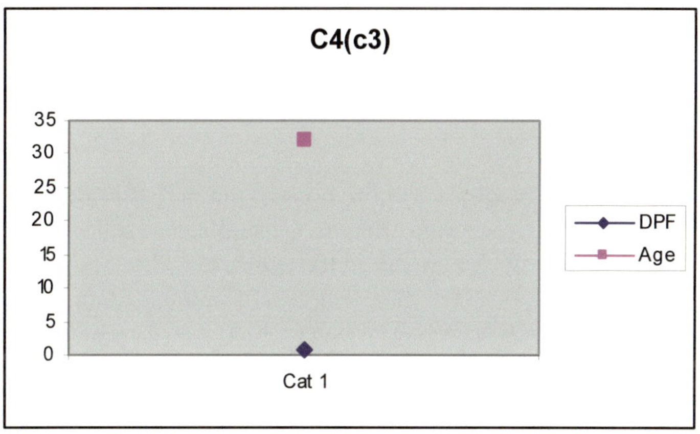

Figure 25. $V_4(v_3)$

The results of set $V_1(v_1,v_2,v_3)$ are interpreted and evaluated which show that the structure of 2D graphs in figure 14 and 15 is identical. The result obtained from these graphs is if attributes 'NPT' and 'PGC' have the variable values then the patient has either diabetes of 'Cat 1' or 'Cat 2'. But the 2D graph in figure 16 shows that if the attributes are of variable values then the patient has 'Cat 2' diabetes. The set $V_2(v_1,v_2,v_3)$ shows that the structure of 2D graphs in figure 18 and 19 is almost the same as 2D graphs in figure 14 and 15. The result obtained from these graphs is if attributes 'DBP' and 'TSFT' have the variable values then the patient has either diabetes of 'Cat 1' or 'Cat 2'. The 2D graph in figure 17 is similar to 2D graph in figure 16, which shows that if the attributes are of variable values then the patient has 'Cat 2' diabetes. The set $V_3(v_1,v_2,v_3)$ illustrates that the structure of 2D graphs in figure 20 and 22 is the same as 2D graphs in figures 14, 15, 18 and 19. The result obtained from these graphs is if attributes 'HSI' and 'BMI' have the variable values then the patient has either diabetes of 'Cat 1' or 'Cat 2'. The 2D graph in figure 21 is similar to 2D graph in figures 16 and 17, which shows that if the attributes are of variable values then the patient has 'Cat 2' diabetes. Finally, the set $V_4(v_1, v_2, v_3)$ demonstrates that the structure of 2D graphs in figure 23 and 24 is the same as 2D graphs in figures 14, 15, 18, 19, 20 and 22. The result obtained from these graphs is if attributes 'DPF' and 'Age' have the variable values then the patient has either diabetes of 'Cat 1' or 'Cat 2'. The 2D graph in figure 25 is similar to 2D graph in figures 16, 17 and 21, which shows that if the attributes are of variable values then the patient has 'Cat 2' diabetes.

Table 24 summarizes the steps to unify the data mining process through the composition of functions for case 2 discussed above.

S	f	$g \circ f$	$h \circ g \circ f$
s_1	$C_1(c_1, c_2, c_3)$	$R_1(r_1, r_2, r_3)$	$V_1(v_1, v_2, v_3)$
s_2	$C_2(c_1, c_2, c_3)$	$R_2(r_1, r_2, r_3)$	$V_2(v_1, v_2, v_3)$
s_3	$C_3(c_1, c_2, c_3)$	$R_3(r_1, r_2, r_3)$	$V_3(v_1, v_2, v_3)$
s_4	$C_4(c_1, c_2, c_3)$	$R_4(r_1, r_2, r_3)$	$V_4(v_1, v_2, v_3)$

Table 24. Composition of the Functions

Thus the knowledge can be extracted from the given dataset S through the unified process of the composition of clustering, classification and visualization followed by interpretation and evaluation of the results which depend on the user's selection according to his business requirements. It also shows that the proposed unified data mining theory is comprehensiveness, precise, consistent and correct which are the prerequisites for a unified theory.

5. Unified Data Mining Tool (UDMTool)

The Unified Data Mining Tool (UDMTool) is a new and better next generation solution which is a unified way of architecting and building software solutions by integrating different data mining algorithms. The figure 26 depicts the architecture of UDMTool.

The figure 26 is an architecture of UDTMTool based on proposed UDMT. The dataset is inputed, there are many types of datasets like, numeric, categorical, multimedia, text and many more, the selection crterion will take the whole dataset, analayises the data and produces 'under-fitted' or 'over-fitted' values of the dataset, on the bases of these values the appropriate data mining algorithms are selected and the data is passed to the unified data mining processes for 'knowledge' as output. The UDMTool has four parts:

i. Datasets
ii. The Selection Criterion (Data Analayiser)
iii. The Unified Data Mining Processes and
iv. Finally, 'the knowledge', as an output.

Let dataset D = {Numeric, Multimedia, Text, Categorical}

Selection criterion S = {VC Dimension, AIC, BIC} The output of S = Over-fitted, Under-fitted}

Unified Process U = {Clustering, Classification, Visualization, Interpretation} [Assume that 'clustering' will be the first step followed by the rest of the steps]

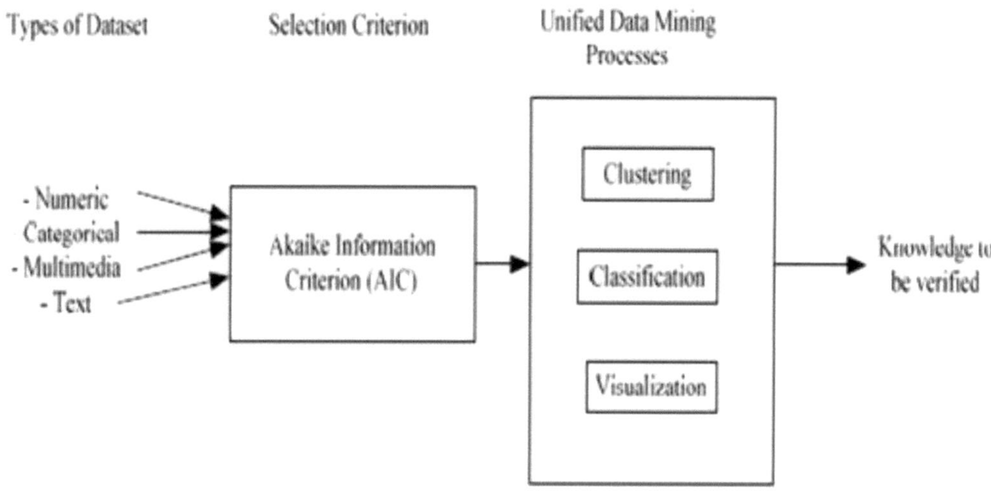

Figure 26. The Architecture of the UDMTool

Knowledge K={Accepted, Rejected} [Accepted means that the required results are according to the business goals and Rejected means that the output is not within the domain of the business goals. The 'knowledge' will be verified by the user, the Model cannot play any role in this regard]

Step 1. Input D
If D # Numeric Stop/Exit
else go to step 2

Step 2. S takes the dataset D and generates the values for S
If over-fitted and under-fitted then again pre-process the inputted dataset D
else create the appropriate vertical partitions of the dataset D and go to step 3

Step 3. One by one take these vertical partitioned datasets
Up = First, create clusters, then classify each cluster, then draw 2D graphs of each cluster, then evaluate and interpret these results and finally produce the 'knowledge' K as output.

Step 4. K = {Accepted, Rejected}
Rejected: Exit/Stop and select another dataset
Accepted: Ok/Stop. The process is successfully completed and the output meets the business goals.

These steps are further illustrated in a flow chart in figure 27.

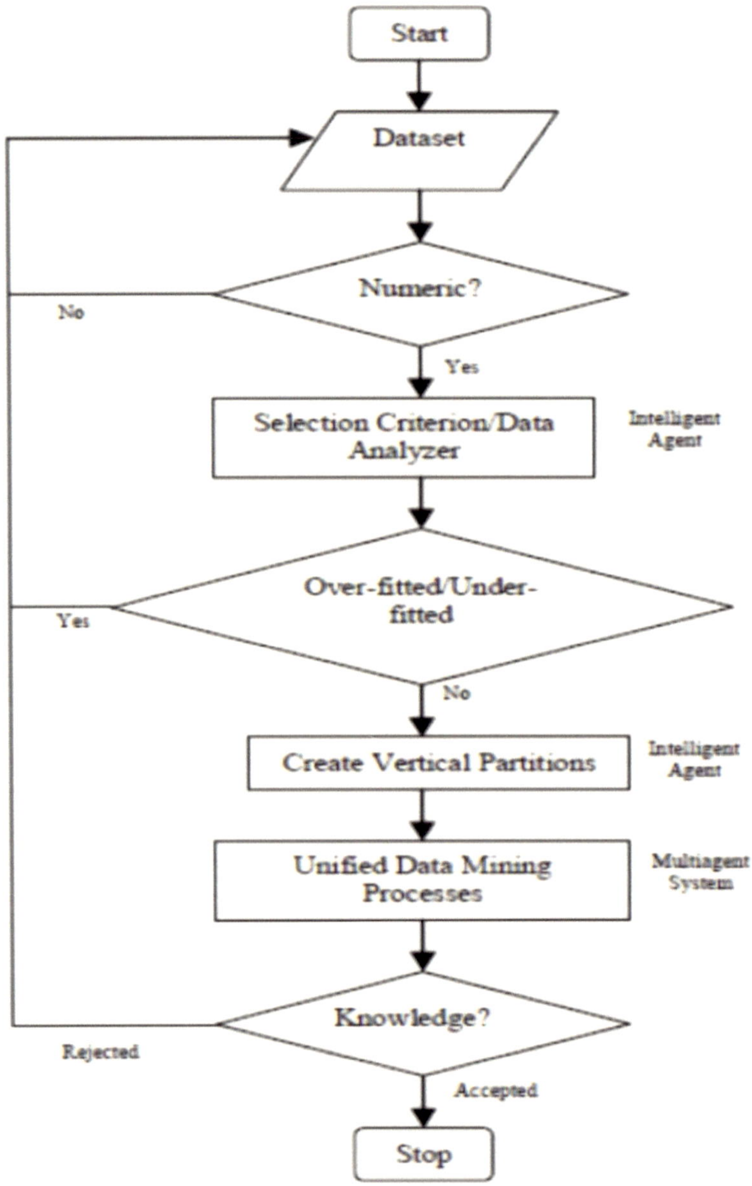

Figure 27. The Flow Chart of the UDMTool

The explanation of the flow chart is: A numeric dataset of 'n' attributes i.e. a data file is the starting point of this flowchart. An intelligent agent takes the dataset and analyzes the data using AIC selection criterion. An agent is for the selection criterion. The under-fitted or over-fitted values of the dataset show the errors in the data. This requires the proper cleansing of the data. The second agent creates the 'm' vertical partitions of the dataset where $m = \frac{n-1}{2}$, where 'n' and 'm' both are non-zero positive integers. Finally, these partitions are taken by a MAS, which unifies the data mining processes such as clustering, classification, visualization and interpretation and evaluation and the 'knowledge' is extracted as output. The knowledge is either accepted or rejected. Thus, multiagent systems (MASs) for unified theory of data mining processes, one agent is for selection criterion and the other agent is for vertical partition of the dataset.

Figure 28 explains the framework of multiagent systems (MASs) used in UDMTool.

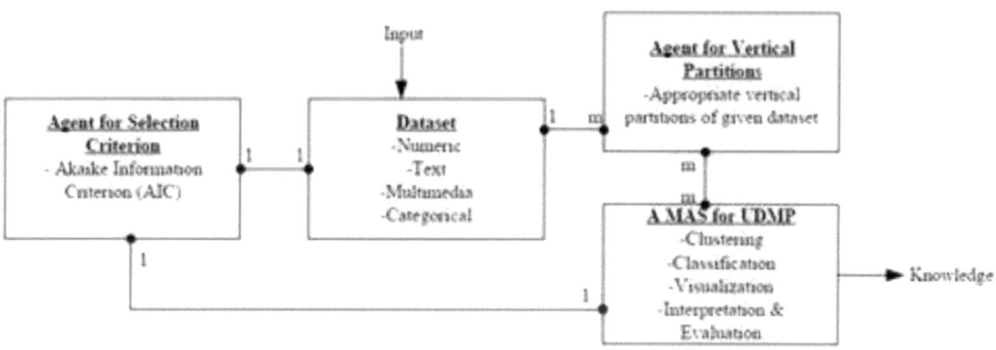

Figure 28. The Framework of MASs of the UDMTool

A well-prepared dataset is a starting input of this framework. First, intelligent agent compute the value model of selection AIC, which is used to select appropriate data mining algorithm and the second intelligent agent creates the vertical partitions, which are the inputs of UDMP. Finally, the knowledge is extracted, which is either accepted or rejected. The framework of UDMTool, a proposed model is shown in figure 29 below. The design is based on *Gaia methodology*, which is used to build models in the analysis and design phase (Wooldridge, M, Jennings, N. R., Kinny, D., 2000). The relationship between dataset and selection criterion is 1:1 i.e. one dataset and one value for model selection and between dataset and vertical partitions is 1:m i.e. more then one partitions are created for one dataset. The relationship between selection criterion and UDMP is 1:1 i.e. one value of selection model will give one data mining algorithm and finally the relationship between vertical partitions and UDMP is m:m i.e. many partitioned datasets are inputs for UDMP and only one result is produced as knowledge.

The function of the UDMTool is demonstrated in figure 29.

The dataset is a starting input of UDMTool, first intelligent agent compute the value of AIC, which is used to pick the right algorithm from unified data mining process, a MAS, for the given dataset. The second algorithm generates the required and appropriate vertical partitions of the given dataset, which are the inputs of MAS. The knowledge is produced in the forms of 2D graph(s) as the final output, which is verified by the user according to his business rules.

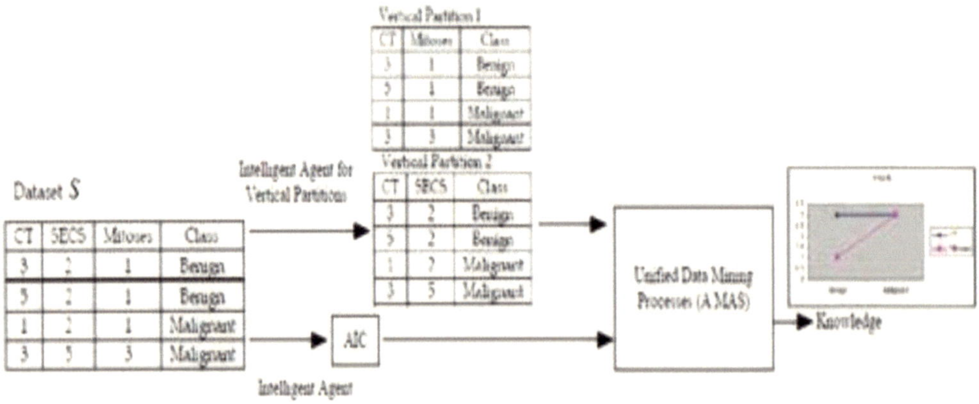

Figure 29. The Function of the UDMTool

The UDMTool is tested on variety of datasets such as 'Diabetes' and 'Breast Cancer', two medical datasets, 'Iris', an agriculture dataset and 'Sales', an account dataset. In this book chapter, we present the results of 'Iris' and 'Sales' datasets. The following figures (2D graphs) are the results and the extracted knowledge from 'Iris', an agriculture dataset using UDMTool:

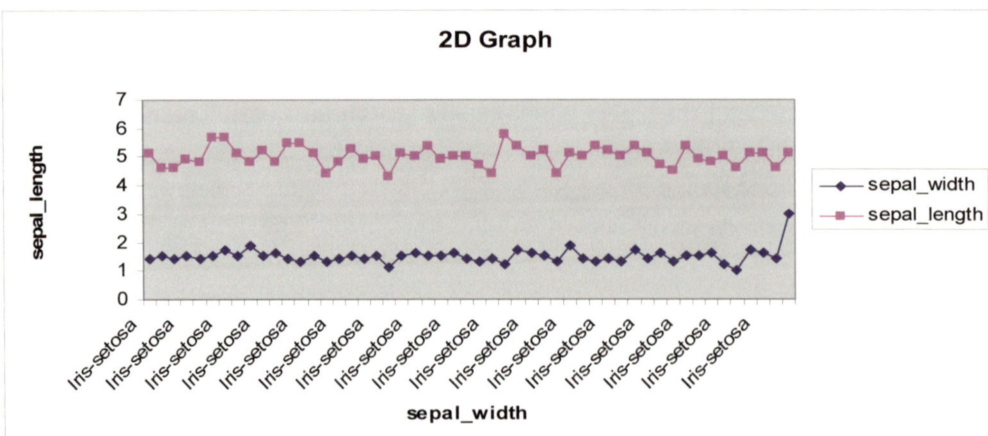

Figure 30. The Graph between 'sepal_length' and 'sepal_width' of 'Iris' dataset

The graph in figure 30 shows that there is no relationship between the attributes 'sepal_width' and 'sepal_length' from the beginning to the end. Both attributes have the distinct values which show the value of attribute 'class' is 'Irissetosa'. Therefore, the result derived from this 2D graph is if these two attributes have no relationship then the class is 'Irissetosa'.

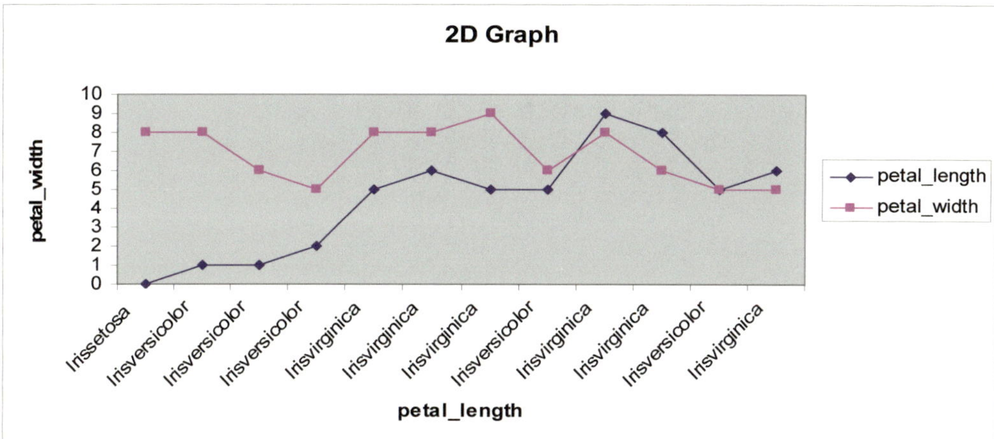

Figure 31. Graph between 'petal_length' and 'petal_width' of 'Iris' dataset

The value of the attributes 'petal_length' and 'petal_width' is almost constant at the beginning and then at the end there is some relationship between the attributes in this graph of figure 31. The graph can be divided into two main regions; the value of the attributes 'petal_length' and 'petal_width' is constant i.e. there is no relationship between the attributes and the attribute 'class' also have the distinct values. In the second region there exists a relationship between the attributes which gives almost the unique value of the attribute 'class' 'Irisvirginica'. The outcome of this graph is that if the value of the attributes is variable then the 'class' is also variable otherwise the value of 'class' is constant which is 'Irisvirginicia'.

The structure of the graph in figure 32 is complex. In the beginning of the graph there is no relationship between the attributes 'petal_length' and 'petal_width', then there exists a relationship between these attributes, again the attributes have distinct values and at the end there is relationship between the attributes. The outcome of this graph is that if there is no relationship between the attributes, the value of attribute 'class' is 'Irisvirginicia' and if there exists a relationship between the attributes then the value of attribute 'class' is 'Irisversicolor'.

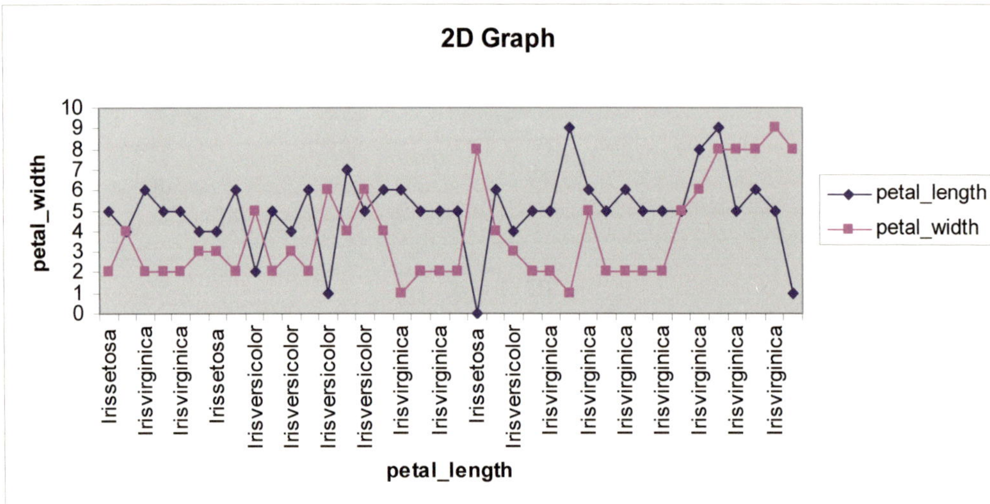

Figure 32. Graph between 'petal_length' and 'petal_width' of 'Iris' dataset

The following figures (2D graphs) are the results and the extracted knowledge from 'Sales', an account dataset using UDMTool:

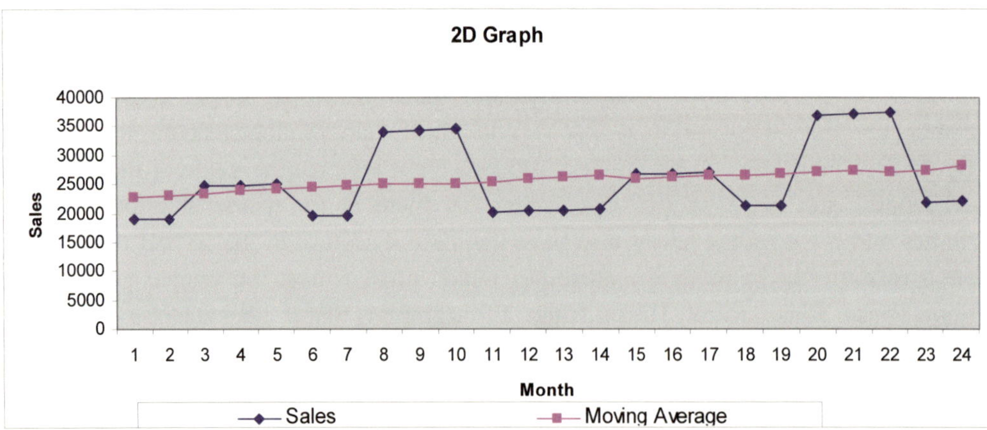

Figure 33. Graph between 'monthly sales' and 'moving average' of 'Sales' dataset

The graph in figure 33 shows a relationship between 'monthly sales' and the 'moving average sales' of the dataset 'Sales'. The graph shows that in the first two months the 'monthly sales' is below is the 'average sales' and then in the next couple of months the 'monthly sales' is almost equal to the 'average sales'. The value of 'monthly sales' is higher then the 'average sales' during 8, 9, 10, 20, 21 and 22 months, the rest of the period shows that either the sales is low or equal to the 'average sales'. The outcome of this graph is that in these twenty four 'months sales' of the company, twelve months the sales is below the expected 'average sales' and in six months the sales is higher then the expected 'average sales' and in the remain six months the sales is equal to the expected 'average sales'.

The graph in figure 34 shows a relationship between 'average sales' and the 'forecast sales' of the dataset 'Sales'. The graph shows that in the beginning the 'average sales' and the 'forecast sales' are equal, in the middle of the graph the 'average sales' is either higher or equal then the 'forecast sales' values. The graph also shows that the gap between two values is quite significant during 20, 21 and 22 months i.e. the value of 'average sales' is much higher then the 'forecast sales' but at the end of the graph both values are again equal. The outcome of this graph is that during this period 'average sales' is higher then the 'forecast sales' values.

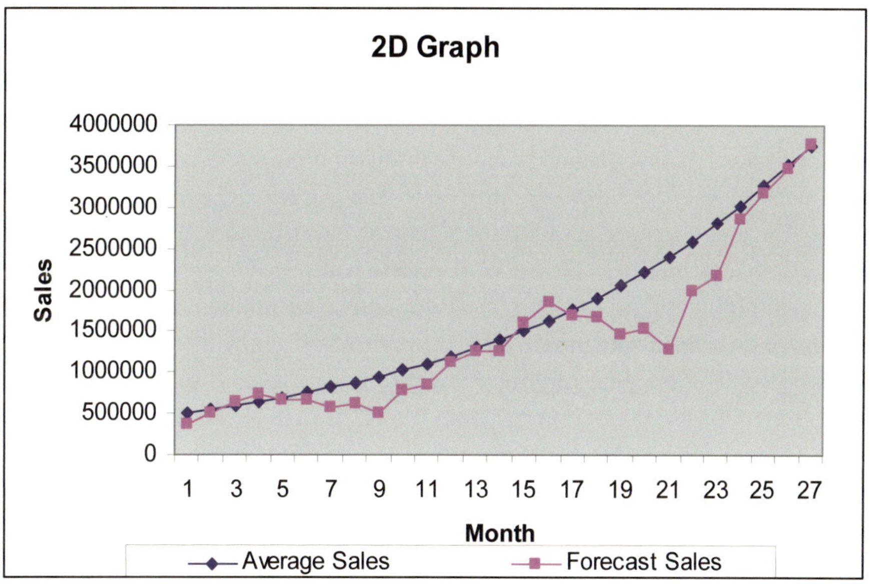

Figure 34. Graph between 'average sales' and 'forecast sales' of 'Sales' dataset

The graph in figure 35 shows a relationship between 'calculated seasonal index' and 'average index' of the dataset 'Sales'. The graph shows that at the beginning the 'calculated seasonal index' is either below or above the 'average index' and the trend remains the same up to the middle of the graph, after this both values are same up to the end of the graph. The 'knowledge' extracted from this graph is that the forecast values of sales are equal to the average sales which shows the trend of profit.

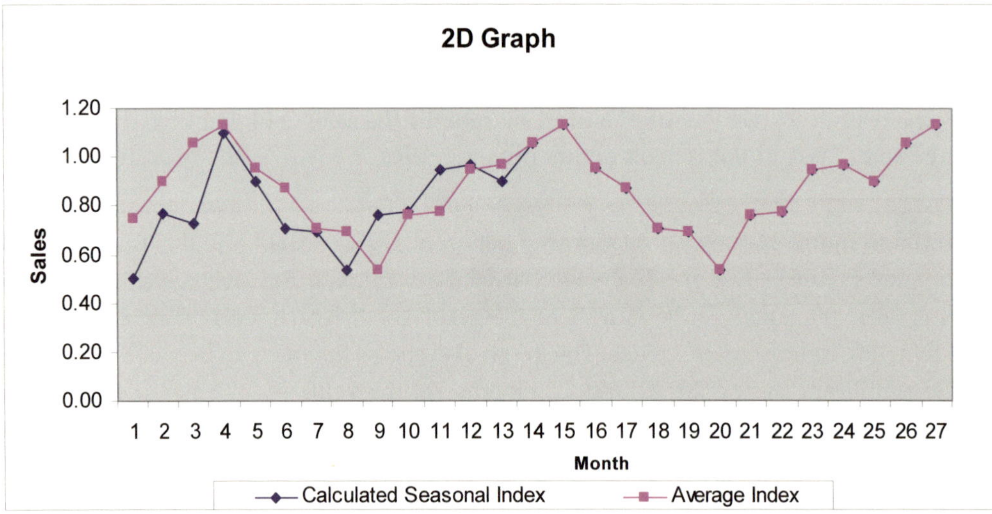

Figure 35. Graph between 'calculated seasonal index' and 'average index' of 'Sales' dataset

6. Conclusion

The book chapter presents a unified data mining theory and then the mathematical formulation of the unified data mining theory (UDMT). The data mining processes; clustering, classification and visualization are unified by means of mathematical functions. The chosen data mining algorithms are proved to be as functions i.e. the algorithms are used as functions. The first function takes the set of data as input, applies K-means clustering data mining algorithm and produces the set of clusters as output. The second function takes the set of clusters as input, applies the C4.5 (Decision Tree) data mining algorithm and produces the set of rules as output and finally the third function takes the set of rules as input, applies data visualization data mining algorithm and produces the set of 2D graphs as output. The functions are the mappings from the set of data to the set of clusters to the set of rules to the set of 2D graphs. From the set of 2D graphs one can interpret and evaluate the results to discover the knowledge i.e. the knowledge is extracted from the given dataset through the unified process of the composition of clustering, classification and visualization followed by interpretation and evaluation of the results. Thus, we attempt to unify the processes of data mining life cycle. In summary we can say, first pass the set of data through the composition of clustering, classification and visualization and then the obtained results are interpreted and evaluated to extract the knowledge. The proposed unified data mining theory covers all the pertinent essentials of the unified theory i.e. generates truly applicable explanations and predictions of the real world problems and does not contradict itself, therefore, we can say that it is comprehensiveness, precise, consistent and correct. The UDMT is tested on variety of datasets and the knowledge is discovered through the unified processes of data mining. On the basis of UDMT, a tool namely; UDMTool, multiagent systems, is developed, which takes dataset as input and produces the knowledge as output. At this stage we can conclude that the results obtained through the UDMT are satisfactory and consistent. For future consideration, more tests can be conducted to validate the proposed UDMT.

Author details

Dost Muhammad Khan
Department of Computer Science & IT, The Islamia University of Bahawalpur, Pakistan;
School of Innovative Technologies & Engineering, University of Technology Mauritius (UTM), Mauritius

Nawaz Mohamudally
Consultancy & Technology Transfer Centre, Manager, University of Technology, Mauritius (UTM), Mauritius

D. K. R. Babajee
Department of Applied Mathematical Sciences, SITE, University of Technology, Mauritius (UTM), Mauritius

Acknowledgement

The first author is thankful to The Islamia University of Bahawalpur, Pakistan for providing financial assistance to carry out this research activity under HEC project 6467/F – II.

7. References

Brog, Xavier., (2011). Unified Theory Foundations, Blaze Labs URL http://blazelabs.com/f-u-intro.asp

Dalton, J., (1808). *A New System of Chemical Philosophy*

Darwin, C., (1859). *On the Origin of Species by Means of Natural Selection, or the Preservation of Favoured Races in the Struggle for Life*

Das, Somenath, (2007). Unified data mining engine as a system of patterns, *Master's Theses*. Paper3440.http://scholarworks.sjsu.edu/etd_theses/3440

Davidson, Ian, (2002). Understanding K-Means Non-hierarchical Clustering, SUNY Albany–Technical Report

Dhillon IS, Guan Y, Kulis B, (2004). Kernel k-means: spectral clustering and normalized cuts, KDD 2004, pp 551–556

Dries. Lou van den. (2007). Mathematical Logic, Math 570, Lecture Notes, Fall Semester 2007

Gray RM, Neuhoff DL, (1998). Quantization, IEEE Trans Inform Theory 44(6):2325–2384

Grossman. Robert, Kasif. Simon, Moore. Reagan, Rocke. David., & Ullman. Jeff, (1998). Data Mining Research: Opportunities and Challenges, *A Report of three NSF Workshops on Mining Large, Massive, and Distributed Data*, (Draft 8.4.5)

Hunt EB, Marin J, Stone PJ, (1996). Experiments in Induction, Academic Press, New York

Jain AK, Dubes RC, (1988). Algorithms for clustering data, Prentice-Hall, Englewood Cliffs

Johnson, P., Ekstedt, M., (2007). In Search of a Unified Theory of Software Engineering, International Conference on Software Engineering Advances (ICSEA 2007)

Khan, Dost Muhammad., & Mohamudally, Nawaz., (2010). A Multiagent System (MAS) for the Generation of Initial Centroids for k-means clustering Data Mining Algorithm based on Actual Sample Datapoints, *Journal of Next Generation Information Technology,* Vol. 1, Number 2, 31 August 2010, pp(85-95), ISSN: 2092-8637

Khan, Dost Muhammad., & Mohamudally, Nawaz., (2010). An Agent Oriented Approach for Implementation of the Range Method of Initial Centroids in K-Means Clustering Data Mining Algorithm, *International Journal of Information Processing and Management,* Volume 1, Number 1, July 2010 (pp 104-113), ISSN: 2093-4009

Khan, Dost Muhammad., & Mohamudally, Nawaz., (2011). An Integration of k-means clustering and Decision Tree (ID3) towards a more Efficient Data Mining Algorithm, Journal of Computing, Volume 3, Issue 12, 2011, pp 76-82, ISSN: 2151-9617

King, G., R. Keohane, and S. Verba, (1994). *Designing Social Inquiry: Scientific Inference in Qualitative Research*, Princeton University Press

Kuhn, T., (1962). *The Structure of Scientific Revolution*, University of Chicago Press

Li, Xining., Ni, JingBo., (2007). Deploying Mobile Agents in Distributed Data Mining, International workshop on High Performance Data Mining and Applications (HPDMA 2007) China

Liu, Bing, (2007). Web Data Mining Exploring Hyperlinks, Contents, and Usage Data, ISBN-13 978-3-540-37881-5, Springer Berlin Heidelberg New York pp. 124 -139

Lloyd SP, (1982). Least squares quantization in PCM. Unpublished Bell Lab. Tech. Note, portions presented at the Institute of Mathematical Statistics Meeting Atlantic City, NJ, September 1957. Also, IEEE Trans Inform Theory (Special Issue on Quantization), vol IT-28, pp 129–137

Lovász. L. , Pelikán. J., Vesztergombi. K. (2003). Discrete Mathematics: Elementary and Beyond, pp. 38, Springer, ISBN: 0-387-95585-2

MacQueen, J.B., (1967). Some Methods for classification and Analysis of Multivariate Observations, *Proceedings of 5-th Berkeley Symposium on Mathematical Statistics and Probability*, Berkeley, University of California Press, p: 281-297

MathWorksheetsGo (2011). Evaluating Functions. at URL: www.MathWorksheetsGo.com

Mendeleev, D., (1869). *Principles of Chemistry*

Mielikäinen, Taneli., (2004). Inductive Databases as Ranking, In: DaWak, Zaragoza, Spain

Mohamudally, Nawaz., Khan, Dost Muhammad. (2011). Application of a Unified Medical Data Miner (UMDM) for Prediction, Classification, Interpretation and Visualization on Medical Datasets: The Diabetes Dataset Case, P. Perner (Ed.): ICDM 2011, LNAI 6870, Springer-Verlag Berlin Heidelberg pp. 78–95

Moore Andrew W., (2001).VC-dimension for characterizing classifiers, Carnegie Mellon University at URL: www.cs.cmu.edu/~awm

Newell, A., (1990). *Unified Theories of Cognition*, Harvard University Press

Newton, I., (1687). *Philosophiae Naturalis Principia Mathematica.*

Peng, Y., Kou, G., Shi, Y., Chen, Z., (2008). A Descriptive Framework for the Field of Data Mining and Knowledge Discovery, International Journal of Information Technology and Decision Making, Vol. 7, Issue: 4, Page 639-682

Peter Stone, & Manuela Veloso (1997). Multiagent Systems: A Survey from a Machine Learning Perspective, URL: http://www.cs.cmu.edu/afs/cs/usr/pstone/public/papers/97MAS-survey/revised-survey.html

Popper K., (1980). *The Logic of Scientific Discovery*, Hutchinson, 1st impression 1959

Quinlan JR, (1979). Discovering rules by induction from large collections of examples, In: Michie D (ed), Expert systems in the micro electronic age. Edinburgh University Press, Edinburgh

Quinlan JR, (1993). C4.5: Programs for machine learning, Morgan Kaufmann Publishers, San Mateo

Sarabjot S. Anand, David A. Bell, John G. Hughes, (1996). EDM: A general framework for Data Mining based on Evidence Theory, Data & Knowledge Engineering 18 (1996) 189-223, *School of Information and Software Engineering, Faculty of Informatics, University of Ulster (Jordanstown), UK*

Schwann, T., (1839). *Mikroskopische Untersuchungen uber die Ubereinstimmung in der Structur und dent Wachsthum der Thiere und Pflanzen*

Singh. Shivanshu K., Eranti. Vijay Kumer., & Fayad. M.E., (2010). Focus Group on Unified Data Mining Engine (UDME 2010): *Addressing Challenges, Focus Group Proposal*

Steinbach M, Karypis G, Kumar V, (2000). A comparison of document clustering techniques. In: Proceedings of the KDD Workshop on Text Mining

Two crows, (1999). Introduction to Data Mining and Knowledge Discovery, ISBN: 1-892095-02-5, Third Edition by Two Crows Corporation

Unified Theory or Theory of Everything (TOE), (2001). URL: http://searchcio-midmarket.techtarget.com/ definition/unified-field-theory

US Census Bureau, (2009). Iris, Diabetes, Vote and Breast datasets at URL: www.sgi.com/tech/mlc/db

Wooldridge, M, Jennings, N. R., Kinny, D., (2000). "The Gaia Methodology for Agent-Oriented Analysis and Design", Kluwer Academic Publishers

Wu. Xindong, Kumar. Vipin, Quinlan., & J. Ross, et al, (2008). Top 10 algorithms in data mining, SURVEYPAPER, *Knowl Inf Syst* (2008) 14:1–37

Yang. Qlang., & Wu. Xindong, (2006). 10 CHALLENGING PROBLEMS IN DATA MINING RESEARCH, *International Journal of Information Technology & Decision Making,* Vol. 5, No. 4 (2006) 597–604

Chapter 2

Selecting Representative Data Sets

Tomas Borovicka, Marcel Jirina Jr., Pavel Kordik and Marcel Jirina

Additional information is available at the end of the chapter

http://dx.doi.org/10.5772/50787

1. Introduction

A training set is a special set of labeled data providing known information that is used in the supervised learning to build a classification or regression model. We can imagine each training instance as a feature vector together with an appropriate output value (label, class identifier). A supervised learning algorithm deduces a classification or regression function from the given training set. The deduced classification or regression function should predict an appropriate output value for any input vector. The goal of the training phase is to estimate parameters of a model to predict output values with a good predictive performance in real use of the model.

When a model is built we need to evaluate it in order to compare it with another model or parameter settings or in order to estimate predictive performance of the model. Strategies and measures for the model evaluation are described in section 2.

For a reliable future error prediction we need to evaluate our model on a different, independent and identically distributed set that is different to the set that we have used for building the model. In absence of an independent identically distributed dataset we can split the original dataset into more subsets to simulate the effect of having more datasets. Some splitting algorithms proposed in literature are described in section 3.

During a learning process most learning algorithms use all instances from the given training set to estimate parameters of a model, but commonly lot of instances in the training set are useless. These instances can not improve predictive performance of the model or even can degrade it. There are several reasons to ignore these useless instances. The first one is a noise reduction, because many learning algorithms are noise sensitive [31] and we apply these algorithms before learning phase. The second reason is to speed up a model response by reducing computation. It is especially important for instance-based learners such as k-nearest neighbours, which classify instances by finding the most similar instances from a training set and assigning them the dominant class. These types of learners are commonly called lazy learners, memory-based learners or case-based learners [14]. Reduction of training sets can be necessary if the sets are huge. The size and structure of a training set needed to correctly estimate the parameters of a model can differ from problem to problem and a chosen instance

INTECH
open science | open minds

©2012 Jirina et al., licensee InTech. This is an open access chapter distributed under the terms of the Creative Commons Attribution License (http://creativecommons.org/licenses/by/3.0), which permits unrestricted use, distribution, and reproduction in any medium, provided the original work is properly cited.

selection method [14]. Moreover, the chosen instance selection method is closely related to the classification and regression method. The process of instance reduction is also called instance selection in the literature. A review of instance selection methods is in section 4.

The most of learning algorithms assumes that the training sets, used to estimate the parameters of a model or to evaluate a model, have proportionally the same representation of classes. But many particular domains have classes represented by a few instances while other classes have a large number of representative instances. Methods that deal with the class imbalance problem are described in section 5.

1.1. Basic notations

In this section we set up basic notation and definitions used in the document.

A population is a set of all existing feature vectors (features). By S we denote a sample set defined as a subset of a population collected during some process in order to obtain instances that can represent the population.

According to the previous definition the term representativeness is closely related. We can define a *representative set* S^* as a special subset of an original dataset S, which satisfies three main characteristics [72]:

1. It is significantly smaller in size compared to the original dataset.
2. It captures the most of information from the original dataset compared to any subset of the same size.
3. It has low redundancy among the representatives it contains.

A training set is in the idealized case a representative set of a population. Any of mentioned methods is not needed if we have representative subset of the population. But we never have itin practise. We usually have a random sample set of the population and we use various methods to make it as representative as possible. We will denote a training set by R.

In order to define a representative set we can define a *minimal consistent subset* of a training set. Given a training set R, we want to obtain a subset $R^* \subset R$ such that R^* is the smallest set of instances such that $Acc(R^*) \cong Acc(R)$, where $Acc(X)$ denotes the classification accuracy obtained using X as a training set [71].

Sets used for an evaluation of a model are the validation set V, usually used for a model selection, and the testing set T, used for model assessment.

2. Model evaluation

The model evaluation is an important but often underestimated part of model building and assessment. When we have prepared and preprocessed data we want to build a model with the ability to accurately predict future observations. We do not want a model that perfectly fits training data, but we need a model that is reliable after deployment in the real use. For this purpose we should have two phases of a model evaluation. In the first phase we evaluate a model **in order to estimate the parameters of the model** during the learning phase. This is a part of the model selection when we select the model with the best results. This phase is also called as the validation phase. It does not necessary mean that we choose a model that best fits a particular set of data. The well learned model captures only the underlying phenomenon, not the noise. A model that captures a noise is called as *over-fitted* [47]. In the second phase we evaluate the selected model **in order to assess the real performance of the model** on new unseen data. Process steps are shown below.

1. Model selection
   (a) Model learning (Training phase)
   (b) Model validation (Validation phase)
2. Model assessment (Testing phase)

2.1. Evaluation methods

During building a model, we need to evaluate its performance in order to validate or assess it as we mention earlier. There are more methods how to check our model, but not all are usually sufficient or applicable in all situations. We should always choose the most appropriate and reliable method for our purpose. Some of common evaluation methods are [83]:

Comparison of the model with physical theory
A comparison of the model with a physical theory is the first and probably the easiest way how to check our model. For example, if our model predicts a negative quantity or parameters outside of a possible range, it points to a poorly estimated model. However, a comparison with a physical theory is not always possible nor sufficient as a quality indicator.

Comparison of model with theoretical or empirical model
Sometimes a theoretical model exists, but may be to complicated for a practical use. In this case, the theoretical model could be used for a comparison or evaluation of the accuracy of the built model.

Collect new data for evaluation
The use of data collected in an independent experiment is the best and the most preferred way for a model evaluation. It is the only way that gives us a real estimate of the model performance on new data. Only new collected data can reveal a bias in a previous sampling process. This is the easiest way if we can easily repeat the experiment and sampling process. Unfortunately, there are situations when we are not capable to collect new independent data for this purpose either due to a high cost of the experiment or another unrepeatability of the process.

Use the same data as for model building
The use the same data for evaluation and for a model building usually leads to an optimistic estimation of real performance due to a positive bias. This is not recommended method and if there is another way it could not be used for the model evaluation at all.

Reserve part of the learning data for evaluation
A reserve part of the learning data is in practise the most common way how to deal with the absence of an independent dataset for model evaluation. As the reserve part selection from the data is usually not a simple task, many methods were invented. Their usage depends on a particular domain. Splitting the data is wished to have the same effect as having two independent datasets. However, this is not true, only newly collected data can point out the bias in the training dataset.

2.1.1. *Evaluation measures*

For evaluating a classifier or predictor there is a large variation of performance measures. However, a measure, good for evaluating a model in a particular domain, could be inappropriate in another domain and vice versa. The choice of an evaluation measure depends on the domain of use and the given problem. Moreover, different measures are used for classification and regression problems. The measures below are shortly described basics for the model evaluation. For more details see [46, 100].

Measures for classification evaluation

The basis for analysing classifier performance is a **confusion matrix**. The confusion matrix describes how well a classifier can recognize different classes. For c classes, the confusion matrix is an $n \times n$ table, which (i, j)th entry indicates the count of instances of the class i classified as j. It means that correctly classified instances are on the main diagonal of the confusion matrix. The simplest and the most common form of the confusion matrix is a two-classes matrix as it is shown in the table 1. Given two classes, we usually use a special terminology describing members of the confusion matrix. Terms *Positive* and *Negative* refer to the classes. *True Positives* are positive instances that were correctly classified, *True Negatives* are also correctly classified instances but of the negative class. On the contrary, *False Positives* are incorrectly classified positive instances and *False Negatives* are incorrectly classified negative instances.

		Predicted	
		Positive	Negative
True	Positive	True Positives (TP)	False Negatives (FN)
	Negative	False Positives (FP)	True Negatives (TN)

Figure 1. Confusion matrix

The first and the most commonly used measure is the **accuracy** denoted as $Acc(X)$. The accuracy of a classifier on a given set is the percentage of correctly classified instances. We can define the accuracy as

$$Acc(X) = \frac{correctly\ classified\ instances}{all\ instances}$$

or in a two-classes case

$$Acc(X) = \frac{TP + TN}{TP + TN + FP + FN} .$$

In order of having defined the accuracy, we can define the **error rate** of a classifier as

$$Err(X) = 1 - Acc(X) ,$$

which is the percentage of incorrectly classified instances.

If costs of making a wrong classification are known, we can assign different cost or benefit to each correct classification. This simple method is known as **costs and benefits** or **risks and gains**. The *cost matrix* has then the structure shown in Figure 2, where λ_{ij} corresponds to the cost of classifying the instance of class i to class j. Correctly classified instances have usually a zero cost ($\lambda_{ii} = \lambda_{jj} = 0$). Given a cost matrix, we can calculate the cost of a particular

		Predicted		
		Class i	...	Class j
True	Class i	λ_{ii}	...	λ_{ij}
	$\vdots$	$\vdots$	$\ddots$	$\vdots$
	Class j	λ_{ji}	...	λ_{jj}

Figure 2. Cost matrix

learned model on a given test set by summing relevant elements of the cost matrix accordingly to the model's prediction [100]. Here, the cost matrix is used as a measure, the costs are ignored during the classification. When a cost matrix is taken into account during learning a classification model, we speak about a cost-sensitive learning, which is mentioned in section 5 in the context of class balancing.

Using the accuracy measure fails in cases, when classes are significantly imbalanced (The class imbalanced problem is discussed in section 5). Good examples could be medical data, where we can have a lot of negative instances (for example 98%) and just a few (2%) of positive instances. It gives an impressive 98% accuracy, when we simply classify all instances as negative, which is absolutely unacceptable for medical purposes. The reason for this is that the contribution of a class to the overall accuracy rate is a function of its cardinality, with the effect that rare positives have an almost insignificant impact on the performance measure [22].

Alternatives for the accuracy measure are:
Sensitivity (also called *True Positive Rate* or *Recall*) - the percentage of truly positive instances that were classified as positive,

$$sensitivity = \frac{TP}{TP + FN} .$$

Specificity (also called *True Negative Rate*) - the percentage of truly negative instances that were classified as negative,

$$specificity = \frac{TN}{TN + FP} .$$

Precision - the percentage of positively classified instances that are truly positive,

$$precision = \frac{TP}{TP + FP} .$$

It can be shown that the accuracy is a function of the sensitivity and specificity:

$$accuracy = sensitivity \cdot \frac{TP + FN}{TP + TN + FP + FN} + specificity \cdot \frac{TN + FP}{TP + TN + FP + FN} .$$

F-measure combines precision and recall. It is generally defined as

$$F_\beta = (1 + \beta^2) \frac{precision \cdot recall}{\beta^2 \cdot precision + \cdot recall}$$

where β specifies the relative importance of precision and recall. The F-measure can be interpreted as a weighted average of the precision and recall. A disadvantage of this measure is that it does not take the true negative rate into account. Another measure, that overcomes disadvantages of the accuracy on imbalanced datasets is the **geometric mean** of class accuracies. For the two-classes case it is defined as

$$gm = \sqrt{\frac{TP}{TP+FN} \cdot \frac{TN}{TN+FP}} = \sqrt{sensitivity \cdot specificity}$$

The geometric mean puts all classes on an equal footing, unfortunately there is no way to overweight any class [22].

The evaluation measure should be appropriate to the domain of use. If is it possible, usually the best way to write a report is to provide the whole confusion matrix. The reader than can calculate the measure which he is most interested in.

Measures for regression evaluation

The measures described above are mainly used for classification problems rather than for regression problems. For regression problems more appropriate error measures are used. They are focused on how close is the actual model to the ideal model instead of looking if the predicted value is correct or incorrect. The difference between known value y and predicted value $f(x_i)$ is measured by so called **loss functions**. Commonly used loss functions (errors) are described bellow.

The **square loss** is one of the most common measures used for regression purposes, is it defined as

$$l(y_i, f(x_i)) = (y_i - f(x_i))^2$$

A disadvantage of this measure is its sensitivity to outliers (because squaring of the error scales the loss quadratically). Therefore, data should be filtered for outliers before using of this measure. Another measure commonly used in regression is the **absolute loss**, defined as

$$l(y_i, f(x_i)) = |y_i - f(x_i)|$$

It avoids the problem of outliers by scaling the loss linearly. Closely similar measure to the absolute loss is the **ϵ-insensitive loss**. The difference between both is that this measure does not penalize errors within some defined range ϵ. It is defined as

$$l(y_i, f(x_i)) = max(|y - f(x)| - \epsilon, 0)$$

The average of the loss over the dataset is called **generalization error** or **error rate**. On the basis of the loss functions described above we can define the **mean absolute error** and **mean squared error** as

$$MAE = \frac{1}{n}\sum_{i=1}^{n}|y_i - f(x_i)|$$

and

$$MSE = \frac{1}{n}\sum_{i=1}^{n}(y_i - f(x_i))^2$$

, respectively. Often used measure is also the **root mean squared error**

$$RMSE = \sqrt{\frac{1}{n}\sum_{i=1}^{n}(y_i - f(x_i))^2}$$

, which has the same scale as the quantity being estimated. As well as the squared loss the mean squared error is sensitive to outliers, while the mean absolute error is not. When a relative measure is more appropriate, we can use the **relative absolute error**

$$RAE = \frac{\sum_{i=1}^{n}|y_i - f(x_i)|}{\sum_{i=1}^{n}|y_i - \bar{y}|}$$

or the **relative squared error**

$$RSE = \frac{\sum_{i=1}^{n}(y_i - f(x_i))^2}{\sum_{i=1}^{n}(y_i - \bar{y})}$$

where $\bar{y} = \frac{1}{n}\sum_{i=1}^{n} y_i$.

2.1.2. Bias and variance

With the most important performance measure - the mean square error, the bias, variance and bias/variance dilemma is directly related. They are described thoroughly in [41]. Due the importance of these characteristics, it is in place to describe them more in detail.

With given statistical model characterized by parameter vector θ we define estimator $\hat{\theta}$ of this model (classification or regression model in our case) as a function of n observations of x and we denote it as

$$\hat{\theta} = \hat{\theta}(x_1, \ldots, x_N)$$

The MSE is equal to the sum of the variance and the squared bias of the estimate, formally

$$MSE(\hat{\theta}) = Var(\hat{\theta}) + Bias(\hat{\theta})^2$$

Thus either bias or variance can contribute to poor performance of the estimator.

The **bias** of an estimator is defined as a difference between the expected value of the method and the true value of the parameter, formally

$$Bias(\hat{\theta}) = E[\hat{\theta}] - \theta = E[\hat{\theta} - \theta]$$

In another words the bias says whether the estimator is correct on average. If the bias is equal to zero, the estimator is said to be unbiased. The estimator can be biased for many reasons, but the most common source of an optimistic bias is using of the training data (or not independent data from the training data) to estimate predictive performance.

The **variance** gives us an interval within which the error appears. For an unbiased estimator the MSE is equal to the variance. It means that even though an estimator is unbiased it still may have large MSE if the variance is large.

Since the MSE can be decomposed into a sum of the bias and variance, both characteristics need to be minimized to achieve good predictive performance. It is common to trade-off some increase in the bias for a larger decrease in the variance [41].

2.2. Comparing algorithms

When we have learned more models and we need to select the best one, we usually use some of described measures to estimate the performance of the model and then we simply choose the one with the highest performance. This is often sufficient way for a model selection. Another problem is when we need to prove the improvement in the model performance, especially if we want to show that one model really outperforms another on a particular learning task. In this way we have to use a test of statistical significance and verify the hypothesis of the improved performance.

The most known and most popular in machine learning is the **paired t test** and its improved version the **k-fold cross-validated pair test**. In paired t test the originial set S is randomly devided into a training set R and a testing set T. Models M_1 and M_2 are trained on the set R and tested on the set T. This process is repeated k times(usually 30 times [28]). If we assume that each partitioning is drawn independently, then also individual error rates can be considered as different and independent samples from a probability distribution, which follow t *distribution* with k degrees of freedom. Our null hypothesis is that the difference in mean error rates is zero. Then the *Student's t test* is computed as follows

$$t = \frac{\sum_{i=1}^{k} (Err(M_1)_i - Err(M_2)_i)}{\sqrt{Var(M_1 - M_2)/k}}$$

Unfortunately the given assumption is less than true. Individual error rates are not independent as well as error rate differences are not independent, because the training sets and the testing sets in each iteration overlaps. The **k-fold cross-validated pair test** mentioned above is build on the same basis. The difference is in the splitting into a training and a testing set, instead of a random dividing. The original set S is splitted into k disjoint folds of the same size. In each iteration one fold is used for testing and remaining $k-1$ folds for training the model. In this approach each test set is independent of the others, but the training sets still overlaps. For more details see [28].

The improved version, **the 5xcv paired t test**, proposed in [28] performs 5 replications of 2-fold cross-validation. In each replication, the original dataset is divided into two subsets S_1 and S_2 and each model is trained on each set and tested on the other set. This approach solves the problem of overlapping (correlated) folds, which led to poorly estimated means and large t values.

Another approaches described in literature are **McNemar's test** [33], **The test for the difference of two proportions** [82] and many others.

Methods described above consider comparison over one dataset, for comparison of classifiers over multiple data sets see [26].

2.3. Dataset comparison

In some cases we need to compare two datasets, if they have the same distributions. For example if we split the original dataset into a training and a testing set, we expect that a representative sample will be in each subset and distributions of the sets will be the same (with a specific tolerance of deviation). If we assess splitting algorithms, one of the criteria will be the capability of the algorithm to divide the original dataset into the two identically distributed subsets.

For comparing datasets distributions we should use a statistical test under the null hypothesis that distributions of the datasets are the same. These tests are usually called **goodness-of-fit** tests and they are widely described in literature [2, 8, 59, 85]. For an univariate case we can compare distributions relatively easily using one of the numerous graphical or statistical tests e.g. histograms, PP and QQ plots, the Chi-square test for a dicrete multinominal distribution or the Kolmogorov-Smirnov non-parametric test. For more details see [87].

A multivariate case is more complicated because generalization to more dimensions is not so straightforward. Generalization of the most cited goodness-of-fit test, the Kolmogorov-Smirnov test, is in [10, 35, 54].

In the case of comparing two subsets of one set, we use a naive approach for their comparison. We suppose that two sets are approximately the same, based on comparing basic multivariate data characteristic. We believe, that for our purpose the naive approach is sufficient. Advantages of this approach are its simplicity and a low computational complexity in comparison with the goodness-of-fit tests. A description of commonly used multivariate data characteristics follows.

The first characteristic is the **mean vector**. Let $\mathbf{x}$ represent a random vector of p variables, and $\mathbf{x}_i = (x_{i1}, x_{i2}, \ldots, x_{ip})$ denote the i-th instance in the sample set, the **sample mean error** is defined as

$$\bar{\mathbf{x}} = \frac{1}{n}\sum_{i=1}^{n} x_i = \begin{pmatrix} \bar{\mathbf{x}}_1 \\ \bar{\mathbf{x}}_2 \\ \vdots \\ \bar{\mathbf{x}}_p \end{pmatrix}$$

where n is the number of observations. Thus $\bar{x}_i$ is the mean of the i-th variable on the n observations. The mean of $\mathbf{x}$ over all possible instances in the population is called **population mean vector** and is defined as a vector of expected values of each variable, formally

$$\boldsymbol{\mu} = E(\mathbf{x}) = \begin{pmatrix} E(x_1) \\ E(x_2) \\ \vdots \\ E(x_p) \end{pmatrix} = \begin{pmatrix} \mu_1 \\ \mu_2 \\ \vdots \\ \mu_p \end{pmatrix}$$

Therefore, $\bar{\mathbf{x}}$ is an estimate of $\boldsymbol{\mu}$.

Second characteristic is the **covariance matrix**. Let $s_{jk} = \frac{1}{n-1}\sum_{i=1}^{n}(x_{ij} - \bar{x}_j)(x_{ik} - \bar{x}_k)$ be a sample covariance between j-th and k-th variable. We define the **sample covariance matrix** as

$$S = \begin{pmatrix} s_{1,1} & s_{1,2} & \cdots & s_{1,p} \\ s_{2,1} & s_{2,2} & \cdots & s_{2,p} \\ \vdots & \vdots & \ddots & \vdots \\ s_{p,1} & s_{p,2} & \cdots & s_{p,p} \end{pmatrix}$$

Because $s_{jk} = s_{kj}$, the covariance matrix is symmetric and there are variances s_j^2, the squares of standard deviations s_j, on the diagonal of the matrix. Therefore, the covariance matrix is also called **variance-covariance** matrix. As for the mean, the covariance matrix over whole population is called **population covariance matrix** and is defined as

$$\Sigma = cov(\mathbf{x}) = \begin{pmatrix} \sigma_{1,1} & \sigma_{1,2} & \cdots & \sigma_{1,p} \\ \sigma_{2,1} & \sigma_{2,2} & \cdots & \sigma_{2,p} \\ \vdots & \vdots & \ddots & \vdots \\ \sigma_{p,1} & \sigma_{p,2} & \cdots & \sigma_{p,p} \end{pmatrix}$$

where $\sigma_{jk} = E[(x_j - \mu_j)(x_k - \mu_k)]$.

The covariance matrix contains $p \times p$ values corresponding to all pairs of variables and their covariances. The covariance matrix could be inconvenient in some cases and therefore it can be desired to have one single number as an overall characteristic. One measure summarising the covariance matrix is called **generalized sample variance** and is defined as the determinant of the covariance matrix

$$generalized\ sample\ variance = |S|$$

The geometric interpretation of the generalized sample variance is a p-dimensional hyperellipsoid centered at $\bar{\mathbf{x}}$.

More details about the multivariate data characteristic can be found in [77].

3. Data splitting

In the ideal situation we have collected more independent data sets or we can simply and inexpensively repeat an experiment to collect new ones. We can use independent data sets for learning, model selection and even an assessment of the prediction performance. In this situation we have not any reason to split any particular dataset. But in situation when only one dataset is available and we are not capable to collect new data, we need some strategy to perform particular tasks described earlier. In this section we review several data splitting strategies and data splitting algorithms which try to deal with the problem of absence of independent datasets.

3.1. Data splitting strategies

When only one dataset is given, several possible ways how to use available data come into consideration to perform tasks described in section 2 (training, validation, testing). We can split available data into two or more parts and use each to perform a particular task. Common practise is to split data into two or three sets:

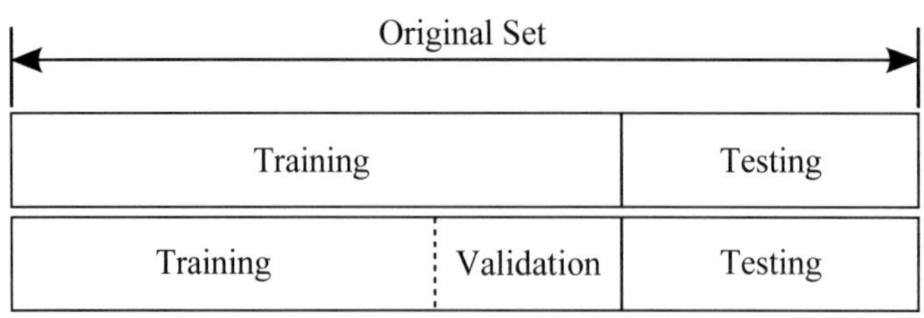

Figure 3. Two and three way splitting

Training set - a set used for learning and estimating parameters of the model.

Validation set - a set used to evaluate the model, usually for model selection.

Testing set - a set of examples used to assess the predictive performance of the model.

Let us define following data splitting strategies according to how data used in a process of model building are available.

The null strategy (*Strategy 0*) is when all available data are used for all tasks. Training, selecting and making an assessment on the same data usually leads to over-fitting of the model and to an over-optimistic estimate of the predictive accuracy. The error estimated on the same set as the model was trained is known as **re-substitution error**.

The strategy motivated by the arrival of new data (*Strategy 1*) uses one set for training and the second set, containing the first set and newly collected data, for the assessment. Merging new collected data with the old data loses the independence of model selection and assessment, which can lead to an over-optimistic estimate of the performance of the model.

The most commonly used strategy is to split data into two sets, a training set and a testing set. The training set (also called the estimation set) is used to estimate the parameters of the model and also for model selection (validation). The testing set is then used to assess the prediction performance of the model (*Strategy 2*).

Another strategy (*Strategy 3*) which splits data into two sets uses one set for learning and the second for model selection and to assess its predictive performance.

The use an independent set for each task is generally recommended. This strategy (*Strategy 4*) splits available data into three sets.

Strategy	Training	Validation	Testing
0	All data	All data	All data
1	Part 1	All data	All data
2	Part 1	Part 1	Part 2
3	Part 1	Part 2	Part 2
4	Part 1	Part 2	Part 3

Table 1. Data usage in different splitting strategies

3.2. Data splitting algorithms

Many data splitting algorithms were proposed. Quality and complexity of algorithms differ and not any approach is superior in general. Data splitting methods and algorithms and their comparison can be found in literature [15, 68, 83, 86]. Some of commonly used algorithms are described bellow.

The holdout method described in [67] is the simplest method that takes an original dataset and splits it randomly into two sets. Common practise is to use one third for testing and the rest for training or half to half. Assuming that the performance of the model increases with the count of seen instances and decreases with the count of left instances apart of the training leads to higher bias and decreases the performance. In other words, both subsets might have different distributions. Moreover, if a dataset is not large enough, and it is usually not, the holdout method is inefficient in the use of data. For example in a classification problem one or more classes might be missing in one of the subsets, which leads to poor estimation of the model as well as to its evaluation. In deal with this some advanced versions use so called stratification. *Stratified sampling* is a probability sampling, where an original dataset is divided into non-overlapping groups called strata, and instances are selected from each strata proportionally to the appropriate probability. It ensures that each class is represented with the same frequency in both subsets. But it still does not prevent inception of the bias in training and testing sets. For better reliability of the error estimation, the methods are repeated and the resulting accuracy is calculated as an average over all iterations. It can positively reduce the bias. The **Repeated holdout** method is also known as Monte Carlo Cross-validation, Random Sub-sampling or Repeated Evaluation Sets.

The most popular resampling method is **Cross-validation**. In **k-fold cross-validation**, the original data set is splitted into k disjoint folds of the same size, where k is a parameter of the method. In each from k turns one fold is used for evaluation and the remaining $k-1$ folds for model learning as shown in Figure 4. As in the repeated holdout method, the resulting accuracy is the average of all turns. As well as holdout method, k-fold cross-validation suffers on a pessimistic bias, when k is small. Increasing the count of folds reduces the bias, but increases the variance of the estimation [41]. Experiments have shown that good results across different domains have the k-fold cross-validation method with ten folds [40], but in general k is unfixed. The k-fold cross-validation is very similar to the repeated holdout method with advantage that all the instances of the original data set are used for learning the model and even for evaluation.

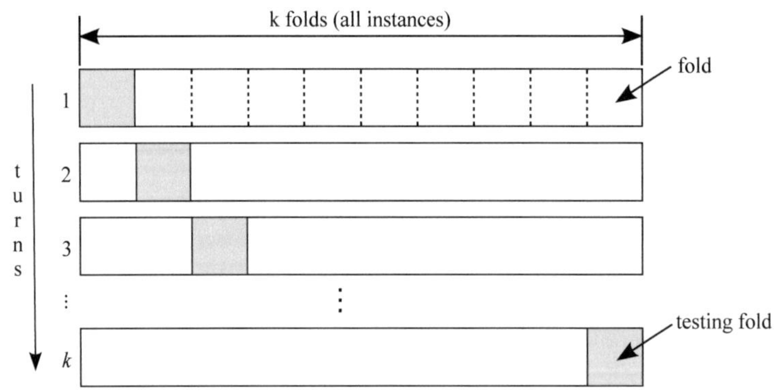

Figure 4. Cross-validation

Leave-one-out cross-validation (LOOCV) is the special case of the k-fold cross-validation in which $k = n$, where n is the size of the original dataset. All test sets have always only one instance. This method makes the best use of data and does not involve any random sub-sampling. According to this, the LOOCV gives nearly unbiased estimates of a model performance but usually with large variability. However, this method is extremely computationally expensive, that makes it often inapplicable.

The **Bootstrap** method was introduced in [89]. The main idea of the method is described as follows. Given a dataset S of size n, generate B bootstrap samples by uniform sampling (*with replacement*), n instances from the dataset. Notice that sampling with replacement allows to select the same instance more than once. After re-sampling, estimate parameters of a model on each bootstrap sample and than estimate a prediction performance of the model on the original dataset. The overall prediction error is given by averaging these B estimates. Process is schematically shown in Figure 5.

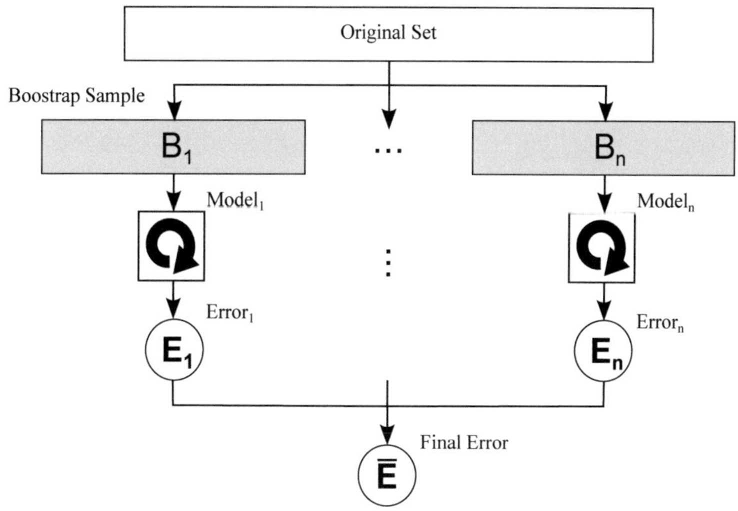

Figure 5. Bootstrap

The most known and commonly used approach is the **.632 bootstrap**. The number 0.632 in the name means the expected fraction of distinct instances of the original dataset appeared in the training set. Each instance has a probability of $1/n$ to being selected from n instances ($(1-1/n)$ to not being selected). It gives the probability of $(1-1/n)^n \approx e^{-1} \approx 0.368$ not to be selected after n samples. In other words, we expect that 63.2% instances of the original dataset will be selected for training and 36.8% remaining instances will be used for testing. The *.632 bootstrap estimate* is defined as

$$Acc(T) = \frac{1}{B}\sum_{i=1}^{B}(0.632 \cdot Acc(B_i)_{B_i'} + 0.368 \cdot Acc(B_i)_T)$$

where $Acc(B_i)_{B_i'}$ is the accuracy of the model built with bootstrap sample B_i as the training set and applied to the test set B_i' and $Acc(B_i)_T$ is the accuracy of the same model applied to the original dataset. Comparison of the bootstrap with other methods can be found in literature [5, 13, 48, 56, 89]. The results show that 0.632 bootstrap estimates have usually low variability but with a large bias in comparison with the cross-validation that gives approximately unbiased estimates, but with a high variability. It is also reported that the 0.632 bootstrap works best for small datasets. Some experiments showed that the .632 bootstrap fails in some cases, for more details see [3, 5, 11, 56].

Kennard-Stone's algorithm (CADEX) [25, 55] is used for splitting data sets into two distinct subsets which cover approximately the same region of the factor space defined by the original dataset. Instead of measuring coverage by an explicit criterion, the algorithm follows two guidelines. The first one is that no instance from one set should be too far from any instance of the other set, and the second one is that the coverage should start on the boundary of the factor space. The instances are chosen sequentially and the aim is to select the instances in each iteration to get uniformly distributed instances over the space defined by original dataset. The algorithm works as follows. Let P be the subset of already selected instances and let Q be the dataset equal to T at the beginning. We define $Dist(p,q)$ as the distance from instance $p \in P$ to instance $q \in Q$ and $\Delta_q(P)$ will be the minimal distance from instance q over the set of already selected instances in P.

$$\Delta_q(P) = arg \min_{p \in P}(Dist(p,q))$$

The algorithm starts with adding two most distant instances from Q to P (it is not necessary to select the most distant instances, they can be any instances, but accordingly to the idea of coverage, we usually choose two most distant instances). In each iteration the algorithm selects an instance from the remaining instances in the set Q using the criterion

$$\Delta_Q(P) = arg \max_{q \in Q} \Delta_q(P)$$

In other words, for each instance remaining in the data set Q find the smallest distances to already selected instances in P and choose the one with the maximal distance among these smallest distances. The process is repeat until enough objects are selected. First iteration of the algorithm is shown in Figure 6(a) and in Figure 6(b) is final result with area covered by each set. Since the algorithm uses distances it is sensitive to the used metrics and eventual outliers. For classification purposes subsets should be selected from the individual classes [24]. Improved version of CADEX named **DUPLEX** is described in [83].

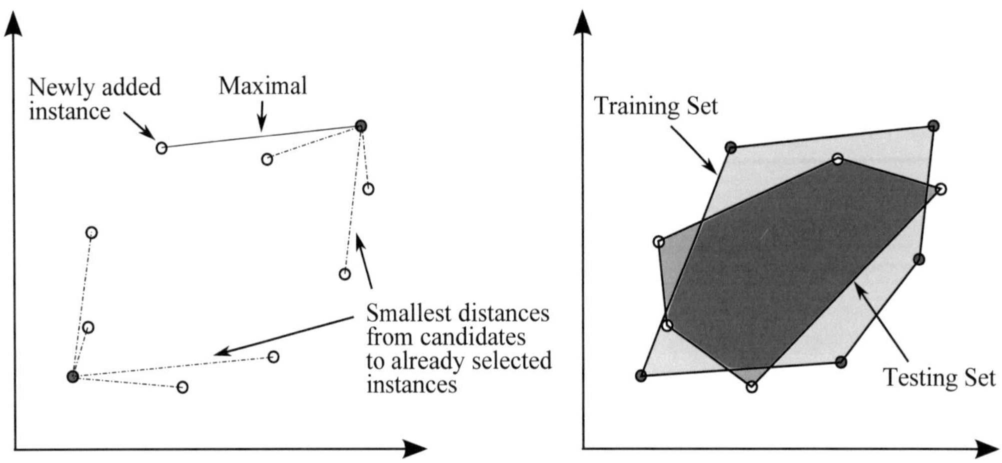

(a) First iteration (b) Factor space coverage

Figure 6. CADEX

Other methods can be considered when we take into account the following assumption. We suppose that two sets P and Q formed by splitting the original dataset S are as similar as possible when sum of distances of all pairs (one instance from the pair is from P and the other from Q) are minimized. Formally

$$d^* = \arg\min_{d} \sum_{\{p,q\} \in S} dist(p,q).$$

To find the optimal splitting to the two sets is computationally very expensive. Two heuristic approaches come to mind. The first is a method based on the **Nearest neighbour** rule. This simple method splits original datasets into two or more datasets by finding the nearest instance (nearest neighbour) of randomly chosen instance and putting each instance into a different subset. The second heuristics finds the **closest pair** (described in [88]) of instances in S and put one instance into P and the second instance into Q. This is repeated until the set T is empty. The result of these algorithms are two disjoint subsets of the original dataset. The question is how properly will this heuristics work in practice.

4. Instance selection

As was mentioned earlier the instance selection is a process of reducing original data set. A lot of instance selection methods have been described in the literature. In [14] it is argued that instance selection methods are problem dependent and none of them is superior over many problems then others. In this section we review several instance selection methods.

According to the strategy used for selecting instances, we can divide instance selection methods into two groups [71]:

Wrapper methods
The selection criterion is based on the predictive performance or the error of a model (commonly, instances that do not contribute to the predictive performance are discarded from the training set).

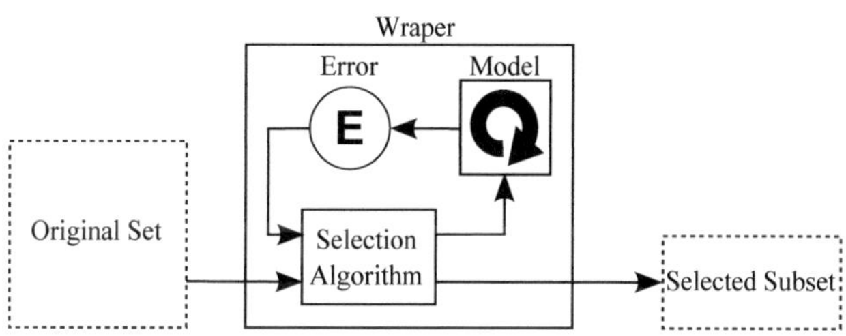

Figure 7. Wraper method

Filter methods
The selection criterion is a function that is not based upon an algorithm used for prediction but rather on features of the instance vector.

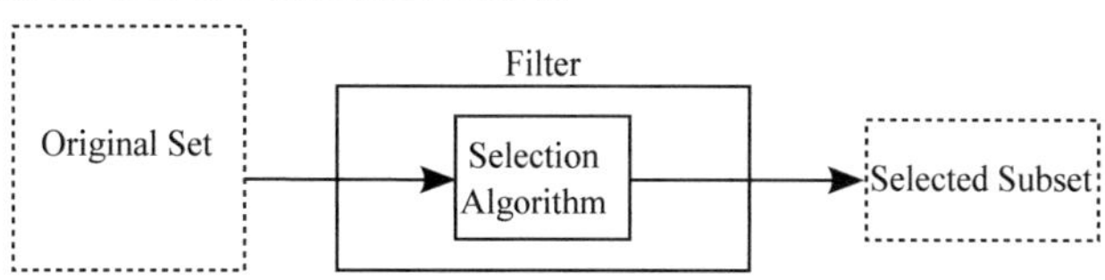

Figure 8. Filter method

Other dividing is also used in literature. Dividing of instance selection methods according to the type of application is proposed in [49]. **Noise filters** are focused on discarding useless instances while **prototype selection** is based on building a set of representatives (prototypes). How instance selection methods create final dataset offers the last presented dividing method. **Incremental methods** start with $S = \emptyset$ and take representatives from T and insert them into

S during the selection process. **Decremental methods** start with $S = T$ and remove useless instances from S during the selection process. **Mixed methods** combine previous methods during the selection process.

A good review of instance selection methods is in [65, 71]. A comparison of instance selection algorithms on several benchmark databases is presented in [50]. Some of instance selection algorithms are described bellow.

4.1. Wrapper methods

The first published instance selection algorithm is probably **Condensed Nearest Neighbour (CNN)** [23]. It is an incremental method starting with new set R which includes one instance per class chosen randomly from S. In the next step the method classifies S using R as a training set. After the classification, each wrongly classified instance from S is added to R (*absorbed*). CNN selects instances near the decision border as shown in Figure 9. Unfortunately, due to this procedure the CNN can select noise instances. Moreover, performance of the CNN is not good [43, 49].

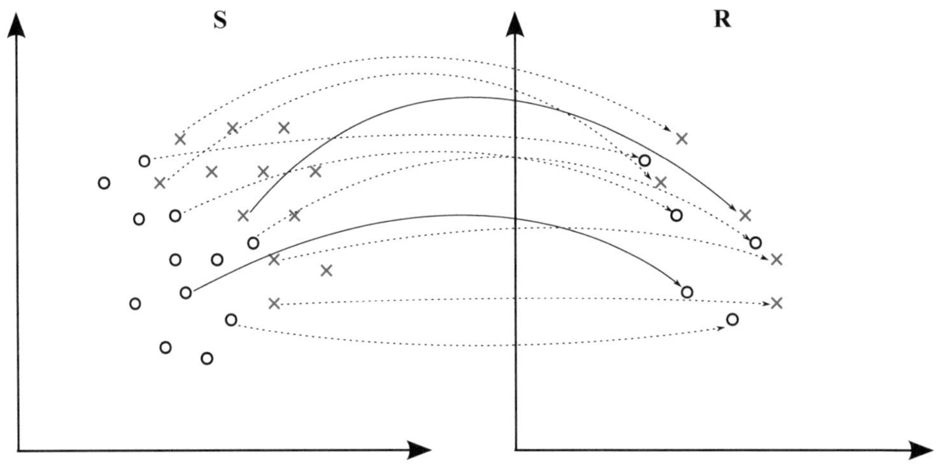

Figure 9. CNN - selected instances

Reduced Nearest Neighbour (RNN) is a modification of the CNN introduced by [39]. The RNN is a decremental method that starts with $R = S$ and removes all instances that do not decrease the predictive performance of a model trained using S.

Selective Nearest Neighbour (SNN) [79] is based on the CNN. It finds a subset $R \subset S$ satisfying that all instances are nearer to the nearest neighbour of the same class in R than to any neighbour of the other class in S.

Generalized Condensed Nearest Neighbour (GCNN)[21] is another instance selection decision rule based on the CNN. The GCNN works the same way as the CNN, but it also defines the following absorption criterion: instance x is absorbed if $\|x - q\| - \|x - p\| > \delta$, where p is the nearest neighbour of the same class as x and q is the nearest neighbour belonging to a different class than x.

Edited Nearest Neighbour (ENN) described in [98] is a decremental algorithm starting with $R = S$. The ENN removes a given instance from R if its class does not agree with the majority class of its neighbourhoods. ENN uses k-NN rule, usually with $k = 3$, to decide about the majority class, all instances misclassified by 3-NN are discarded as shown in Figure 10. An extension that runs the ENN repeatedly until no change is made in R is known as **Repeated ENN (RENN)**. Another modification of the ENN is **All k-NN** published by [90] It is an iterative method that runs the ENN repeatedly for all $k(k = 1, 2, \ldots, l)$. In each iteration misclassified instances are discarded. Another methods based on the ENN are **Multiedit** and **Editing by Estimating Conditional Class Probabilities** described in [27] and [92], respectively.

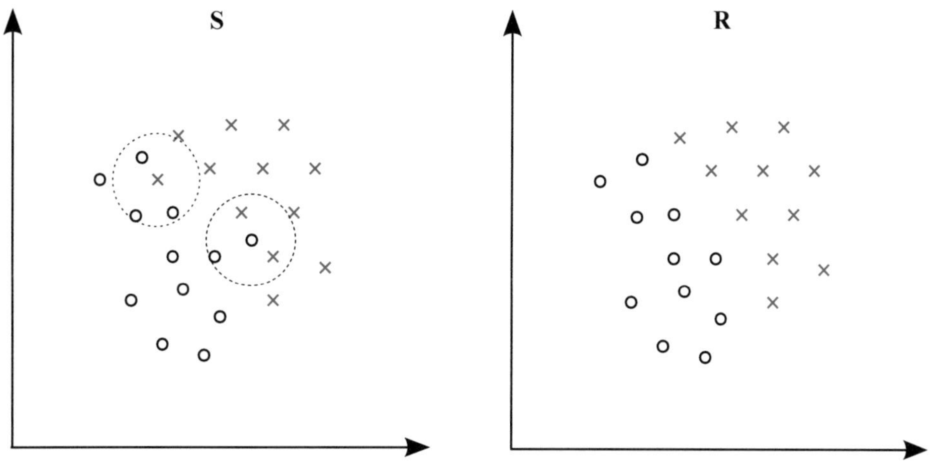

Figure 10. ENN - discarded instances (3-NN)

Instance Based (IB1-3) methods were proposed in [1]. The IB2 selects the instances misclassified by the IB1 (the IB1 is the same as the 1-NN algorithm). It is quite similar to the CNN, but the IB2 does not include one instance per class and does not repeat the process after the first pass through a training set like the CNN. The last version, the IB3, is an incremental algorithm extending the IB2. the IB3 uses a significance test and accepts an instance only if its accuracy is statistically significantly greater than the frequency of its class. Similarly, an instance is rejected if its accuracy is statistically significantly lower than the frequency of its class. Confidence intervals are used to determine the impact of the instance (0.9 to accept, 0.7 to reject).

Decremental Reduction Optimization Procedures (DROP1-5) are instance selection algorithms presented in [99]. These methods use an associate that can be defined by function $Associates(x)$ that collects all instances that have x as one of its neighbours. The DROP1 method removes instances from R that do not change a classification of its associates. The DROP2 is the same as the DROP1 but the associates are taken from the original sample set S instead of considering only instances remaining in R as the DROP1 method. The DROP3 and DROP4 methods run a noise filter first and then apply the DROP2 method. The DROP5 method is another version of the DROP2 extended of discarding the nearest opposite class instances.

Iterative Case Filtering (ICF) are described in [14]. They define $LocalSet(x)$ as a set of cases contained in the largest hypersphere centred at x such that only cases in the same class as x are contained in the hypersphere. They defined property $Adaptable(x, x')$ as $\forall x \in LocalSet(x')$.

It means that instance x can be adapted to x'. Moreover they define two properties based on the adaptable property called *reachability* and *coverage* and defined as follows.

$$Reachability(x) = x' \in S : Adaptable(x', x)$$

$$Coverage(x) = x' \in S : Adaptable(x, x')$$

The algorithm is based on these two properties. At first, the ICF uses the ENN to filter noise instances then the ICF repeatedly computes defined instance properties and in each iteration removes instances that have $|Reachability(x)| > |Coverage(x)|$. The process is repeated until no progress is observed. Another method based on the same properties, the reachability and coverage, was proposed in [104].

Many other methods were proposed in literature. Some of them are based on evolutionary algorithms (EA)[38, 64, 84, 91], other methods use the support vector machine (SVM) [9, 17, 61, 62] or tabu search (TS) [18, 42, 103].

4.2. Filter methods

The **Pattern by Ordered Projections (POP)** method [78] is a heuristic approach to find representative patterns. The main idea of the algorithm is to select only some border instances and eliminate the instances that are not on the boundaries of the regions to which they belong. It uses the function $weakness(x)$, which is defined as the number of times that example x does not represent a border in a partition for every partitions obtained from ordered projected sequences of each attribute, for discarding irrelevant instances that have weaknesses equal to the number of attributes of data set. The weakness of an instance is computed by increasing the weakness for each attribute, where the instance is not near to another instance with different class.

Another method based on finding border instances is the **Pair Opposite Class-Nearest Neighbour (POC-NN)** [75]. The POC-NN calculates the mean of all instances in each class and finds a border instance p_{b1} belonging to the class C_1 as an instance that is the nearest instance to m_2, which is the mean of class C_2. The same way it finds other border instances.

The **Maxdiff kd trees** described in [69] is a method based on *kd trees* [37]. The algorithm builds a binary tree from an original data set. All instances are in the root node and child's nodes are constructed by splitting the node by a pivot, which is a feature with the maximum difference between consecutively ordered values. The process is repeated until no node can be split. Leaves of the tree are the output condensed set.

Several methods are based on clustering. They split an original dataset into n clusters and centres of the clusters are selected as instances [9, 16, 65]. Some extensions were proposed. **The Generalized-Modified Chang algorithm (GCM)** merges the nearest clusters with the same class and uses centres of the merged clusters. **The Nearest Sub-class Classifier** method (NSB) [93] selects more instances (centres) for each class using the Maximum Variance Cluster algorithm [94]. Another method is based on clustering. The **Object Selection by Clustering (OSC)** [4] selects border instances in heterogeneous clusters and some interior instances in homogeneous clusters.

Some prototype filtering methods were proposed in the literature. The first described is **Weighting prototype (WS)**[73] method. The WS method assigns a weight to each prototype

($\forall x \in T$) and selects only those with a larger weight than a certain threshold. The WS method uses a gradient descent algorithm for computing weights of instances. Another published prototype method is **Prototype Selection by Relevance (PSR)**[70]. The PSR computes the *relevance* of each instance in T. The most similar instances in the same class are the most relevant. The PSR selects a user defined portion of relevant instances in the class and the most similar instances belonging to the different class - the border instances.

5. Class balancing

A data set is well-balanced, when all classes are represented with the same proportion, but in practise many domains of classification tasks are characterized by a small proportion of positive instances and a large proportion of negative instances, where the positive instances are usually our points of interest. This problem is commonly known as the class imbalance problem.

Although the performance of a classifier over all instances can be high, we are usually interested in classification of positive instances (true positive rate) only, where the classifier often fails, because it tends to classify all instances into the majority class. To avoid this problem some strategy should be used when a dataset is imbalanced.

Class-balancing methods can be divided into the three main groups according to the strategy of their use. Data level methods are used in preprocessing and usually utilize various ways of re-sampling. Algorithm-level methods modify a classifier or a learning process to solve the imbalance. The last strategy is based on combining various methods to increase the performance.

This chapter gives an overview of class balancing strategies and some particular methods. Two good and detailed reviews were published in [44, 57].

5.1. Data-level methods

The aim of these methods is to change distributions of classes by increasing the number of instances of the minority class (over-sampling), decreasing the number of instances of the majority class (under-sampling), by combinations of these methods or using other advanced sampling ways.

5.1.1. *Under-sampling*

The first and the most naive under-sampling method is **random under-sampling** [52]. The random under-sampling method balances the class distributions by discarding, at random, instances of the majority class. Because of the randomness of elimination, the method discards potentially useful instances, which can lead to a decrease of the model performance.

Several heuristic under-sampling methods have been proposed in literature, some of them are linked with instance selection metods mentioned in section 4. The first described algorithm is **Condensed nearest neighbour (CNN)** [23] and the second is **Wilson's Edited Nearest Neighbour (ENN)**[98]. Both are based on discarding noisy instances.

A method based on the ENN, the **Neighbourhood Cleaning Rule (NCL)** [63], discards instances from the minority and majority class separately. If an instance belongs to the majority class and it is misclassified by its three nearest neighbours' instances (the nearest neighbour rule [23]), then the instance is discarded. If an instance is misclassified in the same way and belongs to the minority class, then neighbours that belongs to the majority class are discarded.

Another method based on the *Nearest Neighbour Rule* is the **One-side Sampling (OSS)** [60] method. It is based on the idea of discarding instances distant from a decision border, since these instances can be considered as useless for learning. The OSS uses 1-NN over the set S (initially consisting of the instances of the minority class) to classify the instances in the majority class. Each misclassified instance from the majority class is moved to S.

The **Tomek Links** [90] focuses on instances near a decision border. Let p,q be instances from different classes and $dist(p,q)$ is the distance between p and q. Pair p,q is called the Tomek link if there is no closer instance of an opposite class to p or q ($dist(p,x) < dist(p,q)$ or $dist(q,x) < dist(p,q)$, where x is the instance of the opposite class than p, respectively q).

5.1.2. Over-sampling

The **random over-sampling** is a naive method, that balances class distributions by replication, at random, instances of the minority class. Two disadvantages of this method were described in literature. The first one, the instance replication increases likelihood of the over-fitting [19] and the second, enlarging the training set by the over-sampling can lead to a longer learning phase and a model response [60], mainly for lazy learners.

The most known over-sampling method is **Synthetic Minority Over-sampling Technique (SMOTE)** [19]. The SMOTE does not over-sample with replacement, instead, it generates "synthetic" instances of the minority class. The minority class is over-sampled by taking each instance of the minority class and its nearest neighbour and placing the "synthetic" instance, at random, along the line joining these instances (Figure 11). This approach avoids over-fitting and causes that a classifier creates larger and less specific decision regions, rather than smaller and more specific ones. The method based on the SMOTE reported better experimental results in *TP-rate* and *F-measure* [45], the **Borderline_SMOTE**. It over-samples only the borderline instances of the minority class.

5.1.3. Advanced sampling

Some advanced re-sampling methods are based on re-sampling of results of the preliminary classification [44].

Over-sampling Algorithm Based on Preliminary Classification (OSPC) was proposed in [46]. It was reported that the OSPC can outperform under-sampling methods and the SMOTE in terms of classification performance [44].

The heuristic method proposed in [96, 97], the **Budget-sensitive progresive sampling algorithm** iteratively enlarges a training set on the basis of performance results from the previous iteration.

A combination of over-sampling and under-sampling methods to improve generalization features of learners was proposed in [45, 58, 63]. A comparison of various re-sampling strategies is presented in [7].

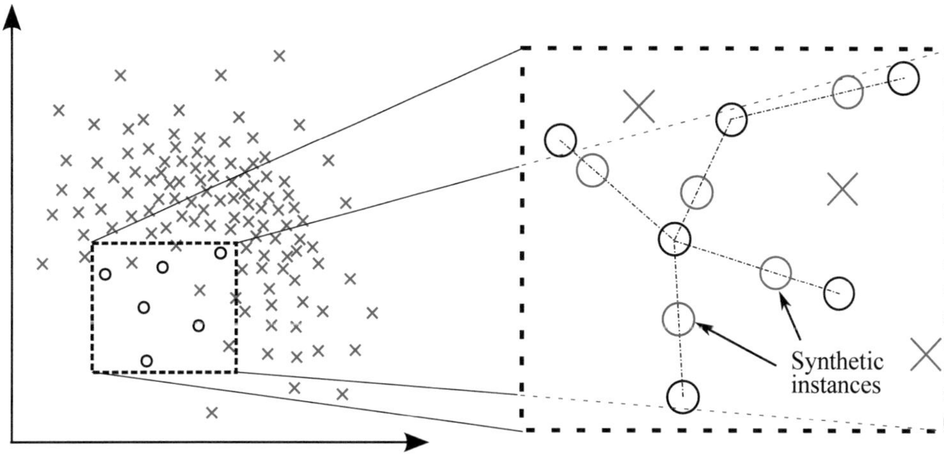

Figure 11. SMOTE - synthetic instances

5.2. Algorithm level methods

Another approach to deal with imbalanced datasets modifies a classifier or a learning process rather than changing distributions of datasets by discarding or replicating instances. These methods are mainly based on overweighting the minority class, discriminating the majority class, penalization for misclassification or biasing the learning algorithm. A short description of published methods follows.

5.2.1. *Algorithm modification*

Ineffectiveness of the over-sampling method when the C4.5 decision tree learner with the default settings is used was reported in [30]. It was noted that under-sampling produces a reasonable sensitivity to changes in misclassification costs and a class distribution when over-sampling produces little or no change in the performance. It was also noted that modifications of C4.5 parameters in relation to the under/over-sampling does have a strong effect on overall performance.

A method that deals with imbalanced datasets by internally biasing the discrimination procedure is proposed in [6]. This method uses a weighted distance function in a classification phase of the k-NN. Weights are assigned to classes such that the majority class has a greater weighting factor than the minority class. This weighting causes that the distance to minority class instances is lower than the distance to instances of the majority class. Instances of the minority class are then used more often when classifying a new instance.

Different approaches using the SVM biased by various ways for dealing with imbalanced datasets were published. The method proposed in [102] modifies a kernel function for this purpose. In [95] it two schemes for controlling the balance between false positives and false negatives are proposed.

5.2.2. *One-class learning*

A one-class learning is an alternative to discriminative approaches that deal with imbalanced datasets. In the one-class learning, a model is built using only target class instances. The model is then learned to recognize these instances, which can be under certain conditions superior to discriminative approaches [51]. Two one-class learning algorithms were studied in literature, particularly the SVM [66, 81] and auto-encoders [51, 66]. An experimental comparison of these two methods can be found in [66]. Usefulness of the one-class learning on extremely unbalanced data sets composed of high dimensional noisy features is showed in [76].

5.2.3. Cost-sensitive learning

A cost-sensitive learning is another commonly used way in the context of imbalanced datasets. A classification model is extended with a cost model in the form of a cost matrix. Given the cost matrix as shown in Figure 2 in section 2 we can define *conditional risk* for making decision α_i about instance x as

$$R(\alpha_i|x) = \sum_j \lambda_{ij} P(j|x)$$

where $P(j|x)$ is a posterior probability of class j being true class of instance x. The goal in a cost-sensitive classification is to minimize the cost of misclassification. This means that the optimal prediction for an instance x is the class i that minimize a conditional risk. Note that the optimal decision can differ from the most probable class [32].

A method which makes classifier cost sensitive, the **MetaCost**, is proposed in [29]. The MetaCost learns an internal cost-sensitive model, then estimates class probabilities and re-labels training instances with their minimum expected cost classes. A new model is built using the relabelled dataset.

The **AdaCost** [34] method based on Adaboost [36] has been made a cost-sensitive by an over-weighting instances from the minority class, which are misclassified. Empirical experiments have shown, that the AdaCost has lower cumulative misclassification costs in comparison with the AdaBoost.

5.3. Ensemble learning methods

Ensemble methods are methods, which use a combination of methods with the aim to achieve better results. Two most known ensemble methods are *bagging* and *boosting*. The bagging (Bootstrap aggregating) proposed in [12] initially generates B bootstrap sets of the original dataset and then builds a classification or regression model using each bootstrap set. Predicted values of these models are combined to predict the final result. In classification tasks it works as follows. Each model has one vote to predict a class, the bagged classifier counts the votes and assigns the class with the most votes. For regression tasks, the predicted value is computed as the average of values predicted by each model.

The boosting, firstly described in [80], is based on the idea a powerful model is created using a set of weak models. The method is quite similar to the bagging. Like the bagging the boosting uses voting for a classification task or averaging for a regression task to predict the output value. However, the boosting is an iterative method. In each iteration a newly built model is influenced by the performance of those built previously. By assigning greater weights to the instances that were misclassified in previous iterations the model pays more attention on these instances.

Another in comparison with bagging and boosting less widely used method is *stacking* proposed in [101]. In the stacking method the original dataset is splitted into two disjoint sets, a training set and a validation set. Several base models are learned on the training set and then applied to the validation set. Using predictions from the validation set as inputs and correct values as the outputs, a higher level model is build. In comparison with the bagging and boosting, the stacking can be used to combine different types of models.

Ensemble methods such the bagging, boosting and stacking often outperform another methods. Therefore, they have been widely studied in recent years and lot of approaches have been proposed. The earlier mentioned **Adaboost** [36] and **AdaCost** [34] are other methods that use the boosting are **RareBoost** [53] or **SMOTEBoost** [20]. A method combining the bagging and stacking to identify the best combination of classifiers is used in [74]. Three agents (Naive Bayes, C4.5, 5-NN) are combined in the approach proposed in [58]. There are many other methods utilizing the mentioned approaches.

6. Conclusion

Several methods for training set re-sampling, instance selection and class balancing, published in literature, were reviewed. All of these methods are very important in processes of construction of training and testing sets. Re-sampling methods allow to split a data set into more subsets in the case of absence of an independent set for model validation or prediction performance assessment. Instance selection methods reduce a training set by removing instances useless for estimating parameters of a model, which can speed up the learning phase and response time, especially for lazy learners. Class balancing algorithms solve the problem of inequality in class distributions.

Acknowledgements

This work was supported by the Institute of Computer Science of the Czech Academy of Sciences RVO: 67985807.

The work was supported by Ministry of Education of the Czech Republic under INGO project No. LG 12020.

Author details

Tomas Borovicka
Faculty of Information Technology and Faculty of Biomedical Engineering at the Czech Technical University, Prague, Czech Republic

Marcel Jirina, Jr.
Faculty of Biomedical Engineering at the Czech Technical University, Prague, Czech Republic

Pavel Kordik
Department of Computer Science and Engineering, FEE, Czech Technical University, Prague, Czech Republic

Marcel Jirina
Institute of Computer Science at the Czech Academy of Sciences, Prague, Czech Republic

7. References

[1] Aha, D., Kibler, D. & Albert, M. [1991]. Instance-based learning algorithms, *Machine learning* 6(1): 37–66.
[2] Anderson, T. & Darling, D. [1954]. A test of goodness of fit, *Journal of the American Statistical Association* pp. 765–769.
[3] Andrews, D. [2000]. Inconsistency of the bootstrap when a parameter is on the boundary of the parameter space, *Econometrica* 68(2): 399–405.
[4] Arturo Olvera-López, J., Ariel Carrasco-Ochoa, J. & Francisco Martínez-Trinidad, J. [2007]. Object selection based on clustering and border objects, *Computer Recognition Systems 2* pp. 27–34.
[5] Bailey, T. & Elkan, C. [1993]. Estimating the accuracy of learned concepts.", *Proc. International Joint Conference on Artificial Intelligence*, Citeseer.
[6] Barandela, R., SÃąnchez, J., Garcia, V. & Rangel, E. [2003]. Strategies for learning in class imbalance problems, *Pattern Recognition* 36(3): 849–851.
[7] Batista, G., Prati, R. & Monard, M. [2004]. A study of the behavior of several methods for balancing machine learning training data, *ACM SIGKDD Explorations Newsletter* 6(1): 20–29.
[8] Bentler, P. & Bonett, D. [1980]. Significance tests and goodness of fit in the analysis of covariance structures., *Psychological bulletin* 88(3): 588.
[9] Bezdek, J. & Kuncheva, L. [2001]. Nearest prototype classifier designs: An experimental study, *International Journal of Intelligent Systems* 16(12): 1445–1473.
[10] Bickel, P. [1969]. A distribution free version of the smirnov two sample test in the p-variate case, *The Annals of Mathematical Statistics* 40(1): 1–23.
[11] Bickel, P. & Freedman, D. [1981]. Some asymptotic theory for the bootstrap, *The Annals of Statistics* 9(6): 1196–1217.
[12] Breiman, L. [1996]. Bagging predictors, *Machine learning* 24(2): 123–140.
[13] Breiman, L. & Spector, P. [1992]. Submodel selection and evaluation in regression. the x-random case, *International Statistical Review/Revue Internationale de Statistique* pp. 291–319.
[14] Brighton, H. & Mellish, C. [2002]. Advances in instance selection for instance-based learning algorithms, *Data mining and knowledge discovery* 6(2): 153–172.
[15] Burman, P. [1989]. A comparative study of ordinary cross-validation, v-fold cross-validation and the repeated learning-testing methods, *Biometrika* 76(3): 503–514.
[16] Caises, Y., González, A., Leyva, E. & Pérez, R. [2009]. Scis: combining instance selection methods to increase their effectiveness over a wide range of domains, *Proceedings of the 10th international conference on Intelligent data engineering and automated learning*, Springer-Verlag, pp. 17–24.
[17] Cano, J., Herrera, F. & Lozano, M. [2003]. Using evolutionary algorithms as instance selection for data reduction in kdd: an experimental study, *Evolutionary Computation, IEEE Transactions on* 7(6): 561–575.

[18] Cerverón, V. & Ferri, F. [2001]. Another move toward the minimum consistent subset: a tabu search approach to the condensed nearest neighbor rule, *Systems, Man, and Cybernetics, Part B: Cybernetics, IEEE Transactions on* 31(3): 408–413.
[19] Chawla, N., Bowyer, K., Hall, L. & Kegelmeyer, W. [2002]. Smote: Synthetic minority over-sampling technique, *Journal of Artificial Intelligence Research* 16: 321–357.
[20] Chawla, N., Lazarevic, A., Hall, L. & Bowyer, K. [2003]. Smoteboost: Improving prediction of the minority class in boosting, *Knowledge Discovery in Databases: PKDD 2003* pp. 107–119.
[21] Chou, C., Kuo, B. & Chang, F. [2006]. The generalized condensed nearest neighbor rule as a data reduction method, *Pattern Recognition, 2006. ICPR 2006. 18th International Conference on*, Vol. 2, IEEE, pp. 556–559.
[22] Cohen, G., Hilario, M., Sax, H. & Hugonnet, S. [2003]. Data imbalance in surveillance of nosocomial infections, *Medical Data Analysis* pp. 109–117.
[23] Cover, T. & Hart, P. [1967]. Nearest neighbor pattern classification, *Information Theory, IEEE Transactions on* 13(1): 21–27.
[24] Daszykowski, M., Walczak, B. & Massart, D. [2002]. Representative subset selection, *Analytica Chimica Acta* 468(1): 91–103.
[25] de Groot, P., Postma, G., Melssen, W. & Buydens, L. [1999]. Selecting a representative training set for the classification of demolition waste using remote nir sensing, *Analytica Chimica Acta* 392(1): 67 – 75.
URL: *http://www.sciencedirect.com/science/article/pii/S0003267099001932*
[26] Demšar, J. [2006]. Statistical comparisons of classifiers over multiple data sets, *The Journal of Machine Learning Research* 7: 1–30.
[27] Devijver, P. & Kittler, J. [1980]. On the edited nearest neighbor rule, *Proc. 5th Int. Conf. on Pattern Recognition*, pp. 72–80.
[28] Dietterich, T. [1998]. Approximate statistical tests for comparing supervised classification learning algorithms, *Neural computation* 10(7): 1895–1923.
[29] Domingos, P. [1999]. Metacost: A general method for making classifiers cost-sensitive, *Proceedings of the fifth ACM SIGKDD international conference on Knowledge discovery and data mining*, ACM, pp. 155–164.
[30] Drummond, C., Holte, R. et al. [2003]. C4. 5, class imbalance, and cost sensitivity: why under-sampling beats over-sampling, *Workshop on Learning from Imbalanced Datasets II*, Citeseer.
[31] Duda, R. & Hart, P. [1996]. *Pattern classification and scene analysis*, Wiley.
[32] Elkan, C. [2001]. The foundations of cost-sensitive learning, *International Joint Conference on Artificial Intelligence*, Vol. 17, LAWRENCE ERLBAUM ASSOCIATES LTD, pp. 973–978.
[33] Everitt, B. [1992]. *The analysis of contingency tables*, Chapman & Hall/CRC.
[34] Fan, W., Stolfo, S., Zhang, J. & Chan, P. [1999]. Adacost: misclassification cost-sensitive boosting, *MACHINE LEARNING-INTERNATIONAL WORKSHOP THEN CONFERENCE-*, Citeseer, pp. 97–105.
[35] Fasano, G. & Franceschini, A. [1987]. A multidimensional version of the kolmogorov-smirnov test, *Monthly Notices of the Royal Astronomical Society* 225: 155–170.
[36] Freund, Y. & Schapire, R. [1995]. A desicion-theoretic generalization of on-line learning and an application to boosting, *Computational learning theory*, Springer, pp. 23–37.
[37] Friedman, J., Bentley, J. & Finkel, R. [1977]. An algorithm for finding best matches in logarithmic expected time, *ACM Transactions on Mathematical Software (TOMS)* 3(3): 209–226.

[38] García, S., Cano, J. & Herrera, F. [2008]. A memetic algorithm for evolutionary prototype selection: A scaling up approach, *Pattern Recognition* 41(8): 2693–2709.

[39] Gates, G. [1972]. The reduced nearest neighbor rule (corresp.), *Information Theory, IEEE Transactions on* 18(3): 431–433.

[40] Geisser, S. [1993]. *Predictive inference: An introduction*, Vol. 55, Chapman & Hall/CRC.

[41] Geman, S., Bienenstock, E. & Doursat, R. [1992]. Neural networks and the bias/variance dilemma, *Neural computation* 4(1): 1–58.

[42] Glover, F. & McMillan, C. [1986]. The general employee scheduling problem. an integration of ms and ai, *Computers & operations research* 13(5): 563–573.

[43] Grochowski, M. & Jankowski, N. [2004]. Comparison of instance selection algorithms ii. results and comments, *Artificial Intelligence and Soft Computing-ICAISC 2004* pp. 580–585.

[44] Guo, X., Yin, Y., Dong, C., Yang, G. & Zhou, G. [2008]. On the class imbalance problem, *Natural Computation, 2008. ICNC'08. Fourth International Conference on*, Vol. 4, IEEE, pp. 192–201.

[45] Han, H., Wang, W. & Mao, B. [2005]. Borderline-smote: A new over-sampling method in imbalanced data sets learning, *Advances in Intelligent Computing* pp. 878–887.

[46] Han, J. & Kamber, M. [2006]. *Data mining: concepts and techniques*, The Morgan Kaufmann series in data management systems, Elsevier.
URL: *http://books.google.cz/books?id=AfL0t-YzOrEC*

[47] Hawkins, D. et al. [2004]. The problem of overfitting, *Journal of chemical information and computer sciences* 44(1): 1–12.

[48] Jain, A., Dubes, R. & Chen, C. [1987]. Bootstrap techniques for error estimation, *Pattern Analysis and Machine Intelligence, IEEE Transactions on* (5): 628–633.

[49] Jankowski, N. & Grochowski, M. [2004a]. Comparison of instances seletion algorithms i. algorithms survey, *Artificial Intelligence and Soft Computing-ICAISC 2004* pp. 598–603.

[50] Jankowski, N. & Grochowski, M. [2004b]. Comparison of instances seletion algorithms i. algorithms survey, *Artificial Intelligence and Soft Computing-ICAISC 2004* pp. 598–603.

[51] Japkowicz, N. [2001]. Supervised versus unsupervised binary-learning by feedforward neural networks, *Machine Learning* 42(1): 97–122.

[52] Japkowicz, N. & Stephen, S. [2002]. The class imbalance problem: A systematic study, *Intelligent data analysis* 6(5): 429–449.

[53] Joshi, M., Kumar, V. & Agarwal, R. [2001]. Evaluating boosting algorithms to classify rare classes: Comparison and improvements, *Data Mining, 2001. ICDM 2001, Proceedings IEEE International Conference on*, IEEE, pp. 257–264.

[54] Justel, A., Peña, D. & Zamar, R. [1997]. A multivariate kolmogorov-smirnov test of goodness of fit, *Statistics & Probability Letters* 35(3): 251–259.

[55] Kennard, R. & Stone, L. [1969]. Computer aided design of experiments, *Technometrics* pp. 137–148.

[56] Kohavi, R. [1995]. A study of cross-validation and bootstrap for accuracy estimation and model selection, *International joint Conference on artificial intelligence*, Vol. 14, LAWRENCE ERLBAUM ASSOCIATES LTD, pp. 1137–1145.

[57] Kotsiantis, S., Kanellopoulos, D. & Pintelas, P. [2006]. Handling imbalanced datasets: A review, *GESTS International Transactions on Computer Science and Engineering* 30(1): 25–36.

[58] Kotsiantis, S. & Pintelas, P. [2003]. Mixture of expert agents for handling imbalanced data sets, *Annals of Mathematics, Computing & Teleinformatics* 1(1): 46–55.

[59] Kruskal, J. [1964]. Multidimensional scaling by optimizing goodness of fit to a nonmetric hypothesis, *Psychometrika* 29(1): 1–27.

[60] Kubat, M. & Matwin, S. [1997]. Addressing the curse of imbalanced training sets: one-sided selection, *MACHINE LEARNING-INTERNATIONAL WORKSHOP THEN CONFERENCE-*, MORGAN KAUFMANN PUBLISHERS, INC., pp. 179–186.
[61] Kuncheva, L. [1995]. Editing for the k-nearest neighbors rule by a genetic algorithm, *Pattern Recognition Letters* 16(8): 809–814.
[62] Kuncheva, L. & Bezdek, J. [1998]. Nearest prototype classification: Clustering, genetic algorithms, or random search?, *Systems, Man, and Cybernetics, Part C: Applications and Reviews, IEEE Transactions on* 28(1): 160–164.
[63] Laurikkala, J. [2001]. Improving identification of difficult small classes by balancing class distribution, *Artificial Intelligence in Medicine* pp. 63–66.
[64] Li, Y., Hu, Z., Cai, Y. & Zhang, W. [2005]. Support vector based prototype selection method for nearest neighbor rules, *Advances in Natural Computation* pp. 408–408.
[65] Liu, H. & Motoda, H. [2002]. On issues of instance selection, *Data Mining and Knowledge Discovery* 6(2): 115–130.
[66] Manevitz, L. & Yousef, M. [2002]. One-class svms for document classification, *The Journal of Machine Learning Research* 2: 139–154.
[67] McLachlan, G. & Wiley, J. [1992]. *Discriminant analysis and statistical pattern recognition*, Wiley Online Library.
[68] Molinaro, A., Simon, R. & Pfeiffer, R. [2005]. Prediction error estimation: a comparison of resampling methods, *Bioinformatics* 21(15): 3301–3307.
[69] Narayan, B., Murthy, C. & Pal, S. [2006]. Maxdiff kd-trees for data condensation, *Pattern recognition letters* 27(3): 187–200.
[70] Olvera-López, J., Carrasco-Ochoa, J. & Martínez-Trinidad, J. [2008]. Prototype selection via prototype relevance, *Progress in Pattern Recognition, Image Analysis and Applications* pp. 153–160.
[71] Olvera-López, J., Carrasco-Ochoa, J., Martínez-Trinidad, J. & Kittler, J. [2010]. A review of instance selection methods, *Artificial Intelligence Review* 34(2): 133–143.
[72] Pan, F., Wang, W., Tung, A. & Yang, J. [2005]. Finding representative set from massive data, *Data Mining, Fifth IEEE International Conference on*, IEEE, pp. 8–pp.
[73] Paredes, R. & Vidal, E. [2000]. Weighting prototypes-a new editing approach, *Pattern Recognition, 2000. Proceedings. 15th International Conference on*, Vol. 2, IEEE, pp. 25–28.
[74] Phua, C., Alahakoon, D. & Lee, V. [2004]. Minority report in fraud detection: classification of skewed data, *ACM SIGKDD Explorations Newsletter* 6(1): 50–59.
[75] Raicharoen, T. & Lursinsap, C. [2005]. A divide-and-conquer approach to the pairwise opposite class-nearest neighbor (poc-nn) algorithm, *Pattern recognition letters* 26(10): 1554–1567.
[76] Raskutti, B. & Kowalczyk, A. [2004]. Extreme re-balancing for svms: a case study, *ACM Sigkdd Explorations Newsletter* 6(1): 60–69.
[77] Rencher, A. [2002]. Methods of multivariate analysis.
[78] Riquelme, J., Aguilar-Ruiz, J. & Toro, M. [2003]. Finding representative patterns with ordered projections, *Pattern Recognition* 36(4): 1009–1018.
[79] Ritter, G., Woodruff, H., Lowry, S. & Isenhour, T. [1975]. An algorithm for a selective nearest neighbor decision rule (corresp.), *Information Theory, IEEE Transactions on* 21(6): 665–669.
[80] Schapire, R. [1990]. The strength of weak learnability, *Machine learning* 5(2): 197–227.
[81] Schölkopf, B., Platt, J., Shawe-Taylor, J., Smola, A. & Williamson, R. [2001]. Estimating the support of a high-dimensional distribution, *Neural computation* 13(7): 1443–1471.

[82] Snedecor, G. & Cochran, W. [1967]. Statistical methods 6th ed, *IOWA State University press, USA. 450pp* .
[83] Snee, R. [1977]. Validation of regression models: methods and examples, *Technometrics* pp. 415–428.
[84] Srisawat, A., Phienthrakul, T. & Kijsirikul, B. [2006]. Sv-knnc: an algorithm for improving the efficiency of k-nearest neighbor, *PRICAI 2006: Trends in Artificial Intelligence* pp. 975–979.
[85] Stephens, M. [1974]. Edf statistics for goodness of fit and some comparisons, *Journal of the American Statistical Association* pp. 730–737.
[86] Stone, M. [1974]. Cross-validatory choice and assessment of statistical predictions, *Journal of the Royal Statistical Society. Series B (Methodological)* pp. 111–147.
[87] Thas, O. [2010]. *Comparing distributions*, Springer.
[88] Thomas H. Cormen, Charles E. Leiserson, R. L. R. C. S. [2009]. *Introduction to Algorithms*, The MIT Press, London, England.
[89] Tibshirani, R. & Efron, B. [1993]. An introduction to the bootstrap, *Monographs on Statistics and Applied Probability* 57: 1–436.
[90] Tomek, I. [1976]. An experiment with the edited nearest-neighbor rule, *IEEE Transactions on Systems, Man, and Cybernetics* (6): 448–452.
[91] Vapnik, V. [2000]. *The nature of statistical learning theory*, Springer Verlag.
[92] Vázquez, F., Sánchez, J. & Pla, F. [2005]. A stochastic approach to wilsonâĂŹs editing algorithm, *Pattern Recognition and Image Analysis* pp. 35–42.
[93] Veenman, C. & Reinders, M. [2005]. The nearest sub-class classifier: a compromise between the nearest mean and nearest neighbor classifier, *Transactions on PAMI* 27(9): 1417–1429.
[94] Veenman, C., Reinders, M. & Backer, E. [2002]. A maximum variance cluster algorithm, *Pattern Analysis and Machine Intelligence, IEEE Transactions on* 24(9): 1273–1280.
[95] Veropoulos, K., Campbell, C. & Cristianini, N. [1999]. Controlling the sensitivity of support vector machines, *Proceedings of the international joint conference on artificial intelligence*, Vol. 1999, Citeseer, pp. 55–60.
[96] Weiss, G. [2003]. *The effect of small disjuncts and class distribution on decision tree learning*, PhD thesis, Rutgers, The State University of New Jersey.
[97] Weiss, G. & Provost, F. [2003]. Learning when training data are costly: The effect of class distribution on tree induction, *J. Artif. Intell. Res. (JAIR)* 19: 315–354.
[98] Wilson, D. [1972]. Asymptotic properties of nearest neighbor rules using edited data, *Systems, Man and Cybernetics, IEEE Transactions on* 2(3): 408–421.
[99] Wilson, D. & Martinez, T. [2000]. Reduction techniques for instance-based learning algorithms, *Machine learning* 38(3): 257–286.
[100] Witten, I., Frank, E. & Hall, M. [2011]. *Data Mining: Practical machine learning tools and techniques*, Morgan Kaufmann.
[101] Wolpert, D. [1992]. Stacked generalization*, *Neural networks* 5(2): 241–259.
[102] Wu, G. & Chang, E. [2003]. Class-boundary alignment for imbalanced dataset learning, *ICML 2003 workshop on learning from imbalanced data sets II*, pp. 49–56.
[103] Zhang, H. & Sun, G. [2002]. Optimal reference subset selection for nearest neighbor classification by tabu search, *Pattern Recognition* 35(7): 1481–1490.
[104] Zhao, K., Zhou, S., Guan, J. & Zhou, A. [2003]. C-pruner: An improved instance pruning algorithm, *Machine Learning and Cybernetics, 2003 International Conference on*, Vol. 1, IEEE, pp. 94–99.

Chapter 3

Similarity Measures and Dimensionality Reduction Techniques for Time Series Data Mining

Carmelo Cassisi, Placido Montalto, Marco Aliotta,
Andrea Cannata and Alfredo Pulvirenti

Additional information is available at the end of the chapter

http://dx.doi.org/10.5772/49941

1. Introduction

A time series is *"a sequence* $X = (x_1, x_2, \ldots, x_m)$ *of observed data over time"*, where m is the number of observations. Tracking the behavior of a specific phenomenon/data in time can produce important information. A large variety of real world applications, such as meteorology, geophysics and astrophysics, collect observations that can be represented as time series.

A collection of time series can be defined as a Time Series Database (*TSDB*). Given a *TSDB*, most of time series mining efforts are made for the similarity matching problem. Time series data mining can be exploited from research areas dealing with signals, such as image processing. For example, image data can be converted to time series: from image color histograms (Fig. 2), where image matching can be applied, to object perimeters for the characterization of shapes [39].

Time series are essentially high-dimensional data [17]. Mining high-dimensional involves addressing a range of challenges, among them: i) the curse of dimensionality [1], and ii) the meaningfulness of the similarity measure in the high-dimensional space. An important task to enhance performances on time series is the reduction of their dimensionality, that must preserve the main characteristics, and reflects the original (dis)similarity of such data (this effect will be referred to as *lower bounding* [11]). When treating time series, the similarity between two sequences of the same length can be calculated by summing the ordered point-to-point distance between them (Fig. 3). In this sense, the most used distance function is the *Euclidean Distance* [13], corresponding to the second degree of general L_p*-norm* [41]. This distance measure is cataloged as a metric distance function, since it obeys to the three

INTECH
open science | open minds

© 2012 Cassisi et al., licensee InTech. This is an open access chapter distributed under the terms of the Creative Commons Attribution License (http://creativecommons.org/licenses/by/3.0), which permits unrestricted use, distribution, and reproduction in any medium, provided the original work is properly cited.

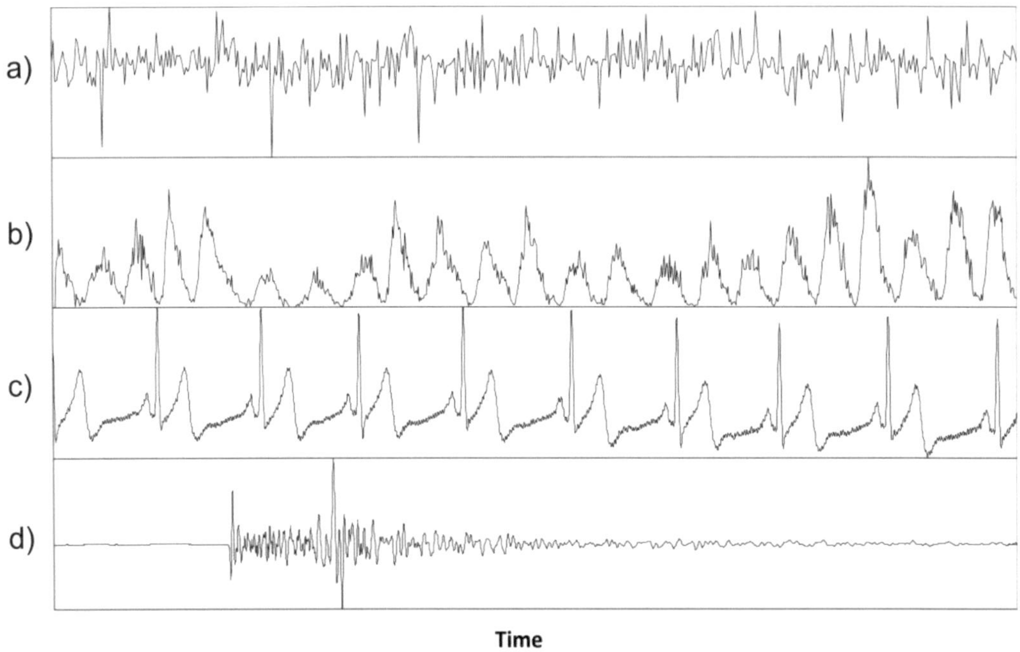

Figure 1. Examples of time series data relative to a) monsoon, b) sunspots, c) ECG (ElectroCardioGram), d) seismic signal.

fundamentals metric properties: *non-negativity*, *symmetry* and *triangle inequality* [29]. In most cases, a metric function is desired, because the triangle inequality can then be used to prune the index during search, allowing speed-up execution for exact matching [28]. In every way, Euclidean distance and its variants present several drawbacks, that make inappropriate their use in certain applications. For these reasons, other distance measure techniques were proposed to give more robustness to the similarity computation. In this sense it is required to cite also the well known *Dynamic Time Warping* (*DTW*) [22], that makes distance comparisons less sensitive to signal transformations as shifting, uniform amplitude scaling or uniform time scaling. In the literature there exist other distance measures that overcome signal transformation problems, such as the *Landmarks similarity*, which does not follow traditional similarity models that rely on point-wise Euclidean distance [31] but, in correspondence of human intuition and episodic memory, relies on similarity of those points (times, events) of "greatest importance" (for example local maxima, local minima, inflection points).

In conjunction to this branch of research, a wide range of techniques for dimensionality reduction was proposed. Among them we will treat only representations that have the desirable property of allowing *lower bounding*. By this property, after establishing a true distance measure for the raw data (in this case the Euclidean distance), the distance between two time series, in the reduced space, results always less or equal than the true distance. Such a property ensures exact indexing of data (i.e. with no false negatives [13]). The following representations describe the state-of-art in this field: spectral decomposition through *Discrete Fourier Transform* (*DFT*) [1]; *Discrete Wavelet Transform* (*DWT*) [7]; *Singular*

Value Decomposition (*SVD*) [24]; *Piecewise Aggregate Approximation* (*PAA*) [19]; *Adaptive Piecewise Constant Approximation* (*APCA*) [6]; *Piecewise Linear Approximation* (*PLA*) [20]; and *Chebyshev Polynomials* (*CHEB*) [29]. Many researchers have also included symbolic representations of time series, that transform time series measurements into a collection of discretized symbols; among them we cite the *Symbolic Aggregate approXimation* (*SAX*) [26], based on *PAA*, and the evolved multi-resolution representation *iSAX 2.0* [35]. Symbolic representation can take advantage of efforts conducted by the text-processing and bioinformatics communities, who made available several data structures and algorithms for efficient pattern discovery on symbolic encodings [2],[25],[36].

The chapter is organized as follows. Section 2 will introduce the similarity matching problem on time series. We will note the importance of the use of efficient data structures to perform search, and the choice of an adequate distance measure. Section 3 will show some of the most used distance measure for time series data mining. Section 4 will review the above mentioned dimensionality reduction techniques.

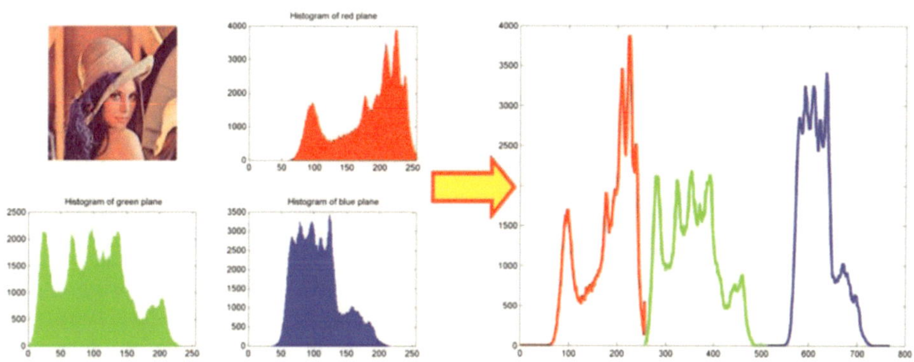

Figure 2. An example of conversion from the RGB (Red, Green, Blue) image color histograms, to a time series.

2. Similarity matching problem

A *TSDB* with *m* objects, each of length *n*, is denoted by $TSDB = \{x_1, x_2, \ldots, x_m\}$, where $x_i = (x_i^{(1)}, x_i^{(2)}, \ldots, x_i^{(n)})$ is a vector denoting the *i*th time series and $x_i^{(j)}$ denotes the *j*th values of x_i, with respect to time. *n* indicates the *dimensionality* of the data set.

The general representation of a *TSDB* is a $m \times n$ matrix:

$$A = \begin{pmatrix} x_1^{(1)} & x_1^{(2)} & \cdots & x_1^{(j)} & \cdots & x_1^{(n)} \\ x_2^{(1)} & x_2^{(2)} & \cdots & x_2^{(j)} & \cdots & x_2^{(n)} \\ \vdots & \vdots & \cdots & \vdots & \cdots & \vdots \\ x_i^{(1)} & x_i^{(2)} & \cdots & x_i^{(j)} & \cdots & x_i^{(n)} \\ \vdots & \vdots & \cdots & \vdots & \cdots & \vdots \\ x_m^{(1)} & x_m^{(2)} & \cdots & x_m^{(j)} & \cdots & x_m^{(n)} \end{pmatrix} = \begin{pmatrix} x_1 \\ x_2 \\ \vdots \\ x_m \end{pmatrix} \tag{1}$$

In many cases, datasets are supported by special data structures, especially when dataset get larger, that are referred as *indexing* structures. Indexing consists of building a data structure I that enables efficient searching within database [29]. Usually, it is designed to face two principal similarity queries: the (i) *k-nearest neighbors* (*knn*), and the (ii) *range query* problem. Given a time series Q in *TSDB*, and a similarity/dissimilarity measure $d(T,S)$ defined for each pair T, S in *TSDB*, the former query deals with the search of the set of first k time series in *TSDB* more similar to Q. The latter query finds the set R of time series that are within distance r from Q. Given an indexing structure I, there are two ways to post a similarity query in time series databases [29]:

- *whole matching*: given a *TSDB* of time series, each of length n, whole matching relates to computation of similarity matching among time series along their whole length.
- *subsequence matching*: given a *TSDB* of m time series $S_1, S_2, \ldots, S_m$, each of length n_i, and a short query time series Q of length $n_q < n_i$, with $0 < i < m$, subsequence matching relates to finding matches of Q into subsequences of every S_i, starting at every position.

Indexing is crucial for reaching efficiency on data mining tasks, such as *clustering* or *classification*, specially for huge database such as *TSDB*s. Clustering is related to the unsupervised division of data into groups (clusters) of similar objects under some similarity or dissimilarity measures. Sometimes, on time series domain, a similar problem to clustering is the *motif discovery* problem [28], consisting of searching main cluster (or motif) into a *TSDB*. The search for clusters is unsupervised. Classification assigns unlabeled time series to predefined classes after a supervised learning process. Both tasks make massive use of distance computations.

Distance measures play an important role for similarity problem, in data mining tasks. Concerning a distance measure, it is important to understand if it can be considered *metric*. A metric function on a *TSDB* is a function $f: TSDB \times TSDB \rightarrow \mathrm{R}$ (where R is the set of real numbers). For all x, y, z in *TSDB*, this function obeys to four fundamental properties:

$$f(x, y) \geq 0 \quad (\textit{non-negativity}) \tag{2}$$

$$f(x, y) = 0 \text{ if and only if } x = y \quad (\textit{identity}) \tag{3}$$

$$f(x, y) = f(y, x) \quad (\textit{symmetry}) \tag{4}$$

$$f(x, z) \leq f(x, y) + f(y, z) \quad (\textit{triangle inequality}) \tag{5}$$

If any of these is not obeyed, then the distance is non-metric. Using a metric function is desired, because the triangle inequality property (Eq. 5) can be used to index the space for speed-up search. A well known framework, for indexing time series, is *GEMINI* (*GEneric Multimedia INdexIng*) [13] that designs fast search algorithms for locating time series that match, in an exact or approximate way, a query time series Q.

It was introduced to accommodate any dimensionality reduction method for time series, and then allows indexing on new representation [29]. *GEMINI* guarantees no false negatives on index search if two conditions are satisfied: (i) for the raw time series, a metric distance measure must be established; (ii) to work with the reduced representation, a specific requirement is that it guarantees the lower bounding property.

3. Similarity measures

A common data mining task is the estimation of similarity among objects. A similarity measure is a relation between a pair of objects and a scalar number. Common intervals used to mapping the similarity are [-1, 1] or [0, 1], where 1 indicates the maximum of similarity.

Considering the similarity between two numbers x and y as :

$$numSim(x,y) = 1 - \frac{|x-y|}{|x|+|y|} \tag{6}$$

Let two time series $X = x_1,\ldots,x_n$, $Y = y_1,\ldots,y_n$, some similarity measures are:

- mean similarity defined as:

$$tsim(X,Y) = \frac{1}{n}\sum_{i=1}^{n} numSim(x_i, y_i) \tag{7}$$

- root mean square similarity:

$$rtsim(X,Y) = \sqrt{\frac{1}{n}\sum_{i=1}^{n} numSim(x_i, y_i)^2} \tag{8}$$

- and peak similarity [15]:

$$psim(X,Y) = \frac{1}{n}\sum_{i=1}^{n}\left[1 - \frac{|x_i - y_i|}{2\max\left(|x_i|,|y_i|\right)}\right] \tag{9}$$

Another common similarity functions used to perform complete or partial matching between time series are the *cross-correlation* function (or *Pearson's correlation* function) [38] and the cosine angle between the two vectors. The cross correlation between two time series x and y of length n, allowing a shifted comparison of l positions, is defined as:

$$r_{XY} = \frac{\sum_{i=1}^{n}\left(x_i - \overline{X}\right)\left(y_{i-l} - \overline{Y}\right)}{\sqrt{\sum_{i=1}^{n}\left(x_i - \overline{X}\right)^2}\sqrt{\sum_{i=1}^{n}\left(y_{i-l} - \overline{Y}\right)^2}} \tag{10}$$

Where $\overline{X}$ and $\overline{Y}$ are the means of X and Y. The correlation r_{XY} provides the degree of linear dependence between the two vectors X and Y from perfect linear relationship ($r_{XY} = 1$), to perfect negative linear relation ($r_{XY} = -1$).

Another way to evaluate similarity between two vectors is the estimation of cosine of the angle between the two vectors X and Y, defined as:

$$\cos(\vartheta) = \frac{X \cdot Y}{\|X\|\|Y\|} = \frac{\sum_{i=1}^{n} x_i y_i}{\sqrt{\sum_{i=1}^{n} x_i^2}\sqrt{\sum_{i=1}^{n} y_i^2}} \quad (11)$$

This measure provides values in range [-1, 1]. The lower boundary indicates that the X and Y vectors are exactly opposite, the upper boundary indicates that the vectors are exactly the same, finally the 0 value indicates the independence.

3.1. Metric distances

Another way to compare time series data involves concept of distance measures. Let be two time series T and S vectors of length n, and T_i and S_i the ith values of T and S, respectively. Let us list the following distance measures. This subsection presents a list of distance functions used in Euclidean space.

1. **Euclidean Distance**. The most used distance function in many applications. It is defined as (Fig. 3):

$$d(T,S) = \sqrt{\sum_{i=1}^{n}(T_i - S_i)^2} \quad (12)$$

2. **Manhattan Distance**. Also called "city block distance". It is defined as:

$$d(T,S) = \sum_{i=1}^{n}\left|T_i - S_i\right| \quad (13)$$

3. **Maximum Distance**. It is defined to be the maximum value of the distances of the attributes:

$$d(T,S) = \max_{0<i\leq n}\left|T_i - S_i\right| \quad (14)$$

4. **Minkowski Distance**. The Euclidean distance, Manhattan distance, and Maximum distance, are particular instances of the Minkowski distance, called also L_p-norm. It is defined as:

$$d(T,S) = \sqrt[p]{\sum_{i=1}^{n}(T_i - S_i)^p} \quad (15)$$

where p is called the order of *Minkowski* distance. In fact, for Manhattan distance $p = 1$, for the Euclidean distance $p = 2$, while for the Maximum distance $p = \infty$.

5. **Mahalanobis Distance**. The Mahalanobis distance is defined as:

$$d(T,S) = \sqrt{(T-S)W^{-1}(T-S)^T} \quad (16)$$

where W is the *covariance* matrix [12].

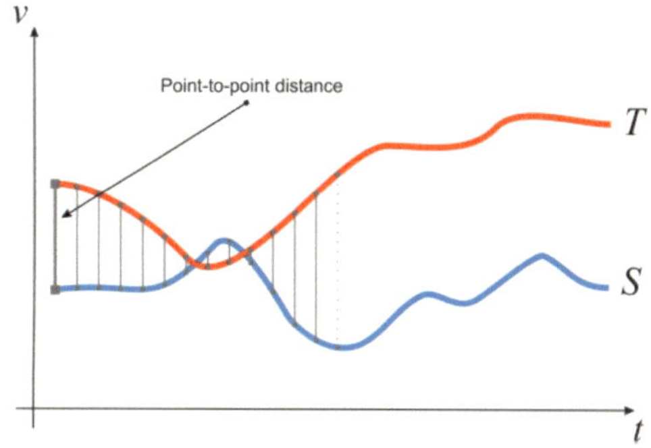

Figure 3. T and S are two time series of a particular variable v, along the time axis t. The Euclidean distance results in the sum of the point-to-point distances (gray lines), along all the time series.

3.2. Dynamic time warping

Euclidean distance is cataloged as a metric distance function, since it obeys to the metric properties: *non-negativity*, *identity*, *symmetry* and *triangle inequality* (Section 2, Eq.2~5). It is surprisingly competitive with other more complex approaches, especially when dataset size gets larger [35]. In every way, Euclidean distance and its variants present several drawbacks, that make inappropriate their use in certain applications:

- It compares only time series of the same length.
- It doesn't handle outliers or noise.
- It is very sensitive respect to six signal transformations: shifting, uniform amplitude scaling, uniform time scaling, uniform bi-scaling, time warping and non-uniform amplitude scaling [31].

Dynamic Time Warping (*DTW*) [22] gives more robustness to the similarity computation. By this method, also time series of different length can be compared, because it replaces the one-to-one point comparison, used in Euclidean distance, with a many-to-one (and viceversa) comparison. The main feature of this distance measure is that it allows to recognize similar shapes, even if they present signal transformations, such as shifting and/or scaling (Fig. 4).

Given two time series $T = \{t_1, t_2, \ldots, t_n\}$ and $S = \{s_1, s_2, \ldots, s_m\}$ of length n and m, respectively, an alignment by *DTW* method exploits information contained in a $n \times m$ distance matrix:

$$distMatrix = \begin{pmatrix} d(T_1,S_1) & d(T_1,S_2) & \cdots & d(T_1,S_m) \\ d(T_2,S_1) & d(T_2,S_2) & & \\ \vdots & & \ddots & \\ d(T_n,S_1) & & & d(T_n,S_m) \end{pmatrix} \tag{17}$$

where $distMatrix(i, j)$ corresponds to the distance of ith point of T and jth point of S $d(T_i, S_j)$, with $1 \le i \le n$ and $1 \le j \le m$.

The *DTW* objective is to find the *warping path* $W = \{w_1, w_2, \ldots, w_k, \ldots, w_K\}$ of contiguous elements on *distMatrix* (with $\max(n, m) < K < m + n - 1$, and $w_k = distMatrix(i, j)$), such that it minimizes the following function:

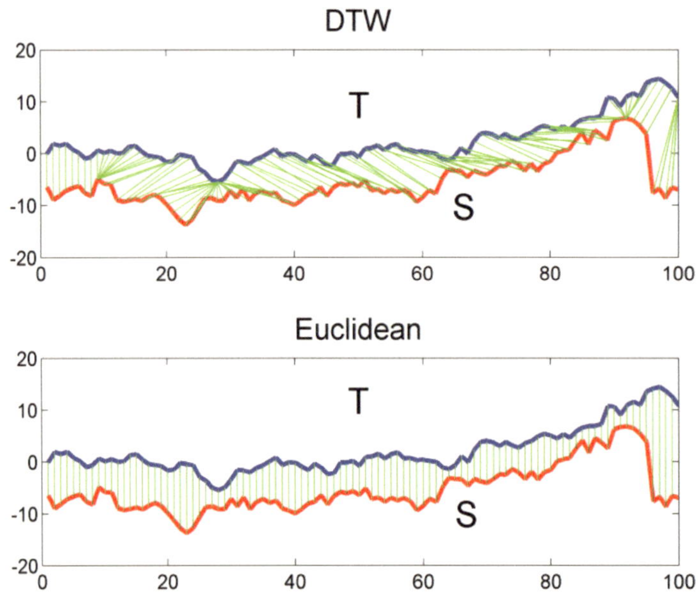

Figure 4. Difference between *DTW* distance and Euclidean distance (green lines represent mapping between points of time series *T* and *S*). The former allows many-to-one point comparisons, while Euclidean point-to-point distance (or one-to-one).

$$DTW(T,S) = \min\left(\sqrt{\sum_{k=1}^{K} w_k}\right) \tag{18}$$

The warping path is subject to several constraints [22]. Given $w_k = (i, j)$ and $w_{k-1} = (i', j')$ with $i, i' \leq n$ and $j, j' \leq m$:

1. **Boundary conditions**. $w_1 = (1,1)$ and $w_K = (n, m)$.
2. **Continuity**. $i - i' \leq 1$ and $j - j' \leq 1$.
3. **Monotonicity**. $i - i' \geq 0$ and $j - j' \geq 0$.

The warping path can be efficiently computed using dynamic programming [9]. By this method, a cumulative distance matrix γ of the same dimension as the *distMatrix*, is created to store in the cell (i, j) the following value (Fig. 5):

$$\gamma(i,j) = d(T_i, S_j) + \min\{\gamma(i-1, j-1), \gamma(i-1, j), \gamma(i, j-1)\} \tag{19}$$

The overall complexity of the method is relative to the computation of all distances in *distMatrix*, that is $O(nm)$. The last element of the warping path, w_K corresponds to the distance calculated with the *DTW* method.

In many cases, this method can bring to undesired effects. An example is when a large number of point of a time series *T* is mapped to a single point of another time series *S* (Fig. 6a, 7a). A common way to overcome this problem is to restrict the warping path in such a way it has to follow a direction along the diagonal (Fig. 6b, 7b). To do this, we can restrict the path enforcing the recursion to stop at a certain depth, represented by a threshold δ. Then, the cumulative distance matrix γ will be calculated as follows:

$$\gamma(i,j)=\begin{cases} d(T_i,S_j)+\min\{\gamma(i-1,j-1),\gamma(i-1,j),\gamma(i,j-1)\} & |i-j|<\delta \\ \infty & otherwise \end{cases} \quad (20)$$

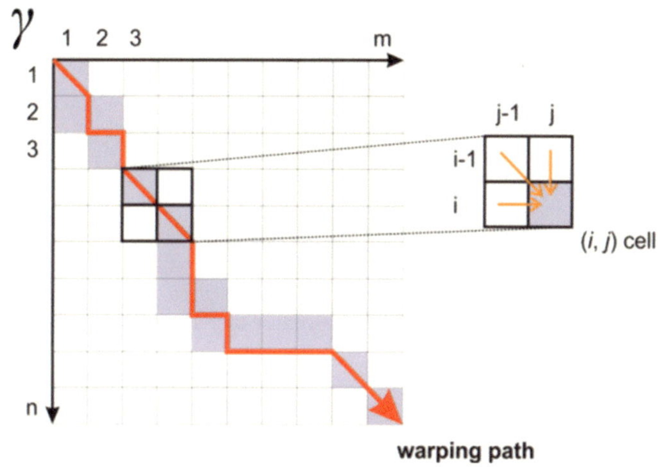

Figure 5. Warping path computation using dynamic programming. The lavender cells corresponds to the warping path. The red arrow indicates its direction. The warping distance at the (i, j) cell will consider, besides the distance between T_i and S_j, the minimum value among adjacent cells at positions: $(i\text{-}1, j\text{-}1)$, $(i\text{-}1, j)$ and $(i, j\text{-}1)$. The Euclidean distance between two time series can be seen as a special case of *DTW*, where path's elements belong to the γ matrix diagonal.

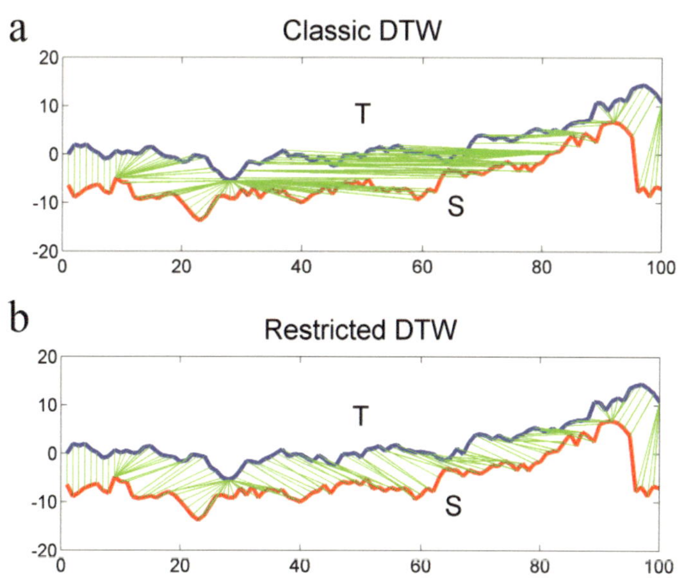

Figure 6. Different mappings obtained with the classic implementation of *DTW* (a), and with the restricted path version using a threshold $\delta = 10$ (b). Green lines represent mapping between points of time series T and S.

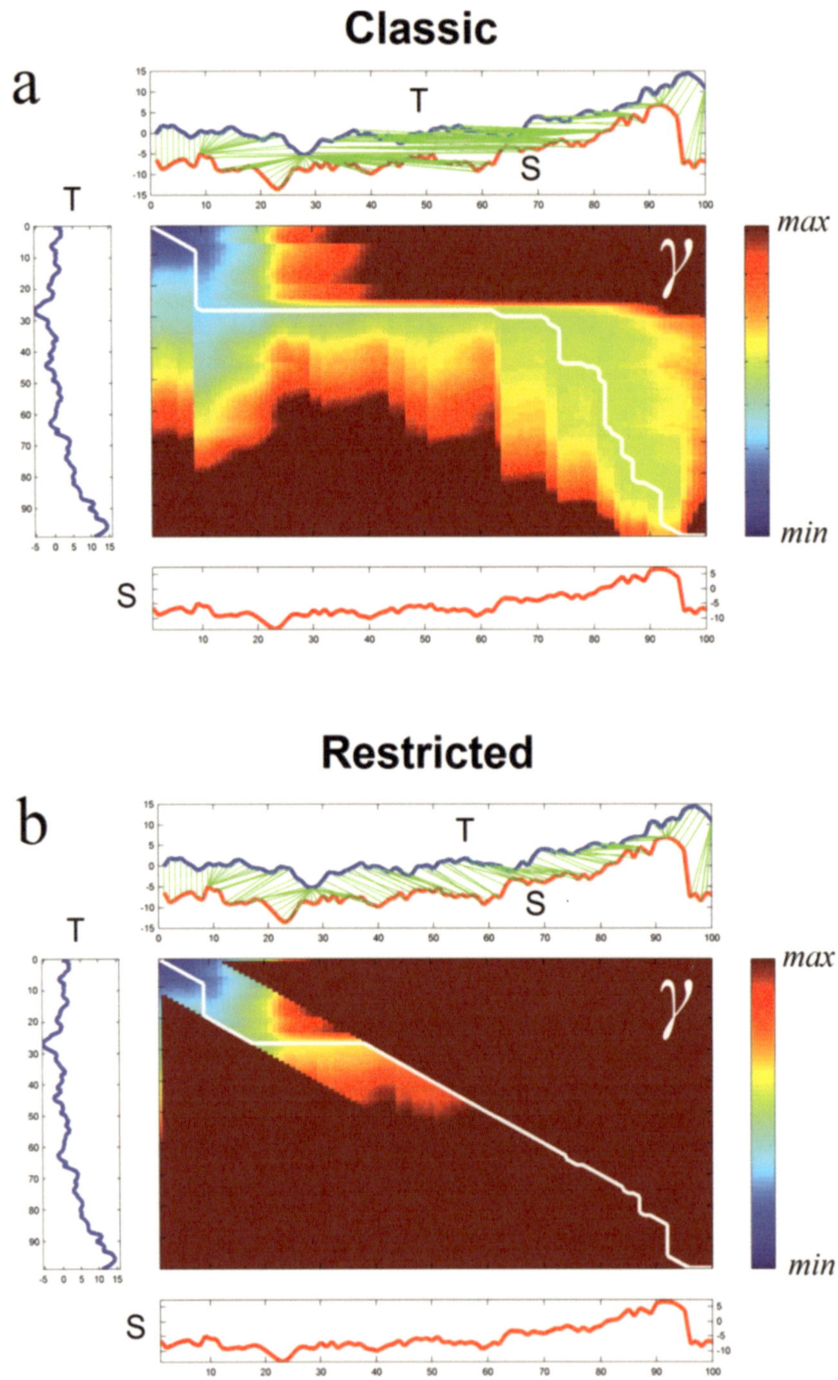

Figure 7. (a) Classic implementation of DTW. (b) Restricted path, using a threshold $\delta = 10$. For each plot (a) and (b): on the center, the warping path calculated on matrix γ. On the top, the alignment of time series T and S, represented by the green lines. On the left, the time series T. On the bottom, the time series S. On the right, the color bar relative to the distance values into matrix γ.

Figure 7a shows the computation of a restricted warping path, using a threshold $\delta = 10$. This constraint, besides limiting extreme or degenerate mappings, allows to speed-up *DTW* distance calculation, because we need to store only distances which are at most δ positions away (in horizontal and vertical direction) from the *distMatrix* diagonal. This reduces the computational complexity to $O((n + m)\delta)$. The above proposed constraint is known also as *Sakoe-Chiba band* (Fig. 8a) [34], and it is classified as global constraint. Another most common global constraint is the *Itakura parallelogram* (Fig. 8b) [18].

Local constraints are subject of research and are different from global constraints [22], because they provide local restrictions on the set of the alternative depth steps of the recurrence function (Eq. 19). For example we can replace Eq. 19 with:

$$\gamma(i,j) = d(T_i, S_j) + \min\{\gamma(i-1,j-1), \gamma(i-1,j-2), \gamma(i-2,j-1)\} \tag{21}$$

to define a new local constraint.

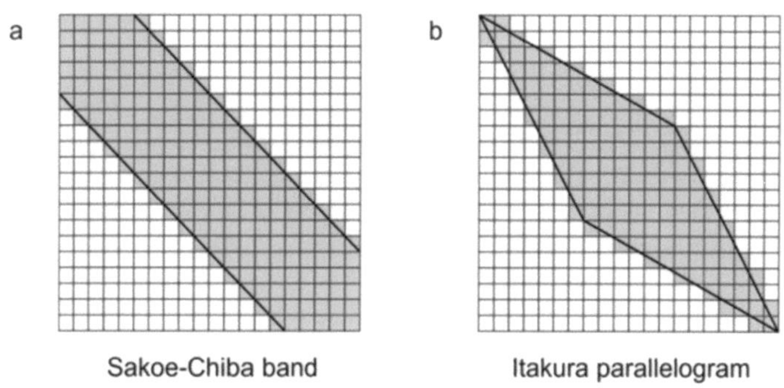

Figure 8. Examples of global constraints: (a) Sakoe-Chiba band; (b) Itakura parallelogram.

3.3. Longest Common SubSequence

Another well known method that takes advantage of dynamic programming to allow comparison of one-to-many points is the *Longest Common SubSequence* (*LCSS*) similarity measure [37]. An interesting feature of this method is that it is more resilient to noise than *DTW*, because allows some elements of time series to be unmatched (Fig. 9). This solution builds a matrix *LCSS* similar to γ, but considering similarity instead of distances. Given the time series T and S of length n and m, respectively, the recurrence function is expressed as follows:

$$LCSS(i,j) = \begin{cases} 0 & i = 0, \\ 0 & j = 0, \\ 1 + LCSS[i-1, j-1] & if \quad T_i = S_j, \\ \max(LCSS[i-1,j], LCSS[i,j-1]) & otherwise \end{cases} \tag{22}$$

with $1 \le i \le n$ and $1 \le j \le m$. Since exact matching between T_i and S_j can be strict for numerical values (Eq. 22 is best indicated for string distance computation, such as the edit distance), a common way to relax this definition is to apply the following recurrence function:

$$LCSS(i,j)=\begin{cases}0 & i=0,\\ 0 & j=0,\\ 1+LCSS[i-1,j-1] & if\left|T_i-S_j\right|<\varepsilon,\\ \max(LCSS[i-1,j],LCSS[i,j-1]) & otherwise\end{cases} \tag{23}$$

The cell *LCSS*(*n*, *m*) contains the similarity between *T* and *S*, because it corresponds to length *l* of the longest common subsequence of elements between time series *T* and *S*. To define a distance measure, we can compute [32]:

$$LCSSdist(T,S)=\frac{n+m+2l}{m+n} \tag{24}$$

Also for LCSS the time complexity is $O(nm)$, but it can be improved to $O((n+m)\delta)$ if a restriction is used (i.e. when $|i-j|<\delta$).

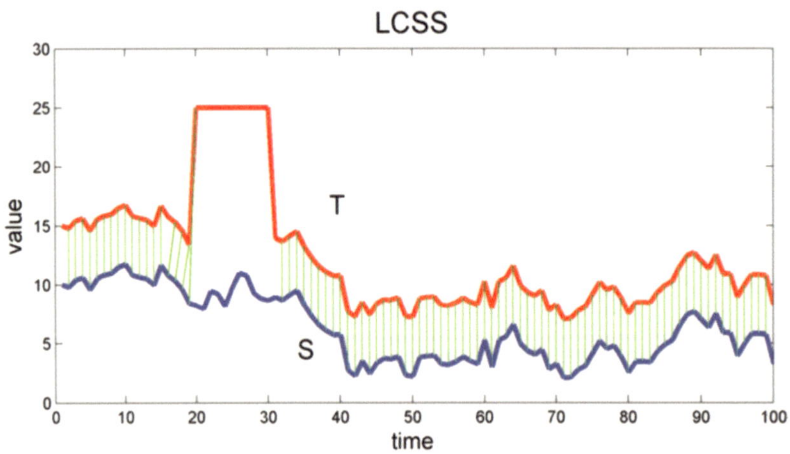

Figure 9. Alignment using *LCSS*. Time series *T* (red line) is obtained from *S* (blue line), by adding a fixed value = 5, and further "noise" at positions starting from 20 to 30. In these positions there is no mapping (green lines).

4. Dimensionality reduction techniques

We have already introduced that a key aspect to achieve efficiency, when mining time series data, is to work with a data representation that is lighter than the raw data. This can be done by reducing the dimensionality of data, still maintaining its main properties. An important feature to be considered, when choosing a representation, is the *lower bounding* property.

Given two raw representations of the time series *T* and *S*, by this property, after establishing a true distance measure d_{true} for the raw data (such as the Euclidean distance), the distance $d_{feature}$ between two time series, in the reduced space, *R*(*T*) and *R*(*S*), have to be always less or equal than d_{true}:

$$d_{feature}(R(T),R(S)) \le d_{true}(T,S) \tag{25}$$

If a dimensionality reduction techniques ensures that the reduced representation of a time series satisfies such a property, we can assume that the similarity matching in the reduced space maintains its meaning. Moreover, we can take advantage of indexing structure such as *GEMINI* (Section 2) [13] to perform speed-up search even avoiding false negative results. In the following subsections, we will review the main dimensionality reduction techniques that preserve the *lower bounding* property.

4.1. DFT

The dimensionality reduction, based on the *Discrete Fourier Transform* (*DFT*) [1], was the first to be proposed for time series. The DFT decomposes a signal into a sum of sine and cosine waves, called *Fourier Series*. Each wave is represented by a complex number known as *Fourier coefficient* (Fig. 10) [29],[32]. The most important feature of this method is the data compression, because the original signal can be reconstructed by means of information carried by the waves with higher Fourier coefficient. The rest can be discarded with no significant loss.

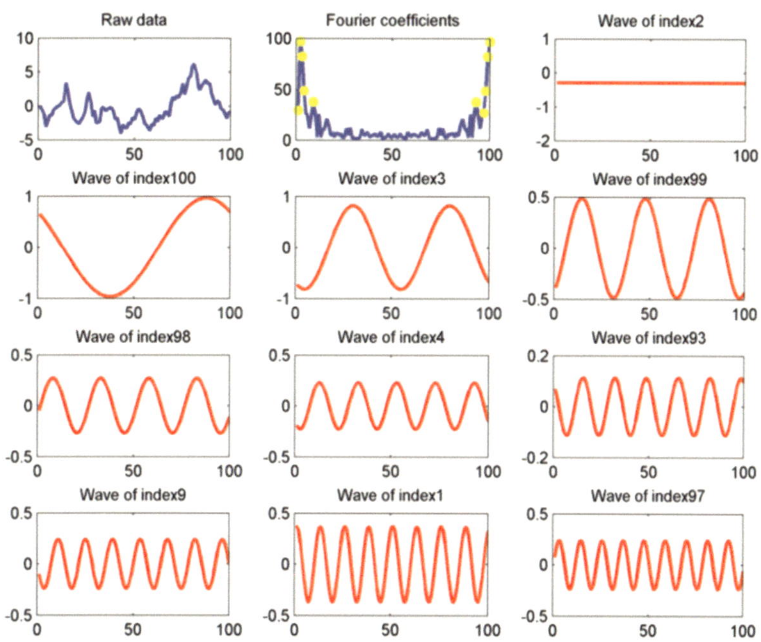

Figure 10. The raw data is in the top-left plot. In the first row, the central plot ("Fourier coefficients" plot) shows the magnitude for each wave (Fourier coefficient). Yellow points are drawn for the top ten highest values. The remaining plots (in order from first row to last, and from left to right) represent the waves corresponding to the top ten highest coefficients in decreasing order, respectively of index {2, 100, 3, 99, 98, 4, 93, 9, 1, 97}, in the "Fourier coefficients" plot.

More formally, given a signal $x = \{x_1, x_2, \ldots, x_n\}$, the n-point *Discrete Fourier Transform* of x is a sequence $X = \{X_1, X_2, \ldots, X_n\}$ of complex numbers. X is the representation of x in the frequency domain. Each wave/frequency X_F is calculated as:

$$X_F = \frac{1}{\sqrt{n}} \sum_{i=1}^{n} x_i e^{-\frac{2\pi ijF}{n}} \quad (j = \sqrt{-1}) \quad F = 1, \ldots, n \tag{26}$$

The original representation of x, in the time domain, can be recovered by the inverse function:

$$x_i = \frac{1}{\sqrt{n}} \sum_{F=1}^{n} X_F e^{-\frac{2\pi ijF}{n}} \quad (j = \sqrt{-1}) \quad i = 1, \ldots, n \tag{27}$$

The energy $E(x)$ of a signal x is given by:

$$E(x) = \|x\|^2 = \sum_{i=1}^{n} |x_i|^2 \tag{28}$$

A fundamental property of *DFT* is guaranteed by the *Parseval's Theorem*, which asserts that the energy calculated on time series domain for signal x is preserved on frequency domain, and then:

$$E(x) = \sum_{i=1}^{n} |x_i|^2 = \sum_{F=1}^{n} |X_F|^2 = E(X) \tag{29}$$

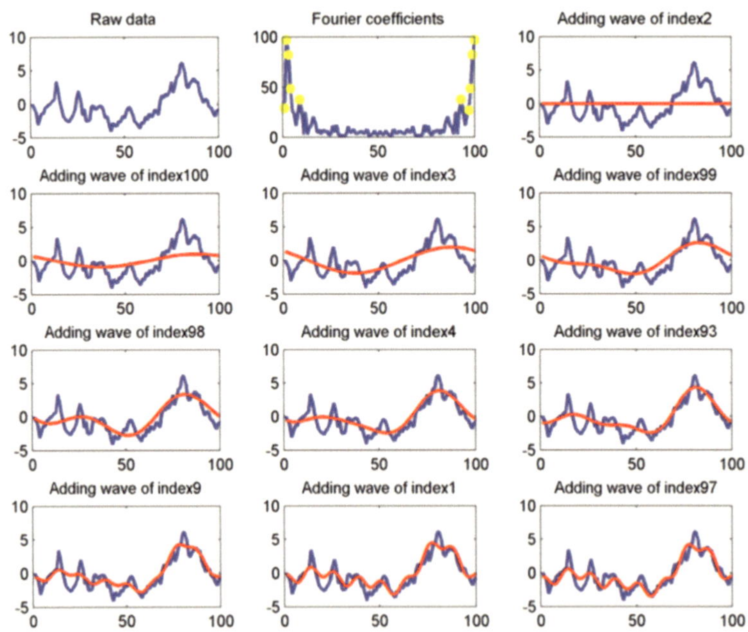

Figure 11. The raw data is in the top-left plot. In the first row, the central plot ("Fourier coefficients" plot) shows the magnitude (Fourier coefficient) for each wave. Yellow points are drawn for the top ten highest values. The remaining plots (in order from first row to last, and from left to right) represent the reconstruction of the raw data using the wave with highest values (of index 2) firstly, then by adding the wave relative to second highest coefficient (of index 100), and so on.

If we use the Euclidean distance (Eq. 12), by this property, the distance $d(x,y)$ between two signals x and y on time domain is the same as calculated in the frequency domain $d(X,Y)$, where X and Y are the respective transforms of x and y. The reduced representation $X' = \{X_1, X_2, \ldots, X_k\}$ is built by only keeping first k coefficients of X to reconstruct the signal x (Fig. 11).

For the Parseval's Theorem we can be sure that the distance calculated on the reduced space is always less than the distance calculated on the original space, because $k \leq n$ and then the distance measured using Eq. 12 will produce:

$$d(X',Y') \leq d(X,Y) = d(x,y) \tag{30}$$

that satisfies the lower bounding property defined in Eq. 25.

The computational complexity of *DFT* is $O(n^2)$, but it can be reduced by means of the *FFT* algorithm [8], which computes the *DFT* in $O(n \log n)$ time. The main drawback of *DFT* reduction technique is the choice of the best number of coefficients to keep for a faithfully reconstruction of the original signal.

4.2. DWT

Another technique for decomposing signals is the *Wavelet Transform* (*WT*). The basic idea of *WT* is data representation in terms of sum and difference of prototype functions, called *wavelets*. The discrete version of *WT* is the *Discrete Wavelet Transform* (*DWT*). Similarly to *DFT*, wavelet coefficients give local contributions to the reconstruction of the signal, while Fourier coefficients always represent global contributions to the signal over all the time [32].

The *Haar* wavelet is the simplest possible wavelet. Its formal definition is shown in [7]. An example of *DWT* based on Haar wavelet is shown in Table 1.

The general *Haar* transform $H_L(T)$ of a time series T of length n can be formalized as follows:

$$A_{L'+1}(i) = \frac{A_{L'}(2i) + A_{L'}(2i+1)}{2} \tag{31}$$

$$D_{L'+1}(i) = \frac{D_{L'}(2i) - D_{L'}(2i+1)}{2} \tag{32}$$

$$H_L(T) = (A_L, D_L, D_{L-1}, \ldots, D_o) \tag{33}$$

where $0 < L' \leq L$, and $1 \leq i \leq n$.

Level (L)	Averages coefficients (A)	Wavelet coefficients (D)
1	10, 4, 6, 6	
2	8, 6	3, 0
3	7	1

Table 1. The *Haar* transform of $T = \{10, 4, 8, 6\}$ depends on the chosen level, and corresponds to merging *Averages coefficients* (column 2) at the chosen level and all *Wavelet coefficients* (column 3) in decreasing order from the chosen level. At level 1 the representation is the same of time series: $H_1(T) = \{10, 4, 6, 6\} + \{\} = \{10, 4, 6, 6\} = T$. At level 2 is $H_2(T) = \{8, 6\} + \{3, 0\} + \{\} = \{8, 6, 3, 0\}$. At level 3 is $H_3(T) = \{7\} + \{1\} + \{3, 0\} = \{7, 1, 3\ 0\}$.

The main drawback of this method is that it is well defined for time series which length n is a power of 2 ($n = 2^m$). The computational complexity of *DWT* using *Haar* Wavelet is $O(n)$. Chan and Fu [7] demonstrated that the Euclidean distance between two time series T and S, $d(T,S)$, can be calculated in terms of their *Haar* transform $d(H(T), H(S))$, by preserving the lower bounding property in Eq. 25, because:

$$d(H(T), H(S)) = \sqrt{2}d(T,S) < d(T,S) \tag{34}$$

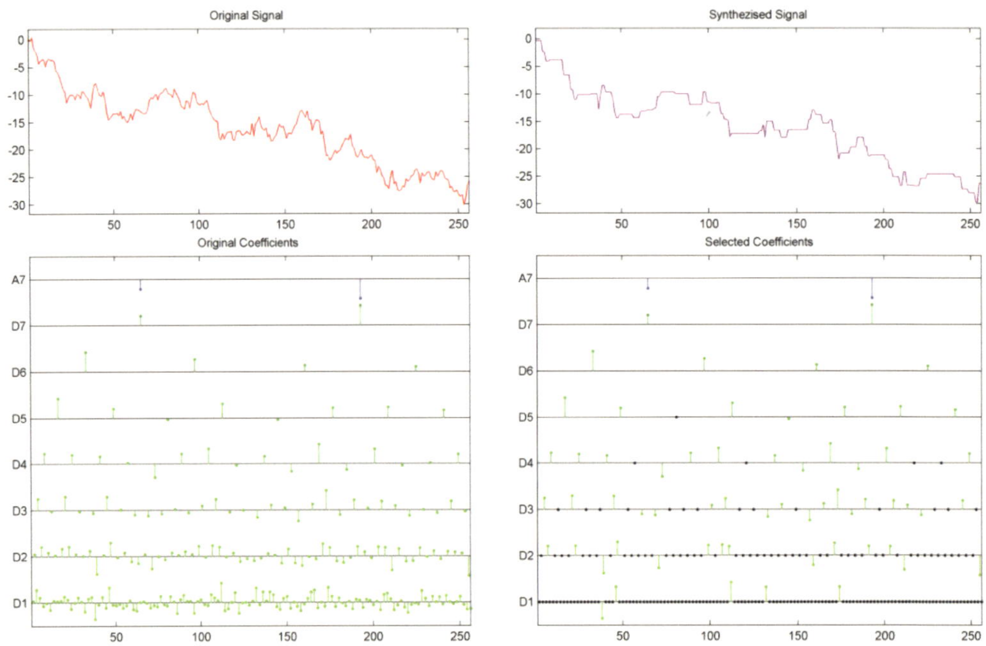

Figure 12. *DWT* using *Haar* Wavelet with *MATLAB Wavelet Toolbox™ GUI tools*. *T* is a time series of length $n = 256$ and it is shown on the top-left plot (*Original Signal*). On the bottom-left plot (*Original Coefficients*) there are all the A_L, represented by blue stems, and $D_{L'}$ coefficients ($L' < L = 7$), represented by green stems (stems' length is proportional to coefficients value). On the top-right plot, the *Synthesized Signal* by selecting only the 64 biggest coefficients, as reported on the bottom-right plot (*Selected Coefficients*): black points represent unselected coefficients.

4.3. SVD

As we have just seen in Section 2, a *TSDB* with m time series, each of length n, can be represented by a $m \times n$ matrix A (Eq. 1). An important result from linear algebra is that A can always be written in the form [16]:

$$A = UWV^T \tag{35}$$

where U is an $m \times n$ matrix, W and V are $n \times n$ matrices. This is called the *Singular Value Decomposition* (*SVD*) of the matrix A, and the elements of the $n \times n$ diagonal matrix W are the *singular values* w_i:

$$W = \begin{pmatrix} w_1 & 0 & \cdots & 0 \\ 0 & w_2 & \cdots & 0 \\ \vdots & \vdots & \ddots & \vdots \\ 0 & 0 & \cdots & w_n \end{pmatrix} \tag{36}$$

V is orthonormal, because $VV^T = V^TV = I_n$, where I_n is the identity matrix of size n. So, we can multiply both sides of Eq. 35 by V to get:

$$AV = UWV^TV \rightarrow AV = UW \tag{37}$$

UW represents a set of n-dimensional vectors $AV = \{X_1, X_2, \ldots, X_m\}$ which are rotated from the original vectors $A = \{x_1, x_2, \ldots, x_m\}$ [29]:

$$\begin{pmatrix} X_1 \\ X_2 \\ \vdots \\ X_m \end{pmatrix} = \begin{pmatrix} U_1 \\ U_2 \\ \vdots \\ U_m \end{pmatrix} \begin{pmatrix} w_1 & 0 & \cdots & 0 \\ 0 & w_2 & \cdots & 0 \\ \vdots & \vdots & \ddots & \vdots \\ 0 & 0 & \cdots & w_n \end{pmatrix} \tag{38}$$

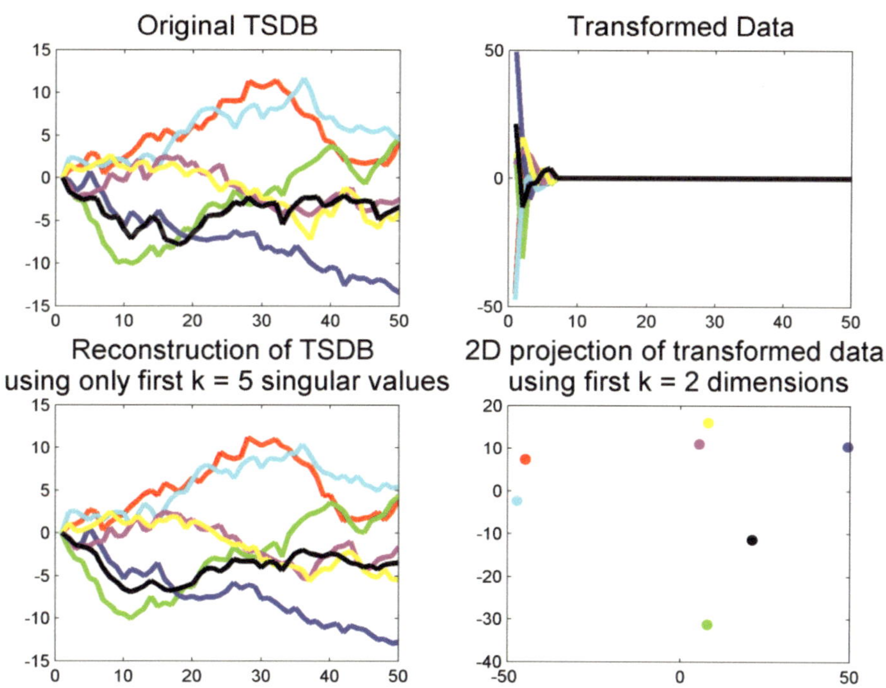

Figure 13. *SVD* for a *TSDB* of m=7 time series of length n=50. It is possible to note in the *transformed data* plot how only first $k < 10$ singular values are significant. In this example we heuristically choose to store only first k=5 diagonal elements of V, and their relative entries in A, U and W, because they represent about 95% of total variance. This permits to reduce space complexity from n to k, still maintaining almost unchanged the information (see the reconstruction on the bottom-left plot).

Similarly to sine/cosine waves for *DFT* (Section 3.1) and to wavelet for *DWT* (Section 3.2), *U* vectors represent basis for *AV*, and their linear combination with *W* (that represents their coefficients) can reconstruct *AV*.

We can perform dimensionality reduction by selecting the first ordered *k* biggest singular values, and their relative entries in *A*, *V* and *U*, to obtain a new *k*-dimensional dataset that best fits original data.

SVD is an optimal transform if we aim to reconstruct data, because it minimizes the reconstruction error, but have two important drawbacks: (i) it needs a collection of time series to perform dimensionality reduction (it cannot operate on singular time series), because examines the whole dataset prior to transform. Moreover, the computational complexity is $O(\min(m^2n, mn^2))$. (ii) This transformation is not incremental, because a new data insertion requires a new global computation.

4.4. Dimensionality reduction via PAA

Given a time series *T* of length *n*, *PAA* divides it into *w* equal sized segments t_i ($1 < i \leq w$) and records values corresponding to the mean of each segment $mean(t_i)$ (Fig. 14) into a vector $PAA(T) = \{mean(t_1), mean(t_2), \ldots, mean(t_w)\}$, using the following formula:

$$mean(t_i) = \frac{w}{n} \sum_{j=\frac{n}{w}(i-1)+1}^{\frac{n}{w}i} t_j \tag{39}$$

When *n* is a power of 2, each $mean(t_i)$ essentially represents an *Averages coefficient* $A_L(i)$, defined in Section 4.2, and *w* corresponds in this case to:

$$w = \frac{n}{2^L} \tag{40}$$

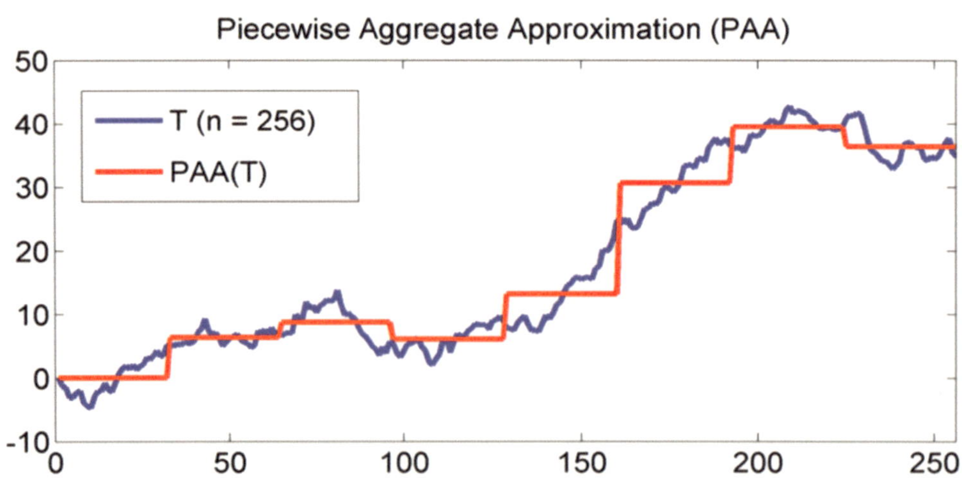

Figure 14. An approximation via *PAA* technique of a time series *T* of length $n = 256$, with $w = 8$ segments.

The complexity time to calculate the mean values of Eq. 39 is $O(n)$. The *PAA* method is very simple and intuitive, moreover it is strongly competitive with other more sophisticated transforms such as *DFT* and *DWT* [21],[41]. Most of data mining researches makes use of *PAA* reduction for its simplicity. It is simple to demonstrate how the distance on raw representation is bounded below by the distances calculated on *PAA* representation (even using Euclidean distance as reference point), satisfying Eq. 25. A limitation of such a reduction, in some contexts, can be the fixed size of the obtained segments.

4.5. APCA

In Section 4.2 we noticed that not all *Haar* coefficients in *DWT* are important for the time series reconstruction. Same thing for *PAA* in Section 4.4, where not all segment means are equally important for the reconstruction, or better, we sometimes need an approximation with no-fixed size segments. *APCA* is an adaptive model that, differently from *PAA*, allows to define segments of variable size. This can be useful when we find in time series areas of low variance and areas of high variance, for which we want to have, respectively, few segments for the former, and many segments for the latter.

Given a time series $T = \{t_1, t_2, \ldots, t_n\}$ of length n, the *APCA* representation of T is defined as [6]:

$$C = \{\langle cv_1, cr_1 \rangle, \ldots, \langle cv_M, cr_M \rangle\}, \quad cr_0 = 0 \tag{41}$$

where cr_i is the last index of the ith segment, and

$$cv_i = mean\left(t_{cr_{i-1}+1}, \ldots, t_{cr_i}\right) \tag{42}$$

To find an optimal representation through the *APCA* technique, dynamic programming can be used [14,30]. This solution requires $O(Mn^2)$ time. A better solution was proposed by Chakrabarti et al. [6], which finds the *APCA* representation in $O(n \log n)$ time, and defines a distance measure for this representation satisfying the lower bounding property defined in Eq. 25. The proposed method bases on *Haar* wavelet transformation. As we have just seen in Section 4.2, the original signal can be reconstructed by only selecting bigger coefficients, and truncating the rest. The segments in the reconstructed signal may have approximate mean values (due to truncation) [6], so these values are replaced by the exact mean values of the original signal. Two aspects to consider before performing APCA:

1. Since *Haar* transformation deals only with time series length $n = 2^p$, we need to add zeros to the end of the time series, until it reaches the desired length.
2. If we held the biggest M Haar coefficients, we are not sure if the reconstruction will return an *APCA* representation of length M. We can know only that the number of segments will vary between M and $3M$ [6]. If the number of segments is more than M, we will iteratively merge more similar adjacent pairs of segments, until we reach M segments.

The algorithm for compute APCA representation can be found in [6].

4.6. Time series segmentation using PLA

As with most computer science problems, representation of data is the key to efficient and effective solutions. A suitable representation of a time series may be *Piecewise Linear Approximation* (*PLA*), where the original points are reduced to a set of segments.

PLA refers to the approximation of a time series *T*, of length *N*, using *K* consecutive segments with *K* much smaller than *n* (Fig. 15). This representation makes the storage, transmission and computation of the data more efficient [23]. In the light of it, *PLA* may be used to support clustering, classification, indexing and association rule mining of time series data (e.g. [10]).

The process of time series approximation using *PLA* is known as segmentation and is related to clustering process where each segment can be considered as a cluster [33].

There are several techniques to segment a time series and they can be distinguished into off-line and on-line approaches. In the former approach an error threshold is fixed by the user, while the latter uses a dynamic error threshold that changes, according to specific criteria, during the execution of the algorithm.

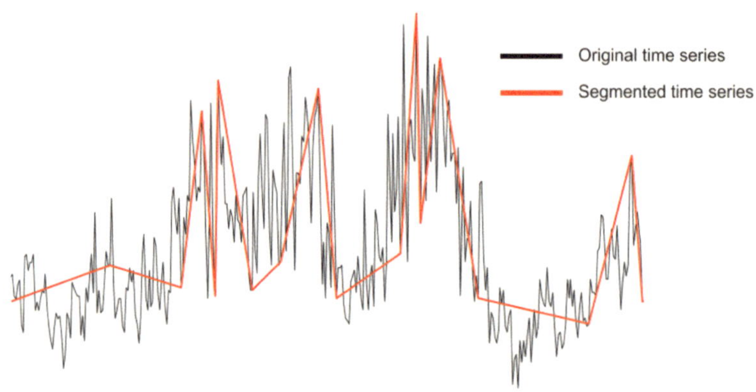

Figure 15. The trend approximation (red line) of the original time series (black line) obtained by *PLA*.

Although off-line algorithms are simple to realize, they are less effective than the on-line ones. The classic approaches to time series segmentation are the sliding window, bottom-up and top-down algorithms. Sliding window is an on-line algorithm and works growing a segment until the error for the potential segment is greater than the user-specified threshold, then the subsequence is transformed into a segment; the process repeats until the entire time series has been approximated by its *PLA* [23]. A way to estimate error is by taking the mean of the sum of the square of vertical differences between the best-fit line and the actual data points. Another commonly used measure of goodness of fit is the distance between the best fit line and the data point furthest away in the vertical direction [23].

In the top-down approach a segment, that represents the entire time-series, is recursively split until the desired number of segment or a error threshold is reached. Dually, the bottom-up algorithm starts from the finest approximation of the time series using *n/2* segments and merging the two most similar adjacent segments until the desired number of segment or an error threshold is reached.

However, an open question is the choice of best k number of segments. This problem involves a trade-off between compression and accuracy of time series representation. As suggested by Salvador et al. [33], the appropriate number of segments may be estimated using evaluation graph. It is defined as a two dimensional plot where x-axis is the number of segments, while y-axis is a measure of the segmentation error. The best number of segments is provided by the point of maximum curvature, also called "knee", of the evaluation graph (Fig. 16).

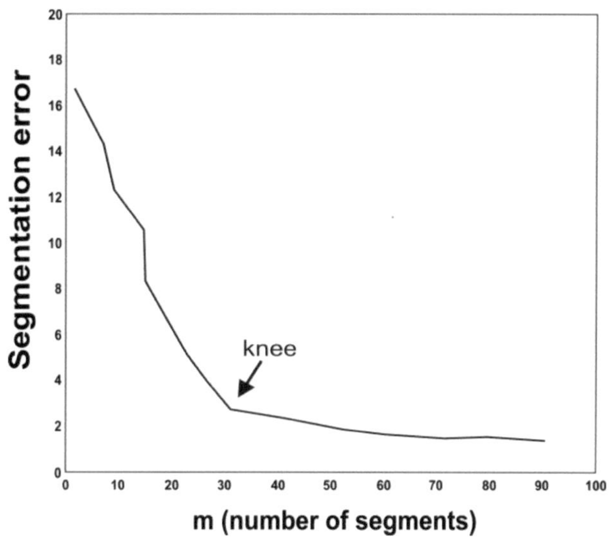

Figure 16. Evaluation graph. The best number of segments is provided by the knee of the curvature.

4.7. Chebyshev Polynomials approximation

By this technique, the reduction problem is resolved by considering the values of the time series T as values of a function f, and approximating it with a polynomial function of degree n which well fits f:

$$P_n(x) = \sum_{i=0}^{n} a_i x^i \tag{43}$$

where each a_i corresponds to coefficients and x^i to the variables of degree i.

There are many possible ways to choose the polynomial: Fourier transforms (Section 4.1), splines, non-linear regressions, etc. Ng and Cai [29] hypothesized that one of the best approaches is the polynomial that minimizes the maximum deviation from the true value, which is called the *minimax* polynomial. It has been shown that the *Chebyshev* approximation is almost identical to the optimal minimax polynomial, and is easy to compute [27]. Thus, Ng and Cai [29] explored how to use the *Chebyshev polynomials* (of the first kind) as a basis for approximating and indexing n-dimensional ($n \geq 1$) time series. The Chebyshev polynomial $CP_m(x)$ of the first kind is a polynomial of degree m ($m = 0, 1, \ldots$), defined as:

$$CP_m(x) = \cos(m \arccos(x)) \quad x \in [-1, 1] \tag{44}$$

It is possible to compute every $CP_m(x)$ using the following recurrence function [29]:

$$CP_m(x) = 2xCP_{m-1}(x) - CP_{m-2}(x) \tag{45}$$

for all $m \geq 2$ with $CP_0(x) = 1$ and $CP_1(x) = x$. Since Chebyshev polynomials form a family of orthogonal functions, a function $f(x)$ can be approximated by the following Chebyshev series expansion:

$$S_{\infty}^{CP}(f(x)) = \sum_{i=0}^{\infty} c_i CP_i(x) \tag{46}$$

where c_i refer to the *Chebyshev coefficients*. We refer the reader to the paper [29] for the conversion of a time series, which represents a discrete function, to an interval function required for the computation of Chebyshev coefficients. Given two time series T and S, and their corresponding vectors of Chebyshev coefficients, C_1 and C_2, the key feature of their work is the definition of a distance function d_{Cheb} between the two vectors, that guarantees the lower bounding property defined in Eq. 25. Since it results:

$$d_{cheb}(C_1, C_2) \leq d_{true}(T_1, T_2) \tag{47}$$

the indexing with Chebyshev coefficients admits no false negatives. The computational complexity of Chebishev approximation is $O(n)$, where n is the length of the approximated time series.

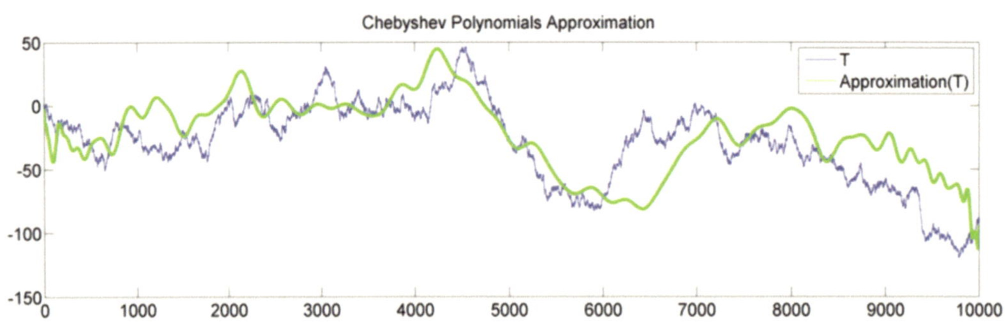

Figure 17. An example of approximation of a time series T of length $n = 10000$ with a Chebyshev series expansion (Eq. 46) where i is from 0 to $k = 100$, using the *chebfun* toolbox for MATLAB (http://www2.maths.ox.ac.uk/chebfun/)

4.8. SAX

Many symbolic representations of time series have been introduced over the past decades. The challenge in this field is to create a real correlation between the distance measure defined on the symbolic representation, and that defined on original time series. *SAX* is the most known symbolic representation technique on time series data mining, that ensures both a considerable dimensionality reduction, and the lower bounding property, allowing enhancing of time performances on most of data mining algorithm.

Given a time series T of length n, and an alphabet of arbitrary size a, *SAX* returns a string of arbitrary length w (typically $w << n$). The alphabet size a is an integer, where $a > 2$. *SAX* method is *PAA*-based, since it transforms *PAA* means into symbols, according to a defined transformation function.

To give a significance to the symbolic transformation, it is necessary to deal with a system producing symbols with equal probability, or with a Gaussian distribution. This can be achieved by normalizing time series, since normalized time series have generally a Gaussian distribution [26]. This is the first assumption to consider about this technique. However, for data not obeying to this property, the efficiency of the reduction is slightly deteriorated. Given the Gaussian distribution, it is simple to determine the "breakpoints" that will produce a equal-sized areas of probability under the Gaussian curve. What follows gives the principal definitions to understand *SAX* representation.

Definition 1. ***Breakpoints***: A sorted list of numbers $B = \beta_1, \ldots, \beta_{a-1}$ such that the area under a $N(0, 1)$ Gaussian curve from β_i to $\beta_{i+1} = 1/a$ (β_0 and β_a are defined as $-\infty$ and ∞, respectively) (Table 2). For example, if we want to obtain breakpoints for an alphabet of size $a = 4$, we have to compute the first (q_1), the second (q_2), and the third (q_3) quartiles of the inverse cumulative Gaussian distribution, corresponding to the 25%, 50% and 75% of the cumulative frequency: $\beta_1 = q_1$, $\beta_2 = q_2$, $\beta_3 = q_3$.

Definition 2. ***Alphabet***: A collection of symbols $alpha = \alpha_1, \alpha_2, \ldots, \alpha_a$ of size a used to transform mean frames into symbols.

$\beta_i \backslash a$	3	4	5	6	7	8
β_1	-0.43	-0.67	-0.84	-0.97	-1.07	-1.15
β_2	0.43	0	-0.25	-0.43	-0.57	-0.67
β_3		0.67	0.25	0	-0.18	-0.32
β_4			0.84	0.43	0.18	0
β_5				0.97	0.57	0.32
β_6					1.07	0.67
β_7						1.15

Table 2. A look-up table for breakpoints used for alphabet of size $2 < a < 9$.

Definition 3. ***Word***: A PAA approximation $PAA(T) = \{mean(t_1), mean(t_2), \ldots, mean(t_w)\}$ of length w can be represented as a word $SAX(T) = \{sax(t_1), sax(t_2), \ldots, sax(t_w)\}$, with respect to the following mapping function:

$$sax(t_i) = \alpha_j, \quad iff \ \beta_{j-1} \le mean(t_i) < \beta_j \quad (0 < i \le w, \quad 1 < j < a) \tag{39}$$

Lin et al. [26] defined a distance measure for this representation, such that the real distance calculated on original representation is bounded below from it. An extension of *SAX* technique, *iSAX*, was proposed by Shieh and Keogh [35] which allows to get different resolutions for the same word, by using several combination of parameters *a* and *w*.

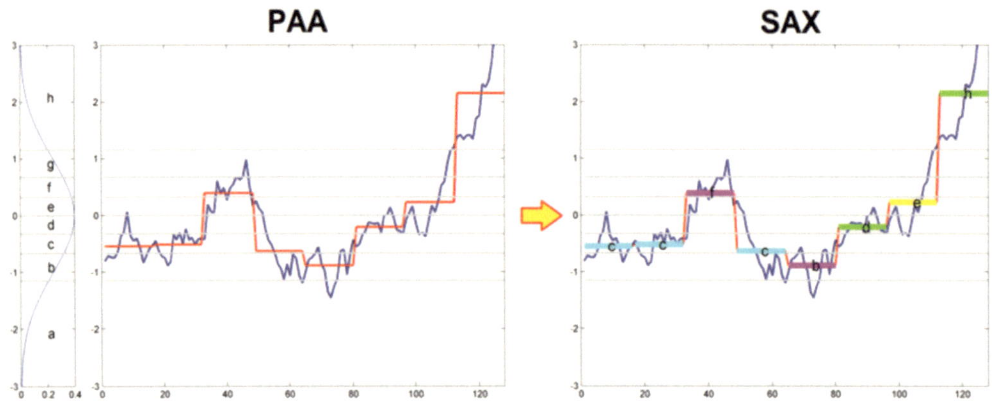

Figure 18. An example of conversion of a time series *T* (blue line) of length $n = 128$, into a word of length $w = 8$, using an alphabet *alpha* = {*a,b,c,d,e,f,g,h*} of size $a = 8$. The left plot refers to the Gaussian distribution divided into equal areas of size $1/a$. *PAA* mean frames falling into two consecutive cutlines (gray lines) will be mapped into the corresponding plotted symbol (colored segments). The *PAA* plot shows the *PAA* representation (red line), while *SAX* plot shows the conversion of *PAA*(*T*) into the word *SAX*(*T*) = {*c,g,e,g,f,g,a,a*}. Images generated by MATLAB and code provided by *SAX* authors [26].

Author details

Placido Montalto, Marco Aliotta and Andrea Cannata
Istituto Nazionale di Geofisica e Vulcanologia, Osservatorio Etneo, Sezione di Catania, Catania, Italy

Carmelo Cassisi* and Alfredo Pulvirenti
Università degli studi di Catania, Dipartimento di Matematica e Informatica, Catania, Italy

5. References

[1] Agrawal, Faloutsos, Swami (1993). "Efficient similarity search in sequence databases". *Proc. of the 4th Conference on Foundations of Data Organization and Algorithms*, pp. 69–84.

[2] Bailey, Elkan (1995). "Unsupervised learning of multiple motifs in biopolymers using expectation maximization". *Machine Learning Journal 21*, 51–80.

[3] Beckmann, Kriegel, Schneider, Seeger (1990). "The R*-tree: An Efficient and Robust Access Method for Points and Rectangles". *Proc. ACM SIGMOD Int. Conf. on Management of Data*, Atlantic City, NJ, pp. 322-331.

[4] Bentley (1975). "Multidimensional binary search trees used for associative searching". *Communications of ACM*. Vol. 18, pp. 509-517.

* Corresponding Author

[5] Cantone, Ferro, Pulvirenti, Reforgiato (2005). "Antipole tree indexing to support range search and k-nearest neighbour search in metric spaces". *IEEE Transactions on Knowledge and Data Engineering*. Vol. 17, pp. 535-550.

[6] Chakrabarti, Keogh, Mehrotra, Pazzani (2002). "Locally adaptive dimensionality reduction for indexing large time series databases". *ACM Trans. Database Syst.* 27, 2, pp 188-228.

[7] Chan, Fu (1999). "Efficient time series matching by wavelets". In *proceedings of the 15th IEEE Int'l Conference on Data Engineering*. Sydney, Australia, Mar 23-26. pp 126-133.

[8] Cooley, Tukey (1965). "An algorithm for the machine calculation of complex Fourier series", *Math. Comput.* 19, 297–301.

[9] Cormen, Leiserson, Rivest (1990). *Introduction to Algorithms*. The MIT Press, McGraw-Hill Book Company.

[10] Di Salvo, Montalto, Nunnari, Neri, Puglisi (2012). "Multivariate time series clustering on geophysical data recorded at Mt. Etna from 1996 to 2003". *Journal of Volcanology and Geothermal Research.*

[11] Ding, Trajcevski, Scheuermann, Wang, Keogh (2008). "Querying and Mining of Time Series Data: Experimental Comparison of Representations and Distance Measures". *VLDB*.

[12] Duda, Hart, Stork (2001). *Pattern Classification*. John Wiley & Sons.

[13] Faloutsos, Ranganthan, Manolopoulos (1994). "Fast subsequence Matching in Time-Series Databases". *SIGMOD Conference*.

[14] Faloutsos, Jagadish, Mendelzon, Milo (1997). "A signature technique for similarity-based queries". In *Proceedings of the SEQUENCES 97* (Positano-Salerno, Italy).

[15] Fink, Pratt (2004). "Indexing of compressed time series". In Mark Last, Abraham Kandel, and Horst Bunke, editors, *Data Mining in Time Series Databases*, pages 43-65. World Scientific, Singapore.

[16] Golub, Van Loan (1996). *Matrix Computations*, 3rd edition. Baltimore, MD: Hopkins University Press.

[17] Han and Kamber (2005). *Data Mining: Concepts and Techniques*. Morgan Kaufmann Publishers, CA.

[18] Itakura (1975). Minimum prediction residual principle applied to speech recognition. *IEEE Trans Acoustics Speech Signal Process*. ASSP 23:52–72

[19] Keogh, Chakrabarti, Pazzani, Mehrotra (2000). "Dimensionality reduction for fast similarity search in large time series databases". *Journal of Knowledge and Information Systems*.

[20] Keogh, Chu, Hart, Pazzani (2001a). An Online Algorithm for Segmenting Time Series. In Proc. IEEE Intl. Conf. on Data Mining, pp. 289-296, 2001.

[21] Keogh, Kasetty (2002). "On the need for time series data mining benchmarks: a survey and empirical demonstration". *Proceedings of the Eighth ACM SIGKDD International Conference on Knowledge Discovery and Data Mining*, pp. 102-111.

[22] Keogh, Ratanamahatana (2002). "Exact indexing of dynamic time warping". In *proceedings of the 26th Int'l Conference on Very Large Data Bases*. Hong Kong. pp 406-417.

[23] Keogh, Chu, Hart, Pazzani (2004). "Segmenting time series: a survey and novel approach". In: Last, M., Kandel, A., Bunke, H. (Eds.), *Data mining in time series database*. World Scientific Publishing Company, pp. 1-21.

[24] Korn, Jagadish, Faloutsos (1997). "Efficiently supporting ad hoc queries in large datasets of time sequences". *Proceedings of SIGMOD '97*, Tucson, AZ, pp 289-300.

[25] Lawrence, Altschul, Boguski, Liu, Neuwald, Wootton (1993). "Detecting subtle sequence signals: A Gibbs sampling strategy for multiple alignment". *Science 262*, 208–14.

[26] Lin, Keogh, Wei, Lonardi (2007). "Experiencing SAX: a novel symbolic representation of time series". Data Mining Knowledge Discovery, 15(2).

[27] Mason, Handscomb (2003). *Chebyshev Polynomials*. Chapman & Hall.

[28] Mueen, Keogh, Zhu, Cash, Westover (2009). "Exact Discovery of Time Series Motifs". *SDM 2009*.

[29] Ng, Cai (2004): "Indexing Spatio-Temporal Trajectories with Chebyshev Polynomials". *SIGMOD 2004*.

[30] Pavlidis (1976). "Waveform segmentation through functional approximation". *IEEE Trans.Comput. C-22*, 7 (July).

[31] Perng, Wang, Zhang, Parker (2000). "Landmarks: a newmodel for similarity-based pattern querying in time series databases". *Proc.2000 ICDE*, pp. 33–42.

[32] Ratanamahatana, Lin, Gunopulos, Keogh, Vlachos, Das (2010): "Mining Time Series Data". *Data Mining and Knowledge Discovery Handbook*, pp. 1049-1077.

[33] Salvador, Chan, (2004). "Determining the number of clusters/segments in hierarchical clustering/segmentation algorithms". *Proceedings of the 16th IEEE International Conference on Tools with Artificial Intelligence*, 2004, pp. 576-584.

[34] Sakoe, Chiba (1978). Dynamic programming algorithm optimization for spoken word recognition. *IEEE Trans Acoustics Speech Signal Process*. ASSP 26:43–49

[35] Shieh and Keogh (2008). "iSAX: Indexing and Mining Terabyte Sized Time Series". *SIGKDD*, pp 623-631.

[36] Tompa, Buhler (2001). "Finding motifs using random projections". *In proceedings of the 5th Int'l Conference on Computational Molecular Biology*. Montreal, Canada, Apr 22-25. pp 67-74.

[37] Vlachos, Kollios, Gunopulos (2002). "Discovering similar multidimensional trajectories". *Proc. 2002 ICDE*, pp. 673–684.

[38] Von Storch, Zwiers (2001). *Statistical analysis in climate research.* Cambridge Univ Pr. ISBN 0521012309.

[39] Wang, Ye, Keogh, Shelton (2008). "Annotating Historical Archives of Images". *JCDL 2008*.

[40] Yang, Shahabi (2004). "A PCA-based similarity measure for multivariate time series". In Proceedings of the 2nd ACM international workshop on Multimedia database, pp. 65-74.

[41] Yi and C. Faloutsos (2000). "Fast Time Sequence Indexing for Arbitrary Lp Norms". *VLDB*.

Chapter 4

Data Mining and Neural Networks: The Impact of Data Representation

Fadzilah Siraj, Ehab A. Omer A. Omer and Md. Rajib Hasan

Additional information is available at the end of the chapter

http://dx.doi.org/10.5772/51594

1. Introduction

The extensive use of computers and information technology has led toward the creation of extensive data repositories from a very wide variety of application areas [1]. Such vast data repositories can contribute significantly towards future decision making provided appropriate knowledge discovery mechanisms are applied for extracting hidden, but potentially useful information embedded into the data [2].

Data mining (DM) is one of the phases in knowledge discovery in databases. It is the process of extracting the useful information and knowledge in which the data is abundant, incomplete, ambiguous and random [3], [4], [5]. DM is defined as an automated or semi-automated exploratory data analysis of large complex data sets that can be used to uncover patterns and relationships in data with an emphasis on large observational databases [6]. Modern statistical and computational technologies are applied to the problem in order to find useful patterns hidden withina large database [7], [8], [9]. To uncover hidden trends and patterns, DM uses a combination of an explicit knowledge base, sophisticated analytical skills, and domain knowledge. In effect, the predictive models formed from the trends and patterns through DM enable analysts to produce new observations from existing data. DM methods can also be viewed as statistical computation, artificial intelligence (AI) and database approach[10]. However, these methods are not replacing the existing traditional statistics; in fact, it is an extension of traditional techniques. For example, its techniques have been applied to uncover hidden information and predict future trends in financial markets. Competitive advantages achieved by DM in business and finance include increased revenue, reduced cost, and improved market place responsiveness and awareness [11]. It has also been used to derive new information that could be integrated in decision support, forecasting and estimation to help business gain competitive advantage [9]. In higher educational institutions, DM can be used in the process of uncovering hidden trends and patterns that help them in forecasting the students' achievement. For instance, by using DM

INTECH
open science | open minds

© 2012 Siraj et al., licensee InTech. This is an open access chapter distributed under the terms of the Creative Commons Attribution License (http://creativecommons.org/licenses/by/3.0), which permits unrestricted use, distribution, and reproduction in any medium, provided the original work is properly cited.

approach, a university could predict the accuracy percentage of students' graduation status, whether students will or will not be graduated, the variety of outcomes, such as transferability, persistence, retention, and course success[12], [13].

The objective of this study is to investigate the impact of various data representations on predictive data mining models. In the task of prediction, one particular predictive model might give the best result for one data set but gives a poor results in another data set although these two datasets contain the same data with different representations [14],[15],[16], [17]. This study focuses on two predictive data mining models, which are commonly used for prediction purposes, namely neural network (NN) and regression model. A medical data set (known as Wisconsin Breast Cancer) and a business data (German credit) that has Boolean targets are used for experimental purposes to investigate the impact of various data representation on predictive DM model. Seven data representations are employed for this study; they are As_Is, Min Max normalization, standard deviation normalization, sigmoidal normalization, thermometer representation, flag representation and simple binary representation.

This chapter is organized as follows. The second section describes data mining, and data representation is described in the third section. The methodology and the experiments for carrying out the investigations are covered in Section 4. The results are the subject of discussion which is presented in Section 5. Finally, the conclusion and future research are presented in Section 6.

2. Data mining

It is well known that DM is capable of providing highly accurate information to support decision-making and forecasting for scientific, physiology, sociology, the military and business decision making [13]. DM is a powerful technology with great potential such that it helps users focus on the most important information stored in data warehouses or streamed through communication lines. DM has a potential to answer questions that were very time-consuming to resolve in the past. In addition, DM can predict future trends and behavior, allowing us to make proactive, knowledge-driven decisions [18].

NN, decision trees, and logistic regression are three classification models that are commonly used in comparative studies [19]. These models have been applied to a prostate cancer data set obtained from SEER (the Surveillance, Epidemiology), and results program of the National Cancer Institute. The results from the study show that NN performed best with the highest accuracy, sensitivity and specificity, followed by decision tree and then logistic regression. Similar models have been applied to detect credit card fraud. The results indicate that NN give better performance than logistic regression and decision tree [20].

3. Data representation

Data representation plays a crucial role on the performance of NN, "especially for the applications of NNs in a real world." In data representation study,[14] used NNs to extrapolate the presence of mercury in human blood from animal data. The effect of different data representations such as *As-is, Category, Simple binary, Thermometer*, and *Flag* on the prediction models are investigated. The study concludes that the *Thermometer* data representation using NN performs extremely well.

[16], [21] used five different data representations (*Maximum Value, Maximum* and *Minimum Value, Logarithm, Thermometer* (powers of 10), and *Binary* (powers of 2)) on a set of data to predict maize yield at three scales in east-central Indiana of the Midwest USA [17]. The data used to consist of weather data and yield data from farm, county and state levels from the year 1901 to 1996. The results indicate that data representation has a significant effect on NN performance.

In another study, [21] investigate the performance of data representation formats such as *Binary* and *Integer* on the classification accuracy of network intrusion detection system. Three data mining techniques such as rough sets, NN and inductive learning were applied on binary and integer representations. The experimental results show that different data representations did not cause significant difference to the classification accuracy. This may be due to the fact that the same phenomenon were captured and put into different representation formats [21]. In addition, the data was primarily discrete values of qualitative variables (system class), and different results could be obtained if the values were continuous variables.

Numerical encoding schemes (*Decimal Normalization and Split Decimal Digit representation*) and bit pattern encoding schemes (*Binary representation, Binary Code Decimal representation, Gray Code representation, Temperature code representation, and Gray Coded Decimal representation*) were applied on Fisher Iris data and the performance of the various encoding approaches were analyzed. The results indicate that encoding approaches affect the training errors (such as maximum error and root mean square error) and encoding methods that uses more input nodes that represent one single parameter resulted in lower training errors. Consequently, [22] work laid an important foundation for later research on the effect of data representation on the classification performance using NN.

[22] conducted an empirical study based on a theoretical provided by [15] to support the findings that input data manipulation could improve neural learning in NN. In addition, [15] evaluated the impact of the modified training sets and how the learning process depends on data distribution within the training sets. NN training was performed on input data set that has been arranged so that three different sets are produced with each set having a different number of occurrences of 1's and 0's. The *Temperature Encoding* is then employed on the three data sets and then being used to train NN again. The results show that by employing *Temperature Encoding* on the data sets, the training process is improved by significantly reducing the number of epochs or iteration needed for training. [15]'s findings proved that by changing input data representation, the performance in a NN model is affected.

4. Methodology

The methodology for this research is being adapted from [14] by using different data representations on the data set, and the steps involved in carrying out the studies are shown in Figure 1 [14]. The study starts with data collection, followed by data preparation stage, analysis and experiment stage, and finally, investigation and comparison stage.

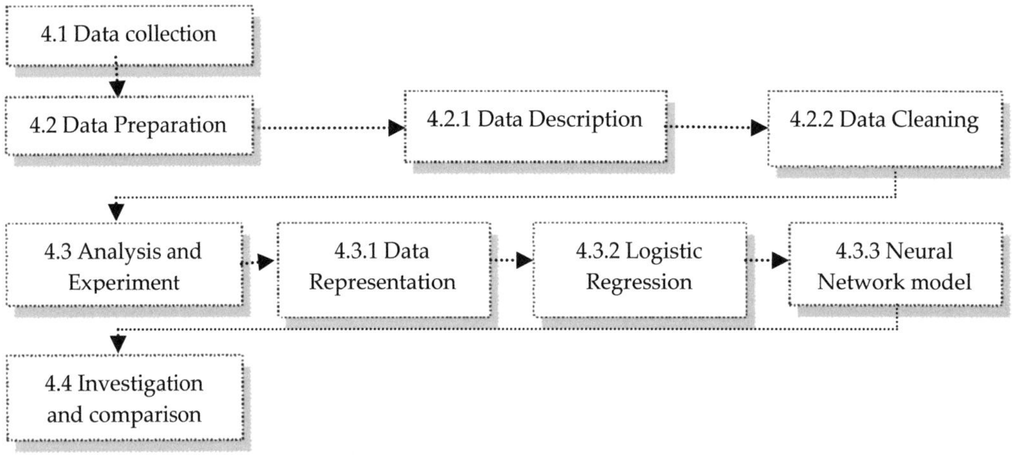

Figure 1. Steps in carrying out the study

4.1. Data collection

At this stage, data sets have been acquired through the UCI machine learning repository which can be accessed at http://archive.ics.uci.edu/ml/ datasets.html. The UCI Machine Learning Repository is a collection of databases, domain theories, and data generators that are used by the machine learning community for conducting empirical studies on machine learning algorithms. Two types of data have been obtained from UCI; they are Wisconsin Breast Cancer data set and German credit data set.

4.2. Data preparation

After the data has been collected in the previous stage, data preparation would be performed to prepare the data for the experiment in the next stage. Each attribute is examined and missing values are treated prior to training.

4.2.1. Data description

In this study, two sets of data are used, namely Wisconsin Breast Cancer and German Credit. Each data set is described in details in the following subsections.

4.2.1.1. Wisconsin breast cancer data set

Wisconsin breast cancer data set is originated from University of Wisconsin Hospitals, Madison donated by Dr. William H. Wolberg. Each instance or data object from the data represents one patient record. Each record comprises of information about Breast Cancer patient whose cancer condition is either benign or malignant. A total of 699 cases in the data set with nine attributes (excluding Sample Code Number) that represent independent variables and one attribute, i.e. Class represent the output or dependent variable.

Table 1 describes the attribute in the data set, code which represents the short form for this attribute, type, which shows the data type for particular attribute, domain, which represents the possible range in the value and the last column, shows the missing values in all attributes in the study. From Table 1, only one attribute has been missing values (a total of 16 instances), and this attribute is Bare Nuclei.

No	Attribute description	Code	Type	Domain	Missing value
1	Sample code number	CodeNum	Continues	Id number	0
2	Clump Thickness	CTHick	Discrete	1 – 10	0
3	Uniformity of Cell Size	CellSize	Discrete	1 – 10	0
4	Uniformity of Cell Shape	CellShape	Discrete	1 – 10	0
5	Marginal Adhesion	MarAd	Discrete	1 – 10	0
6	Single Epithelial Cell Size	EpiCells	Discrete	1 – 10	0
7	Bare Nuclei	BareNuc	Discrete	1 – 10	16
8	Bland Chromatin	BLChr	Discrete	1 – 10	0
9	Normal Nucleoli	NormNuc	Discrete	1 – 10	0
10	Mitoses	Mito	Discrete	1 – 10	0
11	Class:	Cl	Discrete	2 for benign 4 for malignant	0

Table 1. Attribute of Wisconsin Breast Cancer Dataset

Based on the condition of Breast Cancer patients, a total of 65.5% (458) of them has benign condition and the rest (34.5% or 241) is Malignant.

4.2.1.2. German credit dataset

German credit data set classifies applicants as good or bad credit risk based upon a set of attributes specified by financial institutions. The original data set is provided by Professor Hofmann contains categorical and symbolic attributes. A total of 1000 instances have been provided with 20 attributes, excluding the German Credit Class (Table 2). The applicants are classified as good credit risk (700) or bad (300) with no missing value in this data set.

No.	Attribute description	Code	Type	Domain	Missing value
1	Status of existing checking account	SECA	Discrete	1, 2, 3, 4	0
2	Duration in month	DurMo	Continuous	4 - 72	0
3	Credit history	CreditH	Discrete	0, 1, 2, 3, 4	0
4	Purpose	Purpose	Discrete	0, 1, 2, 3, 4, 5, 6, 7, 8, 9, 10	0

No.	Attribute description	Code	Type	Domain	Missing value
5	Credit amount	CreditA	Continuous	250 - 18424	0
6	Savings account/bonds	SavingA	Discrete	1, 2, 3, 4, 5	0
7	Present employment since	EmploPe	Discrete	1, 2, 3, 4, 5	0
8	Instalment rate in percentage of disposable income	InstalRate	Continuous	2 – 4	0
9	Personal status	PersonalS	Discrete	1, 2, 3, 4, 5	0
10	Other debtors / guarantors	OtherDep	Discrete	1, 2, 3	0
11	Present residence since	PresentRe	Discrete	1 – 4	0
12	Property	Property	Discrete	1, 2, 3, 4	0
13	Age in years	Age	Continuous	19 – 75	0
14	Other instalment plans	OtherInst	Discrete	1, 2, 3	0
15	Housing	Housing	Discrete	1, 2, 3	0
16	Number of existing credits at bank	NumCBnk	Discrete	1,2,3	0
17	Job	Job	Discrete	1, 2, 3, 4	0
18	Number of people being liable to provide maintenance for	Numppl	Discrete	1, 2	0
19	Telephone	Telephone	Discrete	1, 2	0
20	Foreign worker	ForgnWor	Discrete	1, 2	0
21	German Credit Class	GCL	Discrete	1 good 2 bad	0

Table 2. Attribute of German Credit Dataset

4.2.2. Data cleaning

Before using the data that has been collected in the previous stage, missing values should be identified. Several methods that could be performed to solve missing values on data, such as deleting the attributes or instances, replacing the missing values with the mean value of a particular attribute, or ignore the missing values. However, which action would be performed to handle the missing values depends upon the data that has been collected.

German credit application data set has no missing values (refer to Table 2); therefore, no action was taken on German credit data set. On the other hand, Wisconsin breast cancer data set has 16 missing values of an attribute Bare Nuclei (see Table 1). Therefore, these missing values have been resolved by replacing the mean value to this attribute. The mean value to this attribute is 3.54, since the data type for this attribute is categorical so the value was rounded to 4. Finally, all the missing values have been replaced by value 4.

4.3. Analysis and experiment

The data representations used for the experiments are described in the following subsections.

4.3.1. Data representation

Each data set has been transformed into data representation identified for this study, namely As_Is, Min Max Normalization, Standard Deviation Normalization, Sigmoidal Normalization, Thermometer Representation, Flag Representation and Simple Binary Representation. In As_Is representation, the data remain the same as the original data without any changes. The Min Max Normalization is used to transform all values into numbers between 0 and 1. The Min Max Normalization applies linear transformation on the raw data, keeping the relationship to the data values in the same range. This method does not deal with any possible outliers in the future value, and the min max formula [25] is written in Eqn. (1).

$$V' = (v - Min(v(i)))/(Max(v(i)) - Min(v(i))) \tag{1}$$

Where V' is the new value, Min(v(i)) is the minimum value in a particular attribute, Max(v(i)) the maximum value in a particular attribute and v is the old value.

The *Standard Deviation Normalization* is a technique based on the mean value and standard deviation function for each attribute on the data set. For a variable v, the mean value **Mean (v)** and the standard deviation Std_dev(v) is calculated from the data set itself. The standard deviation normalization formula [25] is written as in Eqn. (2).

$$V' = \frac{(v - mean(v))}{std\_dev(v)} \tag{2}$$

where

$$meanv(v) = \frac{Sum(v)}{n}$$

std_dev(v)= sqr(sum(v^2)-(sum(v)^2/n)/(n-1))

The *Sigmoidal Normalization* transforms all nonlinear input data into the range between -1 and 1 using a sigmoid function. It calculates the mean value and standard deviation function value from the input data. Data points within a standard deviation of the mean are converted to the linear area of the sigmoid. In addition, outlier points to the data are compacted along the sigmoidal function tails. The sigmoidal normalization formula [25] is given by Eq. (3).

$$V' = \frac{(v - mean(v))}{std\_dev(v)} \tag{3}$$

Where

$$a = \frac{(v - mean(v))}{std_{dev(v)}}$$

$$mean(v) = \frac{Sum(v)}{n}$$

std_dev(v)= sqr(sum(v^2)-(sum(v)^2/n)/(n-1))

In the *Thermometer* representation, the categorical value was converted into a binary form prior to performing analysis. For example, if the range of values for a category field is 1 to 6, thus value 4 can be represented in thermometer format as "111100" [15].

In the *Flag* format, digit 1 is represented in the binary location for the value. Thus, following the same assumption that the range values in a category field is 1 to 6, if the value 4 needs to be represented in *Flag* format, the representation will be shown as "000100." The representation in *Simple Binary* is obtained by directly changing the categorical value into binary. Table 3 exhibits the different representations of Wisconsin Breast Cancer and German Credit data set.

Representations	Wisconsin Breast Cancer	German Credit
As_Is representation	5 4 3	1 6.0 4
Min Max normalization	.0000 .4444 .3333	.0000 .0294 1.000
Standard Deviation normalization	-1.637 .2068 .2836	-1.254 -1.236 1.343
Sigmoidal normalization	-.675 .1102 .149	-.362 .8103 -.576
Thermometer representation	111110000011110	1000100000111111
Flag representation	0000100000000001000	10001000000000100
Simple Binary representation	010101000011000	00010001010000110

Table 3. Various dataset representations

4.3.2. *Logistic regression*

Logistic regression is one of the statistical methods used in DM for non-linear problems either to classify or for prediction. Logistic Regression is one of the parts of statistical models, which allows one to predict a discrete outcome (known as dependent variable), such as group membership, from a set of variables (also known as independent variables) that may be continuous, discrete, dichotomous, or a combination of any of these. The logistic regression aims to correctly predict the category of outcome for individual cases using the most parsimonious model. In order to achieve the goal, a model is created, which comprises of all predictor (independent) variables that are useful in predicting the desired target. The relationship between the predictor and the target is not linear instead; the logistic regression function is usedwhose equation can be written as Eqn. (4) [26].

$$\theta = \frac{\exp\left(\beta_0 + \beta_{1}{}_{X_1} + \ldots + \beta_{k}{}_{x_k}\right)}{1 + \exp\left(\beta_0 + \beta_{1}{}_{X_1} + \ldots + \beta_{k}{}_{x_k}\right)} \quad (4)$$

Where α = the constant from the equation andβ = the coefficient of the predictor variables. Alternatively, the logistic regression equation can be written as Eqn. (5).

$$\log it\left[\theta(x)\right] = \log\left[\frac{\theta(x)}{1-\theta(x)}\right] = \alpha + \left(\beta_0 + \beta_{1}{}_{X_1} + \ldots + \beta_{k}{}_{x_k}\right) \quad (5)$$

Anodd's ratio is formed from logistic regression that calculates the probability or success over the probability of failure. For example, logistic regression is often used for epidemiological studies where the analysis result shows the probability of developing cancer after controlling for other associated risks. In addition, logistic regression also provides knowledge about the relationships and strengths among the variables (e.g., smoking 10 packs a day increases the risk for developing cancer than working in asbestos mine)[27].

Logistic regression is a model which is simpler in terms of computation during training while still giving a good classification performance [28]. The simple logistic regression model has the form as in Eqn. (6), viz:

$$logit(Y) = natural \log(odds) = ln\left(\frac{\pi}{1-\pi}\right) = \alpha + \beta X \quad (6)$$

Taking the antilog of Eqn. (1) on both sides, an equation to predict the probability to the occurrence of the outcome of interest is as follows:

$$\pi = Probability(Y = outcome\ of\ interest\ |X = x, a\ specific\ value\ of\ X) = \frac{e^{\alpha+\beta x}}{1+ e^{\alpha+\beta s}} \quad (7)$$

Where π is theprobability for the outcome of interest or "event," α is the intercept, ß is the regression coefficient, and e = 2.71828 is the base forthe system of natural logarithms X can be categorical or continuous, but Y is always categorical.

For the Wisconsin Breast Cancer dataset, there are ten independent variables and one dependent variable for logistic regression as shown in Figure 2. However, the CodeNum is not included for analysis.

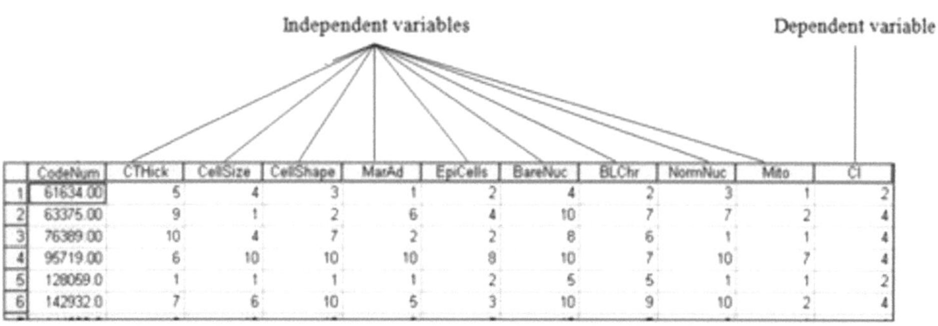

	CodeNum	CTHick	CellSize	CellShape	MarAd	EpiCells	BareNuc	BLChr	NormNuc	Mito	Cl
1	61634.00	5	4	3	1	2	4	2	3	1	2
2	63375.00	9	1	2	6	4	10	7	7	2	4
3	76389.00	10	4	7	2	2	8	6	1	1	4
4	95719.00	6	10	10	10	8	10	7	10	7	4
5	128059.0	1	1	1	1	2	5	5	1	1	2
6	142932.0	7	6	10	5	3	10	9	10	2	4

Figure 2. Independent and dependent variables of Wisconsin Breast Cancer dataset

Similar approach is applied to German Credit dataset.

4.3.3. Neural network

NN or artificial neural network (ANN) are one of the DM techniques; defined as an information-processing system which is inspired from the function of the human brain whose performance characteristics are somehow in common with biologicalNN [30]. It comprises of a large number of simple processing units, called artificial neurons or nodes. All nodes are interconnected by links known as connections.These nodes are linked together to perform parallel distributed processing in order to solve a desired computational taskby simulating the learning process [3].

There are weights associated with the links that represent the connection strengths between two processing units. These weights determine the behavioron the network. The connection strengths determine the relationship between the input and the output for the network, and in a way represent the knowledge stored on the network. The knowledge is acquired by NN through a process of training during which the connection strengths between the nodes are modified. Once trained, the NN keeps this knowledge, and it can be used for the particular task it was designed to do [29]. Through training, a network understands the relationship of the variables and establishes the weights between the nodes.Once the learning occurs, a new case can be loaded over the network to produce more accurate prediction or classification [31].

NN models can learn from experience, generalize and "see through" noise and distortion, and also abstract essential characteristics in the presence of irrelevant data [32]. NN model is also described as a 'black box' approach which has great capacity in predictive modelling. NN models provide a high degree of robustness and fault tolerance since each processing node has primarily local connections[33]. NNs techniques are also advocated as a replacement for statistical forecasting methods because of its capabilities and performance [33], [34], [33]. However, NNs are very much dependent upon the problem at hand.

The techniques of NNs have been extensively used in pattern recognition, speech recognition and synthesis, medical applications (diagnosis, drug design), fault detection, problem diagnosis, robot control, and computer vision [36], [37]. One major application areas of NNs is forecasting, and the NNs techniques have been used as to solve many forecasting problems ([33], [36], [39], [38].

There are two types of perceptron in NN, namely simple or linear perceptron and MLP. Simple perceptron consists of only two layers; the input layer and output layer. MLP consists of at least three layers input layer, hidden layer and output layer. Figure 3 illustrates the two types of perceptron.

The basic operation of NN involves summing its input weights and the activation function is applied to these layers to yield the output. Generally, there are three types of activation functions used in NN, which are threshold function, Piecewise-linear function and Sigmoid function (Figure 4). Among these sigmoid function is the most commonly used in NN.

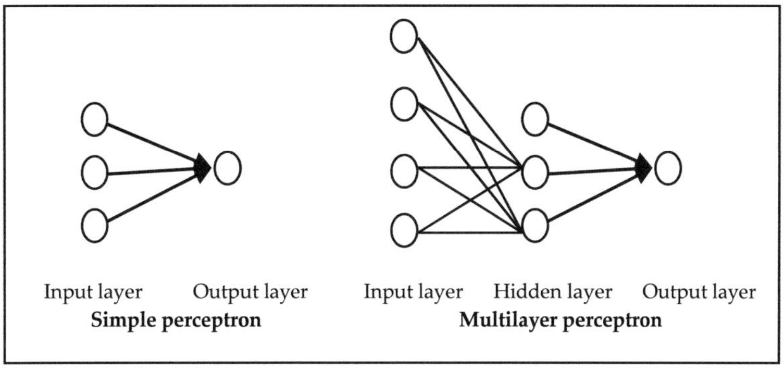

Figure 3. Simple and MLP architecture

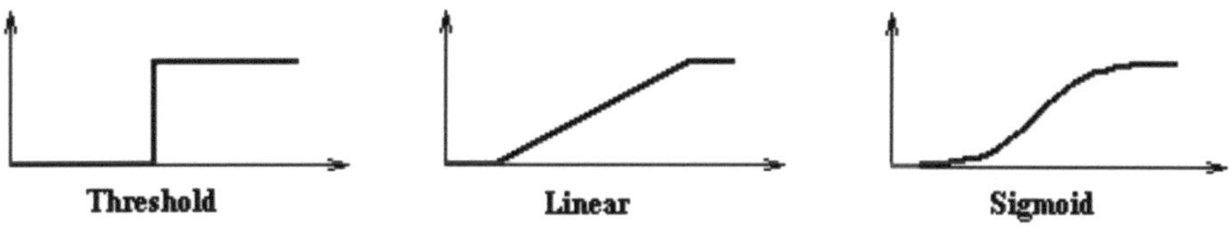

Figure 4. Activation function for BP learning

Multilayer Perceptron (MLP) is one of the most common NN architecture that has been used for diverse applications, particularly in forecasting problems [40]. The MLP network is normally composed of a number of nodes or processing units, and it is organized into a series of two or more layers. The first layer (or the lowest layer) is named as an input layer where it receives the external information while the last layer (or the highest layer) is an output layer where the solution to the problem is obtained. The hidden layer is the intermediate layer in between the input layer and the output layer, and may compose with one or more layers. The training of MLP could be stated as a nonlinear optimization problem. The objective of MLP learning is to find out the best weights that minimize the difference between the input and the output. The most popular training algorithm used in NN is Back propagation (BP), and it has been used in solving many problems in pattern recognition and classification. This algorithm depends upon several parameters such as a number of hidden nodes at the hidden layers 'learning rate, momentum rate, activation function and the number of training to take place. Furthermore, these parameters could change the performance on the learning from bad to good accuracy [23].

There are three stages involved when training the NN using BP algorithm[36]. The first step is the feed forward of the input training pattern, second is calculating the associated error from the output with the input. The last step is the adjustment to the weight. The learning process basically starts with feed forward stage when each of input units receives the input information and sends the information to each of the hidden units at the hidden layer. Each hidden unit computes the activation and sends its signal to each output unit, and applies the activation to form response of the net for given input pattern. The accuracy of NN is provided by a confusion matrix. In a confusion matrix, the information about actual values and the predictive values are illustrated in Table 4. Each row of the matrix represents the actual accounts of a class of target for the actual data, while each column represents the predictive value from the actual data. To obtain the accuracy of NN, the summation of the correct instance will be divided by the summation for all instances. The accuracy of NN is calculated using Eqn. (7).

$$Percentage\ of\ Correct = \left(\frac{Total\ of\ correctly\ predicted\ pattern}{Total\ no.of\ pattern}\right) * 100\% \qquad (7)$$

Based on Table 4, the Percentage of correct is calculated as:

Percentage of Correct = ((48 + 39) / (48 + 2 + 11 + 39)) * 100%

Wrongly predicted

Correctly predicted

Correctly predicted

	Predicted	
Actual	Benign	Malignant
Benign	48	2
Malignant	11	39

Table 4. Confusion matrix

Experiments are conducted to obtain a set of training parameters that gives the optimum accuracy for both data sets. Figure.5 shows general architecture of NN for the Wisconsin Breast Cancer data set. Note that the ID number is not including in the architecture.

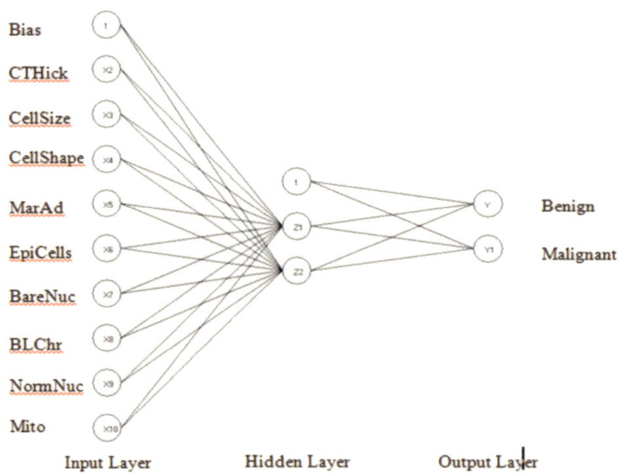

Figure 5. Neural Network architecture for Wisconsin Breast Cancer

Similar architecture can be drawn for German Credit dataset; however, the number of hidden units and output units will be different from the Wisconsin Breast Cancer.

4.4. Investigation and comparison

The accuracy results obtained from previous experiments are compared and investigated further. Two data sets are considered for this study, the Logistic regression and Neural Network. Logistic regression is a statistical regression model for binary dependent variables [24], which is simpler in terms of computation during training while still giving a good classification performance [27]. Figure 6 shows the general steps involve in performing logistic regression and NN experiments using different data representations in this study.

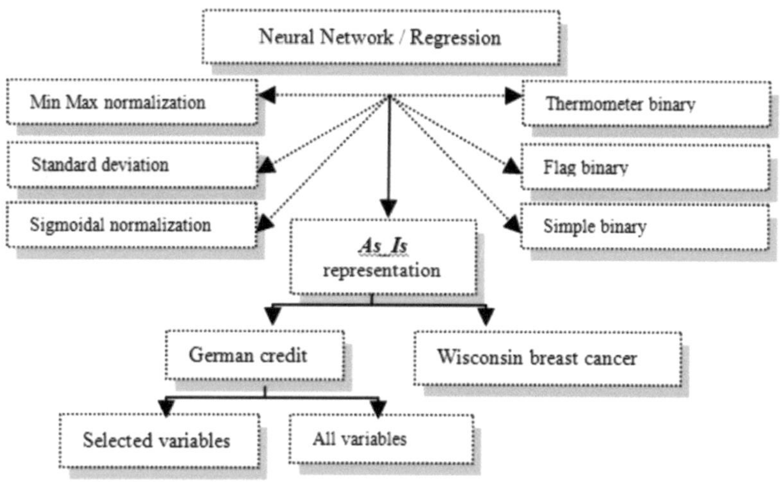

Figure 6. Illustration of Data Representation for NN/ Regression analysis experiments

5. Results

Investigating the prediction performance on different data sets involves many uncertainties for a different data type. In the task of prediction, one particular predictive model might give the best result for one data set but gives the poor results in another data set although these two data sets contain the same data with different representations [14],[15],[16], [17].

Initial experimental results of correlation analysis on Wisconsin Breast Cancer indicate that all attributes (independent variables) has significant correlation with the dependent variable (target). However, German Credit data set indicates otherwise. Therefore, for German Credit data set, two different approaches (all dependent variables and selected variables) were performed in order to complete the investigation.

Based on the results exhibited in Table 5, although NN obtained the same percentage of accuracy, *As_Is* achieved the lowest training results (98.57%, 96.24%). On the other hand, regression exhibits the highest percentage of accuracy for *Thermometre*and *Flag* representation (100%) followed by *Simple Binary* representation.

Referring to the result shown in Figure 7, similar observation has been noted for German Credit data set when **all variables** are considered for the experiments. *As_Is* representation obtained the highest percentage of accuracy (79%) for NN model. For regression analysis,

Thermometer and *Flag,* representation obtained the highest percentage of accuracy (80.1%). Similar to earlier observation on the Wisconsin Breast Cancer dataset. Simple *Binary* representation obtained the second highest percentage of accuracy (79.5%).

	Wisconsin Breast Cancer		
	Neural Network		Regression
	Train	Test	Accuracy
As_Is representation	96.24%	98.57%	96.9%
Min Max normalization	96.42%	98.57%	96.9%
Standard Deviation normalization	96.42%	98.57%	96.9%
Sigmoidal normalization	96.60%	98.57%	96.9%
Thermometer representation	97.14%	98.57%	100.0%
Flag representation	97.67%	98.57%	100.0%
Simple Binary representation	97.14%	98.57%	97.6%

Table 5. Percentage of accuracy for Wisconsin Breast Cancer Dataset

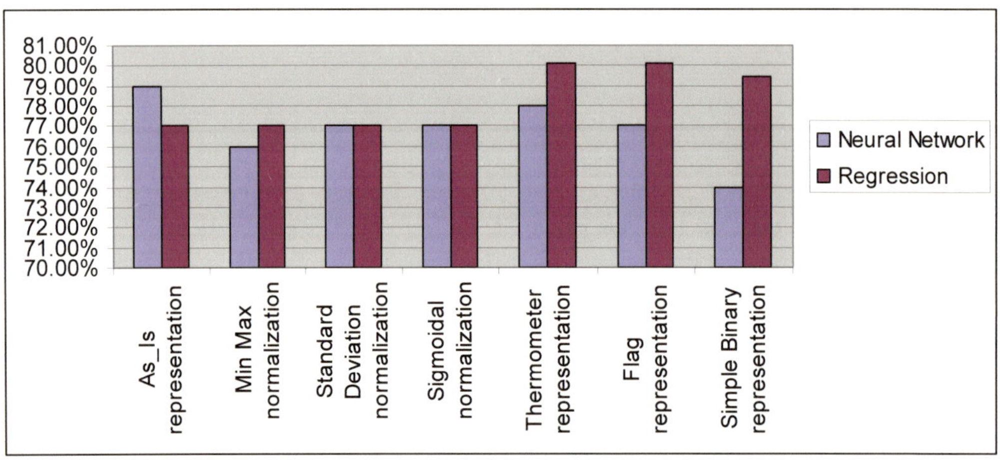

Figure 7. German Credit All Variables accuracy for Neural Network and Regression

When **selected variables** of German Credit data set was tested with NN, the highest percentage accuracy was obtained using *As_Is* representation (80%), followed by *Standard Deviation Normalization* (79%) *Min Max Normalization* (78%) and **Thermometer** (78%) representation. The regression results show similar patterns with results illustrated in Figure. In other words, the data representation techniques, namely *Thermometer* (77.4%) and Flag (77.4%) representations produce the highest and second highest percentage of accuracy for selected variables of German Credit.

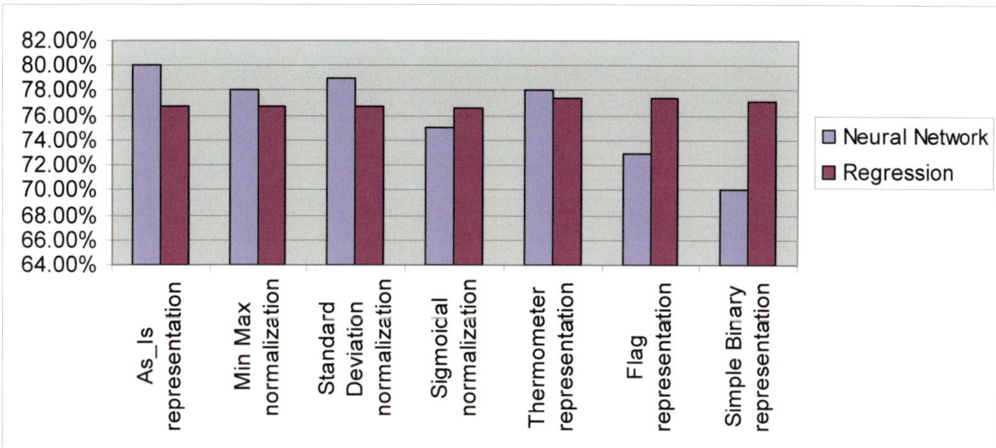

Figure 8. German Credit Selected Variables accuracy for Neural Network and Regression

For brevity, Table 6 exhibits NN parameters that produce the highest percentage of accuracy for Wisconsin Breast Cancer, and German Credit data set using all variables as well as selected variables in the experiments.

Neural Network	Wisconsin Breast lCancer	German credit using all variables	German credit using selected variables
Percentage of Accuracy	**98.57%**	80.00%	79.00%
Input units	9	20	12
Hidden units	2	6	20
Learning rate	0.1	0.6	0.6
Momentum rate	0.8	0.1	0.1
Number of epoch	100	100	100

Table 6. The summary of NN experimental results using *As_Is* representation

The logistic regression and correlation results for Wisconsin Breast Cancer data set are exhibited in Table 7. Note that based on Wald Statistics, variables such as *CellSize, Cellshape, EpiCells, NormNuc* and *Mito* are not significant in the prediction model. However, these variables have significant correlation with Type of Breast Cancer. Thus, the logistic regression independent variables include all variables listed in Table 7.

For German Credit data set, NN obtained the highest percentage of accuracy when all variables are considered for the training (see Table 6). The appropriate parameters for this data set are also listed in the same table. The summary of logistic regression results is shown in Table 8. All shaded variables displayed in Table 8 are significant independent variables for determining whether a credit application is successful or not.

Logistic Regression			**Correlation**	
Variables	B	Sig.	R	p
CTHick	.531	.000		
CellSize	.006	.975	.818(**)	.000
CellShape	.333	.109	.819(**)	.000
MarAd	.240	.036		
EpiCells	.069	.645	.683(**)	.000
BareNuc	.400	.000		
BLChr	.411	.009		
NormNuc	.145	.157	.712(**)	.000
Mito	.551	.069	.423(**)	.000
Constant	-9.671	.000		

Table 7. List of variables included in logistic regression of Wisconsin breast cancer

Note also that variable *age* is not significant to German Credit target. However, its correlation with the target is significant. Therefore, these are variable included in logistic regression equation that represents German credit application.

Regression (Thermometer representation)	**German Credit using all variables (80%)**			
Variables	Logistic Regression		Correlation	
	B	Sig.	R	p
SECA	-.588	000	-.348(**)	.000
DurMo	.025	.005	.206(**)	.000
CreditH	-.384	.000	-.222(**)	.000
CreditA	-.384	.018	.087(**)	.003
SavingA	-.240	.000	-.175(**)	.000
EmploPe	-.156	.029	-.120(**)	.000
InstalRate	.300	.000	.074(**)	.010
PersonalS	-.267	.022	-.091(**)	.002
OtherDep	-.363	.041	-0.003	.460
Property	.182	.046	.141(**)	.000
Age	**-.010**	**.246**	**-.112(**)**	**.000**
OtherInst	-.322	.004	-.113(**)	.000
Forgn Work	-1.216	.047	-.082(**)	.005
Constant	4.391	.000		

Table 8. List of variables included in logistic regression of German Credit dataset

6. Conclusion and future research

In this study, the effect of different data representations on the performance of NN and regression was investigated on different data sets that have a binary or boolean class target. The results indicate that different data representation produces a different percentage of accuracy.

Based on the empirical results, data representation *As_Is*is a better approach for NN with Boolean targets (see also Table 9). NN has shown consistent performance for both data sets. Further inspection of the results exhibited in Table 6 also indicates that for German Credit data set, NN performance improves by 1%. This leads to suggestion that by considering correlation and regression analysis, both NN results using *As_Is* and *Standard Deviation Normalization* could be improved. For regression analysis, *Thermometer, Flag* and *Simple Binary* representations produce consistent regression performance. However, the performance decreases when the independent variables have been reduced through correlation and regression analysis.

As for future research, more data sets will be utilized to investigate further on the effect of data representation on the performance of both NN and regression. One possible area is to investigate which cases fail during training, and how to correct the representation of cases such that the cases will be correctly identified by the model. Studying the effect of different data representations on different predictive models enable future researchers or data mining model's developer to present data correctly for binary or Boolean target in the prediction task.

	German Credit All Variables			German Credit Selected Variables		
	Neural Network		Regn	Neural Network		Regn
	Train	Test		Train	Test	
As_Is representation	77.25	79.00	77.0	75.00	80.00	76.8
Min Max normalization	76.50	76.00	77.0	75.25	78.00	76.8
Standard Deviation normalization	76.75	77.00	77.0	75.13	79.00	76.8
Sigmoidal normalization	76.75	77.00	77.0	74.00	75.00	76.6
Thermometer representation	78.38	78.00	80.1	77.00	78.00	77.4
Flag representation	76.75	77.00	80.1	75.13	73.00	77.4
Simple Binary representation	75.75	74.00	79.5	70.63	70.00	77.1

Table 9. Summary of NN and regression analysis of German Credit dataset

Author details

Fadzilah Siraj, Ehab A. Omer A. Omer and Md. Rajib Hasan

School of Computing, College of Arts and Sciences, University Utara Malaysia, Sintok, Kedah, Malaysia

7. References

[1] C. Li, and G. Biswas, "Unsupervised learning with mixed numeric and nominal data," *IEEE Transactions on Knowledgeand Data Engineering,* vol. 14, no. 4, pp. 673-690, 2002.

[2] A. Ahmad, and L. Dey, "A k-mean clustering algorithm for mixed numeric and categorical data," *Data &KnowledgeEngineering,* vol. 63, no. 2, pp. 503-527, 2007.

[3] Li Kan, LuiYushu, "Agent Based Data Mining Framework for the High Dimensional Environment," Journal of Beijing institute of technology, vol. 14, pp. 113-116, Feb 2004.

[4] Pan Ding, ShenJunyi, "Incorporating Domain Knowledge into Data Mining Process: An Ontology Based Framework," Wuhan University Journal of Natural Sciences, vol. 11, pp. 165-169, Jan. 2006.

[5] XianyiQian; Xianjun Wang; , "A New Study of DSS Based on Neural Network and Data Mining," E-Business and Information System Security, 2009. EBISS '09. International Conference on , vol., no., pp.1-4, 23-24 May 2009 doi: 10.1109/EBISS.2009.5137883

[6] Zhihua, X. (1998) Statistics and Data Mining. *Department of Information System and computer Scince, National University of Singapore.*

[7] Tsantis, L &Castellani, J. (2001) Enhancing Learning Environment Solution-based knowledge Discovery Tools: Forecasting for Self-perpetuating Systematic Reform. JSET Journal 6

[8] Luan, J (2002). Data Mining Application in Higher education. SPSS Executive Report. Retrieved from http://www.crisp-dm.org/CRISPWP.pdf

[9] A. Ahmad, and L. Dey, "A k-mean clustering algorithm for mixed numeric and categorical data," *Data &KnowledgeEngineering,* vol. 63, no. 2, pp. 503-527, 2007.

[10] Fernandez, G., (2003), Data Mining Using SAS Application. CRC press LLC. pp 1-12

[11] Dongsong Zhang; Lina Zhou; , "Discovering golden nuggets: data mining in financial application," *Systems, Man, and Cybernetics, Part C: Applications and Reviews, IEEE Transactions on*, vol.34, no.4, pp.513-522, Nov. 2004 doi: 10.1109/TSMCC.2004.829279

[12] Luan, J (2006). Data Mining and Knowledge Management in Higher education Potential Application.*Proceeding of Air Forum, Toronto, Canada*

[13] Siraj, F., &Abdoulha, M. A. (2009). Uncovering hidden information within university's student enrollment data using data mining. Paper presented at the Proceedings - 2009 3rd Asia International Conference on Modelling and Simulation, AMS 2009, 413-418. Retrieved from www.scopus.com

[14] Hashemi R. R., Bahar, M., Tyler, A. A. & Young, J. (2002). The Investigation of Mercury Presence in Human Blood: An Extrapolation from Animal Data Using Neural Networks. *Proceedings of International Conference: Information Technology: Coding and Computing*. 8-10 April.512-517.

[15] Altun, H., Talcinoz, T. &Tezekiei B. S. (2000). Improvement in the Learning Process as a Function of Distribution Characteristics of Binary Data Set. 10th Mediterranean Electrotechnical Conference, 2000,Vol. 2 (pp. 567-569).

[16] O'Neal, M.R., Engel, B.A., Ess, D.R. &Frankenberger, J.R. (2002). Neural Network prediction of maize yield using alternative data coding algorithms. Biosystems Engineering, 83, 31-45.

[17] Wessels, L.F.A., Reinders, M.J.T., Welsem, T.V. & Nederlof, P.M. (2002). Representation and classification for high-throughput data sets. SPIE-BIOS2002, Biomedial Nanotechnology Architectures and Applications, 4626, 226-237, San Jose, USA, Jan 2002.

[18] Jovanovic, N. Milutinovic, V. Obradovic, Z. (2002). Neural Network Applications in Electrical Engineering. Neural Network Applications in Electrical Engineering,, pp. 53-58.

[19] Delen, D. &Patil, N. (2006). Knowledge Extraction from Prostate Cancer Data.*Proceedings of the 39th Annual Hawaii International Conference, HICSS '06: System Sciences*. 04-07 Jan. Vol. 5 92b-92b.

[20] Shen, A., Tong, R., & Deng, Y. (2007). Application of Classification Models on Credit Card Fraud Detection. International Conference: Service Systems and Service Management, 9-11 June 2007 (pp. 1-4).

[21] Zhu, D., Premkumar, G., Zhang, X. & Chu, C.H. (2001). Data mining for Network Intrusion Detection: A Comparison of Alternative Methods. *Decision Sciences*, 32(4), 635-660.

[22] Jia, J. & Chua, H. C. (1993). Neural Network Encoding Approach Comparison: An Empirical Study. *Proceedings of First New Zealand International Two-Stream Conference on Artificial Neural Networks and Expert Systems*.24-26 November .38-41.

[23] Nawi, N. M., Ransing, M. R. and Ransing R. S. (2006). An Improved Learning Algorithm Based on The Broyden-Fletcher-Goldfarb-Shanno (BFGS) Method For Back Propagation Neural Networks. Sixth International Conference on Intelligent Systems Design and Applications, October 2006, Vol. 1, pp.152-157.

[24] Yun, W. H., Kim, D. H., Chi, S. Y. & Yoon, H. S. (2007). Two-dimensional Logistic Regression. 19th IEEE International Conference, ICTAI 2007: Tools with Artificial Intelligence, 29-31 October 2007, Vol. 2 (pp. 349-353).

[25] Kantardzic, M. (2003). DATA MINING: Concepts, Models, Methods and Algorithms. IEEE Transactions on Neural Networks, 14(2), 464-464.

[26] O'Connor, M., Marquez, L., Hill, T., & Remus, W. (2002). Neural network models for forecast a review. *IEEE proceedings of the 25th Hawaii International Conference on System Sciences*, 4, pp. 494–498.

[27] Duarte, L. M., Luiz, R. R., Marcos, E. M. P. (2008). The cigarette burden (measured by the number of pack-years smoked) negatively impacts the response rate to platinum-based chemotherapy in lung cancer patients. Lung Cancer, 61(2), 244-254.

[28] Ksantini, R., Ziou, D., Colin, B., &Dubeau, F. (2008). Weighted Pseudometric Discriminatory Power Improvement Using a Bayesian Logistic Regression Model Based on a Variational Method. *IEEE Transactions*on Pattern Analysis and Machine Intelligence.

[29] Chiang, L. & Wen, L. (2009). A neural network weight determination model designed uniquely for small data set learning. Expert Systems with Applications.36 (6). 9853-9858

[30] Fausett, L. (1994). Fundamentals Of Neural Networks Architectures, Algorithms, and Applications. Upper Saddle River, New Jersey07458: Prentice Hall.

[31] Lippmann, R.P. (1987). An introduction to Computing with neural neural network.*IEEE Transactions on nets, IEEE ASSP Magazine*, April, pp. 4–22.

[32] Wasserman, P. D. (1989). Neural Computing: Theory and Practice, Van Nostrand-Reinhold, New York.

[33] Marquez, L., Hill, T., O'Connor, M., & Remus, W. (1992). Neural network models for forecast a review. *IEEE proceedings of the 25th Hawaii International Conference on System Sciences*, 4, pp. 494–498.

[34] Siraj, F., &Asman, H. (2002). Predicting Information Technology Competency Using Neural Networks.*Proceedings of the 7th Asia Pacific Decision Sciences Institute Conference*, pp. 249 – 255

[35] Siraj, F. & Mohd Ali, A. (2004). *Web-Based Neuro Fuzzy Classification for Breast Cancer.* Proceedings of the Second International Conference on Artificial Intelligence in Engineering &*Technology, pp. 383 – 387.*

[36] Zhang, D. & Zhou, L. (2004). Discovering Golden Nuggets: Data Mining in Financial Application. IEEE Transactions on Systems, Man, and Cybernetics, Part C: Applications and Review, 34(4), 513-522.

[37] Hung, C. & Tsai, C. F. (2008). Market segmentation based on hierarchical self-organizing map for markets of multimedia on demand. Expert Systems with Applications, 34, 780-787.

[38] Heravi, S., Osborn, D. R., &Brichernhall, C. R. (2004). Linear versus neural network forecasts for European industrial production series. *International Journal of Forecasting, 20 (3), 435-446*

[39] Lam, M. (2004). Neural network techniques for financial performance prediction: integrating fundamental and technical analysis. *Decision Support System, 37 (4),567-581*

[40] De Andre, J., Landajo, M., & Lorca P. (2005). Forecasting business profitability by using classification techniques: A comparative analysis based on a spanish case. *Electric Power Engineering, PowerTech Budapest 99.*

Chapter 5

Inconsistent Decision System: Rough Set Data Mining Strategy to Extract Decision Algorithm of a Numerical Distance Relay – Tutorial

Mohammad Lutfi Othman and Ishak Aris

Additional information is available at the end of the chapter

http://dx.doi.org/10.5772/50460

1. Introduction

Modern numerical protective relays being intelligent electronic devices (IED) are inevitably vulnerable to false tripping or failure of operation for faults in the power system [1]. With regular and rigorous analyses the performance reliability of the digital protective relays can be ascertained, their availability maximized and subsequently their misoperation risks minimized [2]. The precise relay operation analyses would normally be assessing the relay characteristics, evaluating the relay performance and identifying the relay-power system interactions so as to ensure that the protective relays operate in correspond to their predetermined settings [3,4].

Protection engineers would in practice resort to computing technologies for automating the analysis process when the gravity of event data exploration, manipulation and inferencing incapacitate human manageability. The voluminous amount of data to be processed has prompted the need to use intelligent data mining, an essential constituent in the Knowledge Discovery in Databases (KDD) process [5]. This has motivated the adoption of rough set theory to data mine the protective relay event report so as to discover its decision algorithm.

2. Problem statement and objective

The following two pertinent problems are the attributing factors in driving this paper into studying the protective relay operation analysis:

- Inconsistencies in the device's event report particularly found when upon power system fault inception, a protective relay detects and invokes a common combination of tripping conditions in time succession but having two distinct tripping decisions

INTECH
open science | open minds

© 2012 Othman and Aris, licensee InTech. This is an open access chapter distributed under the terms of the Creative Commons Attribution License (http://creativecommons.org/licenses/by/3.0), which permits unrestricted use, distribution, and reproduction in any medium, provided the original work is properly cited.

(classifications). These distinct decisions are one, that upon relay pick-up, trip signal has not been asserted immediately after and the other is when a subsequent trip signal is asserted, after a preset time delay as set by the protection engineer.

- Non-linear nature of relay operation that makes it very difficult to select a group of effective attributes to fully represent relay tripping behavior.

In the grueling manual analysis of relay event report [1,6], the selected attributes hardly provide adequate knowledge in accurately mapping the interclass boundary in the relay decision system due to inconsistency. This characterizes the interclass boundary to be usually "rough". Based on the selected attributes, some relay events close to the boundary are unclassifiable – trip or nontrip. The small overlaps between different relay events make the protective relay operation analysis to be actually a rough classification problem. Thus, rough set theory has been appropriately chosen to resolve this conflict [7].

3. Rough set data mining in dealing with inconsistent numerical distance relay decision system to extract decision algorithm – The fundamental concept

Using rough set theory approach, relay decision rule extraction is naturally a byproduct of the data reduction process involved and easily understood. Rule extraction technique is inherent to the machine learning process of rough set theory. Thus, the inherent capability of rough set theory to discover fundamental patterns in relay data has essentially mooted this study. Using an approximation concept, rough set theory is able to remove data redundancies and consequently generate decision rules. In contrast to crisp sets, a rough set has boundary line cases – events that cannot be certainly classified either as members of the set or of its complement. Rough set theory is an alternative intelligent data analysis tool that can be employed to handle vagueness and inconsistencies [8].

An *information system* (*IS*) also alternatively known as *knowledge representation system* (*KRS*) is a tabulated data set, the rows of which are labeled by *objects* (events) of interest, columns labeled by *attributes*, and the entries are *attribute values* [8]. This data layout fits very well the protective relay event report that is characterized by its attributes of relay multifunctional elements versus sequence of time-stamped events [7].

In the protective relay event report, the *IS* manifestation is more appropriately referred as relay *decision table* or *decision system* (*DS*) as Huang et. al. [9] put it that decision table is characterized by disjoint sets of *condition attributes* ($C \subset Q$) and *decision (action) attributes* ($D \subset Q$). In this regard $Q = C \cup D$ and $C \cap D = \emptyset$. This *DS* is a 4-tuple structure formulated as $DS = \langle U, Q, V, f \rangle$, the elements of which are as follows [8,10,11]:

- U, i.e. the *universe* denoted as $U = \{t_1, t_2, t_3, \ldots, t_m\}$, is a finite set of relay events (t_i's).
- $Q = C \cup D$ is a non-empty finite union set of condition and decision *attributes*,
  - condition attributes ($c_i \subset C$) indicate the internally various multifunctional protective elements and analog measurands,

- decision attribute ($d_i \subset D$) indicates the trip output of the relay, such that q: $U \rightarrow V_q$ for every $q \in Q$.

- $V = U_{q \in Q} V_q$, where V_q is a set of values (*domain*) of the attribute q.
- f: $U \times Q \rightarrow V$ called *information function* is a total function such that $f(t,q) \in V_q$ for every $t \in U$, $q \in Q$. Any pair (q,v) is called *descriptor* in DS, where $q \in Q$ and $v \in V_q$,.

3.1. Relay decision system indiscernibility relation

If a set of attributes $P \subseteq Q = C \cup D$ and $f(t_x,q) = f(t_y,q)$ where t_x, $t_y \in U$, then for every $q \in P$, t_x and t_y are *indiscernible* (indistinguishable) by the set of attributes P in DS. Thus, every $P \subseteq Q$ brings forth a binary relation on U called *P-indiscernibility relation* (or *equivalence relation*) which is denoted by $IND(P)$. This suggests that there will be sets of relay events that are indiscernible based on any selected subset of attributes P. $U|IND(P)$ denotes the family of all *equivalence classes* of relation $IND(P)$. $IND(P)$ and $U|IND(P)$ can be formulated as

$$IND(P) = \{(t_x,t_y) \in U^2 | \forall q \in P, q(t_x) = q(t_y)\}, \tag{1}$$

$$U|IND(P) = \otimes\{q \in P | U | IND(\{q\})\}, \tag{2}$$

where,

$$A \otimes B = \{X \cap Y | \forall X \in A, \forall Y \in B, X \cap Y \neq \emptyset\}. \tag{3}$$

$U|IND(P)$ is also interchangeably referred as *P-basic knowledge* or *P-elementary sets* in DS. P-elementary set including relay event t is denoted as $[t]_{IND(P)}$. The first step in classification with rough sets is the construction of elementary sets [11]. A description of P-elementary set $X \in U|IND(P)$ in terms of values of attributes from P is denoted as $Des_P(X)$, i.e.

$$Des_P(X) = \{(q,v) : f(t,q) = v, \forall t \in X, \forall q \in P\} \tag{4}$$

3.2. Relay decision system set approximation

In the context of protective relay operations, consider $T \subseteq U$ as an arbitrary target set of relay events described (classified) by a particular trip assertion status that is needed to be represented by equivalence classes originating from attribute subset $P \subseteq Q$. P could be a selected condition attribute set $P \subseteq C$ or all condition attributes C reflecting relay multifunctional protective elements while T could be the set of relay events indiscernible with respect to the decision attribute $D = Trip$ having a domain value 'b' for pole-B tripping, for example [7].

The idea of the rough set revolves around the concept of approximation [11]. Thus, by introducing a pair of sets, called the *lower* and *upper approximations* of the target set T using only the information contained within P, the target set T can be *approximated*.

Formally, with a given relay decision system *DS*, each target subset $T \subseteq U$ having equivalence relation *IND*(*P*) is related to two subsets of *T* as follows.

P-lower approximation of *T* expressed as,

$$\underline{P}T = \cup\{X \in U \mid IND(P) : X \subseteq T\}, \tag{5}$$

is defined as the union of all elementary sets in $[t]_{IND(P)}$ which are contained in *T*. For any relay event t_i of the lower approximation of *T* with respect to the set of attributes *P* (i.e., $t_i \in \underline{P}T$), it *positively certain* belongs to *T*.

P-upper approximation of *T* expressed as,

$$\overline{P}T = \cup\{X \in U \mid IND(P) : X \cap T \neq \emptyset\}, \tag{6}$$

is defined as the union of elementary sets in $[t]_{IND(P)}$ which have a non-empty intersection with *T*. For any relay event t_i of the upper approximation of *T* with respect to the set of attributes *P* (i.e., $t_i \in \overline{P}T$), it *may possibly* belong to *T*.

P-boundary of set *T* expressed as,

$$BN_P(T) = \overline{P}T - \underline{P}T \tag{7}$$

is the difference between $\overline{P}T$ and $\underline{P}T$. The set of elements t_i which *cannot be certainly* classified as belonging to *T* using the set of attributes *P* [12].

The following three regions shall be derived from the lower- and upper-approximations as illustrated in Figure 1 [7,10,13].

- $POS_P(T) = \underline{P}T$, described as *P*-positive region of *T*, is the set of relay events which can be classified with certainty in the approximated set *T*.
- $NEG_P(T) = U - \underline{P}T$, described as *P*-negative region of *T*, is the set of relay events which cannot be classified without ambiguity in the approximated set *T* (or classified as belonging to the complement of *T*).
- $BN_P(T) = \overline{P}T - \underline{P}T$, described as *P*-boundary region of *T*, is the set of relay events in which none can be classified with certainty into *T* nor its complement $\overline{T}$ as far as the attributes *P* are concerned. The set *T* is *crisp* if there are no boundary sets, i.e. $BN_P(T) = \emptyset$ (empty set), which otherwise it is *rough*.

3.3. Approximation accuracy and quality

$\alpha_P(T)$, the accuracy of the rough set representation of a target set of relay events *T*, is formulated as [10]

$$\alpha_P(T) = \frac{|\underline{P}T|}{|\overline{P}T|} = \frac{card(\underline{P}T)}{card(\overline{P}T)}\ . \tag{8}$$

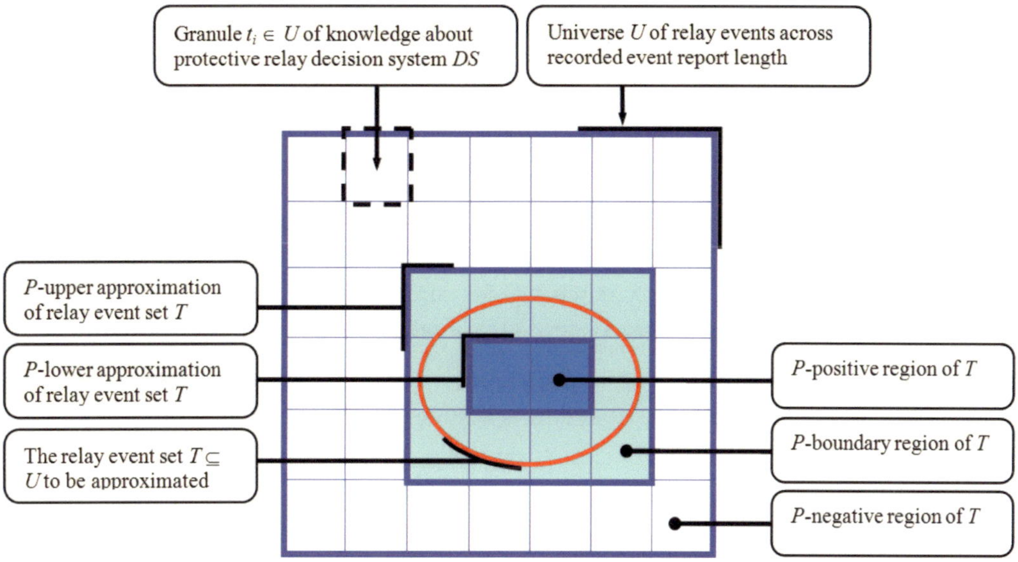

Figure 1. Definition of approximation in rough set theory in the context of protective relay

It provides a measure of how accurate the rough set is in approximating the target set of relay events T by comparing the number of events which can be *positively* placed in P with the number of events that can be *possibly* be placed in P. Noticeably $0 \leq \alpha_P(T) \leq 1$. (Note: *card* (cardinality) of a set is the number of events contained in the set [11]).

Clearly, equal upper and lower approximations, i.e. empty boundary region and that $\alpha_P(T) = 1$, would mean the target set T is said to be *definable* in U since it is perfectly approximated. Regardless of the size of the upper approximation, zero accuracy would mean the lower approximation is empty.

In general, the set T can be defined in U according to one of the following four concepts of definability [14,15]:

- *Roughly definable* T in U given $\underline{P}T \neq \emptyset$ and $\overline{P}T \neq U$ ($\emptyset$ denotes empty set)
- *Externally undefinable* T in U given $\underline{P}T \neq \emptyset$ and $\overline{P}T = U$
- *Internally undefinable* T in U given $\underline{P}T = \emptyset$ and $\overline{P}T \neq U$
- *Totally undefinable* T in U given $\underline{P}T = \emptyset$ and $\overline{P}T = U$

The *quality of approximation* of a target set T is expressed as

$$\gamma_P(T) = \frac{|\underline{P}T|}{U} = \frac{card(\underline{P}T)}{card(U)}, \tag{9}$$

i.e. the ratio of *P-correctly* approximated events to all events in the system.

3.4. The concept of reduct and core in reduction of protective relay attributes

Dependencies between attributes are primarily important in the protective relay data analysis using rough sets approach. The set of attributes $R \subseteq Q$ *depends* on the set of attributes $P \subseteq Q$ in *IS* if and only if $IND(P) \subseteq IND(R)$. This dependency is denoted as $P \rightarrow R$.

This so-called attribute reduction is so performed that the reduced set of attributes provides the same approximation quality as the original set of attributes. If a particular set of attributes is dependent, it is interesting to find *reducts* (all possible minimal subsets of attributes) that lead to the same number of elementary sets as in the case of the whole set of attributes and also to find *core* (the set of all indispensable attributes) [11]. By adopting the fundamental concepts of core and reduct, rough set theory minimizes the subsets of attributes in the relay database but still fully characterizes the inherent knowledge of relay operation behavior.

Reduct is essentially a sufficient set of features of a *DS*, which discerns (differentiates) all events discernible by the original *DS*. Reduct is a subset of attributes $RED \subseteq P$ (where $P \subseteq Q$) such that:

- The reduced attribute set *RED* induces the same equivalence classes as those induced by full attribute set *P*. This is denoted as $[t]_{IND(RED)} = [t]_{IND(P)}$.
- Attribute set *RED* is *minimal* in the sense that $[t]_{IND(RED\text{-}A)} \neq [t]_{IND(P)}$ for any attribute $A \in RED$. This suggests that no attribute can be dispensed from set *RED* without modifying the equivalence classes $[t]_{IND(P)}$ [16].

Core is defined as the set of attributes found to be in common in all reducts. Core is a subset of attributes $CORE \subseteq RED$ (where $RED \subseteq P$ and $P \subseteq Q$) such that:

- It consists of attributes which *cannot be removed* from the *DS* without causing collapse of the equivalence class structure. Formally, $[t]_{IND(RED\text{-}CORE)} \neq [t]_{IND(P)}$ where the above $A \in RED$ in this case is $A \in CORE$.

A *discernibility matrix* with a symmetrical dimension $n \times n$ is constructed to compute reducts and core. n denotes the number of elementary sets and each of the matrix's elements d_{ij} is defined as the set of all attributes which discern elementary sets $[t]_{IND(Pi)}$ and $[t]_{IND(Pj)}$ [17].

3.5. Decision rules interpreted from protective relay event report

Relay *DS* analysis is considered as a supervised learning problem (classification) [13]. A *DS* determines a logical implication called *decision rule* when the conditions specified by condition attributes in each row of *DS* correlate what decisions (trip assertions) are to take effect [18]. Thus, in this study the logical implication is designated as *relay decision rule*. A complete set of relay decision rules can be derived from the relay decision table *DS*. Events in *DS*, i.e. $\{t_1, t_2, t_3, \ldots, t_m\} = U$, identify as labels of relay decision rules.

Formally, let

- $U \mid IND(C)$ be *condition classes* in relay *DS* (a family of all *C*-elementary sets), denoted by X_i $(i = 1, \ldots, k)$,

- $U|IND(D)$ be *decision classes* in relay *DS* (a family of all *D*-elementary sets), denoted by Y_j (j = 1, …, *n*).

Then, $Des_C(X_i) \Rightarrow Des_D(Y_j)$ is called relay *CD-decision rule*. For simplicity, $C \Rightarrow D$. (As aforementioned, $Des_P(X) = \{(q,v) : f(x,q) = v, \forall x \in X, \forall q \in P\}$ which denotes a description of *P*-elementary set $X \in U|IND(P)$ in terms of values of attributes from *P*).

The relay *CD*-decision rules are logical statements read as 'if *C*...then...*D*'. These rule correlate descriptions of condition attributes $C \subset Q$ (for internal multifunctional protective elements, voltages, currents and impedance measurements) to classes of decision attribute $D \subset Q$ (i.e. type of trip assertions).

The set of decision rules for *each* decision class Y_j (j = 1,…, *n*) is denoted by:

$$\{r_{ij}\} = \{Des_C(X_i) \Rightarrow Des_D(Y_j) : X_i \cap Y_j \neq \emptyset, i = 1,\ldots, k\} \tag{10}$$

Decision algorithm in *DS* is used to mean the set of decision rules for *all* decision classes, i.e. *CD-algorithm* [10,18]. In the context of protective relay operation characteristics, a decision algorithm is a collection of relay *CD*-decision rules, thus referred to as *relay CD-decision algorithm* in this study.

Rules having the same conditions but different decisions are *inconsistent* (*nondeterministic, conflicting*); otherwise they are *consistent* (*certain, deterministic, nonconflicting*) [17]. When some conditions are satisfied, deterministic *DS uniquely* describes the decisions (actions) to be made. In a non-deterministic *DS*, decisions are not uniquely determined by the conditions [9]. Formally, it is defined that:

- Relay rule $\{r_{ij}\}$ is *deterministic* in *DS* if and only if $X_i \subseteq Y_j$, and
- Relay rule $\{r_{ij}\}$ is *nondeterministic* in *DS*, otherwise.

The *degree of consistency* (or *degree of dependency*) between the set of attributes *C* and *D* of a relay *CD*-decision algorithm is denoted as $C \Rightarrow_k D$ and can be formally defined as:

$$C \Rightarrow_k D \mid k = \gamma(C, D) = \frac{|POS_C D|}{|U|} \tag{11}$$

(i.e. conceptually similar to the quality of approximation or classification) [10]. In other words, *D depends on C* in a degree of dependency *k* ($0 \le k \le 1$). All the values of attributes from *D depend totally* on (i.e. uniquely determined by) the values of attributes from *C* if $k = 1$, i.e. $C \Rightarrow_1 D$ or simply $C \Rightarrow D$. *D depends partially* in a degree k on *C* if $k < 1$ [17].

It may happen that the set *D* depends on subset *C′* called *relative reduct* and not on the entire set *C*. *C′ is* a relative reduct called *D-reduct of C* if $C' \subseteq C$ is a minimal subset of *C* and $\gamma(C, D) = \gamma(C', D)$ is valid (i.e. similar in dependency). $RED_D(C)$ is used to mean the family of all *D*-reducts of *C* [18]. Putting it simply, the minimal subsets of condition attributes that discern all decision equivalence classes of the relation $U|IND(D)$ discernable by the entire set of attributes are called *D*-reducts [11]. The following notations are, thus, valid:

- If $POS_C(D) = POS_{(C-\{c_i\})}(D)$, an attribute $c_i \in C$ is *D-dispensable* in C. c_i is D-superfluous if it exerts no influence on the lower approximation of D. Otherwise the attribute c_i is *D-indispensable* in C.
- If C is *D-independent*, then all attributes $c_i \in C$ are D-indispensable in C and called the *D-core of* C which is denoted as $CORE_D(C)$.
- The following property is also true for *DS* system as previously defined,

$$CORE_D(C) = \cap RED_D(C) \tag{12}$$

The previous definitions are valid if $D = C$ [18].

- Using a slightly modified discernibility matrix called *D-discernibility matrix of* C, relative reducts can be computed. The set of all condition attributes which discern events t_i and t_j that do not belong to the same equivalence class of the relation $U|IND(D)$ defines the element of D-discernibility matrix of C. The set of all single elements of the D-discernibility matrix of C is the D-core of C [10,11]. Rather than the ordinary reduct of C, D-reduct of C is very much the essence of this paper's study that aspires to derive the relay CD-decision rules (i.e. $C \Rightarrow D$).

4. Discovering decision algorithm of numerical distance protective relay

In order to fairly understand the indiscernibility relation and rules discovery from distance protective relay decision system *DS*, the following tutorial is presented.

4.1. Protective relay decision table

Table 1 illustrates an example of a decision system $DS = \langle U, Q, V, f \rangle$ excerpted from an event report of a protective distance relay. The decision table is a presentation of information function $f: U \times Q \to V$. $C = \{ag, bg, cg, Z1pu, Z2pu, Z3pu, Z4pu, Z1trp, Z2trp, Z3trp, Z4trp\}$ is the set of condition attributes representing the internal multifunctional protective elements. $D = Trip$ is the decision attribute which, essentially, denotes the tripping signal asserted by the relay in response to a particular fault in the power system. The time codes are the events that are analyzed for equivalence relation on the basis of selected subset of attributes P, such that $P \subseteq Q$. The finite set of the attribute *time*'s code forms the universe of interest $U = \{t_1, t_2, t_3, t_4, t_5, t_6, t_7, t_8, t_9, t_{10}, t_{11}, t_{12}, t_{13}, t_{14}, t_{15}, t_{16}, t_{17}, t_{18}, t_{19}, t_{20}, t_{21}\}$.

time(U)		*ag*	*bg*	*cg*	*Z1pu*	*Z2pu*	*Z3pu*	*Z4pu*	*Z1trp*	*Z2trp*	*Z3trp*	*Z4trp*	*Trip*
sec	code	zone	zone	zone	logic	logic	logic	logic	logic	logic	logic	logic	pole
0.4982	t_1	0	0	0	0	0	0	0	0	0	0	0	0
0.4994	t_2	0	0	0	0	0	0	0	0	0	0	0	0
0.5006	t_3	0	0	0	0	0	0	0	0	0	0	0	0
0.5018	t_4	0	1	0	0	1	1	0	0	0	0	0	0
0.5030	t_5	0	2	0	0	1	1	0	0	0	0	0	0
0.5054	t_6	0	2	0	0	1	1	0	0	0	0	0	0

time(U)		*ag*	*bg*	*cg*	*Z1pu*	*Z2pu*	*Z3pu*	*Z4pu*	*Z1trp*	*Z2trp*	*Z3trp*	*Z4trp*	*Trip*
sec	code	zone	zone	zone	logic	logic	logic	logic	logic	logic	logic	logic	pole
0.5066	t_7	0	2	0	0	1	1	0	0	0	0	0	0
0.5498	t_8	0	1	0	1	1	1	0	1	0	0	0	b
0.5510	t_9	0	1	0	1	1	1	0	1	0	0	0	b
0.5522	t_{10}	0	1	0	1	1	1	0	1	0	0	0	b
0.5534	t_{11}	0	0	0	1	1	1	0	0	0	0	0	b
0.5546	t_{12}	0	0	0	1	1	1	0	0	0	0	0	b
0.5558	t_{13}	0	0	0	1	1	1	0	0	0	0	0	b
0.5966	t_{14}	0	0	0	1	1	1	0	0	0	0	0	b
0.5978	t_{15}	0	0	0	1	1	1	0	0	0	0	0	b
0.5990	t_{16}	0	0	0	0	0	1	0	0	0	0	0	b
0.6002	t_{17}	0	0	0	0	0	0	0	0	0	0	0	b
0.6014	t_{18}	0	0	0	0	0	0	0	0	0	0	0	b
0.6026	t_{19}	0	0	0	0	0	0	0	0	0	0	0	b
0.7347	t_{20}	0	0	0	0	0	0	0	0	0	0	0	0
0.7359	t_{21}	0	0	0	0	0	0	0	0	0	0	0	0

Table 1. Excerpt of an event report as a decision table *DS* of a protective distance relay (only ground distance is considered for illustration)

The attribute names are described as follows:

- *ag, bg,* and *cg* are A-G, B-G, and C-G fault detections.
- *Z1pu, Z2pu, Z3pu,* and *Z4pu* are zone 1, 2, 3, and 4 ground distance starts (pick-ups).
- *Z1trp, Z2trp, Z3trp,* and *Z4trp* are zone 1, 2, 3, and 4 ground distance trip signals.

The sets of values (domains) of the particular attributes are as follows:

- V_{ag}, V_{bg}, V_{cg}, = {1, 2, 3, 4}.
- V_{Z1pu}, V_{Z2pu}, V_{Z3pu}, V_{Z4pu}, V_{Z1trp}, V_{Z2trp}, V_{Z3trp}, V_{Z4trp} = {0, 1}.
- V_{Trip} = {a, b, c, 0}, corresponding to tripping signals of phase A, B, C or none.

4.2. Protective relay decision table analysis

From Table 1, the two elementary sets with respect to the decision attribute *D* = {*Trip*} can be deduced as shown in Table 2.

U/D	*Trip*
$\{t_1, t_2, t_3, t_4, t_5, t_6, t_7, t_{20}, t_{21}\} = D_1$	0
$\{t_8, t_9, t_{10}, t_{11}, t_{12}, t_{13}, t_{14}, t_{15}, t_{16}, t_{17}, t_{18}, t_{19}\} = D_2$	b

Table 2. Equivalence classes with respect to decision attribute *D* = {*Trip*}

Six equivalence classes (elementary sets) can be deduced as shown in Table 3 when the full set of attributes C = {*ag, bg, cg, Z1pu, Z2pu, Z3pu, Z4pu, Z1trp, Z2trp, Z3trp, Z4trp*} is considered.

U/C	ag	bg	cg	$Z1pu$	$Z2pu$	$Z3pu$	$Z4pu$	$Z1trp$	$Z2trp$	$Z3trp$	$Z4trp$
$\{t_1, t_2, t_3, t_{17}, t_{18}, t_{19}, t_{20}, t_{21}\}$	0	0	0	0	0	0	0	0	0	0	0
$\{t_4\}$	0	1	0	0	1	1	0	0	0	0	0
$\{t_5, t_6, t_7\}$	0	2	0	0	1	1	0	0	0	0	0
$\{t_8, t_9, t_{10}\}$	0	1	0	1	1	1	0	1	0	0	0
$\{t_{11}, t_{12}, t_{13}, t_{14}, t_{15}\}$	0	0	0	1	1	1	0	0	0	0	0
$\{t_{16}\}$	0	0	0	0	0	1	0	0	0	0	0

Table 3. Equivalence classes with respect to condition attributes $C = \{ag, bg, cg, Z1pu, Z2pu, Z3pu, Z4pu, Z1trp, Z2trp, Z3trp, Z4trp\}$

Within the first equivalence class, $\{t_1, t_2, t_3, t_{17}, t_{18}, t_{19}, t_{20}, t_{21}\}$, the eight events are indiscernible among each other based on the available attributes. In the third and the fourth equivalence classes, $\{t_5, t_6, t_7\}$ and $\{t_8, t_9, t_{10}\}$, the three events within them, based on the available attributes, cannot be distinguished from one another. Similarly, the five events within the fifth equivalence class are also indiscernible from one another. The remaining two events are each discernible (different) from all other events. $[t]_{IND(C)}$ or simply $[t]_C$ can denote these equivalence classes of the C-indiscernibility relation as aforementioned. Each row in Table 3 describes an individual elementary set, whereas the entire Table 3 describes the DS being studied. $U|C$ means that elementary sets of the universe U in the space C are being considered.

The calculations of the C-lower and C-upper approximations and accuracy of classification of D,

$$\underline{C}D_1 = \{t_4\} \cup \{t_5, t_6, t_7\} = \{t_4, t_5, t_6, t_7\} \tag{13}$$

$$\begin{aligned}\underline{C}D_2 &= \{t_8, t_9, t_{10}\} \cup \{t_{11}, t_{12}, t_{13}, t_{14}, t_{15}\} \cup \{t_{16}\} \\ &= \{t_8, t_9, t_{10}, t_{11}, t_{12}, t_{13}, t_{14}, t_{15}, t_{16}\}\end{aligned} \tag{14}$$

$$\begin{aligned}\overline{C}D_1 &= \{t_1, t_2, t_3, t_{17}, t_{18}, t_{19}, t_{20}, t_{21}\} \cup \{t_4\} \cup \{t_5, t_6, t_7\} \\ &= \{t_1, t_2, t_3, t_4, t_5, t_6, t_7, t_{17}, t_{18}, t_{19}, t_{20}, t_{21}\}\end{aligned} \tag{15}$$

$$\begin{aligned}\overline{C}D_2 &= \{t_1, t_2, t_3, t_{17}, t_{18}, t_{19}, t_{20}, t_{21}\} \cup \{t_8, t_9, t_{10}\} \cup \{t_{11}, t_{12}, t_{13}, t_{14}, t_{15}\} \cup \{t_{16}\} \\ &= \{t_1, t_2, t_3, t_8, t_9, t_{10}, t_{11}, t_{12}, t_{13}, t_{14}, t_{15}, t_{16}, t_{17}, t_{18}, t_{19}, t_{20}, t_{21}\}\end{aligned} \tag{16}$$

$$\alpha_C(D_1) = \left|\frac{\underline{C}D_1}{\overline{C}D_1}\right| = \frac{card(\underline{C}D_1)}{card(\overline{C}D_1)} = \frac{4}{12} = 0.33 \tag{17}$$

$$\alpha_C(D_2) = \left|\frac{\underline{C}D_2}{\overline{C}D_2}\right| = \frac{card(\underline{C}D_2)}{card(\overline{C}D_2)} = \frac{9}{17} = 0.53 \tag{18}$$

With classification accuracies of 0.33 and 0.53, the respective elementary sets D_1 and D_2 are roughly definable (vaguely classified) in the DS. This is rather expected. The decision attribute

D = {*Trip*} may remain in a certain domain value for a certain time-sequence of relay events after a particular relay trip trigger according to the protection engineer's preset time duration of signal assertion [7]. This may prevail even though the condition attributes have changed during this duration. This explains the inconsistency found in the CD-algorithm.

The accuracy and quality of overall classification D are:

$$\alpha_C(D) = \frac{\sum_{i=1}^{2} card(\underline{C}D_i)}{\sum_{i-1}^{2} card(\overline{C}D_i)} = \frac{4+9}{12+17} = 0.45 \tag{19}$$

$$\gamma_C(D) = \frac{\sum_{i=1}^{2} card(\underline{C}D_i)}{card(U)} = \frac{4+9}{9+12} = 0.62 \tag{20}$$

i.e. the overall classification with respect to C is rough.

D-reducts and D-core of C can be discovered from the D-discernibility matrix of C by discerning relay events from different equivalence classes in the relation $U|IND(D)$ with respect to the condition attributes C. The D-discernibility matrix that is formed is illustrated in Table 4. It would suffice to consider only the lower diagonal part because of the matrix's symmericalness [11]. Note that even though relay events appearing in the same class in the D-space (for example t_1, t_2, t_3, t_4, t_5, t_6, t_7, t_{20}, t_{21}) are discernible in C-space, they are not discerned between each other with respect to the attributes C. Empty set (Ø) indicates indiscernibility between relay events.

U	t_1	t_2	t_3	t_4	t_5	t_6	t_7	t_8	t_9	t_{10}	t_{11}	t_{12}	t_{13}	t_{14}	t_{15}	t_{16}	t_{17}	t_{18}	t_{19}	t_{20}	t_{21}
t_1	Ø																				
t_2	Ø	Ø																			
t_3	Ø	Ø	Ø																		
t_4	Ø	Ø	Ø	Ø																	
t_5	Ø	Ø	Ø	Ø	Ø																
t_6	Ø	Ø	Ø	Ø	Ø	Ø															
t_7	Ø	Ø	Ø	Ø	Ø	Ø	Ø														
t_8	{bg, Z1pu, Z2pu, Z3pu, Z1trp}	{bg, Z1pu, Z2pu, Z3pu, Z1trp}	{bg, Z1pu, Z2pu, Z3pu, Z1trp}	{Z1pu, Z1trp}	{bg, Z1pu, Z1trp}	{bg, Z1pu, Z1trp}	{bg, Z1pu, Z1trp}	Ø													
t_9	{bg, Z1pu, Z2pu, Z3pu, Z1trp}	{bg, Z1pu, Z2pu, Z3pu, Z1trp}	{bg, Z1pu, Z2pu, Z3pu, Z1trp}	{Z1pu, Z1trp}	{bg, Z1pu, Z1trp}	{bg, Z1pu, Z1trp}	{bg, Z1pu, Z1trp}	Ø	Ø												
t_{10}	{bg, Z1pu, Z2pu, Z3pu, Z1trp}	{bg, Z1pu, Z2pu, Z3pu, Z1trp}	{bg, Z1pu, Z2pu, Z3pu, Z1trp}	{Z1pu, Z1trp}	{bg, Z1pu, Z1trp}	{bg, Z1pu, Z1trp}	{bg, Z1pu, Z1trp}	Ø	Ø	Ø											
t_{11}	{Z1pu, Z2pu, Z3pu}	{Z1pu, Z2pu, Z3pu}	{Z1pu, Z2pu, Z3pu}	{bg, Z1pu}	{bg, Z1pu}	{bg, Z1pu}	{bg, Z1pu}	Ø	Ø	Ø	Ø										

U	t_1	t_2	t_3	t_4	t_5	t_6	t_7	t_8	t_9	t_{10}	t_{11}	t_{12}	t_{13}	t_{14}	t_{15}	t_{16}	t_{17}	t_{18}	t_{19}	t_{20}	t_{21}
t_{12}	{Z1pu, Z2pu, Z3pu}	{Z1pu, Z2pu, Z3pu}	{Z1pu, Z2pu, Z3pu}	{bg, Z1pu}	{bg, Z1pu}	{bg, Z1pu}	{bg, Z1pu}	Ø	Ø	Ø	Ø	Ø									
t_{13}	{Z1pu, Z2pu, Z3pu}	{Z1pu, Z2pu, Z3pu}	{Z1pu, Z2pu, Z3pu}	{bg, Z1pu}	{bg, Z1pu}	{bg, Z1pu}	{bg, Z1pu}	Ø	Ø	Ø	Ø	Ø	Ø								
t_{14}	{Z1pu, Z2pu, Z3pu}	{Z1pu, Z2pu, Z3pu}	{Z1pu, Z2pu, Z3pu}	{bg, Z1pu}	{bg, Z1pu}	{bg, Z1pu}	{bg, Z1pu}	Ø	Ø	Ø	Ø	Ø	Ø	Ø							
t_{15}	{Z1pu, Z2pu, Z3pu}	{Z1pu, Z2pu, Z3pu}	{Z1pu, Z2pu, Z3pu}	{bg, Z1pu}	{bg, Z1pu}	{bg, Z1pu}	{bg, Z1pu}	Ø	Ø	Ø	Ø	Ø	Ø	Ø	Ø						
t_{16}	{Z3pu}	{Z3pu}	{Z3pu}	{bg, Z2pu}	{bg, Z2pu}	{bg, Z2pu}	{bg, Z2pu}	Ø	Ø	Ø	Ø	Ø	Ø	Ø	Ø	Ø					
t_{17}	Ø	Ø	Ø	{bg, Z2pu, Z3pu}	{bg, Z2pu, Z3pu}	{bg, Z2pu, Z3pu}	{bg, Z2pu, Z3pu}	Ø	Ø	Ø	Ø	Ø	Ø	Ø	Ø	Ø	Ø				
t_{18}	Ø	Ø	Ø	{bg, Z2pu, Z3pu}	{bg, Z2pu, Z3pu}	{bg, Z2pu, Z3pu}	{bg, Z2pu, Z3pu}	Ø	Ø	Ø	Ø	Ø	Ø	Ø	Ø	Ø	Ø	Ø			
t_{19}	Ø	Ø	Ø	{bg, Z2pu, Z3pu}	{bg, Z2pu, Z3pu}	{bg, Z2pu, Z3pu}	{bg, Z2pu, Z3pu}	Ø	Ø	Ø	Ø	Ø	Ø	Ø	Ø	Ø	Ø	Ø	Ø		
t_{20}	Ø	Ø	Ø	Ø	Ø	Ø	Ø	{bg, Z1pu, Z2pu, Z3pu, Z1trp}	{bg, Z1pu, Z2pu, Z3pu, Z1trp}	{bg, Z1pu, Z2pu, Z3pu, Z1trp}	{Z1pu, Z2pu, Z3pu}	{Z1pu, Z2pu, Z3pu}	{Z1pu, Z2pu, Z3pu}	{Z1pu, Z2pu, Z3pu}	{Z1pu, Z2pu, Z3pu}	{Z3pu}	Ø	Ø	Ø	Ø	
t_{21}	Ø	Ø	Ø	Ø	Ø	Ø	Ø	{bg, Z1pu, Z2pu, Z3pu, Z1trp}	{bg, Z1pu, Z2pu, Z3pu, Z1trp}	{bg, Z1pu, Z2pu, Z3pu, Z1trp}	{Z1pu, Z2pu, Z3pu}	{Z1pu, Z2pu, Z3pu}	{Z1pu, Z2pu, Z3pu}	{Z1pu, Z2pu, Z3pu}	{Z1pu, Z2pu, Z3pu}	{Z3pu}	Ø	Ø	Ø	Ø	Ø

Table 4. *D*-discernibility matrix of *C*

The discovery of the desired reduct(s) is possible via the formulation of the so-called *discernibility function f(P)* that calculates according to Boolean function operation in which each attribute acts as a Boolean variable [11]. Using the technique introduced by Pawlak [17], a Boolean discernibility function is deduced right off the discernibility matrix in Table 4, i.e.:

$f_C(D)$

$= (bg+Z1pu+Z2pu+Z3pu+Z1trp)\ (Z1pu+Z2pu+Z3pu)\ (Z3pu) \times (Z1pu+Z1trp)\ (bg+Z1trp)\ (bg+Z2pu)\ (bg+Z2pu+Z3pu) \times (bg+Z1pu+Z1trp)\ (bg+Z1pu)\ (bg+Z2pu)\ (bg+Z2pu+Z3pu) \times (bg+Z1pu+Z2pu+Z3pu+Z1trp) \times (Z1pu+Z2pu+Z3pu) \times Z3pu$

$= Z3pu \times (Z1pu+Z1trp)\ (bg+Z1pu)\ (bg+Z2pu) \times (bg+Z1pu)\ (bg+Z2pu) \times (bg+Z1pu+Z2pu+Z3pu+Z1trp) \times (Z1pu+Z2pu+Z3pu) \times Z3pu \rightarrow$ The final Conjunctive Normal Form (CNF)

$= Z3pu\ (Z1pu+Z1trp)\ (bg+Z1pu)\ (bg+Z2pu)$

$= (Z1pu\cdot Z3pu + Z3pu\cdot Z1trp)\ (bg+Z1pu)\ (bg+Z2pu)$

$= (bg\cdot(Z1pu\cdot Z3pu + Z3pu\cdot Z1trp) + Z1pu(Z1pu\cdot Z3pu + Z3pu\cdot Z1trp))\ (bg+Z2pu)$

$= ((bg\cdot Z1pu\cdot Z3pu + bg\cdot Z3pu\cdot Z1trp) + (Z1pu\cdot Z3pu) + (Z1pu\cdot Z3pu\cdot Z1trp))\ (bg+Z2pu)$

= *bg* ((*bg*·*Z1pu*·*Z3pu* + *bg*·*Z3pu*·*Z1trp*) + (*Z1pu*·*Z3pu*) + (*Z1pu*·*Z3pu*·*Z1trp*)) + *Z2pu* ((*bg*·*Z1pu*·*Z3pu* + *bg*·*Z3pu*·*Z1trp*) + (*Z1pu*·*Z3pu*) + (*Z1pu*·*Z3pu*·*Z1trp*))
= (*bg*·*Z1pu*·*Z3pu*) + (*bg*·*Z3pu*·*Z1trp*) + (*bg*·*Z1pu*·*Z3pu*) + (*bg*·*Z1pu*·*Z3pu*·*Z1trp*) + (*bg*·*Z1pu*·*Z2pu*· *Z3pu*) + (*bg*·*Z2pu*·*Z3pu*·*Z1trp*) + (*Z1pu*·*Z2pu*·*Z3pu*) + (*Z1pu*·*Z2pu*·*Z3pu*·*Z1trp*)
→ The final Disjunctive Normal Form (DNF) of $f_C(D)$

Absorption law and eventual expression multiplication are implemented to solve the Boolean expression of $f_C(D)$ [19].

Normalization in its final normal form, the last Boolean expression $f_C(D)$ is recognized as Disjunctive Normal Form (DNF). DNF is analogous to Sum Of Product (SOP) boolean algebra in digital electronics logic. $f_C(D)$ in DNF form is an alternative representation of the *DS* in which all its constituents are the *D*-reducts of *C* (i.e. $RED_D(C)$) [11,17]. Either one of the set of reducts can be used to represent exactly the same data classification as that depicted by the entire set of attributes *C*. The following $RED_D(C)$ of the above final $f_C(D)$ reveals that either one of the *D*-reducts of *C* can be used alternatively to represent exactly the same equivalence relation $U|IND(D)$ of the *DS* as that represented by the whole set of attributes *C*, i.e.,

$$\begin{gathered} RED_D(C) = \{bg, Z1pu, Z3pu\},\ \{bg, Z3pu, Z1trp\},\ \{bg, Z1pu, Z3pu\}, \\ \{bg, Z1pu, Z3pu, Z1trp\},\ \{bg, Z1pu, Z2pu, Z3pu\},\ \{bg, Z2pu, Z3pu, Z1trp\}, \\ \{Z1pu, Z2pu, Z3pu\},\ \{Z1pu, Z2pu, Z3pu, Z1trp\} \end{gathered} \tag{21}$$

The *D*-core of C can be figured out by either:

- Identifying all the single attribute entries in the *D*-discernibility matrix of C [11], which from Table 4, attribute *Z3pu* is the only single attribute entry and thus $CORE_D(C) = \cap RED_D(C) = Z3p$, or
- Taking intersection of all *D*-reducts of *C*, i.e. $CORE_D(C) = \cap RED_D(C) = Z3pu$

Hence, *Z3pu* is the most characteristic attribute that is indispensible in *DS* without reducing the approximation quality of equivalence relation $U|C$ with respect to *D*.

$CORE_D(C) = Z3pu$ does not seem to signify any significance in the behavior of the relay under analysis. Had the reduct analysis been worked out based only on the whole condition attributes *C* (as per the equivalence relation in Table 3, where decision attribute *D* is excluded such as in the case of *IS* instead of *DS*), the core of *C* (i.e. the core of the equivalence relation $U|C$ with respect to *C*) would have been,

$$CORE_{U|C}(C) = \{bg\} \tag{22}$$

This implies the protective relay has been subjected to B-G fault. In reality this fault occurred in distance zone 1 operation characteristic and was picked up by the zone 1 distance element. However, the *D*-core of *C* discovers the indispensability of the condition attribute *Z3pu* as being the core when the decision attribute *D* is considered for the *DS* analysis. Actually, this attribute is entirely insignificant based on the understanding of the manner the distance relay functions. This is simply because of the concurrent nature of the distance relay quadrilateral operation characteristic whereby zone 1 element is encapsulated in zone 2 element and subsequently zone 2 element is encapsulated in zone 3 element. Zone 4 element is on its own separate entity not encapsulated in any zone elements [7]. Thus, by merely considering the exertion of the zone 1 element in case of fault and correspondingly disregarding zones 2, 3 and 4 operation is principally correct. Figure 2 illustrates that a fault occurring in zone 1 is also concurrently shown as present in zones 2 and 3 as well.

To simplify and make the analysis process more sense, an attribute priority of the distance relay operation has to be formulated so that the relay *DS* can be modified as shown Table 5.

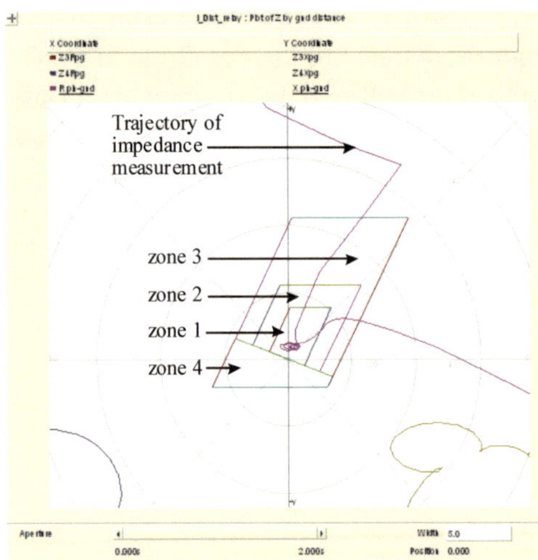

Figure 2. Distance protective relay operation characteristic with impedance measurement

Cases of concurrence	Condition Attributes, $c_i \in C$								Most significant attribute
	Z1pu	*Z2pu*	*Z3pu*	*Z4pu*	*Z1trp*	*Z2trp*	*Z3trp*	*Z4trp*	
Case 1	+	+	+		+				*Z1pu*
Case 1′	+	+	+			*			*Z2pu*
Case 2		+	+			*			*Z2pu*
Case 2′		+	+				*		*Z3pu*
Case 3			+				*		*Z3pu*
Case 4				+				*	*Z4pu*

+ denotes value of attribute equal to "1", i.e. $V_{ci} = 1$ where attribute $c_i \in C$.
* denotes the attribute's value of "1" occurring at possibly different events (rows).

Table 5. Condition attribute priority of the distance relay operation

The absence of relay trip assertion signal in attributes *Z2trp*, *Z3trp*, and *Z4trp* which is represented by the attribute value "0" further justifies the necessity of disregarding attributes *Z2pu*, *Z3pu*, and *Z4pu* for fault in zone 1. This is because, for example, the assertion of attribute *Z1pu* (value of "1") must always be accompanied by the assertion (after and for a preset time duration, i.e. sequence of consecutive events) of the corresponding attribute *Z1trp* in order to be taken into consideration in the analysis. However, in the above example, it is highly likely that attribute *Z2trp* will assert (after and for a preset number of events) in lieu of the attribute *Z1trp* as shown in Table 5 if the relay failed to operate in asserting the attribute *Z1trp* when the attribute *Z1pu* is asserted.

Taking into account the proposition, the *DS* system in Table 1 is then modified prior to reanalysis using rough set as shown in Table 6.

Time (*U*)	*ag*	*bg*	*cg*	*Z1pu*	*Z4pu*	*Z1trp*	*Z2trp*	*Z3trp*	*Z4trp*	*Trip*
t_1	0	0	0	0	0	0	0	0	0	0
t_2	0	0	0	0	0	0	0	0	0	0
t_3	0	0	0	0	0	0	0	0	0	0
t_4	0	1	0	0	0	0	0	0	0	0
t_5	0	2	0	0	0	0	0	0	0	0
t_6	0	2	0	0	0	0	0	0	0	0
t_7	0	2	0	0	0	0	0	0	0	0
t_8	0	1	0	1	0	1	0	0	0	b
t_9	0	1	0	1	0	1	0	0	0	b
t_{10}	0	1	0	1	0	1	0	0	0	b
t_{11}	0	0	0	1	0	0	0	0	0	b
t_{12}	0	0	0	1	0	0	0	0	0	b
t_{13}	0	0	0	1	0	0	0	0	0	b
t_{14}	0	0	0	1	0	0	0	0	0	b
t_{15}	0	0	0	1	0	0	0	0	0	b
t_{16}	0	0	0	0	0	0	0	0	0	b
t_{17}	0	0	0	0	0	0	0	0	0	b
t_{18}	0	0	0	0	0	0	0	0	0	b
t_{19}	0	0	0	0	0	0	0	0	0	b
t_{20}	0	0	0	0	0	0	0	0	0	0
t_{21}	0	0	0	0	0	0	0	0	0	0

Table 6. Modified decision table *DS* to reflect protective relay operation behavior

From Table 6, the elementary sets with respect to the decision attribute *D* = {*Trip*} are still the same as shown in Table 2.

However, the elementary sets with respect to the shrunk condition = {*ag*, *bg*, *cg*, *Z1pu*, *Z4pu*, *Z1trp*, *Z2trp*, *Z3trp*, *Z4trp*} as shown in Table 7 are slightly different from those found with the whole attributes *C* considered (Table 3).

U/C	*ag*	*bg*	*cg*	*Z1pu*	*Z4pu*	*Z1trp*	*Z2trp*	*Z3trp*	*Z4trp*
$\{t_1, t_2, t_3, t_{16}, t_{17}, t_{18}, t_{19}, t_{20}, t_{21}\}$	0	0	0	0	0	0	0	0	0
$\{t_4\}$	0	1	0	0	0	0	0	0	0
$\{t_5, t_6, t_7\}$	0	2	0	0	0	0	0	0	0
$\{t_8, t_9, t_{10}\}$	0	1	0	1	0	1	0	0	0
$\{t_{11}, t_{12}, t_{13}, t_{14}, t_{15}\}$	0	0	0	1	0	0	0	0	0

Table 7. Equivalence classes with respect to modified condition attributes *C* = {*ag, bg, cg, Z1pu, Z4pu, Z1trp, Z2trp, Z3trp, Z4trp*}

The new *D*-discernibility matrix of *C* as in Table 8 will result in new *D*-reducts and *D*-core of *C* when events are discerned with respect to the modified condition attributes *C* between different equivalence classes in the relation $U|IND(D)$. As before, similar consideration is taken in discerning events appearing only in different classes in *D*-space.

U	t_1	t_2	t_3	t_4	t_5	t_6	t_7	t_8	t_9	t_{10}	t_{11}	t_{12}	t_{13}	t_{14}	t_{15}	t_{16}	t_{17}	t_{18}	t_{19}	t_{20}	t_{21}
t_1	Ø																				
t_2	Ø	Ø																			
t_3	Ø	Ø	Ø																		
t_4	Ø	Ø	Ø	Ø																	
t_5	Ø	Ø	Ø	Ø	Ø																
t_6	Ø	Ø	Ø	Ø	Ø	Ø															
t_7	Ø	Ø	Ø	Ø	Ø	Ø	Ø														
t_8	{bg, Z1pu, Z1trp}	{bg, Z1pu, Z1trp}	{bg, Z1pu, Z1trp}	{Z1pu, Z1trp}	{bg, Z1pu, Z1trp}	{bg, Z1pu, Z1trp}	{bg, Z1pu, Z1trp}	Ø													
t_9	{bg, Z1pu, Z1trp}	{bg, Z1pu, Z1trp}	{bg, Z1pu, Z1trp}	{Z1pu, Z1trp}	{bg, Z1pu, Z1trp}	{bg, Z1pu, Z1trp}	{bg, Z1pu, Z1trp}	Ø	Ø												
t_{10}	{bg, Z1pu, Z1trp}	{bg, Z1pu, Z1trp}	{bg, Z1pu, Z1trp}	{Z1pu, Z1trp}	{bg, Z1pu, Z1trp}	{bg, Z1pu, Z1trp}	{bg, Z1pu, Z1trp}	Ø	Ø	Ø											
t_{11}	{Z1pu}	{Z1pu}	{Z1pu}	{bg, Z1pu}	{bg, Z1pu}	{bg, Z1pu}	{bg, Z1pu}	Ø	Ø	Ø	Ø										
t_{12}	{Z1pu}	{Z1pu}	{Z1pu}	{bg, Z1pu}	{bg, Z1pu}	{bg, Z1pu}	{bg, Z1pu}	Ø	Ø	Ø	Ø	Ø									
t_{13}	{Z1pu}	{Z1pu}	{Z1pu}	{bg, Z1pu}	{bg, Z1pu}	{bg, Z1pu}	{bg, Z1pu}	Ø	Ø	Ø	Ø	Ø	Ø								
t_{14}	{Z1pu}	{Z1pu}	{Z1pu}	{bg, Z1pu}	{bg, Z1pu}	{bg, Z1pu}	{bg, Z1pu}	Ø	Ø	Ø	Ø	Ø	Ø	Ø							
t_{15}	Z1pu}	Z1pu}	Z1pu}	{bg, Z1pu}	{bg, Z1pu}	{bg, Z1pu}	{bg, Z1pu}	Ø	Ø	Ø	Ø	Ø	Ø	Ø	Ø						
t_{16}	Ø	Ø	Ø	{bg}	{bg}	{bg}	{bg}	Ø	Ø	Ø	Ø	Ø	Ø	Ø	Ø	Ø					
t_{17}	Ø	Ø	Ø	{bg}	{bg}	{bg}	{bg}	Ø	Ø	Ø	Ø	Ø	Ø	Ø	Ø	Ø	Ø				
t_{18}	Ø	Ø	Ø	{bg}	{bg}	{bg}	{bg}	Ø	Ø	Ø	Ø	Ø	Ø	Ø	Ø	Ø	Ø	Ø			
t_{19}	Ø	Ø	Ø	{bg}	{bg}	{bg}	{bg}	Ø	Ø	Ø	Ø	Ø	Ø	Ø	Ø	Ø	Ø	Ø	Ø		
t_{20}	Ø	Ø	Ø	Ø	Ø	Ø	Ø	{bg, Z1pu, Z1trp}	{bg, Z1pu, Z1trp}	{bg, Z1pu, Z1trp}	{Z1pu}	{Z1pu}	{Z1pu}	{Z1pu}	{Z1pu}	Ø	Ø	Ø	Ø	Ø	
t_{21}	Ø	Ø	Ø	Ø	Ø	Ø	Ø	{bg, Z1pu, Z1trp}	{bg, Z1pu, Z1trp}	{bg, Z1pu, Z1trp}	{Z1pu}	{Z1pu}	{Z1pu}	{Z1pu}	{Z1pu}	Ø	Ø	Ø	Ø	Ø	Ø

Table 8. *D*-discernibility matrix of modified *C*

The Boolean discernibility function is formulated from the discernibility matrix as follows:

$f_C(D)$

$= (bg+Z1pu+Z1trp)\ (Z1pu) \times (Z1pu+Z1trp)\ (bg+Z1pu)\ (bg) \times (bg+Z1pu+Z1trp)\ (bg+Z1pu)\ (bg) \times (bg+Z1pu+Z1trp) \times Z1pu$

$= (Z1pu) \times (Z1pu+Z1trp)\ (bg) \times (bg) \times (bg+Z1pu+Z1trp) \times Z1pu$

$= (Z1pu)\ (bg) \rightarrow$ The final Disjunctive Normal Form (DNF) of $f_C(D)$

There is only one *D*-reduct of *C*, $RED_D(C) = \{bg, Z1pu\}$. As shown in Table 9, it can alternatively be used to represent exactly similar equivalence relation $U|IND(D)$ of the down scaled *DS* as that represented by the whole set of attributes C. The *D*-core of *C* is the set of all single entries of the *D*-discernibility matrix, (or $CORE_D(C) = \cap RED_D(C)$), i.e. $\{bg, Z1pu\}$. In this case, the *D*-core of *C* is similar to *D*-reduct of *C*.

As previously discussed, the possibility of the core inferring the power system state the relay has been subjected to is really prominently singled out now by the new $CORE_D(C) = \{bg, Z1pu\}$. Due the very characteristic of indispensability of core, it is undoubtedly identified that a A-G fault has occurred and consequently the relay's Z1 ground distance element has picked up to get rid of it. This eventually translates into the trip decision having patterns such as that presented by the attribute *Trip* shown all along.

Time (*U*)	*bg*	*Z1pu*	*Trip*
t_1	0	0	0
t_2	0	0	0
t_3	0	0	0
t_4	1	0	0
t_5	2	0	0
t_6	2	0	0
t_7	2	0	0
t_8	1	1	b
t_9	1	1	b
t_{10}	1	1	b
t_{11}	0	1	b
t_{12}	0	1	b
t_{13}	0	1	b
t_{14}	0	1	b
t_{15}	0	1	b
t_{16}	0	0	b
t_{17}	0	0	b
t_{18}	0	0	b
t_{19}	0	0	b
t_{20}	0	0	0
t_{21}	0	0	0

Table 9. Equivalent decision table with respect to $RED_D(C) = \{bg, Z1pu\}$

4.3. Protective relay decision algorithm discovery

As aforementioned, a relay decision algorithm in *DS* called *CD*-decision algorithm manifests as a *CD*-decision table. It comprises a finite set of relay *CD*-decision rules or instructions. The event report of a protective distance relay in the form of a *DS* is a manifestation of relay decision algorithm. In protection system, protection engineers relate relay decision algorithm as relay operation logic. It is envisaged that with rough set theory, the relay operation logic knowledge can be discovered. Later it can be transformed into a knowledge base of a decision support system for determining anticipated relay behavior out of a new test *DS* [7].

Checking whether or not all the relay operation logics (decision rules) are true would enable us to check whether or not a relay decision algorithm is consistent. As aforementioned, consistency is measured by the degree of dependency *k* (or alternatively, dependency is measured by the degree of consistency) [10]. Thus, it is well understood that with the degree of consistency given in Equation (10),

$$k = \frac{card\,POS(C,D)}{card\ (CD - decision\,algorithm)} \tag{23}$$

a relay *CD*-decision algorithm has a degree *k*, i.e. the degree of dependency between condition attributes $C = \{ag, bg, cg, Z1pu, Z4pu, Z1trp, Z2trp, Z3trp, Z4trp\}$ and decision attributes $D = \{Trip\}$.

The relay *CD*-decision rules ($C \rightarrow D$) are:

rule 1: $ag_0\ bg_0\ cg_0\ Z1pu_0\ Z4pu_0\ Z1trp_0\ Z2trp_0\ Z3trp_0\ Z4trp_0 \rightarrow Trip_0$

rule 2: $ag_0\ bg_0\ cg_0\ Z1pu_0\ Z4pu_0\ Z1trp_0\ Z2trp_0\ Z3trp_0\ Z4trp_0 \rightarrow Trip_0$

rule 3: $ag_0\ bg_0\ cg_0\ Z1pu_0\ Z4pu_0\ Z1trp_0\ Z2trp_0\ Z3trp_0\ Z4trp_0 \rightarrow Trip_0$

rule 4: $ag_0\ bg_1\ cg_0\ Z1pu_0\ Z4pu_0\ Z1trp_0\ Z2trp_0\ Z3trp_0\ Z4trp_0 \rightarrow Trip_0$

rule 5: $ag_0\ bg_2\ cg_0\ Z1pu_0\ Z4pu_0\ Z1trp_0\ Z2trp_0\ Z3trp_0\ Z4trp_0 \rightarrow Trip_0$

rule 6: $ag_0\ bg_2\ cg_0\ Z1pu_0\ Z4pu_0\ Z1trp_0\ Z2trp_0\ Z3trp_0\ Z4trp_0 \rightarrow Trip_0$

rule 7: $ag_0\ bg_2\ cg_0\ Z1pu_0\ Z4pu_0\ Z1trp_0\ Z2trp_0\ Z3trp_0\ Z4trp_0 \rightarrow Trip_0$

rule 8: $ag_0\ bg_1\ cg_0\ Z1pu_1\ Z4pu_0\ Z1trp_1\ Z2trp_0\ Z3trp_0\ Z4trp_0 \rightarrow Trip_b$

rule 9: $ag_0\ bg_1\ cg_0\ Z1pu_1\ Z4pu_0\ Z1trp_1\ Z2trp_0\ Z3trp_0\ Z4trp_0 \rightarrow Trip_b$

rule 10: $ag_0\ bg_1\ cg_0\ Z1pu_1\ Z4pu_0\ Z1trp_1\ Z2trp_0\ Z3trp_0\ Z4trp_0 \rightarrow Trip_b$

rule 11: $ag_0\ bg_0\ cg_0\ Z1pu_1\ Z4pu_0\ Z1trp_0\ Z2trp_0\ Z3trp_0\ Z4trp_0 \rightarrow Trip_b$

rule 12: $ag_0\ bg_0\ cg_0\ Z1pu_1\ Z4pu_0\ Z1trp_0\ Z2trp_0\ Z3trp_0\ Z4trp_0 \rightarrow Trip_b$

rule 13: $ag_0\ bg_0\ cg_0\ Z1pu_1\ Z4pu_0\ Z1trp_0\ Z2trp_0\ Z3trp_0\ Z4trp_0 \rightarrow Trip_b$

rule 14: $ag_0\, bg_0\, cg_0\, Z1pu_1\, Z4pu_0\, Z1trp_0\, Z2trp_0\, Z3trp_0\, Z4trp_0 \rightarrow Trip_b$

rule 15: $ag_0\, bg_0\, cg_0\, Z1pu_1\, Z4pu_0\, Z1trp_0\, Z2trp_0\, Z3trp_0\, Z4trp_0 \rightarrow Trip_b$

rule 16: $ag_0\, bg_0\, cg_0\, Z1pu_0\, Z4pu_0\, Z1trp_0\, Z2trp_0\, Z3trp_0\, Z4trp_0 \rightarrow Trip_b$

rule 17: $ag_0\, bg_0\, cg_0\, Z1pu_0\, Z4pu_0\, Z1trp_0\, Z2trp_0\, Z3trp_0\, Z4trp_0 \rightarrow Trip_b$

rule 18: $ag_0\, bg_0\, cg_0\, Z1pu_0\, Z4pu_0\, Z1trp_0\, Z2trp_0\, Z3trp_0\, Z4trp_0 \rightarrow Trip_b$

rule 19: $ag_0\, bg_0\, cg_0\, Z1pu_0\, Z4pu_0\, Z1trp_0\, Z2trp_0\, Z3trp_0\, Z4trp_0 \rightarrow Trip_b$

rule 20: $ag_0\, bg_0\, cg_0\, Z1pu_0\, Z4pu_0\, Z1trp_0\, Z2trp_0\, Z3trp_0\, Z4trp_0 \rightarrow Trip_0$

rule 21: $ag_0\, bg_0\, cg_0\, Z1pu_0\, Z4pu_0\, Z1trp_0\, Z2trp_0\, Z3trp_0\, Z4trp_0 \rightarrow Trip_0$

The two sets of relay decision rules, i.e. rules 1, 2, 3 and rules 16, 17, 18, 19, altogether totaling 7 rules, are inconsistent (false). The positive region of the *CD*-decision algorithm consists of only consistent decision rules 4, 5, 6, 7, 8, 9, 10, 11, 12, 13, 14, 15, 20 and 21 (i.e. *card POS*(*C*,*D*) = 14) and, hence, the degree of dependency is k = 14/21= 0.67. Since there are decision rules in the algorithm that are consistent only by the degree of 0.67 (i.e. false), the relay *CD*-decision algorithm is said to be inconsistent. The decision classes are not all uniquely discernible by conditions of all decision rules in the *CD*-decision algorithm. In other words, there are at least two decision rules having the same conditions but different implications in the decision. This phenomenon is certainly anticipated especially as shown by rules 16, 17, 18, and 19 whereby the decision attribute *Trip* remains in the value "*b*" reflecting the actual distance relay operation behavior. Technically speaking, irrespective of the presence or otherwise of the fault (assertion via attribute "*bg*") and zone 1 element pick-up (assertion via attribute "*Z1pu*"), the relay trip signal remains asserted for a certain preset duration of time [7].

4.4. Protective relay decision algorithm simplification

Algorithm reduction results in simplification of the *CD*-decision algorithm. This is done by investigating whether all condition attributes are necessary to make decisions. Therefore, reducing *CD*-decision algorithm is essentially closely related to the previous discussion on reducing *DS*.

The subset of condition attributes $C' \subseteq C$ is called a reduct of *C* in the *CD*-decision algorithm if the *C′D*-decision algorithm is independent and consistent, i.e. $POS(C',D) = POS(C,D)$. Therefore, the following terms are valid:

- *C′D*-decision algorithm is reduct of *CD*-decision algorithm.
- The set of all reducts of *CD*-decision algorithm is called *RED*(*C*,*D*)
- The set of all indispensible condition attributes in the *CD*-decision algorithm is called the core of the of the *CD*-decision algorithm and, similarly like before, takes on the expression, $CORE(C,D) = \cap RED(C,D)$. (In principle it is similar to the expression $CORE_D(C) = \cap RED_D(C)$).

The modified *DS* in Table 6 had found its only reduct of condition attributes, $RED(C,D) = RED_D(C) = \{bg, Z1pu\}$, in the relay *CD*-decision algorithm. The core had a similar set as that of the reduct, i.e. $CORE(C,D) = \cap RED(C,D) = \{bg, Z1pu\}$. The resulting equivalent *DS* with respect to $RED(C,D) = \{bg, Z1pu\}$ in Table 9 produces a rather simplified version of relay *CD*-decision algorithm, i.e.,

rule 1: $bg_0\ Z1pu_0 \rightarrow Trip_0$

rule 2: $bg_0\ Z1pu_0 \rightarrow Trip_0$

rule 3: $bg_0\ Z1pu_0 \rightarrow Trip_0$

rule 4: $bg_1\ Z1pu_0 \rightarrow Trip_0$

rule 5: $bg_2\ Z1pu_0 \rightarrow Trip_0$

rule 6: $bg_2\ Z1pu_0 \rightarrow Trip_0$

rule 7: $bg_2\ Z1pu_0 \rightarrow Trip_0$

rule 8: $bg_1\ Z1pu_1 \rightarrow Trip_b$

rule 9: $bg_1\ Z1pu_1 \rightarrow Trip_b$

rule 10: $bg_1\ Z1pu_1 \rightarrow Trip_b$

rule 11: $bg_0\ Z1pu_1 \rightarrow Trip_b$

rule 12: $bg_0\ Z1pu_1 \rightarrow Trip_b$

rule 13: $bg_0\ Z1pu_1 \rightarrow Trip_b$

rule 14: $bg_0\ Z1pu_1 \rightarrow Trip_b$

rule 15: $bg_0\ Z1pu_1 \rightarrow Trip_b$

rule 16: $bg_0\ Z1pu_0 \rightarrow Trip_b$

rule 17: $bg_0\ Z1pu_0 \rightarrow Trip_b$

rule 18: $bg_0\ Z1pu_0 \rightarrow Trip_b$

rule 19: $bg_0\ Z1pu_0 \rightarrow Trip_b$

rule 20: $bg_0\ Z1pu_0 \rightarrow Trip_0$

rule 21: $bg_0\ Z1pu_0 \rightarrow Trip_0$

Each relay *CD*-decision rule designation corresponds to the row label in the *DS;* for example, rule 9 corresponding to row label t_9.

The relay *CD*-decision algorithm can be cut down by removing duplicate relay *CD*-decision rules,

rule 1′ (1, 2, 3, 20, 21): $bg_0\ Z1pu_0 \rightarrow Trip_0$

rule 2′ (4): $bg_1\ Z1pu_0 \rightarrow Trip_0$

rule 3′ (5, 6, 7): $bg_2\ Z1pu_0 \rightarrow Trip_0$

rule 4′ (8, 9, 10): $bg_1\ Z1pu_1 \rightarrow Trip_b$

rule 5′ (11, 12, 13, 14, 15): $bg_0\ Z1pu_1 \rightarrow Trip_b$

rule 6′ (16, 17, 18, 19): $bg_0\ Z1pu_0 \rightarrow Trip_b$

From the apparently inconsistent rules 1′ and 6′, i.e. similar conditions but dissimilar decisions, the simplified relay *CD*-decision algorithm reveals pronouncedly its inconsistent nature. This inconsistency may not be desirable in some information system analysis. However, in as far as protective relay operation is concerned, it is interesting to know, among others:

- the time delay between relay pick-up and relay trip signal assertion – traced by identifying the translated time sequence (*DS* row label) from rule 4 (t_4) to rule 8 (t_8),
- the lapsed time of the relay assertion in instructing the circuit breaker to open its contacts – traced by identifying the translated time sequence from rule 8 (t_8) to rule 15 (t_{15}) and eventually to rule 19(t_{19}), and
- the affected pole(s) – determined from the decision attribute *Trip* value.

Decision rules 2′, 3′, 4′, and 5′ are the consistent ones that constitute the positive region of the CD-decision algorithm.

The core *CORE*(*C*,*D*) = {*bg*, *Z1pu*} can be justified why it is so. By dropping the attributes *bg* or *Z1pu,* one step at a time, their indispensability can be seen and whether the positive region that consists of the consistent rules changes can be checked. Different positive region is obtained by removing attribute *bg*:

rule 1′ (1, 2, 3, 20, 21): $Z1pu_0 \rightarrow Trip_0$

rule 2′ (4): $Z1pu_0 \rightarrow Trip_0$

rule 3′ (5, 6, 7): $Z1pu_0 \rightarrow Trip_0$

rule 4′ (8, 9, 10): $Z1pu_1 \rightarrow Trip_b$

rule 5′ (11, 12, 13, 14, 15): $Z1pu_1 \rightarrow Trip_b$

rule 6′ (16, 17, 18, 19): $Z1pu_0 \rightarrow Trip_b$

Likewise, the positive region can be changed as well by removing attribute Z1pu:

rule 1′ (1, 2, 3, 20, 21): $bg_0 \rightarrow Trip_0$

rule 2′ (4): $bg_1 \rightarrow Trip_0$

rule 3′ (5, 6, 7): $bg_2 \rightarrow Trip_0$

rule 4′ (8, 9, 10): $bg_1 \rightarrow Trip_b$

rule 5′ (11, 12, 13, 14, 15): $bg_0 \rightarrow Trip_b$

rule 6′ (16, 17, 18, 19): $bg_0 \rightarrow Trip_b$

Thus, when one by one the said condition attributes is removed, the changes incurred in the positive region of the relay *CD*-decision algorithm concur with the core attributes' indispensability. Thus, the core having both attributes {*bg, Z1pu*} is correct.

4.5. Protective relay decision algorithm minimization

It is subsequently desirable to further minimize the decision rules in the relay *CD*-decision algorithm after the above simplification via reduction of the set of condition attributes. This is achieved by removal of any possibly superfluous decision rules which essentially involves reducing the superfluous values of attributes. In other words, the unnecessary conditions have to be separately removed leaving only the core attribute in each decision rule of the algorithm [10].

The tabulated version of the above simplified relay *CD*-decision algorithm is shown in Table 10.

U	*bg*	*Z1pu*	*Trip*
1′ (1, 2, 3, 20, 21)	0	0	0
2′ (4)	1	0	0
3′ (5, 6, 7)	2	0	0
4′ (8, 9, 10)	1	1	a
5′ (11, 12, 13, 14, 15)	0	1	a
6′ (16,17,18,19)	0	0	a

Table 10. *DS* of simplified *CD*-decision algorithm

In Table 11 the condition attribute of each decision rule in Table 10 is removed one by one. In each removal the resultant rule is cross checked with other rules to find whether they are in conflict (inconsistent). This cross reference with other rules is to figure out whether the remaining condition attribute's value is the same but implication on the decision attribute is different. This process discovers the core attribute(s) that when eliminated causes the corresponding decision rule, or in general the *CD*-decision algorithm, inconsistent and consequently invalid (albeit not necessarily in the relay analysis perspective).

In summary, Table 12 contains cores of each decision rule. The condition attribute having eliminated value can be said as having no effect whatsoever on the *CD*-decision algorithm and may be termed as "don't care". It can be assigned with a value or otherwise. Combining duplicate rules and demarcating separate decision classes, Table 13 is obtained.

For decision attribute *Trip* = 0, one *minimal* set of decision rules is obtained from

$bg_0\, Z1pu_0 \rightarrow Trip_0$

$$bg_1\ Z1pu_0 \rightarrow Trip_0$$

$$bg_2 \rightarrow Trip_0$$

i.e.

$$bg_0\ Z1pu_0 \vee bg_1\ Z1pu_0 \vee bg_2 \quad \rightarrow Trip_0$$

For decision attribute *Trip* = *a*, one minimal set of decision rules is obtained from

$$Z1pu_1 \rightarrow Trip_b$$

$$bg_0\ Z1pu_0 \rightarrow Trip_b$$

i.e.

$$Z1pu_1 \vee bg_0\ Z1pu_0 \rightarrow Trip_b$$

The combined form of the *minimal* *CD*-decision algorithm is

$$bg_0\ Z1pu_0 \vee bg_1\ Z1pu_0 \vee bg_2 \quad \rightarrow Trip_0$$

or,

$$Z1pu_0\ (bg_0 \vee bg_1) \vee bg_2 \rightarrow Trip_0$$

and

$$bg_0\ Z1pu_0 \vee Z1pu_1 \rightarrow Trip_b$$

The final form of *CD*-decision algorithm can now be easily interpreted as follows:

- The decision rule $Z1pu_0\ (bg_0 \vee bg_1) \vee bg_2 \rightarrow Trip_0$ is interpreted as,

  IF $Z1pu = 0$ AND either $bg = 0$ OR $bg = 1$ OR IF $bg = 2$, THEN $Trip = 0$.

  The non-trip assertion ($Trip = 0$) is imminent with either one of the following situations:

  i. when no fault occurs ($bg = 0$) and no relay pick-up ($Z1pu = 0$), or
  ii. when a A-G fault occurs in zone 1($bg = 1$) and no relay pick-up ($Z1pu = 0$), or
  iii. when a A-G fault occurs in zone 2 ($bg = 2$)
- The decision rule $bg_0\ Z1pu_0 \vee Z1pu_1 \rightarrow Trip_b$ is interpreted as,

  IF $Z1pu = 0$ AND $bg = 0$ OR IF $Z1pu = 1$, THEN $Trip = \mathrm{b}$.

  The trip assertion ($Trip = \mathrm{b}$) is imminent with either one of the following situations:

  i. when there is no more fault indication ($bg = 0$) and relay pick-up element has reset ($Z1pu = 0$), or

  ii. when relay pick-up element remains asserted ($Z1pu = 1$)

  Item i. indicates the fact that trip assertion $Trip = \mathrm{b}$ is still present in the face of the fault and relay pick-up resets (i.e. $bg = 0$ and $Z1pu = 0$) suggests that the preset time duration of the trip assertion is taking place.

CD-decision algorithm	Removed attribute *bg*	Removed attribute *Z1pu*	Resultant rule to check	At least one other rule in conflict	Core attribute
rule 1′ (1, 2, 3, 20, 21): $bg_0\ Z1pu_0 \rightarrow Trip_0$	✓		$Z1pu_0 \rightarrow Trip_0$	rule 6′: $Z1pu_0 \rightarrow Trip_b$	*bg*, *Z1pu*
		✓	$bg_0 \rightarrow Trip_0$	rule 5′: $bg_0 \rightarrow Trip_b$	
rule 2′ (4): $bg_1\ Z1pu_0 \rightarrow Trip_0$	✓		$Z1pu_0 \rightarrow Trip_0$	rule 6′: $Z1pu_0 \rightarrow Trip_b$	*bg*, *Z1pu*
		✓	$bg_1 \rightarrow Trip_0$	rule 4′: $bg_1 \rightarrow Trip_b$	
rule 3′ (5, 6, 7): $bg_2\ Z1pu_0 \rightarrow Trip_0$	✓		$Z1pu_0 \rightarrow Trip_0$	rule 6′: $Z1pu_0 \rightarrow Trip_b$	*bg*
		✓	$bg_2 \rightarrow Trip_0$	none	
rule 4′ (8, 9, 10): $bg_1\ Z1pu_1 \rightarrow Trip_a$	✓		$Z1pu_1 \rightarrow Trip_b$	none	*Z1pu*
		✓	$bg_1 \rightarrow Trip_b$	rule 2′: $bg_1 \rightarrow Trip_0$	
rule 5′ (11, 12, 13, 14, 15): $bg_0\ Z1pu_1 \rightarrow Trip_b$	✓		$Z1pu_1 \rightarrow Trip_b$	none	*Z1pu*
		✓	$bg_0 \rightarrow Trip_b$	rule 1′: $bg_0 \rightarrow Trip_0$	
rule 6′ (16, 17, 18, 19): $bg_0\ Z1pu_0 \rightarrow Trip_b$	✓		$Z1pu_0 \rightarrow Trip_b$	rule 1′: $Z1pu_0 \rightarrow Trip_0$	*bg*, *Z1pu*
		✓	$bg_0 \rightarrow Trip_b$	rule 1′: $bg_0 \rightarrow Trip_0$	

Table 11. Eliminating unnecessary condition attribute in decision rules

U	*bg*	*Z1pu*	*Trip*
1′	0	0	0
2′	1	0	0
3′	2	-	0
4′	-	1	b
5′	-	1	b
6′	0	0	b

Table 12. Cores of decision rules

U	*bg*	*Z1pu*	*Trip*
1′	0	0	0
2′	1	0	0
3′	2	-	0
4″ (4′,5′)	-	1	b
6′	0	0	b

Table 13. Cores of decision rules

5. Conclusion

Rough set theory has been proven to be an essentially useful mathematical tool in intelligent data mining analysis of inconsistent and vague protective relay data pattern as evident in the rough classification involved in the assertion of the trip decision attribute. The adoption of rough set theory is managed under supervised learning.

A single *D*-reduct of *C* (i.e. $RED_D(C) = \{bg, Z1pu\}$) has been discovered after formulating the attribute priority of the distance relay operation to trim the *DS*. $RED_D(C)$ can alternatively be used to represent exactly the same equivalence relation $U \mid IND(D)$ represented by the whole set of attributes *C*. Relying on the reduced number of condition attributes represented by $RED_D(C)$, relay analysis that can be achieved at ease.

The *D*-core of *C* (i.e. $CORE_D(C)$ = {*bg*, *Z1pu*}), determined as the set of all single entries of the *D*-discernibility matrix, provides us with a novel technique in inferring the power system state where the relay has been subjected to. The core, because of its indispensability nature, draws our attention undoubtedly to the fact that an B-G fault has occurred and consequently the relay's Z1 ground distance element has picked up to eliminate it. This eventually translates into the trip decision having patterns such as that presented by the attribute *Trip*.

The degree of dependency $k < 1$ of the relay *CD*-decision algorithm justifies our anticipation of rough classification in the distance relay data. This is evidently shown in some of the rules that have the decision attribute *Trip* remain asserted with the value "b" for a certain preset duration of time. This is irrespective of the presence or absence of the fault via the assertion of attribute "*bg*" and zone 1 element pick-up via the assertion of attribute "*Z1pu*").

The *RED*(*C*,*D*) = {*bg*, *Z1pu*} provides us with the discovery of the relay *CD*-decision algorithm in a simple form. By eliminating any possible superfluous decision rules, isolating condition attributes, one value at a time, further minimization of the algorithm can be performed.

Author details

Mohammad Lutfi Othman
Department of Electrical and Electronic Engineering, Faculty of Engineering,
Universiti Putra Malaysia, Serdang, Malaysia

Ishak Aris
Department of Electrical and Electronic Engineering, Faculty of Engineering,
Universiti Putra Malaysia, Serdang, Malaysia

Acknowledgement

This work was supported by the Ministry of Higher Education Malaysia under the 2011 Fundamental Research Grant Scheme with the project code FRGS/1/11/TK/UPM/03/4 and project file code 1057FR.

6. References

[1] Bakar A H A (2001) Disturbance Analysis in TNB Transmission System. Developments in Power System Protection Conference. IEE Publication No.479: 339-442
[2] Kumm J J, Weber M S, Schweitzer E O and Hou D (1994) Philosophies For Testing Protective Relays. 48th Annual Georgia Tech Protective Relaying Conference, Atlanta, Georgia.
[3] Kezunovic, M (2001) Section II: Equipment characteristics. IEEE Tutorial on Automated Fault Analysis. Texas A&M University, College Station, USA, July, pp 5-9.

[4] Kezunovic, M (2001) Section III: Scope of Analysis. IEEE Tutorial on Automated Fault Analysis. Texas A&M University, College Station, USA, July, pp 10-13.
[5] Shapiro G P (1997) Data Mining and Knowledge Discovery: The Third Generation, Foundations of Intelligent Systems. Berlin / Heidelberg: Springer. vol. 1325/1997, pp. 48-49.
[6] Kim G C, Mohd Zin A A and Shukri Z (2005) COMTRADE-Based Fault Information System for TNB Substations. IEEE Proc. Region 10 TENCON, Melbourne, Australia. pp. 1-6.
[7] Othman M L, Aris I, Abdullah S M, Ali M L and Othman M R (2009) Discovering Decision Algorithm from a Distance Relay Event Report. European j. scientific research, 3(1): 30-56.
[8] Pawlak Z (2002) Rough Set and Intelligent Data Analysis. Int. j. information sciences. 147: 1-12.
[9] Huang C L, Li T S and Peng T K (2005) A Hybrid Approach Of Rough Set Theory And Genetic Algorithm For Fault Diagnosis. Int. j. advanced manufacturing technology, Springer-Verlag London, 27(1-2): 119-127.
[10] Pawlak Z (1991) Rough Sets – Theoretical Aspects of Reasoning about Data. Dordrecht/Boston/London: Kluwer Academic Publishers.
[11] Walczak B and Massart D L (1999) Rough Sets Theory: Tutorial", Chemometrics and intelligent laboratory systems. 47(1): 1-16.
[12] Pawlak Z (1995) Rough Set Approach To Knowledge-Based Decision Support. 14th European j. operational research, Jerusalem, Israel, pp. 48–57.
[13] Hor C L and Crossley P A (2006) Substation Event Analysis Using Information from Intelligent Electronic Devices. Int. j. electrical power and energy systems, 28(6): 374-386.
[14] Pawlak Z, Wong S K M and Ziarko W (1988) Rough Sets: Probalistic versus Deterministic Approach. Int. j. man-machine studies. 29: 81-95.
[15] Komorowski J, Pawlak Z, Polkowski L and Skowron A (1999) Rough Fuzzy Hybridization—A New Trend in Decision Making. In: Pal S K, Skowron A, editors. Rough Sets: A Tutorial. New York: Springer.
[16] Ziarko W and Shan N (1995) Discovering Attribute Relationships, Dependencies And Rules By Using Rough Sets. Proceedings of the 28th Annual Hawaii International Conference on System Sciences (HICSS '95), pp. 293–299.
[17] Pawlak Z (2003) Rough Sets. Technical paper, Institute of Theoretical and Applied Informatics, Polish Academy of Sciences, Gliwice, and University of Information Technology and Management, Warsaw, Poland. pp. 1-51.
[18] Pawlak Z (2004) Some Issues on Rough Sets. In: Peters J F et al., editors. Transactions on Rough Sets I LNCS 3100. Verlag, Berlin, Heidelberg: Springer. pp. 1-58.
[19] Skowron A and Rauszer C (1992) The Discernibility Matrices and Functions in Information System. In: Slowinski R, editors. Intelligent Decision Support: Handbook of Applications and Advances of the Rough Sets Theory. Series D: System Theory, Knowledge Engineering and Problem Solving. Dordrecht: Kluwer Academic Publishers. 11, pp. 331-362.

Chapter 6

An Unsupervised Classification Method for Hyperspectral Remote Sensing Image Based on Spectral Data Mining

Xingping Wen and Xiaofeng Yang

Additional information is available at the end of the chapter

http://dx.doi.org/10.5772/50135

1. Introduction

Hyperspectral remote sensing is one of the most significant recent breakthroughs in remote sensing. It obtains image in a large number (usually more than 40), narrow (typically 10 to 20 nm spectral resolution) and contiguous spectral bands to enable the extraction of spectral information at a pixel scale, so it can produce data with sufficient spectral resolution for the direct recognition those materials with diagnostic spectral features [1]. Usually classification method of hyperspectral remote sensing data are divided into two categories [2]: using sub-pixel classification techniques [3] and spectral matching techniques [4]. In the former, the images should not need to atmospheric correction, however, due to higher dimension of hyperspectral image, it will lead to dimensionality disaster and Hughes phenomenon [5, 6] which refer to the fact that with the number of spectral bands increased the sample size required for training set grows exponentially. The solution methods usually are increasing sample size, thus this will cost a lot of human and material resources. Another simple but sometimes effective way to solve this problem is dimension reduction of hyperspectral data, but some useful information will be lost. Furthermore, it is hard to solve mixed pixels. In the latter, matched filtering method is successfully used in information extraction from hyperspectral remote sensing image. It classifies by computing the similarity of the pixel spectrum and the reference spectrum, and it needs no sample data but the image data should be atmospheric corrected beforehand. These methods based on the hypothesis that dark currents of the sensor and path radiation are removed and all spectra data have been calibrated to apparent reflectance. However, it is only the ideal condition for these effects are hard to be removed completely, so some mistakes will be caused due to atmospheric influence, especially for low reflectivity ground objects. This chapter proposed an unsupervised classification for hyperspectral remote sensing image. It can effectively extract

INTECH
open science | open minds

© 2012 Wen and Yang, licensee InTech. This is an open access chapter distributed under the terms of the Creative Commons Attribution License (http://creativecommons.org/licenses/by/3.0), which permits unrestricted use, distribution, and reproduction in any medium, provided the original work is properly cited.

low reflectivity ground objects such as water or vegetation in shadowed area from hyperspectral remote sensing data using spectral data mining. Firstly, extracting more than 40 endmembers from the hyperspectral image using Pixel Purity Index (PPI) and calculating the spectral angle between the pixel spectra and each endmember spectra, the pixel was assigned to the endmember class with the smallest spectral angle. Then, endmember spectra were clustered based on K-mean algorithm. Finally, pixels in the same K-mean result class were combined to one class and the final classification outcome was projected and outputted. Comparing the classification result and field data, they are in accord with each other. This method can produce the objective result with no artificial interference. It can be an efficient information extraction method for hyperspectral remote sensing data.

2. The study area

The study area is located at Heqing county in Yunnan province in southwest of China (25º38'N - 26º30'N; 99º58'E – 100º15'E) (figure 1). It covers mountainous terrain and has big altitude difference. It is situated in the Three Parallel Rivers of Yunnan Protected Areas which is a UNESCO World Heritage Site in China. The Three Parallel Rivers of Yunnan Protected Areas lies within the drainage basins of the upper reaches of three of Asia's great rivers run approximately parallel to one another though separated by higher mountain ranges with peaks over 6,000 meters. They are the Yangtze (Jinsha), Mekong (Lancang) and Salween (Nujiang) rivers, in the Yunnan section of the Hengduan Mountains. After this near confluence area, the rivers greatly diverge: the Nujiang River flows at Moulmein, Burma, into the Indian Ocean, the Mekong south of Ho Chi Minh City, Vietnam, into the South China Sea and the Yangtse impours into the East China Sea at Shanghai. It was awarded World Heritage Site status in 2003 for their richer biodiversity and spectacular topographical diversity [7].

Figure 1. China provincial boundaries and the study area.

3. Remote sensing data

The image investigated in this chapter was obtained by Hyperion sensor boarded on EO-1 satellite in November 11, 2004, and it covers the 0.4 to 2.5 micrometer spectral range with 242 spectral bands at roughly 30m spatial resolution and 10nm spectral resolution over a 7.5 km wide swath from a 705 km orbit. The system has two grating spectrometers; one visible / near infrared (VNIR) spectrometer (approximately 0.4–1.0 micrometers) and one short-wave infrared (SWIR) spectrometer (approximately 0.9–2.5micrometers) (figure 2). Data are calibrated to radiance using both pre-mission and on-orbit measurements. Key Hyperion characteristics are discussed by Green et al. [8]. The image has a total of 242 bands but only 198 bands are calibrated. Because of an overlap between the VNIR and SWIR focal planes, there are only 196 unique channels [8, 9]. Due to water vapor absorption, some bands nearby 0.94, 1.38 and 1.87 micrometers also can not be available. The rest 163 bands can be used in research. Some pre-processing steps are necessary before using image. Firstly, some bad pixel value in original image were replaced by the means of two pixels value beside its two sides; then the image was radiometrically corrected using calibration coefficient; at last, the image was atmospheric corrected using FLAASH model [10]. Figure 3 and figure 4 shows different ground objects spectra before and after atmospheric correction. Shapes of different ground objects spectra after atmospheric correction are similar with shapes of standard laboratory spectra for the same ground object type.

4. Methodology

4.1. Spectral angle mapper (SAM)

Spectral Angle Mapper (SAM) algorithm is successfully used in matched filtering based on hyperspectral remote sensing image [4, 11-18]. It computes the "spectral angle" between the pixel spectrum and the endmember spectrum. When used on calibrated data, this technique is comparatively insensitive to illumination and albedo effects. Smaller angles represent closer matches to the reference spectra. The result indicates the radian of the spectral angle computed using the following equation:

$$\alpha = \cos^{-1}\left(\frac{\sum_{i=1}^{m} t_i r_i}{\left(\sum_{i=1}^{m} t_i^2\right)^{1/2}\left(\sum_{i=1}^{m} r_i^2\right)^{1/2}}\right) \tag{1}$$

Where m=the number of bands.

t_i =pixel spectrum.

r_i =reference spectrum.

α = radian of the spectral angle

Figure 2. Dispaly bands as gray scale (40 = vnir, 93 = swir), Select three bands as RGB (29, 23, 16 = VNIR, 204,150, 93 = SWIR).

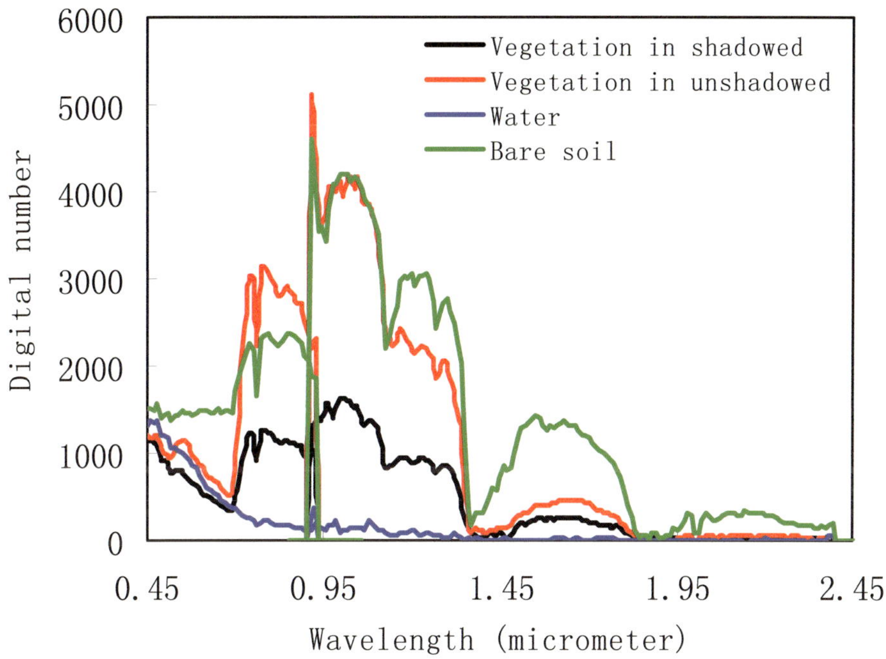

Figure 3. Different ground objects curves before atmospheric correction

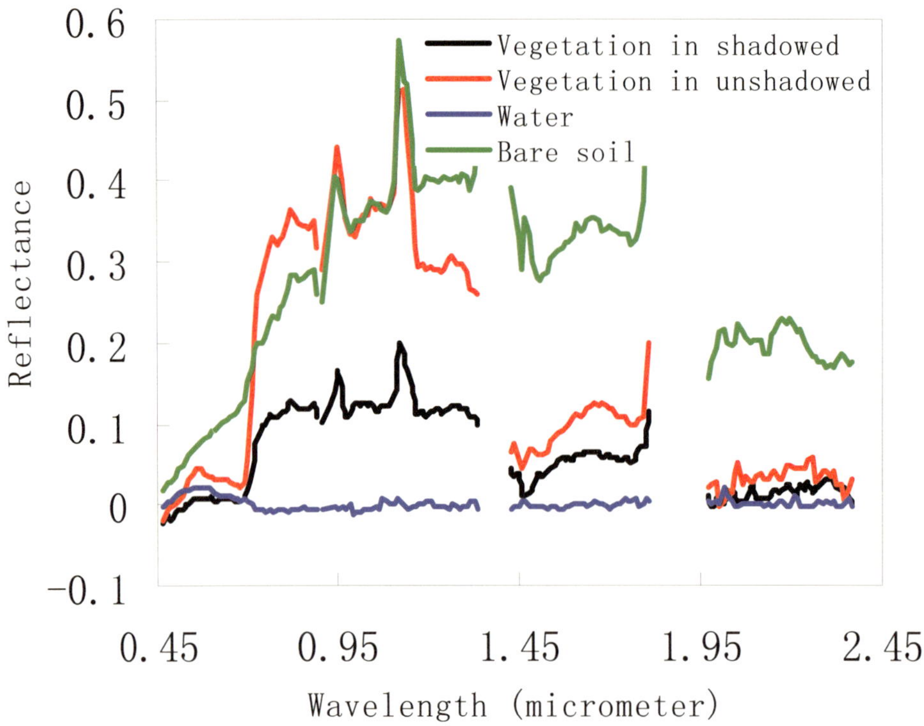

Figure 4. Different ground objects spectra after atmospheric correction.

Usually, a constant threshold is assigned firstly. When α is lower than the constant threshold, that means the pixel spectrum and the reference spectrum are similar with each other, and then assigned the pixel into the reference spectral class.

4.2. Extracting endmembers

The reference spectra can be selected from Spectral libraries, acquired by the handhold spectroradiometer, or extracted from the image itself. The commonly used technique is to extract the reference spectra from the image, for this method has the advantage that endmembers were collected under similar atmospheric conditions and pixel scale. A variety of methods have been used to find endmembers in multispectral and hyperspectral images. Iterated Constrained Endmembers (ICE) is an automated statistical method to extract endmembers from hyperspectral images [19]. [20] found a unique set of purest pixels based upon the geometry of convex sets. Probably Pixel Purity Index (PPI) is the most widely used algorithm [21]. In this chapter, PPI was used to find the most spectrally pure pixels in hyperspectral images as reference spectra. Firstly, the image was applied to a dimensionality analysis and noise whitening using the Minimum Noise Fraction (MNF) transform process [22, 23]. Then, the data are projected onto random unit vectors repeatedly and the total number of each pixel marked as an extreme pixel is noted. At last, the purest pixels in the scene are rapidly identified. In this chapter, 48 endmember spectra were extracted from hyperspectral image.

SAM was used to match each pixel spectrum to 48 endmembers. Figure 5 (b) is the classification result using the constant threshold. Different color represents different classes and black refer to unclassified classes. Comparing figure 5(a) with figure 5(b), it is shown that most vegetation in shadowed region and water are classified into unclassified classes, so some vegetation and water information are lost. One of reason is that the radiance of low reflectivity ground object such as water and vegetation in shadowed area are severely weakened by atmosphere influence when they arrive at the satellite. As is shown from figure 4, the digital numbers value of the vegetation in unshadowed area are 2 times higher than theirs in shadowed region. After atmospheric correction, the reflectance of the vegetation in shadowed area are obviously lower than theirs in unshadowed region, and reflectance in some spectral range (0.46-0.68 and 1.98-2.37 micrometers) are near zero. However, comparing the shape of vegetation spectra in shadowed and unshadowed area, they are similar with each other, so it is possible to identify the low reflectance ground object using SAM algorithm for it is relatively insensitive to illumination and albedo effects, but the constant threshold is not suitable. In this chapter, 48 endmember spectra were used as reference spectra, so the hypothesis that 48 endmember spectra include all land cover type is reasonable. The spectral angle of every pixel was calculated using with all endmembers, and the pixel belongs to the class which has the smallest spectral angle. Figure 5(c) is the processed classification result using adjustable threshold. Comparing with figure 5(b) and figure 5(c), they are the same except unclassified pixel in figure 5(b) which belongs to the certain land cover type in figure 5(c). This method improved the constant threshold SAM classification result, so it is more effective than using constant threshold.

(a) (b) (c)

Figure 5. (a). The hyperspectral image after atmospheric correction. (b). the classification result of SAM using constant threshold. (c). the classification result of SAM using adjustable threshold

4.3. Clustering using K-mean algorithm

Figure 5(c) contains so many classes, and some classes may belong to the same class. In this chapter, these classes were clustered using K-mean algorithm [24], which is a straightforward and effective algorithm for finding clusters in data. It classifies pixels based on features into *k* centroids of group, one for each cluster. These centroids shoud be placed as much as possible far away from each other, then take each point belonging to a given data set which associate to the nearest centroid. The algorithm proceeds as follows. Firstly, the number of classes which the image should be partitioned into is inputted, and *k* records are randomly assigned to be the initial cluster center. Then, for each record, find the nearest cluster center. For each of the *k* clusters, find the cluster centroid, and update the location of each cluster center to the new value of the centroid. Repeat steps until convergence or termination. In this chapter, endmember spectra were clustered using K-mean algorithm and final 5 spectral classed were outputted. Then, classification result using adjustable threshold were merged according the K-mean algorithm result. Final classification result is shown in figure 6. Comparing the classification result and field data, they are in accord with each other.

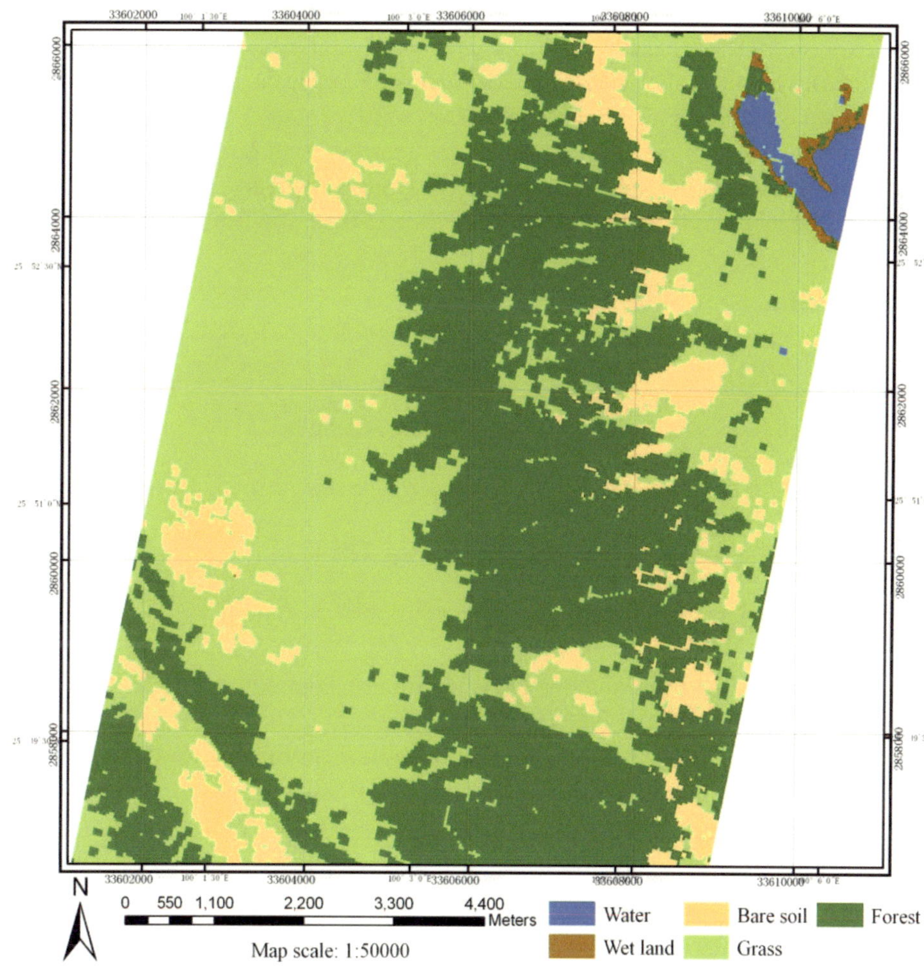

Map Projection: Gauss Kruger 3 Degree, Zone 33, False Easting: 500 kilometer, Central Meridian: 99º.

Figure 6. The classification map of hyperspectral remote sensing image

5. Results and discussions

Matching filter was maturely used in spectral classification in hyperspectral remote sensing image, however, due to atmospheric effect, it is hard to extract low reflectivity ground object. This chapter proposed an unsupervised classification method. Firstly, the hyperspectral remote sensing image was atmospherically corrected. Accuracy atmospheric correction is the key to the classification. Then, endmember spectra were extracted using PPI algorithm, and the image was classified using SAM. Traditionally SAM algorithm used constant threshold. This chapter improved and used adjustable threshold, and the pixel belong to class which has the smallest spectral angle. Finally, the endmember spectra were clustered based on K-mean algorithm and classes were combined according to the K-mean algorithm result. The final classification map was projected and outputted. It is an effective classification method especially for hyperspectral remote sensing image. Users also can adjust the endmember and classes number according to their applications.

Author details

Xingping Wen
Faculty of Land Resource Engineering,
Kunming University of Science and Technology, Kunming, China

Xiaofeng Yang
Research Center for Analysis and Measurement,
Kunming University of Science and Technology, Kunming, China

Acknowledgement

This study was jointly supported by Natural Science Foundation of China (Grant No. 41101343), Natural Science Foundation of China (Grant No. U1133602), China Postdoctoral Science Foundation (20100471687) and the innovation team of ore-forming dynamics and prediction of concealed deposits, Kunming University of Science and Technology, Kunming, China.

6. References

[1] A. F. H. Goetz, G. Vane, J. E. Solomon, and B. N. Rock (1985) Imaging Spectrometry for Earth Remote Sensing, Science, vol. 228, pp. 1147-1153.

[2] F. van der Meer (2006) The effectiveness of spectral similarity measures for the analysis of hyperspectral imagery, International Journal of Applied Earth Observation and Geoinformation, vol. 8, pp. 3-17.

[3] J. J. Settle and N. Drake (1993) Linear mixing and the estimation of ground cover proportions, International Journal of Remote Sensing, vol. 14, pp. 1159-1177.

[4] F. A. Kruse, A. B. Lefkoff, J. W. Boardman, K. B. Heidebrecht, A. T. Shapiro, P. J. Barloon, and A. F. H. Goetz (1993) The Spectral Image-Processing System (SIPS) -

Interactive Visualization and Analysis of Imaging Spectrometer Data, Remote Sensing of Environment, vol. 44, pp. 145-163.
[5] K. Fukunaga and R. R. Hayes (1989) Effects of sample size in classifier design, IEEE Transactions on Pattern Analysis and Machine Intelligence, vol. 11, pp. 873-885.
[6] G. Hughes (1968) On the mean accuracy of statistical pattern recognizers, Information Theory, IEEE Transactions on, vol. 14, pp. 55-63.
[7] Available: http://en.wikipedia.org/wiki/Three_Parallel_Rivers_of_Yunnan_Protected_Areas.
[8] R. O. Green, B. E. Pavri, and T. G. Chrien (2003) On-orbit radiometric and spectral calibration characteristics of EO-1 Hyperion derived with an underflight of AVIRIS and in situ measurements at Salar de Arizaro, Argentina, Geoscience and Remote Sensing, IEEE Transactions on, vol. 41, pp. 1194-1203.
[9] R. Beck (2003) EO-1 User Guide v. 2.3: http://eo1.usgs.gov & http://eo1.gsfc.nasa.gov.
[10] T. Cooley, G. P. Anderson, G. W. Felde, M. L. Hoke, A. J. Ratkowski, J. H. Chetwynd, J. A. Gardner, S. M. Adler-Golden, M. W. Matthew, A. Berk, L. S. Bernstein, P. K. Acharya, D. Miller, and P. Lewis (2002) FLAASH, a MODTRAN4-based atmospheric correction algorithm, its application and validation, in Geoscience and Remote Sensing Symposium, pp. 1414-1418.
[11] R. H. Yuhas, A. F. H. Goetz, and J. W. Boardman (1992) Discrimination among semi-arid landscape endmembers using the spectral angle mapper (SAM) algorithm, in Summaries of the Third Annual JPL Airborne Geoscience Workshop, Pasadena CA, pp. 147-149.
[12] W. M. Baugh, F. A. Kruse, and W. W. Atkinson (1998) Quantitative geochemical mapping of ammonium minerals in the southern Cedar Mountains, Nevada, using the airborne visible/infrared imaging spectrometer (AVIRIS), Remote Sensing of Environment, vol. 65, pp. 292-308.
[13] F. van der Meer (2006) Indicator kriging applied to absorption band analysis in hyperspectral imagery: A case study from the Rodalquilar epithermal gold mining area, SE Spain, International Journal of Applied Earth Observation and Geoinformation, vol. 8, pp. 61-72.
[14] F. Van der Meer, M. Vasquez-Torres, and P. M. Van Dijk (1997) Spectral characterization of ophiolite lithologies in the Troodos Ophiolite complex of Cyprus and its potential in prospecting for massive sulphide deposits, International Journal of Remote Sensing, vol. 18, pp. 1245-1257.
[15] J. Schwarz and K. Staenz (2001) Adaptive Threshold for Spectral Matching of Hyperspectral Data, Canadian Journal of Remote Sensing, vol. 27, pp. 216-224.
[16] E. L. Hunter and C. H. Power (2002) An assessment of two classification methods for mapping Thames Estuary intertidal habitats using CASI data, International Journal of Remote Sensing, vol. 23, pp. 2989-3008.
[17] X. Wen, G. Hu, and X. Yang (2007) Combining the Three Matched Filtering Methods in Mineral Information Extraction from Hyperspectral Data, Journal of China University of Geosciences, vol. 18, pp. 294-296.

[18] X. Wen, G. Hu, and X. Yang (2007) A Simplified Method for Extracting Mineral Information From Hyperspectral Remote Sensing Image Using SAM Algorithm, in 12th Conference of International Association for Mathematical Geology, Geomathematics and GIS Analysis of Resources, Environment and Hazards, Beijing, China, pp. 526-529.
[19] M. Berman, H. Kiiveri, R. Lagerstrom, A. Ernst, R. Dunne, and J. F. Huntington (2004) ICE: a statistical approach to identifying endmembers in hyperspectral images, Geoscience and Remote Sensing, IEEE Transactions on, vol. 42, pp. 2085-2095.
[20] M. E. Winter (1999) Fast autonomous spectral endmember determination in hyperspectral data, in Proceedings of the Thirteenth International Conference on Applied Geologic Remote Sensing, Vancouver, British Columbia, Canada, pp. 337-344.
[21] J. W. Boardman, F. A. Kruse, and R. O. Green (1995) Mapping Target Signatures Via Partial Unmixing of Aviris Data, in Summaries of the Fifth Annual JPL Airborne Earth Science Workshop, Washington, D. C, pp. 23-26.
[22] A. A. Green, M. Berman, P. Switzer, and M. D. Craig (1988) A transformation for ordering multispectral data in terms of imagequality with implications for noise removal, Geoscience and Remote Sensing, IEEE Transactions on, vol. 26, pp. 65-74.
[23] J. W. Boardman (1993) Automated spectral unmixing of AVIRIS data using convex geometry concepts: in Summaries, in Fourth JPL Airborne Geoscience Workshop, Arlington, Virginia, pp. 11–14.
[24] J. MacQueen (1967) Some methods for classification and analysis of multivariate observations, in Proceedings of the Fifth Berkeley Symposium on Mathematical Statistics and Probability, pp. 281-297.

Chapter 7

Visualization Techniques: Which is the Most Appropriate in the Process of Knowledge Discovery in Data Base?

Maria Madalena Dias, Juliana Keiko Yamaguchi,
Emerson Rabelo and Clélia Franco

Additional information is available at the end of the chapter

http://dx.doi.org/10.5772/50163

1. Introduction

Applying visual representation in the KDD process aims to facilitate the understanding over its results. Thus, visualization techniques can be integrated into the process of KDD in three different ways: to preview the data to be analyzed; to help in understanding the results of data mining, or to understand the partial results of the iterations inherent in the process of extracting knowledge [2].

However, the exploration and analysis of data using visualization techniques can bring new and enough knowledge exempting the use of other data mining techniques. Furthermore, the visualization is a powerful tool for conveying ideas, due to the vision plays an important role in human cognition [7].

In the visualization process, it is relevant to consider the choice of the best technique to be used in a certain application or situation. The inadequate use of visualization techniques can generate insufficient or even incorrect results, caused by graphic representation mistakes. In the attempt to solve that kind of problem, an evaluation of visualization techniques was carried out in the representation of data, which is shown in this study. Such evaluation provides subsidies for KDD users and system analysts when searching for the most appropriate visualization.

When visualization techniques are used, first off all, it should be observed the relevant characteristics of the data such as: data type, dimensionality (number of attributes) and scalability (number of records). The tasks that the user can perform during data exploration may also be another factor when deciding for a visualization technique. This paper aims to show how the characteristics of the data can influence the choice of visualization techniques, establishing guidelines to selecting them with the purpose of represent data in the best way.

INTECH
open science | open minds

©2012 Dias et al., licensee InTech. This is an open access chapter distributed under the terms of the Creative Commons Attribution License (http://creativecommons.org/licenses/by/3.0), which permits unrestricted use, distribution, and reproduction in any medium, provided the original work is properly cited.

In the next section, we present what mechanisms were used to find out the parameters which help to select more appropriated visualization techniques. The Keim's classification [26] was considered in associating these parameters with the visualization techniques.

In this paper two approaches about the usage of visualization techniques are presented: when the graphical representation is itself a tool for knowledge discovery [60, 61] and when they are applied on results of data mining, e.g., using K-means algorithm [45]. Here, both approaches are numerated as Approach 1 and Approach 2, respectively.

In the both approaches, the mainly idea is evaluating visualization techniques following some criteria intending to highlight its features according to the represented data. Approach 1 aims to defiine parameters to choose suitable visualization techniques according to the data characteristics. From these parameters, the Approach 2 comes to evaluate them in the data mining context for the clustering task results using the K-means algorithm. The next section presents how these criteria were defined and how the evaluation of visualization techniques were done.

2. Research methodology

The both early mentioned approaches are concerned in detecting the factors which guide the data analyst to choose the best visualization techniques to improve the understanding about data. The Keim's classification of visualization techniques was adopted in both approaches to establish a standard evaluation of visualization techniques. Keim [26] distinguishes five classes of visualization techniques: (1) standard 1D - 3D graphics, (2) iconographic techniques, (3) geometric techniques, (4) pixel-oriented techniques, (5) based on graphs or hierarchical techniques.

The Approach 1 differs from Approach 2 in the focus of application of visualization techniques. In the first one, they were used as a knowledge discovery tool; in the second one, they were applied in KDD process context at data mining stage.

In the Approach 1, the Grounded Theory (GT) methodology was used to identify parameters which are relevant in the choice of visualization techniques. When using GT as a research methodology, you have to do a systematic analysis of the data. In other words, it is necessary adopt procedures for codification of the data collected during the research. There are three stages of coding: open coding, axial and selective coding [1]. These steps can be performed cyclically and without a defined order until the primary collected data become organized in a classification well structured [19]. The organization of identified categories and the meaning of the association among them based an emergent theory that explain why this form of organization was reached and, in addition, brings a new hypothesis [34].

Based on this methodology, the literature related to visualization techniques was used as a data source, in which information about visualization were selected and analyzed. These gathered information were deeply compared until reach at the parameters to be considered to choose visualization techniques. This procedure was the GT's open coding step. These parameters are: data type, user-task type, scalability, dimensionality and position of the attributes in the graph.

Through analysis of relationship among the parameters and the visualization techniques, it was observed that each technique type have a certain configuration of parameters that reflect the characteristics of data and the objectives of the use of visualization. Based on this fact, the theory generation was described in form of guidelines. They serves to choose visualization techniques according to the parameters that influence this choice in function to the characteristics of the data. These guidelines were defined from the association between the identified parameters and the Keim's categories of visualization techniques, performing the GT's axial coding step. The GT's selective coding step is not considered in this approach, because there is not a core category that can be named as the main concept for the final formulation of the theory. Instead, there are a set of factors (parameters and types of techniques) that produce the indicative guidelines for choosing visualization techniques according to the characteristics presented by the dataset analyzed. The Figure 1 shows the association performed among the parameters and each categories of visualization techniques as a result of GT's axial coding.

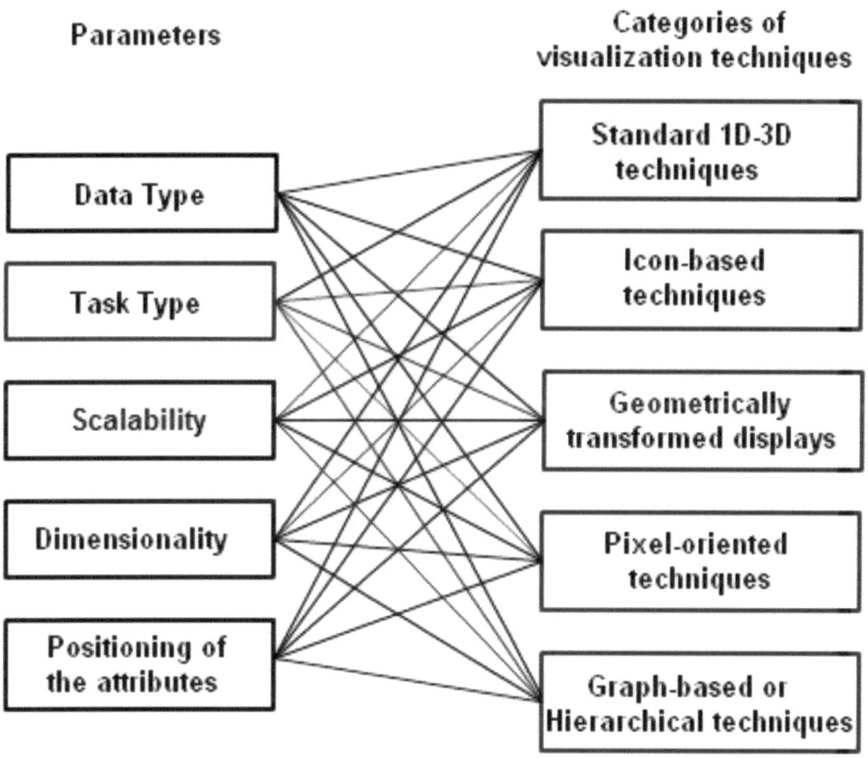

Figure 1. Association among the identified parameters and the categories of visualization techniques defined by [26].

The Approach 2 applies these guidelines to evaluate the best visualization techniques to improve the understanding about the results of clustering task in data mining. For this assay the evaluation technique known as data analysis techniques focusing on Analysis of Characteristics was chosen, as described in [44]. This technique consists of listing the important characteristics of methods, processes or tools and then attributing scores to them - e.g. score 1 (it does not satisfy the need); up to 5 (it satisfies the need completely) - in this case using the visual representation of information visualization techniques. This evaluation is a way to reinforce the applicability of the guidelines obtained from the Approach 1.

In the Approach 2, geometric and iconographical techniques were analyzed because they were appropriate for the projection of results of the K-means algorithm. Two databases (USarrests and Mtcars) were analyzed with this techniques, both available in R language context [48]. The USarrests database contains statistical data on apprehensions carried out to each 100,000 residents in states of the United States of America in 1973, regarding assault, murder and violation. A Mtcars database contains data on fuel consumption and on ten aspects related to the project and performance of 32 vehicles produced from 1973 to 1974. Some matrixes were created in R language, in order to represent databases of high scalability and high dimensionality.

The process of getting the parameters done in the Approach 1 are described in the next section.

3. Getting the parameters

The parameters to consider when selecting visualization techniques emerged from GT's open coding process. The literature related to visualization techniques served as the data source in which we used the key points encoding method [1]. The result of this processes is illustrated in Table 1.

In the first column of this table, the expressions was taken from the main related works, whose references are in the next column, for each one was assigned the concepts, described in the third column. Thus it was possible to identify the parameters: data type, task type, scalability, dimensionality and position of the attributes in the graph, which compose the aspects to be considered in the decision to adopt visualization techniques to represent data.

Data type is a determining factor for choosing visualization techniques. This parameter is also used as a criterion for classification of visualization techniques. Shneiderman [53], for example, classifies data according to the number of attributes (dimensions) and its nature which can be quantitative (numerical data) or qualitative (categorical data). Keim [26] adds to this classification categories that refer to documents or hypertext, algorithms or software, or hierarchical data described by graphs. In this work we considered only the nature of data . Dimensionality is treated separately in this study as a factor for the classfication of visualization techniques, as defined in the encoding process presented in the Section 4.4.

Task type is another criterion to classify visualization techniques. It refers to activities that user or analyst can perform according to goals in the use of a graphical representation as noted in the literature [26, 42, 53, 57]. For practical purposes, the most common tasks were considered in this work, such as:

- Overview data: view the whole data collection;
- Correlation among attributes: the degree of relationship among variables can reveal patterns of behavior and trends;
- Identification of patterns, standards and important characteristics;

Key points	References	Code
Visualization techniques can be classified, among other criteria, by data type	[26, 53]	Data type
Task type is one of the aspects considered in classification of visualization techniques, which provides means of interation between the analyst and the display	[26, 42, 53]	Task type
Visualization techniques are subject to some limitations, such as the amount of data that a particular technique can exhibit	[23, 40, 45]	Scalability
Visualization techniques can also be classified according to the number of attributes	[15, 26, 40, 53]	Dimensionality
In some category of visualization techniques, distribution form of attributes on the chart can influence the interpretation about the representation, such as correlation analysis, in which the relative distance among the plotted attributes is relevant for observation	[2, 21, 28, 40]	Positioning of attributes

Table 1. Key point coding method applied on collected data

- Clusters identification: attributes with similar behavior;
- Outliers detection: data set with atypical behavior in comparison for the rest of data.

Scalability and dimensionality are characteristics to be observed in the data before applying a visualization technique. To facilitate the analysis of these parameters, a convention was established to classify the scalability and dimensionality of data [4, 5, 40].

Thus, as to scalability, data can be classified as small (10^1 to 10^2 = 10 to 100), medium (10^3 to 10^5 = 1000 to 10000) or large volume (10^6 to 10^7 = 1000000 to 10000000), according to the magnitude orders. As to dimensionality (number of attributes), data with up to four attributes are defined as low-dimensional, with five to nine attributes, medium dimensionality and with more than ten attributes, high dimensionality. In this context, the Approach 2 illustrates ahead the limitations of geometric and iconographic techniques in data with varied scalability and dimensionality.

For some types of techniques, such as Stick Figures, Parallel Coordinates, and Mosaics Plot, the position of the attributes or the order of elements representing attributes in a graphic is an important aspect for interpretation of visualizing data. Thus, this parameter is more related to specific techniques or computational tools in which the display is influenced by the order of attributes arranged in the chart.

The next section comprises the guidelines for the choice of the best visualization techniques according to the data characteristics and the technique's purpose. These guidelines were based on parameters established in the Approach 1, which were analyzed below. The

Approach 2 contributes with examples of applicability of these guidelines to represent graphically the results of K-means algorithm over examples of databases.

4. Analysis of the parameters

In Approach 1, the GT's axial coding is the next step after the identification of the parameters. It was done based on analyzes about the relationship between the parameters and categories of visualization techniques, according to the classification suggested by Keim keim02, who distinguishes five classes of techniques: (1) standard 1D-3D graphics; (2) iconographic techniques; (3) geometric techniques; (4) pixel-oriented techniques; and (5) based on graphs or hierarchical techniques.

Standard graphics are commonly used in statistic to view an estimate of certainty about a hypothesis or the frequency distribution of an attribute or to view a data model. For example, Histograms and Scatter Plot.

In pixel-oriented techniques, each value of attribute is mapped to a pixel color and it is placed on the display screen, divided into windows, each corresponding to an attribute. In the end, they are arranged according to different purposes keim02.

Data with a naturally structure of relationships among its elements, as hierarchical or as simple network, may be represented by hierarchical or graph-based techniques, such as: the own graph [38], Cone Trees [9], Treemaps [54], Mosaic Plot [18], Dimensional Stacking [30, 56].

In iconographic techniques, data attributes are mapped into properties of an icon or glyph, which vary depending on the values of attributes. For instance, the icons in format of faces of the Chernoff Faces [8, 13], the icons as stars of the Star Glyphs [39] and the icons in stick shape of the Stick Figures [43].

In geometric techniques, multidimensional data are mapped into a two-dimensional plane providing an overview of all attributes. As examples can be cited Matrix of Scatter Plot [6], 3D Scatter Plot [29] and Parallel Coordinates [20, 21].

In the next sections, each parameter are analyzed in association with categories of visualization techniques in the context of Approach 1, presenting the respective guidelines. Some examples of applicability of the guidelines establishment are presented by the Approach 2.

4.1. Analysis on the data type parameter

Techniques of standard 1D-3D category, generally represents from one to three attributes. In most cases, they are used for analysis of quantitative data. All graphs considered in this class are able to display quantitative data. To represent qualitative data, alternative techniques are more limited. In this case, the histogram is an example whereby is possible to represent these both data type [37].

In literature are found examples of usage of pixel-oriented techniques on quantitative data. Query-independent techniques, for example, were applied to represent temporal data, and query-dependent techniques are commonly used to represent continuous quantitative data

[24]. The author of this technique [25], states that they are not recommended for displaying qualitative data.

Hierarchical or graph-based techniques are ideal for displaying data when they have a structure of relationships among themselves or with a structure of hierarchy or simple network. Data type like as documents, texts (available on web or stored on disk), are likely to be viewed by specific tools found. For example, see [17, 27, 35, 55]. Algorithms and software are also data for which there are visualization tools developed specifically for this data type. For example see [51, 58, 62].

Iconographic techniques are more appropriate for quantitative data because icon features vary with the values of represented attributes. In Chernoff faces, the shapes of each facial properties are changed; in Star Glyph, the components of the star are modified; in Stick Figure, the format of segments are different according to the value of attributes. Qualitative data representation presents more technical difficulties, which can be circumvented by using the appearance properties such as icon color [45].

Geometric techniques are more flexible, being able to represent quantitative and qualitative data. This applies to the Parallel Coordinates technique, which can display attributes of these two data types. Due to the Scatter Plot Matrix is formed by a set of scatter plots, it is more suitable for continuous quantitative data.

In the Approach 2 two databases were used in a data mining process and the R language was applied to illustrate the results through geometric and iconographic visualization techniques. When evaluating the techniques regarding information visualization by using R language, a problem was found in relation to the entry parameter for the qualitative type of datum. R language does not allow that type of data entry in some information visualization. To solve this problem, the code operation, presented by Goldschmidt and Passos [16], in which the qualitative values were substituted by numeric values, was carried out.

All the techniques of information visualization evaluated allow the representation of quantitative data (continuous and discrete). However, for nominal qualitative data, the icon-based techniques evaluated do not enable a good representation.

The insertion of visualization properties may turn the technique of information visualization more effective, when appraised in relation to the characteristic types of qualitative data. In [33] is proposed an ordination of priorities when using the visualization properties, that is, considering the most perceptible and the least perceptible priorities in relation to the types of quantitative and qualitative data (ordinal and nominal). It is possible to add qualitative data by using colors in the visualization components of geometric projection techniques.

The Table 2 summarizes the discussion about the analysis on data type parameter for each class of technique, taking into consideration the nature of data domain.

4.2. Analysis on the task type parameter

Generally, some techniques are better for certain tasks than others. A task type execution depends on whether it is implemented by the tool in use according to the goals in improve the exploitation data activity.

Category	Technique	Quantitative data		Qualitative data	
		continuous	discrete	nominal	ordinal
1D to 3D	Histogram	X	X	X	X
	Box Plot	X			
	Scatter Plot	X			
	Contour Plot	X	X		
Icon-based	Chernoff Faces	X	X		
	Star Glyphs	X	X		
	Stick Figure	X	X		
Geometrically transformed displays	Scatter Plot Matrix	X			
	Parallel Coordinates	X	X	X	X
Pixel oriented	Query-independent techniques	X	X		
	Query-dependent techniques	X	X		
Graph-based orHierarchical	Graph	X	X	X	X
	Cone Tree	X	X	X	X
	Treemap	X	X	X	X
	Dimensional Stacking	X	X	X	X
	Mosaic Plot	X	X	X	X

Table 2. Visualization techniques and the respective data type that they can best represent

Standard 1D-3D techniques serve, in general, to view an estimate of certainty about a hypothesis or the frequency distribution about an attribute, such as the usage of histogram. This class also provides graphs to make comparisons and data classifications (to this case, for example, can be used box plot), and also to determine the correlation between attributes. Different statistical graphs can be used in data analysis, in order to discover patterns and structures in data and identify outliers that can be observed, for example, through using box plot or scatter plot.

Iconographic techniques represent each data entry individually, allowing verification of rules and behavior patterns of the data. Icons with similar properties can be recognized and thus form groups and it be analyzed in particular. A representation with a discrepant format if compared to the other may characterize an outlier. For example, technique of icon-based visualization that works with multidimensional data is the Star Glyphs visualization. Johnson and Wichner [22] stated that this sort of visualization is useful to standardize certain information and they use Star Glyphs to determine the similarity within clusters. Lee et al. [31] also stated that icon-based visualizations are multidimensional points that make use of useful dimensional space to detect clusters and outliers.

Geometric techniques provide a good overview of the data, assigning no priorities to represent its attributes. Furthermore, verification of correlation among them may be more discerning when using techniques of this class, such as the scatter plot matrix. This category of techniques also allows the identification of patterns, rules and behaviors. Therefore, outliers may also be detected, characterized by behaviors outside the common standard. The analyst may choose to analyze a group of data that can be detached using the tool. However, groups are not usually immediately identified by techniques of this class.

Pixel-oriented techniques can be used in the analysis of relationships among data attributes, so rules and patterns may be identified through observing the correlations among them. Furthermore, the pixels can be arranged to finding clusters.

Hierarchical techniques are useful for exploitation of data arranged in a hierarchical or simple relationship. Through techniques of this class is possible to obtain an overview of the data structure and analyze the relationship among the elements. Techniques of this category also allow grouping data, such as Treemaps [54]. Table 3 summarizes the most representative tasks for each class of visualization technique, as previously discussed.

Category	Technique	Tasks				
		overview	correlation	patterns	clustering	outlier
1D to 3D	Histogram			X		X
	Box Plot			X		X
	Scatter Plot		X	X		X
	Contour Plot		X			
Icon-based	Chernoff Faces			X	X	X
	Star Glyphs			X	X	X
	Stick Figure				X	
Geometrically transformed displays	Scatter Plot Matrix		X	X		X
	Parallel Coordinates	X	X	X		X
Pixel oriented	Query-independent techniques		X	X	X	
	Query-dependent techniques		X	X	X	
Graph-based orHierarchical	Graph	X	X			
	Cone Tree	X				
	Treemap	X	X	X	X	
	Dimensional Stacking			X	X	X
	Mosaic Plot	X		X		

Table 3. Most representative tasks for each category of visualization technique

The next section brings an example of analysis on the correlation task using geometrical visualization techniques (matrix of scatter plot and parallel coordinates) done in the Approach 2. It uses the R language to visually represent the results of clustering task of data mining.

4.2.1. Analysis of correlation task into a case study

Correlation is the association or interdependence among the database attributes, used to show if there is or not a relationship among attributes of interest. It is inherent to the association and clustering tasks within the data mining. When referring to correlation, the most emphasized by literature is the visualization of Scatter Plot [10, 11], which supplies a positive or negative correlation measure according to the position of scattering.

The visualization of Scatter Plot supplies a 'cloud' of points in a Cartesian plane, by using axes 'x,y', being very useful to identify the linear correlation [10]. Correlation is identified in visualization according to the position of points. If the points, in the diagram, have a straight increasing line as 'image', it is linear positive, but, on the other hand, if the points form an 'image' as a descending straight line, it is considered linear negative. However, if the points are dispersed, not showing any clear defined 'image', that leads to the conclusion that there is no relationship among the attributes being studied [10, 11].

To show such characteristic, USarrests test database was used in the visualization of the Matrix of Scatter plot, with a function created in the R language, which calculates the correlation, shows the values calculated and builds lines that follow the scattering (the red lines in Figure 2). As it can be observed in that visualization, the correlation is interpreted as a positive correlation when it is found a large correlation coefficient between the attributes 'murder' and 'assault' - it, in other words, the number of deaths increases as the number of assaults increases. A negative correlation is found between the attributes 'assault' and 'urbanpop'.

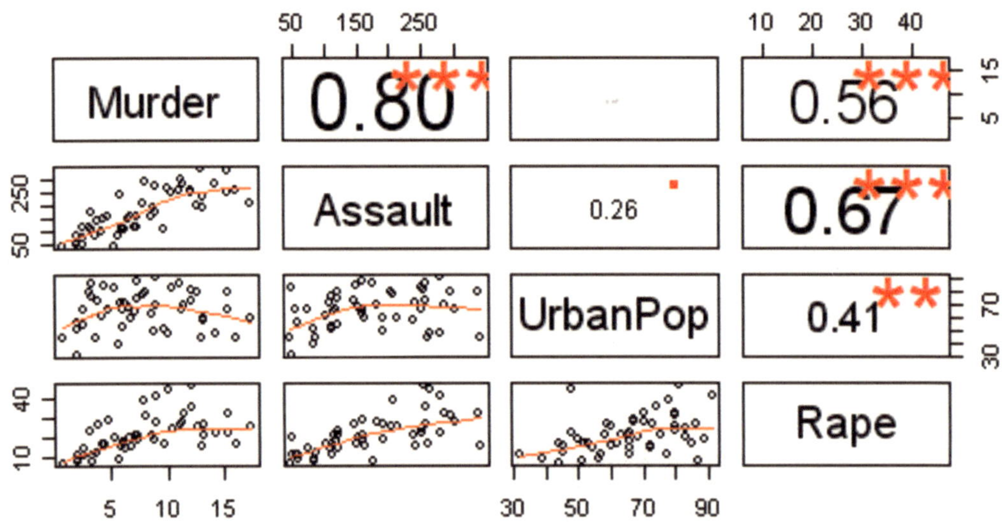

Figure 2. Correlation in the visualization Matrix of Scatter Plot - 'Usarrests' database (R language).

Figure 3 represents the Matrix of Scatter Plot with seven attributes of 'mtcars' database and with the three clusters generated by the K-means algorithm applied to that base. The colors (red, black and green) represent the clusters formed when executing the K-means algorithm. Figure 3 enables to interpret that there is a clear division within the clusters, which is determined by the attribute value named number of cylinders 'cyl'.

Another technique of geometric projection here evaluated was the visualization of Parallel Coordinates that project the relationship among the attributes of the database in bidimensional space. It allows to interpret characteristics as the difference in distribution and the correlation among attributes [20, 59]. Figure 4 represents the visualization of the parallel

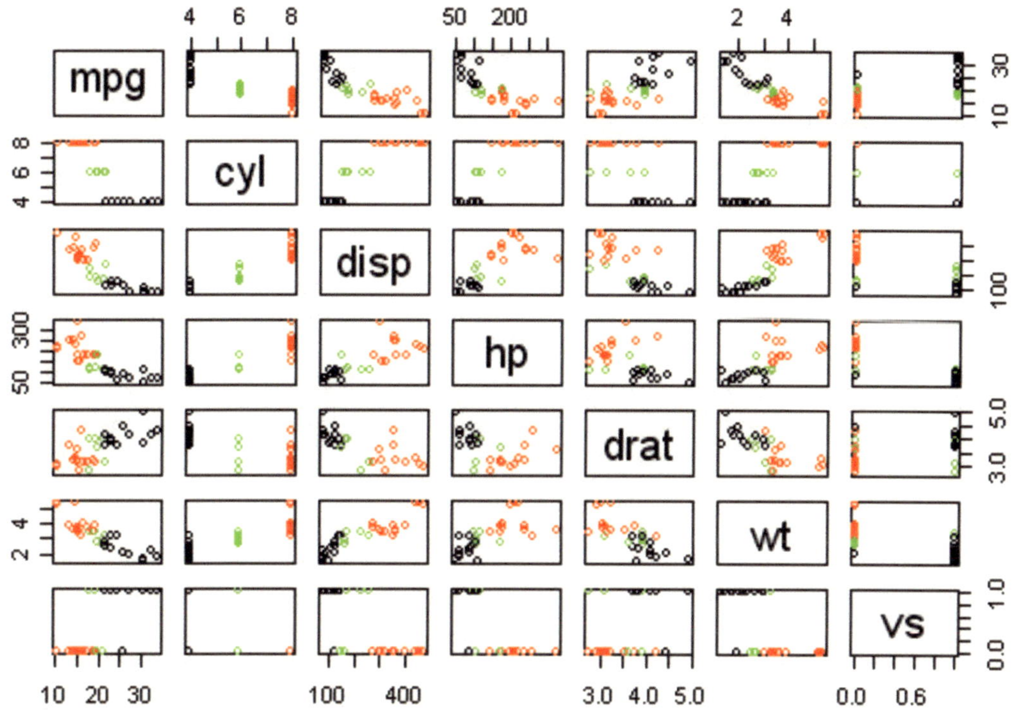

Figure 3. Matrix of Scatter Plot representing the 'Mtcars' database (R language).

coordinates, showing the distribution of records with the attributes of 'Mtcars' test database and the clusters formed by the K-means algorithm through colors (red, green and black).

In Figure 4 it is possible to observe a concentration of colors in the horizontal axes that crosses with the vertical axis of attribute 'cyl' and, which irradiates towards 'disp' and 'hp' vertical axes. It can be concluded that the three clusters generated by the algorithm do not contain the same values for 'cyl' and 'disp' attributes and, the number of cylinders (cyl) is proportional to the values of 'disp' and 'hp' attributes.

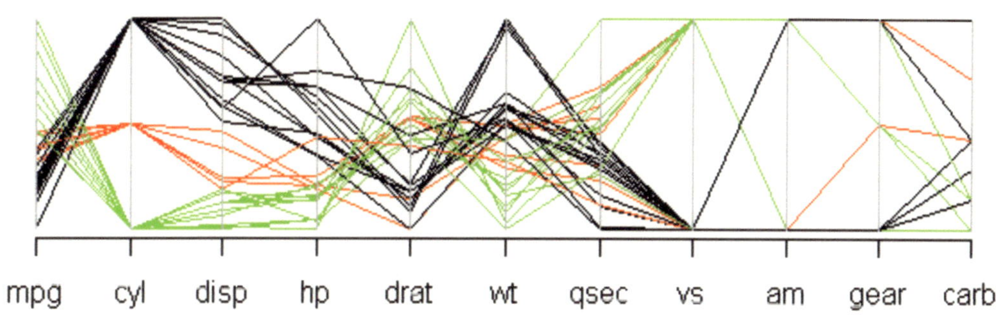

Figure 4. Parallel Coordinates representing the 'Mtcars' database - (R language).

Regarding the icon-based techniques, no type of evaluation was carried out, due to the difficulty to interpret the visualization of correlation characteristic.

4.3. Analysis on the scalability parameter

Implementations of visualization techniques must take in consideration the limits of dimensionality and scalability of data to hold in way that the tool be capable of providing a clear overview of data to the analyst. As described in [3], scalability refers to the computational complexity on the number of records in an array, as well as to the number of attributes. The amount of records that can be simultaneously presented is one of the limitations of the visualization techniques. With high number of records, the result shows a considerable degree of disorder [49].

Standard graphics has low dimensional, because they are intended to represent data with one to three attributes. In addition, they support the view of a small volume of data because, in general, they come from statistical studies, resulting of a sample or of percentages.

Iconographic techniques are able to handle a larger number of attributes in comparison to the standard graphics; however, the visualization generated is best for a small amount of data due to the space occupied by the icons in the screen. This is the same statement found in Approach 2, in which the iconographic techniques evaluated (Star glyphs and Chernoff Faces) were classified as low scalability (support to display an amount of data).

Geometric techniques, in turn, may work with an increased number of dimensions and volume when compared to standard 1D-3D graphics and iconographic techniques. But they are outweighed by the pixel-oriented techniques for their capability to represent the largest volume.

Hierarchical techniques or graph-based techniques are usually used to represent the relationship among data, regardless of dimensionality, which can be high or low, but have the same space constraints like that presented by iconographic techniques, being the visualization clearer if the amount data is not bulky.

However, visualization tools can offer features like zoom, select, filter, among others, to improve the interactivity with the visualization, mitigating the limitations of each technique. Table 4 summarizes, in general, these two parameters, scalability and dimensionality, for each class of visualization technique.

In [23], are presented the limitations of some visualization techniques in relation to the number of records in dataset and these authors state that the visualization of parallel coordinates can represent approximately 1000 records. They also affirm that the geometric techniques quickly reach the limits of what can be considered comprehensible. This happens because there are overlapping records mapped in the same position or close to each other, thus presenting 'blurs', or areas totally filled out. Shimabukuru [52] defends that the visualization of great volumes of data need the integration of the technique with appropriate interaction operations, which can enable the selection and filtering of items considered of interest.

The areas totally filled out, 'blurs' of parallel coordinates, generate incomprehensible visualizations. However, it is possible to notice that the use of colors can help the visualization

Category	Technique	Scalability	Dimensionality
1D to 3D	Histogram	Small	Low
	Box Plot		
	Scatter Plot		
	Contour Plot		
Icon-based	Chernoff Faces	Small	Low to Medium
	Star Glyphs	Small	
	Stick Figure	Medium	
Geometrically transformed displays	Scatter Plot Matrix	Medium	Medium to High
	Parallel Coordinates		
Pixel oriented	Query-independent techniques	Large	Medium to High
	Query-dependent techniques		
Graph-based or Hierarchical	Graph	Small to Medium	High
	Cone Tree	Small to Medium	High
	Treemap	Medium	High
	Dimensional Stacking	Medium	Medium
	Mosaic Plot	Medium	Medium

Table 4. Visualization techniques and their representations of scalability and dimensionality of data

of patterns. The Approach 2 brings an example to show this fact: matrixes with different amounts of records were created and used as entrance parameters in the execution of K-means algorithm. Then, the results obtained were plotted in the technique of parallel coordinates, where the lines represent the matrix attributes, and the colors represent the clusters, as shown in Figure 5a and Figure 5b. The colors appear as blurs, making possible the visualization of the patterns of each cluster.

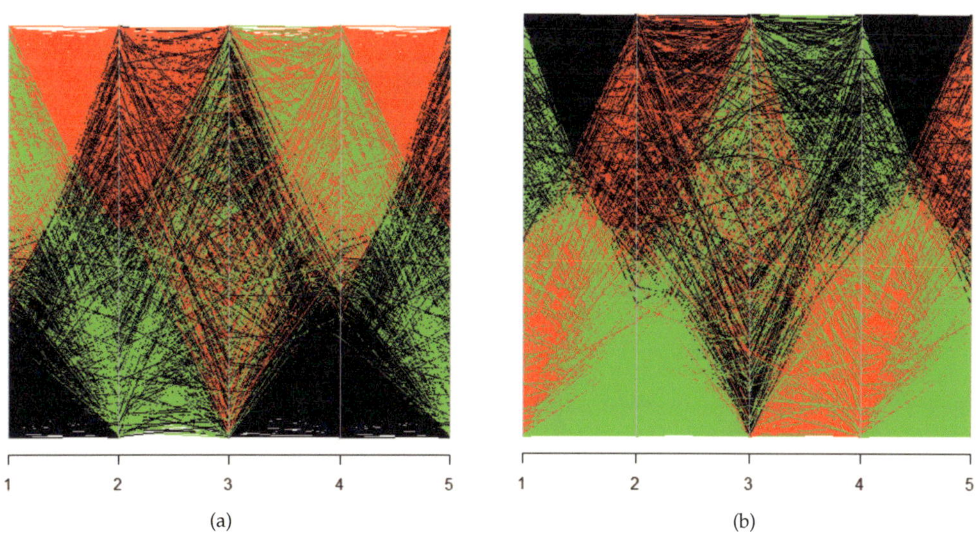

Figure 5. Parallel coordinates: a) 10,000 records, b) 100,000 records

As shown in Figure 5a and Figure 5b, the increase in the number of records from 10,000 to 100,000 generates blurs that show the patterns. In this example, the algorithm has generated three clusters, but, depending on the application domain and on the amount of records, it may be necessary to generate more clusters and, consequently, use a higher number of colors.

To reinforce the difficulty of visualizing a great amount of records by using geometric techniques, Figure 6a, Figure 6b and Figure 6c show the visualization of Scatter Plot in three-dimensional projection (3D Scatter Plot) of matrices with lines size: 100, 1,000 and 10,000, respectively, and with five columns.

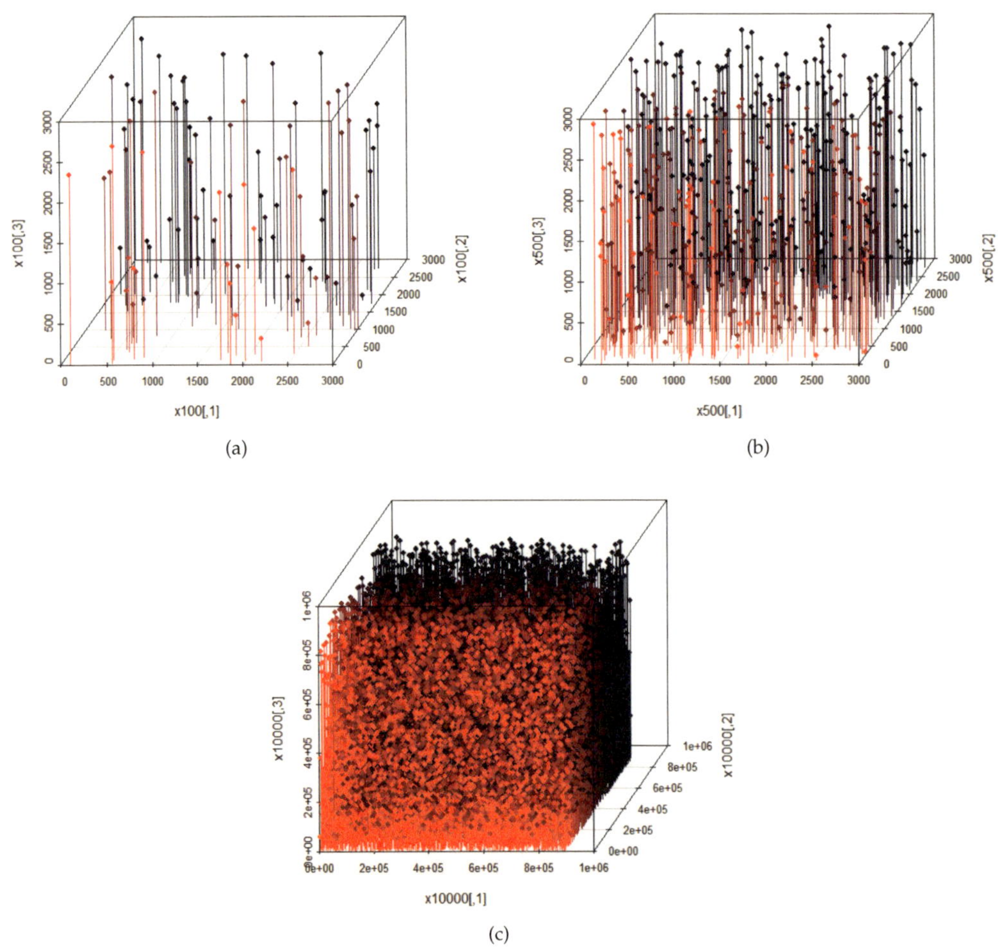

Figure 6. 3D Scatter Plot: a) 100 records, b) 1,000 records, c) 10,000 records

In these figures it is possible to observe that, as the number of records increases, the visualization becomes incomprehensible or difficult to be visualized. The techniques based on icons enable the representation of a small number of records due to the size of the graphical elements [47]. Chernoff Faces is the visualization that has the greatest limitation in relation to scalability, because it just allows the representation of a small amount of records.

According to Shimabukuru [52], the visualization of Stick Figure makes possible to represent great volumes of data. Such visualization technique uses the two dimensions of the screen to map two attributes of data, whereas the other attributes are mapped according to angles and/or segment lengths.

4.4. Analysis on the dimensionality parameter

Dimensionality characteristic is related to the visualization technique capacity of representing attributes. [Keim 02] mentions that, usually, in visualizing information, a great amount of records is used. And each one has many attributes, for instance: a physical experience can be described with five attributes or hundreds of attributes.

In that interpretation, it should be taken into account the capacity of human perception, or the conceptual limit of the dimensionality that, according to Rodrigues [47], may be between low and high dimensionality. However, there is not a consensus on what may be considered low and high dimensionality which standards limits were defined as discussed in the Section 3. Using these conceptual limits as base, several matrixes were created in the Approach 2 with different columns (representing attributes). After the creation, each matrix was plotted in the techniques of information visualization used in this investigation.

The literature revised is unanimous regarding parallel coordinates for representation of multidimensional data [14, 20, 23, 38, 47, 52, 59]. This technique maps each attribute to a line by connecting points in the axes. Figure 7 shows three visualizations using the technique of parallel coordinates, with different amounts of attributes (10, 34 and 100, respectively) but with the same amount (100) of records. The limit of attributes that the parallel coordinates can support is restricted to the resolution of the computer screen. As it can be observed, the increase of attributes can cause blurs, which hinder the visualization, even hindering the recognition of patterns.

The Matrix of Scatter Plot is another technique for visualizing geometric projection, which is able to represent high dimensionality. For the visualization of 3D Scatter Plot, [12] suggest the possibility of using icons for representing data attributes, thus allowing an increase in the number of dimensions to be explored in the visualization. It can be considered that such visualization has good representation in the dimensional characteristic.

The technique of icon-based visualization is one of the most used. In such technique, figures are used as geometric encoders, by taking advantage of attributes, which are perceptible visually, such as color, forms and texture [32].

Chernoff Faces, classified as an icon-based visualization technique, can also be used to visualize multidimensional data. Although such technique is highly useful to exhibit multidimensional data, the records are presented separately, because they do not transmit any information on the real value arrays. However, Chernoff Faces enables to illustrate tendencies and focus on data to be highlighted [50]. Specific literature on the subject does not limit the amount of characteristics that may be used in Chernoff Faces' visualization, but in [22] is suggested using up to 18 attributes. In R language, the function 'faces' enables a maximum representation of 15 attributes.

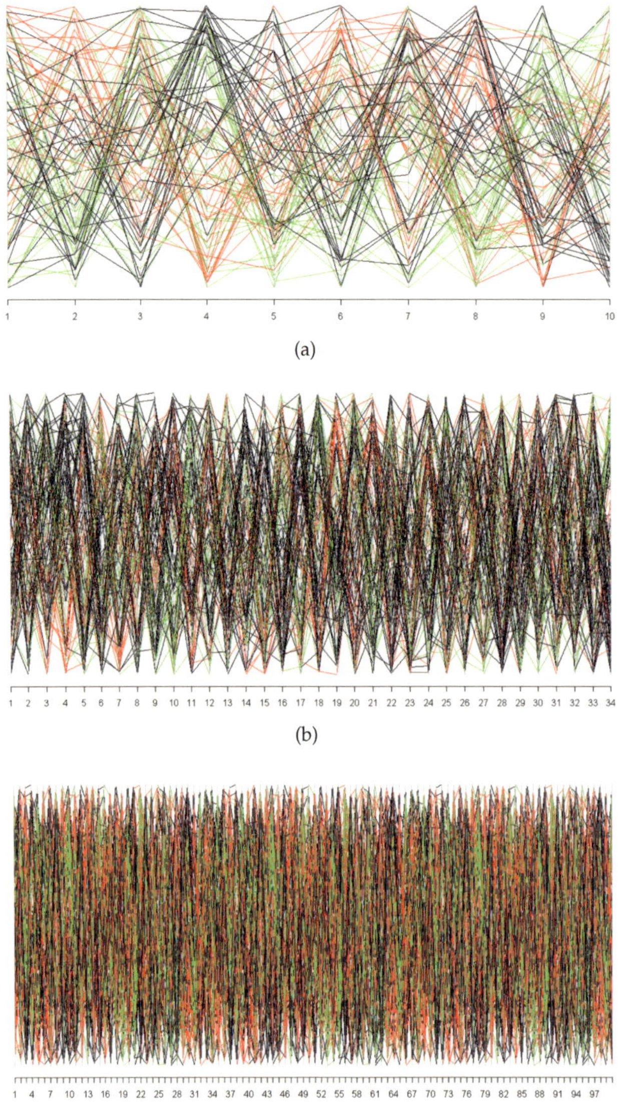

(a) (b) (c)

Figure 7. Parallel Coordinates a) 10 attributes, b) 34 attributes, c) 100 attributes (R language)

Star Glyphs visualization allows a larger number of attributes if compared to Chernoff Faces. That can be seen in Figure 8, which shows that the possibility of representation is around 80 attributes (Figure 8c). However, as shown in Figure 8d, only blurs are visualized when there is a great amount of attributes.

Besides the icon-based visualization techniques described, there is also the Stick Figure visualization that, in spite of representing high scalability, possesses certain limitation regarding dimensionality, which is in the order of approximately a dozen attributes [26].

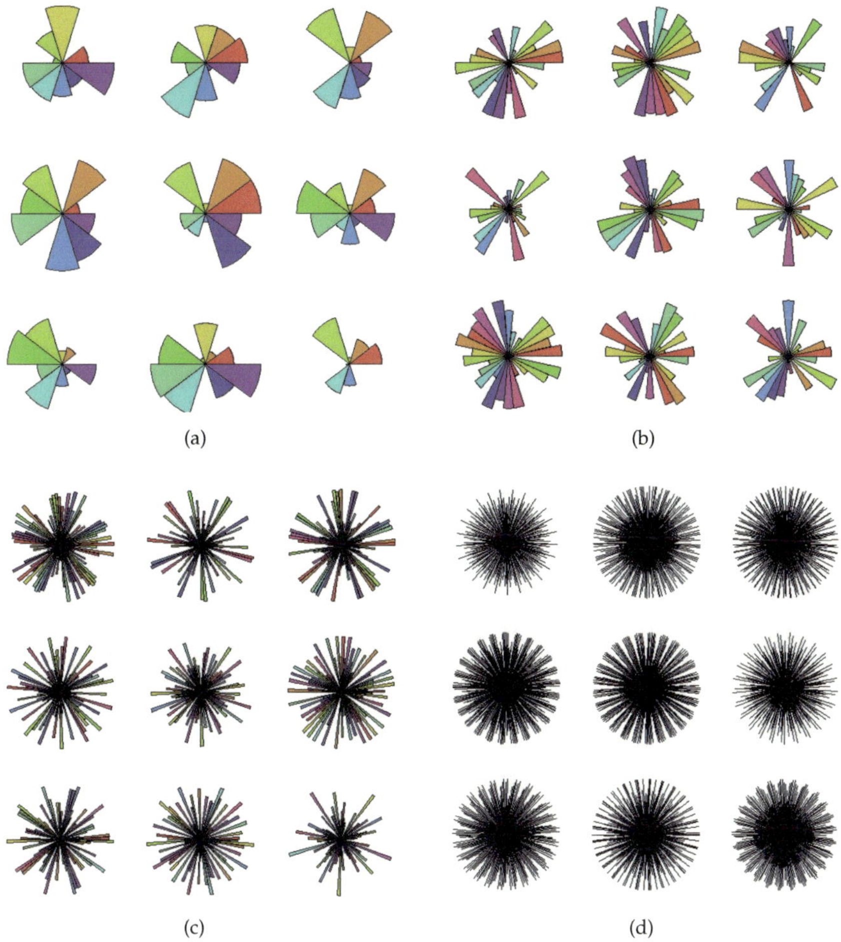

Figure 8. Star Glyphs a) 10 attributes, b) 30 attributes, c) 80 attributes, d) 500 attributes (R language)

4.5. Analysis on the positioning of attributes parameter

Although it is not a parameter directly linked to the characteristics of data, it is an important factor in visual data exploration for some techniques as, among others, Treemaps [54], Mosaic Plots [18], Dimensional Stacking [30]. This parameter depends on the technique or tool used to generate the visualization, which should allow the change of the positions of the attributes in the graph, producing different views that can reveal new patterns.

Thus, the categories of visualization techniques followed by its respective analyzed techniques are described in Table 5. In the third column, it is indicated if the positioning of attribute can influence or not in the interpretation of graphical data representation for this technique.

In general, for 1D-3D standard graphics, positioning of attribute does not change the interpretation of results due to the low dimensionality of the data that might be represented. Moreover, the goal of using techniques of this class is to analyze the behavior of a given attribute, or the correlation among two or three attributes.

Category	Technique	Positioning
1D to 3D	Histogram	It does not influence
	Box Plot	
	Scatter Plot	
	Contour Plot	
Icon-based	Chernoff Faces	It does not influence
	Star Glyphs	It does not influence
	Stick Figure	It influences
Geometrically transformed displays	Scatter Plot Matrix	It does not influence
	Parallel Coordinates	It influences
Pixel oriented	Query-independent techniques	It influences
	Query-dependent techniques	
Graph-based or Hierarchical	Graph	It influences
	Cone Tree	It does not influence
	Treemap	It influences
	Dimensional Stacking	It influences
	Mosaic Plot	It influences

Table 5. Interference of the positioning of attributes and over each visualization techniques

Among the iconographic techniques presented in Table 5, Stick Figures is an example in which the position of the attributes can influence the visual data exploration according to the icon type used, derived from the variation of the mapping of data attributes into icon properties [43, p. 516].

Chernoff faces, in turn, have a fixed structure for its icon, since it corresponds to the human face characteristics and thus, the change of the positioning of attributes is not a relevant aspect for this technique.

But there are studies about which icon properties may be more representative for the interpretation of results, such as the eyes size and the shape of the face are aspects that draw attention [31, 36]. Likewise it is for Star Glyph technique, for which once established the order of the best mapping of attributes [28, 41], it remains the same for all the icons representing a record data per star.

In the works of Inselberg [21] and Wegman [59], it is explained how the position of the attributes in the graph may influences the correlation detection in Parallel Coordinates. Scatteplot Matrix is, on the other hand, composed of a set of Scatter Plots, for this reason nor is influenced by the change of attributes positioning, since their main objective is to evaluate the correlation between attributes.

Keim [24] presents techniques for the placement of pixels on the display, which can influence the interpretation of the visualization to identify patterns and relationships among the represented attributes.

The query-independent technique, for example, may have the pixels arranged by recursive pattern technique. When using the query-dependent technique, the pixels can be arranged in the window using spiral technique [24].

Hierarchical techniques or graph-based techniques are in general influenced by the attributes positioning, due to its elements naturally hold a relationship structure, therefore, the assignment of variables in the graph should be made carefully, especially when there is a hierarchy between the elements. The exception is for the Cone Trees technique, which represents a defined tree structure (as files and directories structures in a hard disk), providing only interactive features such as animation to navigate among the tree nodes [9, 46].

The Approach 2 brings a deeper analysis on the positioning of attributes focusing on the relationship among attributes in geometrical visualization techniques, which is presented below.

4.5.1. Relationship among attributes

Likewise the Matrix of Scatter Plot, another technique of geometric projection that shows the relationship among attributes is the visualization of Parallel Coordinates, which is shown in Figure 9. When generating a plane representation, it transforms multi-varied relationships into bidimensional patterns, being possible to visualize many attributes [59].

The relationship among the attributes it is found on the vertical axes, that means that, closer the axes, better the visualization of the relationship. For example, the attribute named 'assault' related with the attribute 'urban pop' is shown through the position of the horizontal lines that exhibit the meaning in the relationship, as shown in Figure 9a. In the relationship among the attributes 'assault' and 'rape', which are separated by the attribute 'urban pop', it is necessary to create the relationship mentally, or to remove the attribute, according to Figure 9b.

Regarding the icon-based techniques, it was not possible to determine the existence of relationships among attributes, thus turning the evaluation for such a characteristic impossible.

5. Discussion about the results

In the Approach 1, the five parameters (data type, task type, scalability and dimensionality of the data, and position of the attributes in the graph) were identified by means of GT and subsequently they were analyzed in relation to the categories of visualization techniques classified by Keim [26]. Through analysis of relationship among the parameters and the visualization techniques, it was observed that each technique type have a certain configuration of parameters that reflect the characteristics of data and the objectives of the use of visualization as seen below:

- Data type must be the first parameter to be considered. It is the type of data that determines what kind of visualization technique can be prior used. Qualitative data, for example, will be hardly understood if they were represented by a technique developed to represent quantitative data and vice versa.
- The task type to be performed corresponds to the goals of the analyst during the data exploration. For tasks related to statistical analysis, for example, the graphics 1D-3D may be sufficient; for tasks of correlation verification may be used visualization techniques of geometric category, and so on.

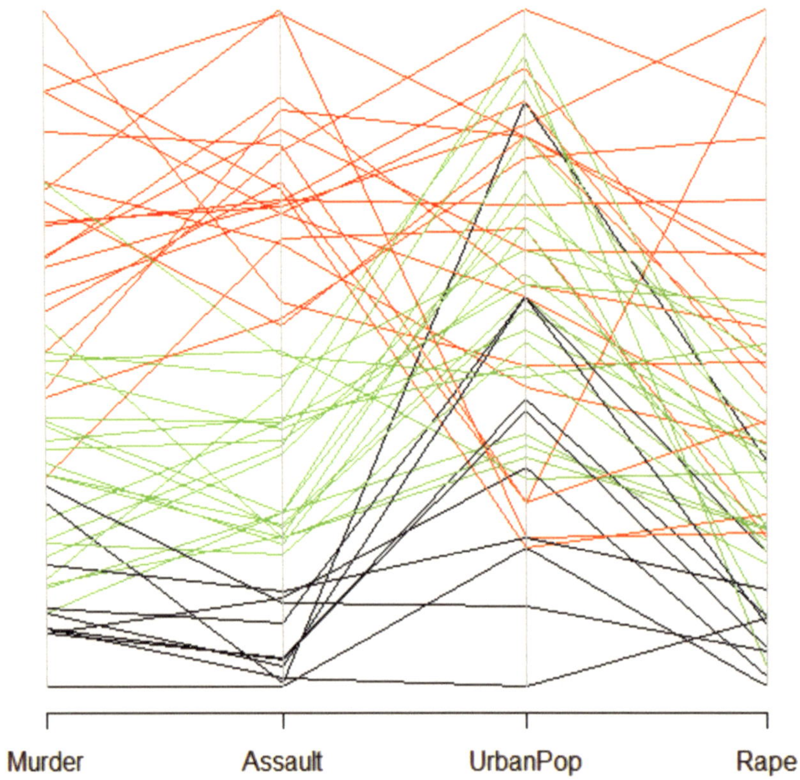

(a)

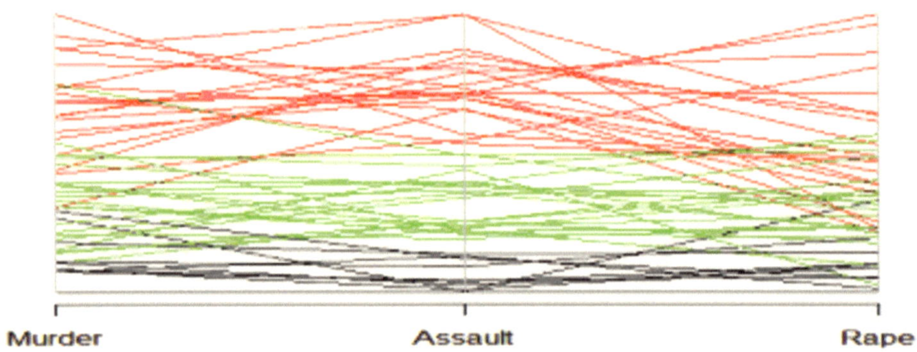

(b)

Figure 9. Parallel Coordinates - 'USarrests' database (R language)

- Both scalability and dimensionality of data are limiting factors for visualization techniques. Although most of them supports multidimensional data, usually these techniques differ in the ability to display a certain amount of dimensionality and volume of data. This is the case of categories of techniques iconographic, geometric and pixel-oriented. However, other ways of interaction can be used during the visual exploration to minimize these limitations, for example, the functions of zooming, selection and filter.

- The positioning of the attributes is a factor more dependent on visualization technique to be used and, hence, on the tool that implements it. For some techniques (such as parallel coordinates and star glyphs), positioning of attributes is important for discovery new patterns or behaviors.

About the Approach 2, the Table 6 shows the results of the Analysis of Characteristics technique [44] by which iconographic and geometric techniques were appraised. The punctuations attributed are subjective, varying of score 1 (it does not satisfy the need) up to 5 (it satisfies the need completely), and it was based on practical experiments carried out in the language R and on the literature studied. In the Table 6 can be seen that the geometric projection techniques were valued by higher punctuations regarding the iconographical techniques for almost all the analyzed characteristics.

	Geometric Projection			Iconographical Techniques		
Characteristics	Matrix of Scatterplot	3D Scatter Plot	Parallel Coordinates	Star Glyphs	Stick Figure	Chernoff Faces
Scalability	5	2	5	1	5	1
Dimensionality	4	3	4	5	3	3
Nominal qualitative data	3	3	3	1	1	1
Ordinal qualitative data	4	3	4	5	5	5
Discreet quantitative data	5	5	5	5	5	5
Continuous quantitative data	5	5	5	5	5	5
Correlation	5	3	3	X	X	X
Relationship among attributes	5	3	3	1	1	1

Table 6. Analysis on characteristics of information visualization techniques

Another important point to consider is the analyst's familiarity with the analyzed data. This is what will awaken new interests or stimulate the user's curiosity during data exploration, forming new hypotheses that can be verified by means of visualizations, or simply comparing the results generated by graphical representations.

6. Conclusion

The aim of this work is minimizing difficulties in the selection of visualization techniques to represent data mining results or even to clarify the data structure throughout the knowledge discovery process. Following this purpose, two approaches were presented: the first one is visualization technique as itself a tool for knowledge discovery, and the second one is visualization techniques applied on results of data mining process.

In the first approach, through Grounded Theory methodology, as soon data have been obtained, they had undergone the coding process that allowed emergence of the concepts that led to the parameters: data type, task type, volume, dimensionality and positioning of the attributes in the graph. Then, each parameter was analyzed in conjunction with visualization techniques, and those most frequently found in the literature were selected, and separated by categories defined in the Keim's taxonomy. Through analysis of this relationship, it was observed that each technique type (1D to 3D standard graphics, icon-based displays, geometrically transformed displays, pixel-oriented displays and graph-based or hierarchical displays) have a certain configuration of parameters that reflect the data characteristics and the objectives of its use.

In the second approach, it was made an evaluation of geometric projection and iconographical information visualization techniques using Analysis of Characteristics technique. However, this technique of evaluation is subjective, because the evaluation reflects the analyst's tendency. For this reason, this evaluation served as an example of applicability of the guidelines established by Approach 1.

It should be noted that the guidelines were established based on two main items: the strongest characteristics of data, identified during the GT's coding phase in the Approach 1, and the features of visualization techniques. This does not mean the invalidation of the use of a visualization technique for other purposes that differ from those established by the guidelines. The meaning of the data analyzed to the analyst is very relevant. As the analyst's familiarity about data increases, greater is his/her incentive to make data exploration to get new hypotheses to be verified by visualizations, or just comparing the results generated by various graphical representations. Thus, the established guidelines intend to be helpful when the analyst is planning to use visualization techniques in the process of extracting knowledge from data.

Acknowledgements

This work was supported by the Fundação Araucária.

Author details

Dias Maria Madalena, Yamaguchi Juliana Keiko, Rabelo Emerson and Franco Clélia
State University of Maringá, Informatic Department, Paraná, Brazil

7. References

[1] Allan G (2003) A critique of using grounded theory as a research method. Electronic Journal of Business Research Methods. j. 2: 1-10.

[2] Ankerst M (2001) Visual Data Mining with Pixel-oriented Visualization Techniques. ACM SIGKDD Workshop on Visual Data Mining, San Francisco, CA.

[3] Barioni C M, Botelho E, Faloustsos C, Razente H, Traina A J M, Traina Jr, C (2011) Data Visualization in RDBMS. Proc. International Conference on Information Systems and Databases, Tokyo, Japan. pp. 367-063.

[4] Beyer K, Goldstein J, Ramakrishnan R, Shaft U (1999) When is "Nearest Neighbor" Meaningful?. Proc. 7th International Conference on Database Theory, Jerusalem, Israel. pp. 217-235

[5] Böhm C, Kriegel H P (2000) Dynamically Optimizing High-Dimensional Index Structures. Proc. 7th International Conference on Extending Database Technology, Konstanz, Germany. pp. 36-50.

[6] Carr D B, Littlefield R J, Nicholson W L, Littlefield J S (1987) Scatterplot matrix techniques for large n. Journal of the American Statistical Association. j. 82:424-436.

[7] Chen C, Härdle W, Unwin A (2008) Handbook of Data Visualization. Springer, 2008. 936 p.

[8] Chernoff H (1973) The use of faces to represent points in k-dimensional space graphically. Journal of the American Statistical Association. j. 68:361-368.

[9] Cockburn A, McKenzie B (2000) An evaluation of cone trees. People and Computers. j. pp. 425-436.

[10] Crespo A A (2011) Estatística Fácil. Saraiva, São Paulo.

[11] Downing, D., Clark, J (2002) Estatística Aplicada. Saraiva, São Paulo.

[12] Ebert D S, Rohrer M R, Shaw D C, Panda P, Kukla M J, Roberts A D (2001) Procedural Shape Generation for Multi-dimensional Data Visualization. Computers & Graphics. j. 24:375-384.

[13] Flury B, Riedwyl H (1981) Graphical representation of multivariate data by means of asymmetrical faces. Journal of the American Statistical Association. j.76:757-765.

[14] Gershon N, Eick S G (1997) Information Visualization. IEEE Computer Graphics and Applications. j. 17:29-31.

[15] Grinstein G, Trutschl M, Cvek U (2001) High dimensional visualizations. Proceedings of the 7th Data Mining Conference-KDD. Citeseer.

[16] Goldschmidt R, Passos E (2005) Data Mining: um Guia Prático. Campus, Rio de Janeiro, Brazil.

[17] Havre S, Hetzler E, Whitney P, Nowell L (2002) Themeriver: Visualizing thematic changes in large document collections. Visualization and Computer Graphics, IEEE Transactions on. j. 8:9-20.

[18] Hofmann H (2003) Constructing and reading mosaicplots. Computational Statistics & Data Analysis. j. 43: 565-580.

[19] Hunter K, Hari S, Egbu C, Kelly J (2005) Grounded Theory: Its Diversification and Application Through two Examples From Research Studies on Knowledge and Value Management.The Electronic Journal of Business Research Methodology. j. 3:57-68. Available:
www.ejbrm.com. Accessed 2010 Feb 14.

[20] Inselberg A, Dimsdale B (1990) Parallel Coordinates: a Tool for Visualizing Multidimensional Geometry. Proc. Conference on Visualization, San Francisco, Los Alamitos. p. 23-26.

[21] Inselberg A (2008) Parallel Coordinates: Visualization, Exploration and ClassiïňĄcation of High-Dimensional Data. In: Chen C, Härdle, W, Unwin A, editors. Handbook of Data Visualization. Springer. pp. 643-680.
[22] Johnson A R, Wichner W D (2011) Applied Multivariate Statistical Analysis. Prentice-Hall, New Jersey.
[23] Keim D, Kriegel H P (1996). Visualization Techniques for Mining Large Databases: a Comparison. IEEE Transactions on Knowledge and Data Engineering. j. 8:923-938.
[24] Keim D (2000). Designing pixel-oriented visualization techniques: Theory and applications. Visualization and Computer Graphics, IEEE Transactions on. j. 6:1-20.
[25] Keim D (2001) Visual exploration of large data sets. Communications of the ACM. j.44:38-44.
[26] Keim D (2002) Information Visualization and Visual Data Mining. IEEE Transactions on Visualization and Computer Graphics. j. 7: 100-107.
[27] Kienreich W, Sabol V, Granitzer M, Klieber W, Lux M, Sarka W (2005) A visual query interface for a very large newspaper article repository. Database and Expert Systems Applications. IEEE Proceedings. Sixteenth International Workshop on. pp. 415-419.
[28] Klippel A, Hardisty F, Weaver C (2009) Starplots: How shape characteristics influence classification tasks. Cartography and Geographic Information Science. j. 36:149-163.
[29] Kosara R, Sahling G, Hauser H (2004) Linking Scientific And Information Visualization With Interactive 3d Scatterplots. International Conference In Central Europe On Computer Graphics, Visualization And Computer Vision Short Communication. j. 12: 133-140.
[30] LeBlanc J, Ward M O, Wittels N (1990) Exploring n-dimensional databases. Proceedings of the 1st conference on Visualization'90. IEEE Computer Society Press. p.237.
[31] Lee M D, Reilly R E, Butavicius M E (2003) An empirical evaluation of chernoff faces, star glyphs, and spatial visualizations for binary data. Proceedings of the Asia-Pacific symposium on Information visualisation. Australian Computer Society, Inc. j. 24: 1-10.
[32] Levkowitz H (1991) Color Icons: Merging Color and Texture Perception for Integrated Visualization of Multiple Parameters. Proc. IEEE International Conference on Visualization, San Diego, USA . pp. 164-170.
[33] Mackinlay J (1986) Automating the Design of Graphical Presentations of Relational Information. ACM Transactions on Graphics. j. 5: 110-141.
[34] Matavire R, Brown I (2008) Investigating the use of "Grounded Theory" in information systems research. SAICSIT '08: Proceedings of the 2008 annual research conference of the South African Institute of Computer Scientists and Information Technologists on IT research in developing countries. j. 139-147.
[35] Mao Y, Dillon J, Lebanon G (2007) Sequential document visualization. IEEE transactions on visualization and computer graphics. pp.1208-1215.
[36] Morris C J, Ebert D S, Rheingans P (2000) Experimental analysis of the effectiveness of features in chernoff faces. Proc Spie Int Soc Opt Eng. Citeseer. 3905:12-17.
[37] Myatt G J (2007) Making sense of data: a practical guide to exploratory data analysis and data mining. Wiley-Blackwell.
[38] Nascimento H A D, Ferreira C B R (2005) Visualização de informações - uma abordagem prática. XXV Congresso da Sociedade Brasileira de Computação, XXIV JAI, São Leopoldo, RS, Brazil.
[39] NIST/SEMATECH (2003) Nistsematech e-handbook of statistical methods. Available: http://www.itl.nist.gov/div898/handbook/. Accessed 2011 Nov 14.

[40] Oliveira M C F, Levkowitz H (2003) From visual data exploration to visual data mining: A survey. IEEE Transactions on Visualization and Computer Graphics. j. 9:378-394.
[41] Peng W, Ward M O, Rundensteiner E A (2004) Clutter reduction in multi-dimensional data visualization using dimension reordering. IEEE Symposium on Information Visualization. pp. 89-96.
[42] Pillat R M, Valiati E R A, Freitas C M D S (2005) Experimental study on evaluation of multidimensional information visualization techniques. Proceedings of the 2005 Latin American conference on Human-computer interaction, ACM. j. pp. 20-30.
[43] Pickett R M, Grinstein G G (1988) Iconographic displays for visualizing multidimensional data. Proc. IEEE Conf. on Systems, Man and Cybernetics. IEEE Press, Piscataway, NJ. 514:519
[44] Pfleeger L S (2004) Engenharia de Software: Teoria e Prática. Pearson Prentice-Hall: São Paulo.
[45] Rabelo E, Dias M M, Franco C, Pacheco R C S (2008) Information Visualization: Which is the most Appropriate Technique to Represent Data Mining Results?. Proceedings of the International Conference on Computational Intelligence for Modelling, Control and Automation, Viena - Austria. pp. 1218-1223.
[46] Robertson G G, Mackinlay J D, Card S K (1991) Cone trees: animated 3d visualizations of hierarchical information. Proceedings of the SIGCHI conference on Human factors in computing systems: Reaching through technology. ACM. pp. 189-194.
[47] Rodrigues J F (2003) Desenvolvimento de um Framework para Análise Visual de Informação Suportando Data Mining. Phd Thesis. Universidade de São Paulo, São Paulo, Brazil.
[48] (2011) The R Project. Available: http://www.r-project.org/. Accessed 2011 Nov 14.
[49] Rundensteiner E A, Ward M O, Yang J, Doshi P R (2002) XmdvTool: Visual Interactive Data Exploration and Trend Discovery of High-dimensional Data Sets. Proc. ACM SIGMOD International Conference on Management of Data, Madison pp.631.
[50] Russo S C, Gros P, Abel P (1999) Visualização Tridimensional de Grandes Volumes de Informação. Proc. Congresso Luso-Moçambicano de Engenharia, Maputo, Mozambique. 2:73-87
[51] Sensalire M, Ogao P, Telea A (2008) Classifying desirable features of software visualization tools for corrective maintenance. Proceedings of the 4th ACM symposium on Software visualization. pp. 87-90.
[52] Shimabukuru H M (2004) Visualizações Temporais em uma Plataforma de Software Extensível e Adaptável. Phd Thesis. Universidade de São Paulo, São Paulo, Brazil.
[53] Shneiderman B (1996) The eyes have it: A task by data type taxonomy for information visualizations. VL'96: Proceedings of the 1996 IEEE Symposium on Visual Languages, Boulder, Colorado. j. pp. 336-343.
[54] Shneiderman B (2006) Discovering business intelligence using treemap visualizations. Technical report, B-Eye: Business Intelligence Network.
[55] Starre L V D, Vries T (2005) Visualizing documents: analysis and evaluation.
[56] Taylor A L, Hickey T J, Prinz A A, Marder E(2006) Structure and visualization of high-dimensional conductance spaces. Journal of neurophysiology. j. 96:891-905.
[57] Valiati E R A (2008) Avaliação de usabilidade de técnicas de visualização de informações multidimensionais. PhD thesis, Universidade Federal do Rio Grande do Sul.

[58] Voinea L, Telea A (2007) Visual data mining and analysis of software repositories. Computers & Graphics. j. 31:410-428.
[59] Wegman E J, Luo Q (2011) High-Dimensional Clustering Using Parallel Coordinates and the Grand Tour. Computing Science and Statistics. j. 28:352-360.
[60] Yamaguchi J K, Dias M M, Franco C (2011) Guidelines For The Choice of Visualization Techniques Applied in the Process of Knowledge Extraction. 13th International Conference on Enterprise Information Systems - ICEIS 2011, Beijing, China. pp. 183-189.
[61] Yamaguchi J K, Dias M M (2011) A Study about Influenceable Parameters in the Choice of Visualization Techniques Based on Grounded Theory. IADIS International Conferences Computer Graphics, Visualization, Computer Vision and Image Processing 2011, Rome, Italy. pp.177-184.
[62] Zeckzer D, Kalcklösch R, Schröder L, Hagen H, Klein T (2008) Analyzing the reliability of communication between software entities using a 3d visualization of clustered graphs. Proceedings of the 4th ACM symposium on Software visualization. pp. 37-46.

Chapter 8

Analysis and Learning Frameworks for Large-Scale Data Mining

Kohsuke Yanai and Toshihiko Yanase

Additional information is available at the end of the chapter

http://dx.doi.org/10.5772/51713

1. Introduction

Recently, lots of companies and organizations try to analyze large amount of business data and leverage extracted knowledge to improve their operations. This chapter discusses techniques for processing large-scale data. In this chapter, we propose two computing frameworks for large-scale data mining:

1. Tree structured data analysis framework, and
2. Parallel machine learning framework.

The first framework is for analysis phase, in which we find out how to utilize business data through trial and error. The proposed framework stores tree-structured data using vertical partitioning technique, and uses Hadoop MapReduce for distributed computing. These methods enable to reduce disk I/O load, and to avoid computationally-intensive processing, such as grouping and combining of records.

The second framework is for model learning phase, in which we create predictive models using machine learning algorithms. The proposed framework is another implementation of MapReduce. The framework is designed to ease parallelization of machine learning algorithms and reduce calculation overheads for iterative procedures. The framework minimizes frequency of thread generation and termination, and keeps feature vectors in local memory and local disk during iteration.

We start with discussion on process of data utilization in enterprise and organization described in Figure 1. We suppose the data utilization process consists of the following phases.

1. Pre-processing phase
2. Analysis phase

INTECH
open science | open minds

©2012 Yanai and Yanase, licensee InTech. This is an open access chapter distributed under the terms of the Creative Commons Attribution License (http://creativecommons.org/licenses/by/3.0), which permits unrestricted use, distribution, and reproduction in any medium, provided the original work is properly cited.

3. Model learning phase
4. Model application phase

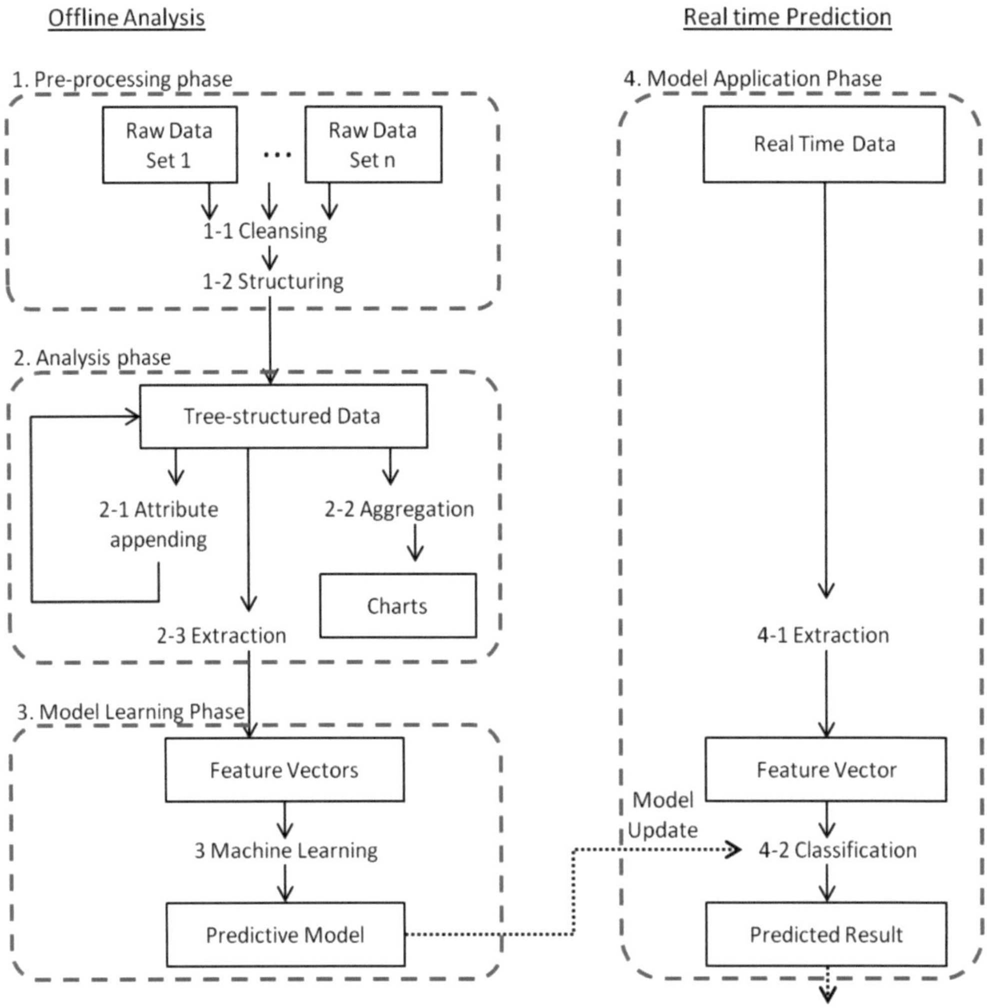

Figure 1. Process of data utilization.

1.1. Pre-processing phase

Pre-processing phase consists of 2 steps:

Step 1-1 Cleansing

Step 1-2 Structuring

Firstly Step 1-1 removes incorrect values and secondly Step 1-2 transforms table-format data into tree-structured data. This pre-processing phase combines raw data from multiple data sources and creates tree-structured data in which records from multiple data sources are "joined".

Figure 2 illustrates an example of tree-structured server logs, in which the log data are grouped by each site at the top level. Site information consists of site ID (e.g. "site001") and a list of server information. Server information consists of server ID (e.g. "serv001"), average CPU usage (e.g. "ave-cpu:84.0%") and a list of detail records. Furthermore, a detail record consists of date (e.g. "02/05"), time (e.g. "10:20"), CPU usage (e.g. "cpu:92%") and memory usage (e.g. "mem:532MB").

```
[(site001
  [(serv001 ave-cpu:84.0%
    [(02/05 10:10 cpu:92% mem:532MB)
     (02/05 10:20 cpu:76% mem:235MB)])
   (serv002 ave-cpu:12.6%
    [(02/05 15:30 cpu:13% mem:121MB)
     (02/05 15:40 cpu:15% mem:142MB)
     (02/05 15:50 cpu:10% mem:140MB)])])
 (site021
  [(serv001 ave-cpu:50.0%
    [(02/05;11:40 cpu:88% mem:889MB)
     (02/05;11:50 cpu:12% mem:254MB)])])]
```

Figure 2. Example of tree-structured data.

If we store the data in table format, data grouping and data combining are repeatedly computed in analysis phase which comes after the pre-processing phase. Data grouping and data combining correspond "group-by" and "join" in SQL respectively. Note that the tree structure keeps the data be grouped and joined. In general when data size is large, the computation cost of data grouping and data combining becomes intensive. Therefore, we store data in tree structure format so that we avoid repetition of these computationally-intensive processing.

1.2. Analysis phase

Analysis phase finds out how to utilize the data through trial-and-error. In most situations the purpose of data analysis is not clear at an early stage of the data utilizatoin process. This is the reason why this early phase needs trial-and-error processes.

As described in Figure 1, the analysis phase consists of 3 independent steps:

Step 2-1 Attribute appending

Step 2-1 Aggregation

Step 2-1 Extraction

This phase iterates Step 2-1 and Step 2-2. The purpose of the iterative process is

- To obtain statistical information and trend,
- To decide what kind of predictive model should be generated, and

- To decide which attributes should be used to calculate feature vectors of the predictive model.

Step 2-1 appends new attributes to tree-structured data by combining existing attributes. We suppose the iteration of attribute appending increases data size by 5-20 times. On the other hand, Step 2-2 calculates statistics of attributes and generates charts that help to grasp characteristics of the data. The calculations of Step 2-2 include mean, variance, histogram, cross tabulation, and so on.

An instance of the iterative process consisting attribute appending and aggregation is the following.

1. Calculate frequencies of CPU usage (Step 2-2)
2. Append a new attribute "average memory usage for each server" (Step 2-1)
3. Calculate standard deviation of a new attribute "average memory usage" (Step 2-2)
4. Append a new attribute "difference of memory usage from its average" (Step 2-1)
5. ...

We usually append more than 10 new attributes into the raw data. Attribute appending increases value and visibility of data, and eases trial-and-error process for finding how to utilize the data.

After the iterative process of attribute appending and aggregation, Step 2-3 extracts feature vectors from tree-structured data, which are used in model learning phase.

1.3. Model learning phase

Model learning phase generates predictive models which are used in real-world operations of enterprises and organizations. The model learning phase uses machine learning techniques, such as SVM (support vector machine) [1] and K-Means clustering [2].

For instance, this phase generates a model that predicts when hardware troubles will happen in IT system. The input of the model is history of CPU usage and memory usage. The output is date and time.

1.4. Model application phase

Model application phase applies the predictive models obtained from the model learning phase into actual business operations. We emphasize the input data is "real time".

As described in Figure 1, the model application phase consists of 2 steps:

Step 4-1 Extraction

Step 4-2 Classification

Step 4-1 extracts a feature vector from real time data. Usually computation of this step is similar to that of Step 2-3. Step 4-2 attaches a predictive label to the input data by using predictive models. For example, this label represents date and time of hardware trouble. The label is used in business operations as an event.

2. Architecture

We propose architecture for large-scale data mining. Figure 3 illustrates our architecture.

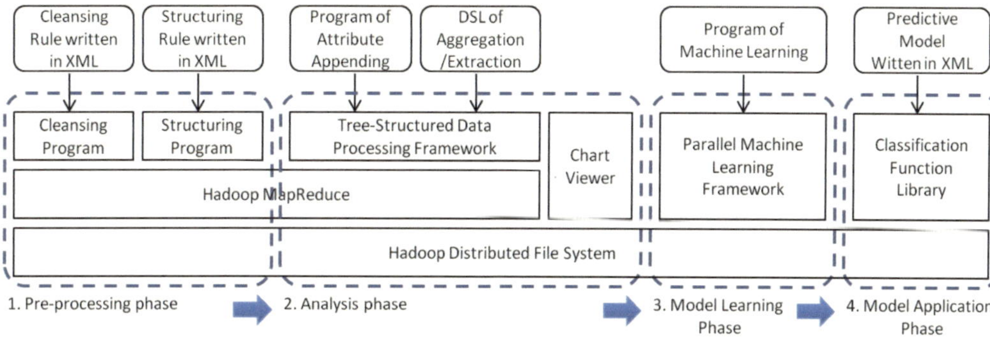

Figure 3. Architecture.

# Phase	Data	Computation	Approach
1 Pre-processing	Table format	I/O-intensive	Hadoop MR
2 Analysis	Tree-structured, large number of attributes	I/O-intensive	Hadoop MR + vertical partitioning + data store in tree-structured format
3 Model learning	Vectors	CPU-intensive	Iterative MR + Hadoop DFS
4 Model application	Steream	Real time	Event driven software

Table 1. Approach of each phase. MR: MapReduce, DFS: Distributed File System.

As discussed in Section 1, we suppose four phases: pre-processing, analysis, model learning and model application. In pre-processing phase, data is in table format and the computation is I/O-intensive. Hadoop MapReduce [3] is appropriate for the pre-processing from the view point of data format and I/O load reduction. Hadoop MapReduce is distributed computing platform based on MapReduce computation model [4, 5]. Hadoop MapReduce consists of three computation phases: Map, Combine and Reduce. Hadoop MapReduce parallelizes disk I/O by reading and writing data in parallel on Hadoop DFS (Distributed File System). Regarding details of Hadoop, refer to the literature [4, 5].

We develop cleansing program and structuring program which run on Hadoop MapReduce. The cleansing program and the structuring program are general-purpose, which means we can use the same programs for all cases. The cleansing program and the structuring program read cleansing rule and structuring rule respectively, and programs run by following the rules written by users as XML files.

In analysis phase, data is tree-structured and the computation is I/O-intensive. In addition, the number of attributes is large since this phase repeatedly appends new attributes. Therefore, key approach is also reduction of I/O load. We propose a method combining Hadoop MapReduce, vertical partitioning and data store in tree-structured format in Section 3. This phase also needs chart viewer that displays result of aggregation of Step 2-2.

On the other hand, I/O load in model learning phase is permissive. Because input of machine learning algorithms is feature vectors whose size is much smaller than that of raw data. The computation in model learning phase is CPU-intensive since machine learning algorithms include iterative calculation for optimization. Section 4 proposes another MapReduce framework for parallel machine learning, in which iterative algorithms are easily parallelized.

In model application phase, data is stream and the computation should be performed in real time. Therefore, we develop event-driven software that runs at the timing of input data coming. The software includes a library of classification function. It reads a predictive model written in PMML [6] that is XML-based language for model description.

We summarize our approaches in Table 1. The rest of this paper focuses on frameworks for analysis phase and model learning phase. Because while new techniques are necessary for efficient computation in the two phases, system for pre-processing and model application is easily implemented by combining existing technologies.

3. Tree-structured data analysis framework

3.1. Mathod

This section proposes a computing framework that performs data analysis on a large amount of tree-structured data. As discussed in Section 1, an early stage of the data utilization process needs trial-and-error processes, in which we repeatedly append new attributes and calculate statistics of attributes. As a result of repetition of attribute appending, the number of attributes increases. Therefore, not only scalability to the number of records but also scalability to the number of attributes is important.

The key approaches of the proposed framework are:

1. To partition tree-structured data in column-wise and store the partitioned data in separated files corresponding to each attribute, and
2. To use Hadoop MapReduce framework for distributed computing.

The method (1) is referred to as "vertical partitioning." It is well known that vertical partitioning of **table format data** is efficient [7]. We propose vertical partitioning of tree-structured data. Figure 4 illustrates the vertical partitioning method. The proposed framework partitions tree-structured data into multiple lists so that each list includes values belonging to the same attribute. Then the framework stores the lists of each attribute in correspoinding files. Note that the file of "Average CPU usage" in Figure 4 includes only values belonging to "Average CPU usage" attribute, and does not include values of any other attributes.

The framework reads only 1-3 attributes required in data analysis out of 10-30 attributes, and restores tree-structured data that consists of only required attributes. In addition, when appending a new attribute, the framework writes only the newly created attribute into files. If we do not use the vertical partitioning technique, it should write all of existing attributes into files. Thus the proposed method reduces amount of input data as well as amount of output data.

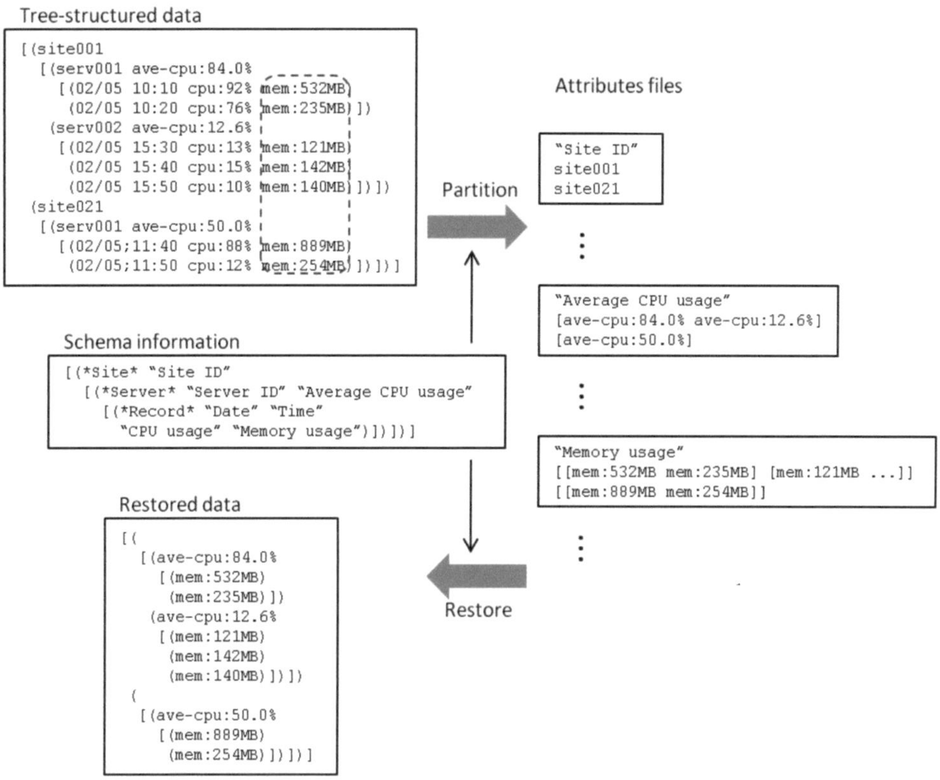

Figure 4. Vertical partitioning of tree-structured data.

3.2. Implementation

The data model of the proposed framework is a recursively-defined tuple.

Tuple: Combination of lists and values. e.g. `("serv002", 13, [(15, 10)])`.

List: Sequence of tuples whose types are the same. e.g. `[("serv001" 4.0) ("serv002" 2.6)]`.

Value: Sscalar, vector, matrix or string. e.g. `"532MB"`.

A round bracket `()` represents a tuple while a square bracket `[]` represents a list. In this paper, elements of a tuple and a list are separated by white spaces.

Figure 5 describes pseudo code of partitioning algorithm. The algorithm partitions tree-structured data into recursive lists by running the function "Partition" recursively. Each list to be generated by the algorithm consists of values belonging to the same attribute.

Similarly Figure 6 describes pseudo code of restoring algorithm. The algorithm restores tree-structured data from divided attribute data. An example of input for the algorithm is shown in Figure 7. S is trimmed schema which excludes attributes unused in analysis computation. D is generated by replacing attribute names in trimmed schema with recursive lists stored in attribute files.

```
Partition(S, D) {
  if S is atom then return [D]
  if S is list then {
    L = []
    foreach di in D:
      append Partition(SOE(S), di) to L
    return transpose of L
  }
  if S is tuple then {
    L = []
    foreach (si, di) in (S, D):
      L = L + Partition(si, di)
  return L
}
```

Figure 5. Pseudo code of partitioning algorithm. S is schema information, D is tree-structured data, The function SOE returns schema of an element of a list.

```
Restore(S, D, d=0) {
  if S is atom then return D
  if S is list then {
    L = []
    foreach (di) in D:
      append Restore(SOE(S), di, d+1) to L
    return transpose L with depth d
  }
  if S is tuple then {
  L = []
  foreach (si, di) in (S, D):
    append Restore(si, di, d) to L
  return L
}
```

Figure 6. Pseudo code of restoring algorithm. An example of the input is shown in Figure 7. The function SOE returns schema of an element of a list.

```
S: [(
     [("Average CPU uage"
      [("Memoery Usage")])])]
D: [(
    [([[ave-cpu:84.0% ave-cpu:12.6%] [ave-cpu:50.0%]])
     [([[[mem:532MB mem:235MB] [mem:121MB ...]] [[mem:889MB mem:254MB]]])])]
```

Figure 7. Example of input of the restoring alogoritthm.

We implemented the partitioning algorithm and the restoring algorithm in Gauche. Gauche is an implementation of computer language Scheme. Users implement programs for attribute appending and aggregation using Gauche. The proposed framework combines user programs with partitioning and restoring programs. Then the combined program runs in parallel on Hadoop Streaming of Hadoop MapReduce 0.20.0. Table 2 summarizes key Hadoop components for implementation of the framework.

Item	Description
Hadoop aggregation package	Used for Combine and Reduce calculation.
CompositeInputFormat class	Used for multiple file input and "Map-side join" [3].
MultipleTextOutputFormat class	Used for multiple file output.

Table 2. Hadoop configuration.

Figure 8 shows an example of user program. The program appends a new attribute "Average memory usage". The variable "new-schema" represents a location of the newly appended attribute in tree structure. The function mapper generates a new tree-structured data including only the attribute to be appended. The framework provides accessors to attributes and tuples, such as "`ref-Server-tuples`" and "`ref-Memory-usage`".

```
(define new-schema
  '(
    [("Average memory usage")])
)

(define (mapper site)
   (tuple
    [foreach (ref-Server-tuples site) (lambda (server)
     (tuple
       (mean (map ref-Memory-usage (ref-Record-tuples server)))
     )]))))
```

Figure 8. Example of user program.

3.3. Evaluation

We evaluated the proposed framework on 6 benchmark tasks.

Task A Calculates average CPU usage for each server and append it as a new attribute into the corresponding tuple of server information. The SQL for the calculation includes "group-by" and "update" if relational database is used instead of the proposed framework.

Task B Calculates difference between CPU usage and average CPU usage for each server. The SQL of the calculation includes "join".

Task C Calculates frequency distribution of CPU usage with interval of 10. The SQL of the calculation includes "group-by".

Task D Calculates difference between CPU usages of two successive detail records and append it as a new attribute into the corresponding tuple of a detail record. It is impossible to express the calculation with SQL.

Task E Searches detail records in which both of CPU usage and memory usage is 100%.

Figure 9 shows the result of evaluation on 90 GB data. We used 19 servers as slave machines for Hadoop: 9 servers with 2-core 1.86 GHz CPU and 3 GB memory, and 10 servers with two of 4-core 2.66 GHz CPU and 8 GB memory. Thus the Hadoop cluster has 98 CPU cores in total. The vertical axis of Figure 9 represents average execution time over 5 runs. The result indicates that the vertical partitioning accelerates the calculations by 17.5 times on the task A and by 12.7 times on the task D. The task A and D require the processing of attribute appending, in which a large amount of tree-structured data is not only read from files, but also written into files. That is the reason why the acceleration on the task A and D is more than that on the other tasks.

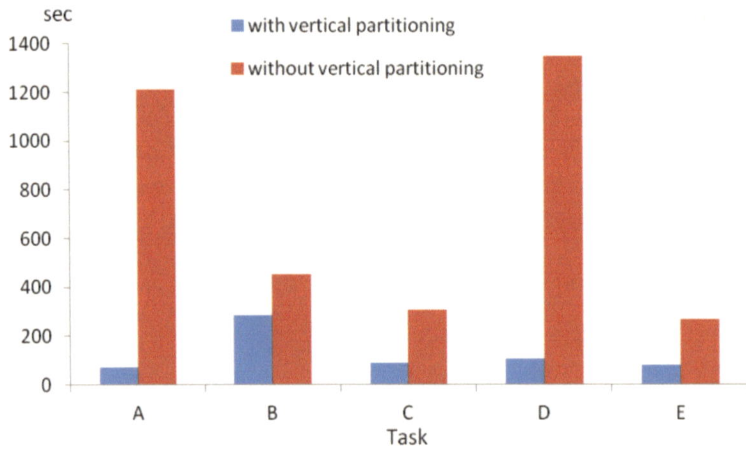

Figure 9. Evalution of the tree-structured data analysis framework.

Table 3 compares the proposed method with MySQL. Both of the proposed framework and MySQL run on a single server, and the size of benchmark data is 891 MB. Note that parallelization is not used in this experiment so that we investigate the effect of vertical partitioning and data store in tree-structured format without the disturbing factor due to parallel computation. We created indexes on columns of primary id, CPU usage and memory usage in MySQL tables. Table 3 shows average and standard deviation of execution times over 5 runs. The performance of the proposed method is comparative or superior to that of MySQL on the task A, B, C and D despite the proposed method is mainly implemented in Gauche. On the other hand, the performance of the proposed method on the task E is inferior to that of MySQL. This is because MySQL finds records that match the condition by using indexes while the proposed framework scans whole data linearly to find out the records. However, the actual execution time of the proposed framework on the task E is permissible since it is not long compared to that on the other tasks.

Task	Proposed method [sec]	MySQL [sec]
A	10.67 ± 0.08	402.72 ± 5.55
B	76.67 ± 0.36	445.48 ± 3.42
C	13.21 ± 0.18	12.89 ± 0.05
D	36.36 ± 0.20	-
E	16.87 ± 0.14	1.34 ± 2.66

Table 3. Comparison of the tree-structured data analysis framework and MySQL using a single server.

As a result of the experiments, we conclude that the proposed framework is efficient for data analysis of a large amount of tree-structured data. The performance can be improved by implementing it using Java, instead of Gauche.

4. Parallel machine learning framework

4.1. Mathod

This section proposes a computing framework for parallel machine learning. The proposed framework is designed to ease parallelization of machine learning algorithms and reduce calculation overheads of iterative procedures.

We start with discussion on a model of machine learning algorithms. Let $D = (x_n, y_n)$ be training data, where x_n is a feature vector with d dimension, y_n is a label. Machine learning algorithm estimates a model M describing D well. In this paper we discuss machine learning algorithms that are describable as an iteration of the following steps:

$$z_n = f(x_n, y_n, M) \quad (1)$$

$$M = r(g([z_0, z_1, ..., z_{N-1}])), \quad (2)$$

where M represents a model to be trained, g is a function which satisfies the following constraint.

$$\forall i < j < ... < k < N, g([z_0, ..., z_{N-1}]) = g([g[(z_0, ..., z_{i-1})], g[(z_i, ..., z_{j-1})], ..., g[(z_k, ..., z_{N-1})]]) \quad (3)$$

For instance, a function that summates elements in an array satisfies the constraints mentioned above. By using the characteristic of g, we re-formulate the steps of machine learning algorithms as follows.

$$M_{i..j} = g([f(x_i, y_i, M), f(x_{i+1}, y_{i+1}, M), ..., f(x_{j-1}, y_{j-1}, M)]) \quad (4)$$

$$M = r(g([M_{0..i}, M_{i..j}, ..., M_{k..N}])) \quad (5)$$

Note that parallelization of the calculation of $M_{i..j}$ is possible since the calculation is independent of other (x_n, y_n).

Consider we use MapReduce for parallelization; Map phase calculates $M_{i..j}$ and Reduce phase calculates M. Although MapReduce fits parallelization of machine learning algorithms described with the above formula, use of Hadoop Mapreduce, that is, the most popular implementation of MapReduce, is unreasonable. Because the implementation of Hadoop MapReduce is optimized so that it performs non-iterative algorithms efficiently. The problems with repeatedly using Hadoop MapReduce are following.

- Hadoop MapReduce does not keep feature vectors in memory devices during iterations.
- Hadoop MapReduce restarts threads of Map and Reduce at every iteration. Initialization overheads of these threads are large compared to computation time of machine learning algorithms.

Consequently, the proposed framework provides another MapReduce implementation for iterative algorithms of machine learning. The key approaches of the framework are follows.

1. It keeps feature vectors in memory devices during iterations. In case data size of feature vectors is larger than memory size, it uses local disk as a cache.
2. It does not terminate threads of Map and Reduce and uses the same threads repeatedly.
3. It controls iterations, read/write and data communication.
4. Users implement only 4 functions: initialization of M, calculation of $M_{i..j}$, update of M and termination condition.
5. It utilizes Hadoop DFS as its file system.

A few MapReduce frameworks for iterative computation have been proposed. Haloop [8] adds the functions of loop control, caching and indexing into Hadoop. However, it restarts threads of Map and Reduce at every iteration like Hadoop. Therefore, the initialization overheads still remain. Twister [10, 11] and Spark [9] reduce the initialization overheads and keep feature vectors in memory devices during iterations. These frameworks perform similarly to the proposed framework if input data size is smaller than total memory size of a computing cluster. However, in case the data size is larger than total memory size, the performance of the proposed framework is superior to that of Twister and Spark since the proposed framework uses local disk as a cache.

4.2. Implementation

We implemented the proposed framework using Java. The framework reads feature vectors and configuration parameters from Hadoop DFS with version of 0.20.2. Figure 10 illustrates the sequence diagram of the proposed framework. The framework consists of a master thread, a Reduce thread and multiple Map threads. The master thread controls the Reduce thread and the Map threads. The Reduce thread controls iterations. The Map threads parallelize calculations of $M_{i..j}$.

Firstly the master thread starts multiple Map threads, which read feature vectors from Hadoop DFS and keep the data in memory and HDD in a local machine during an iteration. Secondly the master thread starts a Rreduce thread. The Map threads and the Reduce thread are not terminated until the iteration ends. Next the Reduce thread initializes M, and then the Map threads calculate $M_{i..j}$ in parallel. The Reduce thread updates M by collecting the calculation results from the Map threads and continue the iteration.

Figure 11 and Figure 12 shows implementation of parallel K-Means algorithms using the proposed framework. We omit initialization of M and termination condition since these implementations are obvious. As shown in Figure 11 and Figure 12, parallelization of the algorithm is easily implemented, and the source code is short. The rest procedures are implemented inside the framework, and users do not have to write codes of data transfer and data read. Thus users are able to focus on core logics of machine learning algorithms.

4.3. Evaluation

We compared the proposed framework with Hadoop. We used Mahout library as implementations of machine learning algorithms on Hadoop [16]. We used 6 servers as slave machines for both of the proposed framework and Hadoop: 4 servers with 4-core 2.8 GHz CPU and 4 GB memory, and 2 servers with two of 4-core 2.53 GHz CPU and 2 GB memory. In

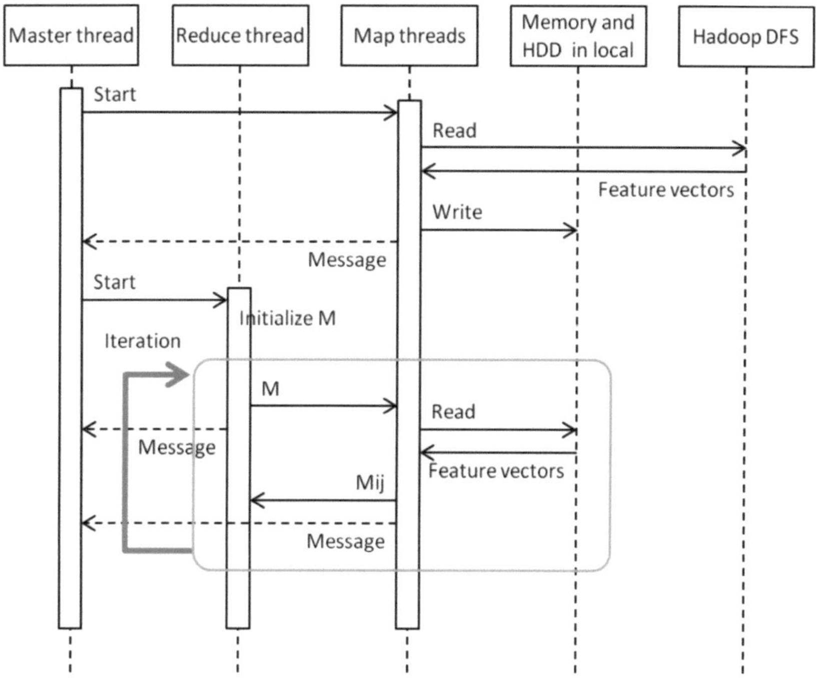

Figure 10. Sequence diagram of parallel machine learning framework

```
class KMeansMapper extends Mapper<KMeansModel> {
  public KMeansModel map(KMeansModel M) {
    KMeansModel Mij = new KMeansModel();
    for (D : x) {
      int cid = argmin_distance(x, M);
      Mij.s[cid].add(x);
      Mij.l[cid] += 1;
    }
    return Mij;
  }
}
```

Figure 11. Implementation of computing $M_{i..j}$ in parallel K-Means algorithm.

the Map phase, 40 Map threads run in parallel. On the other hand, one Reduce thread runs in the Reduce phase. The data size of feature vectors is 1.4 GB. Table 4 shows execution times of one iteration on three machine learning algorithms: K-Means [2], Dirichlet process clustering [12] and IPM perceptron [13, 14]. The values are mean and standard deviation over 10 runs. The result indicates that the proposed framework is 33.8-274.1 times as fast as Mahout.

Figure 13 illustrates scalability of the proposed framework on three machine learning algorithms: K-Means, variational Bayes clustering [15] and linear SVM [1]. The horizontal axes represent the number of Map threads that run in parallel. The vertical axes represent 1 / (execution time), i.e., speed. Figure 13 indicates that the more Map threads in parallel are, the faster the parallelized algorithms run.

```
class KMeansReducer extends Reducer<KMeansModel> {
  public KMeansModel reduce(KMeansModel[] Mijs) {
    KMeansModel M = new KMeansModel();
    for (int cid=0; cid<M.num_of_cluster; cid++) {
      for (Mijs : Mij) {
        M.s[cid].add(Mij.s[cid]);
        M.l[cid] += Mij.l[cid];
      }
      M.centroid[cid] = M.s[cid] / M.l[cid];
    }
    return M;
  }
}
```

Figure 12. Implementation of updating M in parallel K-Means algorithm.

Algorithm	Proposed method [sec]	Mahout [sec]
K-Means	0.93 ± 0.052	31.8 ± 1.49
Dirichlet process clustering	1.14 ± 0.057	67.4 ± 3.87
IPM perceptron	0.11 ± 0.026	30.7 ± 2.00

Table 4. Comparison of the parallel machine learning framework and Mahout on K-Means [2], Dirichlet process clustering [12] and IPM perceptron [13, 14].

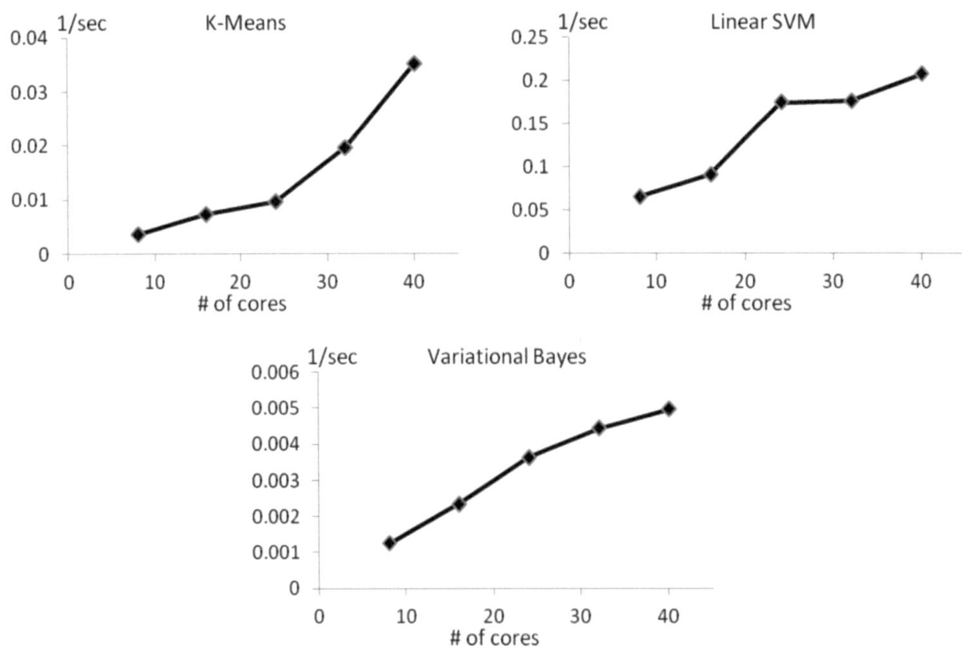

Figure 13. Scalability evaluation of the parallel machine learning framework.

We also applied the framework in order to parallelize a learning algorithm of an acoustic model for speech recognition. The learning algorithm reads voice data and corresponding text data, and generates a Hidden Markov model by using Forward Backward algorithm. We compared performance of the parallelized algorithm with that of single thread implementation using C language. We used 1.0 GB of feature vectors as a input of these programs. The parallelized algrorithm on the proposed framework with 32 parallel Map threads run 7.15 times faster than the single thread implementation. Considering the difference of speed between Java and C language, the proposed framework performs the parallelization well. Consequently, we conclude that the proposed framework is efficient for parallel machine learning.

5. Conclusion

This chapter discussed techniques for processing large-scale data. Firstly we explained that process of data utilization in enterprises and organizations includes (1) pre-processing phase, (2) analysis phase, (3) model learning phase and (4) model application phase. Secondly we described architecture for the data utilization process. Then We proposed two computing frameworks: tree-structured data analysis framework for analysis phase, and parallel machine learning framework for model learning phase. The experimental results demonstrated that our approaches work well.

Future works are follows:

- To implement tree-structured data analysis framework using Java.
- To design original machine learning algorithms which run on the parallel machine learning framework.
- To formulate a framework for model application phase.

Author details

Kohsuke Yanai
Research & Development Centre, Hitachi India Pvt. Ltd.
Central Research Laboratory, Hitachi Ltd.

Toshihiko Yanase
Central Research Laboratory, Hitachi Ltd.

6. References

[1] Chapelle, O. (2007) Training a Support Vector Machine in the Primal. Neural Computation, Vol. 19, No. 5, pp. 1155-1178.
[2] MacQueen, J. B. (1967) Some Methods for Classification and Analysis of MultiVariate Observations. Proc. of the fifth Berkeley Symposium on Mathematical Statistics and Probability, Vol. 1, pp. 281-297.
[3] White, T. (2009) Hadoop: The Definitive Guide. Oreilly & Associates Inc.
[4] Dean, J. and Ghemawat, S. (2004) MapReduce: Simplified Data Processing on Large Clusters. Proceedings of Sixth Symposium on Operating System Design and Implementation (OSD2004), pp. 137-150.

[5] Dean, J. and Ghemawat, S. (2008) MapReduce: simplified data processing on large clusters. Communications of the ACM, Vol. 51, No. 1, pp. 107-113.
[6] Data Mining Group. PMML standard, http://www.dmg.org/v4-1/GeneralStructure.html
[7] Manegold, S., Boncz, P. A., and Kersten, M. L. (2000) Optimizing database architecture for the new bottleneck: memory access. The VLDB Journal, Vol. 9, No. 3, pp. 231-246.
[8] Bu, Y., Howe, B., Balazinska, M., and Ernst, M. D. (2010) HaLoop: Efficient Iterative Data Processing on Large Clusters. Proceedings of the VLDB Endowment, Vol. 3, p. 1.
[9] Zaharia, M., Chowdhury, M., Franklin, M. J., Shenker, S., and Stoica, I. (2010) Spark: Cluster Computing withWorking Sets. HotCloud 2010.
[10] Ekanayake, J. and Pallickara, S.: (2008) MapReduce for Data Intensive Scientific Analysis. Forth IEEE International Conference on eScience, pp. 277-284.
[11] Ekanayake, J., Balkir, A. S., Gunarathne, T., Fox, G., Poulain, C., Araujo, N., and Barga, R. (2009) DryadLINQ for Scientific Analyses. Proceedings of Fifth IEEE International Conference on e-Science (eScience2009).
[12] McCullagh, P. and Yang, J. (2008) How Many Clusters. Bayesian Analysis, Vol. 3, No. 1, pp. 101-120.
[13] McDonald, R., Hall, K., and Mann, G. (2010) Distributed Training Strategies for the Structured Perceptron. Proceedings of Human Language Technologies: The 2010 Annual Conference of the North American Chapter of the ACL, pp. 456-464.
[14] Hall, K. B., Gilpin, S., and Mann, G. (2010) MapReduce/Bigtable for Distributed Optimization. Neural Information Processing Systems Workshop on Leaning on Cores, Clusters, and Clouds.
[15] Corduneanu, A. and Bishop, C. M. (2001) Variational Bayesian Model Selection for Mixture Distributions. Artificial Intelligence and Statistics 2001, pp27-34.
[16] Apache Mahout: Scalable machine learning and data mining. http://mahout.apache.org/

Section 2

Data Mining Applications

Chapter 9

Data Mining Applied to Cognitive Radio Systems

Lilian Freitas, Yomara Pires, Jefferson Morais, João Costa and Aldebaro Klautau

Additional information is available at the end of the chapter

http://dx.doi.org/10.5772/51824

1. Introduction

Cognitive radio (CR) is a novel technology that allows to improve spectrum utilization by enabling opportunistic access to the licensed spectrum band by unlicensed users [2]. This is accomplished through heterogeneous architectures and techniques of dynamic spectrum access. The CR is defined as an intelligent wireless communication system that is aware of its environment and is capable to learn from the environment and adapt its transmission parameters, such as frequency, modulation, transmission power and communication protocols [14].

An important aspect of a cognitive radio is spectrum sensing [10], which involves two main tasks: signal detection and modulation classification. Signal detection refers to detection of unused spectrum (spectrum holes). It is a simpler task and can be done, for example, by comparing the energy in the frequency band of interest with a predetermined threshold. This task is important so that the unlicensed users do not cause interference to licensed users. Modulation classification consists in automatically identifying the modulation scheme (PSK, FM, QAM, etc) of a given communication system with a high probability of success and in a short period of time. The identification of the modulation scheme allows the cognitive radio to demodulate the received signal. In order to accomplish the task of modulation classification, several data mining techniques can be applied, such as artificial neural networks, support vector machine, Bayesian classifiers, etc.

This chapter aims to evaluate different algorithms for classification of modulation signals on spectrum sensing. The features used for classification are based on a well-established technique called cyclostationarity [7, 10]. Based on these features are evaluated the performances of five data mining techniques: naïve bayes, decision tree, k-nearest neighbor (KNN), support vector machine (SVM) and artificial neural networks (ANN). The choice of such techniques was based on the fact that they are the most popular representatives of different learning paradigms.

INTECH
open science | open minds

©2012 Freitas et al., licensee InTech. This is an open access chapter distributed under the terms of the Creative Commons Attribution License (http://creativecommons.org/licenses/by/3.0),which permits unrestricted use, distribution, and reproduction in any medium, provided the original work is properly cited.

2. The problem of modulation classification

A modulation classification system consists of a *front end* and a *back end* or classifier. The *front end* converts the received signal $r(t)$ to a vector $\mathbf{x}[k], k = 1, \ldots, N$ composed of N elements. Having $\mathbf{x}[k]$ as input, the classifier decides the class $y \in \{1, \ldots, C\}$ among C pre-determined modulation schemes. The process is depicted in the diagram below:

$r(t)$ (signal)→ [front end] →$\mathbf{x}[k]$ (features)→ [classifier] →y (class)

The feature selection is a key step in the performance of the classifier. This selection depends on factors such as the modulation type to be classified, the signal to noise ratio, the presence of fading, the frequency offset, etc. This chapter uses the cyclostationarity to extract features of modulation due to its reduced sensibility to noise and interfering signals, and also its ability to extract signal parameters such as the carrier frequency and the symbol rate [7].

In the literature there are numerous works that combine different techniques of extraction features and classifiers to perform the modulation classification, as shown in Table 1.

Ref.	front end	Classifier	Noise/ Interference	SNR (dB) (min:Δ:max)	Modulations	Training/ Testing
[15]	CSS	SVM	AWGN/ freq. offset	-5:2:10	BPSK, 4PAM, 16QAM, 8PSK	500/500
[16]	features derived from amplitude, frequency and phase	neural networks	AWGN	-5:5:20	2ASK, 4ASK, 2FSK, BPSK, QPSK, AM, DSB, SSB, FM OFDM, 16QAM, 64QAM	1200/1200
[18]	cyclic spectrum	neural network and HMM	AWGN	-10:5:10	BPSK, QPSK/QAM, FSK, MSK	several
[13]	spectrogram time-frequency	rule based	AWGN	0:2:12	ASK, FSK, PSK	NE/400
[4]	linear transform of amplitude and phase	joint moments	AWGN/ freq. offset	0:1:5	BPSK, QPSK	NE/100
[20]	wavelet transform	decision threshold	AWGN	0:5:15	FSK,PSK, QAM	NE/1000
[19]	fourth-order cumulant	decision threshold	AWGN/ freq. offset	0:5:20	BPSK, QPSK, 8PSK pi/4 DQPSK	NE/100
[24]	forth-order and sixth-order cumulants	ARBF	not informed	0:5:20	4ASK, 2ASK, 2PSK 4PSK, 16QAM	50/50
[1]	cyclostationarity	neural networks	AWGN/ freq. offset	-10:5:15	BPSK, QPSK FSK, MSK, AM	NE/1000
[11]	Renyi entropy, high order statistics	SVM	AWGN	10 dB	AM, FM, AM-FM QPSK	200/200

Table 1. Examples of different *front end* and *classifier* used in the literature. NA: not available.

These works show good results in the experimental setup in which they were assessed. However, these works are evaluated on different operating conditions (signal-to-noise ratio, type of noise and distortion) and use different modulations. Thus, it is difficult to directly compare the results, or even to reproduce the results presented.

In this chapter, the comparison of main classifiers available in the literature is performed, considering the same operating conditions: five modulation schemes (AM, BPSK, QPSK, BFSK and 16QAM); channel with additive white Gaussian noise (AWGN) and Rayleigh multipath fading; all the modulated signals adopt the same symbol rate, sampling frequency and carrier frequency. For every modulation scheme 1500 samples are generated under each SNR (from -10 dB to 10 dB at intervals of 5 dB), in which 750 samples are used for training, and the other 750 samples for testing.

3. Front end: Cyclostationarity

Cyclostationarity is a technique that extracts features of the signals. Signals are characterized as cyclostationary since their mean and autocorrelation are periodic with some period T. This is

$$M_x(t+T) = M_x(t)$$
$$R_x(t+T, u+T) = R_x(t, u)$$

for all t and u, where $x(t)$ is a signal said to be cyclostationary.

Modulated signals are cyclostationary since they are coupled with several sources of periodicities such as sine wave carriers, pulse trains, repeating spreading, hopping sequences, or cyclic prefixes. These introduced periodicities cause spectral redundancy, which can be measured by the correlation between spectral components of cyclostationary signals. This periodicity appearing in transmitted signal of the users can be used by cognitive radio to detect and identify user signals.

Since the autocorrelation function $R_x(\tau)$ of received signal $x(t)$ is periodic, it can be represented by a Fourier Series, shown in Equation 1,

$$R_x(t+\tau/2, t-\tau/2) = \sum_{\alpha} R_x^{\alpha}(\tau) e^{i2\pi\alpha t} \tag{1}$$

where $R_x^{\alpha}(\tau)$ is the Fourier Series coefficients called *cyclic autocorrelation function* with spectral components at cyclic frequencies α. The Fourier coefficients may be obtained by Equation 2.

$$R_x^{\alpha}(\tau) \triangleq \frac{1}{T}\int_{-T/2}^{T/2} R_x(t+\frac{\tau}{2}, t-\frac{\tau}{2}) e^{-i2\pi\alpha t} dt, \tag{2}$$

The density of spectral correlation is the Fourier Transform of cyclic autocorrelation function $R_x^{\alpha}(\tau)$ and *spectral correlation function* (SCF), $S_x^{\alpha}(f)$, is the density of correlation between spectral components at $(f+\alpha/2)$ and $(f-\alpha/2)$, and is given by Equation 3,

$$S_x^{\alpha}(f) = \lim_{T\to\infty}\lim_{\Delta t\to\infty}\frac{1}{T\Delta t}\int_{-\Delta t/2}^{\Delta t/2} X_T(t, f+\frac{\alpha}{2}) X_T^*(t, f-\frac{\alpha}{2}) dt \tag{3}$$

where $X_T(t, f)$ is the spectral components of received signal $x(t)$ at frequency f with bandwidth $1/T$ as defined in Equation 4.

$$X_T(t, f) = \int_{t-T/2}^{t+T/2} x(u) e^{-i2\pi f u} du \tag{4}$$

The SCF is a three-dimensional function; therefore, to reduce the calculations for the classifier, it is possible to use the peak values of normalized SCF as features to distinguish each modulation, that is, the *cyclic domain profile* (CDP), obtained by Equation 5.

$$I(\alpha) = \max_{k} |S_x^{\alpha}(f)|. \tag{5}$$

In order to illustrate the use of the cyclostationarity technique, Figure 1 shows the estimation of the normalized SCF for BPSK and QPSK modulations respectively. The Figure 2 shows the cyclic domain profile for the BPSK and QPSK modulations. These examples adopted a sampling frequency $f_s = 8192$ Hz, carrier frequency $K = 2048$ Hz, cyclic frequency resolution $\Delta\alpha = 20$ Hz and frequency resolution $\Delta f = 80$ Hz.

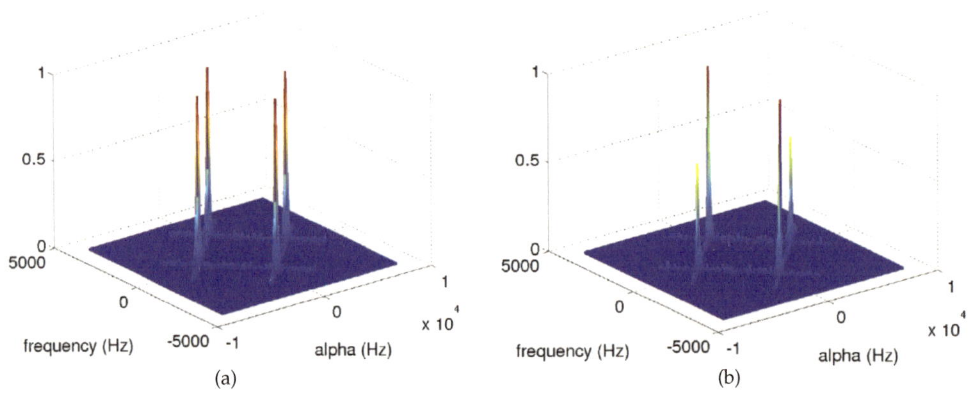

Figure 1. Spectral correlation function. (a) BPSK. (b) QPSK

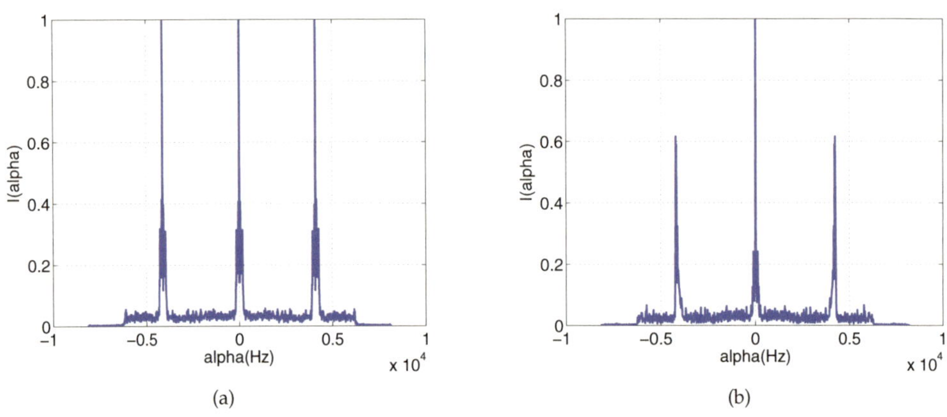

Figure 2. Cyclic domain profile. (a) BPSK. (b) QPSK

Note that different modulations have different CDP, thus these features were used as input to the block classifier. The cyclostationary features of modulated signals have been increasingly considered for use in a large range of applications, including signal detection, classification, synchronization and equalization. Its main advantages are the reduced sensibility to noise and interfering signals, and also its ability to extract signal parameters such as the carrier frequency and the symbol rate [7].

4. Classifiers

4.1. Naïve Bayes

The naïve Bayes classifier is based on Bayes' theorem. This classifier is particularly useful when the input data dimensionality is high. Thus, to represent the classifier in the cognitive radio system, we adopt the nomenclature used in [6], where $P(y|\mathbf{x})$, $P(\mathbf{x}|y)$, $P(y)$ and $P(\mathbf{x})$ are called posterior, likelihood, prior and evidence, respectively, and are related through Bayes' rule,

$$P(y|\mathbf{x}) = \frac{P(\mathbf{x}|y)P(y)}{P(\mathbf{x})}. \tag{6}$$

This classifier attempts to select the label

$$\mathcal{F}(\mathbf{x}) = \arg \max_{y=1...,Y} P(\mathbf{x}|y)P(y), \tag{7}$$

which maximizes the posterior probability. However, neither $P(y)$ nor $P(\mathbf{x}|y)$ is known. Hence, the classifiers use estimates $\hat{P}(y)$ and $\hat{P}(\mathbf{x}|y)$ and maximize

$$\mathcal{F}(\mathbf{x}) = \arg \max_{y=1,...,Y} \hat{P}(\mathbf{x}|y)\hat{P}(y). \tag{8}$$

In most cases, the prior $P(y)$ can be reliably estimated by counting the labels in the training set, i.e., we assume that $\hat{P}(y) = P(y)$. In order to estimate $\hat{P}(\mathbf{x}|y)$ is often the most difficult task. Hence, Bayes classifiers typically assume a parametric distribution $\hat{P}(\mathbf{x}|y) = \hat{P}_{\theta_y}(\mathbf{x}|y)$ where θ_y describes the distribution's parameters to be determined (e.g., the mean and covariance matrix if the likelihood model is a Gaussian distribution).

The naïve Bayes algorithm assumes that the attributes $(x_1, \ldots, x_K)$ of $\mathbf{x}$ are conditionally independent of each other, given y. It means that the algorithm simplifies the representation of $P(\mathbf{x}|y)$, and the estimation problem from the training set. Whereas. In the case where $\mathbf{x} = (x_1, x_2)$, we have:

$$P(\mathbf{x}|y) = P(x_1, x_2|y) = P(x_1|x_2, y)P(x_2|y) = P(x_1|y)P(x_2|y) \tag{9}$$

where $P(x_1, x_2|y) = P(x_1|x_2, y)P(x_2|y)$ is a general property from conditional probability definition, while $P(x_1, x_2|y) = P(x_1|y)P(x_2|y)$ is only valid for conditional independence. Generalizing Equation 9, we have:

$$P(\mathbf{x}|y) = P(x_1, ..., x_K|y) = \prod_{i=1}^{K} P(x_i|y). \tag{10}$$

When training a naïve Bayes classifier, this will produce a probability distribution $P(\mathbf{x}_i|y)$ and $P(y)$ for all values of y, i.e, y_k, $k = 1, \ldots, Y$. To calculate the posterior probability of each class

y, we use Bayes' theorem:

$$p(y_k|\mathbf{x}) = \frac{P(y_k)P(x_1,\ldots,x_K|y_k)}{\sum_j P(y_j)P(z_1,\ldots,x_K|y_j)} \tag{11}$$

Assuming x_i is conditionally independent given y, we can rewrite Equation 10 as:

$$p(y_k|\mathbf{x}) = \frac{P(y_k)\prod_i P(x_i|y_k)}{\sum_j \left(P(y_j)\prod_i P(x_i|y_j)\right)}. \tag{12}$$

Equation 12 is the fundamental equation of a naïve Bayes classifier. Given a new sample $\mathbf{x}$, this equation shows how to calculate the probability for each y. Such calculation depends only on observed attribute values and distributions $P(y)$ and $P(x_i|y)$ estimated from the data training. If it is desired only to the most likely value of y, then we can simplify to

$$\mathcal{F}(\mathbf{x}) = \arg\max_{y_k} P(y_k)\prod_i P(x_i|y_k) \tag{13}$$

or, using the fact that the logarithm is a monotonic function:

$$\mathcal{F}(\mathbf{x}) = \arg\max_{y_k} \left[\log P(y_k) + \sum_i \log P(x_i|y_k)\right]. \tag{14}$$

4.2. Decision tree

A decision tree is a model of predictive machine learning which performs the decision of a new instance based on the value of its various attributes [23]. It consists of a structure where leaf nodes represent tests of one or more attributes. The branches of these nodes are the possible values of these attributes. The terminal nodes are the result of classification. In order to perform the classification of a new instance, a decision tree is created based on the values of the attributes of the training set. This chapter uses the decision tree implemented in the Weka software, called J4.8, which is an implementation of the C4.5 algorithm, which was developed by J. Quinlan [17] and probably the most famous algorithm for the design of decision trees.

A decision tree is formed by a set of classification rules. Each path from the root to a leaf represents one of these rules. The decision tree should be set so that for each observation in the database, there is only one path from root to leaf. Classification rules are composed of an antecedent (precondition) and a consequent (conclusion). An antecedent should be formed by one or more predictive attributes, while the consequent defines the class or classes.

A key issue for building a decision tree is the strategy for the choice of features that can determine the class to which a *sample* belongs. Measures based on entropy are commonly used to address this problem, which measures the randomness of the value of a feature before deciding which feature to use to predict the class.

Decision trees are methods that use a recursive algorithm for successive divisions in a training set. The main problem is then the reliability of estimates of the error used to select the divisions. Despite the fact that estimate obtained with the training data used during the growth of the tree known as "resubstitution error" continues to decrease, generally, the choices of the division in higher levels of the tree does not produce very reliable statistics. Therefore, the quality of the sample directly influences the accuracy of the estimates of the error. Since each iteration of the algorithm divides the set of training data, the internal nodes make decisions from ever smaller samples. This means that the error estimates are less reliable as the tree grows. Thus, *pruning methods* have been used to minimize this problem and avoid *overfitting* [6, 23].

Basically, there are two classes of methods in pruning a decision tree: a post-pruning and pre-pruning. In this chapter the *post-prune* method is used, which consists in allowing the tree to grow to a maximum size, i.e., until the leaf nodes that have minimal impurity, for subsequent application of the pruning.

4.3. SVM classifier

A support vector machine (SVM) is a class of learning algorithms based on statistical learning theory, which implements the principle of structural risk minimization [21]. The goal of an SVM classifier is to find a maximum margin hyperplane in a feature space. A hyperplane function is to be a decision surface such that the margin of separation between examples of one class and another is at a maximum [5].

More specifically, a SVM is a binary classifier given by

$$f(\mathbf{x}) = \sum_{m=1}^{M} \alpha_m \mathcal{K}(\mathbf{x}, \mathbf{x}_m) + c,$$

where $\mathcal{K}(\mathbf{x}, \mathbf{x}_m)$ is the kernel function between the test vector $\mathbf{x}$ and the m-th training example $\mathbf{x}_m$, with $c, \alpha_m \in \Re$. The effectively used examples have $\alpha_m \neq 0$ and are called *support vectors*. In the literature, several possibilities of kernels are presented in applications involving pattern recognition, such as linear, Gaussian, polynomial, sigmoid and radial basis functions.

A SVM with a linear kernel $\mathcal{K}(\mathbf{x}, \mathbf{x}_m) = \langle \mathbf{x}, \mathbf{x}_m \rangle$ given by the inner product between $\mathbf{x}$ and $\mathbf{x}_m$ can be converted to a perceptron $f(\mathbf{x}) = \langle \mathbf{a}, \mathbf{x} \rangle + c$, where $\mathbf{a} = \sum_{m=1}^{M} \alpha_m \mathbf{x}_m$ is pre-computed.

Therefore, linear SVMs were adopted in this chapter due to their lower computational cost when compared to non-linear SVMs with kernels such as the Gaussian [5]. To combine the binary SVMs $f_b(\mathbf{x}), b = 1, \ldots, B$, to obtain $F(\mathbf{x})$ this work adopted the *all-pairs* error-correcting output code (ECOC) matrix with Hamming decoding [3], where the winner class is the one with the majority of "votes". Note that an alternative to all-pairs, which uses $B = 0.5C(C-1)$ SVMs, is the one-vs-all ECOC that uses $B = C$ SVMs [12].

4.4. Artificial neural networks

Artificial neural networks (ANN) are parallel distributed systems composed of simple processing units called *neurons* that compute some mathematical function, usually nonlinear. Such units are arranged in one or more layers and interconnected by so-called synaptic weights. The intelligent behavior of ANN comes from the interactions between the processing units of the network.

A neuron consists of a sum of weights and inputs, and an activation function. The weight of the connections are set by a rule of training, according to the patterns presented. In this chapter, a neural network was used called multilayer perceptrons with the backpropagation algorithm for training, which has shown good results in classification problems.

The algorithm multilayer perceptron backpropagation (also called the generalized Delta Rule) consists in a process of supervised learning using a predetermined set of pairs of input and output to adjust the weights in the network using an error correction scheme held in propagation cycles [6, 9]. The backpropagation is divided into two phases: the *first step* is forward the input vector from the first through the last layer and to compare the output value to the desired value. The *second phase* consists of backwarding the error based on the last layer through the input layer by adjusting the weights of the neurons of the hidden layers. After adjusting all the weights of network, is given one more set of examples is given, ending a epoch. This process is repeated until the error is acceptable for the training set, referred to as the convergence time of the network.

The performance of a multilayer perceptron neural network during training depends on the following parameters [9]:

- *Initialization of weights.* The weights of the connections between neurons can be initialized randomly or uniformly.
- *Learning rate.* The learning rate controls the speed of learning, increasing or decreasing the set of weights performed at each iteration during training. Intuitively, its value must be greater than 0 and less than 1. If the learning rate is too small, learning will take place very slowly. Where the rate is very large (greater than 1), the correction would be greater than the observed error, causing the neural network learning point exceeding its greatest value, making the training process unstable.
- *Transfer function parametrization.* Also known as threshold logic, this function is the one which defines and sends out the value passed by the neuron activation function. The activation function can take many forms and methods. The best known are the following: linear function, sigmoid function and exponential function.

4.5. KNN

The classifiers that simply store the training data are called "lazy" classifiers, or known as IBL (instance based learning) [23]. The k-nearest neighbor (KNN) is a method of this family and stores examples in memory as points in n-dimensional space defined by n attributes that describe the examples [6]. Thus, for each new example to classify, KNN uses the training data to determine the examples in the database that are "nearest" to the example in the analysis. With each new example to be classified, a sweep in the training data, is made, which causes a large computational effort.

Suppose a training set with N examples. Let $\mathbf{x} = (x_1, \ldots, x_k)$ be a new example, not yet classified. In order to classify it, calculate distances by a measure of similarity between $\mathbf{x}$ and all examples in the training set and consider the K closest examples (with the lowest distance) for $\mathbf{x}$. The example $\mathbf{x}$ is classified according to the most frequent class y among the K examples found.

The distance between two examples is calculated by a measure of similarity. A popular measure of similarity is the Euclidian distance [6]. This measure calculates the square root of the sum of the squares of the differences between the vectors $\mathbf{x}$ and $\hat{\mathbf{x}}$:

$$d(\mathbf{x}, \hat{\mathbf{x}}) = \sqrt{\sum_{i=1}^{K} (x_i - \hat{x}_i)^2} \tag{15}$$

This chapter uses the Euclidean distance. Based on this metric, the KNN searches the "nearest neighbors" to classify new examples.

5. Results

The simulations aim to evaluate the reliability of cyclostationarity technique for feature extraction and and to compare the performance of data mining techniques like naïve bayes, decision tree, KNN, SVM and ANN, under various conditions. The signals were modulated using AM, BPSK, QPSK, BFSK and 16-QAM modulations. The signals were propagated through two types of channel models: AWGN channel and an AWGN and multipath fading channel. The signal-to-noise ratio (SNR) was varied randomly from -10 to 10 dB as part of the simulation. In both channel models, carrier frequency $f_c = 2.4$ GHz, sampling period T_s= 0.167 ns, square-root raised cosine with roll-off factor $r = 0.1$, number of symbols $Nsymbol = 100$, FFT points $Nfft = 512$ was used.

In order to implementation of the classifiers we used the WEKA software [22], which is a collection of machine learning algorithms for data mining tasks. Weka is open source software issued under the General Public License. We adopted the following settings for the classifiers:

- **Naïve Bayes**: The naïve Bayes used a normal distribution for numeric attributes, and the parameter K (*UseKernelEstimator*) set to False, which corresponds to the standard naive Bayes.

- **KNN**: In the configuration we adopted the KNN search algorithm of neighbors based on Euclidean distance.

- **J4.8**: The J4.8 has been configured with automatic selection for the confidence factor parameter C. Thus, the results presented represent the best result achieved for confidence factor values which varied between [0.1, 0.25 and 0.5];

- **SVM**: The SVM has been configured with linear kernel (K = 0), with the cost parameter C ranging from [2, 1, 0.5 and 0.25] and degree of the kernel D = 3.

- **ANN**: We adopted a neural network multilayer perceptron with learning algorithm backpropagation, the number of neurons in the hidden layer ranging from [60, 110, 130 and 160] neurons, learning rate ranging between a rate of [0.1, 0.5 and 0.9], and time varying between [0.1, 0.2 and 0.4].

5.1. Sample complexity

The first experiment aimed to analyze the accuracy of classifiers with the variation in the number of samples used in the training phase. This analysis was performed using the sample complexity curves [8].

The sample complexity curve aims to determine how many samples are required for the classifier to achieve a certain level of performance. The abscissa represents the number of samples in the training set and the ordinate represents the percentage of correct classifications obtained in the test phase. It should be noted that only the number of samples of the training set varies, while the number of samples in the test phase remains fixed.

The classifiers were trained with different numbers of samples, varying between [50, 150, 300, 450, 750 and 1000] samples of each modulation. In the test phase, 1000 samples were used for each modulation. Figure 3 through Figure 6 show the results obtained for a multipath fading channel, configured with Doppler frequency FD = 50 Hz and AWGN.

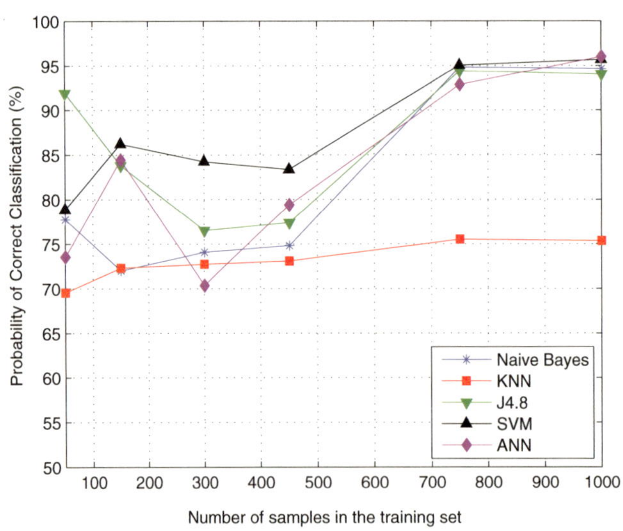

Figure 3. Sample complexity for SNR = -10 dB.

Through an analysis of sample complexity curves, it was decided to work with 750 training samples of each modulation, since this number had a good performance for the different classifiers which were evaluated.

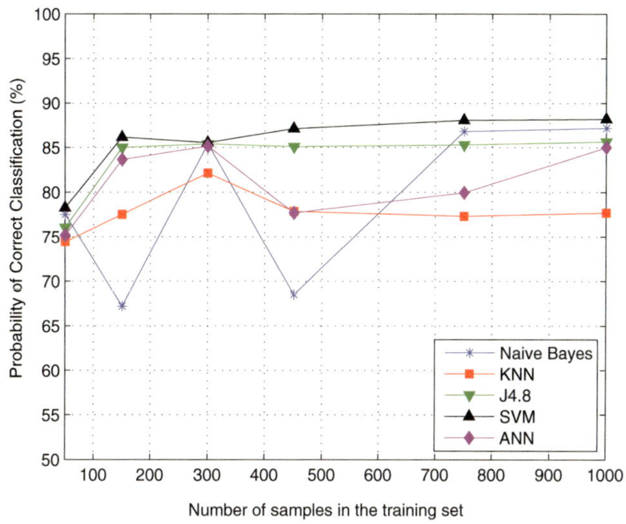

Figure 4. Sample complexity for SNR = -5 dB.

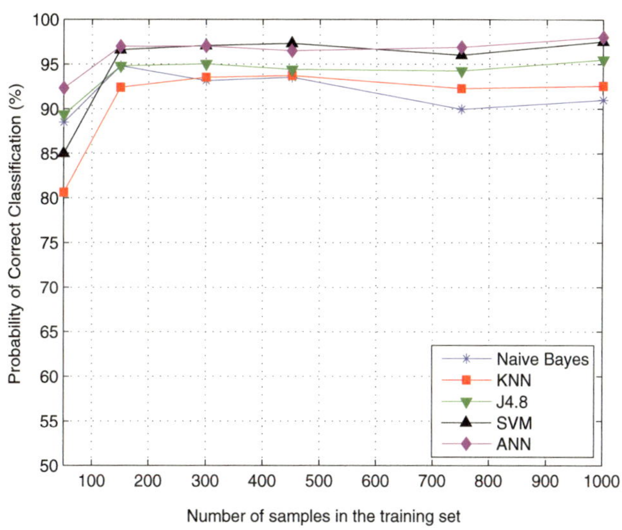

Figure 5. Sample complexity for SNR = 5 dB.

5.2. Simulation result of AWGN channel

In this scenario, the SNR is varied from a range of -15 to 15 dB range. The training, testing and validation sets were composed of 750 different samples of each modulation. The classifiers were trained and tested with the same values of SNR. Figure 7 shows the results for the classification of AM, BPSK, QPSK and BFSK modulations.

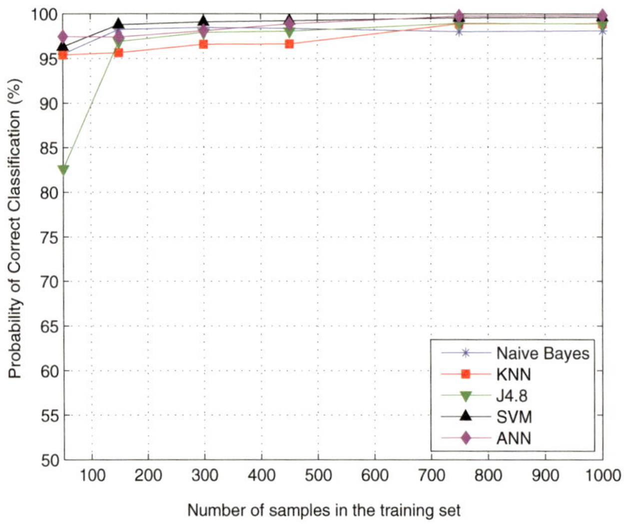

Figure 6. Sample complexity for SNR = 10 dB.

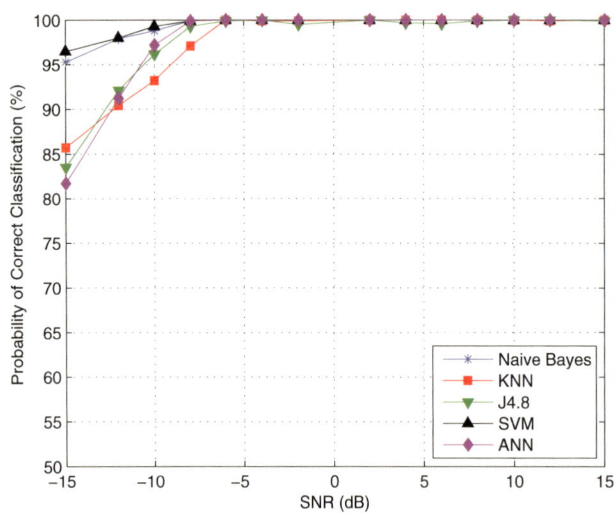

Figure 7. Performance of classifiers in a AWGN channel.

The results show that for SNR values greater than -5 dB, all classifiers presented excellent performance with nearly 100% correct classification. Among the evaluated classifiers, the SVM had a higher percentage of correct classification, even for SNR values lower than -5 dB.

Table 2 allows the analysis of the performance of classifiers in the worst case, i.e., SNR = -15 dB. The results show that the greater number of errors occurs in the classification of QPSK and BPSK modulations, mainly by KNN (with 14.3 % errors) and decision tree J4.8 (16.5 % errors) classifiers.

Modulations	N. Bayes	J4.8	KNN	SVM	ANN
AM	100	100	100	100	100
BPSK	90.0	67.6	85.2	92.8	79.2
QPSK	91.2	67.2	58.0	93.2	47.6
BFSK	100	99.2	99.6	100	100

Table 2. Performance of classifiers in SNR = -15 dB.

Table 3 shows the confusion matrix of the J4.8 classifier considering a SNR = -15 dB. It is observed that at low SNR, the classification error occurs to distinguish the QPSK and BPSK modulation, due to distortions in their features. Figure 8 shows the profiles of the BPSK and QPSK modulations in SNR = -15 dB and 15 dB.

Classifier as ->	AM	BPSK	QPSK	BFSK
AM	750	0	0	0
BPSK	3	507	237	3
QPSK	3	243	504	0
BFSK	6	0	0	744

Table 3. Confusion matrix of the J4.8 classifier, SNR = -15 dB.

In order to analyze the degree of generalization of the classifiers, two experiments were realized. In the first, the number of samples in training set was fixed at 750 samples for each modulation with SNR = 5 dB. The number of samples in the test set was varied with SNR values from -15 to 15 dB. The goal was to evaluate the performance of classifiers when tested with SNR values for which they were not trained. The results are shown in Figure 9. It is observed that SVM and ANN presented the best performance, which can be seen, for example, comparing the performance of classifiers in SNR = -5 dB.

The second experiment was to train classifiers with SNR values from -15 to 15 dB. Then the classifiers were tested with specific values of SNR, which are indicated on the axis of abscissa in Figure 9.

In this experiment, the performance of the classifiers obtained a considerable increase. The ANN and SVM classifiers presented the best performance; on the other hand, the naïve Bayes classifier had the worst performance.

Classifiers	Correct class. (%)
Naïve Bayes	89.1
KNN	91.9
J4.8	92.7
SVM	97.5
ANN	100

Table 4. Performance of classifiers when trained and tested with different SNR values.

In the literature there are studies indicating that the classification of QAM using cyclostationarity is difficult due to the fact that high-order QAM modulations do not exhibit periodicity of 2nd order, or in some cases, exhibit similar characteristics of QPSK

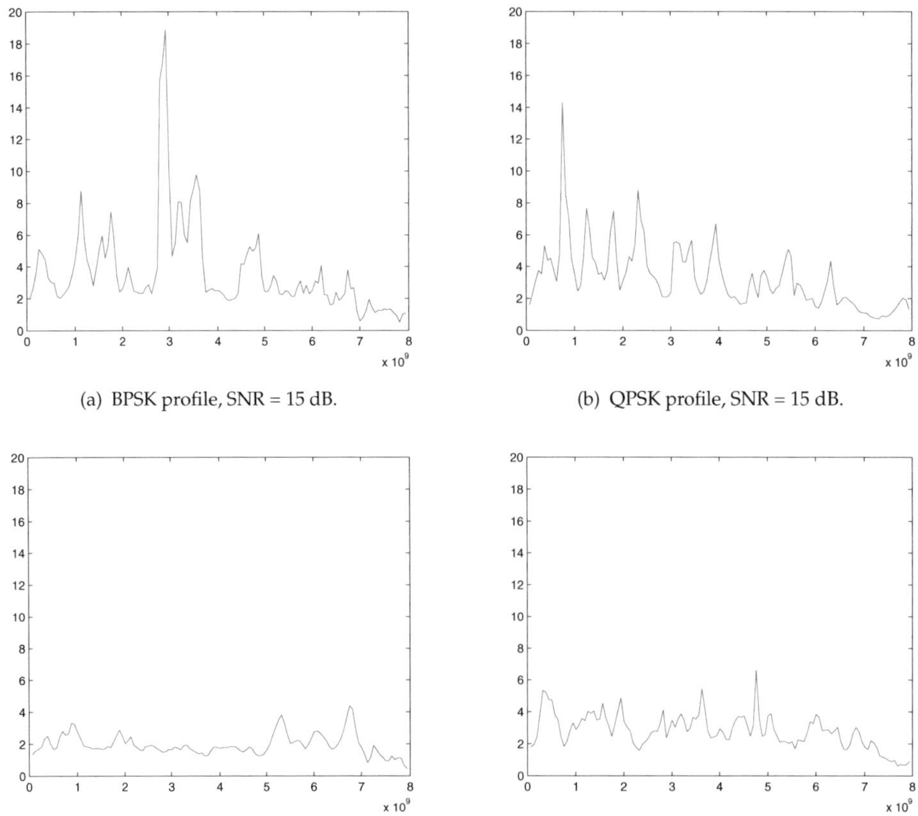

(a) BPSK profile, SNR = 15 dB.

(b) QPSK profile, SNR = 15 dB.

(c) BPSK profile, SNR = -15 dB.

(d) QPSK profile, SNR = -15 dB.

Figure 8. Profiles of the BPSK and QPSK modulations.

modulation [1]. The results that follow show the performance of classifiers to classify the 16-QAM modulation. Figure 10 allows comparison of the performance of classifiers when the 16-QAM modulation is included.

The results show that at low SNR, the performance of the classifiers decreases, when included the 16-QAM modulation. However, with increasing SNR, the performance of the classifiers is close to 100% of a correct classification.

In general, the SVM classifier obtained the best results, which can be justified by their robustness, due to its mathematical formulation based on the search of the optimal solution. The naïve Bayes, despite being a simplistic method, also performed well, better than some classifiers already recognized as an ANN and KNN.

6. Simulation result of a multipath rayleigh fading and AWGN channel

Figure 11 through Figure 13 show the results for SNR values from -15 to 15 dB and Doppler frequency FD = [50, 150 and 300] Hz. Modulations used were AM, BPSK, QPSK, BFSK and 16-QAM.

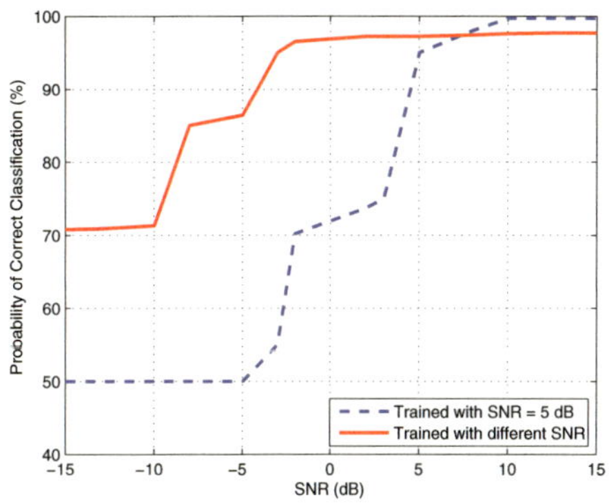

(a) Naïve Bayes

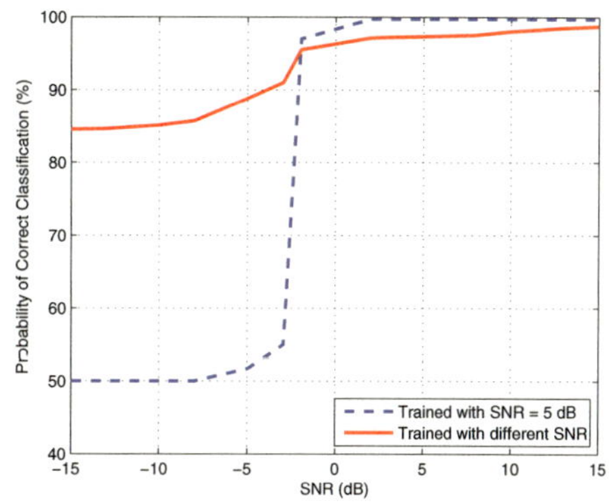

(b) KNN

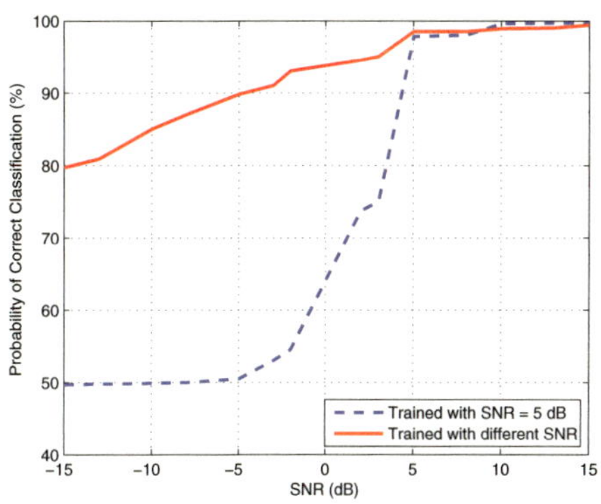

(c) Decision tree J4.8

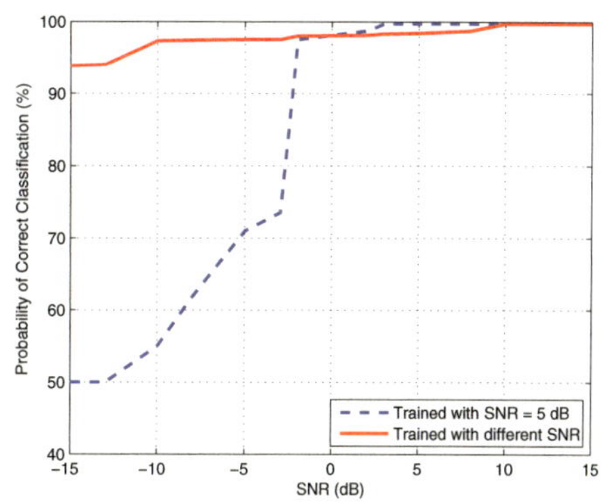

(d) SVM

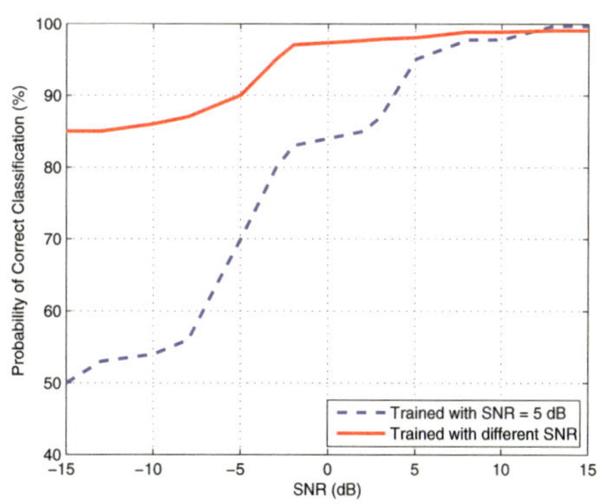

(e) ANN

Figure 9. Performance of classifiers when trained and tested with different SNR values. Abscissa indicates the SNR adopted for the test set.

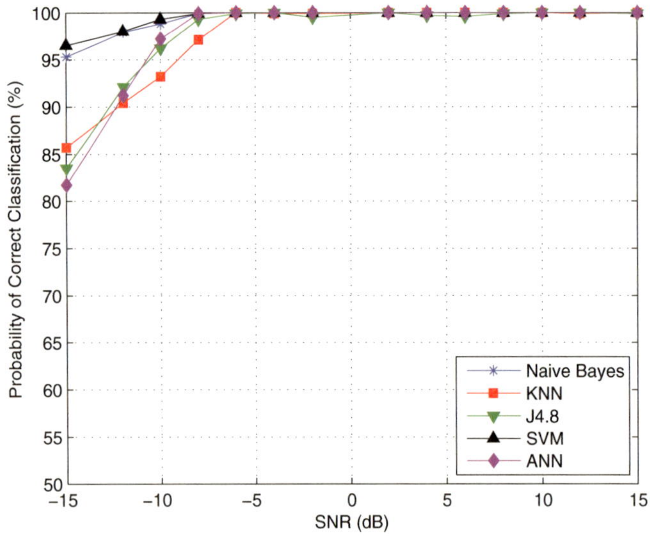

(a) Without the 16-QAM modulation.

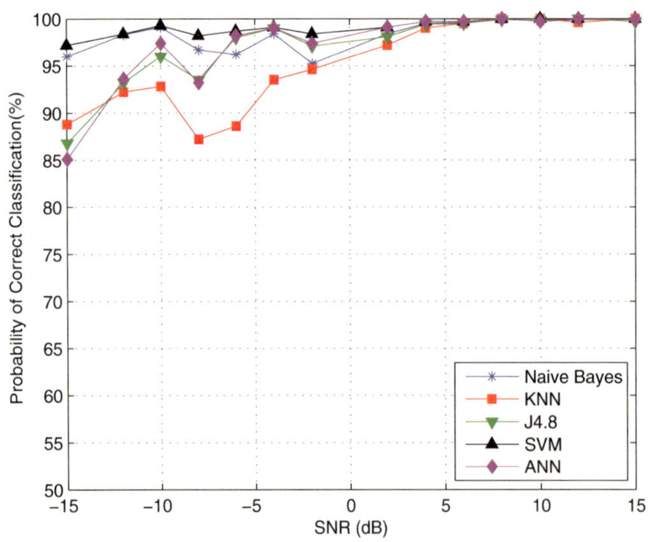

(b) With the 16-QAM modulation.

Figure 10. Performance of the classifiers for the classification of 16-QAM modulation.

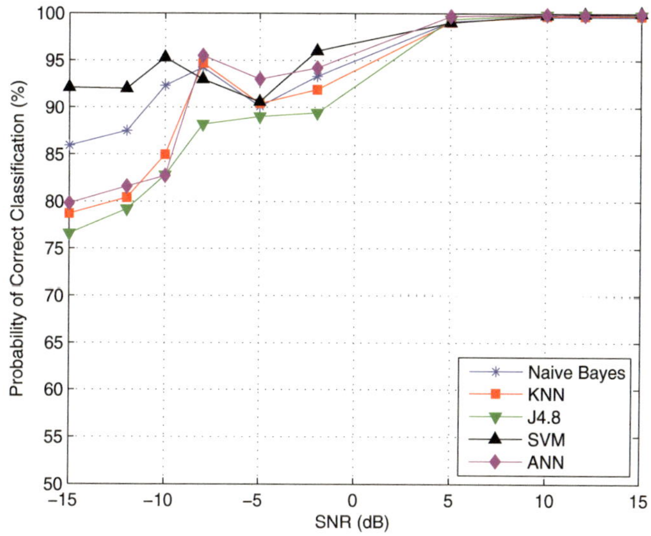

Figure 11. Performance of classifiers. Rayleigh fading channel, FD=50 Hz.

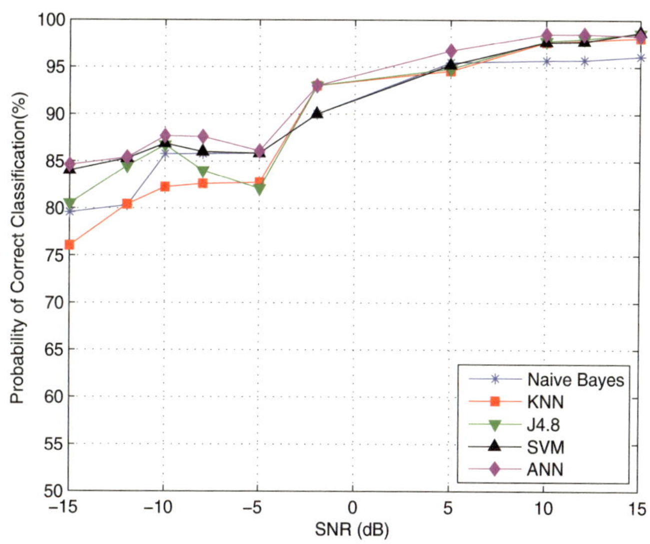

Figure 12. Performance of classifiers. Rayleigh fading channel, FD=150 Hz.

The results show that in general, all the classifiers had good performance. However, the decision tree KNN and J4.8 proved very susceptible to noise, especially for SNR values between -15 dB and 5 dB.

Furthermore, comparison between the Rayleigh and AWGN channels shows that there was a decrease in the performance of the classifiers. In the experiments, it was used a uniform procedure was used for selection of models of classifiers (i.e., not invested much in the tune

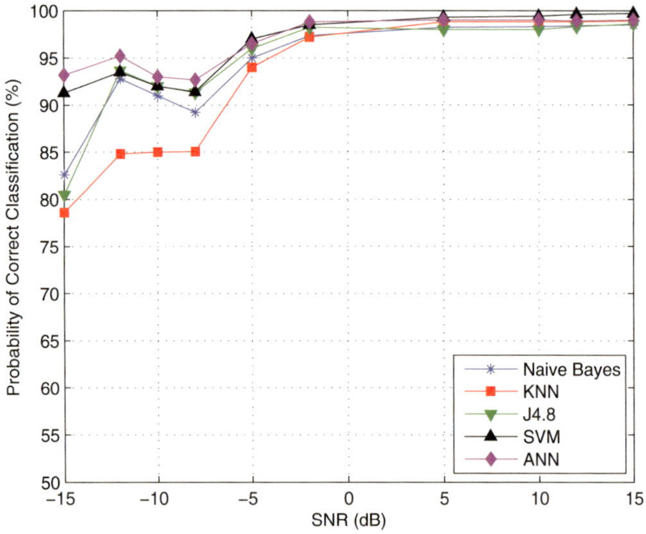

Figure 13. Performance of classifiers. Rayleigh fading channel, FD=300 Hz.

of a specific classifier). This may explain the variation in results for AWGN and multipath fading. A more detailed investigation about the parameters of classifiers such as SVM and ANN would probably improve the results.

7. Conclusions

This chapter discussed the task of modulation classification in cognitive radio. The modulation classification becomes fundamental, since this information allows the RC to adapt its transmission parameters for the spectrum to be shared efficiently, without causing interference to other users. A modulation classifier was implemented based on the characteristics of cyclostationarity of modulated signals. The performance of five data mining techniques were evaluated: naïve Bayes, decision tree J4.8, KNN, SVM, and ANN. In this evaluation, the signal classifications were performed to classifier AM, BPSK, BFSK, QPSK and 16-QAM modulations. An environment with multipath Rayleigh fading and AWGN was adopted.

Simulation results show that it is possible to classify the incoming signals, even at very low SNR, if the The cyclostationarity technique proved an effective technique for feature extraction, even in environments with low SNR. The SVM classifier with a linear kernel presented the best results, even in a fading multipath configuration.

The evaluation of algorithms for modulation classification proposed may serve as a starting point for researchers who want to compare results systematically.

Author details

Lilian C. Freitas and João Costa
Applied Electromagnetism Laboratory (LEA), Federal University of Pará (UFPA), Belém – PA – Brazil

Yomara Pires, Jefferson Morais and Aldebaro Klautau
Signal Processing Laboratory (LaPS), Federal University of Pará (UFPA), Belém – PA – Brazil

8. References

[1] A. Fehske, J. Gaeddert, J. R. [2005]. A new approach to signal classification using spectral correlation and neural networks, *DySPAN* pp. 144–150.

[2] Akyildiz, I., Lee, W., Vuran, M. C. & Mohanty, S. [2006]. Next generation/dynamic spectrum access/cognitive radio wireless networks: A survey, *Computer Networks: The International Journal of Computer and Telecommunications Networking* 50: 2127–2159.

[3] Allwein, E., Schapire, R. & Singer, Y. [2000]. Reducing multiclass to binary: A unifying approach for margin classifiers, *Journal of Machine Learning Research* pp. 113–141.

[4] D. Shimbo; I. Oka; S. Ata; [2007]. An improved algorithm of modulation classification for digital communication signals based on wavelet transform, *Radio and Wireless Symposium, 2007 IEEE* 03: 567–570.

[5] Cristianini & Shawe-Taylor, J. [2000]. *An introduction to support vector machines and other kernel-based learning methods*, Cambridge University Press.

[6] Duda, R., Hart, P. & Stork, D. [2001]. *Pattern classification*, Wiley.

[7] Gardner, W. A. & Spooner, C. M. [1992]. Signal interception: Performance advantages of cyclic-feature detectors, *IEEE Transactions on Communications* 40: 149–159.

[8] Hastie, T., Tibshirani, R. & Friedman, J. [2001]. *The elements of statistical learning*, Springer Verlag.

[9] Haykin, S. [2001]. *Redes Neurais: Principios e Prática. 2. Ed.*, Porto Alegre: Bookman.

[10] Haykin, S., Thomson, D. & Reed, J. [2009]. Spectrum sensing for cognitive radio, *Proceedings of the IEEE* 97: 849–877.

[11] Kadambe, S. & Jiang, Q. [2004]. Classification of modulation of signals of interest, *Digital Signal Processing Workshop, 2004 and the 3rd IEEE Signal Processing Education Workshop. 2004 IEEE 11th* pp. 226–230.

[12] Klautau, A., Jevtić, N. & Orlitsky, A. [2003]. On nearest-neighbor ECOC with application to all-pairs multiclass SVM, *J. Machine Learning Research* 4: 1–15.

[13] Lynn, T. J. & Sha'amerr, A. [2007]. Automatic analysis and classification of digital modulation signals using spectogram time frequency analysis, *International Symposium on Communications and Information Technologies, 2007. ISCIT '07.* pp. 916–920.

[14] Mitola, J. & Maguire, G. Q. [1999]. Cognitive radio: making software radios more personal, *Personal Communications, IEEE* 6(4): 13–18.
URL: *http://dx.doi.org/10.1109/98.788210*

[15] Muller, F., Cardoso, C. & Klautau, A. [2011]. A front end for discriminative learning in automatic modulation classification, *Communications Letters, IEEE* 15(4): 443 –445.

[16] Popoola, J. & van Olst, R. [2011]. A novel modulation-sensing method, *Vehicular Technology Magazine, IEEE* 6(3): 60 –69.

[17] Quinlan, J. [1993]. *C4.5: Programs for Machine Learning*, Morgan Kaufmann.

[18] Ramkumar, B. [2009]. Automatic modulation classification for cognitive radios using cyclic feature detection, *Circuits and Systems Magazine, IEEE* 9(2): 27 –45.

[19] Shen, L., Li, S., Song, C. & Chen, F. [2006]. Automatic modulation classification of mpsk signals using high order cumulants, *8th International Conference on Signal Processing, 2006* 01.
[20] Si, L.-L. M. X.-J. [2007]. An improved algorithm of modulation classification for digital communication signals based on wavelet transform, *IEEE Transactions on Aerospace and Electronic Systems* 03: 1226–1231.
[21] Vapnik, V. [1995]. *The nature of statistical learning theory*, Springer Verlag.
[22] Weka [n.d.]. http://www.cs.waikato.ac.nz/ml/weka.
[23] Witten & Frank, E. [2005]. *Data mining: practical machine learning tools and techniques with java implementations*, Morgan Kaufmann.
[24] Xiaorong;, H. T. J. [2004]. Modulation classification using arbf networks, *7th International Conference on Signal Processing, ICSP 04.* 03: 1809 – 1812.

Chapter 10

Short-Term Energy Price Prediction Multi-Step-Ahead in the Brazilian Market Using Data Mining

José C. Reston Filho, Carolina de M. Affonso and Roberto Célio L. de Oliveira

Additional information is available at the end of the chapter

http://dx.doi.org/10.5772/48472

1. Introduction

The electricity price tend to be very volatile due to weather conditions, fuel price, economic growth and many others factors [1]. As a consequence, electricity markets participants face high risks in bilateral contracts and short-term market. With regard to short-term market, generators sell energy at variable pool prices while their fuel cost are fixed. Also, distributors supply energy to most of their costumers at an annual fixed tariff, but they have to purchase electricity at a variable pool price. Then, a reliable tool to forecast electricity price is absolutely crucial for risk management in energy markets.

Many papers have proposed hybrid models to energy price prediction. The benefit of the hybrid model is to combine strengths of the techniques providing a robust model capable of capturing the nonlinear nature of the complex time series, producing more accurate forecasts. Reference [2] provides a hybrid methodology that combines both ARIMA and Artificial Neural Network (ANN) models for predicting short-term electricity prices. In [3], a novel technique to forecast day-ahead electricity prices is presented based on Self-Organizing Map neural network (SOM) and Support Vector Machine (SVM) models. Reference [4] proposes a novel price forecasting method based on wavelet transform combined with ARIMA and GARCH model.

The major data mining functions that are developed in research communities include summarization, association, prediction and clustering. This work deals with the energy price prediction problem multi-step-ahead in the Brazilian market. The ARIMA model is used to predict the variables that affect the short-term energy price (exogenous input), instead of predicting the energy price directly as in [2]. The results obtained with the

INTECH
open science | open minds

© 2012 Filho et al., licensee InTech. This is an open access chapter distributed under the terms of the Creative Commons Attribution License (http://creativecommons.org/licenses/by/3.0), which permits unrestricted use, distribution, and reproduction in any medium, provided the original work is properly cited.

methodology proposed are compared with the traditional ARIMA techniques. The historical data are from January 2006 to December 2009.

Some papers have already proposed the use of exogenous input to predict the energy price [5,6]. However, no work has been reported so far with energy price prediction models for the Brazilian market. Regarding the Brazilian market, most of the papers deal with risk analysis, optimal contract portfolio, and load prediction [7,8,9,10]. The main contribution of this chapter lies in the application of energy price forecasting methodologies applied to the Brazilian market, which adopts the tight pool model with unique characteristics of energy price behavior.

Another contribution of this study is to consider price spikes in the data base, and treat them equally as the normal prices. A price that is much higher than the normal price is usually considered as price spike. Most energy price forecast methods remove price spikes as noise and deal only with the normal prices, or build two different prediction models separately for both normal prices and spikes [5,11,12].

The next sections of this chapter are organized as follows. Section 2 describes the main features and peculiarities of the Brazilian electricity market. The proposed methodology and important aspects of data-preparation are addressed in Section 3. Section 4 presents the results and Section 5 presents the main conclusions.

2. The Brazilian System

The Brazilian System system has an installed capacity of 91GW where 82% corresponds to hydro generation, 15.2% to thermal generation, 2.19% to nuclear power and only 0.64% corresponds to biomass and wind generation [13].

The hydro system is characterized by large reservoirs with multi-year regulation capacity, arranged in complex cascades over several river basins.

Brazil still has an undeveloped hydro potential of 145,000 MW. Then, it is expected that the system remains predominantly hydro in the future.

The country is fully interconnected by a 80,000 km meshed grid, with voltages levels from 230 kV to 765 kV ac, plus two 600 kV dc links connecting the binational Itaipu hydro power plant to the main grid.

The National System Operator (ONS) is responsible to operate, supervise and control power generation and transmission grid in the Brazilian system. The Electrical Energy Commercialization Chamber (CCEE) is the body responsible for energy market transactions, such bilateral and short-term market contracts.

The Brazilian National Interconnected System (SIN) has four geoelectric submarkets organized by regions: North, Northeast, South and Center-west/Southeast. These markets can import/export energy from/to each other.

2.1. Tight Pool model

In general, there are two types of power pool arrangements: loose pool and tight pool. In the loose pool model there is no common dispatch center and each company in the group has its own dispatch center. The generation dispatch is carried out through auctions where generators and demand agents bid for price and quantities. Then, agents are paid at the same price, the market-clearing price, defined by the equilibrium between supply and demand.

In a tight pool model the generation dispatch is centralized by an Independent System Operator (ISO) in order to maximize the energy production by the system as a whole. The Brazilian system adopts the tight pool model with the dispatch centralized by the ONS due to the predominance of the hydro generation. This model is adopted to make efficient use of hydroelectric reservoir. The water is stored during the "wet" years (favorable inflow energy) in order to increase energy production in the dry years, reducing the generation from thermal power plants.

In the Brazilian model, hydro plants are dispatched with basis on their expected opportunity costs ("water values") calculated by a multi-stage stochastic optimization model (Stochastic Dual Dynamic Programming - SDDP) considering several inflow scenarios with uncertainties [14].

The SDDP model minimizes the marginal price of the system operation considering the immediate benefit of using water in the reservoirs (immediate cost) and the future benefits of its storage (future cost), measured in terms of the economy expected by the use of fuel in thermal units [15]. Then, the spot price used in the short-term market is not calculated from the equilibrium between demand and supply, but from the Lagrange multipliers of the stochastic dispatch model instead.

2.2. Short-term spot market

Wholesale energy markets have a structure organized by a long term market (forward or bilateral contracts) and a spot market. In long term contracts sellers and buyers of energy negotiate freely the terms of volume, price and duration. A spot market represents the short term 24-hour look-ahead market condition in which prices and generation dispatch are defined.

Since generators and loads does not bid prices in the Brazilian market, the market settlement is an accounting procedure controlled by CCEE, given by the difference between the energy produced and the energy volumes registered in financial forward contracts.

Positive or negative differences are settled in the spot market through the spot price, which is named PLD (Settlement Price for the Differences). Figure 1 illustrates this commercialization process. The PLD price is determined by a stochastic optimization model and is limited by a minimum and maximum price. It is computed on a weekly basis for each load level (low, medium and high) in each submarket (North, Northeast, Center-west/Southeast and South).

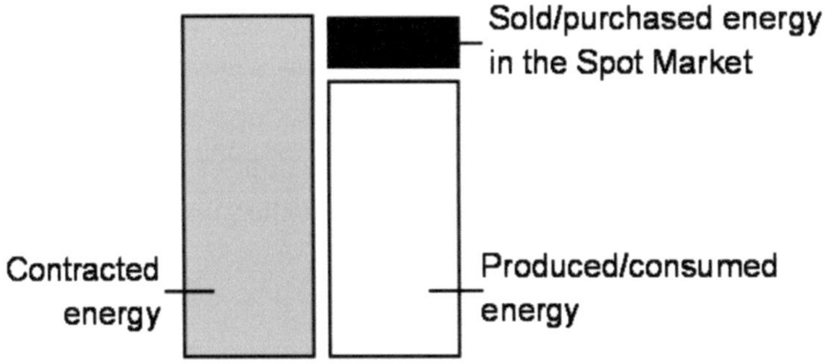

Figure 1. Commercialization process in the Spot Market [17].

2.3. Exogenous input

In general, forecasting loads and prices in the wholesale markets are mutually intertwined activities since the main variable that drives the price is the power demand [16]. For this reason, the demand has been the most commonly examined explanatory variable in price forecasting studies. However, the Brazilian market is a tight pool model with no price bids from producers and consumers. The Brazilian short-term energy price (PLD) is obtained from optimization models. Then the demand does not respond to energy price variations.

On the other side, the Brazilian short-term energy price is strongly dependent on the water level and inflow energy in reservoirs of the hydropower plants, since hydroelectric generation is predominant in Brazil. The result is that Brazilian short-term energy price is very volatile and dependent on the system's hydrological conditions.

Table 1 shows the exogenous input used in this study to forecast the short-term electricity price to the Brazilian market. These inputs are selected based on the methodology used by the Brazilian Independent System Operator. According to then, the most important variables involved in the computation of the PLD are variables related to hydrological conditions, system power load and fuel prices of thermal units [17].

Exogenous Input	Definition	Unit
HyGen	Total hydro generation	MWmed
TherGen	Total thermal generation	MWmed
Load	System power load	MWmed
StEn	Stored energy in reservoirs	% MLT*
InEn	Inflow energy in reservoirs	% MLT*

Table 1. Exogenous Input (*MLT: long-term average - historical average of 79 years)

Figure 2 shows linear correlation graphs of the input attributes from the proposed hybrid model to South region. It is possible to note that the variables do not exhibit a linear relation between them, which justifies its use in the prediction with hybrid model. The same behavior was observed to the other regions.

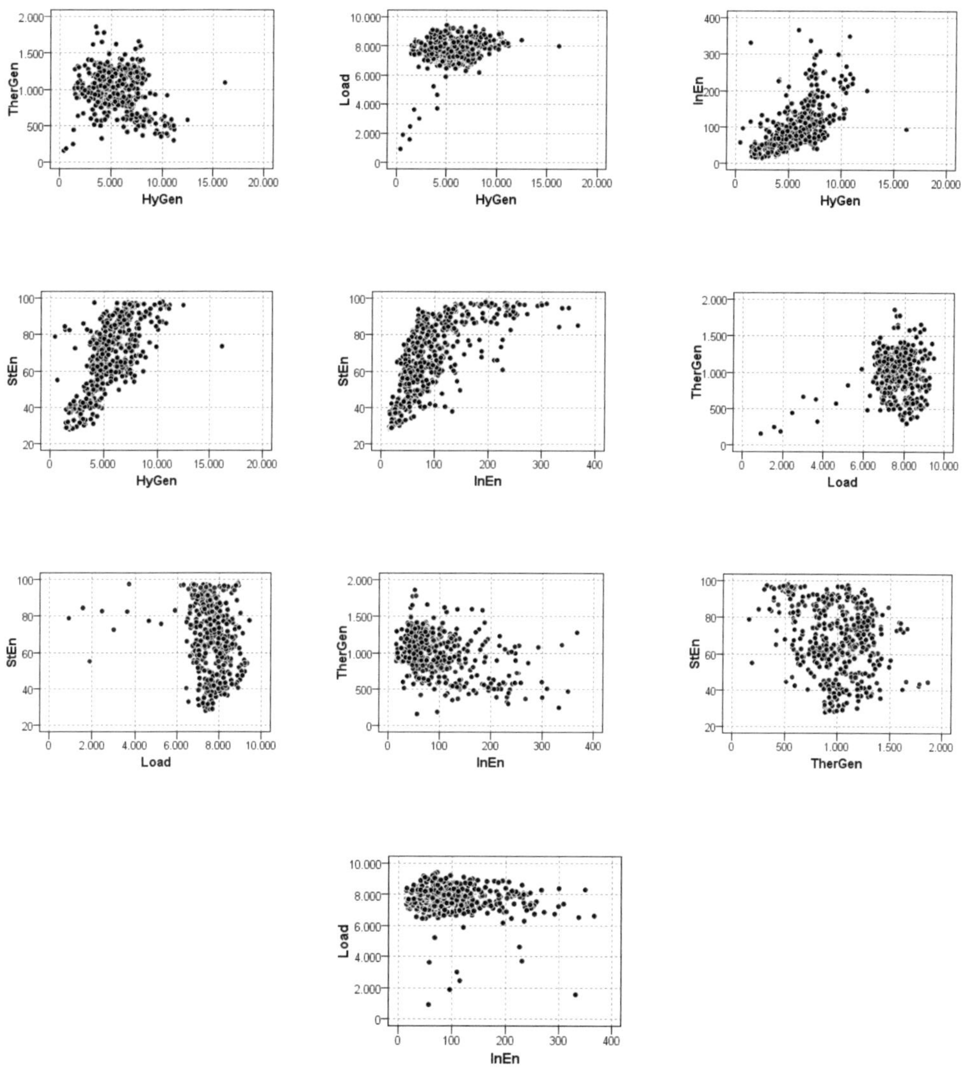

Figure 2. Linear correlation graphs of the input attributes from the proposed hybrid model to South region.

Figure 3 shows the behavior of PLD, storage energy and inflow energy from May 2006 through April 2007 to the Center-west/Southeast region.

This region is characterized by two distinct seasons: dry, which falls between May and November, and wet, which falls between December and April.

During the dry season the inflow energy is lower, and tends to increase during the wet season. Stored energy also presents this behavior with a delayed relationship. Also, PLD tends to be higher during the dry season due to the use of the thermal power plants.

The strong relationship between these variables reinforces the need to use then as exogenous input to forecast the short-term electricity price to the Brazilian market.

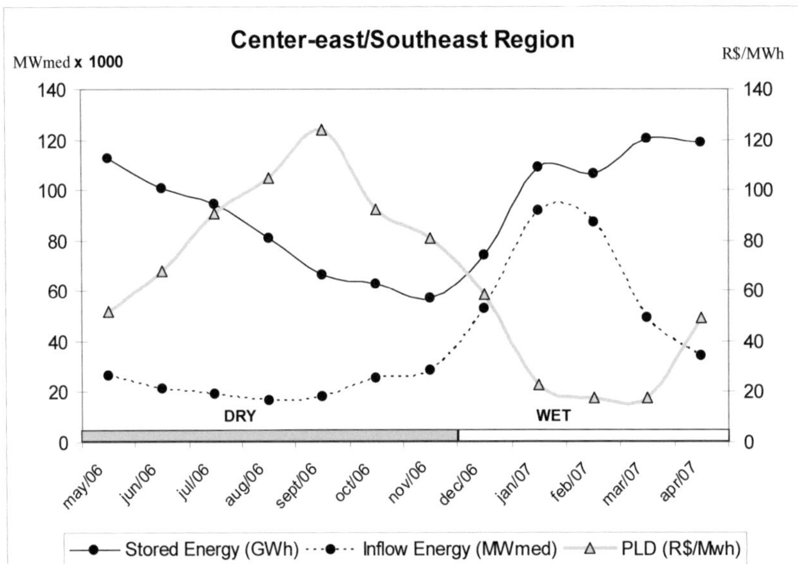

Figure 3. Relationship between PLD, stored energy and inflow energy.

3. Proposed hybrid model

The behavior of the short-term energy price may not be easily captured by stand-alone models since time series data may include a variety of characteristics such as seasonality and heteroskedasticity. A hybrid model having both linear and nonlinear modeling abilities could be a good alternative for predicting energy price data. Figure 4 shows the flowchart of the proposed hybrid model. The main steps of the algorithm are presented below and the details will be discussed next. This study uses the data mining software SPSS Clementine to develop and test the proposed methodology [18].

Step 1. Create a large data base composed by historical data of the short-term energy price and the attributes that affect the short-term energy pricing – exogenous input (U_i): stored energy, inflow energy, hydro generation, thermal generation and power load. These are the exogenous input.

Step 2. Forecast the linear relationship of the exogenous input (U_i) 12-steps-ahead (12 weeks ahead) with the ARIMA model.

Step 3. Apply PCA and Balacing in data preparation process to reduce the dimension of the input vectors and choose the better learning set before training the first ANN.

Step 4. Forecast the non-linear relationship from the exogenous input (U_i) 12-steps-ahead (12 weeks ahead) with the ANN model.

Step 5. Apply again the PCA and Balacing in data preparation process to the second ANN.

Step 6. Forecast the short-term energy price 12-steps-ahead (12 weeks ahead) with the ANN model.

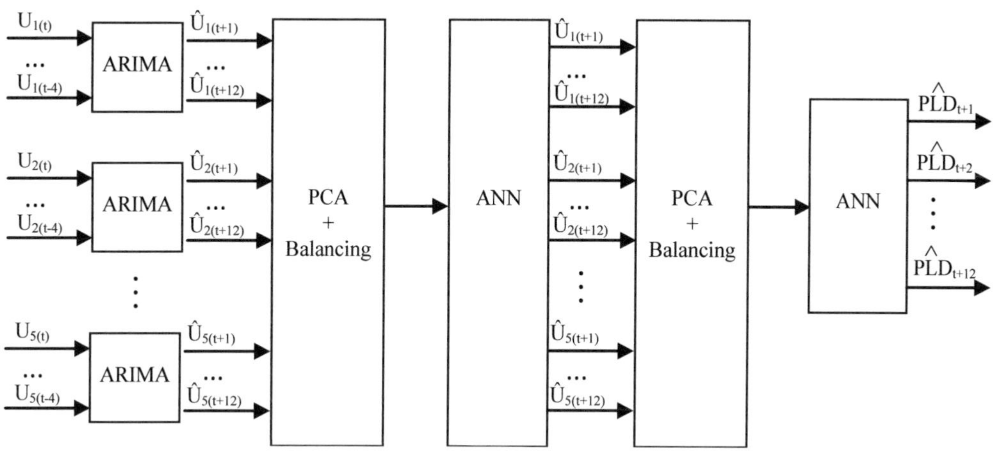

Figure 4. Flowchart of the proposed hybrid model.

3.1. Autoregressive Integrated Moving Average (ARIMA)

The ARIMA (autoregressive integrated moving average) model predicts a value in a response time series as a linear combination of its own past values, past errors, and current and past values of other time series [19].

An ARIMA model, usually referred as ARIMA (p,d,q), can be described by equation (1):

$$\phi P(q-p)\Delta dy(k) = \theta 0 + \theta q(q-q)V(k) \tag{1}$$

where p and q are the order of the parameters ϕ and θ respectively, $\theta 0$ is the model constant and the operator q-p delays the sample of p steps. Δd is the differencing operator given by:

$$D = 1 - q-1 \tag{2}$$

The ARIMA modeling approach involves the following four steps: model identification, parameter estimation, diagnostic checking and forecast future outcomes based on the known data. Identification of the general form of a model includes appropriate differencing of the series to achieve stationary and normality. Then, the temporal correlation structure of the transformed data is identified by examining its autocorrelation (ACF) and partial autocorrelation (PACF) functions [20].

The second step is the estimation, which can be done using an iterative procedure to minimize the prediction error, such as least square method [21].

The third step is the diagnostic checking to investigate the adequacy of the model. Tests for white noise residuals (uncorrelated and normally distributed around a zero mean) indicate whether the residual series contains additional information that might be utilized by a more complex model. The last step is forecast future outcomes based on the known data.

3.2. Artificial Neural Networks (ANN)

Neural networks are flexible computing frameworks for modeling a broad range of nonlinear problems [22]. It can be considered a black box that is able to predict an output pattern when it recognizes a given input pattern. ANN makes no prior assumptions concerning the data distribution. A neural network can be trained by the historical data of a time series in order to capture the characteristics of this time series. The model parameters (connection weights and node biases) will be adjusted iteratively by a process of minimizing the forecast errors. The algorithm used in this work is the Backpropagation algorithm and the ANN architecture is the multilayer perceptron (multilayer feed-forward network). This neural network is widely used and consists of an input layer, hidden layers and an output layer of neurons.

3.3. Data preparation

The historical data used to create the database are available on Brazilian Electrical Energy Commercialization Chamber website [17] and in the National System Operator website [13]. The exogenous input data were on a daily basis and the PLD data was on a weekly basis. Thus, all data was first standardized to a weekly basis, consuming a lot of effort. Then, a large database was constructed for each one of the four submarkets (North, Northeast, South and Center-west/Southeast) for the period from April 2001 to December 2009.

The variables used to create the database to each submarket are the PLD as the goal attribute, and the exogenous input as input variables (total hydro and thermal generation, system power load, stored energy and inflow energy in reservoirs). Figure 5 shows the time series data to the South region.

In data mining, the data set is usually cleaned before applying forecasting algorithms. It means that price spikes (outliers) are usually removed as noise to avoid very large forecasting errors introduced by the outliers. In this work, we chose not to eliminate any noise or discrepant samples. The decision was to create an estimation model also capable to map price spikes since they have significant impact on the electricity market. The idea is that the prediction model can be used in a risk analysis tool, where the exact value of the energy price is not as important as its rage of variation.

The Principal Component Analysis (PCA) technique is applied to reduce the dimension of the input vectors eliminating data highly correlated (redundant) [23]. In addition, analysis of rare events is performed since some pattern occurs less often than others. As an example, Figure 6 shows the histogram of the PLD series. Most price scenarios are very low and only a few are high. However, models built with neural networks algorithms are very sensitive to imbalanced data sets. Then, balancing data sets is necessary to equilibrate the bias in the learning process [24].

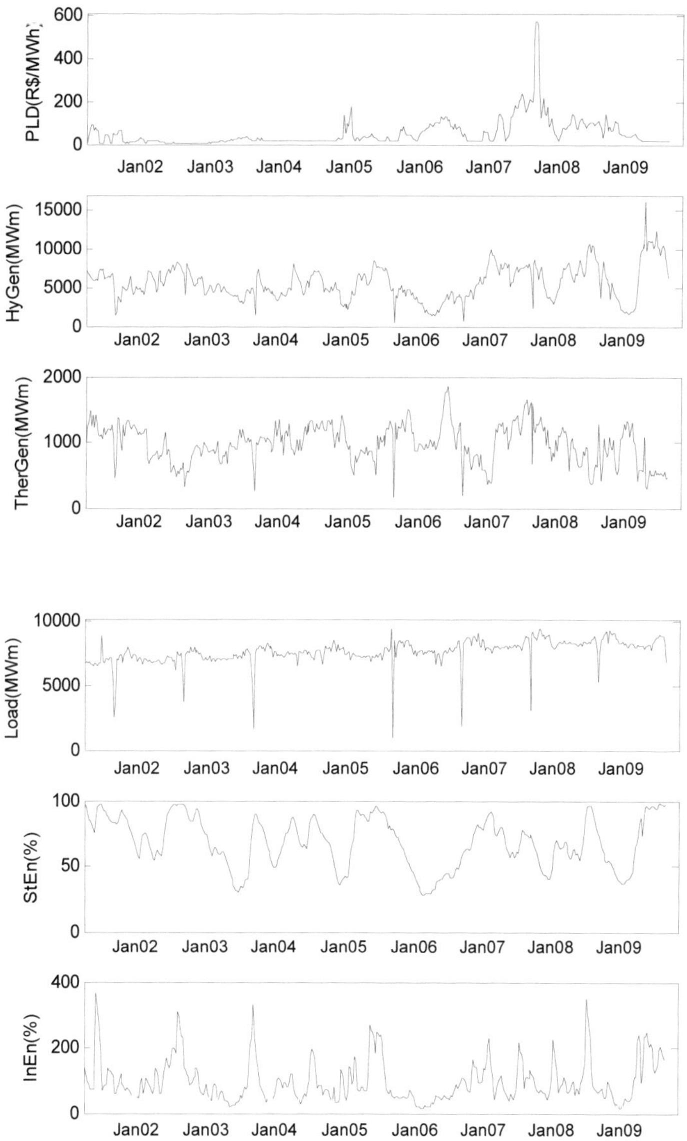

Figure 5. Time series data to South region.

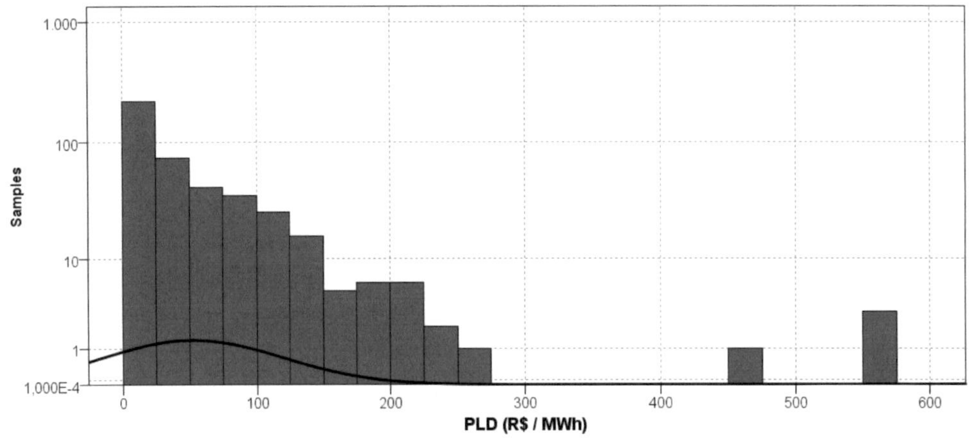

Figure 6. Histogram of the PLD series to South region.

4. Results

The proposed hybrid model was applied to the Brazilian electricity market. Several tests were made to identify the neural network architecture that produces best generalization accuracy for each attribute (short-term energy price PLD, hydro generation, thermal generation, power load, stored energy and inflow energy in reservoirs) varying the number of hidden layers and number of neurons. Best results were obtained with the ANN configuration presented in Table 2, using hyper tangent function in all layers. The same architecture is used to predict the PLD to all regions (North, Northeast, South and Center-west/Southeast). The data set is divided considering the training set with 80% of the data and the test set with the remaining 20% of the data.

Layers	Number of Neurons
Input layer	5
Hidden layer 1	20
Hidden layer 2	15
Hidden layer 3	10
Output layer	1

Table 2. Artificial Neural Networks Architecture.

The results are compared with the ARIMA traditional techniques. Some accuracy measures commonly used are employed in this study to analyze the results: the mean square error (MSE), standard deviation and linear correlation. Table 3 gives a statistical comparison of the short-term energy price prediction obtained from the ARIMA and the hybrid model for each region with both training and test set. The hybrid model provides better results for both training and test set, with lower error, lower standard deviation and higher linear correlation.

North region		
	ARIMA	**Hybrid**
Mean Square Error	18.78	10.589
Standard Deviation	22.37	15.719
Linear Correlation	0.894	0.987
Northeast region		
	ARIMA	**Hybrid**
Mean Square Error	13.12	10.587
Standard Deviation	23.39	21.231
Linear Correlation	0.915	0.964
Center-west / Southeast region		
	ARIMA	**Hybrid**
Mean Square Error	11.33	8.292
Standard Deviation	22.65	11.305
Linear Correlation	0.942	0.995
South region		
	ARIMA	**Hybrid**
Mean Square Error	13.308	11.048
Standard Deviation	26.489	14.754
Linear Correlation	0.935	0.98

Table 3. Performance of the proposed hybrid model.

Figure 7 shows the absolute error obtained for the ARIMA model and the hybrid model to regions North, Northeast, Center-west/Southeast and South. The hybrid model presented superior results. It is important to mention that better results were obtained applying the proposed methodology to predict energy prices with less steps-ahead. However, for practical issues related to the Brazilian market design, which has unique features, the prediction to 12-steps ahead (12 weeks) is more suitable to risk management practices.

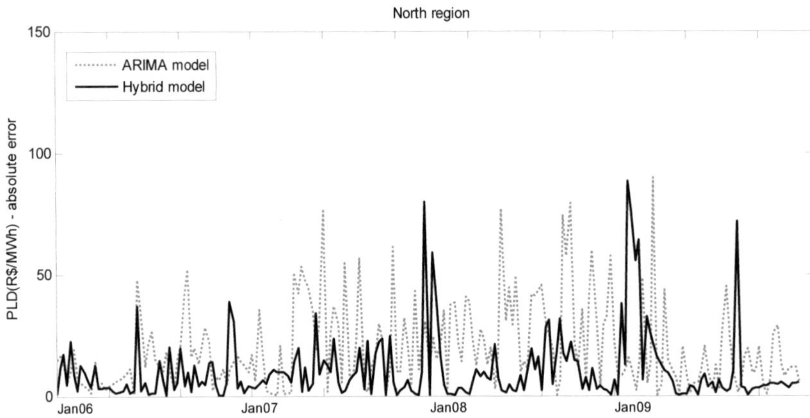
North region
150
100
50
0
ARIMA model
Hybrid model
PLD(R$/MWh) - absolute error
Jan06
Jan07
Jan08
Jan09

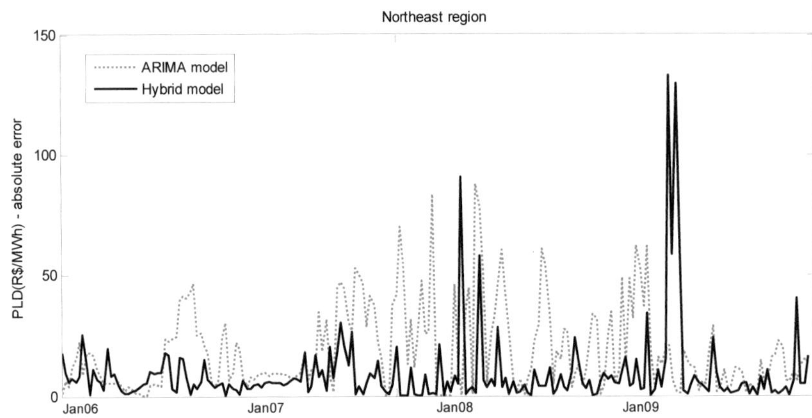
Northeast region
150
100
50
0
ARIMA model
Hybrid model
PLD(R$/MWh) - absolute error
Jan06
Jan07
Jan08
Jan09

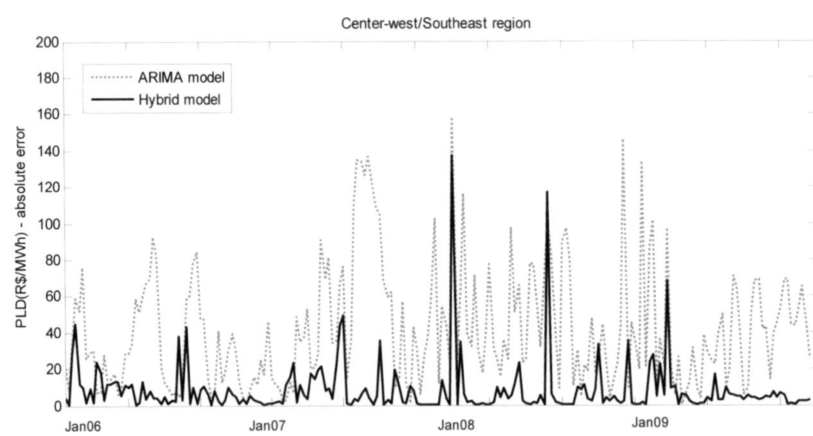
Center-west/Southeast region
200
180
160
140
120
100
80
60
40
20
0
ARIMA model
Hybrid model
PLD(R$/MWh) - absolute error
Jan06
Jan07
Jan08
Jan09

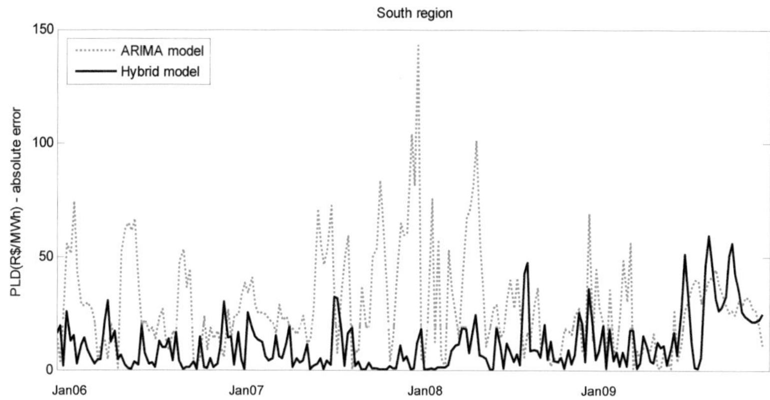

Figure 7. Absolute error obtained for ARIMA and Hybrid model.

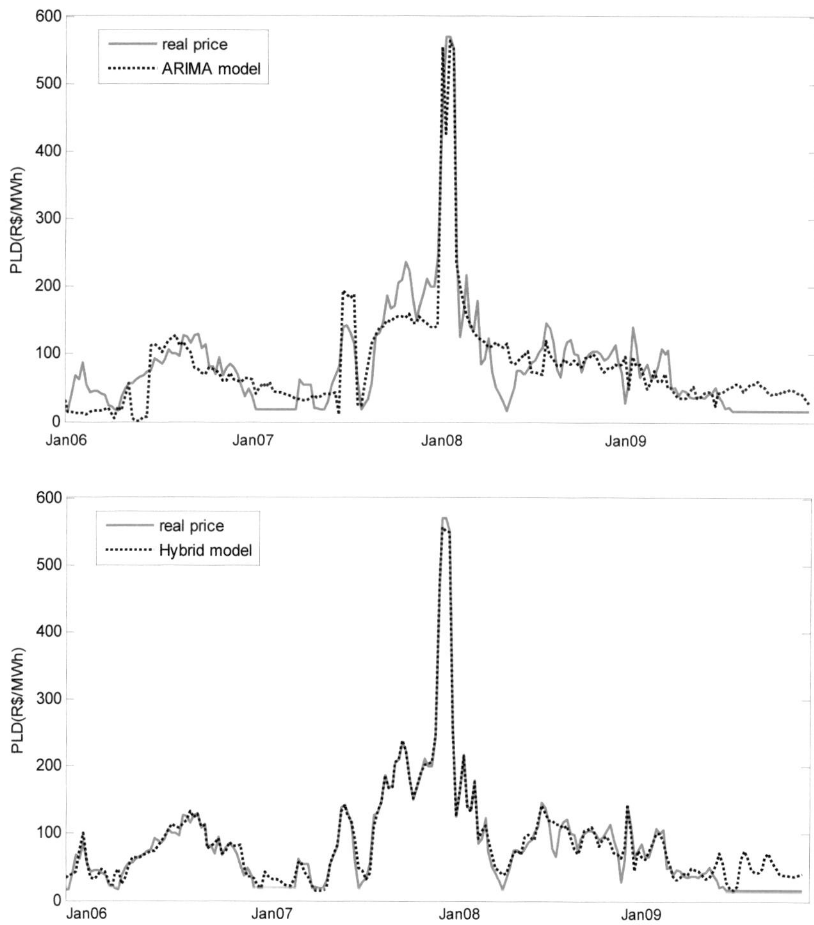

Figure 8. Short-term energy price observed and predicted by the ARIMA and hybrid model to South region.

Figure 8 shows the observed and predicted short-term energy price (PLD) obtained from the ARIMA and hybrid model to South region. The results show that the hybrid model produces better predictions than the ARIMA model. Also, the proposed hybrid model has a strong ability of predicting spikes. Note that this accuracy is obtained with serious insufficient data containing spikes, and spikes are caused by many stochastic events that cannot be entirely considered in the model. Furthermore, the price prediction is being made to 12-steps ahead (12 weeks), which represents a considerable time. For these reasons, we can say that the results are sufficiently good.

5. Conclusions

In this chapter, a hybrid model combining ARIMA and ANN with exogenous input is proposed for short-term energy price prediction in the Brazilian market. The ARIMA model is used to predict the variables that affect the short-term energy price (exogenous input), instead of predicting the energy price directly. This methodology is encouraged by the way energy price is computed in the Brazilian market by National System Operator. The exogenous input are: stored energy, inflow energy, hydro generation, thermal generation and power load. These are the most important attributes involved in the computation of the short-run marginal cost.

After the time series of the exogenous input are predicted, a second ANN is used to forecast the energy price multi-step ahead (12-weeks-ahead). In order to guarantee ANN generalization capacity, a data preparation process is first applied, which includes Principal Component Analysis (PCA) and balancing (analysis of rare patterns of occurrences). Software SPSS Clementine was used to develop and test the proposed methodology. The results obtained with the proposed methodology are compared with the ARIMA traditional techniques.

The results show that the proposed hybrid method performs the short-term electricity price prediction 12- steps ahead with high accuracy. This work provides a valuable contribution for price forecasting in the Brazilian market that can help market participants in their risk management practices.

Author details

José C. Reston Filho
Federal University of Pará (UFPA), Belém, Pará, Brasil

Carolina de M. Affonso
Institute of Technology - ITEC, Federal University of Pará (UFPA), Belém, Pará, Brasil

Roberto Célio L. de Oliveira
Institute of Technology - ITEC, Federal University of Pará (UFPA), Belém, Pará, Brasil

Acknowledgement

This work was supported in part by FAPEAM – AM, Brazil.

6. References

[1] Shahidehpour M, Alomoush M (2001) Restructured Electrical Power Systems: Operation, Trading, and Volatility. New York: Marcel Dekker. 489p.

[2] Areekul P, Senjyu T, Toyama H, Yona A (2010) A Hybrid ARIMA and Neural Network Model for Short-Term Price Forecasting in Deregulated Market. IEEE Transactions on Power Systems. 25:524–530.

[3] Niua D, Liua Da, Dash Wub D (201) A soft computing system for day-ahead electricity price forecasting. Applied Soft Computing. 10: 868–875.

[4] Tan Z, Zhang J, Wangb J, Xu J (2010) Day ahead electricity price forecasting using wavelet transform combined with ARIMA and GARCH models. Applied Energy. 87: 3606–3610.

[5] Conejo A J, Plazas M A, Espinola R, Molina A B (2005) Day-ahead electricity price forecasting using wavelet transform and ARIMA models. IEEE Transactions on Power Systems. 20: 1035-1042.

[6] Amjady N, Keynia F (2008) Day ahead price forecasting of electricity markets by a miked data model and hybrid forecast method. International Journal of Electrical Power Energy Systems. 9: 533-546.

[7] Marzano L G B, Melo A C G, Souza R C (2003) An Approach for Portfolio Optimization of Energy Contracts in the Brazilian Electric Sector. Proc. 2003 IEEE Bologna Powertech Conf. Bologna-Italy.

[8] Barroso L A, Rosenblatt J, Guimarães A, Bezerra B, Pereira M V (2006) Auctions of Contracts and Energy Call Options to Ensure Supply Adequacy in the Second Stage of the Brazilian Power Sector Reform. Proc. 2006 IEEE Power Engineering Society General Meeting Conf. Montreal- Canada.

[9] Soares L J, Medeiros M C(2008) Modeling and forecasting short-term electricity load: A comparison of methods with an application to Brazilian data. International Journal of Forecasting. 24: 630–644.

[10] Leme R C, Turrioni J B, Balestrassi P P, Zambroni de Souza A C, Santos P S (2008) A Study of Electricity Price Volatility for the Brazilian Energy Market. 5th International Conference on European Electricity Market – EEM. Lisboa-Portugal.

[11] Amjady N, Keynia F (2011) A new prediction strategy for price spike forecasting of day-head electricity markets. Applied Soft Computing. 11: 4246-4256.

[12] Lu X, Dong Z I, Li X (2005) Electricity market price spike forecast with data mining techniques. Electric Power Systems Research. 73:19–29.

[13] National System Operator (ONS) [Online]. Available: http://www.ons.com.br

[14] Granville S, Oliveira G C, Thomé L M, Campodónico N, Latorre M L, Pereira M, Barroso L A (2003) Stochastic Optimization of Transmission Constrained and Large Scale Hydrothermal Systems in a Competitive Framework. in Proc. 2003 IEEE General Meeting. Toronto-Canada.

[15] Lino P, Barroso L A, Fampa M, Pereira M V, Kelman R (2003) Bid-Based Dispatch of Hydrothermal Systems in Competitive Markets. Annals of Operations Research. 120: 81-97.

[16] Mandal P, Senjyu T, Funabashi T (2006) Neural networks approach to forecast several hour ahead electricity prices and loads in deregulated market. Energy Conversion and Management. 47: 2128-2142.
[17] Brazilian Electrical Energy Commercialization Chamber (CCEE) [Online]. Available: http://www.ccee.org.br
[18] SPSS, Data Mining, Statistical Analysis Software. [Online]. Available: http://www.spss.com
[19] Box G E P, Jenkins G M, Reinsel G C (1976) Time Series Analysis, Forecasting and Control. New Jersey: Holden-Day. 784p.
[20] Mishra A K, Desai V R (2005) Drought forecasting using stochastic models. Stochastic Environmental Research Risk Assessment. 19: 326–339.
[21] Morettin P A, Toloi C M C (2006) Análise de Séries Temporais. São Paulo: Edgard Blucher. 538p.
[22] Haykin S (1994) Neural Networks: A Comprehensive Foundation. New York: Macmillan. 842p.
[23] Nisbet R, Elder J, Miner G (2009) Handbook of Statistical Analysis & Data Mining Applications. Oxford: Academic Press (Elsevier).824p.
[24] Olson D L (2005) Data Set Balancing. Lecture Notes in Computer Science-Data Mining and Knowledge Management. 3327: 71-80.

Chapter 11

Electricity Load Forecasting Using Data Mining Technique

Intan Azmira binti Wan Abdul Razak, Shah bin Majid,
Mohd Shahrieel bin Mohd. Aras and Arfah binti Ahmad

Additional information is available at the end of the chapter

http://dx.doi.org/10.5772/48657

1. Introduction

Accurate load forecasting is become crucial in power system operation and planning [1-3]; both for deregulated and regulated electricity market. Electric load forecasting can be divided into three categories that are short term load forecasting, medium term load forecasting and long term load forecasting. The short term load forecasting predicts the load demand from one day to several weeks. It helps to estimate load flows that can prevent overloading and hence lead to more economic and secure power system . The medium term load forecasting predicts the load demand from a month to several years that provides information for power system planning and operations. The long term load forecasting predicts the load demand from a year up to twenty years and it is mainly for power system planning [1].

A variety of methods including neural networks [2], time series [1], hybrid method [3,4] and fuzzy logic [5] have been developed for load forecasting. The time series techniques have been widely used because load behaviour can be analyzed in a time series signal with hourly, daily, weekly, and seasonal periodicities. Besides, it is able to deal with non stationary data to reflect the variation of variables [4].

However, for a huge power system covering large geographical area such as Peninsular Malaysia, a single forecasting model for the entire Malaysia would not satisfy the forecasting accuracy; due to the load and weather diversity[6]. Thus, this research will cater these conditions whereby five models of SARIMA (Seasonal ARIMA) Time Series [7,8] were developed for five day types.

2. Problem statement

Electric load forecasting is very important in power system operation such as during start-up and shut-down schedules of generating units as well as for overhaul planning [2] and

INTECH
open science | open minds

© 2012 Razak et al., licensee InTech. This is an open access chapter distributed under the terms of the Creative Commons Attribution License (http://creativecommons.org/licenses/by/3.0), which permits unrestricted use, distribution, and reproduction in any medium, provided the original work is properly cited.

spot market energy pricing [4]. In normal working condition, system generating capacity should meet load requirement to avoid adding generating units and importing power from the neighbouring network [9].

This research applied ARIMA time series approach to forecast future load in Peninsular Malaysia. Time series method that was introduced by Box and Jenkins is a sequence of data points that measured typically at successive times and time intervals [10].

3. Data mining with SARIMA time series

Before proceeding the forecasting process, load data need to be analyzed. Table 1 shows the average maximum and minimum demand, average energy and peak hour per day within a week. From the analysis, it can be concluded that the load characteristic among the days in a week is different. The average energy for Monday is slightly lower compared to Tuesday, Wednesday and Thursday. On the other hand, the average energy for those three days is fairly around 255MWh so that they can be clustered in a category. The average energy for Friday shows the lowest value within weekdays while the energy used for weekend is much lower than the consumption on weekdays. Comparing energy consumed on weekend, there is more consumption on Saturday rather than Sunday. Hence, the forecast will be conducted based on five day types that are:

Type 1 : Monday
Type 2 : Tuesday, Wednesday, Thursday
Type 3 : Friday
Type 4 : Saturday
Type 5 : Sunday

Day	Average Maximum Demand (MW)	Average Minimum Demand (MW)	Average Energy (MWh)	Peak Hour
Monday	12 442	7 842	249.06	3.00 – 4.30 pm
Tuesday	12 484	8 526	254.89	
Wednesday	12 508	8 565	255.95	
Thursday	12 436	8 543	255.03	
Friday	11 884	8 463	246.23	
Saturday	10 718	8 122	227.26	11.30am – 12.00pm
Sunday	10 116	7 605	211.01	8.00 – 9.00 pm

Table 1. Load data analysis within a week

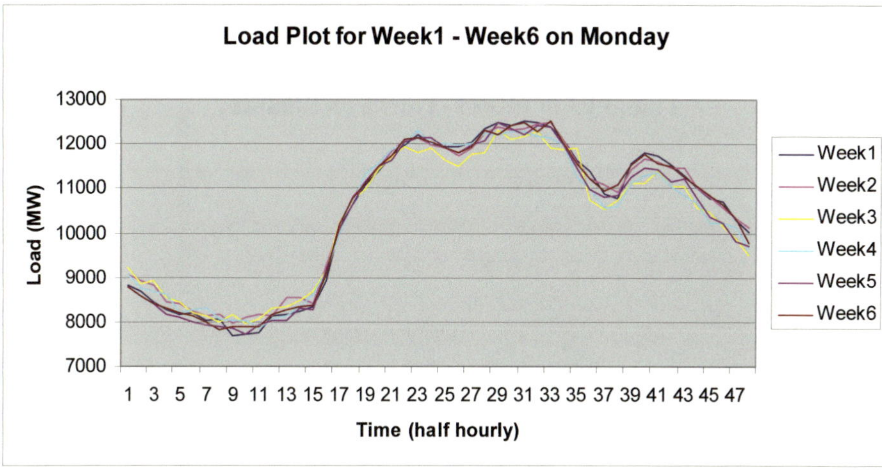

Figure 1. Load Plot for Monday

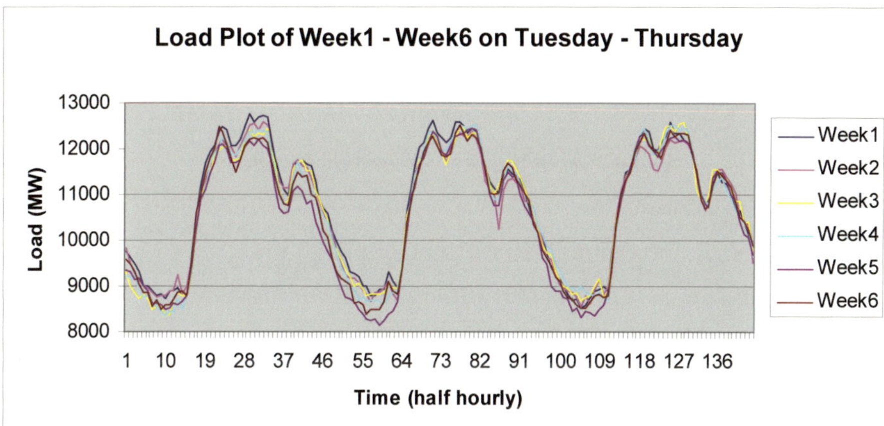

Figure 2. Load Plot for Tuesday, Wednesday and Thursday

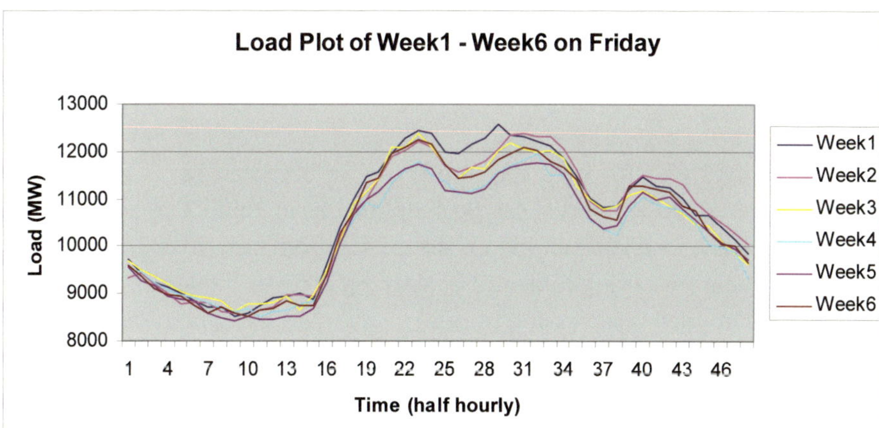

Figure 3. Load Plot for Friday

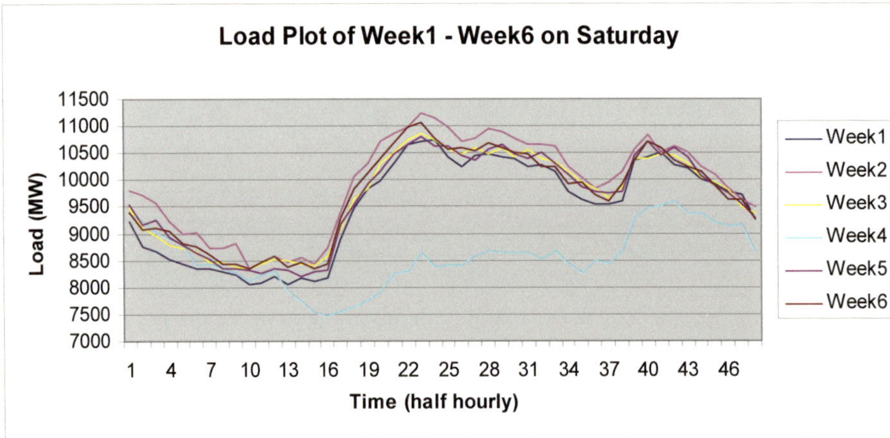

Figure 4. Load Plot for Saturday

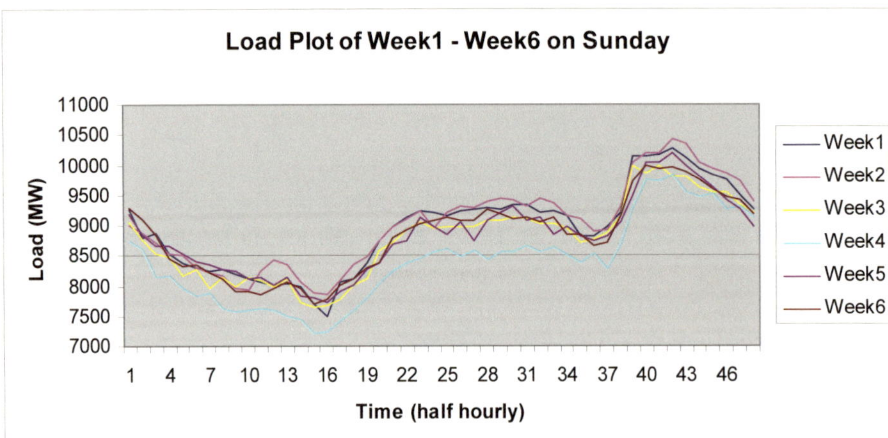

Figure 5. Load Plot for Sunday

Apart from that, load plot for each day types can be observed as in Figure 1-5. Their characteristic for certain time interval can be simplified as in Table 2 (a) and (b). Referring Table 2(a) for weekday, load consumption is decreasing from time 20.00 till 00.00 and 00.30 till 04.00 where people are having some rest or sleeping at night. However, starting 04.00 till 17.00 the load consumption is increasing because people start using home appliances and go to work. The load consumption for 17.00 till 19.00 shows slight decrease as people come back to home. The next an hour show the load consumption increasing where people spend some time watching television or having a dinner. However, there are bit differences of people activities during weekend that affect load consumption.

Time	Monday	Tuesday – Thursday	Friday
00.30 – 04.00	9 100 – 8 000	9 800 – 8 800	9 300 – 8 500
04.00 – 17.00	8 000 – 12 500	8 800 – 12 600	8 500 – 12 300
17.00 – 19.00	12 500 – 11 100	12 600 – 11 100	12 300 – 10 800
19.00 – 20.00	11 000 – 11 700	11 100 – 11 700	10 800 – 11 600
20.00 – 00.00	11 700 – 10 100	11 700 – 10 200	11 600 – 10 000

(a) Weekday

Time	Saturday	Sunday
00.30 - 08.00	9 800 – 8 400	9 000 – 7 900
08.00 – 12.00	8 400 – 11 300	08.00 – 16.00: 7 900 – 9 400 16.00 – 18.00: 9 400 – 8 900
12.00 – 18.00	11 300 – 9 800	
18.00 – 21.00	9 800 – 10 600	8 900 – 10 400
21.00 – 00.00	10 600 – 9 500	10 400 – 9 400

(b) Weekend

Table 2. Load consumption per day (MW)

Five models of SARIMA were developed in Minitab which represents the five day types. ARIMA; Autoregressive Integrated Moving Average involves the filtering steps in constructing the ARIMA model until only random noise remains. ARIMA model can be classified as seasonal or non-seasonal model. The series with seasonal repeating pattern is categorized as seasonal model or seasonal ARIMA (SARIMA) while the series with random series or no seasonal repeating trend is called as non-seasonal pattern. At least four or five seasons of the data are needed to fit the SARIMA model. Instead, ARIMA modeling identifies an acceptable model by some steps which are differencing, autocorrelation and partial autocorrelation functions. A non-seasonal ARIMA model is known as an ARIMA (p, d, q) model while a seasonal ARIMA model is named as ARIMA (P, D, Q) model where P or P is the number of autoregressive term (AR), d or D is the number of non-seasonal differences and q or Q is the number of lagged forecast errors in the prediction equation (MA). Appropriate ARIMA model is determined by identifying the p, d, q and P, D, Q parameters [10].

During modelling an ARIMA, the first step is determining whether the series has a trend or not. Trend analysis determines the seasonality and stationary. The second step is determining period for the seasonal model; by plotting spectral plot in MATLAB or ACF from Minitab. Usually the period is already known and it can be seen from ACF but spectral plot will prove that assumption. The third step involved is data transformation (if any) by Box-Cox plot; depending on the value of λ as shown in Table 3.

Value of λ	Transformation
-1.0	$\frac{1}{x_t}$
-0.5	$\frac{1}{\sqrt{x_t}}$
0	$\ln x_t$
0.5	$\sqrt{x_t}$
1.0	X_t

Table 3. Box-Cox Transformation

The last step is identifying the p, d, q and P, D, Q parameters. It started by determining the order of differencing needed to stationarize the series [10]. Normally the lowest order of differencing leads time series to fluctuates around a well-defined mean value and the spikes of ACF and PACF decays fairly rapidly to zero. After chosen appropriate order of differencing, AR and MA terms are then identified to determine whether the AR and MA terms are needed to correct any autocorrelation that remains in the differenced series.

Apart from that, the best fit of the model must meet these specifications:

a. -1.96 ≥ t-value ≥ 1.96
b. The lowest standard deviation
c. Chi-Square at Lag-12 is acceptable
d. -1 ≤ Parameter's coefficient ≤ 1

Some equations related to ARIMA model are shows in (1) to (4).

The order of d can be expressed in terms of the backshift operator B as:

$$\nabla^d = (1-B)^d \tag{1}$$

The seasonal backshift operator;

$$B^S z_t = z_{t-S} \tag{2}$$

Where
S = seasonal period,
Z_t = transformed data at time *t*

The seasonal difference operator;

$$\nabla_S^D = (1-B^S)^D \tag{3}$$

Combining (1) and (3) yields:

$$Y_t = (1-B)^d (1-B^S)^D z_t \tag{4}$$

Where Y_t = differenced data at time t

4. SARIMA modelling

4.1. ARIMA model for monday

The load data on Monday for six weeks had been plotted by trend analysis. Figure 6 shows that the data is seasonal and non-stationary so the period of the data must be identified. It can be done by plotting spectral plot in MATLAB as shown in Figure 7.

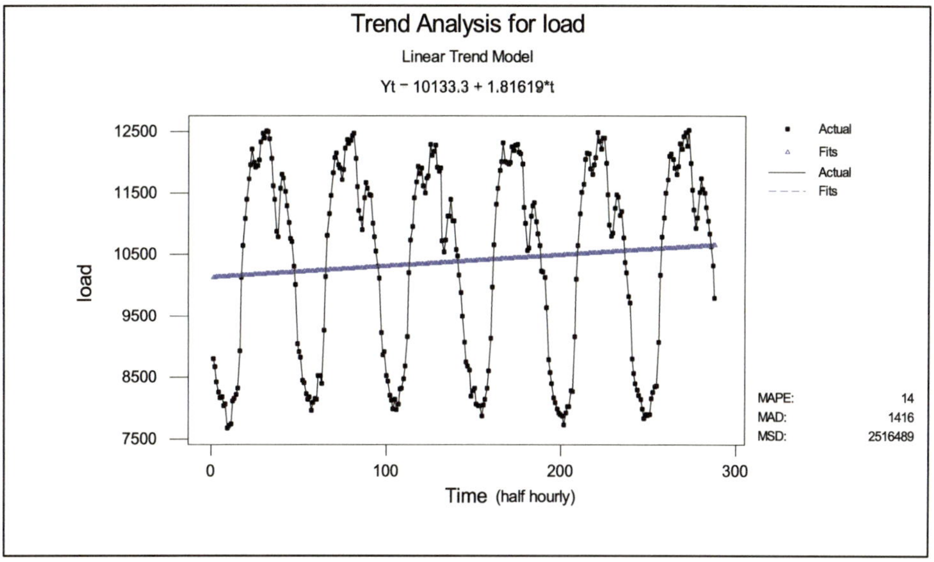

Figure 6. Trend analysis for Monday

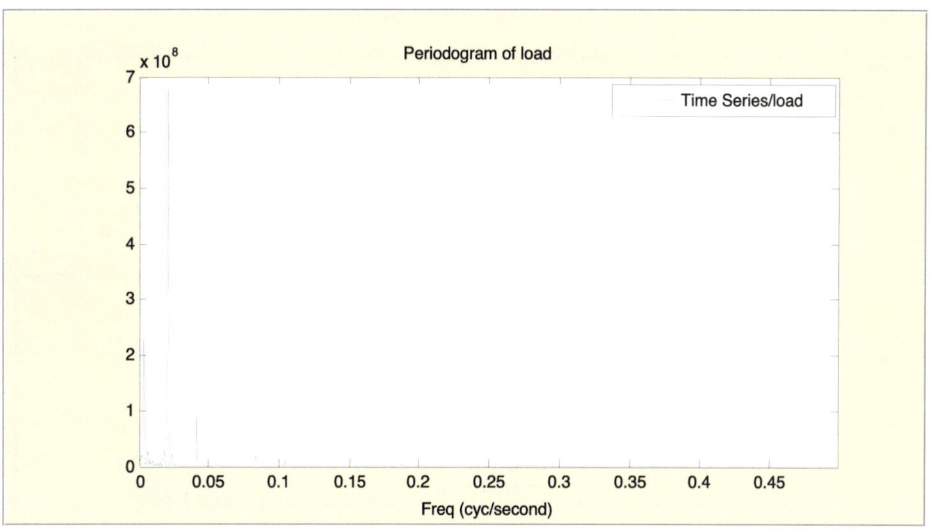

Figure 7. Spectral plot

Figure 7 shows that the graph had no aliasing or crossing on x-axis; meaning that the data is suitable for an analysis. The period is determined by;

$$T = 1/f \tag{5}$$

Where T = period, and f = frequency

From Figure 8, the frequency was 0.0208 thus the period was approximately 48. This value was determined based on the half hourly load and is valid for all day types. Since the data was not stationary, the actual data must be transformed; depending on the value of λ.

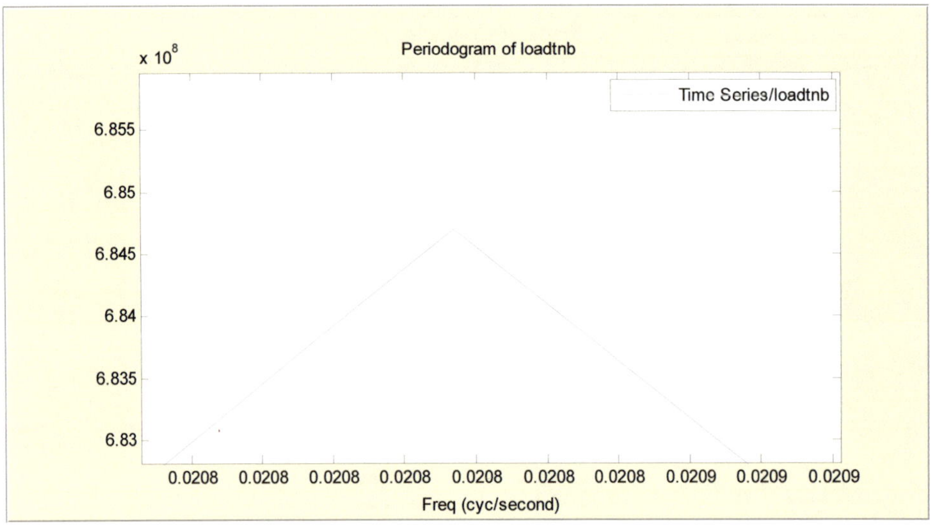

Figure 8. Enlarged view of spectral plot

Figure 9 shows the Box-Cox Plot for Monday where the value of λ = 0.562 so the rounded value is 0.5. Hence the actual data was transformed to $\sqrt{X_t}$.

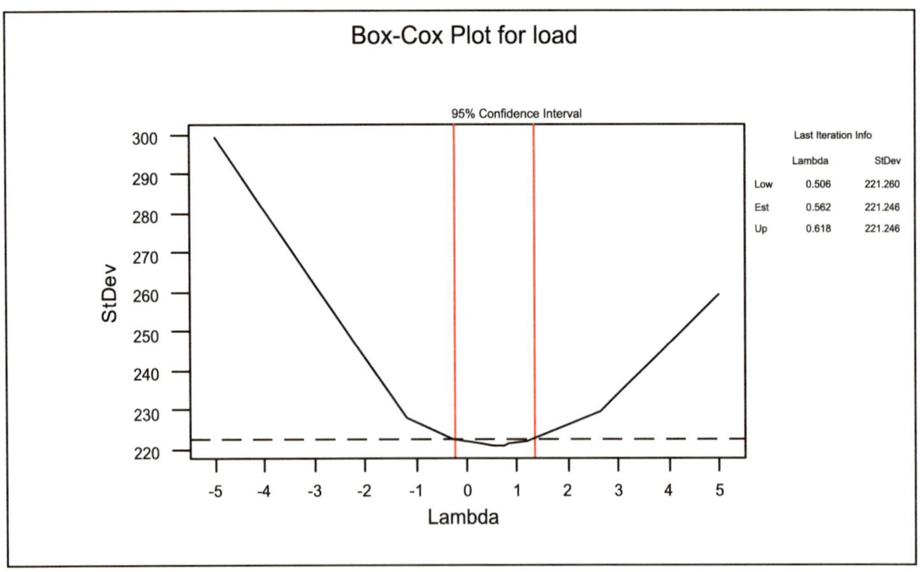

Figure 9. Box-Cox plot for Monday

Figure 10 show bad ACF (sine-cosines' phenomenon) and PACF when all parameters are zero. It is important to ensure that all the spikes are within the boundary to be a stationary model. Then the ARIMA parameters were identified and the selected model was ARIMA $(2,1,1)(0,1,1)_{48}$.

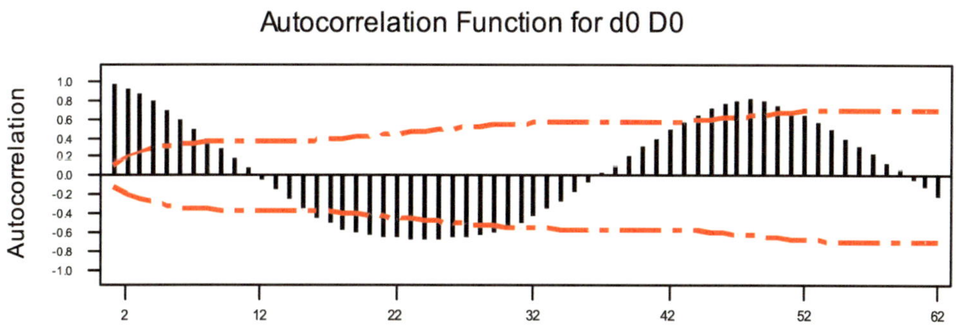

Lag	Corr	T	LBQ
1	0.98	16.57	277.31
2	0.93	9.24	528.78
3	0.86	6.80	746.52
4	0.78	5.37	926.57
5	0.69	4.35	1068.78
6	0.60	3.52	1174.48
7	0.49	2.79	1247.06
8	0.39	2.14	1292.28
9	0.28	1.53	1316.26
10	0.18	0.95	1325.67
11	0.07	0.38	1327.16
12	-0.04	-0.22	1327.65
13	-0.15	-0.81	1334.66
14	-0.26	-1.39	1355.16
15	-0.36	-1.92	1395.02
16	-0.45	-2.36	1457.14
17	-0.52	-2.68	1541.13
18	-0.58	-2.91	1645.09
19	-0.62	-3.03	1765.22
20	-0.65	-3.08	1897.12
21	-0.67	-3.06	2036.54
22	-0.68	-3.00	2180.29
23	-0.68	-2.93	2326.72
24	-0.68	-2.86	2474.92
25	-0.68	-2.78	2622.91
26	-0.68	-2.68	2768.93
27	-0.67	-2.58	2911.02
28	-0.65	-2.45	3045.37
29	-0.62	-2.28	3167.60
30	-0.57	-2.08	3273.68
31	-0.52	-1.85	3359.97
32	-0.44	-1.57	3424.26
33	-0.36	-1.27	3466.91
34	-0.27	-0.94	3490.73
35	-0.17	-0.61	3500.69
36	-0.08	-0.27	3502.61
37	0.02	0.07	3502.74
38	0.11	0.39	3507.03
39	0.21	0.72	3521.35
40	0.30	1.04	3551.77
41	0.39	1.36	3603.74
42	0.48	1.65	3681.80
43	0.56	1.92	3789.80
44	0.64	2.14	3929.11
45	0.70	2.33	4099.26
46	0.76	2.47	4298.02
47	0.80	2.54	4518.19
48	0.81	2.52	4746.75
49	0.79	2.42	4967.23
50	0.75	2.25	5166.45
51	0.70	2.05	5338.03
52	0.63	1.83	5479.66
53	0.56	1.60	5590.48
54	0.48	1.36	5672.23
55	0.39	1.11	5727.82
56	0.31	0.86	5761.74
57	0.22	0.62	5779.39
58	0.13	0.38	5785.97
59	0.05	0.13	5786.77
60	-0.04	-0.12	5787.45
61	-0.13	-0.37	5794.05
62	-0.22	-0.62	5812.18

ACF Plot for ARIMA $(0,0,0)(0,0,0)_{48}$

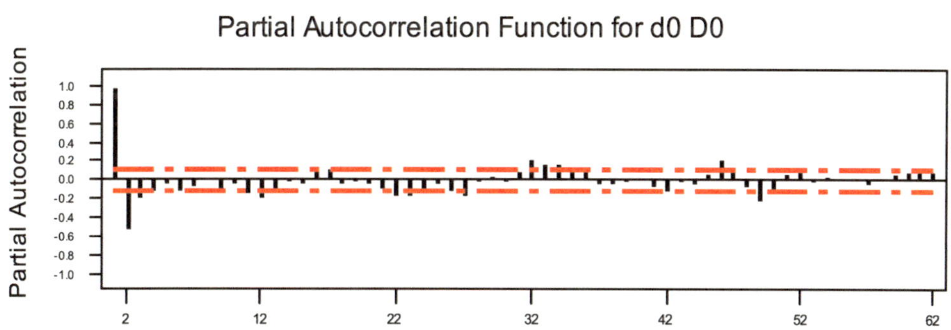

Lag	PAC	T
1	0.98	16.57
2	-0.53	-9.01
3	-0.19	-3.29
4	-0.12	-2.05
5	-0.05	-0.78
6	-0.14	-2.37
7	-0.09	-1.51
8	0.01	0.21
9	-0.10	-1.65
10	-0.06	-1.08
11	-0.15	-2.58
12	-0.21	-3.60
13	-0.09	-1.53
14	-0.02	-0.28
15	-0.06	-1.00
16	0.11	1.79
17	0.11	1.95
18	-0.06	-0.97
19	-0.02	-0.34
20	-0.06	-1.01
21	-0.10	-1.64
22	-0.18	-2.97
23	-0.17	-2.90
24	-0.16	-2.77
25	-0.06	-1.00
26	-0.12	-1.97
27	-0.17	-2.97
28	-0.03	-0.46
29	0.02	0.37
30	-0.02	-0.27
31	0.08	1.29
32	0.20	3.47
33	0.16	2.64
34	0.15	2.52
35	0.08	1.39
36	0.08	1.33
37	-0.05	-0.81
38	-0.06	-1.00
39	-0.03	-0.57
40	0.00	0.05
41	-0.07	-1.20
42	-0.13	-2.28
43	-0.02	-0.38
44	-0.06	-1.03
45	0.05	0.84
46	0.20	3.33
47	0.12	2.02
48	-0.08	-1.35
49	-0.23	-3.93
50	-0.15	-2.50
51	0.05	0.82
52	0.12	2.04
53	-0.03	-0.54
54	0.02	0.28
55	-0.01	-0.12
56	-0.01	-0.17
57	-0.05	-0.86
58	-0.01	-0.21
59	0.05	0.82
60	0.06	1.09
61	0.07	1.27
62	0.08	1.31

Figure 10. ACF and PACF for Monday

Figure 11-12 shows good ACF and PACF where the spikes decay fairly rapidly to zero. There was strong autocorrelation at lag-48 that shows the period of the data. All these steps were repeated for other day types.

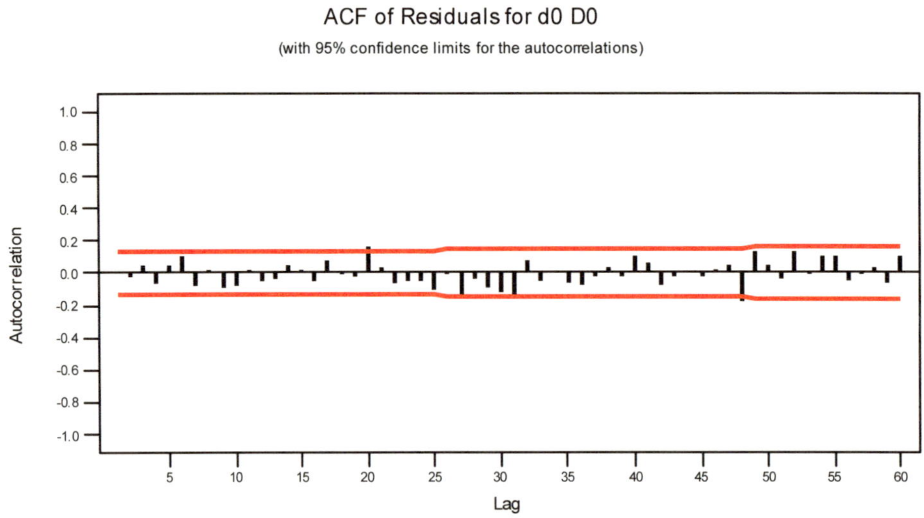

Figure 11. ACF Plot for ARIMA $(2,1,1)(0,1,1)_{48}$ on Monday

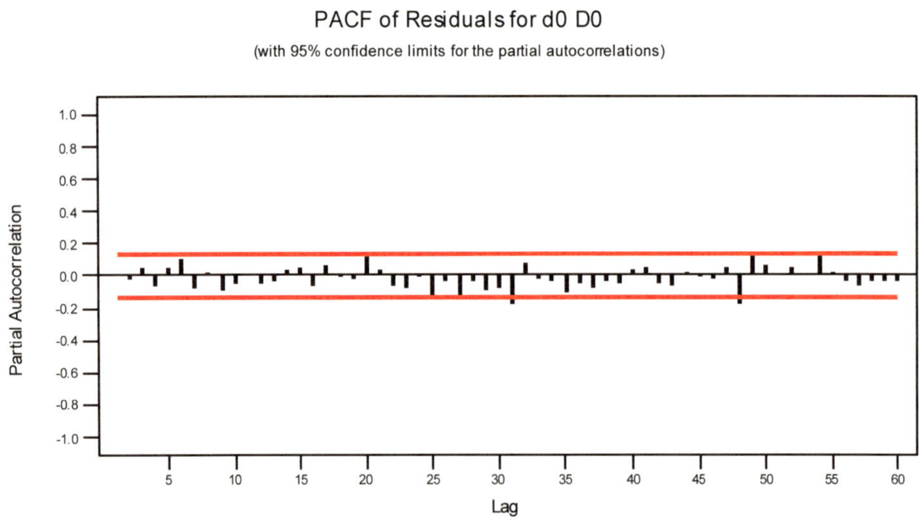

Figure 12. PACF Plot for ARIMA $(2,1,1)(0,1,1)_{48}$ on Monday

4.2. ARIMA model for Tuesday, Wednesday and Thursday

The steps taken for modelling ARIMA for this second model were repeated as for Monday. The trend analysis for Tuesday, Wednesday and Thursday was plotted followed by Box-Cox plot. The value of λ is 0.45 thus the rounded value is 0.5. After the data had been transformed to $\sqrt{X_t}$, the fitted ARIMA model was ARIMA $(1,1,1)(0,1,1)_{48}$.

Figure 13 and 14 show good ACF and PACF for selected ARIMA model where less spikes were found outside the boundary.

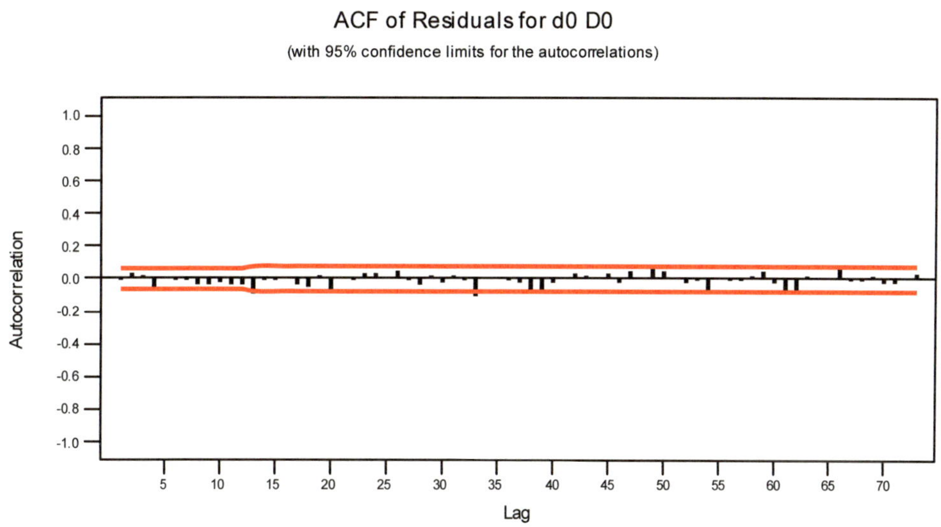

Figure 13. ACF Plot for Tuesday, Wednesday and Thursday

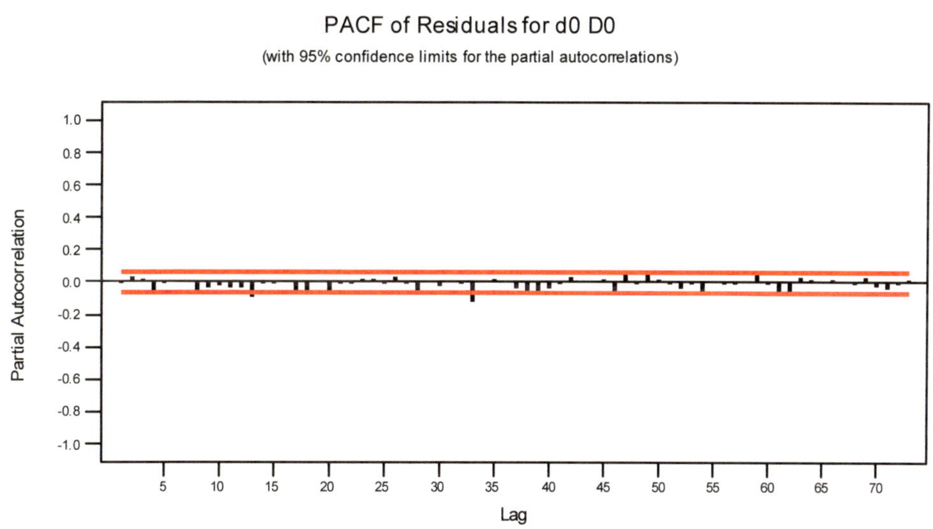

Figure 14. PACF Plot for Tuesday, Wednesday and Thursday

4.3. ARIMA model for Friday

The steps taken for modelling ARIMA for this third model were repeated as for two previous models. The trend analysis for Friday was plotted followed by Box-Cox plot. The trend analysis showed that the data is seasonal and non-stationary thus it must be transformed. Box-Cox plot showed that the value of λ is -0.112 and the rounded value is 0. The data was transformed to $ln\ X_t$ and the selected model is ARIMA $(0,1,1)(0,1,1)_{48}$.

Figure 15 and 16 show good ACF and PACF for Friday model with no spikes outside the boundary.

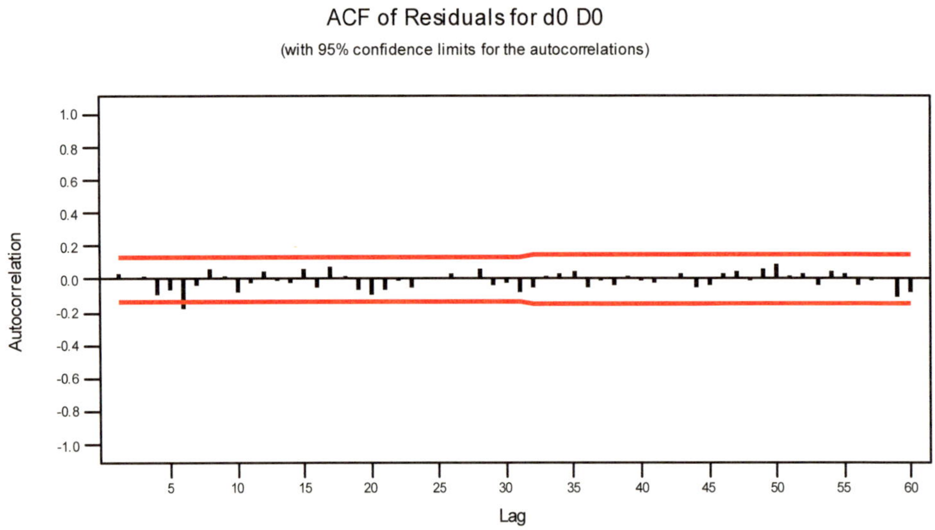

Figure 15. ACF Plot for Friday

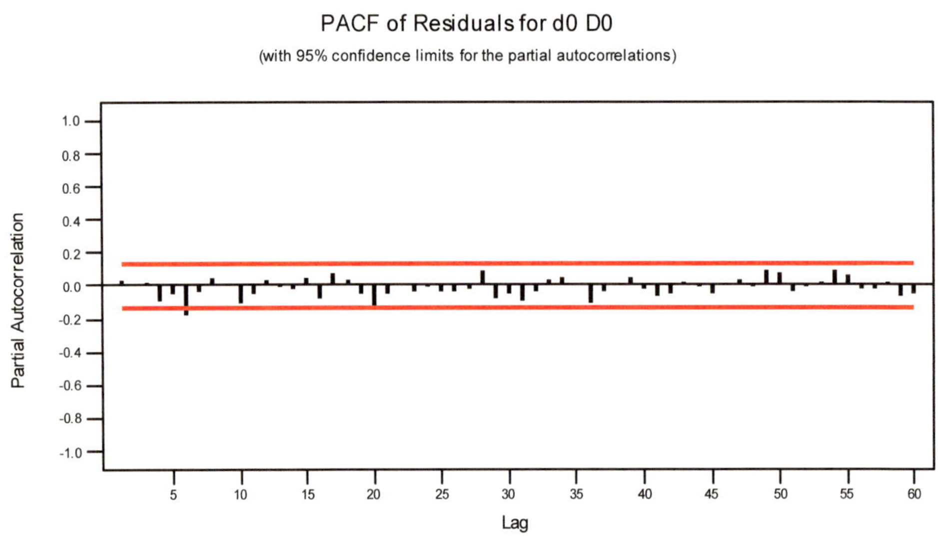

Figure 16. PACF Plot for Friday

4.4. ARIMA model for Saturday

The steps taken for modelling ARIMA for this fourth model were repeated as for three previous models. The trend analysis for Saturday was plotted followed by Box-Cox plot. The trend analysis showed that the data is seasonal and non-stationary thus it must be transformed. Box-Cox plot showed that the value of λ is 0.113 and the rounded value is 0.

After the actual data had been transformed to $ln\ X_t$, the selected model was ARIMA $(2,1,1)(0,1,1)_{48}$.

Figure 17-18 show good ACF and PACF for Saturday with ARIMA model selected.

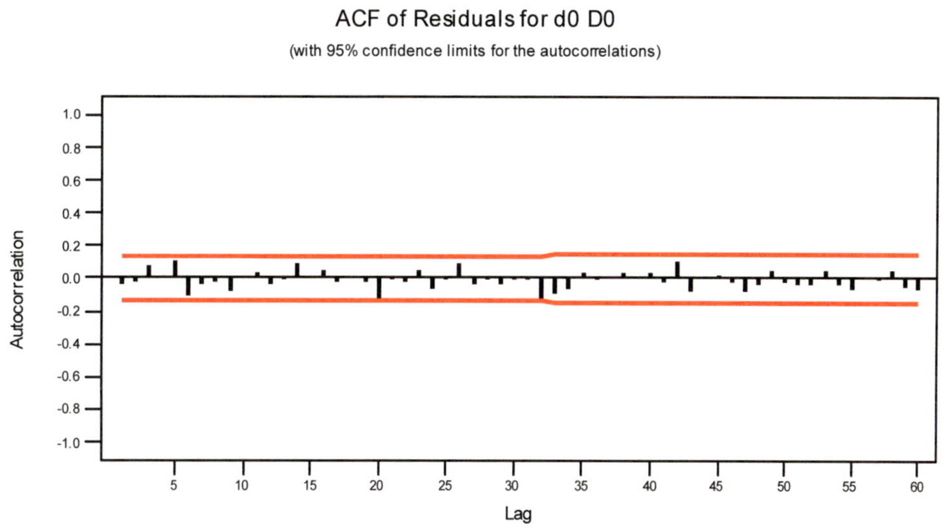

Figure 17. ACF Plot for Saturday

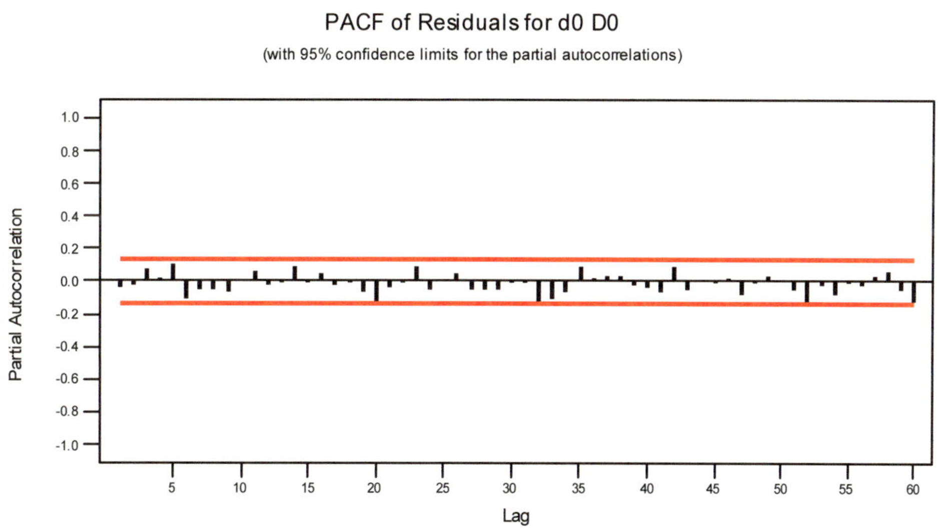

Figure 18. PACF Plot for Saturday

4.5. ARIMA model for Sunday

The steps taken for modelling ARIMA for this fifth model were repeated as for four previous models. The trend analysis for Sunday was plotted followed by Box-Cox plot. The trend analysis showed that the data is seasonal and non-stationary thus it must be transformed. Box-Cox plot showed that the value of λ is 0.225 and the rounded value is 0. After the actual data had been transformed to *ln* X_t, the selected model was ARIMA $(0,1,1)(0,1,1)_{48}$.

Figure 19-20 show good ACF and PACF for the fitted model. The plots show less spikes outside the boundary after a differencing and good selection of p, P, q and Q.

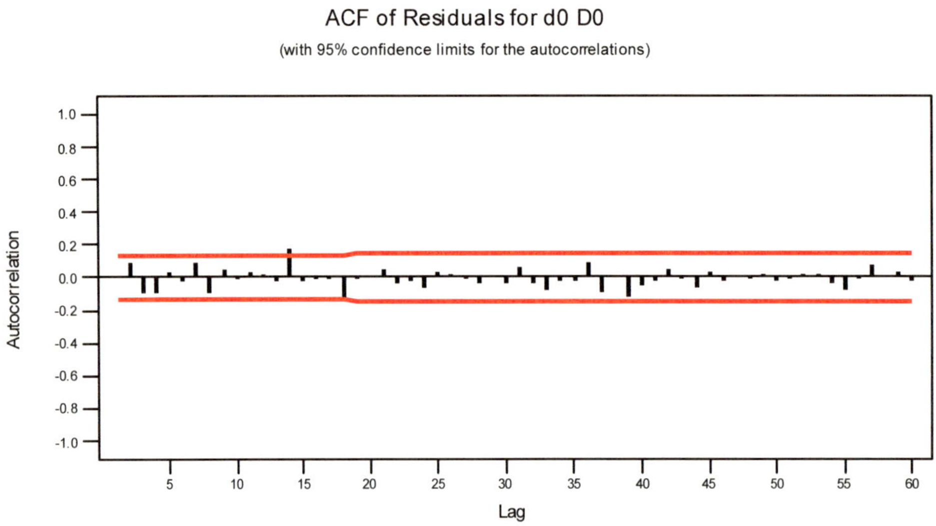

Figure 19. ACF Plot for Sunday

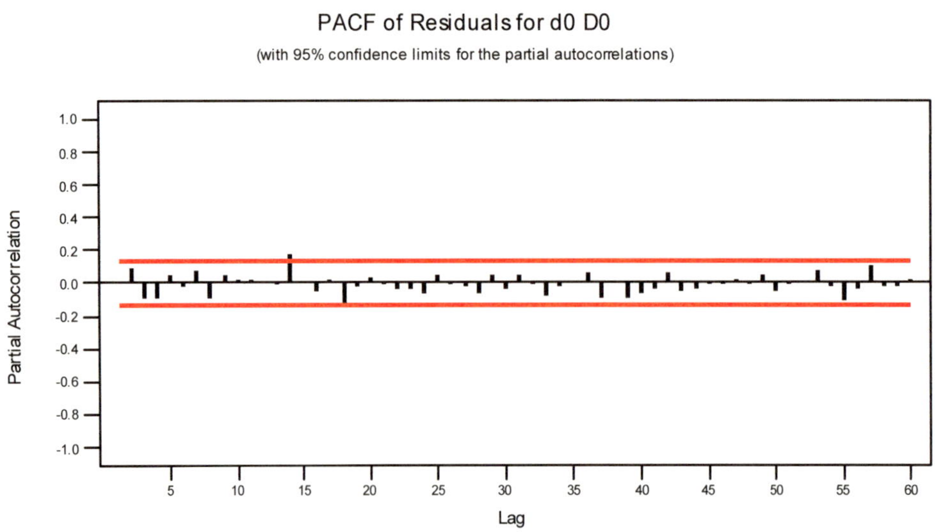

Figure 20. PACF Plot for Sunday

5. Result and analysis

The forecasting was held for 48 points that represent a day ahead for each day types. Table 4-8 show model specifications for all day types. Referring to t-values for all models, they satisfied the condition -1.96 ≥ t-value ≥ 1.96. Besides, good standard deviations shown for all models as well as Chi-Square at Lag-12 are also acceptable. The parameters' coefficients also fulfil the condition within the range of -1 and 1.

Parameters' Coefficient	t-value	Standard Deviation	Chi-Square at Lag-12	DF
AR 1 -0.3879	-2.98	82.9448	10.9	8
AR 2 -0.2675	-2.86			
MA 1 0.3717	2.86			
SMA 48 08382	13.87			

Table 4. Model Specification for Monday

Parameters' Coefficient	t-value	Standard Deviation	Chi-Square at Lag-12	DF
AR 1 0.1962	3.23	226.319	9.8	9
MA 1 0.6848	15.20			
SMA 48 0.9120	41.80			

Table 5. Model Specification for Tuesday, Wednesday and Thursday

Parameters' Coefficient	t-value	Standard Deviation	Chi-Square at Lag-12	DF
MA 1 0.4878	8.73	0.0355914	14.4	10
SMA 48 0.6243	11.01			

Table 6. Model Specification for Friday

Parameters' Coefficient	t-value	Standard Deviation	Chi-Square at Lag-12	DF
AR 1 0.4083	2.33	0.0632711	10.1	8
AR 2 0.3241	5.16			
MA 1 0.6491	3.59			
SMA 48 0.7511	13.48			

Table 7. Model Specification for Saturday

Parameters' Coefficient	t-value	Standard Deviation	Chi-Square at Lag-12	DF
MA 1 0.5746	10.81	0.0596651	11.9	10
SMA 48 0.6823	11.77			

Table 8. Model Specification for Sunday

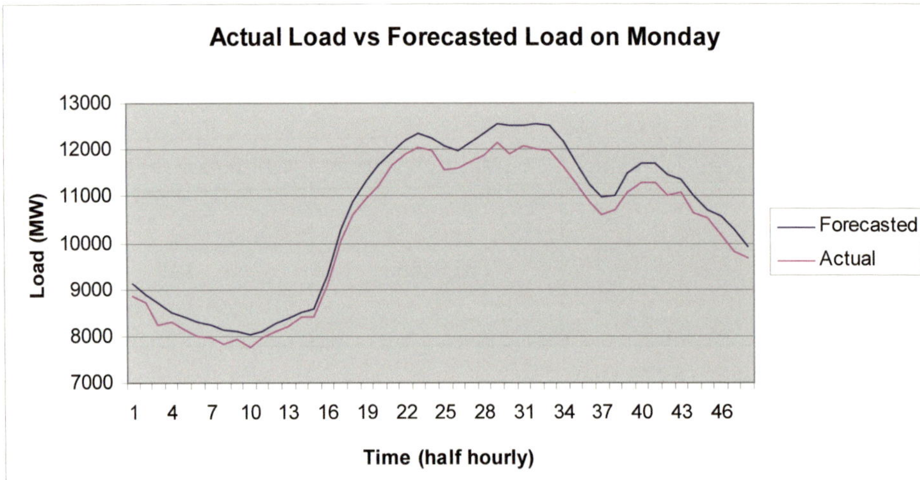

Figure 21. Actual load vs. forecasted load on Monday

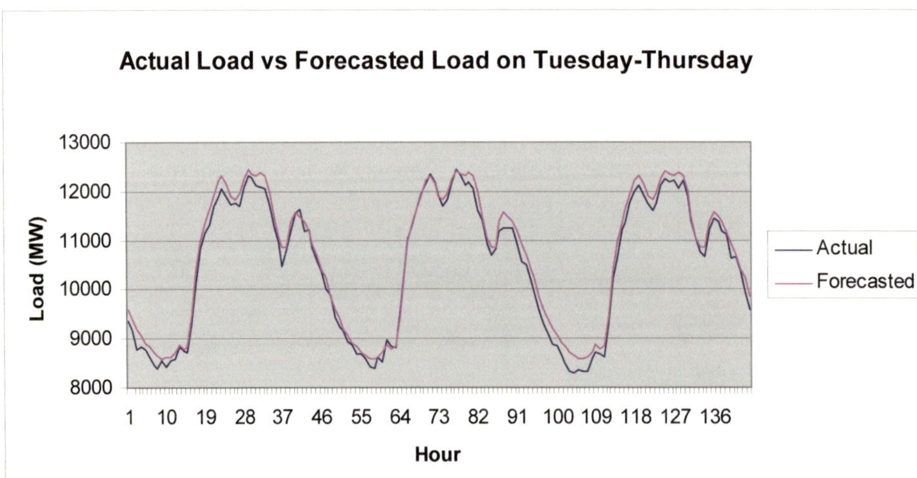

Figure 22. Actual load vs. forecasted load on Tuesday, Wednesday and Thursday

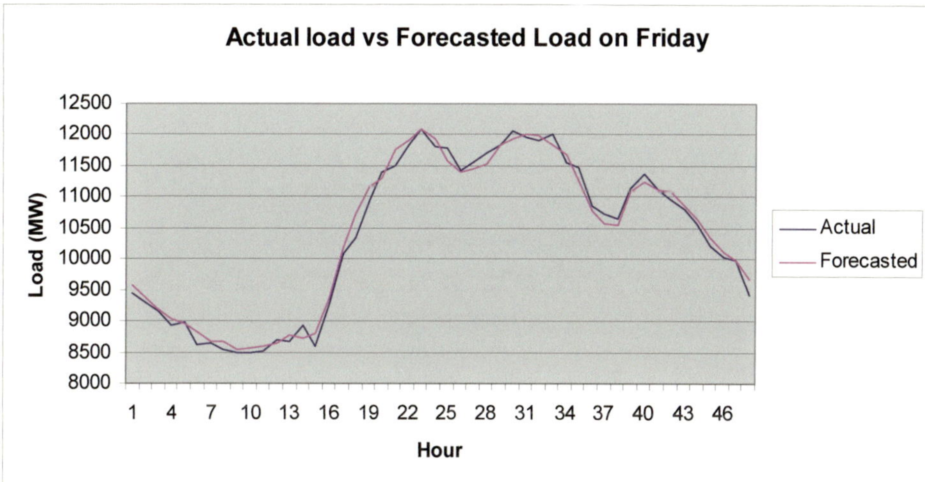

Figure 23. Actual load vs. forecasted load on Friday

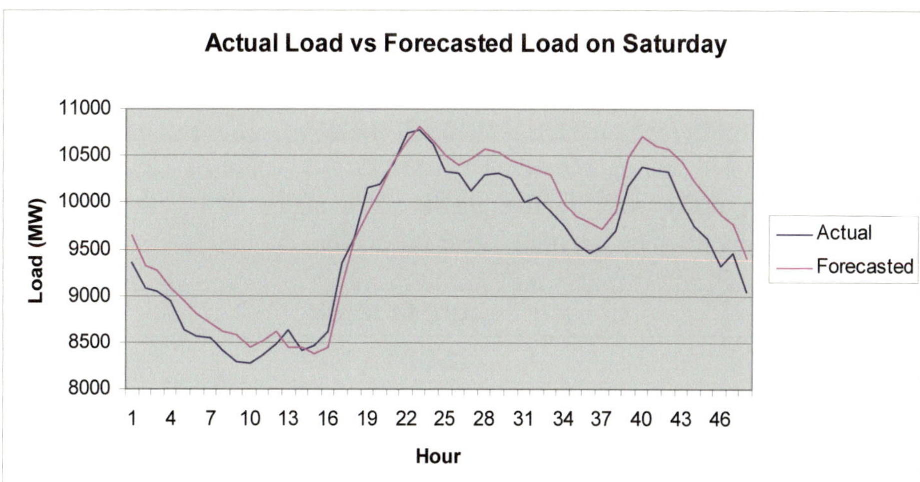

Figure 24. Actual load vs. forecasted load on Saturday

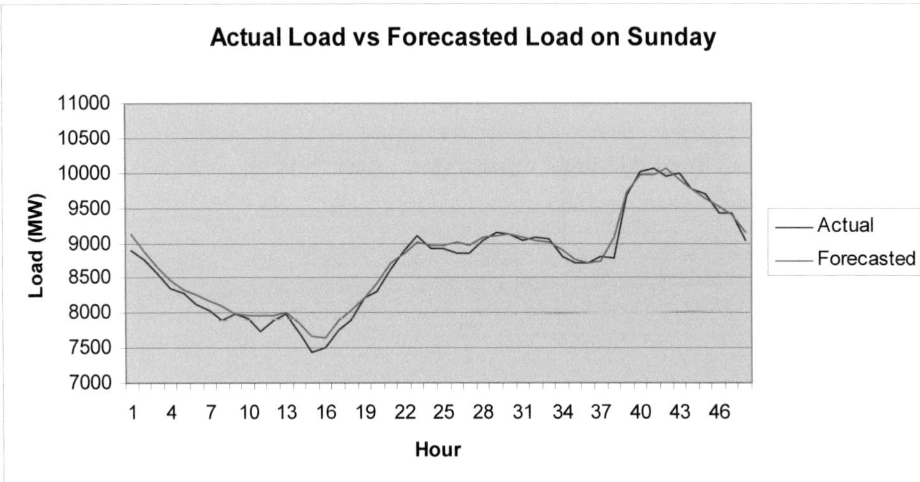

Figure 25. Actual load vs. forecasted load on Sunday

Figure 21-25 show the plots of forecasted load vs. actual load. The forecasted load plot are seems to be close as actual load plot. Mean Absolute Percentage Error (MAPE) for all day types were calculated as in (7):

$$\text{MAPE}\,(\%) = \frac{1}{N}\left[\frac{\left|Z'_t - x_t\right|}{x_t}\right] \times 100\% \tag{6}$$

Where Z't = Forecasted Load,
Xt = Actual Load
N = Forecasting number

Table 9 shows the ARIMA models and their MAPEs for all day types. It can be seen that the difference order (d and D) for all models is 1which is the lowest order and the best selection. The result is considered as accurate when the MAPE is lower than 1.5% as shown for Tuesday –Thursday, Friday and Sunday models. The higher MAPE for Monday and Saturday models may caused by load or weather fluctuation.

Day	ARIMA Model	MAPE
Monday	$(2,1,1)(0,1,1)_{48}$	3.26064%
Tuesday -Thursday	$(1,1,1)(0,1,1)_{48}$	1.62094%
Friday	$(0,1,1)(0,1,1)_{48}$	1.11833 %
Saturday	$(2,1,1)(0,1,1)_{48}$	2.41944 %
Sunday	$(0,1,1)(0,1,1)_{48}$	1.07158 %

Table 9. Forecasting result for all day types

6. Conclusion

From the data analysis, load data was clustered to five day types and hence five models of SARIMA are designed. Each forecasting model is developed for each day except for Tuesday, Wednesday and Thursday which clustered as a model. Forecasting method is held by Time Series - SARIMA where it is one of data mining methods which require enough experience on determining its parameter (p,d,q,P,D,Q). Sometimes it is needs for trial and error during identifying the parameters. However, the MAPEs obtained for each day types were ranging from 1% to 3%. This new approach had improved the accuracy of forecasting compared to traditional approach of ARIMA that use only a model for all days in a week.

7. Further research

Additional input variables can be included in the forecasting process such as weather data, customers' classes and event day; instead of only the load data. Besides, other methods may be implemented such as Neural Network, Fuzzy Logic as well as hybrid method [11].

Author details

Intan Azmira binti Wan Abdul Razak*,
Mohd Shahrieel bin Mohd. Aras and Arfah binti Ahmad
Faculty of Electrical Engineering, UTeM, Malacca, Malaysia

Shah bin Majid
Faculty of Electrical Engineering, UTM, Johor, Malaysia

Acknowledgement

I wish to express my gratitude to honorable University (**Universiti Teknikal Malaysia Melaka- UTeM**) especially to Faculty of Electrical Engineering for give the financial as well as moral support. My special thanks also fall to Mr. Fuad Jamaluddin from Utility of Malaysia for his valuable advice and help during completion of this research. Also to all my research members that give full commitments and cooperation.

8. References

[1] I. Azmira, A. Razak, S. Majid, and H.A. Rahman, "Short Term Load Forecasting Using Data Mining Technique," *Energy Conversion and Management*, 2008, pp. 139-142.
[2] "Application of Pattern Recognition and Artificial Neural Network to Load Forecasting in Electric Power System," *Pattern Recognition*, 2007.
[3] P. Qingle and Z. Min, "Very Short-Term Load Forecasting Based on Neural Network and Rough Set," *Network*, 2010, pp. 1132-1135.

* Corresponding Author

[4] J.C. Hwang and C.S. Chen, "Customer Short Term Load Forecasting by Using Arima Transfer Function Model," *Electrical Engineering*, pp. 317-322.

[5] B. Ye, N.N. Yan, C.X. Guo, and Y.J. Cao, "Identification of Fuzzy Model for Short-Term," *Evolution*, 2006, pp. 1-8.

[6] S. Fan, Y.-kang Wu, W.-jen Lee, and C.-yin Lee, "Different Geographical Distributed Loads," *Systems Research*, 2011, pp. 1-8.

[7] Y.H. Kareem and A.R. Majeed, "Sulaimany Governorate Using SARIMA .," *Building*, 2006, pp. 1-5.

[8] "Robust Estimation of Sarima Models : Application to Short-Term Load Forecasting Yacine Chakhchoukh , Patrick Panciatici Versailles , France," *Signal Processing*, 2009, pp. 77-80.

[9] J.K. Basu, D. Bhattacharyya, and T.-hoon Kim, "Use of Artificial Neural Network in Pattern Recognition," *Engineering*, vol. 4, 2010, pp. 23-34.

[10] H.L. Willis, *Power Distribution Planning Reference Book*, North Carolina,USA: Marcel Dekker, Inc., 2004.

[11] L. Xuemei, D. Lixing, and D. Yuyuan, "Hybrid Support Vector Machine and ARIMA Model in Building Cooling Prediction," *Built Environment*, 2010.

Chapter 12

Mining and Adaptivity in Automated Teller Machines

Ghulam Mujtaba Shaikh and Tariq Mahmood

Additional information is available at the end of the chapter

http://dx.doi.org/10.5772/48317

1. Introduction

Since the past few years, the banking sector has seen a considerable application of diverse technologies for its daily operations. The most significant of such technologies has been the introduction of Automated Teller Machines (ATMs). A typical ATM is shown in Figure 1. Initially, ATMs were used only for dispensing cash, but now offer round-the-clock services for a diverse number of operations, e.g., electronic transfer of funds, paying bills, viewing past transactions of bank accounts, changing the ATM sign-in credentials etc [9]. For using ATM services, the bank issues its customer an ATM card and a PIN code. The customer inserts the card into the ATM terminal, and enters the PIN code. If the bank authenticates the PIN code, then the customer can use the ATM services. The first ATM was installed in 1967 by Barclay's Bank in the USA, and now there is hardly any bank in the world which operates without an ATM. Till March 2012, the current number of ATMs is estimated around

Figure 1. A typical Automated Teller Machine (ATM)

INTECH
open science | open minds

©2012 Mujtaba and Mahmood, licensee InTech. This is an open access chapter distributed under the terms of the Creative Commons Attribution License (http://creativecommons.org/licenses/by/3.0), which permits unrestricted use, distribution, and reproduction in any medium, provided the original work is properly cited.

2.3 million[1]. Also, both the number of ATM terminals and the ATM transactions are expected to grow exponentially in the near future [8].

Notwithstanding their popularity, a major limitation of ATMs is that customers often have to wait in queue, due to a large ATM usage time of other customers [22]. This trend frequently occurs with old people, who can spend considerable time at ATMs understanding the content of the interfaces, due to their cognitive and visual disabilities [17]. Such a situation is likely to frustrate the other customers in the queue, considering that the typical ATM usage time can be considered between 20 seconds to 60 seconds [10, 17][2]. Moreover, a study conducted on the elderly ATM users of Israel [22] found that these users require ATM interfaces which present content in a simpler manner with easy-to-understand jargon. This calls for designing usable (simple) ATM interfaces which can assist customers in completing their transactions more efficiently. In fact, ATMs currently support a *fixed* interaction process with their customers. Specifically, each bank selects a set of services which will be offered by its ATMs. Each time the user enters her PIN, these same services are displayed to her. The user selects her desired service, with each service being typically offered on a separate interface. For instance, Figure 2 shows the ATM interface of the Bank of America[3] offering the available services, and Figure 3 shows the ATM interface for the "Balance Inquiry" service.

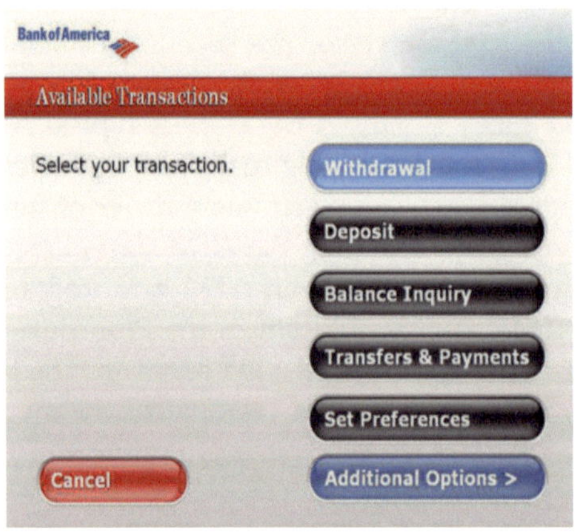

Figure 2. An ATM interface of Bank of America showing some of the offered services

Each time any customer enters her PIN, she is always shown the screen in Figure 2. However, suppose that a majority of customers use only the "Balance Inquiry" and "Deposit" operations, and we show a screen with only these operations, along with the "Additional Options" button for the remaining operations. Then, viewing lesser options could reduce the usage time for a majority of customers, along with making the interfaces more usable. Similarly, if many customers inquire their current balance, showing this balance autonomously to the user can reduce their usage time (as they won't have to request for it explicitly). Finally, the rapid accumulation of ATM transaction data makes it possible to *mine* this data, in order to extract interesting information regarding the usage patterns of ATM customers [4]. This information can be used to make the ATM usage process more

[1] https://www.atmia.com/mig/globalatmclock/

[2] http://www.me.utexas.edu/ jensen/or_site/computation/unit/stoch_anal/marp_add/marp_add.html

[3] https://www.bankofamerica.com/

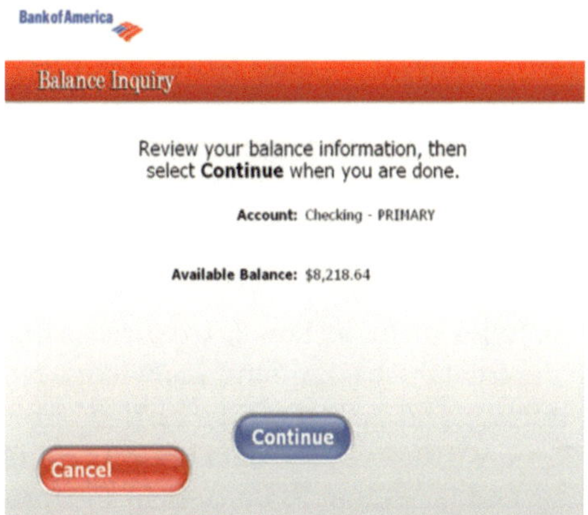

Figure 3. An ATM interface of Bank of America for the "Balance Inquiry" service

adaptive, i.e., one that caters for the customers' behavior. These requirements call for the design of *adaptive* ATM interfaces, which are more usable, attempt to reduce the usage time of customers, hence enhancing the customer satisfaction along with having a positive impact on customer relationship management [4]. Generating efficient transactions implies lesser waiting times (and frustration) for customers in the queue. We note that currently, no concrete work exists that involves the application of data mining techniques to ATM transactions. In fact, only simple statistics are being computed to answer minor queries of the bank managers, e.g., number of customers who used a particular ATM on some day, total amount of withdrawl on a given day etc.

In this work, we propose a set of five adaptive ATM interfaces, which are adapted to the behavior of an ATM customer population. For this, we obtain an ATM transaction dataset for an international bank in Kuwait, a Middle-Eastern country[4]. We initially pre-process this dataset to ensure data quality for the mining activity. Then, we mine it using the technique of "process mining" [1], i.e., mining of the ATM usage process, through the Process Miner (ProM) tool. Our results show that the customers frequently use only some ATM operations. Specifically, withdrawal is performed most frequently, followed by purchase, and balance inquiry options. A majority of customers perform these operations repeatedly, and also one after the other. We also obtain the distribution of the withdrawn amount, with respect to individual customers, the location (ATM terminal) of withdrawl, and the time of the withdrawl. These data reveal that individual customers withdraw specific amounts at specific timestamps. We also identify heavy traffic ATMs, as well as usage times of peak customer activity, on which our five adaptive interfaces can be applied to reduce the usage time.

In the first interface, we show only the ATM operations that are frequently used by the customers. In the second interface, we show only those amounts that are frequently withdrawn by the customers. In the third interface, we query the customer explicitly about performing another withdrawl. In the fourth interface, we display the customer's current balance on several screens autonomously. Finally, in the fifth interface, we query the customer explicitly about viewing her purchase history. In order to acquire the opinion of the customers regarding these interfaces, we conducted an online questionnaire (survey), that was filled by

[4] We will not mention the name of this bank for the sake of privacy.

216 users who were representative ATM customers. A large majority of these users believed that the first, second and fourth interfaces could reduce their usage time, and were willing to evaluate these interfaces in real-time. Moreover, our work has been approved by the State Bank of Pakistan, which is Pakistan's banking authority[5]. We are currently implementing four of our interfaces for a Pakistani bank. We note that a part of this work was published in two papers [14, 15] in the International Conference of Information and Communication Technologies in 2011[6].

This chapter is structured as follows. In Section 2, we discuss the state-of-the-art related to our work. In Section 3, we describe the background knowledge related to the ProM tool, i.e., the description of process mining, and how it can be carried out in ProM through a specific XML format. Then, in Section 4, we describe the data pre-processing tasks that we applied on our ATM transaction dataset, and in Section 5, we present the results of mining this dataset. In Section 6, we illustrate and describe our five adaptive ATM interfaces, and in Section 7, we present the results of our real user ATM survey. Finally, in Section 8, we conclude our work, and present the limitations of our adaptive interfaces along with the future work.

2. Related work

Perhaps the work most related to our approach is [12, 13]. Here, the author proposes the design and implementation of a software agent called the Personal Bank Teller (PBT). The PBT is associated with an ATM card, and personalizes (adapts) the ATM interaction for the customer, irrespective of the time and location of ATM access. It attempts to show the customer's frequently-used ATM operations towards the top of the screen, so that they are more in focus. Also, those amounts are shown towards the top which are withdrawn more frequently. These are similar behaviors to our first and second adaptive interfaces, respectively (Section 1). However, PBT operates by simply calculating the probability of access of a given operation, or amount. Our adaptive interfaces are based on more robust mining methods, and focus also on a more usable (simpler) display by removing less frequently used operations or amounts. Moreover, PBT has a smaller scope because it doesn't employ the roles of our third, fourth and fifth adaptive interfaces.

Moreover, in [8], the authors perform a questionnaire-based survey to acquire the opinions of customers regarding ATM usage in Pakistan. They show that more customers prefer using ATM services when they are provided in the national language, and also, when they are available near the customers' residences. This survey provides a motivation for international banks to open their branches in sub-urban (rural) locations in Pakistan, which can provide ATM terminals connected both locally (within Pakistan) and internationally. The scope of our work is expansive as compared to [8], because we are mining the actual ATM transactions to extract usage patterns of customers, along with a questionnaire-based survey. Also, our goal is more critical: we are not catering for the language requests of the customers, but rather, attempting to minimize their ATM usage time.

On a related note, in [19], the authors have employed data mining techniques to discover useful information concerning Customer Relationship Management (CRM) in the banking

[5] http://www.sbp.org.pk/
[6] http://icict.iba.edu.pk/

sector. The results show that retaining old customers is very important because it costs 7 to 10 times more to make a new customer rather than to retain an old one. In comparison, although we are not aiming to directly optimize CRM, we believe that building adaptive ATM interfaces will positively influence CRM, e.g., customers will use ATM services more often if these services are adapted to their behaviors and preferences. Another work related to our approach is a research survey [7], which mentions that building and maintaining profiles of customers will increase banking transactions. It also concludes that the usage of data mining tools is essential for efficient banking functionality, which provides a strong support and motivation for our work. Moreover, we believe that we are also (indirectly) profiling different customers according to their behaviors, e.g., those who make frequent withdrawls, those who check their current balance regularly, at a given location and time.

Along with this, several enterprises are conducting simple statistical analysis on ATM transactions to increase customer satisfaction. For instance, the enterprise Prognosis [20] has implemented the ATM Transaction Manager, which provides business intelligence-related transaction statistics to enhance the transaction throughput for ATM customers. By using data warehousing techniques, it can uncover reasons for fallacies such as excessive denials of ATM services, transaction failures and slow response times. Also, the enterprise ESQ Business Services [6] has implemented the Automated Trailer Machine Transaction Analyzer (ATMTA), which provides continuous real-time monitoring of ATM transactions to perform important tasks such as dynamic calculation of transaction time, generation of user activity reports, identifying user traffic across diverse ATMs etc. Although these solutions are important, they do not involve mining of ATM transactions to extract relevant information regarding the customers' behavior. In other words, they do not adapt to what the customers are doing, in order to provide them with a more usable ATM interaction experience.

The work done in the domain of process mining [1] is also related to our approach. Given a particular domain, process mining is the branch of data mining that discovers models of processes from the event logs of this domain. In our work, the event logs are the ATM transactions, and the process is that of ATM usage by the customers. We process mine our transaction dataset through the ProM tool (Section 3). In this context, the following works will assist the reader in understanding that ProM has been applied in diverse domains, and its outputs have been extremely beneficial for these domains. In [21], the authors apply process mining to the domain of software development, in order to determine whether the evolution process of a software proceeds according to its documentation (or deviates from it), as the project progresses. The authors hypothesized that such deviations could occur towards the end of the project, when the time constraints become more severe. However, the results of mining reject this hypothesis, and showed that the throughput time of software development is longer when a particular process of development is not followed. Furthermore, process mining has been used to bridge the gap between customers' expectations about commercial products and the actual performance of the products [5]. Here, the process of usability of a particular product is mined, in order to acquire useful information about the product's usage. For instance, if the users have previous knowledge about the product, then their usability performance will be typically good for a first use of this product. Finally, in [11], the authors apply process mining to the domain of health care in order to obtain meaningful information about the patients' care flows, i.e., the process of treatment (health care) imparted to the patients. The authors apply ProM to a real-life oncology process (of a metropolitan hospital), and show that the mining outputs can be used to improve the efficiency and efficacy of existing care flows.

3. Process mining and ProM tool

In this section, we will describe the techniques of process mining, and the method through which it can be carried out within the ProM tool.

3.1. Background on process mining

Process mining [1, 23] is a data mining technique for extracting useful knowledge from event logs in information systems. An event log logs different events as they occur within a particular process of the system. For instance, consider a computer system that keeps track of the actions of user on an E-Commerce portal. Then, it could log events such as "the start of user session", "user buys a product", "user views top-10 products", "end of user session" etc. Process mining discovers useful information regarding the process available in the event logs. For instance, in the car repair example, process mining can reveal that a particular part of a car engine is repaired most frequently, and mostly through two specific repair operations. The following points describe process mining in detail:

- Each event refers to an instance of a process, also called a *process instance*,
- Each event can have an originator (the actor initiating the activity),
- Each event is identified by a particular activity; activities are associated with cases, and
- Each event can have a timestamp.

Process mining discovers causalities amongst events by using three state-of-the-art methodologies, i.e., finite state machines, Markovian framework, and neural networks [2].

3.2. Background on ProM tool

ProM is an open-source tool for process mining [24]. It provides a vast variety of process mining plug-ins. A given plug-in implements one or more data mining algorithms. ProM reads files in a particular XML format, called MXML (described below). For creating an MXML file, we need an *audit trail entry*, which is an event that occurs at a particular time stamp. Each audit trail entry should refer to one unique activity. It also contains the description of the event, and refers to a process instance or a case. Also, each process instance belongs to one specific process. The MXML file format is described in Figure 4. At the root (top), there exists a WorkflowLog element, which can contain optional Data and Source elements, along with a number of Process elements. A Data element can log textual data. It comprises a set of Attribute elements. A Source element records information about the system which originated the event log (under analysis). The Process element depicts a particular process in the system, and a ProcessInstance depicts a process instance. An AuditTrailEntry element may refer to an activity (WorkflowModelElement), a type of the event (labeled as Eventtype), a timestamp (Timestamp), or a person that started (or managed) the activity (Originator). In order to convert our event logs into MXML format, we employ the Nitro tool [3]. Through Nitro, we load the event data, select the cases, activities, time stamps and the originator entities in this data, and convert it to MXML.

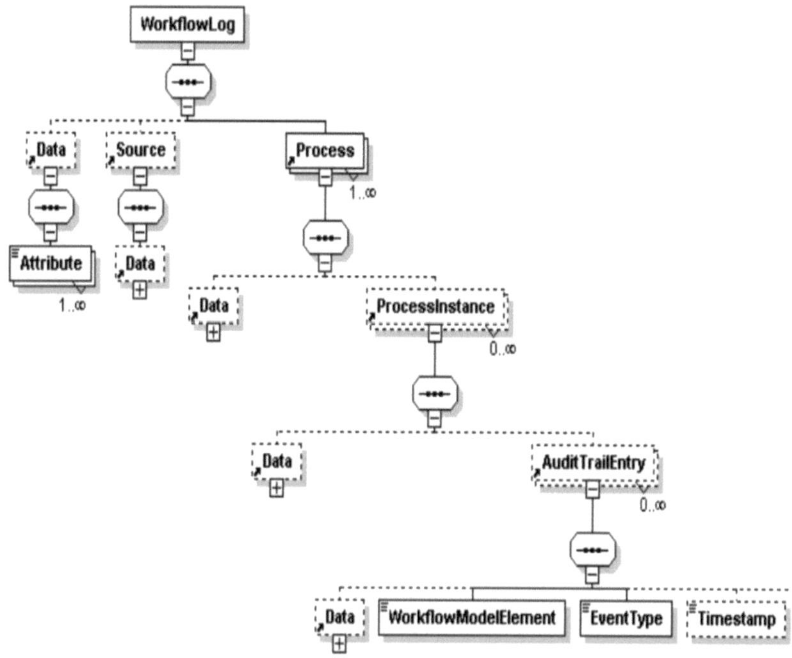

Figure 4. MXML File Format (adapted from [23])

4. Data collection and data cleaning

As mentioned in Section 1, we employ an ATM transaction dataset of an international bank based in Kuwait. This dataset originally consisted of approximately 10 million transactions conducted by 5000 customers. In order to minimize the computational cost involved in data mining, we sampled this dataset using random sampling technique [4]). Our sample dataset consisted of 2 million transactions for 676 customers. These transactions are recorded from 17th September 2009 (17-09-2009) to 1st December 2010 (01-12-2010). They are represented by 45 attributes (columns) and are stored in Microsoft Excel format. In order to select a reduced (more reasonable) set of attributes, we applied *data cleaning* techniques to the sampled transaction dataset [4]. Specifically, we deleted the redundant attributes, e.g., there is both a name and a unique ID available for the customer, from which we selected only the ID. Moreover, some attributes are irrelevant for our analysis. For instance, each transaction is assigned a tracking number for data archival; this is irrelevant because we are focusing on the customers' usage patterns. Also, there were several attributes which contained missing values, i.e., data for these attributes was not logged completely, e.g., an audit number (assigned to each transaction) was not available for each transaction. We also performed the Pearson's and Chi-squared co-relation test to detect co-related numerical and categorical attributes, respectively. If two attributes were positively co-related, we considered only one of them [4]. In summary, we ignored all columns that were redundant, irrelevant, contained missing values, or were (pair-wise) positively co-related.

After data cleaning, we were left with 9018 transactions of 276 different customers, represented over 10 attributes. We describe these attributes as follows (for a given performed transaction):

1. *PAN*: Stores the ATM card number,
2. *Cust_Code*: Stores a unique code of the customer,
3. *Proc_Code*: Stores the type of transaction, e.g., withdrawl, deposit, balance inquiry etc.,
4. *DateTime*: Stores the time stamp,
5. *Amount*: Stores the amount being withdrawn or deposited,
6. *Response_Code*: Stores the possible responses to the transaction, e.g., approved, denied, invalid pin code entry etc.,
7. *Terminal_ID*: Stores the ID of the ATM cabin at which the transaction was performed,
8. *Terminal_Loc*: Stores the name of the location where the ATM cabin is installed,
9. *Acquiring_ID*: Stores the ID of the bank which has installed the ATM cabin, and
10. *Authorizer_ID*: Stores the ID of the bank whose card is being used for transactions (since card holders of different banks can use the ATM).

We converted our cleaned transaction dataset into MXML using Nitro. We chose the *PAN* attribute as the Case attribute of the MXML format, *Cust_Code* as the Originator attribute, *Proc_Code* as the Activity attribute, and *DateTime* as the Timestamp attribute (Section 3.2). The ProcessInstance tag identifies a particular transaction, i.e., a process instance. Moreover, the AuditTrailEntry tag specifies the detail of one particular action being performed by the customer, e.g., a "withdrawal", which is specified by the WorkflowModelElement tag. Besides this, the EventType tag represents the type of an event, which we have set as default to "start", i.e., a transaction has started. When a transaction finishes, i.e., when the customer takes a final action, the EventType is "complete", i.e., the transaction has finished. Finally, the Originator tag represents the *Cust_Code*, i.e., the particular customer doing the transaction.

5. Process mining results

In this section, we employ eight ProM plug-ins to mine useful knowledge from our ATM MXML file. We recall from Section 1 that our aim is to use this knowledge to develop adaptive ATM interfaces, which have a tendency to minimize the ATM usage time for a population of customers, particularly at heavy traffic ATMs. We discuss our results in the following eight sub-sections.

5.1. Generic transaction distribution

We initially acquired the frequency distribution of the different ATM transactions, i.e., the number of transactions conducted for a given ATM operation. We note that a pattern or an event that occurs frequently is deemed interesting for data mining purposes [4]. The generic transaction distribution of our dataset is shown in Table 1. We see that customers perform 10 different ATM operations. In order of decreasing frequency, these include the withdrawal of money, purchase of products, balance inquiry (query for the current account balance), open-ended credit (acquiring loan as a credit on account), cash deposit (in the customer's own account), PIN validation (on inserting the ATM card), mini-statement request (a short version of the bank statement), open-ended cash (acquiring loan as cash), statement request, and PIN change (request to change PIN code). Also, the frequencies of withdrawl (5213), purchase

S. No.	Transaction	Frequency
1	Withdrawl	5213
2	Purchase	1916
3	Current Balance Inquiry	1064
4	Open-Ended Credit	338
5	Own-Account Cash Deposit	201
6	PIN Validation	131
7	Mini-Statement Request	101
8	Open-Ended Cash	34
9	Statement Request	10
10	PIN Change	10

Table 1. Generic Distribution of ATM Transaction Dataset (adapted from [15])

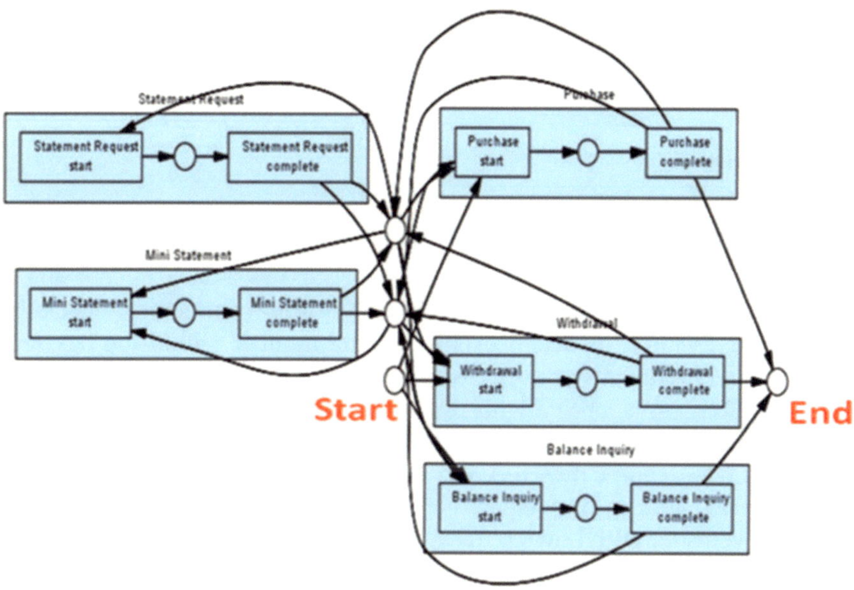

Figure 5. Generic process of ATM transactions mined by the Alpha++ algorithm (adapted from [15])

(1916) and balance inquiry (1064) are quite large as compared to those of other operations. Due to these large frequencies, we conclude that the withdrawl, purchase and balance inquiry operations are most important, and we will learn an adaptive ATM behavior regarding these operations only.

5.2. Alpha++ algorithm

In order to acquire further information regarding the ATM usage, we employ the Alpha++ algorithm plug-in. This plug-in mines the generic process that is implicitly present in the event logs (MXML file). This process is represented as dependencies (directed arcs) between events [1]. Figure 5 shows the output of the Alpha++ algorithm for our ATM transaction dataset. The generic ATM process comprises 5 (out of 10) transactions, i.e., withdrawl, balance inquiry, purchase, mini-statement request, and statement request. Each transaction has a "start" and "complete" event, signaling the start and end of this transaction. These events are represented collectively as a blue rectangle. The circles outside the rectangles represent junctions of process flow for modeling dependencies between events. We have labeled the starting junction as "Start", which represents the start of a transaction (after PIN authorization). Also, we have labeled the terminating junction as "End", which represents the end of a transaction. From "Start", customers either performed a purchase, withdrawl or a balance inquiry. Moreover, customers have requested for the bank statement and the mini-statement, after withdrawl and after a purchase. After this, customers can again perform withdrawl, balance inquiry or purchase. Finally, the "End" junction shows that customers terminate their transactions only after performing one of these three transactions. In summary, customers generally perform withdrawl, balance inquiry and purchase operations, sometimes repeatedly, and follow these up by sometimes viewing their bank statements. This result confirms our statement that withdrawl, balance inquiry and purchase are the more important ATM operations. In order to acquire further details about the sequence of usage (dependencies) of these operations, we employ the Heuristic Miner plug-in (next section).

5.3. Heuristic miner

The Heuristic Miner is a ProM plug-in which uses heuristics to provide mathematical details about the dependencies illustrated by the Alpha++ algorithm [1]. This information is displayed in a graphical structure called the heuristic net, which is very similar to a directed cyclic graph. The heuristic net for our ATM transaction dataset is shown in Figure 6. Here, each box represents a particular event, and the number within the box represents the frequency of this event. Also, a directed arc from event A to event B indicates that B occurred after A. Each arc is labeled with two numbers (one above the other). The upper number indicates the likelihood (probability) that B occurs *immediately* after A, i.e., the user performs no other transaction between A and B. The lower number indicates the frequency with which B occurred after A. As compared to Alpha++, the heuristic net shows the "Start" and "Complete" events for withdrawl, purchase and balance inquiry only. In other words, it ignores the transactions concerning the bank statement requests, possibly due to the smaller frequency of these operations.

From Figure 6, we see that a total of 2732 withdrawals have been performed, out of which 2044 have been performed one after another, 309 have been performed after balance inquiry, and 269 after a purchase. The likelihood of these transactions is very high, i.e., 1, 0.997 and 0.996 respectively. Moreover, balance inquiry was performed 565 times, out of which 186 were performed one after another, 221 after a withdrawl, and 129 after a purchase. These transactions also have a high likelihood, i.e., 0.997, 0.995 and 0.992 respectively. Finally, purchase was performed 858 times, out of which 438 were performed after one another, 353 after a withdrawl, and 59 after a balance inquiry. The likelihood of these transactions is high, i.e., 0.999, 0.997 and 0.983 respectively. These statistics reveal that customers have a strong tendency to repeat their previous operation, particularly withdrawl and purchase. The largest repetition occurs for the withdrawl operation, followed by purchase and balance inquiry.

Also, customers tend to perform different operations in a sequence, albeit with a reduced frequency as compared to their repetitive behavior. More notably, customers tend to withdraw

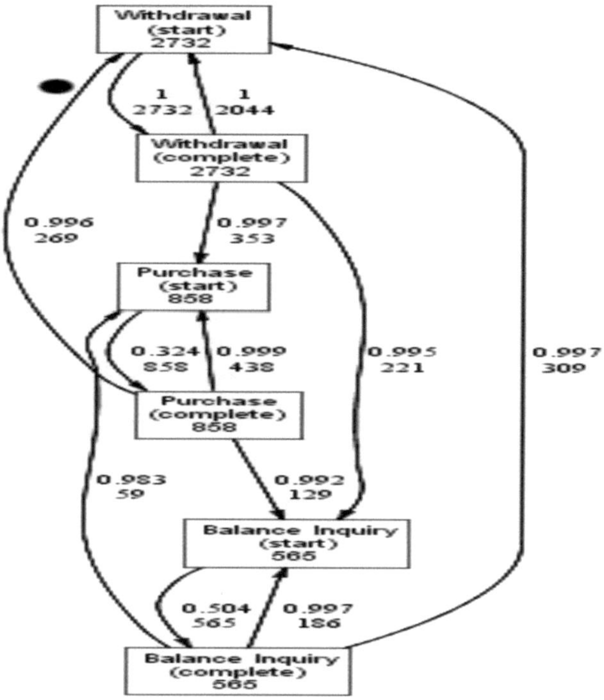

Figure 6. Heuristic net for the ATM transaction dataset (adapted from [15])

money after a balance inquiry or a purchase, and to inquire the balance after a withdrawl or a purchase. Finally, we note that users performed several transactions between starting and completing a purchase (likelihood=0.324), or the balance inquiry (likelihood=0.504). However, users completed their withdrawl operations immediately after starting them (likelihood=1). These results confirm that withdrawl, balance inquiry and purchase are the most important operations. Customers perform them repeatedly, as well as one after the other. If only these operations are shown to the customer, she might spend lesser time browsing through the ATM options, and on a simpler interface. We now employ a series of ProM plug-ins to further investigate the actions of the customers regarding these operations.

5.4. Originator by task matrix

ProM allows us to obtain the distribution of transactions for each individual customer, through the "Originator by Task Matrix" plug-in. A snapshot of this distribution is shown in Figure 7. The left-most column is the ID of the customer followed by the frequencies of balance inquiry, purchase and withdrawl respectively. These figures indicate the customers who have carried out a particular transaction maximum, or minimum, number of times. For instance, the first customer has performed balance inquiry and purchase the maximum number of times (126 and 22 time respectively), while the second one has performed withdrawl the maximum number of times (22). Although everyone has made a withdrawl, there are customers who haven't performed either balance inquiry and/or purchase.

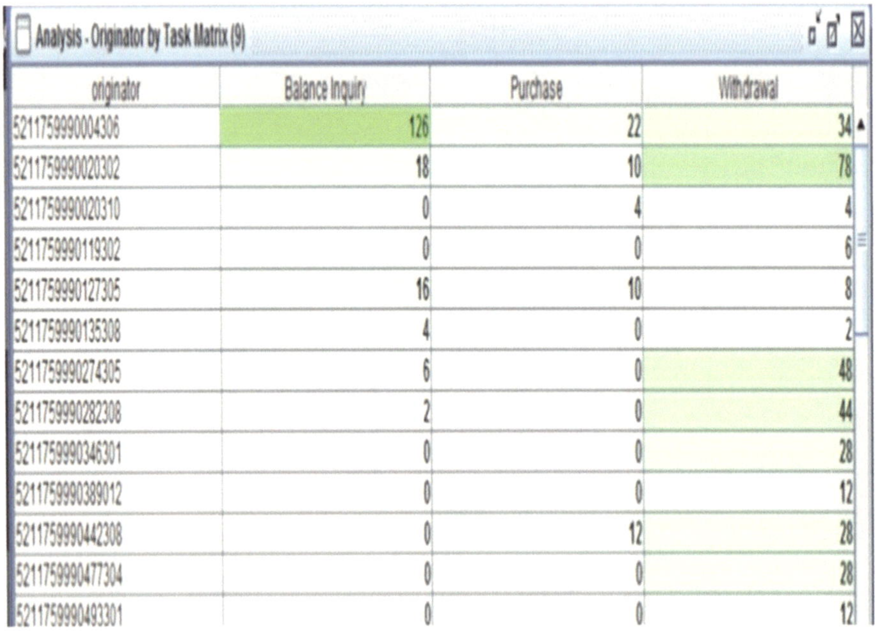

Analysis - Originator by Task Matrix (9)

originator	Balance Inquiry	Purchase	Withdrawal
5211759990004306	126	22	34
5211759990020302	18	10	78
5211759990020310	0	4	4
5211759990119302	0	0	6
5211759990127305	16	10	8
5211759990135308	4	0	2
5211759990274305	6	0	48
5211759990282308	2	0	44
5211759990346301	0	0	28
5211759990389012	0	0	12
5211759990442308	0	12	28
5211759990477304	0	0	28
5211759990493301	0	0	12

Figure 7. Distribution of withdrawl, balance inquiry, and purchase for several customers (adapted from [15])

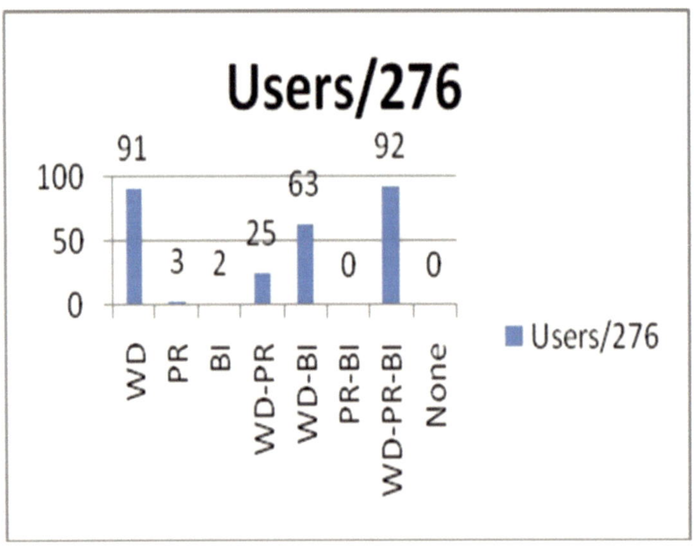

Figure 8. Transaction-based Customer Distribution (adapted from [15])

5.5. Transaction-based customer distribution

To acquire further details about this behavior, we determine the frequency of customers who have performed one or more operations, either individually or collectively (together). These statistics are shown in Figure 8. The y-axis represents the number of customers. On the x-axis, WD, PR and BI represent customers who have made a withdrawl, purchase,

Timestamp	Count	Location	Min_Amnt	Max_Amnt
12:00 AM TO 01:00 AM	120	L1	1	500
01:00 AM TO 02:00 AM	81	L1	1	300
02:00 AM TO 03:00 AM	64	L2	1	185
03:00 AM TO 04:00 AM	34	L2	2	350
04:00 AM TO 05:00 AM	9	L3	1	615
05:00 AM TO 06:00 AM	38	L3	1	820
06:00 AM TO 07:00 AM	36	L4	1	1000
07:00 AM TO 08:00 AM	77	L4	1	500

Table 2. Location-based withdrawl distribution (adapted from [15])

and balance inquiry respectively. Also, WD-PR, WD-BI, PR-BI, and WD-PR-BI represent customers who have made a withdrawl and purchase together, a withdrawl and balance inquiry together, a purchase and balance inquiry together, and all three operations together, respectively. Finally, the label "None" represents those customers who didn't perform any transaction. From Figure 8, we see that every customer performs one or more transactions. Also, withdrawl was performed by 91 customers, purchase by 3 customers and balance inquiry by 2 customers. Viewing the operations collectively, 92 customers perform all three operations, 25 make withdrawl and purchase together, while 63 make withdrawl and balance inquiry together. Also, no one performs purchase and balance inquiry together. These results show that a majority of the customers either perform all three operations collectively, or only the withdrawl operation. Based on this, we deem the withdrawl operation to be the most important one for the sake of designing an adaptive ATM behavior. To this end, we will now mine three separate distributions regarding withdrawl.

5.6. Location-based withdrawl distribution

We also acquired the withdrawl distribution based on the location of ATM terminals, shown in Table 2. In our transaction dataset, we have withdrawl information of 16 ATM locations in Kuwait. In order to avoid a length analysis, we show a snapshot of the withdrawl distribution for four locations only, i.e., L1, L2, L3 and L4 (column 'Location')[7]. We have grouped the withdrawls according to one-hourly time periods (column 'Timestamp'). For each time period, we show the number of customers who have made a withdrawl in this period (column 'Count'), and the minimum and maximum amounts withdrawn in this period (columns 'Min_Amnt' and 'Max_Amnt'). We can see that, at L1, around 200 customers access the ATM between 12 AM and 2 AM, and withdraw between 1 KD - 500 KD. At L2, around 100 customers access the ATM between 2 AM and 4 AM, and withdraw between 1 KD - 350 KD. Similarly at L3, around 50 customers access the ATM between 4 AM and 6 AM, and withdraw between 1 KD - 820 KD. Finally, at L4, around 100 customers access the ATM between 6AM and 8AM, and withdraw between 1 KD - 1000 KD. These statistics reveal the overall withdrawl behavior of customers at a given ATM location. Using them, we can also calculate the *usage rate* of an ATM, i.e., the number of withdrawls (operations) performed in a given timestamp. For instance, there might be heavy usage traffic at some ATM from 1300-1400 (during lunch

[7] The actual names of the location are kept anonymous.

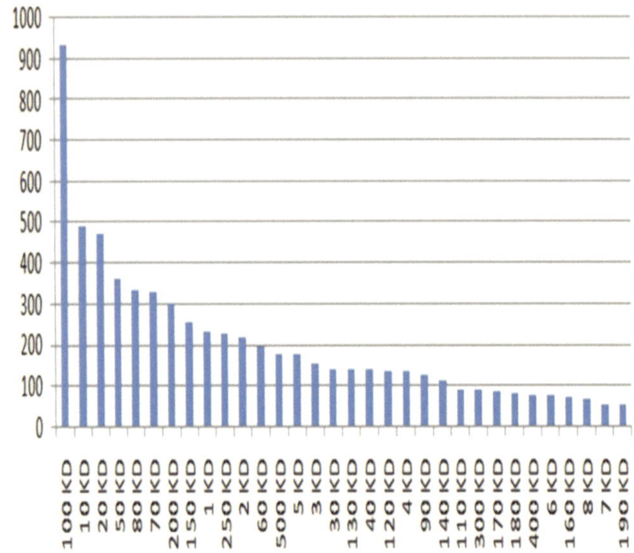

Figure 9. Distribution of the amount withdrawn by customers, KD = Kuwaiti Dinar (adapted from [15])

break), because users collectively perform 80 withdrawls in this interval. These statistics can help us in identifying heavy traffic ATMs, at which a large number of withdrawls are being performed daily, at various timestamps of peak activities. Then, an adaptive ATM behavior can be employed at these timestamps in order to minimize the ATM usage time.

5.7. Amount-based withdrawl distribution

Using another ProM plug-in, we acquired the distribution of the amount withdrawn by the customers. The results are shown in Figure 9. Here, the X-axis shows the amount in Kuwaiti Dinar (KD)[8], and the Y-axis shows the frequency of the withdrawn amount. The distribution shows that 100 KD has been withdrawn a maximum number of times (around 900), while amounts of 10 KD and 20 KD have been withdrawn around 500 times. Moreover, the amounts of 50 KD, 70 KD, 80 KD and 200 KD have been withdrawn between 300 - 350 times. Customers have also withdrawn more than 100 KD, and very small amounts, e.g., 1KD and 2KD, as well. In other words, we can acquire the top-N frequent amounts being withdrawn by customers. If only these amounts are shown to a customer at peak activity times, she will have to browse lesser options on a simpler interface, possibly reducing her usage time.

5.8. Customer-based withdrawl distribution

Finally, we acquired the withdrawl distribution for each individual customer. This provides more detail, as compared to the generic distribution shown in Figure 8. For instance, Figure 10 shows the withdrawl distribution for two customers including timestamps of withdrawls. Let's assume that the distribution on the left and right belongs to Customer A and Customer

[8] Dinar is the currency of Kuwait

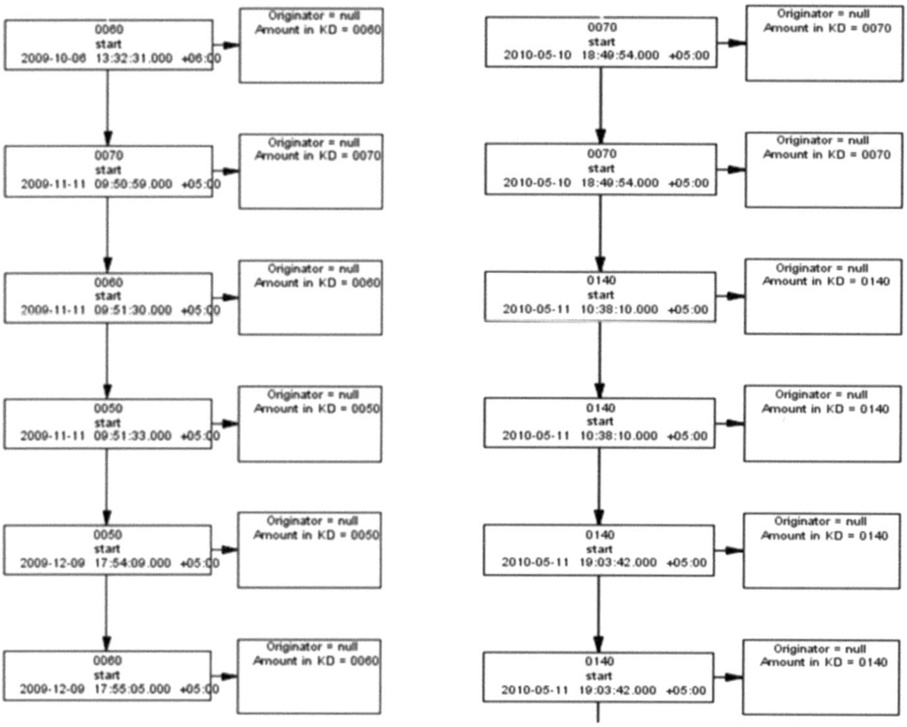

Figure 10. Withdrawl distribution for two individual customers

B respectively [9]. We can see that, from October 2009 to December 2009, Customer A has withdrawn 60 KD, 70 KD, 60 KD, 50 KD, 50 KD and finally 60 KD, in this order. These withdrawls have been made in the mornings, afternoons and evenings. Also Customer B has withdrawn only two different amounts, i.e., 70 KD and 140 KD, over a period of two days in May 2010. These withdrawls have been made in the mornings and evenings. Until now, we have talked about developing adaptive interfaces for a customer population. However, using the customer-based withdrawl statistics, we can develop adaptive interfaces for each customer individually. This, however, is part of our future work (Section 8).

6. Adaptive ATM interfaces

In this section, we use our ProM results to describe and illustrate five adaptive ATM interfaces. In doing so, we will use the Pakistani currency PKR (Pakistani Rupees) rather than Kuwaiti Dinar (KD). Let us initially summarize our ProM results (abbreviated with 'R') as follows:

- **R1:** Withdrawl is the most frequent operation performed by customers, followed by purchase and balance inquiry,
- **R2:** These operations are frequently repeated, with withdrawl having the highest repetition frequency,

[9] Customers are identified by their ATM card number, which we keep confidential.

- **R3:** These operations are also performed in a sequence (one after another); sequences containing withdrawl have the highest frequency,
- **R4:** A majority of customers perform only the withdrawl operation,
- **R5:** A majority of customers withdraw only specific amounts,
- **R6:** It is possible to obtain the rate of the withdrawl operation at a given location (ATM terminal).
- **R7:** A majority of customers perform withdrawl, balance inquiry and purchase collectively.

Recall that our primary goal is to reduce the ATM usage time for the customers (Section 1). This can be achieved particularly at locations with heavy usage traffic. Due to R6, we can easily identify such ATMs. For instance, ATMs installed near a large corporate environment, or a busy thoroughfare, can witness heavy traffic at peak activity times, e.g., from 0900 to 1000, 1330-1530, 1900-2100 etc. We now define five adaptive ATM interfaces which can be employed at heavy traffic ATM's:

1. **Interface 1:** This shows only the most frequently used ATM operations to the customer,
2. **Interface 2:** This shows only the most frequently withdrawn amounts to the customer,
3. **Interface 3:** This queries the customers regarding their willingness to perform another withdrawl (after a withdrawl)?
4. **Interface 4:** This shows the customer's current balance on several screens autonomously,
5. **Interface 5:** This queries the customers regarding their consent to view the purchase history (or not)?

Let us discuss these interfaces separately.

6.1. Interface 1

As can be seen from R1, R2, R3 and R4, customers frequently use only a subset of the ATM operations. At a heavy traffic ATM, we can only show these specific operations to the user, once she logs on to her account. The remaining operations can then be accessed through some other option. Such an interface is shown in Figure 11. Here, the screen only shows the "Cash Withdrawl" and "Balance Inquiry" operations, while "Other Operations" allows access to the remaining ATM operations. Showing lesser options leads to more usable interfaces, as customers can avoid the cognitive effort required in browsing through all ATM operations, which are typically 5-10 in number (Figure 2). Also, in relationship with the principles of usability, online customers prefer to view a smaller number of text options [16]. We believe that both these factors will lead to a reduction in the ATM usage time.

6.2. Interface 2

As can be seen from R4 and R5, customers frequently use the withdrawl operation, and withdraw only specific amounts. Typically a pre-defined set of amounts is displayed to every customer by default, which could be 5-10 in number. On the other hand, if we show only the frequently-withdrawn amounts, it is possible that the overall usage time at a heavy

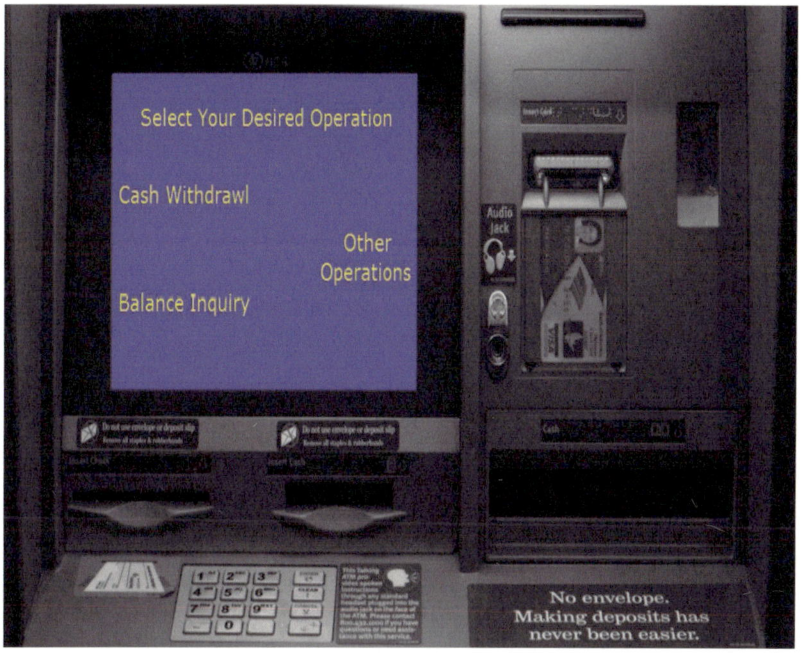

Figure 11. Adaptive Interface 1 showing only the frequently used options to the customer

Figure 12. Adaptive Interface 2 showing only the frequently withdrawn amounts to the customer

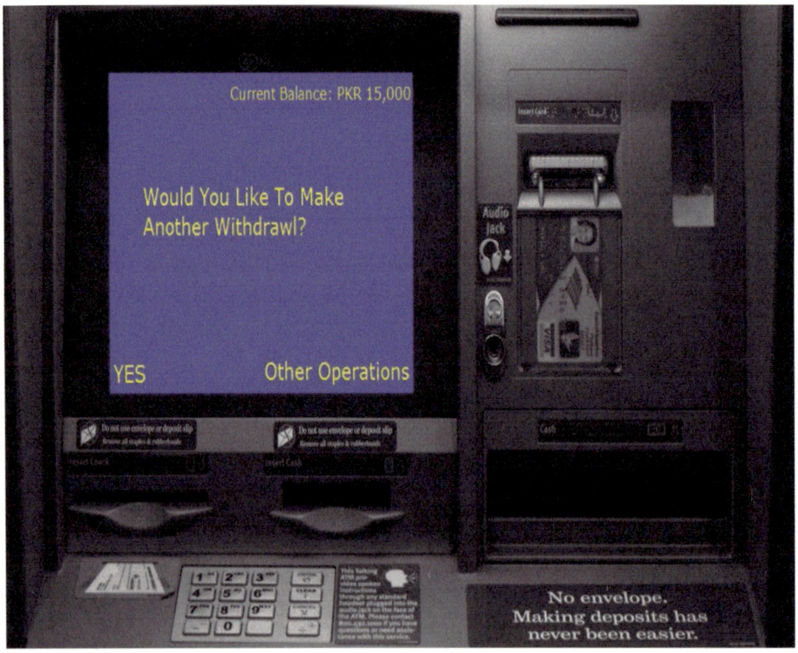

Figure 13. Adaptive Interface 3 querying the customer directly about performing another withdrawl

traffic ATM will be reduced, in a given time frame. Such an interface is shown in Figure 12. Here, the screen shows amounts of PKR (Pakistani Rupees) 2500, 4000, 7000, 10000 and 15000, which could be the top-5 frequently withdrawn amounts. Note that we have the flexibility of showing top-N amounts. In order to withdraw other amounts, customers can select "Other Amounts". We believe that such an interface can assist a majority of users in quickly selecting their desired amount. For instance, in Pakistan, there are not many ATMs which display the withdrawl amount of PKR 7000. At a given ATM, if 80% of customers want to withdraw this amount, they have to select "Other Amounts" and then type this amount. This process could consume from 10-30 seconds, because the response time of ATMs could be slow [18]. So, showing PKR 7000 in the initial withdrawl amounts could minimize this time delay considerably. Similarly to Interface 1, Interface 2 is also a usable interface showing lesser amount of text (amounts).

6.3. Interface 3

As can be seen from R2 and Section 5.3, a large number of customers who withdraw money, follow it up by making another withdrawl. In essence, customers can perform withdrawls in a sequence. In a typical scenario, customers have to return to the main ATM menu (showing all the operations) after a withdrawl, and then re-select withdrawl from this menu. This process could consume from several seconds to half a minute, depending on the ATM's response time [18]. If we can autonomously query the customer about performing another withdrawl, she can avoid wasting this time. Such an interface is shown in Figure 13. Once the user has completed a withdrawl, we can show this interface to her. If she selects "YES", the withdrawl amounts will be displayed to her (as in Figure 12). Otherwise, she can select "Other

Figure 14. Adaptive Interface 4 showing the current balance before a withdrawl

Operations" (the balance being shown towards the top-right will be explained in next section). Interface 3 is another example of a usable interface: it contains a small amount of text which can be read clearly.

6.4. Interface 4

As can be seen from R3 and Section 5.3, customers tend to perform a balance inquiry after a withdrawl operation and also after a purchase. This requires accessing the main menu and selecting "Balance Inquiry". We have seen that this could consume up to half a minute, depending on the ATM response times. This time could be saved if the ATM displays the current balance autonomously for the customer. This could be done on several screens. For instance, Figure 14 shows a balance of PKR 2,50000 (at the top-right corner) when the user logs on to her account. Also, Figure 15 shows a balance of PKR 1,20000 just before a withdrawl operation, and Figure 13 shows a balance of PKR 15,000 just after a withdrawl operation. In all these interfaces, we cater for the privacy of customers by displaying the balance in smaller fonts size, and in a corner of the screen. This would prevent other customers from viewing the balance (clearly) over the shoulder of the customer. This situation could occur in open-space ATMs (Figure 16), but not in ATMs installed within cabins (Figure 17).

6.5. Interface 5

Our final adaptive interface (Interface 5) is regarding the purchase behavior of customers. Note that a purchase is made by an ATM card in some market, but not at an ATM machine. From R1, R2, and R3, we can see that purchasing is a frequent operation, occurs repeatedly, as well as after a withdrawl and a balance inquiry. After a purchase is made, customers

Figure 15. Adaptive Interface 4 showing the current balance after a withdrawl

Figure 16. An ATM installed in an open space

could be interested in viewing their purchase history, which is detailed in the bank statement. Customers typically access the bank statement from the main menu, which could consume time. In order to minimize this time, we can autonomously query the customer to view her purchase history when she logs on (Figure 18), and when she logs out (Figure 19). Similarly to Interface 3, Interface 5 is also a usable interface containing a small amount of clearly-legible text. One final comment is concerning R7; there exists a user majority which performs withdrawl, balance inquiry and purchase collectively. To cater for this trend, we have proposed Interface 4 and Interface 5, which attempt to reduce usage time regarding

Figure 17. An ATM Cabin

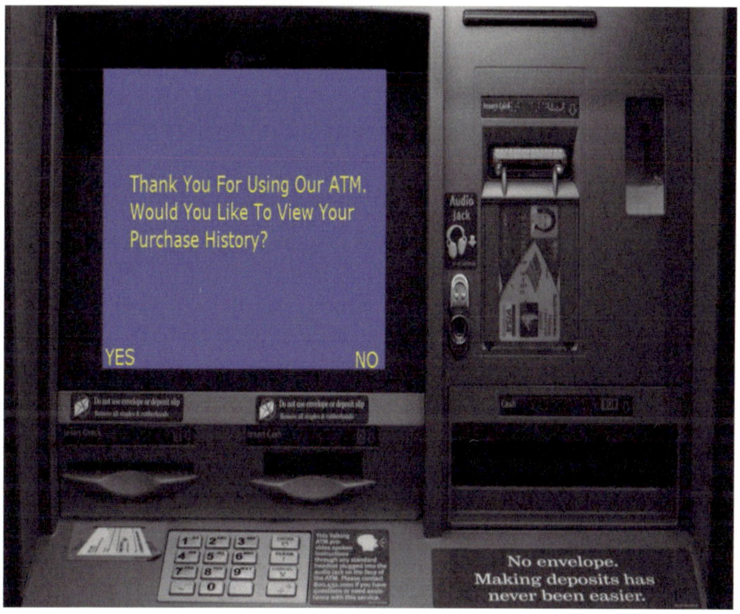

Figure 18. Adaptive Interface 5 autonomously querying the customer about viewing her purchase history, at logout

balance inquiry and purchase respectively. Note that we have proposed Interface 2 and Interface 3 for the majority of users who perform only the withdrawl operation.

7. ATM usage questionnaire and results

We have described five different types of adaptive ATM interfaces. We believe that these interfaces could considerably reduce the ATM usage time at heavy traffic ATMs. We also have the flexibility to apply these interfaces at specific timestamps related to heavy traffic, for instance, during lunch breaks, or in the evenings. In order to acquire the opinions of the ATM customers regarding these interfaces, we conducted an online survey (questionnaire)

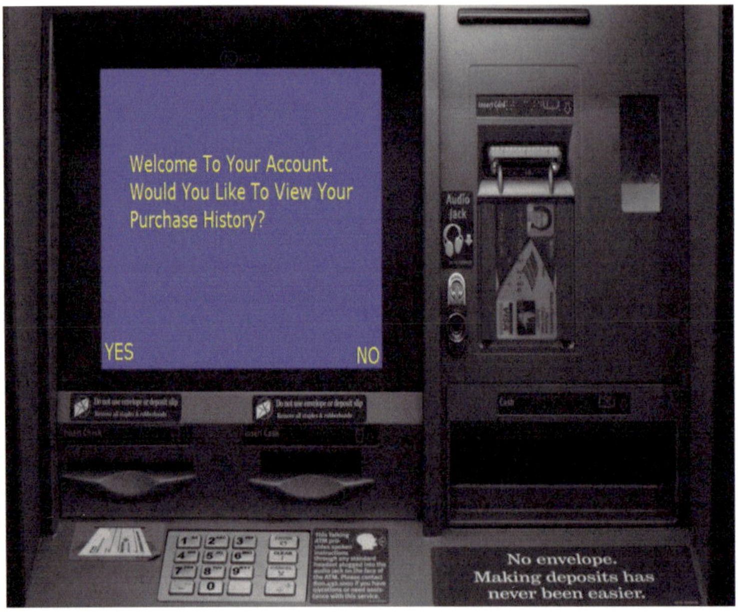

Figure 19. Adaptive Interface 5 autonomously querying the customer about viewing her purchase history, at login

comprising 15 statements[10]. In all, 216 users completed the questionnaire, over a period of two months (from 1st December 2011 to 24 January 2012). They provided three types of data regarding ATM usage, which we analyze in the following three sub-sections.

7.1. Basic analysis

Some basic analysis about the users is listed below:

- 81% of the users were males and 19% were females,
- 71% of the users were employed (either permanently or part-time),
- 80% of the users were Pakistani residents with the remaining 20% residing internationally,
- 94% of the users owned an ATM card; half of the users owned one card, and 45% owned two or more cards, and
- 63% of the users use ATM for 30 seconds to 1 minute, while 21% take 30 seconds or less. Around 15% of the users take more than a minute.

Based on these statistics, our users can be considered representative of the typical ATM users: they comprise both males and females, are both employed and non-employed, and are located across different countries. They own one or more ATM cards, and use ATM services for typical ATM usage times [10, 17].

[10] Available online at https://docs.google.com/a/nu.edu.pk/spreadsheet/viewform?formkey=dEtpa0FvRTRxTEZZOFNnRTZaOHdjb1E6MQ#gid=0

7.2. Analysis regarding ATM usage

We acquired further details from the users regarding their ATM usage, which are listed below:

- 75% of the users are satisfied with their ATM usage, while only 3% are dissatisfied,
- Users are satisfied due to several reasons, i.e., ATMs are much faster as compared to manual bank transactions (82%), avoid interaction with bank personnel (64%), are more accessible (64%), and facilitate the usage of the same ATM card at ATMs of different banks (58%),
- Users are dissatisfied due to several reasons, i.e., ATMs are mostly out of service (67%), are insecure (44%), and charge high fees on the usage of ATMs of other banks (30%). More importantly, around 30% of users believe that old people take too much time using ATMs, while another 30% get frustrated by waiting in queues to use ATM.

Generally speaking, around 60% of the users are dissatisfied due to more time taken by other customers in using ATMs. *This provides a concrete motivation for the application of our work, i.e., applying adaptive approaches to ATM usage processes to minimize the ATM usage time.* Concerning the issue of insecurity, users feel more insecure in using open-space ATMs; 70% of the users believe that they will feel more secure using ATM's installed in cabins. Based on this, *we believe that our adaptive approach can serve the users in a better way if it were applied inside ATM cabins only.*

7.3. Analysis regarding adaptive ATM interfaces

Finally, we acquired opinions of the users regarding our adaptive ATM interfaces, which are listed below.

- We inquired about Interface 4, i.e., whether (or not) users would prefer the system to show the current balance on several screen simultaneously. 75% of the users want to view the balance in this way, but under secure conditions, in which people in the queue won't get a chance to view the balance over the customer's shoulder; this condition can be easily satisfied by using ATM cabins.
- We inquired about Interface 1, i.e., whether (or not) users would prefer to view only frequently used ATM operations. Around 38% of users are willing to view frequent operations (because it will save time), while a similar percentage of users is not. However, the remaining 25% of users, although indecisive, are willing to give it a try. Overall, around 65% of users are willing to view frequent operations.
- We inquired about Interface 2, , i.e., whether (or not) users would prefer to view only frequently-withdrawn amounts. 35% of users are willing to view these amounts but around 50% believe that showing all amounts is the better option. However, around 20% of (indecisive) users are willing to give it a try. In essence, more than half of the users believe that showing Interface 2 could be a good option.
- We inquired about the need of heavy traffic ATMs to assist users in completing their ATM transactions more efficiently. Around 70% of users believe that this need should be satisfied, particularly in hours of peak activities.

In conclusion, a majority of users are willing to adopt Interface 1, Interface 2, and Interface 4. Also, users think these interfaces should be shown in ATM cabins witnessing typical heavy traffic. Note that we deliberately didn't query the users regarding Interface 3 and Interface 5. We didn't query regarding Interface 5 because, in Pakistan, ATM customers do not typically make many purchases using ATM cards[11]. Regarding Interface 3, we didn't consider the opinion of the users as important; as system designers, we decided in advance to implement Interface 3 whenever a majority of withdrawls are found to occur repeatedly (one after another).

8. Conclusions and future work

In this paper, we have applied process (data) mining techniques on a transaction dataset of Automated Teller Machines (ATMs). Based on the results, we have proposed a set of five *adaptive* ATM interfaces, which can reduce the ATM usage time at heavy traffic ATMs and particularly at peak activity hours. Our interfaces have the potential to reduce the frustration of the users waiting at ATM queues, display much simpler (usable) screens (e.g., for old people), and can have a positive impact on customer relationship management. The first interface shows only the most frequently-used ATM operations, and the second one shown only the most frequently-withdrawn amounts. The third interface queries the user explicitly for another withdrawl (after the current withdrawl is completed), and the fourth one autonomously outputs the balance inquiry on several screens. Finally, the fifth interface queries the user explicitly for showing her purchase history. Interfaces 1, 2, 3 and 5 are examples of usable (simpler) interfaces containing lesser amounts of text. They can reduce the cognitive effort required by old people in using ATMs, possibly reducing their ATM usage time. In order to acquire the opinions of the customers regarding our interfaces, we conducted a real-user survey. The survey consisted of 15 statements which were filled by 216 respondents. The results show that a large majority of representative ATM users (more than 70%) are willing to employ the first, second and fourth interfaces[12].

Our work has been approved by the State Bank of Pakistan, the primary authority which manages all banking operations in Pakistan. We are currently applying process mining on the dataset of a Pakistani bank. Our preliminary results show that several of our interfaces can be applied on the ATMs of this bank in heavy traffic hours. We will test these interfaces on an ATM testbed, which is provided by the multi-national company Transaction Processing Systems[13]. Moreover, our interfaces are currently adapted to the behavior of a customer population. Specifically, we mined the transaction dataset of around 250 customers, and suggested interfaces which are applicable for a majority of these customers. As part of the future work, we plan to propose a set of adaptive interfaces for each customer *individually*, i.e., we will mine the sequence of operations for each user separately, and use the results to propose the adaptive interfaces. For instance, for one customer, our second adaptive interface can show withdrawl amount of PKR 5000, 10000, and 20,000. For another customer, these amounts could be PKR 6000, 8000 and 10000.

---

[11] We have observed this trend from our personal experience lasting over several years; we have no statistics to prove this claim.

[12] We didn't query the users regarding the other two interfaces.

[13] http://www.tpsonline.com/

Acknowledgements

We acknowledge the assistance provided by Transaction Processing Systems in helping us to acquire the ATM transaction data sets, and also for providing the testbed for testing our interfaces.

Author details

Ghulam Mujtaba Shaikh
Sukkur Institute of Business Administration, Department of Computer Science, Airport Road, Sukkur, Pakistan

Tariq Mahmood
National University of Computer and Emerging Sciences, Department of Computer Science, Shah Lateef Town, National Highway, Karachi, Pakistan

9. References

[1] Aalst, W. [1998]. The application of petri nets to workflow management, *The Journal of Circuits, Systems and Computers*, Vol. 8, pp. 21–66.

[2] Cook, J. E. & Wolf, A. L. [1998]. Discovering Models of Software Processes from Event-Based Data, *ACM Transactions on Software Engineering and Methodology* 7: 215–249. URL: *http://citeseerx.ist.psu.edu/viewdoc/summary?doi=10.1.1.46.5456*

[3] Fluxicon [2011]. Nitro flux capactitor, http://fluxicon.com/blog/2010/09/nitro/.

[4] Han, J. & Kamber, M. [2006]. *Data Mining: Concepts and Techniques*, The Morgan Kaufmann Series in Data Management Systems, 2 edn, Morgan Kaufmann.

[5] Hofstra, P. [2009]. *Analysing the effect of consumer knowledge on product usability using process mining techniques*, Master's thesis, Technische Universiteit Eindhoven.

[6] Inc., E. B. S. [2011]. Atmta, http://www.esq.com/products-a-solutions/category/4-atm-transaction-analyzer.

[7] Keane, J. [1997]. High performance banking, *Seventh International Workshop on Research Issues in Data Engineering, 1997.*, pp. 66–69.

[8] Khawaja, K. & Manarvi, I. [2009]. Evaluating customer perceptions towards atm services in financial institutions; a case study of pakistani banks, *International Conference on Computers and Industrial Engineering, CIE 2009*, pp. 1440–1445.

[9] LevelFour [2011]. Is a new business and technology model required for atm channel.

[10] Luca, A. D., Langheinrich, M. & Hussmann, H. [2010]. Towards understanding atm security: a field study of real world atm use, *SOUPS*.

[11] Mans, R., Schonenberg, M., Song, M., van der Aalst, W. & Bakker, P. [2008]. Process mining in health care, *International Conference on Health Informatics (HEALTHINF'08)*, Funchal, Maldeira, Portugal, pp. 118–125.

[12] Morgan, J. [2012a]. A conceptual model for personalising an automated teller machine, http://usabilityetc.com/articles/atm-conceptual-model/.

[13] Morgan, J. [2012b]. Learning user preferences to personalise smart card applications, http://usabilityetc.com/articles/learning-user-preferences/.

[14] Mujtaba, G. & Mahmood, T. [2011a]. Adative automated teller machines - part i, *Proceedings of the 4th International Conference on Information and Communication Technologies*, pp. 1–6.

[15] Mujtaba, G. & Mahmood, T. [2011b]. Adative automated teller machines - part ii, *Proceedings of the 4th International Conference on Information and Communication Technologies*, pp. 6–12.

[16] Nielsen, J., Molich, R., Snyder, C. & Farrell, S. [2001]. *E-Commerce User Experience*, Nielsen Norman Group.

[17] Noonan, T. [2000]. Barriers to using automatic teller machines: A review of the useability of self-service banking facilities for australians with disabilities, *Australian Human Rights and Equal Opportunity Commission* pp. 61–101.

[18] Perakh, A. V. [2010]. *ATM (Automated Teller Machine) Business Basics*, 2 edn, Cashflow ATM, Inc.

[19] Ping, Z. L. & Liang, S. Q. [2010]. Data mining application in banking-customer relationship management, *Computer Application and System Modeling (ICCASM)*.

[20] Prognosis [2011]. Atm/pos products, integrated research limited, http://www.prognosis.com/products _and_solutions/atm_/_pos_monitoring/products/page__1550.aspx.

[21] Rigat, J. [2009]. *Data mining analysis of defect data in software development process*, Master's thesis, Technische Universiteit Eindhoven.

[22] Tarakanov-Plax, A. [2004]. Use and non-use of automatic teller machines by older people in israel, *Gerontechnology* 3(2): 107–110.

[23] van Dongen, B. F., de Medeiros, A. K. A., Verbeek, H. M. W., Weijters, A. J. M. M. & van der Aalst, W. M. P. [2005]. The prom framework: A new era in process mining tool support, *ICATPN*, pp. 444–454.

[24] van Dongen, B. F. & van der Aalst, W. M. P. [2005]. A meta model for process mining data, *CAiSE WORKSHOPS*, pp. 309–320.

Chapter 13

The Performance Evaluation of Speech Recognition by Comparative Approach

R.L.K. Venkateswarlu, R. Raviteja and R. Rajeev

Additional information is available at the end of the chapter

http://dx.doi.org/10.5772/50640

1. Introduction

For more than five decades, Automatic speech recognition has been the area of active research. This problem was thoroughly studied with the advent of digital computing and signal processing. Increased awareness of the advantages of conversational systems led to the development of this problem. Speech recognition has wide applications and includes voice-controlled appliances fully featured speech-to-text software, automation of operator-assisted services and voice recognition aids for the handicapped.

There are four main approaches in speech recognition:

The acoustic –phonetic approach, The pattern recognition approach, The artificial intelligence approach and Neural network approach. Hidden Markov Model(HMM) and Gaussian Mixture models are also adopted in ASR.

Speech recognition has a big potential in becoming an important factor of interaction between human and computer in the near future. A successful speech recognition system has to determine features not only present in the input pattern at one point in time but also features of the input pattern changing over time (Berthold, M.R, Benyettou). In the speech recognition domain, the first model used by weibel is based on multilayer perceptron using Time Delay Neural network. But this model was the hard time processing. For new applications, the adjustment of parameters became a laborious stain.

RBF networks don't require a special adjustment and with regard to the Time delay Neural network the training time becomes shorter. But RBF problem is the shift invariant in time [Berthold,M.R].

The NN approach for SR can be divided into two main categories: Conventional neural networks and recurrent neural networks. The main rival to the multilayer perceptron is RBF

INTECH
open science | open minds

© 2012 Venkateswarlu et al., licensee InTech. This is an open access chapter distributed under the terms of the Creative Commons Attribution License (http://creativecommons.org/licenses/by/3.0), which permits unrestricted use, distribution, and reproduction in any medium, provided the original work is properly cited.

which is becoming an increasingly popular neural network with diverse applications. Traditional statistical pattern classification techniques became inspiration for RBF networks.

In RBF network, process is performed in the hidden layer which is its unique feature. The patterns in the input space form clusters. The distance from the cluster center can be measured if the centers of these clusters are known. Further this distance measure is made non-linear so that it gives a value close to 1 if a pattern is in an area that is close to a cluster center. Serious rivals to MLP are RBF networks which are statistical feed-forward networks. The learning mechanisms in these networks are not biologically plausible- they have not been taken by some researchers who insist on biological anologies.

2. Present work

In the dependent mode, the sequence of sound units from the speech signal can be determined so that the linguistic message in the form of text can be decoded from the speech signal.

The steps used in the present speech recognition system are discussed below:

2.1. Speech dataset design

To design the system, five different speech datasets were used that consists of speech of both male and female. The recordings which are used in this work, were made with 8 bits and 11 KHz via a headset microphone in a closed room. The following speech dataset is chosen for speech recognition system.

The basic unit for sentence parsing and understanding is word. In order to identify the sentences, the words must be identified properly. The following dataset which consists of words that are made up of both consonants and vowels is chosen. The dataset composed of 6 words is tabulated in Table 1.

Words	passion	galaxy	marvellous
Pronunciation	pas·sion	gal·ax·y	mar·vel·ous
Words	manifestation	almighty	pardon
Pronunciation	man·i·fes·ta·tion	al·might·y	par·don

Table 1. Words with pronunciation

2.2. Speech database design

Speech Database Six different speakers (2 male and 4 female) are allowed to utter 6 words of speech dataset 4. So the speech database consists of 216 .wav files.

2.3. Preprocessing

Using good quality recording equipment, the speech signals are recorded in a low noise environment. The signals are sampled at 11KHz frequency. When the input data is surrounded by silence, reasonable results can be achieved in isolated word recognition.

2.4. Speech processing

The speech signal also contains data that is unnecessary like noise and non speech, which need to be removed before feature extraction. The resulting speech signals will be passed through an endpoint detector to determine the beginning and the ending of a speech data.

2.5. Sampling rate

Samples at sampling rate 11KHz are chosen to represent all speech sounds.

2.6. Windowing

A window length of 0.015 is selected for the given 12Mel frequency coefficients for time 0.005 seconds by the Praat object software tool.

2.7. Soft signal

The analog signal captured is converted into a smoothened analog signal by speech preprocessing which can be readily accessed by machine.

2.8. Front – End analysis

The speech signal exists as pressure variations in air. These pressure variations are converted into an electric current related to pressure by using microphone. In humans, the pressure variations are converted by ear into a series of nerve impulses which are then transmitted to the brain. For speech recognition task, selection of features is very important. For achieving good results, good features are required. Proper identification of features for speech recognition task and a strategy to extract these features from speech signal is the basic problem in speech recognition.

2.9. Feature extractor

The object of feature extractor is to transform an input in the signals space to an output in a feature space by using priori knowledge in order to achieve some desired criteria (Rabiner, 1993). The feature extractor (FE) block is designed in speech recognition in order to reduce the complexity of the problem before the next stage starts to work with data. Its aim is to use a priori knowledge to transform an input in the signal space to an output in a feature space to achieve some desired criteria. If lots of clusters present in a high dimensional space are to be classified, then FE transforms that space such that classification becomes easier.

2.9.1. LPCC analysis

Linear predictive coding (LPC) is a tool used in audio signal processing and also for speech processing which represents the spectral envelope of a digital speech signal in compressed form with the information of a linear predictive mode. The speech signal is analyzed by LPC by estimating the formants, their effects are removed and intensity and frequency of the remaining buzz are estimated. The process of removing the formants is known as inverse filtering. After the subtraction of the filtered modeled signal, the remaining signal is called the residue. This residue signal, the formants and the number which represents the intensity and frequency of the buzz are stored or transmitted elsewhere. The speech signal is synthesized by LPC by reversing the process using the buzz parameters and the residue in order to produce a source signal. This process is done on short chunks of the speech signal, as it varies with time, which are called frames. 30 to 50 frames per second are required for intelligible speech with good compression. LPC is one of the most powerful speech analysis techniques. LPC is the most useful method for encoding good quality speech at a low bit rate. It provides extremely accurate estimates of speech parameters. Since a very small error can distort the whole spectrum, LPC has to be tolerant of transmission errors. A small error might make the prediction filter unstable.

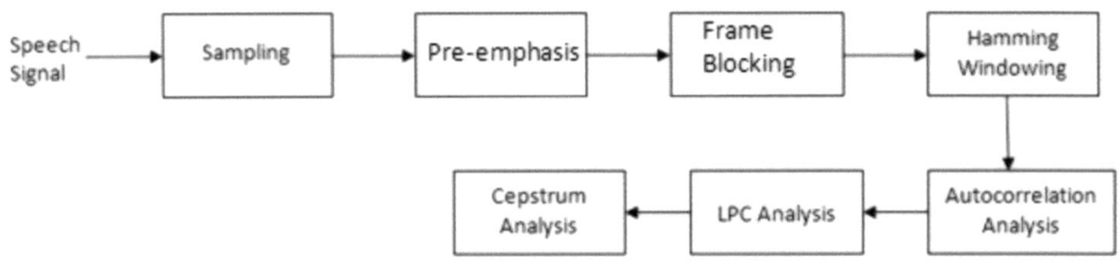

Figure 1. Feature Extractor schematic diagram for LPCC analysis

2.9.1.1. Speech sampling

Higher sampling frequency or more sampling precision is needed to achieve higher recognition accuracy. Commercial speech recognizers typically use comparable parameter values and achieve impressive results. It is not necessary to increase the sampling rate beyond 11,025 Hz or the sampling precision higher than 8 bits.

2.9.1.2. Pre-emphasis

The speech waveform which is digitized has a high dynamic range and it suffers from additive noise. So pre-emphasis is applied to spectrally flatten the signal so as to make it less susceptible to finite precision effects in the processing of speech.The most widely used pre-emphasis is the fixed first-order system. The calculation of pre-emphasis is shown as follows.

$$H(z) = 1 - az^{-1} \quad 0.9 \leq a \leq 1.0$$

The most common value for a is 0.95 (Deller et at; 1993). A Pre-Emphasis can be expressed as

$$\hat{s}(n) = s(n) - 0.95\, s\,(n-1)$$

2.9.1.3. Frame blocking

The speech signal is dynamic or time-variant in the nature. According to Rabiner (1993), the speech signal is assumed to be stationary when it is examined over a short period of time. In order to analyze the speech signal, it has to be blocked into frames of N samples, with adjacent frames being separated by M samples. If $M \leq N$, then LPC spectral estimates from frame to frame will be quite smooth. On the other hand if $M > N$ there will be no overlap between adjacent frames.

2.9.1.4. Windowing

Each frame is windowed in order to minimize the signal discontinuities or the signal is tapered to zero at the starting and ending of each frame.If window is defined as w(n), then the windowed signal is

$$\tilde{x}(n) = x(n)w\,(n), 0 \leq n \leq N-1$$

A typical window used is the Hamming window, which has the form

$$w(n) = 0.54 - 0.46\cos\left(\frac{2n}{N-1}\right), 0 \leq n \leq N-1$$

The value of the analysis frame length N must be long enough so that tapering effects of the window do not seriously affect the result.

2.9.1.5. Autocorrelation analysis

Auto correlation analysis can be used to find fundamental frequency or a pitch of the signal. It can also be used for finding repeating patterns in a signal or identifying the missing fundamental frequency. The technique relies on finding the co-relation between the signal and a delayed version of itself. Each frame of windowed signal is next auto correlated to give

$$R(n) = \sum_{x=0}^{N-1-m} \tilde{x}\,(n)\,\tilde{x}(n+m), m = 0,1,2,\ldots,P.$$

Where, the highest autocorrelation value, P is the order of the LPC analysis. The selection of p depends primarily on the sampling rate

2.9.1.6. LPC analysis

The next processing step is the LPC analysis which converts each frame of autocorrelation coefficients R into the LPC parameters. The LPC parameters can be the LPC coefficients. This method of converting autocorrelation coefficients to LPC coefficients is known as Durbin's method. Levinson-Durbin recursive algorithm is used for LPC analysis.

$$E_0 = R(0)$$

$$k_i = \left[R(i) - \sum_{j-1}^{i-1} a_j^{i-1}\, R(i-j)\right] / E_{i-1,}\ 1 \leq i \leq p$$

$$a_i^i = k_i$$

$$a_i^i = a_i^{i-1} - k_i a_{i-j}^{i-1}, 1 \leq j \leq i-1$$

$$E_i = (1 - k_1^2)E_{i-1}$$

The above set of equations is solved recursively for i = 1,2, p, where p is the order of the LPC analysis. The k_i are the reflection or PARCOR coefficients. The a_j are the LPC coefficients. The final solution for the LPC coefficients is given as

$$a_j = a_j^{(p)}, 1 \leq j \leq P$$

2.9.1.7. Cepstrum analysis

The parametric representations are divided into two groups- those based on the Fourier spectrum and those based on the linear prediction spectrum. The first group comprises the mel-frequency cepstrum coefficients (MFCC) and the linear frequency cepstrum coefficients (LFCC). The second group includes the linear prediction coefficients (LPC), Reflection coefficients (RC) and cepstrum coefficients derived from the linear prediction coefficients (LPCC). Linear Predictive Cepstral coefficients are extension to LPC.

2.9.1.8. Implementation of LPCC

After capturing the speech for the speech datasets with the microphone, the speech signals are captured in .wavfiles (sound objects), these sound objects are converted into mono to get mono sound objects. These mono objects are re-sampled at 11kHz with precision of 50 samples. These objects are subject to prediction order of 16, Window length is chosen as 0.025 with time steps 0.005 and pre-emphasis frequency is maintained at 50 kHz. The LPC (autocorrelation) co-efficients are converted into Linear frequency cepstral co-efficients by using Praat object software tool.

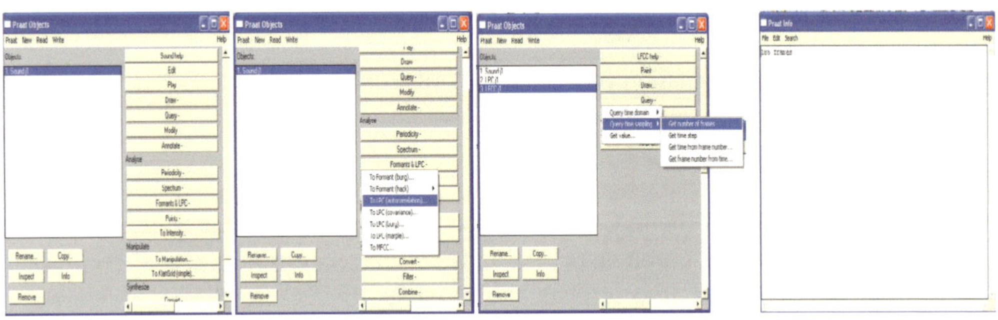

Figure 2. LPCC Feature Extraction for Sound object

2.9.2. MFCC analysis

The Mel frequency Cepstral co-efficients (MFCC) are the most widely used features in speech recognition today. The Mel scale was developed by Stevens and Volkman [1940] as a result of a study of the human auditory perception. It was used by Mermelstein and Davis [1980], to extract features from the speech signal for improved recognition accuracy. MFCC'S are one of the more popular parameterization methods used by researchers in the speech technology. It is capable of capturing the phonetically important characteristics of speech. The coefficients are largely independent, allowing probability densities to be modeled with the diagonal co-variances matrices. Mel scaling has been shown to offer better discrimination between phones, which is an obvious help in recognition. It has good discriminating properties.

MFCC'S are based on the known variation of the human ears critical band widths with frequency to capture the phonetically important characteristics of speech, filters spaced linearly at low frequencies and logarithmically at high frequencies have been used. This is expressed in the mel-frequency scale. Mel –frequency scale is linear frequency spacing below 1000 Hz and a logarithmic spacing above 1000Hz. The process of computing MFCC is shown in figure.

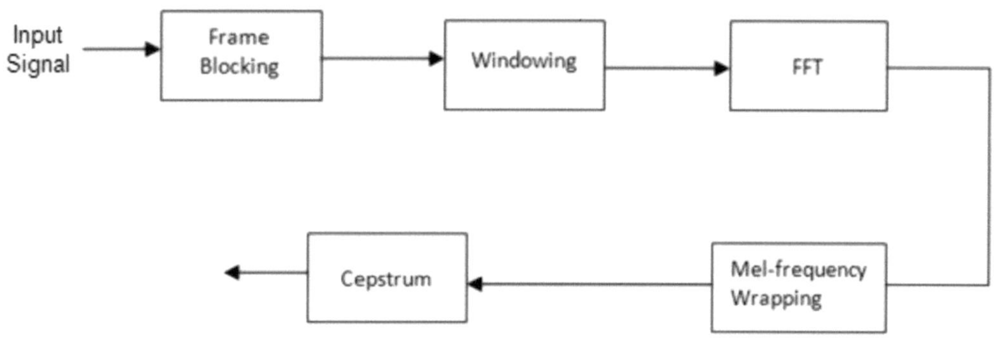

Figure 3. Feature Extractor schematic diagram for MFCC analysis

2.9.2.1. Blocking of frames

In this step, the continuous speech signal is blocked into frame of N samples with adjacent frames being separated by M (M<N). The first frame consists of the first N samples. The second frame begins M samples after the first frame and overlaps it by N-M samples. Similarly third frame begins 2M samples after the first frame and overlaps it by N-2M samples. This process continues until all the speech is accounted for within one of more frames.

2.9.2.2. Windowing of speech signal

The next step is to window each frame. Each frame is windowed in order to minimize the signal discontinuities at the starting and ending of the frame. Also spectral distortion is minimized by using the window for tapering the signal to zero at he beginning and ending of each frame. If window is defined as w(n), 0<n<N, where N is the number of samples in each frame then the result of windowing is

$$\mathrm{y_1(n)} = \mathrm{x_1(n)w(n)}, 0 < n < N - 1$$

Typically the hamming window has the form

$$\mathrm{w(n)} = 0.54 - 0.46 \cos\ (2\pi \mathrm{n/N} - 1), 0 < N < N - 1$$

2.9.2.3. Fast Fourier transform (FFT)

Fast fourier transform converts each frame of N sample from the time domain into the frequency domain. The FFT is a fast algorithm to implement the discrete Fourier Transform (DFT) which is defined on the set of N samples (x_n).

2.9.2.4. Mel-frequency warping

It is shown that human perception of the frequency contents of sound for speech signals does not follow a linear scale. The actual frequency 'f' measured in Hz a subjective pitch is measured on a scale called the mel scale. The mel scale is a linear frequency spacing below 1000Hz and a logarithmic spacing above 1000Hz. The approximate formula to compute the mels for a given frequency f in kHz is mel (F) = 2595 x log 10 (1+ f/700).

The MFCC analysis is carried out in two steps.

2.9.2.5. Filter bank analysis on Mel frequency scale

Mel Filter is an object that represents an acoustic time- frequency representation of a sound. The power spectral density $P(f, t)$ expressed in dBs is sampled into a number of points around equally spaced times t_i and frequencies f_i on a mel frequency scale. A mel filter object is created for every selected sound object by band filtering in the frequency domain as follows:

Divide a sound into frames according to a certain window length and time step. A filter bank is simulated with N filters. Apply the following algorithm for every selected sound object with a bank of filters.

Step 1. Apply a Gaussian window to the sound frame
Step 2. Convert the windowed frame into a Spectrum object
Step 3. Convert the spectral amplitudes to energy values by squaring the real and imaginary parts and multiplying by df, the frequency distance between two successive frequency points in the spectrum. Since the Spectrum object only contains positive frequencies, multiply all energy values, except the first and the last frequency, by another factor of 2 to compensate for negative frequencies
Step 4. For each of the N filters in the filter bank: determine the inner product of its filter function with the energies as determined in the previous step. The result of each inner product is the energy in the corresponding filter
Step 5. Convert the energies in each filter to power by dividing by the window length
Step 6. Correct the power, due to the windowing of the frame, by dividing by the integral of the squared windowing function
Step 7. Convert all power values to dB's according to 10 * log10 (power / 4 10-10)

Filter functions which are in triangular shape are used on a linear frequency scale. These functions depends on three parameters the lower frequency f_l, the central frequency f_c and the higher frequency f_h.The distances $f_c - f_l$ and $f_h - f_c$ are the same for each filter and are equal to the distance between the f_c's of successive filters on mel scale.

$$H(f) = 0 \text{ for } f \leq f_l \text{ and } f \geq f_h$$

$$H(f) = \frac{(f - f_i)}{(f_c - f_i)} \text{ for } f_l \leq f \leq f_c$$

$$H(f) = (f_h - f)/(f_h - f_c) \text{ for } f_c \leq f \leq f_h$$

2.9.2.6. Cepstrum

The cepstral representation of the speech spectrum provides a good representation of the local spectral properties of the signal for the given frame analysis. The Mel filter values are converted as Mel frequency cepstral coefficients in this stage.

This transformation was first used by Davis and Mermelstein (1980). From the discrete cosine transform of the filter bank spectrum (in dB), μ frequency cepstral coefficients are obtained by using the following relation

$$c_i = \sum_{j=1}^{N} P_j \cos(i\pi/N(j - 0.5))),$$

Where N represents the number of filters and P_j the power in dB in the jth filter.

2.9.2.7. Implementation of MFCC

After capturing the speech for the speech dataset with the microphone, the speech signals are captured in .wav files (sound objects). These sound objects are converted into mono to get mono sound objects. These objects are applied to MFCC with 12 coefficients, window length 0.015, time step 0.005, the filter – bank parameters are chosen as follow:

The coefficient of 1st filter is taken as 100 mels the distance between filters is maintained as 100 mels.

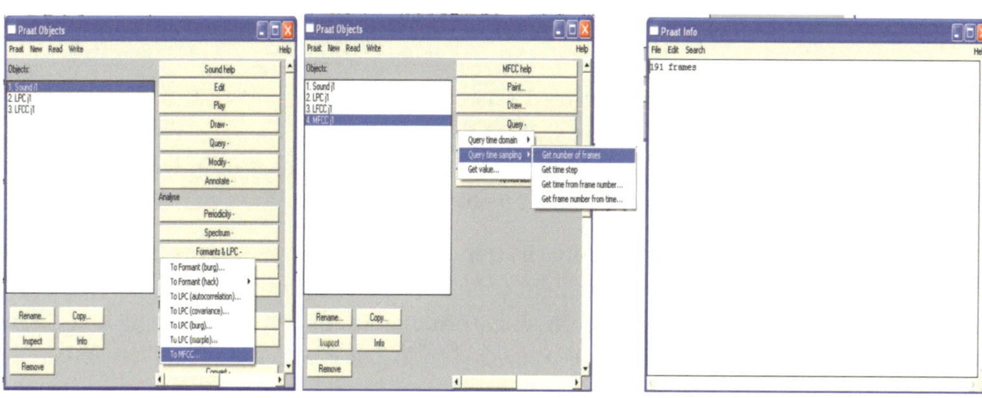

Figure 4. MFCC Feature Extraction for Sound object

3. Recognition methodology

In multi-class mode, each classifier identifies whether the set of input features which are derived from the current signal, belongs to a specific class of numbers or not. Also it tries to identify exactly to which class it belongs.

3.1. Classifiers used

3.1.1. Multilayer perceptron architecture

The demonstration of the limitations of single-layer neural neural networks was a significant factor in the decline of interest in neural networks in the 1970's. The discovery (by several researches independently) and wide spread dissemination of an effective general method of training a multilayer neural network [Rumelhart, Hinton, & Williams, 1986a, 1986b; McClelland & Rumelhart, 1988] played a major role in the reemergence of neural networks as a tool for solving a wide variety of problems. In this, we shall discuss this training method, known as backpropagation (of errors) or the generalized delta rule. It is simply a gradient descent method to minimize the total squared error of the output computed by the net. According to Laurene Fausett, the training of a network by a backpropagation involves three stages: the feed forward of the input training pattern, the calculation and backpropagation of the associated error, and the adjustment of the weights. After training, application of the net involves only the computations of the feed forward phase. Even if training is slow, a trained net can produce its output very rapidly. Numerous variations of backpropagation have been developed to improve the speed of the training process. A multilayer neural network with one layer of hidden units (the Z units) is shown in figure. The output units (the Y units) and the hidden units also may have biases (as shown). The biases on a typical output unit Y_k is denoted by $w0_k$; the bias on a typical hidden unit Zj is denoted v0j. These bias terms act like weights on connections from units whose output is always 1. (These units are shown in Figure but are usually not displayed explicitly.) Only the direction of information flow for the feed forward phase of operation is shown. During the backpropagation phase of learning, signals are sent in the reverse direction.

3.1.1.1 Backpropagation algorithm

According to Laurene Fausett, during feed forward, each input unit (X_i) receives an input signal and broadcasts this signal to the each of the hidden units $Z_1,....,Z_p$. Each hidden unit then computes its activation and sends its signal (z_j) to each output unit. Each output unit (Y_k) computes its activation (y_k) to form the response of the net for the given input pattern.

During training, each output unit compares its computed activation y_k with its target value t_k to determine the associated error for that pattern with that unit. Based on this error, the factor δ_k (k = 1 ,...., m) is computed. δ_k is used to distribute the error at output unit Y_k back to all units in the previous layer (the hidden units that are connected to Y_k). It is also used (later) to update the weights between the output and the hidden layer. In a similar manner, the factor δ_j (j= 1,....., p) is computed for each hidden unit Z_j. It is not necessary to propagate the error back to the input layer, but δj is used to update the weights between the hidden layer and the input layer.

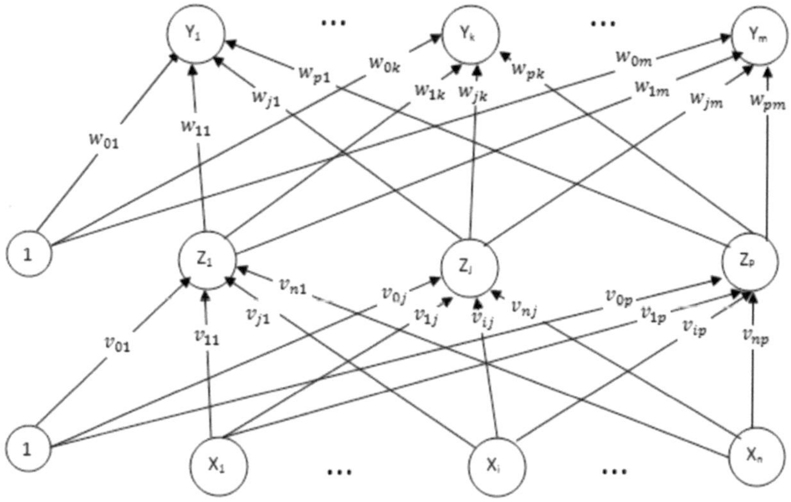

Figure 5. Backpropagation neural network with one hidden layer.

After all of the δ factors have been determined, the weights for all layers are adjusted simultaneously. The adjustment to the weight w_{jk} (from hidden unit Z_j to output unit Y_k) is based on the factor δ_k and the activation z_j of the hidden unit Z_j. The adjustment to the weight v_{ij} (from input unit X_i to hidden unit Z_j) is based on the factor δ_j and the activation xi of the input unit.

Training Algorithm

The training algorithm is as follows:

Step 0. Initialize weights.

(Set to small random values)

Step 1. While stopping condition is false, do Steps 2-9.
Step 2. For each training pair, do Steps 3-8.

Feed forward:

Step 3. Each input unit (X_i, i = 1,……,n) receives input signal xi and broadcasts this signal to all units in the layer above (the hidden units).
Step 4. Each hidden unit (Zj, j = 1,…….,p) sums its weighted input signals,

$$z\_in_j = v_{oj} + \sum_{i=1}^{n} x_i v_{ij},$$

applies its activation function to compute its output signal,

$$z_j = f(z\_in_j),$$

and sends this signal to all units in the layer above (output units).

Step 5. Each output unit (Y_k, k = 1,.......,m) sums its weighted input signals,

$$y\_in_k = w_{ok} + \sum_{j=1}^{p} z_j w_{jk},$$

applies its activation function to compute its output signal,

$$y_k = f(y\_in_k),$$

Backpropagation of error:

Step 6. Each output unit (Y_k, k = 1,.......,m) receives a target pattern corresponding to the input training pattern, computes its error information term.

$$\delta_k = (t_k - y_k)f'(y\_in_k)$$

calculates its weights correction term (used to update w_{jk} later),

$$\Delta w_{jk} = \alpha \delta_k z_j,$$

calculates its bias correction term (used to update w_{ok} later),

$$w_{ok} = \alpha \delta_k,$$

Step 7. Each hidden unit (Z_j, j = 1,.......,p) sums its delta inputs (from units in the layer above),

$$\delta\_in_j = \sum_{k=1}^{m} \delta_k w_{jk},$$

multiples by the derivative of its activation function to calculate its error information term,

$$\delta_j = \delta\_in_j f'(z\_in_j),$$

calculates its weight correlation term (used to update v_{ij} later),

$$\Delta v_{ij} = \alpha \delta_j x_i,$$

and calculates its bias correlation term (used to update v_{oj} later),

$$\Delta v_{oj} = \alpha \delta_j.$$

Update weights and biases:

Step 8. Each output unit (Y_k, k = 1,...,m) updates its bias and weights (j = 0, ...,p):

$$w_{jk}(new) = w_{jk}(old) + \Delta w_{jk}$$

Each hidden unit (Z_j, j = 1,...,p) updates its bias and weights (i = 0,...,n):

$$v_{ij}(new) = v_{ij}(old) + \Delta v_{ij}$$

Step 9. Test stopping condition.

3.1.1.2. Quick propagation

Quick propagation is an extension to Newton's method. This is used as an optimization to backpropagation. This is useful for decreasing the magnitude of the gradient and for changing the sign in between two steps. In order to determine the weight for the next step a parabolic estimate of the MSE is used. We can compute the derivatives in the direction of each weight by using Quick propagation. A direct step of the error minimum is attempted after computing the first gradient with regular backpropagation.

After computing the first gradient with regular back-propagation, a direct step of the error minimum is attempted by

$$\Delta x(t) = \frac{f'\big((t)\big)}{f'\big((t-1)\big) - f'\big((t)\big)} \Delta x(t-1)$$

3.1.1.3. Delta-Bar-Delta algorithm

Delta-Bar-Delta algorithm can be used to control the learning rates. This is possible with the possible sign changes of an exponential average gradient. The learning rates can be increased by adding a constant value rather than multiplying it.

Hence,

Choose some small initial value for every $\eta_{ji}(0)$.

Adapt the learning rates:

$$\eta_{ji}(n) = \eta_{ji}(n-1) + u, \text{if } \frac{\partial \xi}{\partial w_{ji}}(n) * \frac{\partial \xi}{\partial w_{ji}}(n-1) \geq 0$$

$$\eta_{ji}(n) = \eta_{ji}(n-1) * d, \text{if } \frac{\partial \xi}{\partial w_{ji}}(n) * \frac{\partial \xi}{\partial w_{ji}}(n-1) \leq 0$$

$$\eta_{ji}(n) = \eta_{ji}(n-1), \text{else.}$$

In particular it is difficult to find a proper u. Small values may result in slow adaptations while big ones endanger the learning process. As small values result in slow adaptations while big ones are dangerous for learning process. Vivid values are chosen for u and d. They are respectively u(5.0, 0.095, 0.085, 0.035) and d(0.9, 0.85, 0.666).

3.1.1.4. Conjugate gradient method

A se of Vectors {sj} is conjugate with respect to a positive definite matrix (e.g., the Hessaian) if sTj Hsi=0 where j ≠i. What this expression says is that the rotation by Hof the vector sj. In the n-dimensional Euclidean space Rn there are an infinite number of conjugate vector sets. It is easy to show that the eigenvectors of the Hessian form a conjugate set and can then be used to search the performance surface. The problem is that understanding the Hessian, which is not a practical assumption. However, there is a way to find a conjugate set of vectors that does not require knowledge of the Hessian. The idea is to express the conditions for a conjugate vector set as a function of difference in consecutive gradient directions as

$$(\nabla j(i) - \nabla j(i-1))T\ s(j) = 0 \quad i \neq j$$

For this expression to be true, the minimum of the gradient of J(i) in the direction s(j) is needed, so the algorithm works as follows.

Start with the gradient-descent direction, s(0) = -∇J(0). Search the minimum along this direction. Then construct a vector s(j) that is orthogonal to the set of vectors {∇J(0), ∇J(1), ... ∇J(j 1)}, which can be accomplished by

$$S(j) = -\nabla J(j) + \alpha\ s(j-1)$$

There are basically three well-known ways to find α namely, the Fletcher-Reeves, the Polak-Ribiere, or the Hestenes-Steifel formulas, which are equivalent for quadratic performance surfaces and are given respectively by

$$\alpha j = \frac{\nabla JT(j)\nabla J(j)}{\nabla JT(j-1)\nabla J(j-1)} \quad \alpha j = \frac{[\nabla J(j) - \nabla J(j-1)]T\ \nabla J(j)}{\nabla JT(j-1)\nabla J(j-1)}$$

$$\alpha j = \frac{[\nabla J(j) - \nabla J(j-1)]T\ \nabla J(j)}{\nabla JT(j-1)s(j-1)}$$

In quadratic performance surfaces, the above value can be find the minimum in n iterations, where n is the size of the search space. The minimization along the line can be accomplished for quadratic performance surfaces. The problem is that, for nonquadratic performance surfaces such as the one found in neurocomputing, quadratic termination is not guaranteed and the line search does not have an analytic solution.

The lack of quadratic termination can be overcome by executing the algorithm for n iterations and then resetting it to the current gradient direction. The problem of the lines search is more difficult to solve. There are two basic approaches: direct search or the scaled conjugate method [Shepherd 1997]. The first involves multiple cost-function evaluations and estimations to find the minimum, which complicates the mechanics of the algorithm. The scaled conjugate is more appropriate for neural network implementations. It uses Eq. 4B.1 and avoids the problem of nonquadratic surfaces by messaging the Hessian so as to guarantee positive definiteness, which is accomplished by H+λI, where I is the identity matrix. We get

$$\mu j = -\nabla J\ Tj\ sj / sTjHjsj + \lambda\ |sj|/2$$

Any one may think that this method is more computationally expensive than search, because of the Hessian matrix. But in fact, this is not the case, since there are fast methods to estimate the product of a vector by the Hessian (the product has only n components). The perturbation method can be used to estimate the product [LeCun, Simard, and Pearlmutter 1993]:

$$sT\ (\nabla J) = \frac{[\nabla J(w + \varepsilon s) - \nabla J(w)]}{\varepsilon} + 0(\varepsilon)$$

Or use an analytic approach due to Pearlmutter [1994]. Both methods are compatible with backpropagation.

λ can be solved by using trial and error method. Notice that for large λ the denominator becomes approximately λ | |s| |2. In this case one can use gradient descent, which is known to be convergent to the minimum (albeit slowly). When the error decreases, then λ should again be decreased to fully exploit the potential of the local quadratic information of the performance surface.

3.1.1.5.Implementing multilayer perceptron with Trajan 6.0 demonstrator

Select the speaker (word) whose training and testing recognition rate is required. Create custom neural network training with output (dependent) variable as desired one and input (independent) as target one. Choose the network type as MLP. Train MLP with quick backpropagation in phase one with 100 number of epochs and with learning rate of 0.01. Train MLP with Conjugate gradient learning algorithm in phase two with conjugate gradient learning with 500 number of epochs.

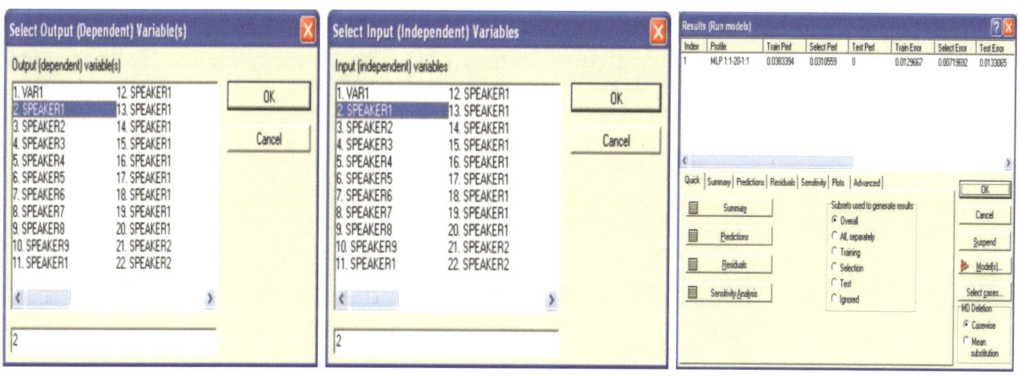

Figure 6. Estimating MLP speaker recognition rate with Trajan

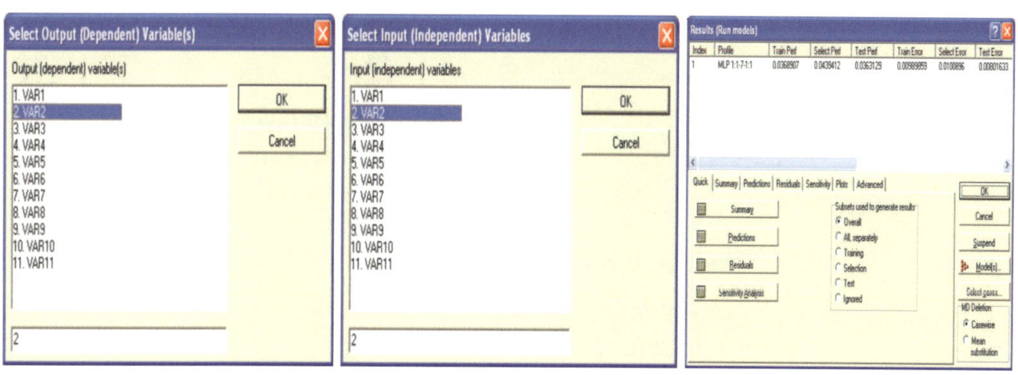

Figure 7. Estimating MLP word recognition rate with Trajan

3.2. Radial basis function architecture

Radial basis function networks are a special case of multilayer perceptrons. The cells compute their activation not through a sigmoid function but according to a Euclidean similarity measure between patterns. The network uses radial basis functions as activation functions. These networks are used in function approximation, time series prediction and control.

Radial basis function networks typically has a two-layer feed forward architecture. The first layer maps an input feature vector to a set of hidden nodes or centers that constitute a basis for the input pattern space. The basis functions of this hidden layer produce a localized response to an input pattern. The second layer implements a linear mapping from the activation of the centers to the output nodes corresponding to different pattern classes. Hence the network carries out a non linear transformation by forming a linear combination of the basic functions. The basic function taken is Gaussian function. For each input pattern, the RBF network computes nodal outputs that are estimates of Bayesian Probabilities. Organization of RBF is shown in figure.

The training of an RBF network is a hybrid phase i.e. it is made up of an unsupervised phase followed by a supervised phase. As MLPs, RBF networks can be used for classification and function approximation tasks. They keep the pattern classification performances of other ANNs with a much lower training computation cost. These networks also feature good generalization capabilities.

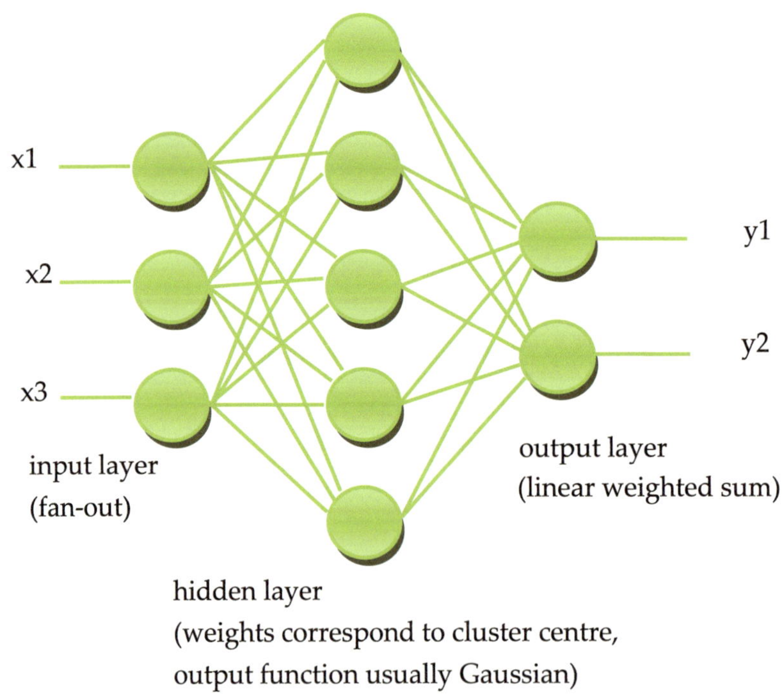

Figure 8. Radial Basis Function Neural Network Architecture

3.2.1. Training algorithm for an RBFN with fixed centers

The training algorithm for the radial basis function network is given below. The important aspect of the radial bais function network is the usage of activation function for computing the output.

Activation Function

Radial basis function uses Gaussian activation function. The response of such function is non-negative in all value of x. The function is defined as

$$f(x) = \exp(-x^2)$$

Its derivative is given by

$$f'(x) = -2x\exp(-x^2) = -2xf(x)$$

The radial basis function is different from the back propagation network in the Gaussion function it uses. The training algorithm for the network is given as follows:

Step 1. Initialize the weights (set to small random values)
Step 2. While stopping is false do Step 3 – 10.
Step 3. For each input do Step 4 – 9.
Step 4. Each input unit (x_i ,i = 1,. . . . n) receives input signals to all units in the layer above(hidden unit).
Step 5. Calculate the radial basis function.
Step 6. Choose the centres for the radial basis functions. The centres are chosen from the set of input vectors. A sufficient number of centers have to be selected in order to ensure adequate sampling of the input vector space.
Step 7. The output of an unit $v_i(x_i)$in the hidden layer.

$$v_i(x_i) = e\left(-\sum_{j=1}^{r}\left[x_{ji} - \widehat{x_{j1}}\right]^2 / \sigma_1^2\right)$$

Where

x_{ji} is center of RBF unit for input variables.
σ_i is width of the RBF unit.
X_{ji} is j^{th} variable of input pattern.
Step 8. Initialize the weights in the output layer of the network to some small random value.
Step 9. Calculate the output of the neural network

$$y_{net} = \sum_{i=1}^{H} w_{im} v_i(x_i) + w_0$$

Where,

H is number of hidden layer nodes (RBF function)
Y_{net} is output value of mth node in output layer for the nth incoming pattern.
W_{im} is weight between i^{th} RBF unit and m^{th} output node
W_o is biasing term at n^{th} output node.
Step 10. Calculate error and test stopping condition.

3.2.1.1. Isotropic

Select the deviation same for all units. Select these deviations heuristically in order to reflect the number of the centres and the space of the volume that they occupy(Haykin, 1994).

3.2.1.2. K-Nearest neighbor

Set each unit's deviation individually to the mean distance to its K-nearest neighbors (Bishop, 1995). Deviations are kept smaller in the space whose area is tightly packed whereas deviations are kept higher for sparse areas by interpolation. The output layer can be optimized after centres and deviations are set. The output layer can be optimized by using Pseudo-inverse (Singular-value decomposition) algorithm (Haykin, 1994; Golub and Kahan, 1965).

3.2.1.3. Implementing the radial basis function with Trajan 6.0 demonstrator

The Trajan 6.0 demonstrator accepts column formatted ASCII files. Use the Browse. Create custom neural network training with input data file as independent variables. Choose the network type as RBF. Choose the output (dependent) variable as the desired one. Select input (independent) variable as target one. Train RBF with the algorithm 3.2.1 with quick propagation. Training cases are sampled at Radial assignment. The Radial spread is set to the value 1, Isotropic is scaled by 1. K- nearest neighbour chosen as 10.

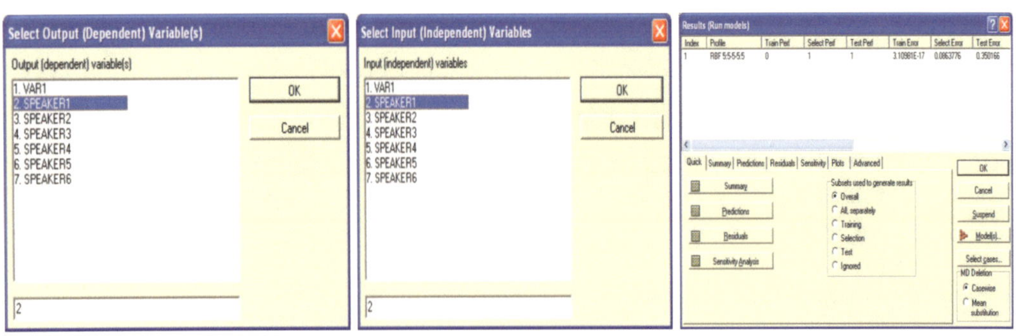

Figure 9. Estimating RBF speaker performance with Trajan

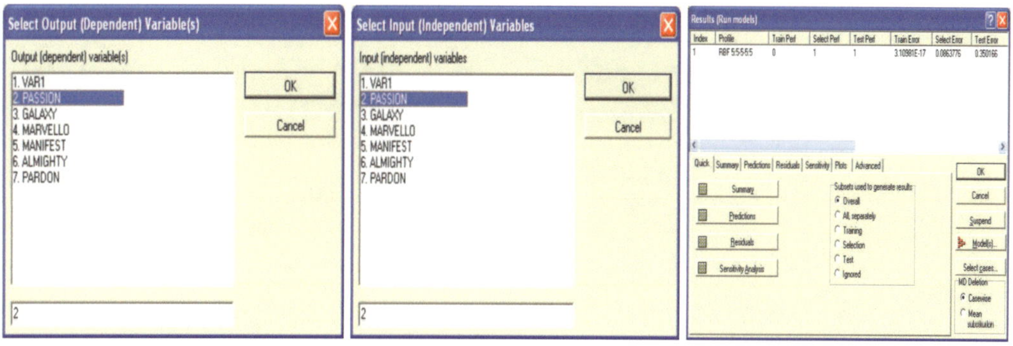

Figure 10. Estimating RBF word performance with Trajan

4. Results and discussions

The speaker and word identification rates for each speaker with the features LPCC and MFCC are obtained for both conventional and proposed systems in order to find maximum speaker and word identification rates for both training and testing the classifiers MLP and RBF. The results are presented in tables 2-3 and its analysis is presented in graph.

4.1. Estimating speaker identification rates

The experiment is carried out with 6 speakers (2 male,4 female)taking continuous speech and sound proof closed room. The system is trained continuously using high quality microphone with vocabulary size of 216 .wav files in constrained spoken input format.

Speakers	LPCC Training (%)	LPCC Testing (%)	MFCC Training (%)	MFCC Testing (%)
Speaker 1	90	85	92	90
Speaker 2	89	89	94	92
Speaker 3	93	90	90	88
Speaker 4	88	85	93	89
Speaker 5	91	90	94	91
Speaker 6	92	91	91	85

Table 2. Speaker identification rate with Multilayer perceptron

Speakers	LPCC Training (%)	LPCC Testing (%)	MFCC Training (%)	MFCC Testing (%)
Speaker 1	96	93	97	95
Speaker 2	94	91	99	98
Speaker 3	98	94	99	99
Speaker 4	97	95	97	98
Speaker 5	99	93	99	97
Speaker 6	95	92	98	96

Table 3. Speaker identification rate with Radial basis function

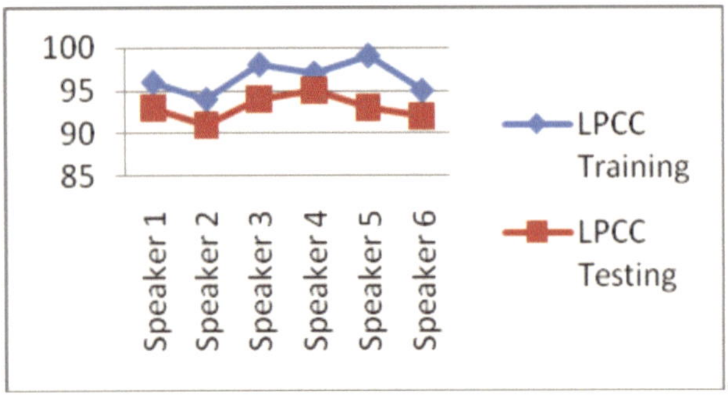

Figure 11. LPCC speaker identification rate with proposed system

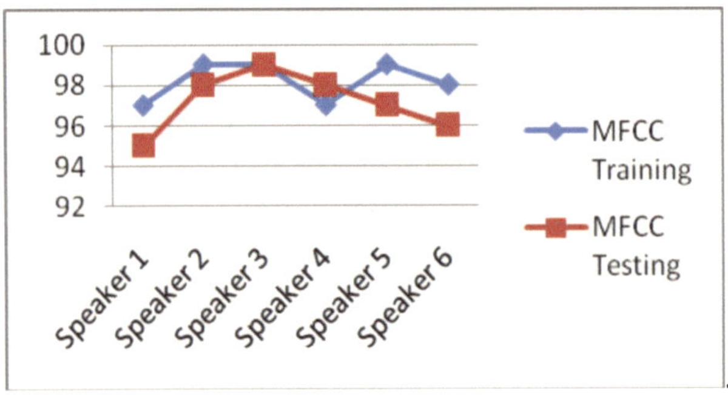

Figure 12. MFCC speaker identification rate with proposed system

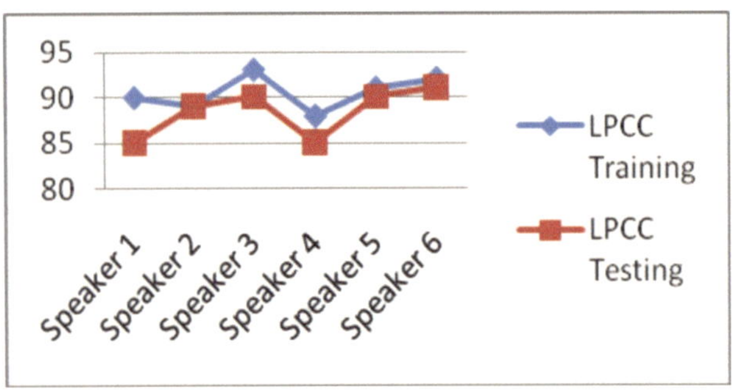

Figure 13. LPCC speaker identification rate with conventional system

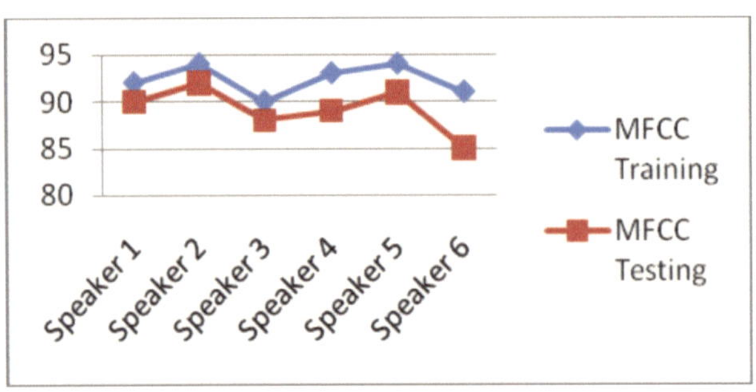

Figure 14. MFCC speaker identification rate with conventional system

4.1.1. *Discussion*

The LPCC training identification rate for speakers dominates the testing identification rate for all the speakers with proposed system. The MFCC training identification rate for speakers dominates the testing speaker identification rate for all the speakers except for speaker 4 and for the speaker 3 both the performances are same with proposed system. The LPCC training identification rate for speakers dominates the testing identification rate for all the speakers and for the speaker 2 both the performances are same with conventional system. The MFCC training identification rate for speakers dominates the testing speaker identification rate for all the speakers with conventional system. In the combination of MLP and RBF algorithms, the maximum identification of speakers is found in the range of 95% -99% for proposed system where as for the conventional system it is in the range of 89%-92%.

4.2. Estimating word identification rates

4.2.1. *Discussion*

For the proposed system, the highest recognition rate is obtained for Marvellous and Almighty with LPCC feature. For the conventional system, the highest recognition rate is obtained for Passion, Galaxy, Almighty and Pardon with LPCC feature. For the proposed system, the highest recognition rate is obtained for Galaxy, Almighty and Pardon with MFCC feature. For the conventional system, the highest recognition rate is obtained for Galaxy, Manifestaion, Almighty and Pardon respectively with MFCC feature. In the combination of MLP and RBF algorithms, the maximum identification of words is found in the range of 97%-99% for proposed system where as for the conventional system it is in the range of 94%-95%.

Feature Extraction	WIPS (%)		WICS (%)		WIPS-WICS (%)
	RBF Testing		MLP Testing		Difference
LPCC	Passion	94	Passion	91	3
	Galaxy	93	Galaxy	91	2
	Marvellous	95	Marvellous	90	5
	Manifestaion	91	Manifestaion	89	2
	Almighty	95	Almighty	91	4
	Pardon	94	Pardon	91	3

Table 4. Word identification rate for Multilayer perceptron and Radial basis function with LPCC

Feature Extraction	WIPS (%)		WICS (%)		WIPS-WICS (%)
MFCC	RBF Testing		MLP Testing		Difference
	Passion	97	Passion	94	3
	Galaxy	99	Galaxy	95	4
	Marvellous	98	Marvellous	94	4
	Manifestaion	97	Manifestaion	95	2
	Almighty	99	Almighty	95	4
	Pardon	99	Pardon	95	4

Table 5. Word identification rate for Multilayer perceptron and Radial basis function with MFCC

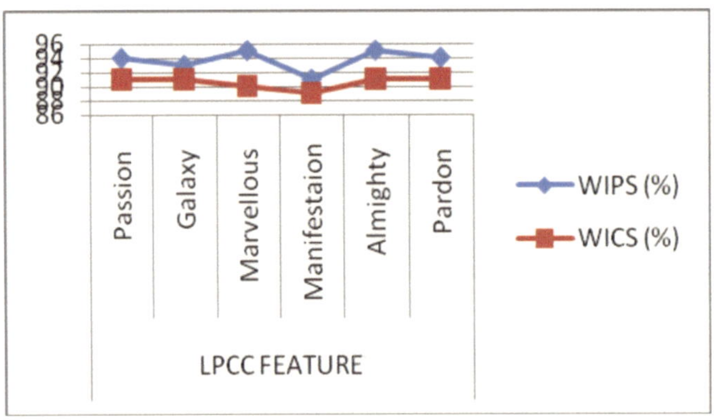

Figure 15. Word identification rate for conventional and proposed system with LPCC

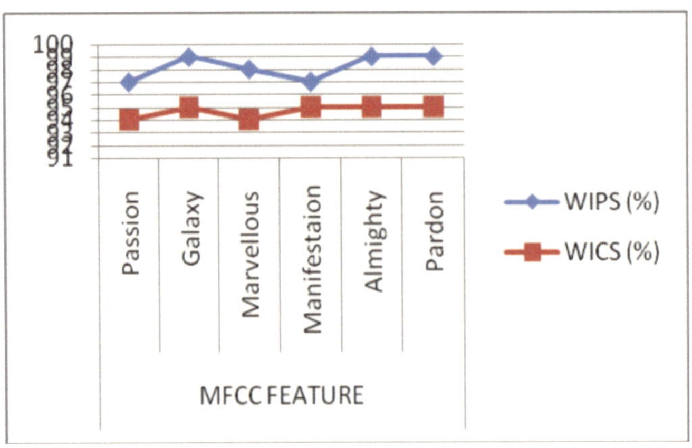

Figure 16. Word identification rate for conventional system and proposed system with MFCC

4.3. Testing results for conventional system

The recognition accuracy for training and testing set with the feature LPCC and MFCC for Letter recognition for conventional system (WRCS) is presented in Table 6 and its analysis is presented in graph form shown in Fig 17.

Feature	Recognition in accuracy (%)	
	Training	Testing
LPCC	97	94
MFCC	99	95

Table 6. Recognition accuracy for conventional System with MLP classifier

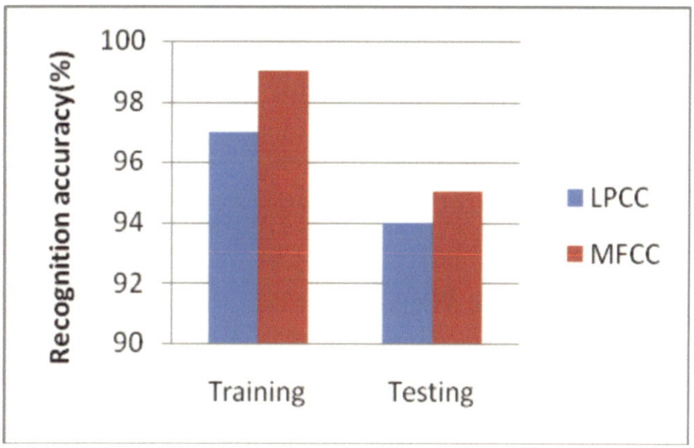

Figure 17. Recognition accuracy for conventional system with MLP classifier

From Table 6 and Fig 17, it is found that the highest recognition accuracy is obtained with MFCC feature both in training and testing. The training phase dominates the testing phase with both the features LPCC and MFCC.

4.4. Testing results for proposed system

From Table 7 and Figure 18, it is found that the highest recognition accuracy is obtained with MFCC feature both in training and testing. The training phase dominates testing phase with both the features LPCC and MFFC. The recognition accuracy for training and testing set with the features LPCC and MFCC for word recognition for proposed system(WRPS) is presented in Table 7 and its analysis is presented in graph form shown in Fig 18.

Feature	Recognition in accuracy (%)	
	Training	Testing
LPCC	99.9	98
MFCC	100	99

Table 7. Recognition accuracy for proposed System with RBF classifier

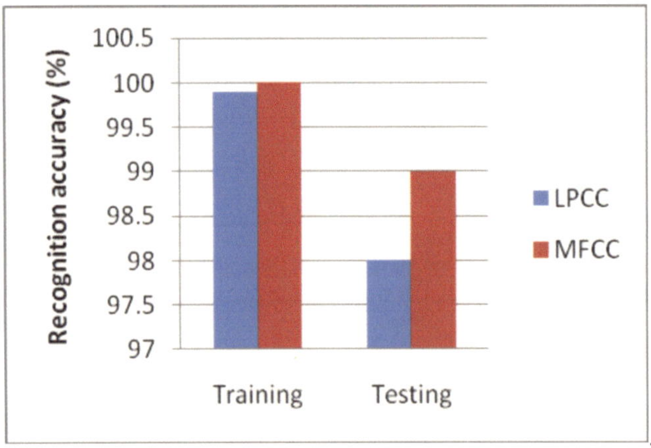

Figure 18. Recognition accuracy for conventional system with RBF classifier

4.5. Comparison of Performance for word recognition for proposed system (WRPS) and Word recognition for conventional system (WRCS) according to features

The comparison of performance for WRPS and WRCS according to feature is presented in Table 8 and analyzed in Fig 19. The comparison of performance is presented for testing the results.

Feature	Recognition in accuracy (%)		
	WRPS	WRCS	WRPS - WRCS
LPCC	98	94	4
MFCC	99	95	4

Table 8. Comparison of performance for WRPS and WRCS according to features.

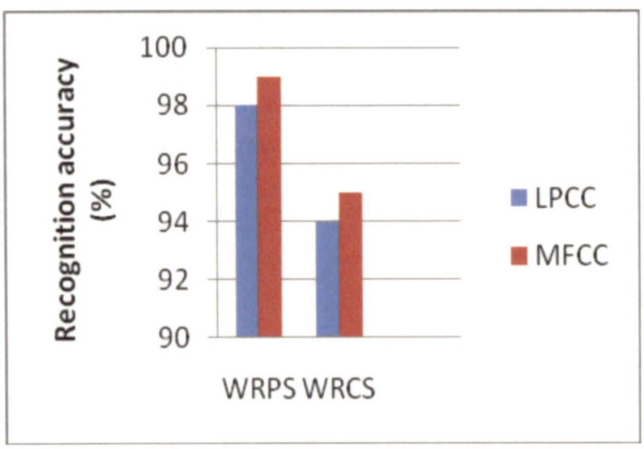

Figure 19. Comparison of performance for WRPS and WRCS according to features

From Table 8 and Fig 19, the following observations are made

1. For both WRCS and WRPS, the highest recognition accuracy is obtained with MFCC.
2. WRPS has the highest accuracy than WRCS for every test sets.

It is shown that WRPS out perform the WRCS in every test set according to features. From the tests, MFCC out performs LPCC.

The comparison of performance for speaker recognition for proposed system (SRPS) and speaker recognition for conventional system (SRCS) according to features is presented in Table 9. The comparison of performance is presented for testing the results.

Feature	Testing System	Mean (%)	Mode (%)	Median (%)	Min (%)	Max (%)	Standard deviation	Variance	Co-Efficient of variation	Skewness	Correlation coefficient
LPCC	SRCS	88.3	89.5	90	85	91	2.27	5.15	2.57	-0.75	-0.25
	SRPS	93	93	93	91	95	1.290	1.66	1.79	0.1	
MFCC	SRCS	93.59	88.35	93	90	92	1.2	1.44	2.3	0.23	-0.01
	SRPS	87.56	92	89.22	85	91	1.39	1.93	1.34	1.23	

Table 9. Comparative study of different feature recognition techniques of Multilayer perceptron and Radial basis function

In testing the speaker performance with both the features LPCC and MFCC, the proposed system is negatively correlated with the conventional system. The value of Co-efficient of variation for both the features LPCC and MFCC of the proposed system is less than the conventional system. Hence the proposed system is more efficient than the conventional system.

5. Conclusion

For the recognition of isolated words, it has been shown that the Radial basis function Neural network is suitable. Word recognition is carried out in speaker dependent mode. In this mode, trained data and tested date are chosen to be same. As the first 16 in the cepstrum represent most of the formant information 16 Linear Predictive cepstral coefficients and Mel frequency cepstral coefficients with 16 parameters are chosen. From the experimental results, it is found that RBF classifier performs better than MLP classifier. It is found that speaker 6 average performance is the best performance in training MLP classifier and speaker 2 average performance is the best performance in training RBF classifier. It is found that average speaker 4 performance is the best performance in testing MLP classifier and speaker 1 average performance is the best performance in testing RBF classifier. The real time factor for the proposed speech recognition system is found as less than 1.

6. Future scope

Besides improving the FE block and devising a more robust recognizer, the scope of the problem should be broadened to larger vocabularies, continuous speech and more speakers

Author details

R.L.K.Venkateswarlu*
Dean of Research, Research and Development Wing, Sasi Institute of Technology and Engineering Tadepalligudem, India

R. Raviteja and R. Rajeev
R.L.K. Institute of Mathematics, Rajahmundry, Andhra Pradesh, India

7. References

Al-Alaoui, M.A., Mouci, R., Mansour M.M., Ferzli, R., , 2002: A Cloning Approach to Classifier Training, IEEE Transactions on Systems, Man and Cybernetics – Part A: Systems and Humans, vol.32, no.6, pp.746- 752).

Benyettou, A., 1995: Acoustic Phonetic Recognition in the Arabex System. Int. Work Shop on Robot and Human Communication, ATIP95.44, Japan.

Berthold, M.R., 1994: A Time Delay Radial Basis Function for Phoneme Recognition. Proc. Int. Conf. on Neural Network, Orlando, USA.

Gurney, K., 1997: An Introduction to Neural Networks, UCL Press, University of Sheffield, pp.no 234.

Kandil N, Sood V K, Khorasani K and Patel R V, 1992: Fault identification in an AC–DC transmission system using neural networks, IEEE Transaction on Power System, 7(2):812–9.

Laurene, Fausett., 2009: Fundamentals of Neural Networks Architectures, Algorithms and Applications, Pearson Education and Dorling Kindersly Publishing Inc., India, pp.no.467.

Morgan, D. and Scolfield, C., 1991: Neural Networks and Speech Processing, Kluwer Academic Publishers, pp.no.391.

Park D C, El-Sharakawi M A and Ri Marks II, 1991: Electric load forecasting using artificial neural networks, IEEE Trans Power System, 6(2), pp 442–449.

Picton, P. 2000: Neural Networks, Palgrave, NY .pp.no 195.

Rabiner, L. and Juang, B. -H., 1993: Fundamentals of Speech Recognition, PTR Prentice Hall, San Francisco, NJ. pp.no 507.

Tan Lee, P. C. Ching, L.W. Chan, 1998: Isolated Word Recognition Using Modular Recurrent Neural Networks, Pattern Recognition, vol. 31, no. 6, pp. 751-760.

---

* Corresponding Author

Chapter 14

Data Mining from Remote Sensing Snow and Vegetation Product

Gao Jie

Additional information is available at the end of the chapter

http://dx.doi.org/10.5772/45732

1. Introduction

Snow is an important research interest in international cryosphere research. In China, cold region account for 43% of the total area (Yang et al., 2000). The area of stable snow where snow cover duration is greater than 60 days is approximately $420\times10^4 km^2$. In West China, the recharge to spring freshet from winter snow is a necessary regulation for spring drought (Qin et al., 2006). However, larger area but sparser stations in West China lead to a shortage of observations. Especially for snow, most of the regions where snow-dominated are located in mountainous regions that are quite inconvenient for people to establish observatory stations. All these result in a poor representative of station observations (Li, 1995). Therefore, application of Remote Sensing is absolutely necessary for snow research (Gao et al., 2010).

The data received and released by the Moderate-resolution Imaging Spectroradiometer (MODIS) with a spatial resolution of 250m, 500m and 1000m have been widely used for research. Huang et al (2007) combined Geographic Information System (GIS) and station observations to analyze the precision of snow identification of two types of MODIS snow products: MOD10A1 (daily snow cover data) and MOD10A2 (8-day snow cover data) in Northern Xinjiang area. 8-day data is proved to better eliminate the influence of amount of clouds and with a mean precision of snow identification about 87.5%. Wen et al (2006) assessed the seasonal variation of snow extent in parts of Nyainqntanglha Range (4720-5850m) based on MODIS data, and proved it feasible to monitor snow extent by MODIS data in this region. Zhang et al (2005) revealed that snow-cover area and snow line altitude change obviously with climate change in Qilian Mountains by adopting NOAA-AVHRR, EOS-MODIS data and station observation between May and August, 1997-2004. Han et al (2007) analyzed the feedback of regional snow-cover to climate in Northeast China during 2000-2005 by MODIS products.

INTECH
open science | open minds

© 2012 Jie, licensee InTech. This is an open access chapter distributed under the terms of the Creative Commons Attribution License (http://creativecommons.org/licenses/by/3.0), which permits unrestricted use, distribution, and reproduction in any medium, provided the original work is properly cited.

Snowmelt hydrological model focus on snowmelt runoff processes and used to quantify snow-related variables in snow water equivalent (SWE). Anderton et al. (2002) developed a grid-based distributed energy balance snowmelt model and used distributed SWE as initial boundary condition. Bell and Moore (1999) developed an elevation-dependent snowmelt forecasting model, and used PACK snowmelt module, which conceptualizes snow storage to 'dry' and 'wet' snow reservoirs with different outflow rates. These methods provide a simple but quantitative relation between snow and water. However, both distributed SWE and reservoir calculate snow as water amount rather than its real state, hardly simulate the spatial pattern of snow covered area, and how it evolves with time. In fact, spatial distribution of snow is very important for hydrological cycle in snowmelt-dominated regions. Whether soil is covered by snow or not is a necessary boundary input for hydrological modelling. It determines the energy balance by albedo, inform whether rainfall runoff generation or snowmelt runoff.

Different factors dominate snow distribution at different scales. At macro-scales (10km–1000km), latitude, elevation, and water bodies primarily control spatial variation of snow. Terrain characteristics and vegetation cover determine at meso-scales (100m–10km), interception, sublimation, and wind redistribution dominate at micro-scales (10m–100 m) (McKay & Gray, 1981; Pomeroy et al., 2002; Liston, 2004). Based on the results of experiments, topographic factors (Marchand & Killingtveit, 2005) and vegetation cover (Jost et al., 2007) are considered to be the most important variables to explain snow pattern at the watershed-scale.

Among all the topographic factors, elevation provides a significant positive correlation with the spatial pattern of snow (Daugharty & Dickinson, 1982; D' Eon, 2004; Varhola et al., 2010) because orographic cooling influence the accumulation and ablation processes of snow (Hendrick et al., 1971; Sloan et al., 2004). Linear lapse rate is regularly observed in mid-latitude mountainous regions (Hantel et al., 2000). Most often, the global mean lapse rate of approximately 6.5°/1000m is common used (Barry, 1992; Li & Williams, 2008). Bell and Moore (1999) adopted 5.9°/1000m in upland British. Based on a statistics of 27-year time series in 7 stations, temperature lapse rate in Eastern Tibet is 6.3°C per 1000 meters, a little smaller than that of 7.0°C per 1000m reported for Colorado Rocky Mountains (Williams et al., 2011; Gao et al., 2012).

Vegetation offers a negative indicator of snow distribution. Calculated from a physically based formulation, interception is closely related to vegetation cover (Hedstrom and Pomeroy, 1998; Pomeroy, 2002). Interception by canopies and increased sublimation reduce snow accumulation on the ground (Essery et al., 2003). In forested area, the amount of snow is 40% lower than in nearby clear-cut reference sites (Winker et al., 2005). Presence of snow affects both length of growing season, and primary plant production (Buus-Hinkler et al., 2006). Long snow-covered periods will shorten vegetative season, for snow-cover prevents the initiation of growing season until it disappears from vegetated areas (Palacios, 1997; Buus-Hinkler et al., 2006). Normalized Difference Vegetation Index (NDVI), an index of vegetation greenness derived from remote sensing data (Jia et al., 2004) is frequently employed. NDVI-related researches in cold regions are frequently conducted. Ones reveal the inter-annual (Myneni et al., 1997; Hope et al., 2003) and intra-seasonal variability of NDVI. Different latitudes (Hope et al., 2004) and vegetation types (Jia et al., 2004) are also assessed. Buus-Hinkler et al. (2006) monitored Snow-NDVI relations at Zackenberg in high Arctic Northeast Greenland at both high spatial and high temporal resolution, and developed a semi-empirical model to calculate snow-cover extent and NDVI. They contributed to establish a detailed relation between vegetation and snow in High Arctic areas. However, less work has been done to relate the spatial patterns of snow cover and NDVI together, and to the altitude in Alpine areas.

In our study, remote sensing data play a critical role in our data mining. Elevation as a variable is considered in spatial distribution of snow, vegetation will be used as a reference, or an indicator. We investigate: (1) quantification of SCA (Snow-Cover Area per unit area of elevation band) – Elevation relations and NDVI-Elevation relations; (2) comparisons among Snow-Elevation-Vegetation relations, to obtain a better understanding of snow-covered area vary with elevation, and the relation to vegetation.

2. Study area and data source

Yangbajain Basin locates at 90°00′E–90°45′E, 29°30′N–30°30′N, southwest of Lhasa River Basin, Tibet China, and southeast of Nyainqntanglha Range. It covers an area of 2665 km^2 and elevation ranges from 3855 to 6970 m (Fig. 2). Permanent snow and glacier develop in this area because of the high altitude and cold weather. Alpine meadow, shrub, and rock cover this mountainous, continental, mid-latitude region.

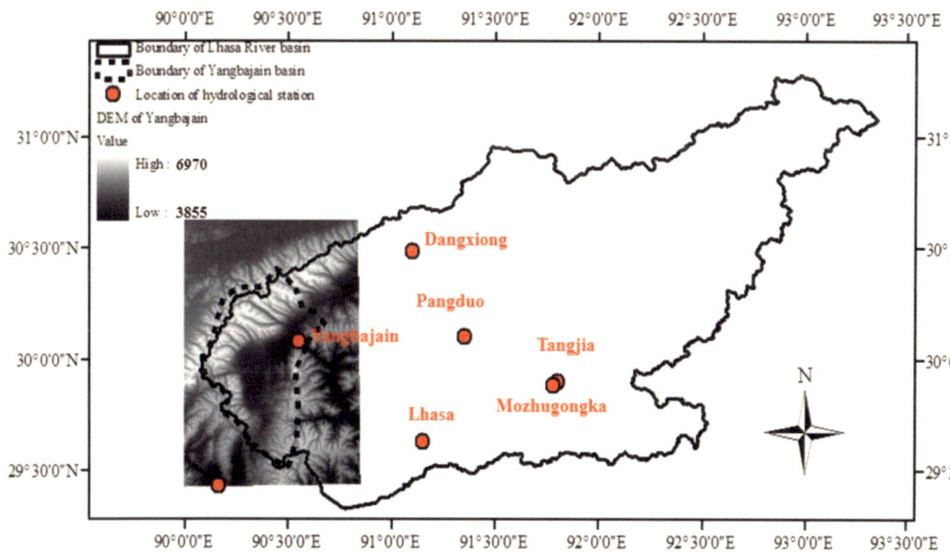

Figure 1. An overview of the study area

Yangbajain Hydrological Station (90°33′E, 30°5′N) is located at the outlet of Yangbajain Basin with an elevation of 4250 m. According to temperature records of the station from

2003 to 2008, annual precipitation in the area averages 505.2 mm, 87.4% of which falls in the summer season from June to September. Monthly air temperature from June to August is above 10°C, with five months: January, February, March, November, and December, having temperatures below 0°C. Monthly average temperature at different elevation bands based on observations at Yangbajain station and interpolated with lapse rate of 6.3°C/1000m are shown in Table 1, elevation bands with air temperature above 0°C are marked in orange, which might indicate an intensive vegetative growth.

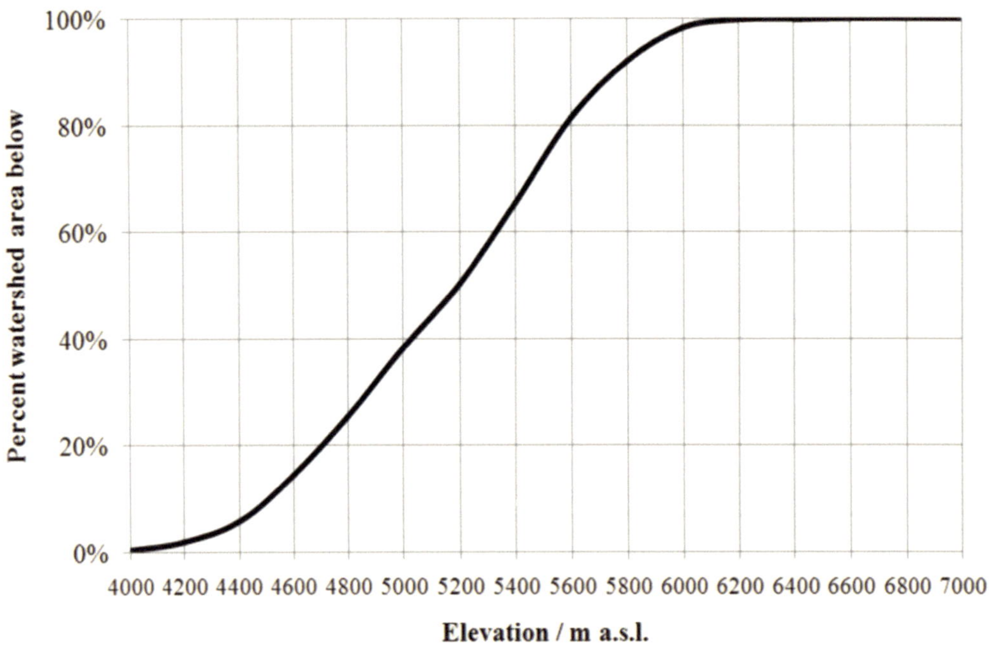

Figure 2. Area-elevation curve for Yangbajain Basin

To examine the relation between SCA and elevation (SCA-Elevation) and Vegetation-Elevation relation, three types of dataset are required:

1. MODIS snow product: MYD10A2 (MODIS/Aqua Snow Cover 8-Day L3 Global 500 m SIN Grid V005) with a resolution of 500 m.
2. MODIS vegetation product: MYD13A1 dataset (MODIS/Aqua Vegetation Indices L3 Global 500 m SIN Grid V005) with a spatial resolution of 500 m and a temporal resolution of 16 days.

Digital Elevation Data (DEM) released by Shuttle Radar Topography Miss (SRTM) version 2 with a resolution of about 90 m.Table 1. Monthly average temperature at different elevation band based on observations at Yangbajain station and interpolated with lapse rate of 6.3°C/1000m.

H (m)	4000	4200	4400	4600	4800	5000	5200	5400	5600	5800	6000	6200	6400	6600	6800	7000
Month	Monthly average temperature (°C) at different elevation band based on observation and lapse rate 6.3°C/1000m															
Jan	-3.2	-4.5	-5.7	-7.0	-8.2	-9.5	-10.8	-12.0	-13.3	-14.5	-15.8	-17.1	-18.3	-19.6	-20.8	-22.1
Feb	-2.3	-3.6	-4.8	-6.1	-7.3	-8.6	-9.9	-11.1	-12.4	-13.6	-14.9	-16.2	-17.4	-18.7	-19.9	-21.2
Mar	1.8	0.5	-0.7	-2.0	-3.2	-4.5	-5.8	-7.0	-8.3	-9.5	-10.8	-12.1	-13.3	-14.6	-15.8	-17.1
Apr	5.0	3.7	2.5	1.2	0.0	-1.3	-2.6	-3.8	-5.1	-6.3	-7.6	-8.9	-10.1	-11.4	-12.6	-13.9
May	9.5	8.2	7.0	5.7	4.5	3.2	1.9	0.7	-0.6	-1.8	-3.1	-4.4	-5.6	-6.9	-8.1	-9.4
Jun	13.0	11.7	10.5	9.2	7.9	6.7	5.4	4.2	2.9	1.6	0.4	-0.9	-2.1	-3.4	-4.7	-5.9
Jul	13.7	12.5	11.2	9.9	8.7	7.4	6.2	4.9	3.6	2.4	1.1	-0.1	-1.4	-2.7	-3.9	-5.2
Aug	13.4	12.1	10.9	9.6	8.4	7.1	5.8	4.6	3.3	2.1	0.8	-0.5	-1.7	-3.0	-4.2	-5.5
Sep	11.4	10.1	8.9	7.6	6.3	5.1	3.8	2.6	1.3	0.0	-1.2	-2.5	-3.7	-5.0	-6.3	-7.5
Oct	6.2	4.9	3.7	2.4	1.2	-0.1	-1.4	-2.6	-3.9	-5.1	-6.4	-7.7	-8.9	-10.2	-11.4	-12.7
Nov	0.1	-1.2	-2.4	-3.7	-5.0	-6.2	-7.5	-8.7	-10.0	-11.3	-12.5	-13.8	-15.0	-16.3	-17.6	-18.8
Dec	-2.6	-3.9	-5.1	-6.4	-7.6	-8.9	-10.2	-11.4	-12.7	-13.9	-15.2	-16.5	-17.7	-19.0	-20.2	-21.5

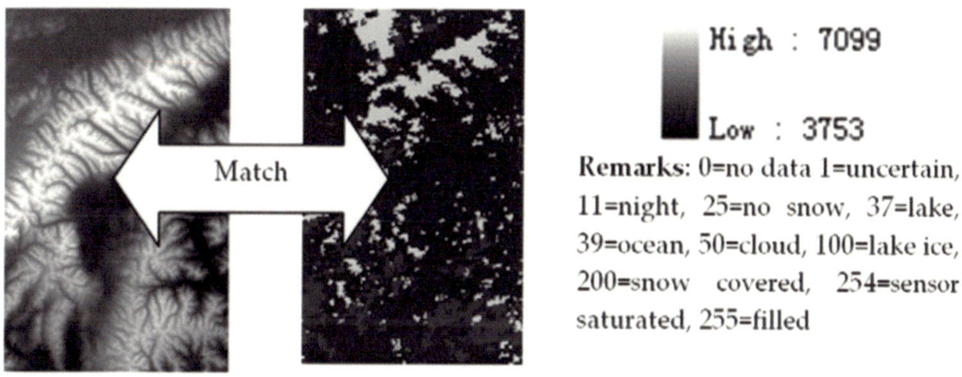

Figure 3. *An example of DEM(left) data and MODIS(right) in gif format*All these datasets are available from https://wist.echo.nasa.gov/. The hdf files of snow product from July 2002 to January 2009, and vegetation product from 2003 to 2005 are adopted in this chapter, except for January 2004 which was unavailable.

The study area involves h25v05 and h25v06 blocks, 226 rows, 150 columns, 33900 grids. The original data are on a Sinusoidal projection. MODIS Reprojection Tools (MRT) provided by NASA is applied for re-projection, mosaic, and extraction. The command: hdftool and hdfread in Matlab is useful for processing the data in hdf format. Programs on C++ language are made to match the DEM and MODIS data (Fig. 3), calculating the average elevation of all the DEM pixels within one MODIS grid. As the spatial resolution of DEM is about 90m, and that of MODIS product is approximately 500m, every MODIS grid has 30 DEM pixels. Thus, we know the elevation for each grid in 6-year MODIS snow products with a time interval of 8-day and 3-year MODIS NDVI products with time interval of 16 days.

MODIS snow grids blurred by cloud are removed under the assumption that average snow cover percentage of cloud-affected grids is similar to average level of the ones without clouds. Finally, every grid in that 6-year/3-year time series contains three types of property: with/without snow, NDVI, and elevation.

3. Temporal distribution of snow and vegetation coverage

Intra-seasonal snow cycle in different elevation zone

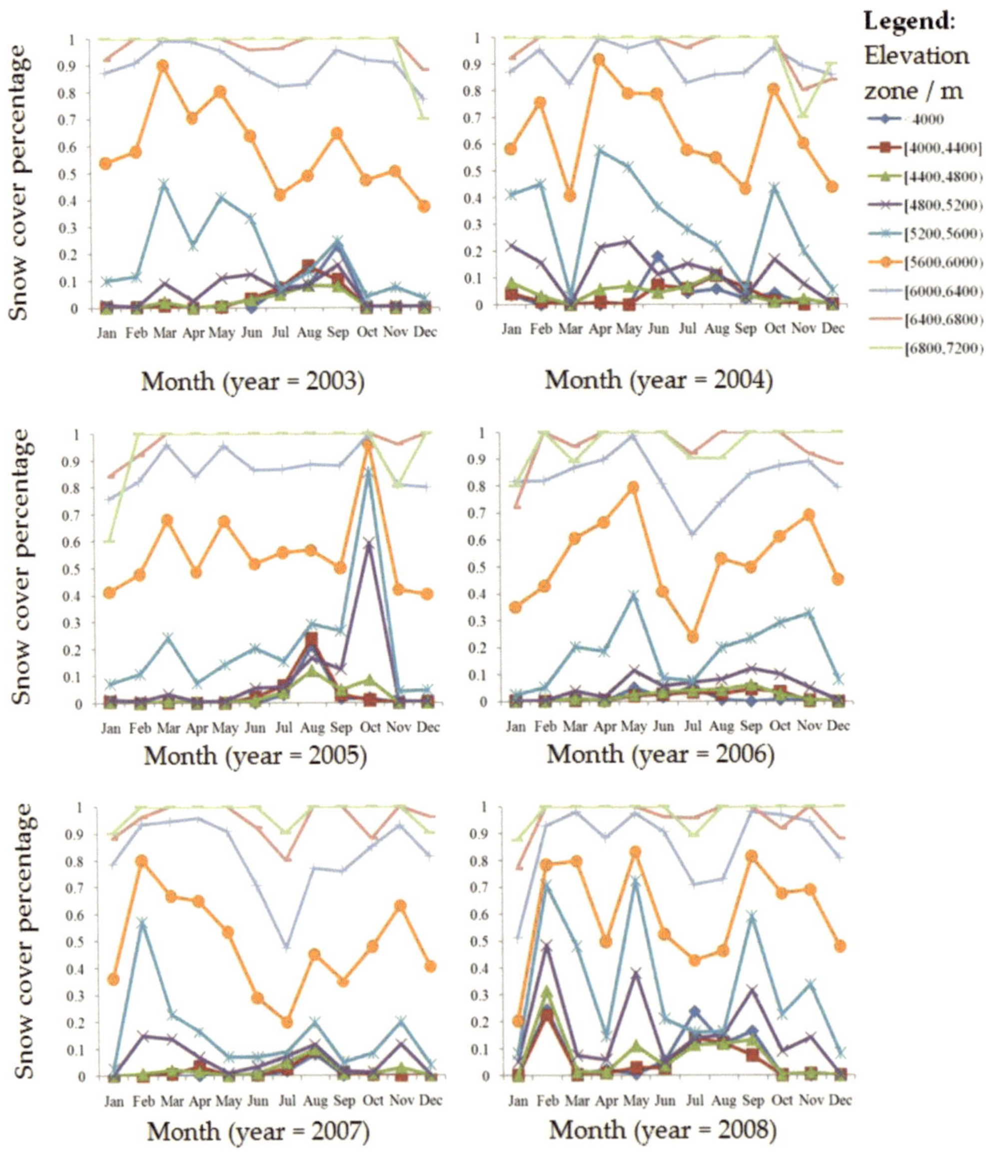

Figure 4. Snow covered and depletion curve in different elevation band from 2003 to 2008

The regions below 4800 m have lower snow coverage, less than 20%. The region above 6400 m is covered by glaciers and permanent snow with snow coverage of more than 70%. In the elevation band between 5600 and 6400 m, the SCA varies but remains 20% at minimum. This is sometimes influenced by the temperature in warm seasons. Seasonal snow covers elevation band between 4800 and 5600 m, and is largely affected by precipitation in winter. The lack of precipitation may lead to snow-free.

Intra-seasonal NDVI variation in different elevation zone

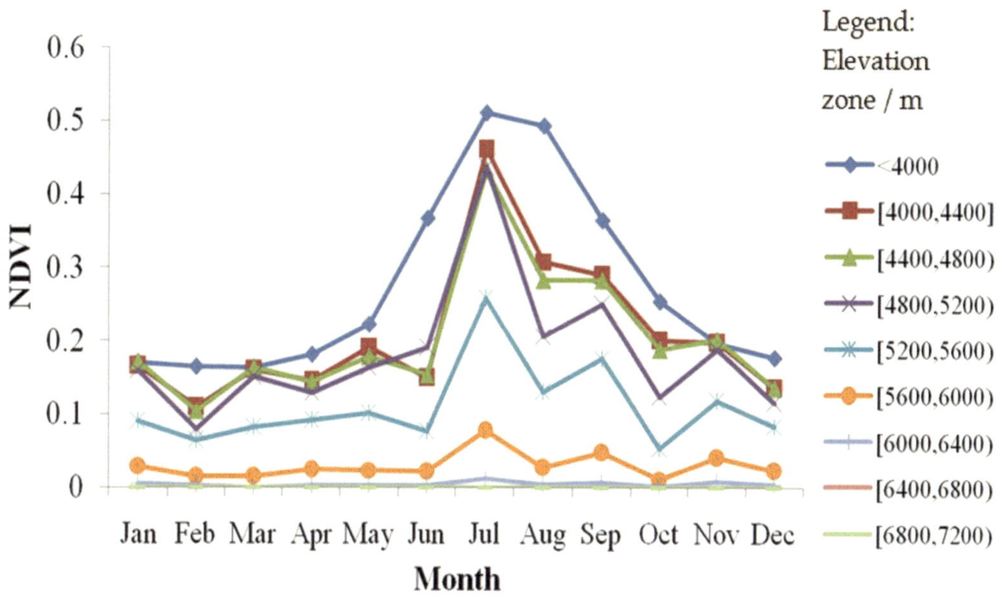

Figure 5. Monthly mean NDVI in different elevation band

A significant seasonality of vegetation is detected in elevations below 5200 m. NDVI values gradually increase from June to July when peak NDVI (>0.3) happens and then decreases. For high elevations (>6000 m), NDVI values remain less than 0.01 during the whole year.

Precipitation and temperature analysis

Precipitation and temperature are considered to be the primary factors which influence snow distribution (Hope et al., 2003), especially winter precipitation and summer temperature. Based on monthly meteorological records from 2003 to 2008, air temperature stays above 0°C from April to October. Figure 6 depicts the monthly temperature anomaly from April to October which indicates melting temperature, while Figure 7 presents the precipitation in January, February, March, November, and December which indicates winter snowfall.

Obvious positive monthly temperature anomalies are recorded in April, August, and October of 2003, May and September of 2004, April and from June to September in 2005, from June to August in 2006, all the warm months except August in 2007 and April of 2008. Furthermore, the decline of SCA occurs within those months, especially in the elevation zone of [5600, 6400] m.a.s.l.

Higher precipitation in February and March of 2007 and 2008 is observed with the total amount of 10.8 and 13.0 mm, respectively. These values are much more than those during the same time of the other four years, which lead to a larger snow-cover percentage at the beginning of those two years. Shortage of snowfall in March 2004 results in the absence of snow below 5600 m.

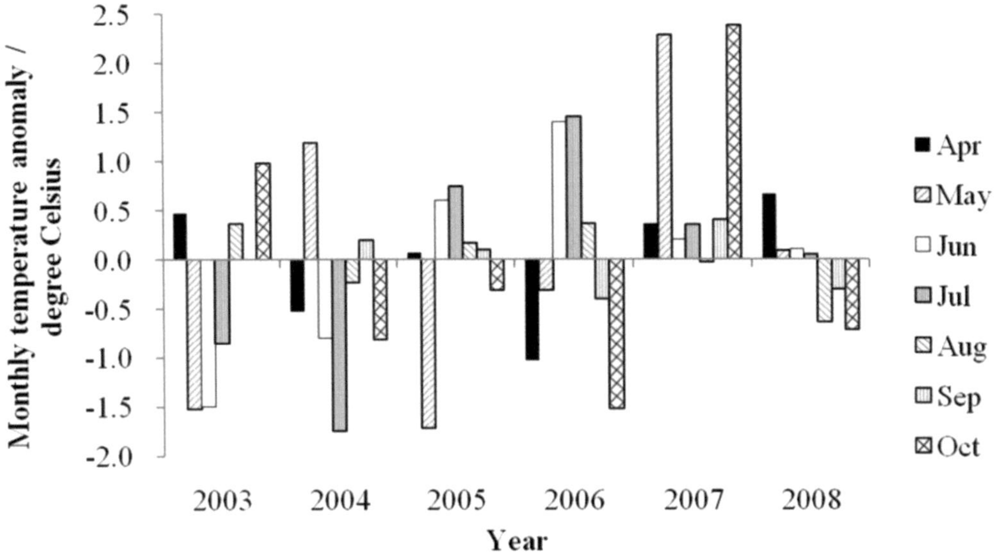

Figure 6. Monthly temperature anomaly from April to Octorber between 2003 and 2008

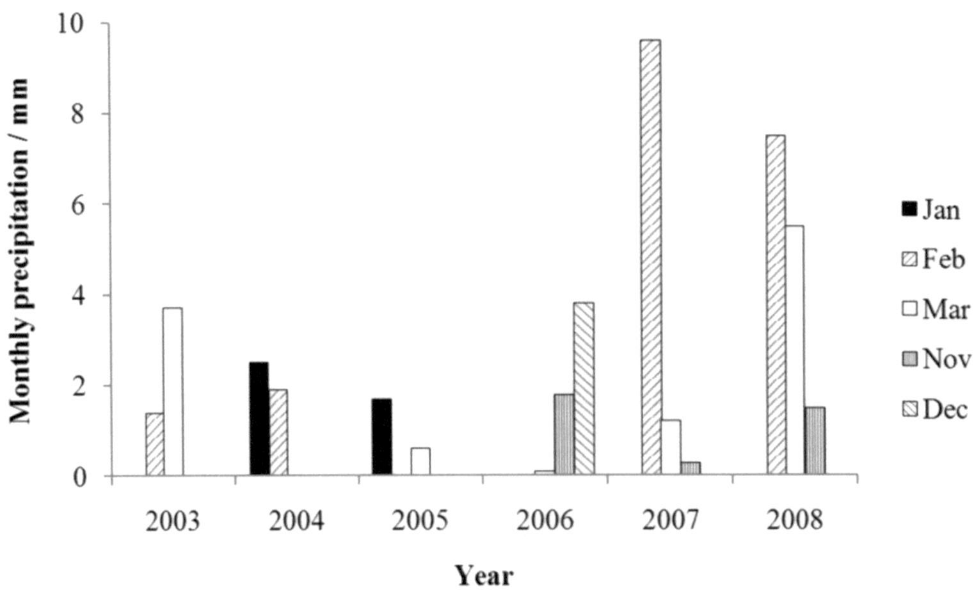

Figure 7. Monthly precipitation from 2003 to 2008 in January, February, March, November, and December

4. Spatial distribution of snow and vegetation coverage

Under a given elevation interval, we sort all the MODIS grids into different elevation band. Therefore, snow cover percentage in one elevation band is counted from the information of with/without snow in the MODIS grids belong to that band. And average NDVI is calculated in that elevation band. In this way, SCA-Month/NDVI-Month relations in different elevation bands are transferred to SCA-Elevation/NDVI-Elevation relations in different months.

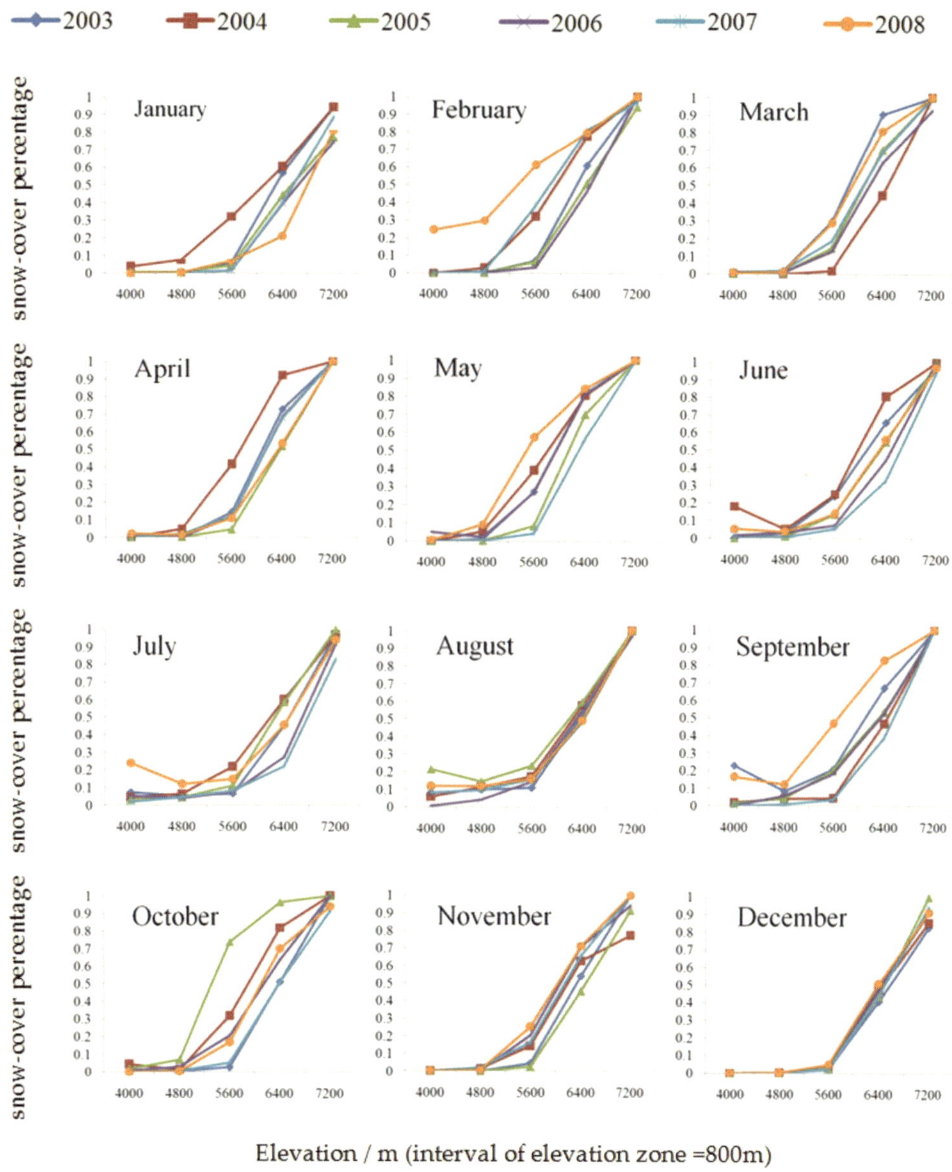

Figure 8. Relation between snow-cover percentage and elevation from January to December during 2003-2008 with an elevation interval of 800 m

Generally, if resolution permitting, the division of a finer elevation interval will help to reveal the results in detail. The resolution of MODIS and DEM are 500 and 90 m, respectively. With a similar magnitude of resolution in both vertical and horizontal directions, the elevation intervals of 800, 400, and 200 m are chosen.

First, we use the elevation intervals 800 and 400 m to discover the relation of SCA-Elevation from 2003 to 2008. Then a comparison between SCA-Elevation and NDVI-Elevation is made based on elevation interval of 200 m from 2003 to 2005.

Two groups are depicted with elevation band intervals equal to 400 and 800 m. In each group, there are 12 figures denoting the 12 months in a year. In each figure, six lines represent the relations of SCA-Elevation in each year from 2003 to 2008 (shown in Fig. 8 and Fig. 9).

The legend is as follows: different shapes denote different years from 2003 to 2008:

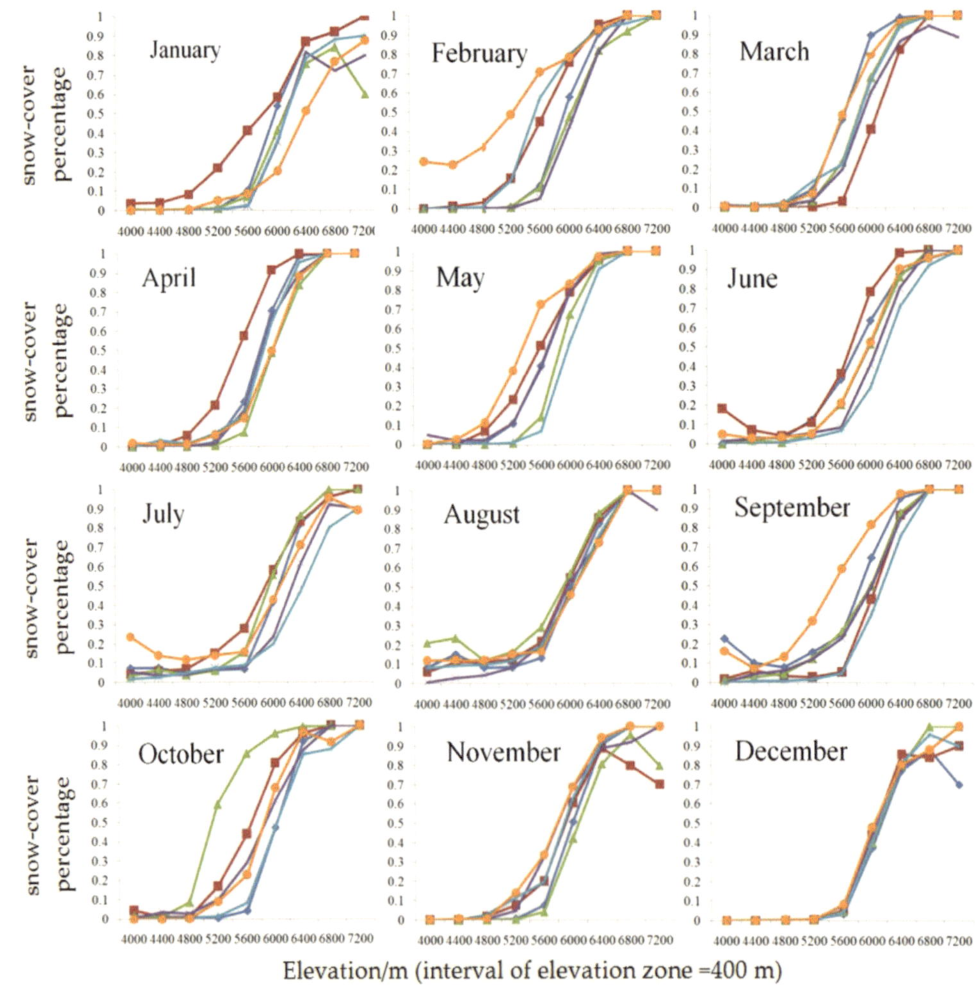

Figure 9. Relation between snow-cover percentage and elevation from January to December during 2003–2008 with an elevation interval of 400 m

The following can be concluded:

1. Based on the division with an elevation interval of 800 m, an obvious positive relation between SCA and elevation is presented. This relation could be considered to be a three-segmented line (Fig. 8) with a slow increase below 5600 m, followed by a rapid rise between 5600 and 6400 m, and finally a lagging growth above 6400 m.
2. If 400 m is used as the elevation interval, the three-segmented line evolves into a smooth "S"-shaped curve in all the months and years (Fig. 9). This is expressed as follows:

$$\frac{dS}{dh} > 0 \tag{1}$$

where S is the ratio of SCA per unit area of elevation zone (Snow-cover percentage).

There exists a critical elevation h_c, which seems to be between 5000 and 6000 m from Fig. 6:

$$\begin{aligned} &if\ h < h_c,\ \frac{dS^2}{d^2h} > 0 \\ &if\ h > h_c,\ \frac{dS^2}{d^2h} < 0 \end{aligned} \tag{2}$$

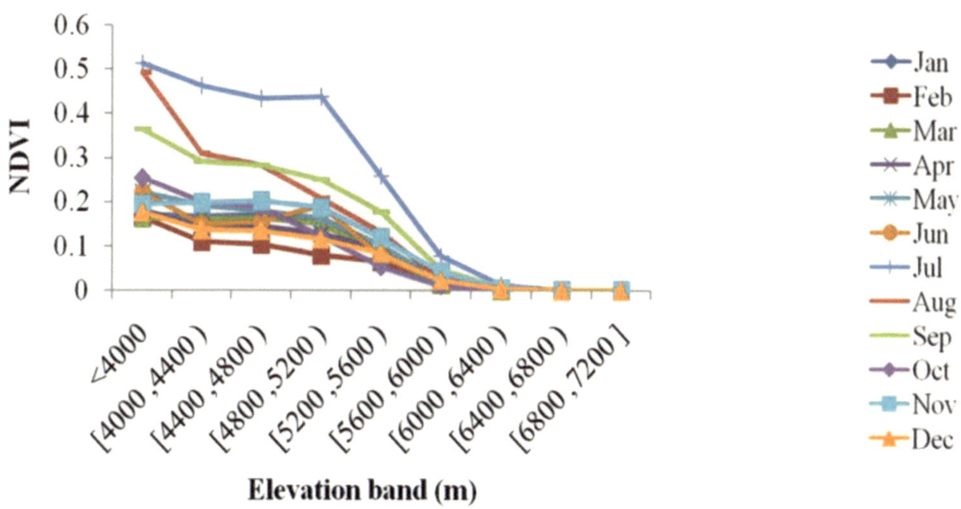

Figure 10. Relation between monthly NDVI and elevation from 2003 to 2005 with an elevation interval of 400 m

The relation of NDVI-Month at different elevation zones (Fig. 5) is converted to the relation of NDVI-Elevation in different months (Fig. 10). A pair of similar but reversed graphs of SCA-Elevation and NDVI-Elevation is preliminarily derived.

5. Correlation between SCA-elevation and NDVI-elevation

In this section, a finer interval of 200 m is adopted for elevation division in order to provide an insight into the relation among SCA-NDVI-Elevation. SCA-Elevation and NDVI-Elevation are obtained during the same time period of 2003-2005. For each elevation band, the expected values of snow-cover percentage (E(S)) and NDVI (E(ndvi)) and standard deviation of snow-cover percentage (σ(S)) and NDVI (σ(ndvi)) are derived from 12-month data. The values of E(S)±σ(S) and E(ndvi)±σ(ndvi) are used to represent the variability of SCA and NDVI within a year for every elevation band.

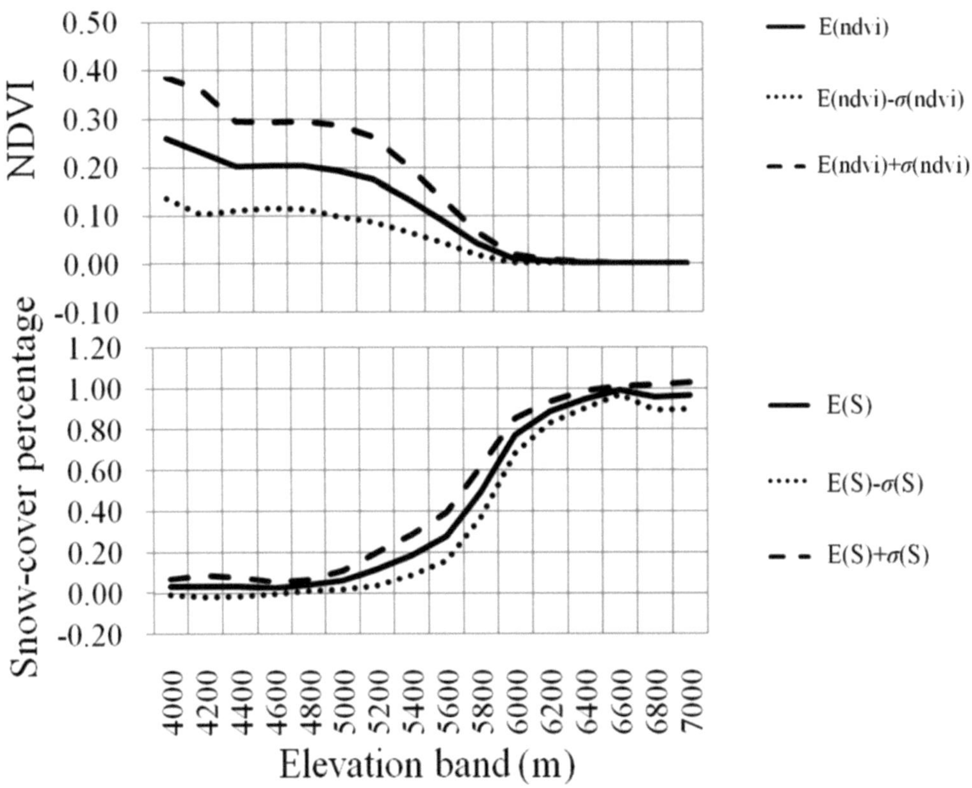

Figure 11. Relation among Snow-covered percentage, NDVI and elevation with an elevation interval of 200 m (h =200m). They look like each other, but reversed.

From Fig. 11, SCA increases, while vegetation cover decreases as elevation rises. Although a linear relationship between temperature and elevation is commonly used as "lapse rate", and both snow and vegetation are closely related to temperature, neither Snow-Elevation nor Vegetation-Elevation seems to be linear, as shown in Fig. 11. Furthermore, as elevation increases, both snow and vegetation follow the changing style of being gradually varying, rapidly varying and gradual varying again.

For variance:

Vegetation takes on a significant seasonality at low elevation, which leads to a high variance ($max\{\sigma$(ndvi)$\}$= 0.13, at the elevation band of [4000,4200] meters above sea level (m.a.s.l)) at low elevation sites. As elevation increases, the seasonal variability decreases (shown in Fig. 12). In the SCA-Elevation curve, a high variability with maximum of σ(S) (= 0.12) occurs at the elevation band of [5600, 5800] m.a.s.l, where air temperature keeps above 0°C only in summer months (June, July, August) (shown in Table 1) (shown in Fig. 13). It suggests that there is sufficient snow because it is always cold enough to maintain snow in winter season, while hot enough to melt snow during summer season. Those contribute to high variability in snow regime. It also indicates that during summer season snowmelt strongly influence underlaying surface and snow regime in this region, which result in an intensive interaction between snow and vegetation in this region, such as the interception of vegetation could reduce snow accumulation and prolonged snow-covered periods would shorten vegetative growing season.

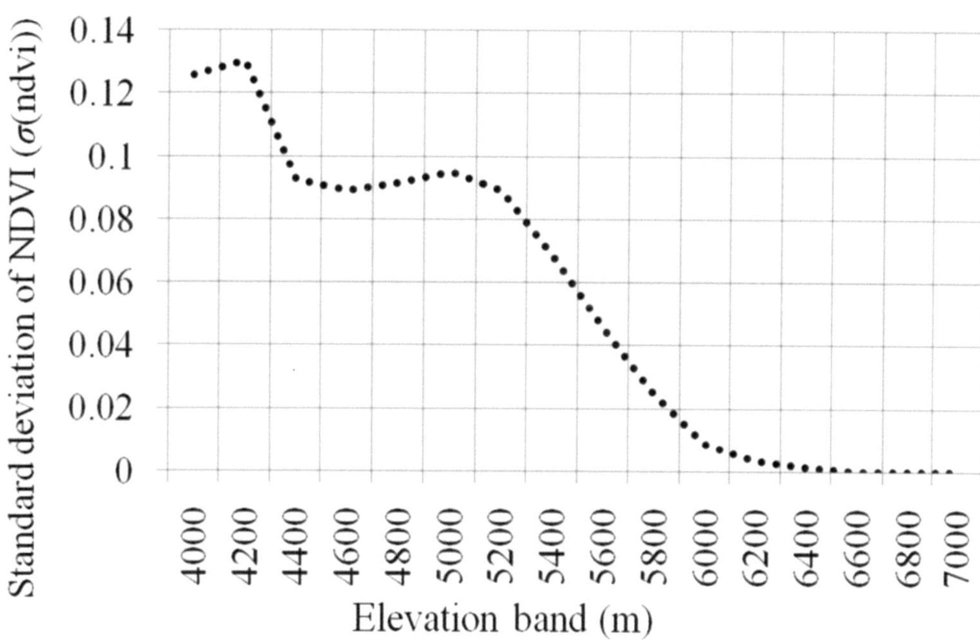

Figure 12. Variability of NDVI in a year. Variability increases as elevation decreases, which indicates an obvious seasonality for vegetation at low elevation sites, where vegetation grows well. As elevation increases, the seasonality diminishes.

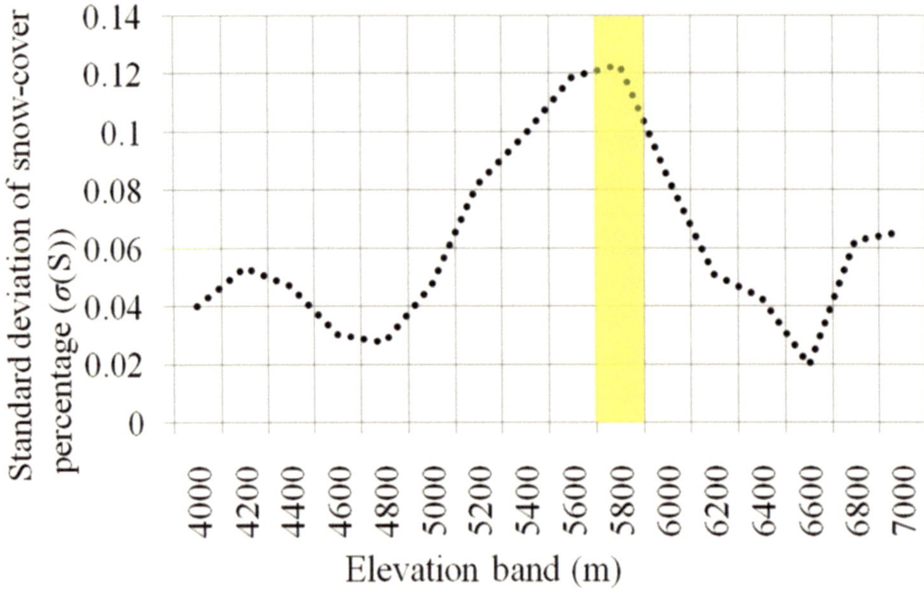

Figure 13. Variability of snow-cover percentage in a year

For expected value:

Knowledge in second derivative could offer a quantitative analysis. Second derivative illustrates how the rate of change proceeds for a given system. It could also be reflected by the curvature or concavity of a graph. A positive second derivative is illustrated by an upward curve (concave up), whereas a negative second derivative is denoted by a downward curve (concave down). The point switch from concave up to concave down is an inflection point. Based on the definition of the second derivative,

$$\begin{aligned} f''(S) &= \lim_{h\to 0}\frac{\dfrac{f(S+h)-f(S)}{h}-\dfrac{f(S)-f(S-h)}{h}}{h} \\ &= \lim_{\Delta h\to 0}\frac{f(S+h)-2f(S)+f(S-h)}{h^2} \end{aligned} \tag{3}$$

Here, $f(S+h)$ represents the snow-cover percentage / NDVI at upper elevation band, $f(S)$ is the snow-cover percentage / NDVI at middle elevation band, and $f(S-h)$ denotes the snow-cover percentage / NDVI at lower band.

The expression on the right only involves two variables: S (snow-cover percentage / NDVI) and h (elevation interval). As elevation interval is set to 200 m, we adopt the equation $f(S+h)$-$2f(S)+f(S-h)$ to calculate the second derivative.

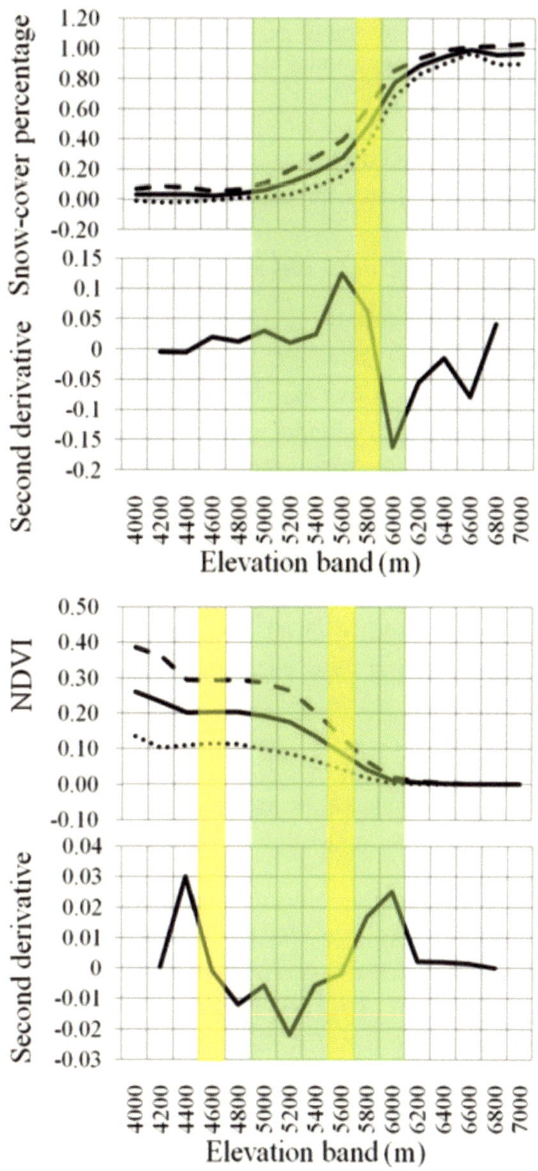

Figure 14. Second derivatives of SCA-elevation curve and NDVI-elevation curve

The second derivative demonstrates one inflection point in SCA-Elevation curve and two inflection points in NDVI-Elevation curve. As shown in Fig. 14, SCA-Elevation curve varies from concave up to concave down, with inflection point in the band of [5600, 5800] m.a.s.l. It suggests an accelerated growth below 5600 m and decelerated growth above 5800 m. Two inflection points in the band of [4400, 4600] and [5400, 5600] m.a.s.l divide NDVI-Elevation curve into three segments, from concave up to concave down then to concave up again:

1. ≤4400 m, vegetation decelerated decreases as elevation increase;
2. In the bands of [4600, 5400] m.a.s.l, vegetation acceleration decreases as elevation increase;
3. ≥5600 m, vegetation decelerated decreases as elevation increase.

According to Section 3, less than 20% of the area below 4800 m is seasonally covered by snow, where air temperature keeps above 0°C for more than 6 months (see Table 1). In the regions above 6000m, NDVI value is less than 0.01 and air temperature remains below 0°C during the whole year (see Table 1). Therefore, the coincident regions [4800, 6000] m.a.s.l for both snow and vegetation are meaningful and highlighted (Fig. 14).

Within the bands of [4800, 6000] m.a.s.l, the negative NDVI-Elevation curve varies from concave down to concave up with an inflection point in the band of [5400, 5600] m.a.s.l. On the other hand, the positive SCA-Elevation curve changes from concave up to concave down with an inflection point in the band of [5600, 5800] m.a.s.l. A nearly completed reversed relation between NDVI-elevation and snow-elevation is obtained.

6. Conclusion

Based on the Snow-Vegetation-Elevation relation derived from MODIS snow and MODIS vegetation products with a spatial resolution of 500 m, we discovered the following:

1. A positive relation between snow and elevation exists because temperature decreases as elevation increases. However, the quantification of SCA-Elevation relation derived in Yangbajain Basin, a branch of Lhasa River Basin, Tibet, China, demonstrates an "S"-shaped curve. This means that the SCA-Elevation does not follow the supposed linear shape of temperature lapse rate to elevation.
2. Phenological traits of vegetation are closely related to temperature, followed by elevation. However, a complex nonlinear relation between NDVI (an index of vegetation greenness) and elevation is also discovered.

Combined with the analysis on temporal distribution of snow and vegetation in Section 3, the elevation zone of [4800, 6000] m.a.s.l seems sensitive to both snow and vegetation in our study area. Furthermore, within this elevation zone, both SCA-Elevation and NDVI-Elevation present an "S" shape, initially having an accelerated variation followed by a decelerated one, but in reversed directions. The inflection point of Vegetation-Elevation is located between 5400 and 5600 m, and that of Snow-Elevation is between 5600 and 5800 m. It reveals that the NDVI-Elevation relation could be an indication of Snow-Elevation relation. In fact, there is really a very close interaction between snow and vegetation, such as interception of vegetation could reduce snow accumulation and long snow-covered periods would shorten vegetative growing season (Palacios, 1997; Buus-Hinkler et al., 2006). That is why the inflection of NDVI-Elevation almost coincide with inflection of Snow-Elevation relation, which could help to develop the linear Snow-Temperature-Elevation relation into a more complex function for a better model input.

1. It is also consistent with the point that the forest cover is the most highly correlated variable with snow cover (Varhola, 2010) at meso-scales (100–10 km), but mainly in snow-vegetation sensitive elevation. At relatively high elevations such as from 801 to 1069m accounting for a maximum about 1000m and >851/1200 in southeast British Columbia (D' Eon, 2004), or >6000 m/6970 m for Yangbajain Basin, greater snow versus reduced vegetation make the NDVI-Snow indication meaningless.
2. This book chapter provides a quantitative method to detect the Snow-NDVI-Elevation relation. It is a simple method that could be adopted in other watersheds for more comparisons and new findings.

Author details

Gao Jie
Hydrochina Corporation,
Beijing,
China

7. References

Anderton, S. P., White, S. M., & Alvera, B. (2002). Micro-scale spatial variability and the timing of snow melt runoff in a high mountain catchment. *Journal of Hydrology*, 268: 158-176.

Barry, R. G. (1992). *Mountain Weather and Climate, 2nd edn*. Routledge, London: 402.

Bell, V. A., & Moore, R. J. (1999) .An elevation-dependent snowmelt model for upland Britain. *Hydrological Processes*, 13: 1887-1903.

Buus-Hinkler, J., Hansen, B. U., Tamstorf, M. P., & Pedersen, S. B. (2006). Snow-vegetation relations in a high arctic ecosystem: inter-annual variability inferred from new monitoring and modeling concepts. *Remote Sens. Environ*. 105, 237-247.

D' Eon, R. (2004). Snow depth as a function of canopy cover and other site attributes in a forested ungulate winter range in southeast British Columbia. *BC J. Ecosyst. Manage.* 3, 1-9.

Daugharty, D., & Dickinson, B. (1982). Snow distribution in forested and deforested landscapes in New Brunswick, Canada. *Proceedings of the 39th Eastern Snow Conference, Reno*, NV, April 19-23, 1982:10-19.

Essery, R.L., Pomeroy, J.W., Parvianen, J., & Storck, P. (2003). Sublimation of snow from coniferous forests in a climate model. *J. Climate*. 16, 1855-1864.

Gao, J., Wang, G. Q., Fu, X. D., Wang, H., & Gong, T. L. (2010). A research on spatial and temporal distribution of snow cover in Yangbajain Basin of Lhasa River Basin based on MODIS snow product. *Proceedings of The international conference on multimedia technology——Special Workshop on Geoscience and Remote Sensing*, Ningbo, China:1131-1137.

Gao, J., Williams, W. M., Fu, X. D., Wang, G. Q., & Gong, T. L. (2012). Spatiotemporal distribution of snow in Eastern Tibet and the response to climate change. *Remote Sensing of Environment*, doi:10.1016/j.rse.2012.01.006.

Han, Q. H., Wang, P. C., Wang, Y. K., Wang, J. K., Chen, W. M. & Gao, J. (2007). Characters of winter snow-cover and climate in Northeast China revealed by MODIS products, *Journal of Nanjing Institute of Meteorology*. 30, 3: 396-401. (In Chinese)

Hantel, M., Ehrendorfer, M., & Haslinger, A. (2000). Climate sensitivity of snow cover duration in Austria. *International Journal of Climatology*, 20(6): 615-640.

Hedstrom, N.R., & Pomeroy, J.W. (1998). Measurements and modeling of snow interception in the boreal forest, *Hydrol. Proc.* 12, 1611-1625.

Hendrick, R.L., Filgate, B.D., & Adams, W.M. (1971). Application of environment analysis to watershed snowmelt. *J. Appl. Meteorol.* 10, 418-429.

Hope, A.S., Boynton, W.L., Stow, D.A., & Douglas, D.C. (2003). Interannual growth dynamics of vegetation in the Kuparuk River watershed, Alaska based on the Normalized Difference Vegetation Index. *Int. J. Remote Sens.* 24, 3413-3425.

Hope, A.S., Pence, K.R., & Stow, D.A. (2004). NDVI from low attitude aircraft and composited NOAA AVHRR data for scaling Arctic ecosystem flux. *Int. J. Remote Sens.* 25, 4237-4250.

Huang, X. D., Zhang, X. D., Li, X. & Liang, T, G. (2007). Accuracy Analysis for MODIS Snow Products of MOD10A1 and MOD10A2 in Northern Xinjiang Area, *Journal of Glaciology and Geocryology*. 29, 5: 722-729. (In Chinese)

Jia, G. J., Epstein, H. E., & Walker, D. A. (2004). Controls over intra-seasonal dynamics of AVHRR NDVI for the Arctic tundra in northern Alaska. *Int. J. Remote Sens.* 25, 1547-1564.

Jost, G., Weiler, M., Gluns, D.R., & Alila, Y. (2007). The influence of forest and topography on snow accumulation and melt at the watershed-scale. *J. Hydrol.* 347, 101-115.

Li, P. J. (1995). Distribution of snow cover over the high Asia. *Journal of Glaciology and Geocryology*, 17, 4: 292-295. (In Chinese)

Li, X. G., & Williams, M. W. (2008). Snowmelt runoff modelling in an arid mountain watershed, Tarim Basin, China. *Hydrological Processes*, 22(19): 3931-3940.

Liston, G.E. (2004). Representing subgrid snow cover heterogeneities in regional and global models. *J. Climate*. 17, 1381-1397.

Ma, H., & Cheng, G.D. (2003). A test of Snowmelt Runoff Model (SRM) for the Gongnaisi River basin in the western Tianshan Mountains, China. *Chin. Sci. Bull.* 48(20), 2253-2259.

Marchand, M.D., & Killingtveit, A. (2005). Statistical probability distribution of snow depth at the model sub-grid cell spatial scale. *Hydrol. Proc*,19, 355-369.

McKay, G.A., & Gray, D.M. (1981). *The distribution of snowcover. In: Handbook of Snow: Principles, Processes, Management and Use*, Gray D M, Male D H (eds). Pergamon Press: Toronto; 153-190.

Myneni, R.B., Keeling, C.D., Tucker, C.J., Asrar, G., & Nemani, R.R. (1997). Increased plant growth in the northern high latitudes from 1981 to 1991. *Nature*, 386, 698-702.

Palacios, D., & García Sánchez-Colomer, M. (1997). The distribution of high mountain vegetation in relation to snow cover: Penalara, Spain. *Catena*. 30, 1-40.

Williams, M.W., Rebecca, T., Barnes, R. T., Parman, J. N., Freppaz, M., & Hood, E. (2011). Stream Water Chemistry along an Elevational Gradient from the Continental Divide to the Foothills of the Rocky Mountains. *Vadose Zone Journal*, doi:10.2136/vzj2010.0131, 10:900-914

Pomeroy, J., Gray, D., Hedstrom, N., & Janowicz, J. (2002). Precipitation of seasonal snow accumulation in cold climate forests, *Hydrol. Proc*. 16, 3543-3558.

Qin, D. H., Xiao, C. D., Ding, Y. J., Yao, T. D., Bian, L. G., Ren, J. W., Wang, N. L., Liu, S. Y. & Zhao, L. (2006). Progress on cryospheric studies by international and Chinese communities and perspectives, *Journal of Applied Meteorological Science*. 17, 6: 649-656. (In Chinese)

Sloan, W. T., Kilsby, C. G., & Lunn, R. (2004). Incorporating topographic variability into a simple regional snowmelt model. *Hydrological Processes*, 18: 3371-3390.

Varhola, A., Coops, N.C., Weiler, M., & Moore, R.D. (2010). Forest canopy effects on snow accumulation and ablation: An integrative review of empirical results. *J. Hydrol*. 392, 219-233.

Wen, J., Dai, M., Deroin, J. P., Wang, Z. J., & Humber, L. (2006). Extent and depth of snow cover over the Nyaingentanghla Range derived from ASAR and MODIS data, *Journal of Glaciology and Geocryology*. 28, 1: 54-61. (In Chinese)

Winkler, R. D., Spittlehouse, D. L., & Golding, D. L. (2005). Measured differences in snow accumulation and melt among clearcut, juvenile, and mature forest in southern British Columbia. *Hydrol. Proc*. 19, 51-62.

Yang, Z. N., Liu, X. R. & Zeng, Q. Z. (2000). *Hydrology in Chinese cold region*. Beijing: science press. (In Chinese)

Zhang, J., Han, T. & Wang, J. (2005). Changes of snow-cover area and snowline altitude in the Qilian Mountains, 1997-2004, *Journal of Glaciology and Geocryology*. 27, 5: 649-654. (In Chinese)

Chapter 15

Mining Complex Network Data for Adaptive Intrusion Detection

Dewan Md. Farid, Mohammad Zahidur Rahman
and Chowdhury Mofizur Rahman

Additional information is available at the end of the chapter

http://dx.doi.org/10.5772/48308

1. Introduction

Intrusion detection is the method of identifying intrusions or misuses in a computer network, which compromise the confidentiality and integrity of the network. Intrusion Detection System (IDS) is a security tool used to monitor network traffic and detect unauthorized activities in the network [23, 28, 30]. A security monitoring surveillance system, which is an intrusion detection model based on detecting anomalies in user behaviors was first introduced by James P. Anderson in 1980 [1]. After that several intrusion detection models based on statistics, Markov chains, time-series, etc proposed by Dorothy Denning in 1986. At first host-based IDS was implemented, which located in the server machine to examine the internal interfaces [35], but with the evolution of computer networks day by day focus gradually shifted toward network-based IDS [20]. Network-based IDS monitors and analyzes network traffics for detecting intrusions from internal and external intruders [26, 27, 34]. A number of data mining algorithms have been widely used by the intelligent computational researchers in the large amount of network audit data for detecting known and unknown intrusions in the last decade [3, 9, 18, 32, 33]. Even for a small network the amount of network audit data is very large that an IDS needs to examine. Use of data mining for intrusion detection aim to solve the problem of analyzing the large volumes of audit data and realizing performance optimization of detection rules.

There are many drawbacks in currently available commercial IDS, such as low and unbalanced detection rates for different types of network attacks, large number of false positives, long response time in high speed network, and redundant input attributes in intrusion detection training dataset. In general a conventional intrusion detection dataset is complex, dynamic, and composed of many different attributes. It has been successfully tested that not all the input attributes in intrusion detection training dataset may be needed for training the intrusion detection models or detecting intrusions [31]. The use of redundant attributes interfere with the correct completion of mining task, increase the complexity of detection model and computational time, because the information they added is contained in

INTECH
open science | open minds

©2012 Farid et al., licensee InTech. This is an open access chapter distributed under the terms of the Creative Commons Attribution License (http://creativecommons.org/licenses/by/3.0), which permits unrestricted use, distribution, and reproduction in any medium, provided the original work is properly cited.

other attributes [7]. Ideally, IDS should have an intrusion detection rate of 100% along with false positive of 0%, which is really very difficult to achieve.

Applying mining algorithms for adaptive intrusion detection is the process of collecting network audit data and convert the collected audit data to the format that is suitable for mining. Finally, developing a clustering or classification model for intrusion detection, which provide decision support to intrusion management for detecting known and unknown intrusions by discovering intrusion patterns [4, 5].

2. Intrusion detection

Intrusion detection is the process of monitoring and analyzing the network traffics. It takes sensor data to gather information for detecting intrusions from internal and external networks [6], and notify the network administrator or intrusion prevention system (IPS) about the attack [19, 24]. Intrusion detection is broadly classified into three categories: misuse, anomaly, and hybrid detection model [10]. Misuse detection model detects attacks based on known attack patterns, which already stored in the database by using pattern matching of incoming network packets to the signatures of known intrusions. It begins protecting the network immediately upon installation and produces very low FP, but it requires frequently signature updates and cannot detect new intrusions. Anomaly based detection model detects deviations from normal behaviors to identify new intrusions [22]. It creates a normal profile of the network and then any action that deviated from the normal profile is treated as a possible intrusion, which produces large number of false positives. Hybrid detection model combines both misuse and anomaly detection models [2]. It makes decision based on both the normal behavior of the network and the intrusive behavior of the intruders. Table 1 shows the comparisons among misuse, anomaly, and hybrid detection models.

Characteristics	Misuse	Anomaly	Hybrid
Detection Accuracy	High (for known attacks)	Low	High
Detecting New Attacks	No	Yes	Yes
False Positives	Low	Very high	High
False Negatives	High	Low	Low
Timely Notifications	Fast	Slow	Rather Fast
Update Usage Patterns	Frequent	Not Frequent	Not Frequent

Table 1. Comparisons of Detection Models.

Detection rate (DR) and false positive (FP) are the most important parameters that are used for performance estimation of intrusion detection models [8]. Detection rate is calculated by the number of intrusions detected by the IDS divided by the total number of intrusion instances present in the intrusion dataset, and false positive is an alarm, which rose for something that is not really an attack, which are expressed be equation 1 and 2.

$$DetectionRate, DR = \frac{TotalDetectedAttacks}{TotalAttacks} * 100 \quad (1)$$

$$FalsePositive, FP = \frac{TotalMisclassifiedProcess}{TotalNormalProcess} * 100 \quad (2)$$

Also precision, recall, overall, and false alarm have been used to measure the performance of IDS [21, 25] from table 2, precision, recall, overall, and false alarm may be expressed be equation 3 to 6.

Parameters	Definition
True Positive (TP) or Detection Rate (DR)	Attack occur and alarm raised
False Positive (FP)	No attack but alarm raised
True Negative (TN)	No attack and no alarm
False Negative (FN)	Attack occur but no alarm

Table 2. Parameters for performances estimation of IDS.

$$Precision = \frac{TP}{TP + FP} \tag{3}$$

$$Recall = \frac{TP}{TP + FN} \tag{4}$$

$$Overall = \frac{TP + TN}{TP + FP + FN + TN} \tag{5}$$

$$FalseAlarm = \frac{FP + FN}{TP + FP + FN + TN} \tag{6}$$

2.1. Intrusion detection dataset

The data generated by IDS contain information about network topology, hosts and other confidential information for this reason intrusion detection dataset cannot be shared in public domain. Whereas it is not difficult task to generate a large set of intrusion detection alets by running IDS in a private or Internet-exposed network. For generating intrusion detection dataset only major challenge is to labeling the network data, because network data are unlabeled and it is not clear which attacks are false positives and which are true positives. The KDD 1999 cup benchmark intrusion detection dataset is the most popular dataset for intrusion detection research, a predictive model capable of distinguishing between intrusions and normal connections, which was first used in the 3rd International Knowledge Discovery and Data Mining Tools Competition for building a network intrusion detector [29]. A simulated environment was set up by the MIT Lincoln Lab to acquire raw TCP/IP dump data for a local-area network (LAN) to compare the performance of various IDS that is the part of KDD99 dataset. Examples in KDD99 dataset represent attribute values of a class in the network data flow, and each class is labelled either normal or attack. For each network connection 41 attributes are in KDD99 dataset that have either discrete or continuous values. These attributes are divided into three groups: basic features , content features, and statistical features of network connection.

The classes in KDD99 dataset are mainly categorized into five classes: normal, denial of service (DoS), remote to user (R2L), user to root (U2R), and probing. Normal connections are generated by simulated daily user behaviours. Denial of service computes power or memory of a victim machine too busy or too full to handle legitimate requests. Remote to user is an attack that a remote user gains access of a local user or account by sending packets to a machine over a network communication. User to root is an attack that an intruder begins with the access of a normal user account and then becomes a root-user by exploiting various vulnerabilities of the system. Probing is an attack that scans a network to gather information or find known vulnerabilities. In KDD99 dataset the main four attacks are divided into 22 different attacks that tabulated in table 3 and table 4 shows the number of training and testing examples for each major class.

4 Main Attack Classes	22 Attacks Classes
Denial of Service (DoS)	back, land, neptune, pod, smurf, teardrop
Remote to User (R2L)	ftp_write, guess_passwd, imap, multihop, phf, spy, warezclient, warezmaster
User to Root (U2R)	buffer_overflow, perl, loadmodule, rootkit
Probing	ipsweep, nmap, portsweep, satan

Table 3. Different types of attacks in KDD99 Dataset.

Attack Types	Training Examples	Testing Examples
Normal	97278	60592
Denial of Service	391458	237594
Remote to User	1126	8606
User to Root	52	70
Probing	4107	4166
Total Examples	494021	311028

Table 4. Number of training and testing examples in KDD99 dataset.

3. Combining naïve Bayesian and Decision Tree

In this section, we present the hybrid learning algorithms, NBDTAID (naïve Bayesian with Decision Tree for Adaptive Intrusion Detection) [14], ACDT (Attacks Classificaton using Decision Tree) [13], and Attribute Weighting with Adaptive NBTree Algorithm [11, 15] for intrusions classification in intrusion detection problem. Presented algorithms are performed balance detections and keep FP at acceptable level for different types of network intrusions. It has been successfully tested that by combining the properties of naïve Bayesian classifier and decision tree classifier, the performance of intrusion detection classifier can be enhanced.

3.1. Adaptive intrusion classifier

Naïve Bayesian with Decision Tree for Adaptive Intrusion Detection (NBDTAID) performs balance detections and keeps FP at acceptable level in intrusion detection. NBDTAID eliminates redundant attributes and contradictory examples from training data, and addresses some mining difficulties such as handling continuous attribute, dealing with missing attribute values, and reducing noise in training data [14].

Given a training data $D = \{t_1, \cdots, t_n\}$ where $t_i = \{t_{i1}, \cdots, t_{ih}\}$ and the training data D contains the following attributes $\{A_1, A_2, \cdots, A_n\}$ and each attribute A_i contains the following attribute values $\{A_{i1}, A_{i2}, \cdots, A_{ih}\}$. The attribute values can be discrete or continuous. Also the training data D contains a set of classes $C = \{C_1, C_2, \cdots, C_m\}$. Each example in the training data D has a particular class C_j. The algorithm first searches for the multiple copies of the same example in the training data D, if found then keeps only one unique example in the training data D (suppose all attribute values of two examples are equal then the examples are similar). Then the algorithm discreties the continuous attributes in the training data D by finding each adjacent pair of continuous attribute values that are not classified into the same class value for that continuous attribute. Next the algorithm calculates the prior $P(C_j)$ and conditional $P(A_{ij}|C_j)$ probabilities in the training data D. The prior probability $P(C_j)$ for each class is estimated by counting how often each class occurs in the training data D. For each attribute A_i the number of occurrences of each attribute value A_{ij} can be counted to determine $P(A_i)$. Similarly, the conditional probability $P(A_{ij}|C_j)$ for each attribute values A_{ij} can be estimated by counting how often each attribute value occurs in the class in the training data D. Then the algorithm classifies all the examples in the training data D with these prior $P(C_j)$ and conditional $P(A_{ij}|C_j)$ probabilities. For classifying the examples, the prior and conditional probabilities are used to make the prediction. This is done by combining the effects of the different attribute values from that example. Suppose the example e_i has independent attribute values $\{A_{i1}, A_{i2}, \cdots, A_{ip}\}$, we know $P(A_{ik}|C_j)$, for each class C_j and attribute A_{ik}. We then estimate $P(e_i|C_j)$ by

$$P(e_i|C_j) = P(C_j) \prod_{k=1}^{p} P(A_{ij}|C_j) \tag{7}$$

To classify the example, the algorithm estimates the likelihood that e_i is in each class. The probability that e_i is in a class is the product of the conditional probabilities for each attribute value with prior probability for that class. The posterior probability $P(C_j|e_i)$ is then found for each class and the example classifies with the highest posterior probability for that example. After classifying all the training examples, the class value for each example in training data D updates with Maximum Likelihood (ML) of posterior probability $P(C_j|e_i)$.

$$C_j = C_i \rightarrow P_{ML}(C_j|e_i) \tag{8}$$

Then again the algorithm calculates the prior $P(C_j)$ and conditional $P(A_{ij}|C_j)$ probabilities using updated class values in the training data D, and again classifies all the examples of training data using these probabilities. If any of the training example is misclassified then the algorithm calculates the information gain for each attributes $\{A_1, A_2, \cdots, A_n\}$ in the training data D.

$$Info(D) = -\sum_{j=1}^{m} \frac{freq(C_j, D)}{|D|} log_2 \left(\frac{freq(C_j, D)}{|D|} \right) \tag{9}$$

$$Info(T) = -\sum_{i=1}^{n} \frac{|T_i|}{|T|} info(T_i) \tag{10}$$

$$InformationGain(A_i) = Info(D) - Info(T) \tag{11}$$

And chooses one of the best attributes A_i among the attributes $\{A_1, A_2, \cdots, A_n\}$ from the training data D with highest information gain value, Then split the training data D into sub-datasets $\{D_1, D_2, \cdots, D_n\}$ depending on the chosen attribute values of A_i. After the algorithm estimates the prior and conditional probabilities for each sub-dataset $D_i = \{D_1, D_2, \cdots, D_n\}$ and classifies the examples of each sub-dataset D_i using their respective probabilities. If any example of any sub-dataset D_i is misclassified then the algorithm calculates the information gain of attributes for that sub-dataset D_i, and chooses the best attribute A_i with maximum information gain value from sub-dataset D_i, and split the sub-dataset D_i into sub-sub-datasets D_{ij}. Then again calculates the prior and conditional probabilities for each sub-sub-dataset D_{ij}, and also classifies the examples of sub-sub-datasets using their respective probabilities. The algorithm will continue this process until all the examples of sub/sub-sub-datasets are correctly classified. When the algorithm correctly classifies all the examples then the prior and conditional probabilities for each datasets are preserved for future classification of unseen examples. The main procedure of the algorithm is described in Algorithm 1.

Algorithm 1 NBDTAID Algorithm

Input: Training Data, D.
Output: Adaptive Intrusion Detection Model, $AIDM$.
Procedure:

1: Search the multiple copies of same example in D, if found then keeps only one unique example in D.
2: For each continuous attributes in D find the each adjacent pair of continuous attribute values that are not classified into the same class value for that continuous attribute.
3: Calculate the prior probabilities $P(C_j)$ and conditional probabilities $P(A_{ij}|C_j)$ in D.
4: Classify all the training examples using these prior and conditional probabilities,

$$P(e_i|C_j) = P(C_j)\prod_{k=1}^{p} P(A_{ij}|C_j)$$

5: Update the class value for each example in D with Maximum Likelihood (ML) of posterior probability,

$$P(C_j|e_i); C_j = C_i \rightarrow P_{ML}(C_j|e_i)$$

6: Recalculate the prior $P(C_j)$ and conditional $P(A_{ij}|C_j)$ probabilities using updated class values in D.
7: Again classify all training examples in D using updated probability values.
8: If any training examples in D is misclassified then calculate the information gain for each attributes $A_i = \{A_1, A_2, \cdots, A_n\}$ in D using equation 11.
9: Choose the best attribute A_i from D with the maximum information gain value.
10: Split dataset D into sub-datasets $\{D_1, D_2, \cdots, D_n\}$ depending on the attribute values of A_i.
11: Calculate the prior $P(C_j)$ and conditional $P(A_{ij}|C_j)$ probabilities of each sub-dataset D_i.
12: Classify the examples of each sub-dataset D_i with their respective prior and conditional probabilities.
13: If any example of any sub-dataset D_i is misclassified then calculate the information gain of attributes for that sub-dataset D_i, and choose one best attribute A_i with maximum gain value, then split the sub-dataset D_i into sub-sub-datasets D_{ij}. Then again calculate the probabilities for each sub-sub-dataset D_{ij}. Also classify the examples in sub-sub-datasets using their respective probabilities.
14: Continue this process until all the examples are correctly classified.
15: Preserved all the probabilities of each dataset for future classification of examples.

3.2. Intrusions Classification using Decision Tree

Attacks Classificaton using Decision Tree (ACDT) for anomaly based network intrusion detection [13] addresses the problem of attacks classification in intrusion detection for classifying different types of network attacks.

In a given dataset, first the ACDT algorithm initializes the weights for each example of dataset; W_i equal to $\frac{1}{n}$, where n is the number of total examples in dataset. Then the ACDT algorithm estimates the prior probability $P(C_j)$ for each class by summing the weights that how often each class occurs in the dataset. Also for each attribute, A_i, the number of occurrences of each attribute value A_{ij} can be counted by summing the weights to determine $P(A_{ij})$. Similarly, the conditional probabilities $P(A_{ij}|C_j)$ are estimated for all values of attributes by summing the weights how often each attribute value occurs in the class C_j. After that the ACDT algorithm uses these probabilities to update the weights for each example in the dataset. It is performed by multiplying the probabilities of the different attribute values from the examples. Suppose the example e_i has independent attribute values $\{A_{i1}, A_{i2}, \cdots, A_{ip}\}$. We already know $P(A_{ik}|C_j)$, for each class C_j and attribute A_{ik}. We then estimate $P(e_i|C_j)$ by

$$P(e_i|C_j) = P(C_j) \prod_{k=1}^{p} P(A_{ij}|C_j)$$

To update the weight, the algorithm estimate the likelihood of e_i in each class C_j. The probability that e_i is in a class is the product of the conditional probabilities for each attribute value. The posterior probability $P(C_j|e_i)$ is then found for each class. Now the weight of the example is updated with the highest posterior probability for that example. Finally, the algorithm calculates the information gain by using updated weights and builds a tree for decision making. Algorithm 2 describes the main procedure of learning process:

Algorithm 2 ACDT Algorithm

Input: Dataset, D.
Output: Decision Tree, T.
Procedure:

1: Initialize all the weights in D, $W_i = \frac{1}{n}$, where n is the total number of the examples.
2: Calculate the prior probabilities $P(C_j)$ for each class C_j in D.

$$P(C_j) = \frac{\sum_{C_i} W_i}{\sum_{i=1}^{n} W_i}$$

3: Calculate the conditional probabilities $P(A_{ij}|C_j)$ for each attribute values in D.

$$P(A_{ij}|C_j) = \frac{P(A_{ij})}{\sum_{C_i} W_i}$$

4: Calculate the posterior probabilities for each example in D.

$$P(e_i|C_j) = P(C_j) \prod_{k=1}^{p} P(A_{ij}|C_j)$$

5: Update the weights of examples in D with Maximum Likelihood (ML) of posterior probability $P(C_j|e_i)$;

$$W_i = P_{ML}(C_j|e_i)$$

6: Find the splitting attribute with highest information gain using the updated weights, W_i in D.
7: T = Create the root node and label with splitting attribute.
8: For each branch of the T, D = database created by applying splitting predicate to D, and continue steps 1 to 7 until each final subset belong to the same class or leaf node created.
9: When the decision tree construction is completed the algorithm terminates.

3.3. Attribute Weighting with Adaptive NBTree

This subsection presents learning algorithms: Attribute Weighting Algorithm and Adaptive NBTree Algorithm for reducing FP in intrusion detection [11]. It is based on decision tree based attribute weighting with adaptive naïve Bayesian tree (NBTree), which not only reduce FP at acceptable level, but also scale up DR for different types of network intrusions. It estimate the degree of attribute dependency by constructing decision tree, and considers the depth at which attributes are tested in the tree. In NBTree nodes contain and split as regular decision tree, but the leaves contain naïve Bayesian classifier. The purpose of this subsection is to identify important input attributes for intrusion detection that is computationally efficient and effective.

3.3.1. Attribute Weighting Algorithm

In a given training data, $D = \{A_1, A_2, \cdots, A_n\}$ of attributes, where each attribute $A_i = \{A_{i1}, A_{i2}, \cdots, A_{ik}\}$ contains attribute values and a set of classes $C = \{C_1, C_2, \cdots, C_n\}$, where each class $C_j = \{C_{j1}, C_{j2}, \cdots, C_{jk}\}$ has some values. Each example in the training data contains weight, $w = \{w_1, w_2, \cdots, w_n\}$. Initially, all the weights of examples in training data have equal unit value that set to $w_i = \frac{1}{n}$. Where n is the total number of training examples. Estimates the prior probability $P(C_j)$ for each class by summing the weights that how often each class occurs in the training data. For each attribute, A_i, the number of occurrences of each attribute value A_{ij} can be counted by summing the weights to determine $P(A_{ij})$. Similarly, the conditional probability $P(A_{ij}|C_j)$ can be estimated by summing the weights that how often each attribute value occurs in the class C_j in the training data. The conditional probabilities $P(A_{ij}|C_j)$ are estimated for all values of attributes. The algorithm then uses the prior and conditional probabilities to update the weights. This is done by multiplying the probabilities of the different attribute values from the examples. Suppose the training example e_i has independent attribute values $\{A_{i1}, A_{i2}, \cdots, A_{ip}\}$. We already know the prior probabilities $P(C_j)$ and conditional probabilities $P(A_{ik}|C_j)$, for each class C_j and attribute A_{ik}. We then estimate $P(e_i|C_j)$ by

$$P(e_i|C_j) = P(C_j) \prod P(A_{ij}|C_j) \tag{12}$$

To update the weight of training example e_i, we can estimate the likelihood of e_i for each class. The probability that e_i is in a class is the product of the conditional probabilities for each attribute value. The posterior probability $P(C_j|e_i)$ is then found for each class. Then the weight of the example is updated with the highest posterior probability for that example and also the class value is updated according to the highest posterior probability. Now, the algorithm calculates the information gain by using updated weights and builds a tree. After the tree construction, the algorithm initialized weights for each attributes in training data D. If the attribute in the training data is not tested in the tree then the weight of the attribute is initialized to 0, else calculates the minimum depth, d that the attribute is tested at and initialized the weight of attribute to $\frac{1}{\sqrt{d}}$. Finally, the algorithm removes all the attributes with zero weight from the training data D. The main procedure of the algorithm is described in Algorithm 3.

3.3.2. Adaptive NBTree Algorithm

Given training data, D where each attribute A_i and each example e_i have the weight value. Estimates the prior probability $P(C_j)$ and conditional probability $P(A_{ij}|C_j)$ from the given

Algorithm 3 Attribute Weighting Algorithm

Input: Training Dataset, D.
Output: Decision tree, T.
Procedure:

1: Initialize all the weights for each example in D, $w_i = \frac{1}{n}$, where n is the total number of the examples.

2: Calculate the prior probabilities $P(C_j)$ for each class C_j in D.

$$P(C_j) = \frac{\sum_{C_i} W_i}{\sum_{i=1}^{n} W_i}$$

3: Calculate the conditional probabilities $P(A_{ij}|C_j)$ for each attribute values in D.

$$P(A_{ij}|C_j) = \frac{P(A_{ij})}{\sum_{C_i} W_i}$$

4: Calculate the posterior probabilities for each example in D.

$$P(e_i|C_j) = P(C_j) \prod P(A_{ij}|C_j)$$

5: Update the weights of examples in D with Maximum Likelihood (ML) of posterior probability $P(C_j|e_i)$;

$$W_i = P_{ML}(C_j|e_i)$$

6: Change the class value of examples associated with maximum posterior probability,

$$C_j = C_i \rightarrow P_{ML}(C_j|e_i)$$

7: Find the splitting attribute with highest information gain using the updated weights, W_i in D.

$$InformationGain =$$

$$\left(-\sum_{j=1}^{k} \frac{\sum_{i=C_i} W_i}{\sum_{i=1}^{n} W_i} log \frac{\sum_{i=C_i} W_i}{\sum_{i=1}^{n} W_i} \right) - \left(\sum_{i=1}^{n} \frac{\sum_{i=C_{ij}} W_i}{\sum_{i=C_i} W_i} log \left(\sum_{i=C_{ij}} W_i \right) \right)$$

8: T = Create the root node and label with splitting attribute.

9: For each branch of the T, D = database created by applying splitting predicate to D, and continue steps 1 to 8 until each final subset belong to the same class or leaf node created.

10: When the decision tree construction is completed, for each attribute in the training data D: If the attribute is not tested in the tree then weight of the attribute is initialized to 0. Else, let d be the minimum depth that the attribute is tested in the tree, and weight of the attribute is initialized to $\frac{1}{\sqrt{d}}$.

11: Remove all the attributes with zero weight from the training data D.

training dataset using weights of the examples. Then classify all the examples in the training dataset using these prior and conditional probabilities with incorporating attribute weights into the naïve Bayesian formula:

$$P(e_i|C_j) = P(C_j)\prod_{i=1}^{m} P(A_{ij}|C_j)^{W_i} \tag{13}$$

Where W_i is the weight of attribute A_i. If any example of training dataset is misclassified, then for each attribute A_i, evaluate the utility, $u(A_i)$, of a spilt on attribute A_i. Let $j = argmax_i(u_i)$, i.e., the attribute with the highest utility. If u_j is not significantly better than the utility of the current node, create a NB classifier for the current node. Partition the training data D according to the test on attribute A_i. If A_i is continuous, a threshold split is used; if A_i is discrete, a multi-way split is made for all possible values. For each child, call the algorithm recursively on the portion of D that matches the test leading to the child. The main procedure of the algorithm is described in Algorithm 4.

Algorithm 4 Adaptive NBTree Algorithm

Input: Training dataset D of labeled examples.
Output: A hybrid decision tree with naïve Bayesian classifier at the leaves.
Procedure:

1: Calculate the prior probabilities $P(C_j)$ for each class C_j in D.

$$P(C_j) = \frac{\sum_{C_i} W_i}{\sum_{i=1}^{n} W_i}$$

2: Calculate the conditional probabilities $P(A_{ij}|C_j)$ for each attribute values in D.

$$P(A_{ij}|C_j) = \frac{P(A_{ij})}{\sum_{C_i} W_i}$$

3: Classify each example in D with maximum posterior probability.

$$P(e_i|C_j) = P(C_j)\prod_{i=1}^{m} P(A_{ij}|C_j)^{W_i}$$

4: If any example in D is misclassified, then for each attribute A_i, evaluate the utility, $u(A_i)$, of a spilt on attribute A_i.
5: Let $j = argmax_i(u_i)$, i.e., the attribute with the highest utility.
6: If u_j is not significantly better than the utility of the current node, create a naÃŕve Bayesian classifier for the current node and return.
7: Partition the training data D according to the test on attribute A_i. If A_i is continuous, a threshold split is used; if A_i is discrete, a multi-way split is made for all possible values.
8: For each child, call the algorithm recursively on the portion of D that matches the test leading to the child.

4. Clustering, boosting, and bagging

In this section, we present IDNBC (Intrusion Detection through naïve Bayesian with Clustering) algorithm [12], Boosting [16], and Bagging [17] algorithms for adaptive intrusion detection. The Boosting algorithm considers a series of classifiers and combines the votes of each individual classifier for classifying intrusions using NB classifier. The Bagging algorithm ensembles ID3, NB classifier, and k-Nearest-Neighbor classifier for intrusion detection, which improves DR and reduces FP. The purpose of this chapter is to combines the several classifiers to improve the classification of different types of network intrusions.

4.1. Naïve Bayesian with clustering

It has been tested that one set of probability derived from data is not good enough to have good classification rate. This subsection presents algorithm namely IDNBC (Intrusion Detection through naïve Bayesian with Clustering) for mining network logs to detect network intrusions through NB classifier [12], which clusters the network logs into several groups based on similarity of logs, and then calculates the probability set for each cluster. For classifying a new log, the algorithm checks in which cluster the log belongs and then use that cluster probability set to classify the new log.

Given a database $D = \{t_1, t_2, \cdots, t_n\}$ where $ti = \{t_{i1}, t_{i2}, \cdots, t_{ih}\}$ and the database D contains the following attributes $\{A_1, A_2, \cdots, A_n\}$ and each attribute A_i contains the following attribute values $\{A_{i1}, A_{i2}, \cdots, A_{ih}\}$. The attribute values can be discrete or continuous. Also the database D contains a set of classes $C = \{C_1, C_2, \cdots, C_m\}$. Each example in the database D has a particular class C_j. The algorithm first clusters the database D into several clusters $\{D_1, D_2, \cdots, D_n\}$ depending on the similarity of examples in the database D. A similarity measure, $sim(t_i, t_l)$, defined between any two examples, t_1, t_2 in D, and an integer value k, the clustering is to define a mapping $f : D \rightarrow \{1, \cdots, K\}$ where each t_i is assigned to one cluster K_j. Suppose for two examples there is a match between two attribute values then the similarity becomes 0.5. If there is a match only in one attribute value, then similarity between the examples is taken as 0.25 and so on. Then the algorithm calculates the prior probabilities $P(C_j)$ and conditional probabilities $P(A_{ij}|C_j)$ for each cluster. The prior probability $P(C_j)$ for each class is estimated by counting how often each class occurs in the cluster. For each attribute A_i the number of occurrences of each attribute value A_{ij} can be counted to determine $P(A_i)$. Similarly, the conditional probability $P(A_{ij}|C_j)$ for each attribute values A_{ij} can be estimated by counting how often each attribute value occurs in the class in the cluster. For classifying a new example whose attribute values are known but class value is unknown, the algorithm checks in which cluster the new example belongs and then use that cluster probability set to classify the new example. For classifying a new example, the prior probabilities and conditional probabilities are used to make the prediction. This is done by combining the effects of the different attribute values from that example. Suppose the example e_i has independent attribute values $\{A_{i1}, A_{i2}, \cdots, A_{ip}\}$, we know the $P(A_{ik}|C_j)$, for each class C_j and attribute A_{ik}. We then estimate $P(e_i|C_j)$ to classify the example, the probability that e_i is in a class is the product of the conditional probabilities for each attribute value with prior probability for that class. The posterior probability $P(C_j|e_i)$ is then found for each class and the example classifies with the highest posterior probability for that example. The main procedure of the algorithm is described in Algorithm 5.

Algorithm 5 IDNBC Algorithm

Input: Database, D.
Output: Intrusion Detection Model.
Procedure:

1: **for each** example $t_i \epsilon D$, check the similarity of examples: $sim(t_i, t_l)$;
2: Put examples into cluster: $D_i \leftarrow t_i$;
3: **for each** cluster D_i, calculate the prior probabilities:

$$P(C_j) = \frac{\sum t_{i \to C_j}}{\sum_{i=1}^{n} t_i}$$

4: **for each** cluster D_i, calculate the conditional probabilities:

$$P(A_{ij}|C_j) = \frac{\sum_{i=1}^{n} A_{i \to C_j}}{\sum t_{i \to C_j}}$$

5: **for each** cluster D_i, store the prior probabilities, $S_1 = P(C_j)$; and conditional probabilities, $S_2 = P(A_{ij}|C_j)$;
6: For classifying new example, check in which cluster the example belongs and then use that cluster probability set to classify the example.

4.2. Boosting

Adaptive intrusion detection using boosting and naïve Bayesian classifier [16], which considers a series of classifiers and combines the votes of each individual classifier for classifying an unknown or known intrusion. This algorithm generates the probability set for each round using naïve Bayesian classifier and updates the weights of training examples based on the misclassification error rate that produced by the training examples in each round.

Given a training data $D = \{t_1, \cdots, t_n\}$, where $t_i = \{t_{i1}, \cdots, t_{ih}\}$ and the attributes $\{A_1, A_2, \cdots, A_n\}$. Each attribute A_i contains the following attribute values $\{A_{i1}, A_{i2}, \cdots, A_{ih}\}$. The training data D also contains a set of classes $C = \{C_1, C_2, \cdots, C_m\}$. Each training example has a particular class C_j. The algorithm first initializes the weights of training examples to an equal value of $w_i = \frac{1}{n}$, where n is the total number of training examples in D. Then the algorithm generates a new dataset D_i with equal number of examples from training data D using selection with replacement technique and calculates the prior $P(C_j)$ and class conditional $P(A_{ij}|C_j)$ probabilities for new dataset D_i.

The prior probability $P(C_j)$ for each class is estimated by counting how often each class occurs in the dataset D_i. For each attribute A_i the number of occurrences of each attribute value A_{ij} can be counted to determine $P(A_i)$. Similarly, the class conditional probability $P(A_{ij}|C_j)$ for each attribute values A_{ij} can be estimated by counting how often each attribute value occurs in the class in the dataset D_i. Then the algorithm classifies all the training examples in training data D with these prior $P(C_j)$ and class conditional $P(A_{ij}|C_j)$ probabilities from dataset D_i. For classifying the examples, the prior and conditional probabilities are used to make the prediction. This is done by combining the effects of the different attribute values from that example. Suppose the example e_i has independent attribute values $\{A_{i1}, A_{i2}, \cdots, A_{ip}\}$, we know $P(A_{ik}|C_j)$, for each class C_j and attribute A_{ik}. We then estimate $P(e_i|C_j)$ by using equation 14.

$$P(e_i|C_j) = P(C_j) \prod_{k=1}^{p} P(A_{ij}|C_j) \quad (14)$$

To classify the example, the probability that e_i is in a class is the product of the conditional probabilities for each attribute value with prior probability for that class. The posterior probability $P(C_j|e_i)$ is then found for each class and the example classifies with the highest posterior probability value for that example. The algorithm classifies each example t_i in D with maximum posterior probability. After that the weights of the training examples ti in training data D are adjusted or updated according to how they were classified. If an example was misclassified then its weight is increased, or if an example was correctly classified then its weight is decreased.

To updates the weights of training data D, the algorithm computes the misclassification rate, the sum of the weights of each of the training example t_i in D that were misclassified. That is,

$$error(M_i) = \sum_{i}^{d} W_i * err(t_i) \quad (15)$$

Where $err(t_i)$ is the misclassification error of example t_i. If the example t_i was misclassified, then is $err(t_i)$ 1. Otherwise, it is 0. The misclassification rate affects how the weights of the training examples are updated. If a training example was correctly classified, its weight is multiplied by error $(\frac{M_i}{1-error(M_i)})$. Once the weights of all of the correctly classified examples are updated, the weights for all examples including the misclassified examples are normalized so that their sum remains the same as it was before. To normalize a weight, the algorithm multiplies the weight by the sum of the old weights, divided by the sum of the new weights. As a result, the weights of misclassified examples are increased and the weights of correctly classified examples are decreased. Now the algorithm generates another new data set D_i from training data D with maximum weight values and continues the process until all the training examples are correctly classified. Or, we can set the number of rounds that the algorithm will iterate the process. To classify a new or unseen example use all the probabilities of each round (each round is considered as a classifier) and consider the class of new example with highest classifier's vote. The main procedure of the boosting algorithm is described in Algorithm 6.

4.3. Bagging

Classification of streaming data based on bootstrap aggregation (bagging) [17] creates an ensemble model by using ID3 classifier, naïve Bayesian classifier, and k-Nearest-Neighbor classifier for a learning scheme where each classifier gives the weighted prediction.

Given a dataset D, of d examples and the dataset D contains the following attributes $\{A_1, A_2, \cdots, A_n\}$ and each attribute A_i contains the following attribute values $\{A_{i1}, A_{i2}, \cdots, A_{ih}\}$. Also the dataset D contains a set of classes $C = \{C_1, C_2, \cdots, C_m\}$, where each example in dataset D has a particular class C_j. The algorithm first generates the training dataset D_i from the given dataset D using selection with replacement technique. It is very likely that some of the examples from the dataset D will occur more than once in the training dataset D_i. The examples that did not make it into the training dataset end up forming the test dataset. Then a classifier model, M_i, is learned for each training examples d from

Algorithm 6 Boosting Algorithm

Input: D, Training data D of labeled examples t_i.
Output: A classification model.
Procedure:

1: Initialize the weight $w_i = \frac{1}{n}$ of each example t_i in D, where n is the total number of training examples.
2: Generate a new dataset D_i with equal number of examples from D using selection with replacement technique.
3: Calculate the prior probability $P(C_j)$ for each class C_j in dataset D_i:

$$P(C_i) = \frac{\sum t_{i \to C_j}}{\sum_{i=1}^{n} t_i}$$

4: Calculate the class conditional probabilities $P(A_{ij}|C_j)$ for each attribute values in dataset D_i:

$$P(A_{ij}|C_j) = \frac{\sum_{i=1}^{n} A_{i \to C_j}}{\sum t_{i \to C_j}}$$

5: Classify each training example t_i in training data D with maximum posterior probabilities.

$$P(e_i|C_j) = P(C_j) \prod_{k=1}^{p} P(A_{ij}|C_j)$$

6: Updates the weights of each training examples $t_i D$, according to how they were classified. If an example was misclassified then its weight is increased, or if an example was correctly classified then its weight is decreased. To updates the weights of training examples the misclassification rate is calculated, the sum of the weights of each of the training example $t_i D$ that were misclassified: $error(M_i) = \sum_i^d W_i * err(t_i)$; Where $err(t_i)$ is the misclassification error of example t_i. If the example t_i was misclassified, then is $err(t_i)$ 1. Otherwise, it is 0. If a training example was correctly classified, its weight is multiplied by $(\frac{M_i}{1-error(M_i)})$. Once the weights of all of the correctly classified examples are updated, the weights for all examples including the misclassified examples are normalized so that their sum remains the same as it was before. To normalize a weight, the algorithm multiplies the weight by the sum of the old weights, divided by the sum of the new weights. As a result, the weights of misclassified examples are increased and the weights of correctly classified examples are decreased.
7: Repeat steps 2 to 6 until all the training examples t_i in D are correctly classified.
8: To classify a new or unseen example use all the probability set in each round (each round is considered as a classifier) and considers the class of new example with highest classifier's vote.

training dataset D_i. The algorithm builds three classifiers using ID3, naïve Bayesian (NB), and k-Nearest-Neighbor (kNN) classifiers.

The basic strategy used by ID3 classifier is to choose splitting attributes with the highest information gain first and then builds a decision tree. The amount of information associated with an attribute value is related to the probability of occurrence. The concept used to quantify information is called entropy, which is used to measure the amount of randomness from a data set. When all data in a set belong to a single class, there is no uncertainty, and then the entropy is zero. The objective of decision tree classification is to iteratively partition the given data set into subsets where all elements in each final subset belong to the same class. The entropy calculation is shown in equation 16. Given probabilities $p_1, p_2, \cdots, p_s$ for different classes in the data set

$$Entropy : H(p_1, p_2, \cdots, p_s) = \sum_{i=1}^{s}(p_i log(\frac{1}{p_i})) \tag{16}$$

Given a data set, D, $H(D)$ finds the amount of entropy in class based subsets of the data set. When that subset is split into s new subsets $S = D_1, D_2, \cdots, D_s$ using some attribute, we can again look at the entropy of those subsets. A subset of data set is completely ordered and does not need any further split if all examples in it belong to the same class. The ID3 algorithm calculates the information gain of a split by using equation 17 and chooses that split which provides maximum information gain.

$$Gain(D, S) = H(D) - \sum_{i=1}^{s} p(D_i)H(D_i) \tag{17}$$

The naïve Bayesian (NB) classifier calculates the prior probability, $P(C_j)$ and class conditional probability, $P(A_{ij}|C_j)$ from the dataset. For classifying an example, the NB classifier uses these prior and conditional probabilities to make the prediction of class for that example. The prior probability $P(C_j)$ for each class is estimated by counting how often each class occurs in the dataset D_i. For each attribute A_i the number of occurrences of each attribute value A_{ij} can be counted to determine $P(A_i)$. Similarly, the class conditional probability $P(A_{ij}|C_j)$ for each attribute values A_{ij} can be estimated by counting how often each attribute value occurs in the class in the dataset D_i.

The k-Nearest-Neighbor (kNN) classifier assumes that the entire training set includes not only the data in the set but also the desired classification for each item. When a classification is to be made for a test or new example, its distance to each item in the training data must be determined. The test or new example is then placed in the class that contains the most examples from this training data of k closest items.

After building classifiers using ID3, NB, and kNN, each classifier, M_i, classifies the training examples and initialized the weight, W_i of each classifier based on the accuracies of percentage of correctly classified examples from training dataset. To classify the testing examples or unknown examples each classifier returns its class prediction, which counts as one vote. The proposed bagged classifier counts the votes with the weights of classifiers, and assigns the class with the maximum weighted vote. The main procedure of the bagging algorithm is described in Algorithm 7.

Algorithm 7 Bagging Algorithm

Input:
D, a set of d examples.
$k = 3$, the number of models in the ensemble.
Learning scheme (ID3, naïve Bayesian classifier, and k-Nearest-Neighbor).
Output: A composite model, $M*$.
Procedure:

1: Generate a new training dataset D_i with equal number of examples from a given dataset D using selection with replacement technique. Same example from given dataset D may occur more than once in the training dataset D_i.
2: **for** i = 1 to k **do**
3: Derive a model or classifier, M_i using training dataset D_i.
4: Classify each example d in training data D_i and initialized the weight, W_i for the model, M_i, based on the accuracies of percentage of correctly classified example in training data D_i.
5: **endfor**

To use the composite model on test examples or unseen examples:

1: **for** i = 1 to k **do**
2: Classify the test or unseen examples using the k models.
3: Returns a weighted vote (which counts as one vote).
4: **endfor**
5: $M*$, counts the votes and assigns the class with the maximum weighted vote for that example.

5. Experimental results

The experiments were performed by using an Intel Core 2 Duo Processor 2.0 GHz processor (2 MB Cache, 800 MHz FSB) with 1 GB of RAM.

5.1. NBDTAID evaluation

In order to evaluate the performance of NBDTAID algorithm for network intrusion detection, we performed 5-class classification using KDD99 intrusion detection benchmark dataset [14]. The results of the comparison of NBDTAID with naïve Bayesian classifier and ID3 classifier are presented in Table 5 using 41 input attributes, and Table 6 using 19 input attributes. The performance of NBDTAID algorithm using reduced dataset (12 and 17 input attributes) increases DR that are summarized in Table 7.

Method	Normal	Probe	DOS	U2R	R2L
NBDTAID (DR %)	99.72	99.25	99.75	99.20	99.26
NBDTAID (FP %)	0.06	0.39	0.04	0.11	6.81
naïve Bayesian (DR %)	99.27	99.11	99.69	64.00	99.11
naïve Bayesian (FP %)	0.08	0.45	0.04	0.14	8.02
ID3 (DR %)	99.63	97.85	99.51	49.21	92.75
ID3 (FP %)	0.10	0.55	0.04	0.14	10.03

Table 5. NBDTAID Algorithm: Comparison of the results using 41 attributes.

Method	Normal	Probe	DOS	U2R	R2L
NBDTAID (DR %)	99.84	99.75	99.76	99.47	99.35
NBDTAID (FP %)	0.05	0.28	0.03	0.10	6.22
naïve Bayesian (DR %)	99.65	99.35	99.71	64.84	99.15
naïve Bayesian (FP %)	0.05	0.32	0.04	0.12	6.87
ID3 (DR %)	99.71	98.22	99.63	86.11	97.79
ID3 (FP %)	0.06	0.51	0.04	0.12	7.34

Table 6. NBDTAID Algorithm: Comparison of the results using 19 attributes.

Class Value	12 Attributes	17 Attributes
Normal	99.98	99.95
Probe	99.92	99.93
DoS	99.99	99.97
U2R	99,38	99.46
R2L	99.55	99.69

Table 7. Performance of NBDTAID algorithm using reduced dataset.

5.2. ACDT evaluation

The results of the comparison of ACDT, ID3, and C4.5 algorithms using 41 attributes are tabulated in Table 8 and using 19 attributes are tabulated Table 9 [13].

Method	Normal	Probe	DoS	U2R	R2L
ACDT (DR %)	98.76	98.21	98.55	98.11	97.16
ACDT (FP %)	0.07	0.44	0.05	0.12	6.85
ID3 (DR %)	97.63	96.35	97.41	43.21	92.75
ID3 (FP %)	0.10	0.55	0.04	0.14	10.03
C4.5 (DR %)	98.53	97.85	97.51	49.21	94.65
C4.5 (FP %)	0.10	0.55	0.07	0.14	11.03

Table 8. Comparison of ACDT with ID3 and C4.5 using 41 Attributes.

Method	Normal	Probe	DoS	U2R	R2L
ACDT (DR %)	99.19	99.15	99.26	98.43	98.05
ACDT (FP %)	0.06	0.48	0.04	0.10	6.32
ID3 (DR %)	98.71	98.22	97.63	86.11	94.19
ID3 (FP %)	0.06	0.51	0.04	0.12	7.34
C4.5 (DR %)	98.81	98.22	97.73	56.11	95.79
C4.5 (FP %)	0.08	0.51	0.05	0.12	8.34

Table 9. Comparison of ACDT with ID3 and C4.5 using 19 Attributes.

5.3. Adaptive NBTree evaluation

Firstly, we used attribute weighting algorithm to perform attribute selection from training dataset of KDD99 dataset and then we used adaptive NBTree algorithm for classifier construction [11]. The performance of our proposed algorithm on 12 attributes in KDD99 dataset is listed in Table 10.

Classes	Detection Rates (%)	False Positives (%)
Normal	100	0.04
Probe	99.93	0.37
DoS	100	0.03
U2R	99,38	0.11
R2L	99.53	6.75

Table 10. Performance of adaptive NBTree algorithm on KDD99 Dataset.

Table 11 and Table 12 depict the performance of naïve Bayesian (NB) classifier and C4.5 algorithm using the original 41 attributes of KDD99 dataset. Table 13 and Table 14 depict the performance of NB classifier and C4.5 using reduces 12 attributes.

Classes	Detection Rates (%)	False Positives (%)
Normal	99.27	0.08
Probe	99.11	0.45
DoS	99.68	0.05
U2R	64.00	0.14
R2L	99.11	8.12

Table 11. Performance of NB classifier on KDD99 Dataset.

Classes	Detection Rates (%)	False Positives (%)
Normal	98.73	0.10
Probe	97.85	0.55
DoS	97.51	0.07
U2R	49.21	0.14
R2L	91.65	11.03

Table 12. Performance of C4.5 algorithm on KDD99 Dataset.

Classes	Detection Rates (%)	False Positives (%)
Normal	99.65	0.06
Probe	99.35	0.49
DoS	99.71	0.04
U2R	64.84	0.12
R2L	99.15	7.85

Table 13. Performance of NB classifier using 12 attributes.

Classes	Detection Rates (%)	False Positives (%)
Normal	98.81	0.08
Probe	98.22	0.51
DoS	97.63	0.05
U2R	56.11	0.12
R2L	91.79	8.34

Table 14. Performance of C4.5 algorithm using 12 attributes.

We compare the detection rates among Support Vector Machines (SVM), Neural Network (NN), Genetic Algorithm (GA), and adaptive NBTree algorithm on KDD99 dataset that tabulated in Table 15.

	SVM	NN	GA	Adaptive NBTree
Normal	99.4	99.6	99.3	99.93
Probe	89.2	92.7	98.46	99.84
DoS	94.7	97.5	99.57	99.91
U2R	71.4	48	99.22	99.47
R2L	87.2	98	98.54	99.63

Table 15. Comparison of several algorithms with adaptive NBTree algorithm.

5.4. IDNBC evaluation

The performance of IDNBC algorithm tested by employing KDD99 benchmark network intrusion detection dataset, and the experimental results proved that it improves DR as well as reduces FP for different types of network intrusions are tabulated in Table 16 [12].

Method	Normal	Probe	DoS	U2R	R2L
IDNBC (DR %)	99.66	99.24	99.62	99.19	99.08
IDNBC (FP %)	0.08	0.86	0.09	0.18	7.85
NB (DR %)	99.27	99.11	99.69	64.00	99.11
NB (FP %)	0.08	0.45	0.05	0.14	8.02

Table 16. Performance of IDNBC algorithm with naïve Bayesian classifier.

5.5. Boosting evaluation

We tested the performance of Boosting algorithm with k-Nearest-Neighbor classifier (kNN), Decision Tree classifier (C4.5), Support Vector Machines (SVM), Neural Network (NN), and Genetic Algorithm (GA) by employing on the KDD99 benchmark intrusion detection dataset [16] that is tabulated in Table 17.

Method	Normal	Probe	DoS	U2R	R2L
Boosting Algorithm	100	99.95	99.92	99.55	99.60
kNN	99.60	75.00	97.30	35.00	0.60
C4.5	98.49	94.82	97.51	49.25	91.26
SVM	99.40	89.2	94.7	71.40	87.20
NN	99.60	92.7	97.50	48.00	98.00
GA	99.30	98.46	99.57	99.22	98.54

Table 17. Comparison of the results for the intrusion detection problem (Detection Rate %).

It has been successfully tested that effective attributes selection improves the detection rates for different types of network intrusions in intrusion detection. The performance of boosting algorithm on 12 attributes in KDD99 dataset is listed in Table 18.

Attack Types	DR (%)	FP (%)
Normal	100	0.03
Probing	99.95	0.36
DoS	100	0.03
U2R	99.67	0.10
R2L	99.58	6.71

Table 18. Boosting on reduce KDD99 dataset.

5.6. Bagging evaluation

The presented bagging algorithm was tested on the KDD99 benchmark intrusion detection dataset that is tabulated in Table 19 [17].

Method	Normal	Probe	DoS	U2R	R2L
ID3	99.63	97.85	99.51	49.21	92.75
NB	99.27	99.11	99.69	64.00	99.11
kNN	99.60	75.00	97.30	35.00	0.60
Bagging Algorithm	100	99.92	99.93	99.57	99.61

Table 19. Comparison of the results on KDD99 dataset using bagging (Detection Rate %).

6. Conclusions and future work

The work presented in this chapter has explored the basic concepts of adaptive intrusion detection employing data mining algorithms. We focused on naïve Bayesian (NB) classifier and decision tree (DT) classifier for extracting intrusion patterns from network data. Both NB and DT are efficient learning techniques for mining the complex data and already applied in many real world problem domains. NB has several advantages. First, it is easy to use. Second, unlike other learning algorithms, only one scan of the training data is required. NB can easily handle missing attribute values by simply omitting that probability when calculation the likelihoods of membership in each class. On the other side, the ID3 algorithm to build a decision tree based on information theory and attempts to minimize the expected number of comparisons. The basic strategy used by ID3 is to choose splitting attributes with the highest information gain. The amount of information associated with an attribute value is related to the probability of occurrence. Having evaluated the mining algorithms on KDD99 benchmark intrusion detection dataset, it proved that supervised intrusion classification can increased DR and significantly reduced FP. It also proved that data mining for intrusion detection works, and the combination of NB classifier and DT algorithm forms a robust intrusion-processing framework. Algorithms such as NBDTAID, ACDT, Attribute Weighting with Adaptive NBTree, IDNBC, Boosting, and Bagging presented in this chapter can increase the DR and significantly reduce the FP in intrusion detection. The future works focus on improving FP for R2L attacks and ensemble with other mining algorithms to improve the DR for new network attacks.

Acknowledgements

Support for this research received from the National Science & Information and Communication Technology (NSICT), Ministry of Science and Information & Communication Technology, Government of Bangladesh, Department of Computer Science and Engineering, Jahangirnagar University, Bangladesh, and Department of Computer Science and Engineering, United International University, Bangladesh.

Author details

Dewan Md. Farid and Mohammad Zahidur Rahman
Department of Computer Science and Engineering, Jahangirnagar University, Bangladesh

Chowdhury Mofizur Rahman
Department of Computer Science and Engineering, United International University, Bangladesh

7. References

[1] Anderson, J. P. [1980]. Computer security threat monitoring and surveillance, *Technical report 98-17, James P. Anderson Co., Fort Washington, Pennsylvania, USA* .

[2] Aydin, M. A., Zaim, A. H. & Ceylan, K. G. [2009]. A hybrid intursion detection system design for computer network security, *Computers & Electrical Engineering* 35(3): 517–526.

[3] Bankovic, Z., Stepanovic, D., Bojanic, S. & Talasriz, O. N. [2007]. Improving network security using genetic algorithm approach, *Computers & Electrical Engineering* 33(5-6): 438–541.

[4] BarbarÃą, D., Couto, J., Jajodia, S. & Wu, N. [2001]. ADAM: A tested for exploring the use of data mining in intrusion detection, *Special Interest Group on Management of Data (SIGMOD)* 30(4): 15–24.

[5] Barbara, D., Couto, J., Jajodia, S., Popyack, L. & Wu, N. [2001]. ADAM: Detecting intrusion by data mining, *In Proc. of the 2001 IEEE Workshop on Information Assurance and Security, United States Military Academy, West Point* pp. 11–16.
[6] Bass, T. [2000]. Intrusion detection systems and multi-sensor data fusion, *Communications of the ACM* 43(4): 99–105.
[7] Chebrolu, S., Abraham, A. & Thomas, J. P. [2004]. Feature deduction and ensemble design of intrusion detection systems, *Computer & Security* 24(4): 295–307.
[8] Chen, R. C. & Chen, S. P. [2008]. Intrusion detection using a hybrid support vector machine based on entropy and TF-IDF, *International Journal of Innovative Computing, Information, and Control (IJICIC)* 4(2): 413–424.
[9] Chen, W. H., Hsu, S. H. & Shen, H. P. [2005]. Application of SVM and ANN for intrusion detection, *Computers & Operations Research* 32(10): 2617–1634.
[10] Depren, O., Topallar, M., Anarim, E. & Ciliz, M. K. [2006]. An intelligence intrusion detection system for anomaly and misuse detection in computer networks, *Expert Systems with Applications* 29: 713–722.
[11] Farid, D. M., Darmont, J. & Rahman, M. Z. [2010]. Attribute weighting with adaptive nbtree for reducing false positives in intrusion detection, *International Journal of Computer Science and Information Security (IJCSIS)* 8(1): 19–26.
[12] Farid, D. M., Harbi, N., Ahmmed, S., Rahman, M. Z. & Rahman, C. M. [2010]. Mining network data for intrusion detection through naïve bayesian with clustering, *In Proc. of the International Conference on Computer, Electrical, System Science, and Engineering (ICCESSE 2010), Paris, France* pp. 836–840.
[13] Farid, D. M., Harbi, N., Bahri, E., Rahman, M. Z. & Rahman, C. M. [2010]. Attacks classification in adaptive intrusion detection using decision tree, *In Proc. of the International Conference on Computer Science (ICCS 2010), Rio De Janeiro, Brazil* pp. 86–90.
[14] Farid, D. M., Harbi, N. & Rahman, M. Z. [2010]. Combining naïve bayes and decision tree for adaptive intrusion detection, *International Journal of Network Security and Its Applications (IJNSA)* 2(2): 12–25.
[15] Farid, D. M., Hoa, N. H., Darmont, J., Harbi, N. & Rahman, M. Z. [2010]. Scaling up detection rates and reducing false positives in intrusion detection using nbtree, *In Proc. of the International Conference on Data Mining and Knowledge Engineering (ICDMKE 2010), Rome, Italy* pp. 186–190.
[16] Farid, D. M., Rahman, M.-Z. & Rahman, C. M. [2011a]. Adaptive intrusion detection based on boosting and naïve bayesian classifier, *International Journal of Computer Applications (IJCA)* 24(3): 12–19. Published by Foundation of Computer Science, New York, USA.
[17] Farid, D. M., Rahman, M. Z. & Rahman, C. M. [2011b]. An ensemble approach to classifier construction based on bootstrap aggregation, *International Journal of Computer Applications (IJCA)* 25(5): 30–34. Published by Foundation of Computer Science, New York, USA.
[18] Forn, C. & Lin, C. Y. [2010]. A triangle area based nearset neighbors approach to intrusion detection, *Pattern Recognition* 43(1): 222–229.
[19] Foster, J. J. C., Jonkman, M., Marty, R. & Seagren, E. [2006]. Intrusion detection systems, *Snort Intrusion detection and Prevention Toolkit* pp. 1–30.
[20] Heberlein & Let, A. [1990]. A network secutiry mnitor, *In Proc. of the IEEE Computer Society Symposium, Research in Security and Privacy* pp. 296–303.

[21] Helmer, G., Wong, J. S. K., Honavar, V. & Miller, L. [2002]. Automated discovery of concise predictive rules for intrusion detection, *Journal of Systems and Software* 60(3): 165–175.

[22] Jinquan, Z., Xiaojie, L., Tao, L., Caiming, L., Lingxi, P. & Feixian, S. [2009]. A self-adaptive negative selection algorithm used for anomaly detection, *Progress in Natural Science* 19(2): 261–266.

[23] Patch, A. & Park, J. M. [2007]. An overview of anomaly detection techniques: Existing solutions and latest technological trends, *Computer Netwroks* 51(12): 3448–3470.

[24] Paxson, V. [1999]. Bro: A system for detecting network intruders in real-time, *Computer Networks* pp. 2435–2463.

[25] Provost, F. & Fawcett, T. [2001]. Robust classification for imprecise environment, *Machine Learning* 42(3): 203–231.

[26] Rexworthy, B. [2009]. Intrusion detections systems âĂŞ an outmoded network protection model, *Network Security* 2009(6): 17–19.

[27] Seredynski, F. & Bouvry, P. [2007]. Anomaly detection in TCP/IP networks using immune systems paradigm, *Computer Communications* 30(4): 740–749.

[28] Teodoro, P. G., Verdijo, J. D., Fernandez, G. M. & Vazquez, E. [2009]. Anomaly-based network intrusion detection: Techniques, systems and challenges, *Computers & Security* 28(1-2): 18–28.

[29] *The KDD Archive. KDD99 cup dataset* [1999]. http://kdd.ics.uci.edu/databases/kddcup99/kddcup99.html.

[30] Tsai, C. F., Hsu, Y. F., Lin, C. Y. & Lin, W. Y. [2009]. Intrusion detection by machine learning: A review, *Expert Systems with Applications* 36(10): 11994–12000.

[31] Tsymbal, A., Puuronen, S. & Patterson, D. W. [2003]. Ensemble feature selection with the simple bayesian classification, *Information Fusion* 4(2): 87–100.

[32] Wang, W., Guan, X. & Zhang, X. [2008]. Processing of massive audit data streams for real-time anomaly intrusion detection, *Computer Communications* 31(1): 58–72.

[33] Wu, H. C. & Huand, S. H. S. [2010]. Neural network-based detection of stepping-stone intrusion, *Expert Systems with Applications* 37(2): 1431–1437.

[34] Wuu, L. C., Hung, C. H. & Chen, S. F. [2007]. Building intrusion pattern miner for Snort network intrusion detection system, *Journal of Systems and Software* 80(10): 1699–1715.

[35] Yeung, D. Y. & Ding, Y. X. [2003]. Host-based intrusion detection using dynamic and static behavioral models, *Pattern Recognition* 36: 229–243.

Chapter 16

BotNet Detection: Enhancing Analysis by Using Data Mining Techniques

Erdem Alparslan, Adem Karahoca and Dilek Karahoca

Additional information is available at the end of the chapter

http://dx.doi.org/10.5772/48804

1. Introduction

Recent years revealed that computers are not used only for scientific and business oriented purposes. Individuals of diverse ages, lifestyles, educations and psychologies are living more and more in a virtual reality. This virtual reality affects person's daily activities and habits. In the past, individuals have been used computers only to access knowledge. But nowadays they not only access knowledge, but also share their lives, make money, give or diffuse their opinions and act social. Computers are interfaces for individuals in their virtual social lives. The Internet is the living place of this virtual sociality with its opportunities, capabilities and facilities but also with threats. As the popularity of the Internet increases, the number of attackers who abuse the NET for their nefarious purposes also increases.

The increasing capability of detecting suspicious Internet activities oriented the attackers to a different and sophisticated attack methodology. Coordinated attacks are the attacks realized by more than one, related and co-influenced computer nodes. They make the attackers available to behave in an untraceable Internet activity. The untraceable feature of coordinated attacks is just what hackers/attackers demand to compromise a computer or a network for their illegal activities. Once an attack is initiated by a group of computer nodes having different locations controlled by a malicious individual or controller, it may be very hard to trace back to the origin due to the complexity of the Internet. For this reason, the growing size of events and threats against legitimate Internet activities such as information leakage, click fraud, denial of service (DoS) and attack, E-mail spam, etc., has become a very serious problem nowadays (Liu, Xiao, Ghaboosi, Hongmei, & Zhang, 2009).

The coordinated network attacks are realized by using infected victim computers. Those victims controlled by coordinated attackers are called zombies or bots which derives from the word "robot." The term "bot" is the general terminology of the software applications running automated tasks over the Internet ("Wikipedia - Internet Bot," n.d.). Botnet is a self-

INTECH
open science | open minds

© 2012 Alparslan et al., licensee InTech. This is an open access chapter distributed under the terms of the Creative Commons Attribution License (http://creativecommons.org/licenses/by/3.0), which permits unrestricted use, distribution, and reproduction in any medium, provided the original work is properly cited.

propagating, self-organizing, and autonomous framework that is under a command and control (C2 or C&C) infrastructure. Generally, to compromise a series of systems, the botnet's master (also called as herder or perpetrator) will remotely control bots to install worms, Trojan horses, or backdoors on them. Majority of those zombie computers are running Microsoft Windows operating systems. The process of stealing host resources to form a Botnet is so called "scrumping"(Liu et al., 2009; "Wikipedia - Botnet," n.d.).

Because of their network-based, coordinated and controlled nature Botnets are one of the most dangerous species of the Internet attacks nowadays. Deriving their power both in their cumulative bandwidth and their access capabilities, botnets can cause severe network outages through massive distributed denial-of-service attacks. The threat of this outage can cost enterprises large amounts in extortion fees (Strayer, Lapsely, & Walsh, 2008). According to the recent Symantec's research report, botnets have become one of the biggest security threats. According to the report a large volume of malicious activities from distributed-denial-of-service (DDoS) attacks to spamming, phishing, identity theft and DNS server spoofing can be realized by using the distributed power of botnets (W. Lu, Rammidi, & Ghorbani, 2011). Also one of the largest spam filter companies, SpamHaus,2 has estimated that already in 2004, 70% of spam was sent out via such networks (NISCC, 2005) (Seewald & Gangsterer, 2010). According to the US FBI and public trackers, at least a million bots are known to exist like ShadowServer and the true number is likely to be much higher. The number of bots is also still growing at an exponential rate (Seewald & Gangsterer, 2010).

Botnets are as powerful as they can diffuse on new hosts by infecting them via well-known security holes. One can be infected by clicking a link on a website, opening an attachment of an e-mail or only viewing them, surfing on a website by a browser which has a security weakness. Secure computers are not exactly protected from botnet dissemination. 0-day vulnerabilities are used to attack secured / patched computers. There are some indications that botnet operators invest in R&D to find specific zero-day vulnerabilities, aiming at exploiting them at leisure.

2. Classification of Botnets

Because of their distributed architecture, botnets are quietly different from other types of malwares. Botnets can spread over millions of computers as worms can do. Unlike worms, zombie nodes in a botnet can work cooperated and be managed from a command and control center. Because of this distributed architecture, botnets cannot be classified as other malware types. Many works try to summarize the taxonomy of botnets. The main classification areas of botnets are the topology of C&C architecture used, the propagation mechanism, the exploitation strategy and available set of commands used by perpetrator.

2.1. Classification based on C&C topology

Command and control topologies of botnets are studied in various researches aiming to detect preventive measures for each kind of infrastructure. Detecting the organization of a malicious network may help preventing them.

IRC based botnets are the preliminary types of botnets which are still effective and usable for attackers. IRC is a text based instant messaging protocol over the Internet. It works on client-server architecture but it is also suitable for distributed environments. In most cases interconnected IRC servers communicate each other and each has own subscribers. Thus, a subscriber on an IRC server may communicate with others if IRC servers are interconnected and are on the same channel. This interconnection between the IRC servers is called multiple IRC (mIRC). IRC-based bots use this infrastructure for malicious purposes by managing access lists, moving malicious files, sharing clients, sharing channel information and so on. A typical IRC based botnet is shown in Fig. 1 Victim machine is the compromised internet host which runs the executable bot triggered by a specific command from IRC server. Once a bot is installed on a victim host, it will make a copy into a configurable directory and let the malicious program to start with the operating system. A secured channel set up by the attacker to manage all the bots is called control channel. IRC server may be a compromised machine or even a legitimate service provider. Attacker is the one controls botnet. As in Fig. 1 attacker opens a private IRC channel on an ordinary IRC server. After spreading malwares on victim computers attacker waits bots to subscribe his own private IRC channel. Then he gives commands and controls the botnet infrastructures for his malicious purposes (Puri, 2003).

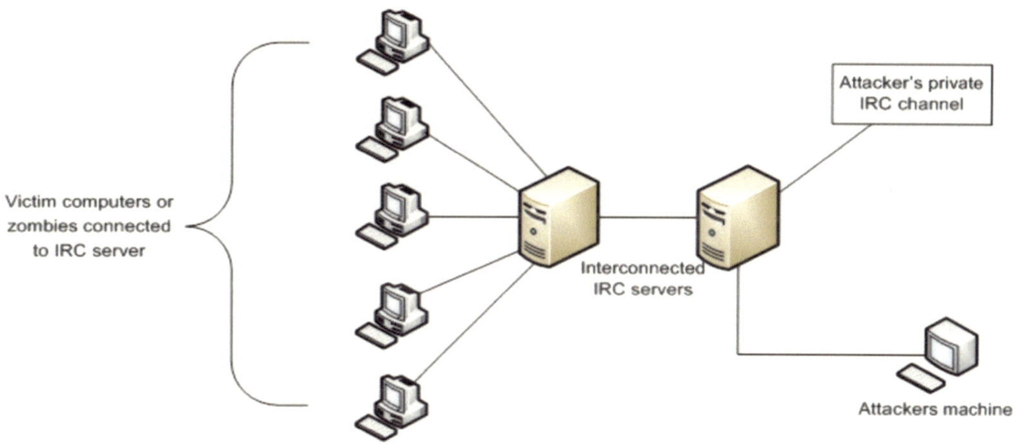

Figure 1. IRC-based botnets (Feily, Shahrestani, & Ramadass, 2009)

However the majority of botnet studies focus on IRC based C&C architecture, P2P based C&C architecture can spread easier and hide itself from intrusion detection techniques. In fact, using P2P networks to control victim hosts is not a novel technique. A P2P spreading worm named Slapper, infected Linux system by DoS attack in 2002. One year after, another

P2P-based bot, Dubbed Sinit appeared. In 2004, Phatbot was using P2P system to send commands to the other compromised hosts. Currently, Storm Worm (Holz, M, & Dahl, 2008) may be the most wide-spread P2P bot over the Internet. Many P2P networks have a central server or a list of peers who can be contacted to add a new peer. Centralized nature of this kind of P2P networks requires a bootstrap procedure which presents a weakness for P2P networks. To overcome this problem authors in (P. Wang, Sparks, & Cou, 2008) presented specific hybrid P2P botnet architecture. Hybrid P2P botnet architecture has servant and client bots who behave as clients and as servers in a traditional P2P file sharing network. Servant bots are connected to each other and form the backbone structure of the botnet. An attacker or botmaster can inject his commands into any hosts of the botnet. Each bot knows only its directed neighbors and transmits the command to its neighbors. If one bot is detected by intrusion detection systems only its neighbors are affected. The hybrid architecture for P2P botnets delivers some new capabilities: (1) it requires no bootstrap procedure; (2) only a limited number of bots nearby the captured one can be exposed; (3) an attacker can easily manage the entire botnet by issuing a single command (Liu et al., 2009).

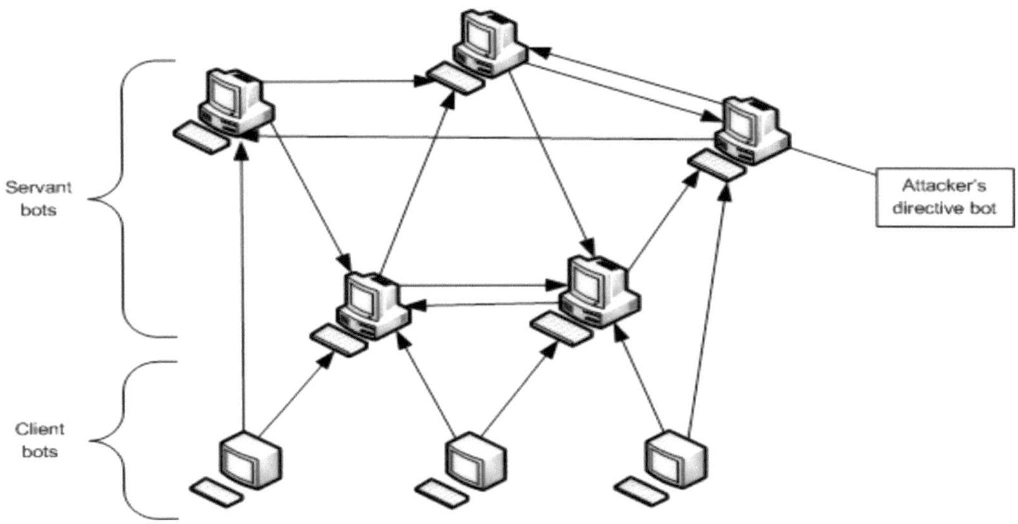

Figure 2. P2P-based botnets(P. Wang et al., 2008)

Another type of C&C mechanism widely used is http-based botnets. In http-based botnets, bots and C&C center communicate each other by using http protocol in an encrypted communication channel. In Chiang&Lloyd (2007), an http-based spam bot module in Rustock rootkit is analyzed by using a well-known analysis tool IDA Pro to find the encryption key. The paper summarizes that a typical routine for the spam bot to send a spam is as following:

i. The bot asks the controller for local processes/files to kill and delete.
ii. The controller sends back system information.
iii. The bot asks for SMTP servers.
iv. The bot gets failure responses from the SMTP servers.
v. The bot gets spam message
vi. The bot gets target email addresses.

In Nazario (2007), an HTTP-based DDoS bot, BlackEnergy is analyzed. The bot is only used for DDoS attacks. However, the bot does not have any exploit activities, so it cannot be captured by Honeynet.

Clickbot, a low-noise click fraud bot is discussed in (Daswani & Stoppelman, 2007). Clickbot propogates its client side malware by e-mail attachments. The bot also use http protocol for command and control (Zhu et al., 2008).

3. Botnet attacks

Botnets are often used for DDoS attacks. Because of their distributed and hard to detect nature, denial of service attacks can be impressively applied by using botnets. Besides, botnets are also used to perform spamming, malware spreading, sensitive information leakage, identity fraud, click fraud. They are very valuable instruments of getting Advanced Persistent Threats (APT) for critical organizations.

"Denial of Service" (DoS) attacks are very powerful threats for organizations. They are inevitable when performed by a distributed environment, so called Distributed DoS or DDoS. Botnets are often used for DDoS attacks to consume network bandwidth of victim system from wide range of IP addresses. The victim system cannot add source IP addresses to the blacklist, because they act as a regular end-user. Evidence reveals that most commonly implemented by botnets are TCP SYN and UDP flooding attacks (Freiling, Holz, & Wicherski, 2005). Exploring the bots in a managed honeypot is one of the most effective prevention mechanisms, which will be discussed in the following chapters.

The internet security industry mostly concern spamming activities. According to recent researches %70 to %90 of the world's spam mailing traffic is caused by botnets. Researchers in (Pappas, 2008; Sroufe, Phithakkitnukkon, & Dantu, 2009) report that once the SOCKS v4/v5 proxy (TCP/IP RFC 1928) on a zombie computer is opened by a malicious bot, the bot can easily use this machine for its nefarious tasks, mostly spamming. On the other hand some types of bots can gather spamming e-mail delivery list from perpetrator. Therefore such a bot can be used for sending massive spam mails. In (Brodsky & Brodsky, 2007) a distributed content independent spam classification system, called Trinity, is proposed against spamming from botnets. According to the Trinity, one can assume that if a computer sends thousands of e-mails at the same time, this computer is probably hosting malicious bot software; so that any e-mail from this host can be considered as a spam. Many researches are performed to discover the aggregate behavior of botnet spamming. In Xie et al. (2008). have designed spam signature generation framework named AutoRE. Their analysis shows that botnet host sending patterns, such as the number of recipients per email, connection rates, and the frequency of sending to invalid users are clusterable and their sending times are synchronized.

Some bots may sniff not only the network traffic passing from victims IP interfaces but also the command data of operating system to retrieve sensitive information like usernames, passwords, and identities. According to the evidences, new generation bots are getting more sophisticated than the predecessors. They can quickly scan the entire system to retrieve corporate or financial data and send this sensitive information to the bot master. They rarely affect the performance of host machine, so that they are very hard to be caught. Keylogger bots listen to the keyboard activities to gather such sensitive information like usernames, passwords, and identities (Feily et al., 2009).

Botnets are also can be used to generate and send phishing mails to the victim individuals. Phishing mail includes legitimate-like URLs and asks the receiver to submit personal or confidential information. This kind of attack is called identity theft. Ordinary mail servers can identify phishing mails by denoting sender IP address. By using botnet's distributed processing facility attacker may send e-mails from ordinary individual's computer which is not listed in mail server phishing blacklists (Erbacher, Marshall, Cutler, & Banerjee, 2008).

With the help of botnet, attackers or bot masters are able to install advertisement add-ons and browser helper objects (BHOs) for business purpose. Attackers may use botnets to click periodically on specific hyperlinks and thus promote the click-through rate (CTR) artificially.

4. Botnet analysis

Botnet researches are mostly performed to detect and prevent bot activities. Detecting a botnet often needs advanced analyzing capabilities which are related to the selected data for analysis track and the characteristics of issues performed. In this part, we will consider the types of analysis according to the characteristics and application data performed.

4.1. Classification based on behavior

4.1.1. Active analysis

Active approaches in botnet analysis cover all kinds of analysis techniques which makes bot master, directly or indirectly informed about botnet analysis / detection activity. Capturing bot malware and deactivating its malicious parts is a well-known active analysis type. Honeypots and honeynets are other active analysis methods performed in botnet detection and prevention. At first sight, while active approaches may seem useful, they have a big disadvantage of being easily detected. Once this happens, bot master will inevitably adapt and circumvent any actions taken against botnets (Zhu et al., 2008).

A good example of active analysis is the study of Dagon et al. (2006). The model that they proposed bases time zone information of victim computers. They assume that the individual users switch off or do not use their machines during the night. They use a DNS redirection technique to redirect known IRC Command & Control servers to IP addresses under their control. In six months they redirected approximately 50 botnets. Another work performed one year ago, was analyzing botnet connectivity structures and proposing botnet classification taxonomy based of their connectivity schemes.

4.1.2. Passive analysis

Passive approaches analyze traffic which the botnet generates without corrupting or modifying it. The analysis mainly focuses on secondary effects of botnet traffic such as broken packets resulting from a distant DDoS attack. Darknets are good examples of passive analysis. They capture and analysis packages instead of using a machine which appears vulnerable (low interaction honeypot), or actually is vulnerable (high interaction honeypot) for attracting botnet attacks, malware, or spam. The bot master assumes that the IP simulated by darknet is empty; so that the TCP call is not responded by anyone. Both honeypot types, low or high interaction, can be detected by perpetrators. Low interaction honeypots are only basically simulates some services and give basic responses coming to specific service ports. The emulation is incomplete, so the perpetrator can easily detect the honeypot emulator by sending a little sophisticated command. On the other hand we know that high interaction honeypots can be detected by fingerprinting the operating system after successfully compromised it. Passive systems are more complex to implement but in the other hand they have the big advantage that they cannot be detected by intruder; because if perpetrator sends a message to a darknet, he will not get a SYN response. So a darknet is absolutely gives the same sense as an unused IP address to an intruder (Zhu et al., 2008; Seewald&Gangsterer, 2010).

Dhamankar and King propose a system detecting botnet by guessing protocol types without reference to the content transferred (Dhamankar & King, 2007). Guessing the protocol types can also detect encrypted botnet traffic for peer-to-peer networks. This approach is a good example of passive analysis, because this approach does not make any changes in original flow. It works only by mirroring the network flow data.

In another research, Collins et al. proposes a network quality metric based on spatiotemporal ratio of botnets. This means the proportion of bots among all IP address for a specific time and specific subnets. Their aim was predicting future bots according to the past botnet distribution (Seewald & Gangsterer, 2010).

4.2. Classification based on used data

4.2.1. Analysis Based on IDS Data

Krugel et al. define intrusion detection as "the process of identifying and responding to malicious activities targeted at computing and network resources". An intrusion attempt, also named as attack, denotes the sequence of actions to gain control of the system. Intrusion Detection System (IDS) discriminates intrusion attempts from normal system usage.

Intrusion detection systems are basically classified into two categories: Misuse-based IDS and Anomaly-based IDS. A misuse-based IDS, also known as signature-based or knowledge-based IDS, detects malicious traffic by comparing new data with a knowledge base or signatures of known attacks. The system delivers an alarm if a previously known intrusion pattern is detected. Misuse-base systems like Snort use pattern matching algorithms in packet payload analysis. It is obvious that misuse-based systems analyze not only the traffic flow of the network; they also analyze payload data of the flow. Misuse-based intrusion detection systems are highly accurate systems. But they need to pay attention on up to date the signature base of the system. They are also ineffective for detecting new intrusion types and zero day threats. On the other hand anomaly-based IDS, also known as behavior-based IDS, compare input data with the expected behavior of the system. However behavior based systems can detect unknown attacks because of their anomaly based nature; they may give false positive alarms. For example flash crowd situation is not a malicious situation but it can be considered as a denial of service attack by an anomaly / behavior based system.

4.2.2. Analysis based on flow data

The growing number of attacks and the rapid extension rates in network bandwidth are very important challenges for intrusion detection systems. IDS researchers assess the payload-based IDSs processing capability to lie between 100 Mbps and 200 Mbps when commodity hardware is used, and close to 1 Gbps when dedicated hardware is employed (Feily et al., 2009; Zhu et al., 2008). Famous tools like Snort and Bro consume high resource when they deal with huge amount of payload data of in today high speed networks. Besides, encrypted traffic is another challenge for payload based detection systems.

Given these problems above, flow based solutions are more comfortable than intrusion detection systems. Flows are monitored by specialized accounting modules usually placed in network routers. Flow-based solutions will analyze these flows to detect attacks. They analyze markedly lower amount of data than payload based intrusion detection systems. Netflow ("Cisco Netflow," n.d.) data is approximately %0.1 to %0.5 of overall data consuming on the network. Flow information tells about the following attributes:

- Source address: The originator of the traffic
- Destination address: The receiver of the traffic
- Ports: Characterizing the application of the traffic
- Class of service (COS): Examining the priority of the traffic
- Interfaces: Defining the usage of the traffic by the network device
- Tallied packets and bytes: To calculate packet and byte characteristics of the traffic

Date flow start	Duration	Proto	Src IP Addr:Port		Dst IP Addr:Port	Flags	Tos	Packets	Bytes	pps	bps	Bpp	Flows
2011-12-27 14:59:51.000	0.000	TCP	SOH [illegible]:80	-> SOH	[illegible]:61414	.A...F	0	1	54	0	0	54	1
2011-12-27 14:58:33.000	59.000	TCP	SOH [illegible]:80	-> SOH	[illegible]:32812	.AP...	0	6	2236	0	303	372	1
2011-12-27 14:59:44.000	5.000	TCP	SOH [illegible]:443	-> SOH	[illegible]:64067	.AP...	164	13	13144	2	21030	1011	1
2011-12-27 14:59:52.000	0.000	TCP	SOH [illegible]:80	-> SOH	[illegible]:53103	.AP...	0	1	200	0	0	200	1
2011-12-27 14:59:57.000	0.000	TCP	SOH [illegible]:80	-> SOH	[illegible]:46756	.AP...	0	1	522	0	0	522	1
2011-12-27 14:56:04.000	208.000	TCP	SOH [illegible]:80	-> SOH	[illegible]:61787	.A....	164	475	719150	2	27659	1514	1
2011-12-27 14:59:54.000	0.000	TCP	SOH [illegible]7.248.125.23:80	-> SOH	[illegible]:58525	.A....	0	1	1514	0	0	1514	1
2011-12-27 14:59:32.000	0.000	UDP	SOH [illegible]:25165	-> SOH	[illegible]:53	......	0	1	89	0	0	89	1

Figure 3. Sample netflow data(*"Cisco Netflow," n.d.)*

The sample flow data in Figure 3 is captured within Cisco Netflow procedures. Data consist of date information of the flow, duration, protocol used, source IP and port, destination IP and port, some denoting TCP / UDP flags like S for SYN or A for ACK, type of service value (TOS) in the interval 0-255, number of packets in the flow, total amount of bytes transferred by the flow, packets per seconds of the flow, transferred bits per second, average bytes per each packet of the flow.

As seen in Figure 3, network flow data does not care about payload information of the communication. In other words, network flow analysis is getting only meta-information of the communication as an input. Thus, it is obvious that flow-based analysis is therefore a logical choice for high-speed and intense networks.

Some researches claim that flow-based analysis may be insufficient in comparison to IDS based or signature based analysis. Flow measurements are aggregated information directly comfortable for data mining algorithms. Therefore they cannot give the chance of detecting malicious activities wrapped in the payload of the communication (Abdullah, Lee, Conti, & Copeland, 2005; Lu, Tavallaee, & Ghorbani, 2009). However the sustainability of the network can be monitored in real time by flow-based analysis. Besides some algorithms like time series can be used to get normal profiles of the inspected network and can detect any inharmonious anomaly activities for the detected profiles.

5. Botnet detection

In recent years, network security researchers are struggling with botnet detection and tracking as a major research topic. Different solutions have been proposed which can be classified under mainly two topics. The first approach basically uses honeypots and honeynets which can be considered as an active analysis. While the solutions in (Valeur, Vigna, Kruegel, & Kemmerer, 2004) have been initial honeynet-based solutions, many papers discussed detecting and tracking botnets for different honeynet configurations. The second approach, based on passive network monitoring and analysis, can be classified as signature-based, DNS-based, anomaly-based and mining-based (Feily et al., 2009; Seewald & Gangsterer, 2010). These two approaches and sub classifications are detailed below.

5.1. Honeypots and honeynets

A honeypot can be defined as an "environment where vulnerabilities have been deliberately introduced to observe attacks and intrusions"(Pouget & Dacier, 2004). They have a strong ability to detect security threats, to collect malware signatures and to understand the motivation and technique behind the threat used by perpetrator. In a wide-scale network, different size of honeypots form honeynet. Usually, honeynets based on Linux operating systems are preferred because of their ability richness and of toolbox contents.

Honeypots are classified as high-interaction and low-interaction according to their emulation capacity. A high-interaction honeypot can simulate almost all aspects of a real operating system. It gives responses for known ports and protocols as in a real zombie computer. On the other hand, low-interaction honeypots simulate only important features of a real operating system. High-interaction honeypots allow intruders to gain full control to the operating system; however low-interaction honeypots do not. Honeypots are also classified according to their physical state. Physical honeypot is a real machine running a real operating system. Virtual honeypot is an emulation of a real machine on a virtualization host.

The value of a honeypot is determined by the information obtained from it. Monitoring the network traffic on a honeypot lets us gather information that is not available to network intrusion detection systems (NIDS). For example, we can log the key strokes of an interactive session even if encryption is used to protect the network traffic. NIDS require signatures of known attacks to detect malicious behavior, and often fail to detect compromises that were unknown before deployment. On the other hand, honeypots can detect vulnerabilities that are not found yet. For example, we can detect compromise by observing network traffic on the honeypot even if the cause of the exploit has never been seen before (Pouget & Dacier, 2004).

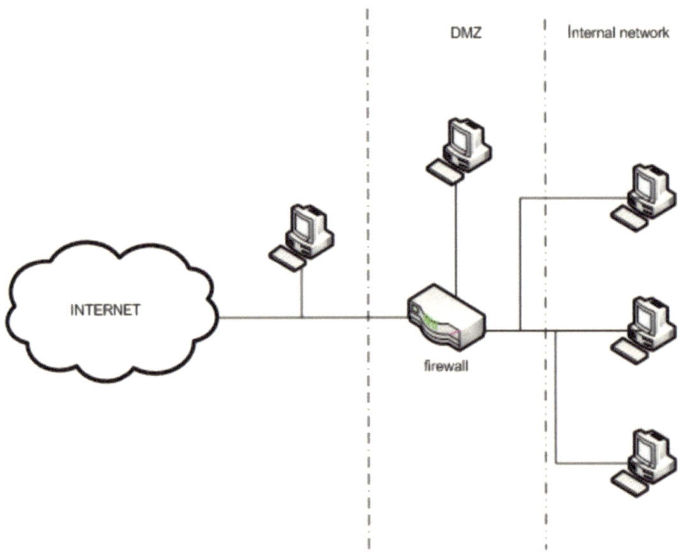

Figure 4. Potential Honeypot Traps *(Pouget & Dacier, 2004)*

Figure 4 depicts sample positioning styles of honeypots. Honeypots can be positioned as a computer in secure corporate network, as a computer in demilitarized zone or as a computer outside of the corporate network. Each position represents a different level of security. Internal network computers are hard to reach but after contamination of a malicious code, these computers may be very harmful for the corporation. Besides DMZ computers have some security restrictions rather than an outside computer but less than an internal computer. Outside computers are hard to reach an useful for DDoS, spamming and other types of attacks.

As honeypots and honeynets are very popular in detecting and preventing threats, intruders are seeking new ways of protecting honeypot traps. Some feasible techniques are used by intruders like detecting VMWare or other emulator virtual machines, detecting incoherent responses from bots. Gu et al. (2007), have successfully identified honeypots using intelligent probing. They used public internet threat report statistics. In addition, Krawetz (2004) have presented a commercial spamming tool, called "Send-Safe's Honeypot Hunter", which is capable of anti-honeypot function. Zou and Cunninqham have proposed a system to detect and eliminate honeypot traps in P2P networks.

5.2. Signature based detection techniques

Malware executable signatures are widely used for detecting and classifying malware threats. Signatures based on known malwares have a discriminating power on classification of executables running on an operating system. Rule based intrusion detection systems like Snort are running by using known malware signatures. They monitor the network traffic and detect sign of intrusions. The detection may be according to the signatures of executable malwares or according to the signatures of malicious network traffic generated by malware. However, signature-based detection techniques can be used for detection of known botnets. Thus, this solution is not useful for unknown bots.

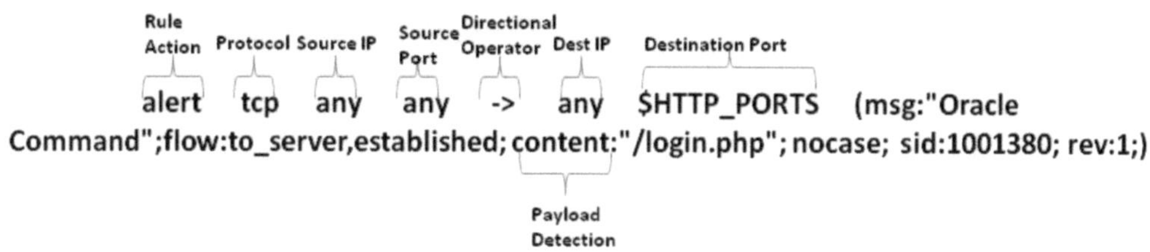

Figure 5. Example rule for Snort IDS *(Xie et al., 2008)*

In Figure 5 an example rule configuration for Snort IDS is given. It is obvious that payload information of network traffic is transformed and embedded into the signature or rule. The IDS detects malicious traffic fitting the communication parameters defined by the rule.

In a wide-scale network there may exists many kinds of intrusion detection systems, firewalls or other perimeter protection devices and systems. Each of these systems generates threat alerts. The alerts generated from diverse source of systems must be correlated to improve accuracy and avoid false positive alarms. Alert correlation is a process that analyzes the alerts produced by multiple intrusion detection systems and provides a more succinct and high-level view of intrusion attempts. Gu et al. (2007) propose a framework, "BotHunter", to correlate IDS based detection alerts. They use a network dialog correlation matrix. Each IDS dialog is inserted into the matrix after pruned or evaluated by BotHunter. The system is based on a weighted score threshold system. Each IDS dialog has a weight and after the correlation the total weight of correlated events is calculated by the system. The system then decides whether the correlated event is a malicious activity or not. Thus, false positive rates are lowered to an acceptable rate.

Valeur et al. (2004) have suggested a very comprehensive and detailed framework for intrusion detection alert correlation. Their system was based on the most complete set of components in the correlation process. In their suggested framework sensor alerts are normalized and pre-processed according to a Sensor Ontology Database. After the preparation tasks alerts are fused and verified. The connected alerts are consolidated in an attack session and a multistep alert correlation is performed on the consolidated attack session. After a prioritization, intrusion reports are delivered to the security administrator (Valeur et al., 2004).

The model proposed by Andersson, Fong, & Valdes (2002) and Valdes & Skinner (2000) present a correlation process in two phases. The first phase aggregates low-level events using the concept of attack threads. The second phase uses a similarity metric to fuse alerts into meta-alerts, in an attempt to provide a higher-level view of the security state of the system.

5.3. Anomaly based detection techniques

Exploring new botnet detection techniques based on network behavior is a considerable research area for botnet researchers. Anomaly based botnet detection, tries to detect bot activities based on several network behavior anomalies such as unexpected network latencies, network traffic on unusual and unused ports, high volumes of traffic for a mid-class network or unusual system behaviors that could indicate the existence of malicious parties in the network (Feily et al., 2009).

Karasaridis, Rexroad, & Hoeflin (2007) proposed an algorithm for detection and characterization of botnets using passive analysis. Their approach was based on flow data in transport layer. This algorithm can also detect encrypted botnet communications, because the algorithm that they used does not care about the encrypted payload data of network flow.

Binkley & Singh (2006) presented an algorithm based on statistical techniques for detection of on campus botnet servers. Proposed algorithm is derived from two experimental flow tuples that collect statistics based on four types of layer-7 IRC commands: PRIVMSG, JOIN, PING, and PONG.

Recently, Gu & Zhang (2008) proposed a system, BotSniffer, to detect botnet Command and Control channels by using both network behavior anomalies and network channel similarities. Their approach is very simple and useful: The bot clients have to reveal same network behavior anomalies and they also communicate with C&C server by the same network behavior characteristics, simultaneously. Hence, it employs several correlation analysis algorithms to detect spatial-temporal correlation in network traffic with a very low false positive rate.

Some other entropy based solutions to detect network behavior anomalies are also proposed by researchers. These approaches are not only to detect botnets and malicious network traffics. They are proposed for general purposes which also include security oriented ones like botnet detection.

5.4. DNS based detection techniques

As mentioned in the first section, a typical bot activity resumes by getting commands and execution parameters of commands from command and control center. Thus bots are bound to send DNS queries to know the IP address of the command and control center. C&C servers have generally a distributed nature in present botnets. Hence they have to use dynamic DNS (DDNS) entries with short time to live to hide them from intrusion detection/prevention systems. Thus, it is possible to detect botnet DNS traffic by monitoring the DNS activities and detecting unusual or unexpected DNS querying.

DNS based techniques are quietly similar to other anomaly based detection techniques. They are commonly based on detection of anomalous DNS network traffic generated by bot computers.

Dagon (2005) proposed an algorithm to identify botnet C&C server addresses by monitoring abnormally high or temporarily intense DDNS queries. This approach is nearly the same as Kristoff's approach (Kristoff, 2004) and both of them are usually useful. But sometimes many important web sites can use short time to live values. Because of naïve nature of this approach many important false positive cases may occur.

Kim et al. (Inhwan, Choi, & Lee, 2008) proposed a methodology for security advisers and administrators providing meaningful visual information do detect botnets. The proposed system is based on DNS traffic which is only a small piece of total network traffic. Hence, this methodology is also comfortable for real time analysis.

Choi, Lee, Lee, & Kim (2007) suggested a system monitoring DNS traffic to detect botnet sub-structures which form a group activity in DNS queries simultaneously. They have identified unique attributes of DNS traffic which help to form groups according to the relevance of these unique features for diverse nodes of network. Their anomaly based approach is more robust than the previous approaches because of detecting botnet flows regardless the type and hierarchy of the botnet structure.

In 2009, Manasrah et al. proposed a system to classify DNS queries and detect malicious DNS activities. The system is based on a simple mechanism which monitors the DNS traffic and detects the abnormal DNS traffic issued by the botnet. Their approach is based on the fact that botnets appear as a group of hosts periodically (Manasrah, Hasan, Abouabdalla, & Ramadass, 2009).

5.5. Data mining based detection techniques

Anomaly based techniques are mostly based on network behavior anomalies such as high network latency, activities on unused ports. However C&C traffic usually does not reveal anomalous behavior. It is mostly hard to differentiate C&C traffic from usual traffic behavior. At this point of view pattern recognition and machine learning based data mining techniques are very useful to extract unexpected network patterns.

Firstly it can be useful to introduce a research of preprocessing tasks of anomaly and data mining based botnet detection systems. Davis and Clark introduce a review of known preprocessing tasks for anomaly based and mining based intrusion detection techniques (Davis & Clark, 2011).

Strayer et al. (2008) suggested a mechanism to detect botnet C&C traffic by a passive analysis applied on network flow information. Their approach is based on flow characteristics such as duration, bytes per packet, bits per second, TCP flags and pushed packets in the flow. The proposed system has a preprocessing phase for flows reducing the set by a factor of about 37, from 1.337.098 to 36.228. They used J48 decision trees, naïve Bayes and Bayesian net algorithms to classify network flows.

Masud, Gao, Khan, & Han (2008) proposed another mining based passive analysis to identify botnet traffic. Their approach is based on correlating multiple log files obtained from different points of the network. The system is not only to detect IRC-based botnet but also applicable for non-IRC botnets. The method is also effective because of its passive and regardless of payload nature. Hence, it is applicable for intense networks and also effective for encrypted communication.

Lu et al. (2011) proposed a system to detect botnet communication patterns based on n-gram feature selection analyzing both payload and flow. They first classify the network traffic into different applications by using traffic payload signatures. Secondly they perform a clustering for each application community to detect anomalous behavior based on the n-gram features extracted the content of network flows. Their approach is payload-aware and hard to execute on a large scale network.

Recently Wang, Huang, Lin, & Lin (2011) proposed a behavior-based botnet detection system based on fuzzy pattern recognition techniques. Their motivation is based on identifying bot-relevant domain names and IP addresses by inspecting the network traces. They used fuzzy pattern recognition techniques with 4 membership functions: (1) generating failed network connection; (2) generating failed DNS queries; (3) having similar DNS query intervals; (4) having similar payload sizes for network communications.

BotMiner (Gu, Perdisci, Zhang, & Lee, 2008), an improvement of BotSniffer (Gu & Zhang, 2008), is a recent and successful solution to detect bot activities. The proposed technique is based on clustering similar communication traffic and similar malicious traffic. After clustering normal and abnormal activity patterns, it correlates these two cross clusters to identify the host that share the same communication pattern and malicious activity pattern. Thus it can be possible to identify botnet structures embedded in the network. BotMiner can detect real-world botnets including IRC-based, HTTP-based, and P2P botnets with a very low false positive rate.

Gu et al. proposed BotHunter (Gu et al., 2007) to detect malware infection by using correlation of intrusion detection dialogs. The system monitors both inbound and outbound network traffic and correlates anomalous flow and unexpected payload information. BotHunter not only uses data mining techniques. Rule based engines and statistical engines are also embedded in BotHunter.

Additionally some graph based solutions are performed to detect botnet sub-graph structures. BotGrep (Nagaraja, Mittal, Hong, Caesar, & Borisov, 2010) is a recent and effective solution to detect bots by using structured graph analysis. For modern bot structures, because of their distributed C&C architecture, detecting sub-graph network is a very useful and convenient way of intrusion detection.

6. Conclusion

This survey aimed to discover the recent state of botnet research in academia. A progressive survey technique is followed which starts with botnet definition, proceeds with attack types caused by botnets and well-known botnet classifications and ends with diverse types of detection techniques.

According to the orientation of recent studies on botnet detection, we can assert that data mining and machine learning based approaches may have an important contribution on detecting malicious bot structures on a wide-scale network. Botnet detection techniques are classified into two classes according to the types of information they use: network flow information and payload information. Increasing network speeds, growing sizes of payload information streaming on the network complicates payload-base analysis in wide-scale networks. Hence, flow based methods are more convenient as they only attend to discover network flow information which can be understood as meta-information of a network flow without payload.

Data mining and machine learning techniques are easily applicable on network flow information. Flow data have a structured and related nature, which do not require massive preprocessing tasks. Besides, flow information implies patterns inside, which makes data mining algorithms convenient and effective for analysis.

Author details

Erdem Alparslan
Bahçeşehir University Software Engineering Department, Turkey
Center of Research for Advanced Technologies of Informatics and Information Security, Turkey

Adem Karahoca
Bahçeşehir University Software Engineering Department, Turkey

Dilek Karahoca
Bahçeşehir University Software Engineering Department, Turkey

7. References

Abdullah, K., Lee, C., Conti, G., & Copeland, J. A. (2005). Visualizing Network Data for Intrusion Detection. the Sixth Annual IEEE SMC (pp. 100-108).

Andersson, D., Fong, M., & Valdes, A. (2002). Heterogeneous Sensor Correlation: A Case Study of Live Traffic Analysis. IEEE Information Assurance Workshop.

Bethencourt, J., Franklin, J., & Vernon, M. (2005). Mapping internet sensors with probe response attacks. 14th Conference on USENIX Security Symposium (pp. 193-208).

Binkley, J. R. (2006). Anomaly-based Botnet Server Detection. FloCon 2006.
Binkley, J. R., & Singh, S. (2006). An algorithm for anomaly-based botnet detection. SRUTI 2006. Retrieved from http://static.usenix.org/events/sruti06/tech/full_papers/binkley/binkley_html
Brodsky, A., & Brodsky, D. (2007). A distributed content independent method for spam detection. 1 stWorkshop on Hot Topics in Understanding Botnets.
Chiang, K., & Lloyd, L. (2007). A case study of the rustock rootkit and spam bot. First workshop on hot topics in understanding botnets.
Choi, H., & Lee, H. (2012). Identifying botnets by capturing group activities in DNS traffic. Computer Networks, (56), 20-33.
Choi, H., Lee, H., Lee, H., & Kim, H. (2007). Botnet Detection by Monitoring Group Activities in DNS Traffic. 7th IEEE International Conference on Computer and Information Technology (CIT 2007), 715-720. Ieee. doi:10.1109/CIT.2007.90
Cisco Netflow. (n.d.). Retrieved from http://www.cisco.com/en/US/products/ps6601/products_ios_protocol_group_home.htm l
Dagon, D. (2005). Botnet Detection and Response, The Network is the Infection. OARC Workshop.
Daswani, N., & Stoppelman, M. (2007). the Google Click Quality, and S. Teams. The anatomy of clickbot. First workshop on hot topics in understanding botnets.
Davis, J. J., & Clark, A. J. (2011). Data preprocessing for anomaly based network intrusion detection: A review. Computers & Security, 30(6-7), 353-375. Elsevier Ltd. doi:10.1016/j.cose.2011.05.008
Dhamankar, R., & King, R. (2007). Protocol identification via statistical analysis (PISA). Black Hat.
Dietrich, C., Rossow, C., Bos, H., & Steen, M. V. (2008). On Botnets that use DNS for Command and Control. kerstin.christian-rossow.de. Retrieved from http://kerstin.christian-rossow.de/publications/dnscnc2011.pdf
Erbacher, R. F., Marshall, J., Cutler, A., & Banerjee, P. (2008). A Multi-Layered Approach to Botnet Detection. Sensors (Peterborough, NH), 42.
Feily, M., Shahrestani, A., & Ramadass, S. (2009). A Survey of Botnet and Botnet Detection. 2009 Third International Conference on Emerging Security Information, Systems and Technologies, 268-273. Ieee. doi:10.1109/SECURWARE.2009.48
François, J., Wang, S., Bronzi, W., State, R., & Engel, T. (2011). BotCloud : Detecting Botnets Using MapReduce. International Workshop on Information Forensics and Security (WIFS), 2011 IEEE (pp. 1-6).
Freiling, F., Holz, T., & Wicherski, G. (2005). Botnet tracking: exploring a root-cause methodology to prevent distributed denial-of-service attacks. th European Symposium on Research in Computer Security (ESORICS '05).
Gu, G., & Zhang, J. (2008). BotSniffer: Detecting botnet command and control channels in network traffic. 15th Annual Network and Distributed System Security Symposium (NDSS'08). Retrieved from http://users.csc.tntech.edu/~weberle/Fall2008/CSC6910/Papers/17_botsniffer_detecting_ botnet.pdf

Gu, G., Perdisci, R., Zhang, J., & Lee, W. (2008). BotMiner: Clustering Analysis of Network Traffic for Protocol and Structure Independent Botnet Detection. SS'08 Proceedings of the 17th conference on Security symposium.

Gu, G., Porras, P., Yegneswaran, V., Fong, M., & Lee, W. (2007). BotHunter : Detecting Malware Infection Through IDS-Driven Dialog Correlation. SS'07 Proceedings of 16th USENIX Security Symposium.

Holz, T., M, S., & Dahl, F. (2008). Measurement and mitigation of peer-to-peer-based botnets: a case study on storm worm. 1st Usenix Workshop on Large-Scale Exploits and Emergent Threats (pp. 1-9).

Inhwan, K., Choi, H., & Lee, H. (2008). Botnet Visualization using DNS Traffic. WISA 08.

Karasaridis, A., Rexroad, B., & Hoeflin, D. (2007). Wide-scale Botnet Detection and Characterization. USENIX Workshop on Hot Topics in Understanding Botnets.

Krawetz, N. (2004). Anti-Honeypot technology. IEEE Security and Privacy, 2, 76-79.

Kristoff, J. (2004). Botnets. 32nd Meeting of the North American Network Operators Group.

Liu, J., Xiao, Y., Ghaboosi, K., Hongmei, D., & Zhang, J. (2009). Botnet: Classification, Attacks, Detection, Tracing and Preventing Measures. Journal on Wireless Communication and Networking.

Lu, W., Rammidi, G., & Ghorbani, A. A. (2011). Clustering botnet communication traffic based on n-gram feature selection. Computer Communications, 34, 502-514.

Lu, W., Tavallaee, M., & Ghorbani, A. A. (2009). Automatic Discovery of Botnet Communities on Large-Scale Communication Networks. 4th International Symposium on Information, Computer, and Communications Security (pp. 1-10).

Manasrah, A. M., Hasan, A., Abouabdalla, O. A., & Ramadass, S. (2009). Detecting Botnet Activities Based on Abnormal DNS traffic. Journal of Computer Science and Information Security, 6(1), 97-104.

Masud, Mohammad, Al-khateeb, T., & Khan, L. (2008). Flow-based identification of botnet traffic by mining multiple log files. , 2008. DFmA 2008., 200-206. Retrieved from http://ieeexplore.ieee.org/xpls/abs_all.jsp?arnumber=4784437

Masud, MM, Gao, J., Khan, L., & Han, J. (2008). Peer to peer botnet detection for cyber-security: a data mining approach. CSIIRW 08. Retrieved from http://dl.acm.org/citation.cfm?id=1413185

Nagaraja, S., Mittal, P., Hong, C.-yao, Caesar, M., & Borisov, N. (2010). BotGrep : Finding Bots with Structured Graph Analysis. 19th USENIX Security Symposium (pp. 1-24).

Nazario, J. (2007). Blackenergy ddos bot analysis.

Pappas, K. (2008). Back to basics to fight botnets. Communications News, 45, 5-12.

Pouget, F., & Dacier, M. (2004). Honeypot based forensics. Asia Pacific Information technology Security Conference (AusCERT '04).

Puri, R. (2003). Bots and botnets: an overview.

Roschke, S., Cheng, F., & Meinel, C. (2010). A Flexible and Efficient Alert Correlation Platform for distributed IDS. Network and System Security.

Seewald, A., & Gangsterer, W. (2010). On the detection and identification of botnets. Computers & Security, 29, 45-58.

Sperotto, A., & Pras, A. (2010, May). Flow-based intrusion detection. 12th IFIP/IEEE International Symposium on Integrated Network Management (IM 2011) and Workshops. Ieee. Retrieved from

http://ieeexplore.ieee.org/lpdocs/epic03/wrapper.htm?arnumber=5990529
Sperotto, A., Schaffrath, G., Sadre, R., Morariu, C., Pras, A., & Stiller, B. (2010). An Overview of IP Flow-Based Intrusion Detection. IEEE Communications Surveys, 12(3), 343-356. doi:10.1109/SURV.2010.032210.00054
Sroufe, P., Phithakkitnukkon, S., & Dantu, P. (2009). Email shape analysis for spam botnet detection. 6th IEEE Consumer Communications and Networking Conference (CCNC '09) (pp. 1-2).
Strayer, W., Lapsely, D., & Walsh, R. (2008). Botnet detection based on network behavior. Botnet Detection (pp. 1-24). Springer. Retrieved from http://www.springerlink.com/index/N77M076734522777.pdf
Valdes, A., & Skinner, K. (2000). An Approach to Sensor Correlation. Recent Advances in Intrusion Detection.
Valeur, F., Vigna, G., Kruegel, C., & Kemmerer, R. (2004). Comprehensive approach to intrusion detection alert correlation. IEEE Transactions on Dependable and Secure Computing, 1(3), 146-169. doi:10.1109/TDSC.2004.21
Villamarín-salomón, R., & Brustoloni, J. C. (2008). Identifying Botnets Using Anomaly Detection Techniques Applied to DNS Traffic. Communications Society, (1), 476-481.
Villamarín-salomón, R., & Brustoloni, J. C. (2009). Bayesian bot detection based on DNS traffic similarity. 2009 ACM symposium on Applied Computing (pp. 2035-2041). Retrieved from http://dl.acm.org/citation.cfm?id=1529734
Wang, K., Huang, C.-Y., Lin, S.-J., & Lin, Y.-D. (2011). A fuzzy pattern-based filtering algorithm for botnet detection. Computer Networks, (55), 3275-3286.
Wang, P., Sparks, S., & Cou, C. (2008). An advanced hybrid peerto- peer botnet. 1st Workshop on Hot Topics in Understanding Botnets (p. 2).
Wikipedia - Botnet. (n.d.). Retrieved from
Wikipedia - Internet Bot. (n.d.). Retrieved from http://en.wikipedia.org/wiki/Internet%0Abot
Wurzinger, P., Bilge, L., Holz, T., Goebel, J., Kruegel, C., & Kirda, E. (2009). Automatically Generating Models for Botnet Detection. ESORICS 09 (pp. 232-249).
Xie, Y., Yu, F., Achan, K., & Panigraghy, R. (2008). Spamming botnets: signatures and characteristics. ACM SIGCOMM Conference on Data Communication (SIGCOMM '08).
Yen, T.-F., & Reiter, M. (2008). Traffic Aggregation for Malware Detection. 5th international conference on Detection of Intrusions and Malware.
Zeidanloo, H. R., & Manaf, A. A. (2010). Botnet Detection by Monitoring Similar Communication Patterns. Journal of Computer Science, 7(3), 36-45.
Zeidanloo, H. R., Zadeh, H. M. J., M, S., & Zamani, M. (2010). A Taxonomy of Botnet Detection Techniques. Industrial Engineering, 158-162. Retrieved from http://www.mendeley.com/research/a-taxonomy-of-botnet-detection-techniques/
Zhu, Z., Lu, G., Chen, Y., Fu, Z. J., Roberts, P., & Han, K. (2008). Botnet Research Survey. 2008 32nd Annual IEEE International Computer Software and Applications Conference, 967-972. Ieee. doi:10.1109/COMPSAC.2008.205

Chapter 17

Improving Decision Support Systems with Data Mining Techniques

Adela Bâra and Ion Lungu

Additional information is available at the end of the chapter

http://dx.doi.org/10.5772/47788

1. Introduction

1.1. Definition and characteristics of decision support system

The Decision Support System concept goes back a long time, the definition varies depending on the evolution of information technologies and, of course, on the point of view of those who issues such a definition.

Looking through several definition we can find that Moore and Chang defined the DSS as "an extensible system, capable of ad-hoc analysis and decision modeling, focused on future planning and used at unplanned and irregular timestamps" [10]. Also Carlson and Sprague cited by [3] define decision support systems as being "interactive systems that help decedent makers use data and models in resolving unstructured and semi-structured economical problems".

In 1998 Turban defines a decision support system as "an interactive, flexible and adaptable system, exclusively designed to offer support in solving unstructured or semi-structured managerial problems, aiming to improve the decisional process. The system uses data (internal and external) and models, providing a simple and easy-to-use interface, thus, allowing the decision maker control over the decision process. The DDS offers support in all decision process's stages". [9]

In this context, studies show that the process of defining a Decision Support System has started from the idea of how the objectives of a DDS can be achieved, how a DDS's components can be identified, the features that are provided to the end user and from the perception of what such a system is capable of doing (offering support in decision making processes, in solving structured and unstructured problems).

Holsapple and Whinston, in the [5], specify five characteristics of a decision support system: contains a knowledge base that describes certain facets of the decision maker's universe (for

INTECH
open science | open minds

© 2012 Bâra and Lungu, licensee InTech. This is an open access chapter distributed under the terms of the Creative Commons Attribution License (http://creativecommons.org/licenses/by/3.0), which permits unrestricted use, distribution, and reproduction in any medium, provided the original work is properly cited.

example, the way certain activities of the decision-making process); has the ability of purchasing and managing descriptive knowledge, as well as other types of knowledge (procedures, rules etc.); has the ability of presenting ad-hoc knowledge in a periodic report format; has the ability of selecting a subset of knowledge for viewing purposes or for deriving other knowledge, mandatory in the decision making process; is able to interact directly with the decision maker, allowing choosing flexible solution and knowledge management.

In conclusion, considering all the definitions mentioned above, some of the most important characteristics of the DDSs are: uses data and models; enhances the learning process; grows the efficiency of the decision making process; offers support in the decision making process and allows the decision maker control over the entire process; offers support in all stages of the decision making process; offers support for decision makers in solving structured or un-structured problems; offers support for a user or for a group of users etc.

1.2. Data mining techniques in decision support systems

In order to make a decision, the managers need knowledge. In case of massive data amounts, issues may occur because of data analysis and necessary knowledge extract. Data is analyzed through an automated process, known as Knowledge Discovery in data mining techniques.

Data mining can be defined as a process of exploring and analysis for large amounts of data with a specific target on discovering significantly important patterns and rules. Data mining helps finding knowledge from raw, unprocessed data. Using data mining techniques allows extracting knowledge from the data mart, data warehouse and, in particular cases, even from operational databases.

In this context, data mining gets an important role in helping organizations to understand their customers and their behavior, keeping clients, stocks anticipation, sale policies optimization as well as other benefits which bring a considerable competitive advantage to the organization.

The main purpose of these techniques is to find patterns and hidden (but relevant) relations that might lead to revenue increase. The essential difference between data mining techniques and the conventional database operation techniques is that, for the second ones, the database becomes passive and is only being used for large amounts of data population, therefore helping in future finding of that specific data. Alternatively, the database is not passive anymore, being able to serve useful information regarding the business plans put in discussion.

Regarding data mining studies, two major types of them exists. One of them is represented by the hypothesis testing, which assumes exposing a theory regarding the relation between actions and their results. The second type of study is represented by the knowledge discovery. For this type of analysis, relations between data warehouse existing data are tracked. This can be done by using data viewing tools or by using fundamental statistical analysis, such as correlation analysis.

Data mining techniques reside from classic statistical calculation, from database administration and from artificial intelligence. They are not a substitute for traditional statistical techniques, but an extension of graphical and statistical techniques.

Data mining uses a large variety of statistical algorithms, shape recognition, classification, fuzzy logic, machine learning, genetic algorithms, neural networks, data viewing etc., from which we can mention regression algorithms, decision algorithms, neural networks, clustering analysis.

Regression algorithms. Regression represents a basic statistical method. In the case of data mining, it is also an important analysis tool, used in classification applications through logical regressions as well as forecasted reports measured using the least square or other methods. Non-linear data can be transformed into useful linear data and analyzed using linear regressions. The universal test for data mining classification is the coincidence index matrix. It is primarily focused on data classification abilities of the model. For continuous regressions, class inflection points must be identified. The applications of the methods into solving business problems are multiple.

Decision trees. In data mining technology, decision trees represent rules tree-view structures, also known as joining rules. The trees' creation mechanism of the trees consists in collecting all the variables the analyst assumes might help the decision making and analyzing them considering their influence into result estimation.

The algorithm automatically determines which of the variables are the most relevant, based on the ease of data sorting. The decision tree algorithms are applied in Business data mining in areas like: loan request classification, applicants ranking for various positions.

Neural networks. This is one of the most commonly used data mining method. It consists of taking sets of observations and placing them in a relational system through arc-connected nodes. This idea derives from the way neurons act inside the human brain. Neural networks are usually structured in at least three layers, having a constant structure allowing reflection of complex non-linear relations. Each entry data has a node in the first layer, while the last layer represents the output data – the result. In order to classify the neural network model, the last layer (containing the output) has a corresponding node for each category. In most of the cases, this type of networks also have a mid node layer (hidden) which adds complexity to the model. The obtained results are compared to the targeted ones, and the difference is re-entered in the system for node's cost adjustments. The process keeps looping until the network correctly classifies the input data (at a tolerance level).

Clustering analysis. One of the most general forms of this type of analysis allows the algorithm to determine the number of subsets. Partitioning is mainly used for defining new variable categories, which divide raw data in a precise number of regions (k-means clustering). Considering a random number of centers (k), data is associated to the center which is the closest to it. The basic principle of this analysis is to identify the average characteristic for different indicators in sets of data. Thus, new observations can be measured by reporting the deviation from the average. This analysis is often the base technique applied in a data mining study, being used in client segmentation and, implicitly, taking a segment-oriented action.

1.3. The process of developing a DSS using data mining techniques

Developing Decision Support Systems involves time, high-costs and human resources efforts and the success of the system can be affected by many risks like: system design, data quality, and technology obsolescence. The decision support systems objective is to assist the managers and executives to make decision regarding the benefit of investment, budgeting cash flows and financial planning, especially in the case of public funds.

Presently, many institutions invest in building organizational data warehouses and data marts in order to increase the performance and the efficiency of the analytical reporting activity. Also, there are several expensive tools and software that can be used to analyze the trends and to predict some future characteristics and evolution of the business. Some of these tools analyze data from the statistic perspective or by using neural networks. In our opinion, in order to build an efficient decision support system there must be combined several techniques and methods that can improve the performance and the accuracy of the analysis from two major perspectives: historical data and forecasts. This requirement can be obtain by combining data warehousing, OLAP, data mining and business intelligence tools for analyzing and reporting into a flexible architecture that must contains: A data model's level where an ETL process must be apply to clean and load data into a data warehouse or data marts; An application level with analytical models where multidimensional reporting like OLAP and data mining techniques can be combined to for historical and forecast analysis; An interface level where dashboards and reports can be build with business intelligence tools.

In the chapter it will be presented the consideration regarding to design the DSS's architecture and there will be described the methods and ways for data mining integration into a data warehouse environment. In the paper [6], the authors propose a series of development stages for business intelligence systems: *feasibility study, project planning, analysis, design, development and release into production.*

These stages can be adapted and applied in decision support systems, but during the development cycle it is mandatory that differences between general system modeling and decision support systems modeling must be treated separately, in order to obtain a successful business requirements of implementing the specifications.

Stage 1. The feasibility study consists of identifying the requirements and business opportunities and proposing solutions of improving the decision making process. Each of the proposed solutions must be justified by the implied costs and benefits.

Stage 2. Project planning consists of evaluating project sustainability possibilities, indentifying existent infrastructure components and future needs. The result of these activities concludes with *the project plan*. After its validation and approval, the effective start of the project can begin.

Stage 3. Business requirements analysis. *This stage focuses on detailing and analyzing on priority the initial requirements* of the organizational management team. Usually, the requirements are indentified based on interviews conducted by managers and the project staff. These requirements might suffer slight changes during the project, but the development team must make the managers aware of the capabilities and limitations of a DSS, therefore reducing the risk of un-feasible business requirements to occur.

Data analysis – the biggest challenge of a decision support system development project – consists of identifying necessary data, analyzing its content and the way it relates to other data. Data analysis is focused on business analysis rather than system analysis performed in traditional methodologies. It is preceded by a data cleaning activity.

Data cleaning implies transforming and filtering data sources in order to be used in building the destination module – the analysis module. This process is done by: identifying necessary data from the functional modules; analyzing the content of the selected data sources; selecting the appropriate data for the project; implementation of data filtering related specifications; selecting the tools to be used in the filtering / cleaning process. During the source selection process, a few key aspects must be taken into consideration: data integrity, precision, accuracy and data format. These facets are critical in regards to the success of the new ETL process.

Metadata analysis is an important activity in which all the identified requirements would be transformed depending on the metadata structure, and stored in a metadata dictionary. A metadata dictionary contains contextual information on the data implied in the project. The system analysis phase can end by *building a prototype* which will be presented to the managers and project staff for functional specifications' validation. The existence of quick development tools allow building new interfaces based on the analysis model.

An important step in this stage is *choosing the technologies used* in the prototype's development and, later on, in the final system. Based on a comparative analysis over advantages and disadvantages brought by each of the technologies on the project, different approaches might be taken into consideration: usage of data warehouses, including OLAP (Online Analytical Processing) functionalities, usage of knowledge extract algorithms, data source integration tools or, on a final phase and assuming a parallel approach on building the system has been taken, usage of applications integration tools.

Stage 4. System design. *Database / data warehouse design.* According to the system's requirements, the necessary data will be stored both on a detailed level as well as on aggregate level, therefore relational, object-oriented or multi-dimensional data storage approaches might be taken. During this sub-phase, the logical data model is refined and detailed and the physical model of the new system is developed in order to satisfy the reporting and analysis requirements of the managers.

While on "Data analysis", the process has been oriented to data sources (*data-in* or *data-entry*) coming from operational modules, in this phase the targets or data destinations (*data-out*) are set aiming on reports, analysis and queries. Therefore, a list of best practices must be taken into consideration:

Due to the above mentioned aspects, we recommend that the storage, management and data processing solution to consist of a centralized data warehouse on an organizational level. Following logical and physical criteria, the data warehouse can be divided into data marts on departmental level, thus being easier to maintain and developed by separate teams, following the same set of specifications.

The ETL (extract / transform / load) process design – this phase is the most complex one in the project's lifecycle and is directly dependant on the data sources' quality.

We recommend the integration of all the destination databases in a single environment and building the ETL process on it, avoiding a separation of each destination module, thus mitigating the risk of distinct data marts. The strategy of building data marts in the same environment is also viable, but only on the condition that these are already integrated. The important fact here is that the ETL process must remain the same for all levels (the *share one coordinated process* principle).

The design of the ETL process needs a series of pre-requisite stages: preliminary processing of data sources, in order to have a standardized format, data reconciliation and redundancy and inconsistency elimination of data.

The steps to be taken in creating an ETL process are the following:

1. *Creation of transformation specifications* (mapping) of the sources in regards to the specific destinations. This may be done as a matrix or as transformation diagrams.
2. *Choosing and testing the ETL tools to be used.* At the moment, a series of ETL process modeling and implementation tools exist on market, but choosing one of them would depend on the features they provide and on the support of data source integration inside the same transformation process.
3. *The ETL process design* – several extract and transform operators are used, depending on the data model (sorting, aggregation, joining, dividing operators, etc.). The process can be split into sub-processes that would run separately in order to minimize the execution time. The execution flow of the process will be modeled using flow diagrams.
4. *ETL programs design.* Depending on the program in which the data is loaded, three phases of data loading are applied:
   - initial load – the initial load of destinations with current operational data
   - historical load – the initial load of destinations with archived historical data
   - incremental load – regular loading of destinations with current data coming from operational systems
5. *Choosing the environment for running the ETL process* – represents the decision over using a dedicated server / machine or the process would be divided and run decentralized. The decision depends on the available resources and on the processing time, as well as on the timelines that the process is scheduled to run.

The results of these activities is materialized in the data mapping documentation, the flow diagram / diagrams of the ETL process, the transformation programs documentation and the process execution specifications.

Metadata repository design – if the repository is acquired and a predefined template is used, then, in this sub-stage, slight changes may occur according to the requirements identified in the metadata analysis sub-stage, but, if the option has been to build a proprietary repository, then the metadata logical model will be implemented for the new system, based on the data storage options: a relational, object-oriented or multidimensional model will be implemented.

If the option was for building a proprietary warehouse, we consider that centralization and standardization of it would represent a good strategy into a more facile administration. The activities performed in this stage are materialized in the detailed logical model and the metadata physical model.

Stage 5. Building the system. The technologies that are used for decision support systems' development are part of the business intelligence technologies category and consist of: technologies for data warehouse data organization, OLAP (On-Line Analytical Processing) analysis systems, data mining algorithms, extract, transform and load (ETL) tools, CASE (Computer-Aided Software Engineering) modeling tools and web technologies.

Stage 6. System implementation. Represents the stage when the system is being delivered, training sessions are held for implied managers / business owners, the necessary technical support is provided, data loading procedures are run, the application is installed and the performance is being tracked.

The stage ends with the release of the system into production (commercial go-live) and with the delivery of the utilities and final project documentation, the user guides and presentation manuals for the application.

1.4. The DSS architecture

Depending on the requirements indentified in the analysis phase, all of these technologies can be merged and combined, creating reliable decision support system architecture. The field literature (for example in [2], [3], [4]) proposes a typical decision support system architecture that contains distinct levels which use the above mentioned technologies in order to be created.

In [3], the definition provided by Bonczek and Holsapple, the main components of a decisional system are emphasized: a DSS is described as being "a system composed of three interacting modules: *the user interface* (Dialog Management), *the data management component* (Data Management), *the model management component* (Model Management)". In [4] it is identified four core components that form a decision support system: *the interface,* often considered to be the most important component, *the database system* which includes all the databases and the database management systems (DBMS) of the organization, *the model system* containing the analytical, mathematical and statistical models and *the communication component*, composed of the core network and the mobile devices.

The DSS architecture can also be seen from a development level point of view, from bottom to top, pyramidal, having three layers: bottom-tier middle-tier and top-tier, the connection of all these layers being made on the telecom layer. Thus, DSS architecture might be composed of the following levels:

Level I (bottom-tier) – data management. It is composed of data, metadata, DBMS (database management systems), data warehouses, data dictionaries and metadata dictionaries. At this level, data coming from several different systems must be integrated and the main techniques used for this process are replication, federalization or data migration, together with data warehouse loading. Data coming from operational databases and external sources are extracted using interface-type applications, known as gateways, running on DBMS and allowing client-applications to generate server-side executable SQL code. During the extract and data processing, different tools can be used – filtering, predefined procedures etc. Data cleaning and transformations is strongly dependent on the data sources and on the quality of it. Several sources may be put in discussion: files, databases, e-mails, internet and unconventional sources.

This sub-stage focuses on implementing the ETL designed requirements, running and testing them.

At this architectural level, in order to load data in a data warehouse, a series of tasks is mandatory:

- Collecting and extracting data from the data sources that have been identified during the analysis phase, according to the management's business requirements. A source data warehouse (staging area) can be created in order to load all the necessary data which then must be processed and loaded into another destination warehouse. This process, most often, transforms raw data for compliance with the internal format of the warehouse;
- Data cleaning and transformation to assure data accuracy and to confirm data can be used for analysis;
- Loading data in the destination warehouse.

This process is extremely important for the success of the future decision support system, thus a faulty design could lead to the failure of the DSS. Subsequently, a method for data refresh must be taken into consideration as time passes. Therefore, the ETL process must be automatically run on accurate timestamps defined during the design and analysis stages. The destination warehouse data will be used at higher levels of the system. If the chosen approach has been to build a new data warehouse (custom development) instead of purchasing a predefined solution, the metadata dictionaries used by the components and utilities of the system must be build and adapted to the solution, integrated and the connection interfaces between the user and the metadata centralized dictionary and the dictionaries used by each component separately must also be developed. Thus, the structure of the dictionary is created and the data will be loaded according to the logical and physical models already designed.

Level II (middle-tier) – model management or analysis level. This is the level where data is processed and the necessary information for decision making is extracted. This level contains data analysis, simulation and forecast models, in order to respond to the high level business requirements. On this level, the core components are: *the model base, the model database management system, the meta-models, the model management and execution server*.

For creating this level, *OLAP technology* can be used. It is based on multidimensional data representation and allows quick and interactive data analysis by using roll-up, drill-down, slice or dice operations.

If the business requirements requires, at this level, *knowledge extract algorithms using data mining algorithms* can be designed and implemented. These algorithms assure data transformation into knowledge using statistical analysis or artificial intelligence techniques and allowing the identification of correlations, rules and knowledge in order to support the decision making process. In order to integrate the analysis and models resulted from different sub-system types, several application integration technologies could be used: application servers that implement middleware models, service-oriented architecture (SOA), Java platforms.

Extracting knowledge from data (Data Mining) – very often, the success of a DSS is determined by the discovery of new facts and data correlations and not by building reports that just presents data. In order to fulfill these requirements, data mining techniques must be applied, together with knowledge extract from the organizational data, such as: clustering, forecasting, predictive modeling and classification.

In this context, an analysis regarding the data mining applicability domains, the specific algorithms to be used and the teams that would develop these initiatives must be done as a mandatory task.

The tasks to be performed are:

1. *Domain and applicability objective setting for data mining techniques* – specific requirements that cannot be resolved through other methods are analyzed, as well as the opportunity of applying data mining techniques and the way they would solve the problem
2. *Data collecting* – a validation is preformed in order to check the existence of the loaded data; if not, new data sources are set and previous steps regarding data design need re-validation
3. *Data consolidation and cleaning* – when data is not loaded in the correct format, cleaning processes are applied. The ETL processes implemented in Stage II may change due to these additional requirements.
4. *Data setup* – data mining algorithms use setup steps by formatting and loading data, in order to be compliant to the agreed techniques.
5. *Building the analytical model* – the step focuses on implementing the data mining algorithms and the specifications for the learning and testing stages
6. *Result interpretation* – according to the agreed requirements and objectives, a validation of the results must be performed. The measured values are interpreted and it is decided whether they can be used by managers.
7. *Result validation* – the measured values are compared to the expected ones, accepted deviations and errors are set based on statistics or comparative analysis and why these

deviations have occurred. If the result can be used, they are presented to the managers (business owners) for the final validation.
8. *Analytical model monitoring* – the performance of the model is tracked in a timeline already defined in the requirements phase.

After applying data mining techniques, a complete database is obtained and will be used by specific programs, as well as the analysis model specifications.

Level III (top-tier) – The interface or the presentation layer. Represents the level where the interaction with the users takes place, where the managers and the persons involved in the decision making process can communicate with the system and can analyze the presented results. The user interface must be specially designed so that this type of users will easily interact with the system. This level is composed of *queries and reports generating tools, dynamic analysis tools* (data viewing using different perspectives, post-implementation evolution analysis, forecasting, data correlations), *data publishing and data presenting tools* in a simple, intuitive and flexible way for the end-users. On this level, the *human resource* can be found, represented by *decision makers* which interact with the system through its interfaces. In the last few years, a growing share in the development of decision support system interfaces is taken by the *portal-based web technologies*. Business Intelligence portals hold the most important position in creating specialized, flexible, user-friendly and accessible interfaces, allowing users a good end-to-end experience, nice graphical appearance, report integration options and graphic tools, obtained in the previous stages.

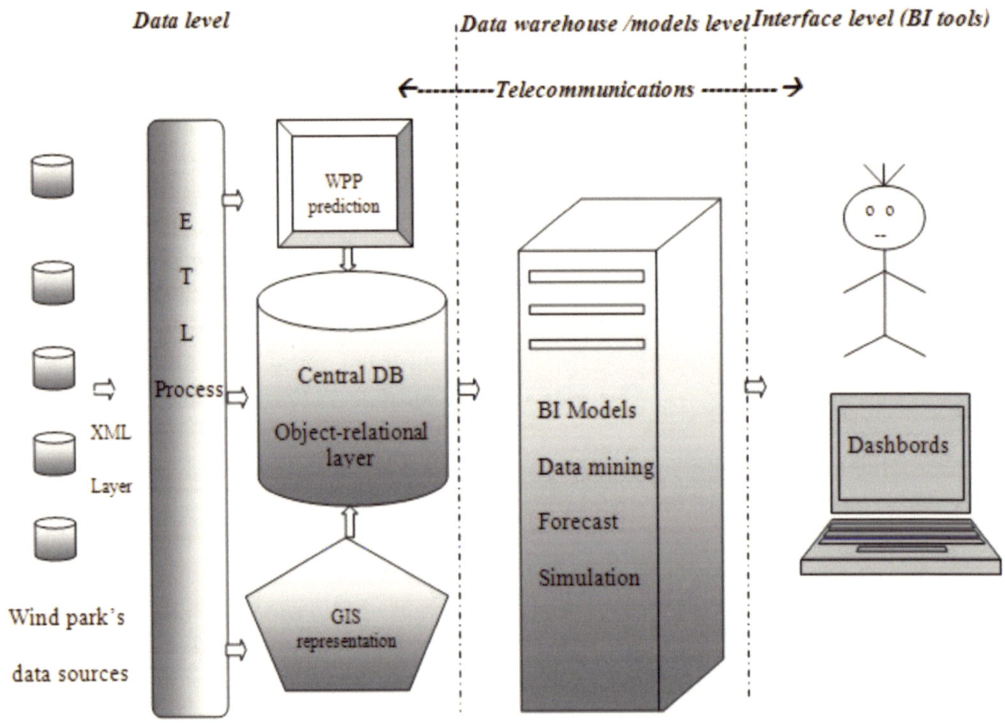

Figure 1. The DSS architecture used for WPP systems

Level IV – Telecommunications. Represents the level that allows interconnecting all the previous levels and may contain web servers, computer networks, communication devices, distributed platforms, GRID technologies and mobile communication platforms.

Based on these steps and DSS' architecture, in the following sections we propose a conceptual model that can be implemented in the case study in which the National Power System's (NPS) activity was analyzed, especially the wind power pants' production and wind energy integration into the NPS.

The architecture is explained in [1] where all the components are presented in detail. The entire case study consider the characteristics of wind power plants, the ways to integrate the energy produced and the impact on decision-making system from the technical point of view (the characteristics and impact on reserve power), financial, commercial, environmental, legal (by analyzing the issues raised by access to the electric wind power). The next section present only the methods applied to predict and determine the wind energy based on data mining techniques and the results obtained for some of the algorithms.

2. Case Study: applying data mining for forecasting the wind power plants' energy production

2.1. The problem formulation: the characteristics of wind energy production

Setting a wind farm is particularly important because its energy production depends to a several meteorological factors of that site. The main criteria for determining the location of wind generating units are wind speed and direction, orography and terrain conditions, environmental conditions, distance from the electricity grid, substations and connection conditions, access to equipment and personal interference human activities (tourism, proximity to settlements, roads, railways, airports), electromagnetic interference, conditions on land use and relationships with local authorities the power of its consumers.

But the main natural factor, wind speed, records significant fluctuations even within hours. Optimal range of wind speeds that produce wind turbines' energy ranges from 3 to 25 m / s If the wind speed falls below this limit or exceeding 27 m / s, the turbines stop. Even for an area such as Dobrogea (where the area is windy) the wind speed in certain areas of land varies significantly. Therefore, to determine if the location is suitable it is necessary to measure the meteorological factors, such as wind speed and direction, temperature and pressure, etc.

From the above mentioned in the investment phase is particularly important to determine the energy produced by wind sources in order to choose the type of wind generator and location of each production station and also in the operational phase to achieve good production forecasts. But forecasts in wind power plants (WPP) still records significant deviations from the real values of energy products due to the inability of present systems to correctly estimate the wind speed. The problem becomes more complex because the forecasts obtained are used to establish the energy resources necessary to cover any gaps in the energy system. It is well known that rapid availability of power is questionable or expensive. If the forecast of wind energy from wind sources is more accurate the more it reduces the power system reserves. The role of a good prognosis is particularly important because it reduces the costs of ensuring safe operation National Power System (NPS) and therefore has no significant increases in energy prices as a result of these reserves.

But the most important problem, which depends on the amount of energy reserves, and return on investment in wind power, is the component on which these wind power plants are based, namely the wind. From Figure 2 one can see large fluctuations of the wind recorded by an anemometer within 24 h at a height of 50 m

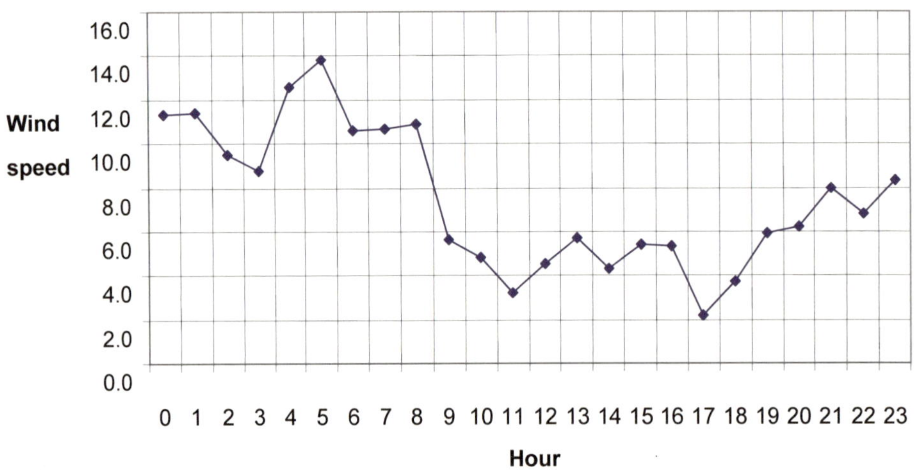

Figure 2. Wind speeds measured within 24 h in a location in Dobrogea area

Wind energy production is conditioned by other factors, some of which are characterized by low predictability, such as the effect of shading, soil orography, the power, losses to the point of connection, etc. Currently, there are several informational systems used for the prediction of energy but the accuracy of these systems is still quite low. This can be seen analyzing the notifications forwarded by the wind power energy production within 7 days (Figure 3).

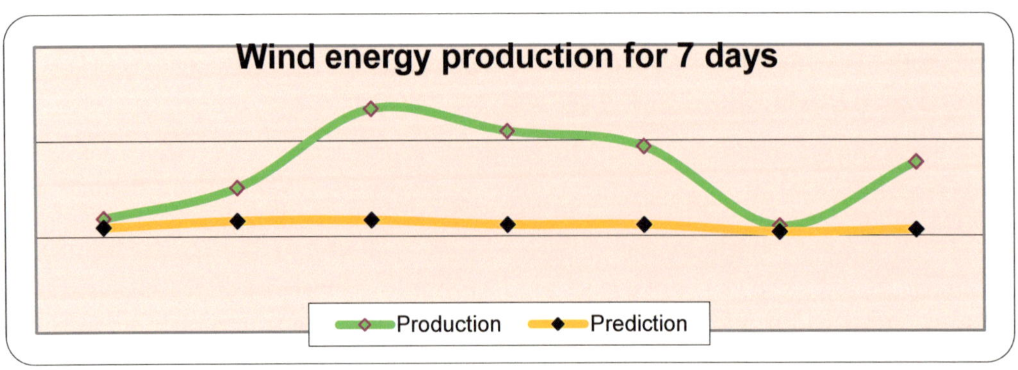

Figure 3. Comparison of energy prediction and actual wind production (source [8])

These problems regarding the low prediction accuracy and of data integration from various equipment and local systems, energy efficiency analysis, lead to the need to develop solutions for a better predictive power as products, but also to support decision making in this area.

A better prediction cannot be achieved by classical statistical methods, and this is the reason for requiring the use of modern techniques like data mining. In these considerations we have been analyzed in the following section, in detail, the main algorithms that can be applied to predict the wind.

2.2. Proposing an effective model for predicting wind energy

For building and testing the data mining algorithms we'll use Oracle Data Miner (ODM) software tool developed by Oracle Corporation that provides a friendly interface for data analysis and validation results. Oracle Data Miner provides several tools (wizards) for the data processing and for the stages of preparation, training, testing and evaluation required in data mining technology.

Oracle Data Miner implements the following types of algorithms [7]:

- Predictive models or supervised training: classification algorithms, regression algorithms and selection of important attributes;
- Descriptive models or unsupervised learning: clustering, association rules, extraction algorithms for new attributes based on existing ones;
- Models for multimedia (TEXT) and bio-informatics (BLAST).

For all the algorithms the data preparation is required. In our case study the data were measured and recorded from 10 to 10 minutes between 09.11.2009 - 28.02.2010. The values recorded at height of 50 m count 16,037 records. The minimum value recorded in this period is 0 m / s, maximum value of 24.8 m / s and average 6.9 m / s.

From the set consisting of the 16,037 records of wind speed at 50 m height, about 2500 were lower or equal to 3.5 m / s - start speed of a wind generator (GGE). In approx. 1100 cases wind recorded a speed exceeding 12 m / s Approximately 8,800 measured values were lower than average speed, and about 7200 values above average wind speed (6.9 m / s).

For the algorithms, the source table entries were imported and divided into three sets for each stage that will be completed. Thus these sets of records will be inserted in three tables, namely: *wind_build, wind_test, wind_apply* (Figure 4).

Each table contains information on different time intervals in which measurements are made as follows: for table for learning are considered records of the period 09.11 - 15.01 (about 10,000 records), the table for the testing process are considered records of the period 16.01 - 15.02 (about 4600 records), and for evaluation the table contains records in period 16.02 - 23.02 (about 1100 records). Tables can be viewed directly in Oracle Data Miner interface by accessing data sources.

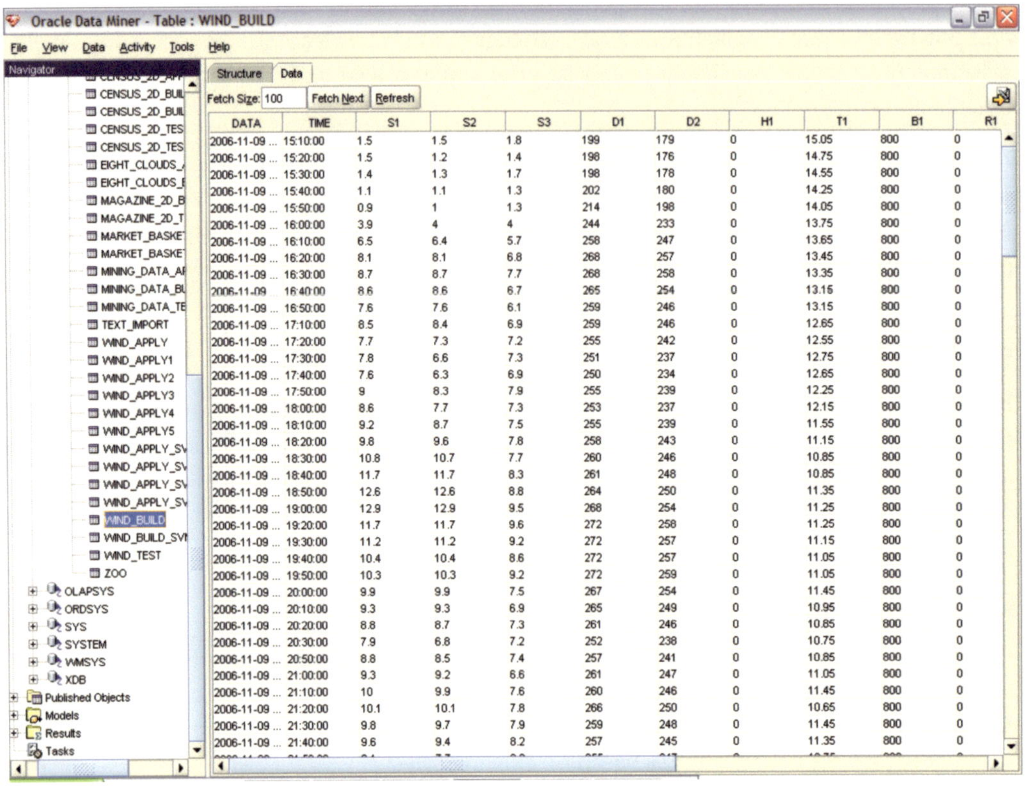

DATA	TIME	S1	S2	S3	D1	D2	H1	T1	B1	R1
2006-11-09 ...	15:10:00	1.5	1.5	1.8	199	179	0	15.05	800	0
2006-11-09 ...	15:20:00	1.5	1.2	1.4	198	176	0	14.75	800	0
2006-11-09 ...	15:30:00	1.4	1.3	1.7	198	178	0	14.55	800	0
2006-11-09 ...	15:40:00	1.1	1.1	1.3	202	180	0	14.25	800	0
2006-11-09 ...	15:50:00	0.9	1	1.3	214	198	0	14.05	800	0
2006-11-09 ...	16:00:00	3.9	4	4	244	233	0	13.75	800	0
2006-11-09 ...	16:10:00	6.5	6.4	5.7	258	247	0	13.65	800	0
2006-11-09 ...	16:20:00	8.1	8.1	6.8	268	257	0	13.45	800	0
2006-11-09 ...	16:30:00	8.7	8.7	7.7	268	258	0	13.35	800	0
2006-11-09	16:40:00	8.6	8.6	6.7	265	254	0	13.16	800	0
2006-11-09 ...	16:50:00	7.6	7.6	6.1	259	246	0	13.15	800	0
2006-11-09 ...	17:10:00	8.5	8.4	6.9	259	246	0	12.65	800	0
2006-11-09 ...	17:20:00	7.7	7.3	7.2	255	242	0	12.55	800	0
2006-11-09 ...	17:30:00	7.8	6.6	7.3	251	237	0	12.75	800	0
2006-11-09 ...	17:40:00	7.6	6.3	6.9	250	234	0	12.65	800	0
2006-11-09 ...	17:50:00	9	8.3	7.9	255	239	0	12.25	800	0
2006-11-09 ...	18:00:00	8.6	7.7	7.3	253	237	0	12.15	800	0
2006-11-09 ...	18:10:00	9.2	8.7	7.5	255	239	0	11.55	800	0
2006-11-09 ...	18:20:00	9.8	9.6	7.8	258	243	0	11.15	800	0
2006-11-09 ...	18:30:00	10.8	10.7	7.7	260	246	0	10.85	800	0
2006-11-09 ...	18:40:00	11.7	11.7	8.3	261	248	0	10.85	800	0
2006-11-09 ...	18:50:00	12.6	12.6	8.8	264	250	0	11.35	800	0
2006-11-09 ...	19:00:00	12.9	12.9	9.5	268	254	0	11.25	800	0
2006-11-09 ...	19:20:00	11.7	11.7	9.6	272	258	0	11.25	800	0
2006-11-09 ...	19:30:00	11.2	11.2	9.2	272	257	0	11.15	800	0
2006-11-09 ...	19:40:00	10.4	10.4	8.6	272	257	0	11.05	800	0
2006-11-09 ...	19:50:00	10.3	10.3	9.2	272	259	0	11.05	800	0
2006-11-09 ...	20:00:00	9.9	9.9	7.5	267	254	0	11.45	800	0
2006-11-09 ...	20:10:00	9.3	9.3	6.9	265	249	0	10.95	800	0
2006-11-09 ...	20:20:00	8.8	8.7	7.3	261	246	0	10.85	800	0
2006-11-09 ...	20:30:00	7.9	6.8	7.2	252	238	0	10.75	800	0
2006-11-09 ...	20:50:00	8.8	8.5	7.4	257	241	0	10.85	800	0
2006-11-09 ...	21:00:00	9.3	9.2	6.6	261	247	0	11.05	800	0
2006-11-09 ...	21:10:00	10	9.9	7.6	260	246	0	11.45	800	0
2006-11-09 ...	21:20:00	10.1	10.1	7.8	266	250	0	10.65	800	0
2006-11-09 ...	21:30:00	9.8	9.7	7.9	259	248	0	11.45	800	0
2006-11-09 ...	21:40:00	9.6	9.4	8.2	257	245	0	11.35	800	0

Figure 4. The records prepared for data mining

After the data preparation step, we applied the following algorithms: Naïve Bayes with an error rate of about 8%, decision tree with a 1% error rate, regression with error rate of 43% and after analyzing the results we modified the regression model and obtained a significant increase in prediction accuracy from 57.68% to 93.72%. The steps and the results are presented in the next sections.

2.2.1. Naïve Bayes results

We'll further present how to apply the Naïve Bayes (NB) algorithm on the measured data to analyze the target attribute E-01. Attribute E-01 has two values: 1 – the turbine produces energy when wind speed is within the range 3.5 to 25 m / s and 0 otherwise.

By applying the NB algorithm will forecast whether or not the turbine will produce energy depending on weather conditions.

It will go through three distinct phases:

- The learning stage consists in applying the algorithms NB on the *wind_build* table data set and build the analysis model;
- The test phase, the model built in the previous step is tested on the table *wind_test*;

- The validation phase, the model built on data set is applied on *wind_apply* table to check the results obtained from the algorithm.

The learning stage. In this stage we applied the templates of analysis to build the model on the table *wind_build*.

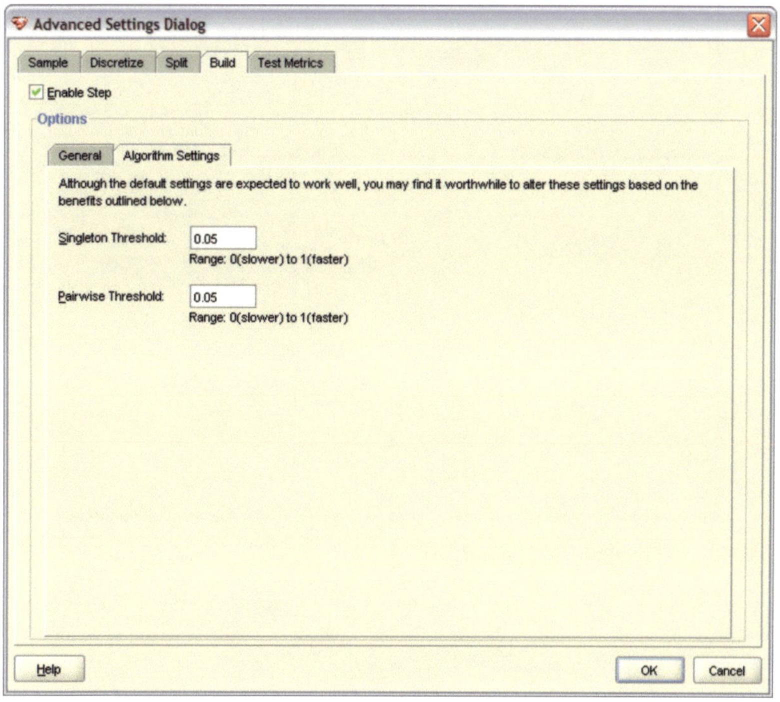

Figure 5. Setting the parameters for the implementation of Naive Bayes algorithm

For this scope a number of steps are required to configure the Oracle Data Miner algorithm parameters, such as setting the model name (*NB_wind_build*), source table, and minimum thresholds for the interpretation of outliers (Figure 5). In our case, is considered the minimum threshold of 5% - only data above this threshold will be considered on the basis of learning (for example, large fluctuations of wind speed are observed at high variations of temperatures whose incidence is rare).

We obtained a 88.6% accuracy of predictions with the NB algorithm.

The test phase. After building the NB model for our data set, we applied the testing algorithm. The results are shown in Figure 6.

The validation phase. To validate the results we considered three sets of validation data (figure 7): table wind_apply with data during 16-23.02.2010 period, wind_apply1 table with data from 24 h (from 02/24/2010) and wind_apply2 table with data from 24h (02/25/2010).

The accuracy of predictions obtained for the three sets is: 91% for table wind_apply (104 erroneous predictions of 1152 records), 99% for table wind_apply1 (1 prediction error of 144 records), 91% for table wind_apply2 (13 of erroneous predictions of 144 records).

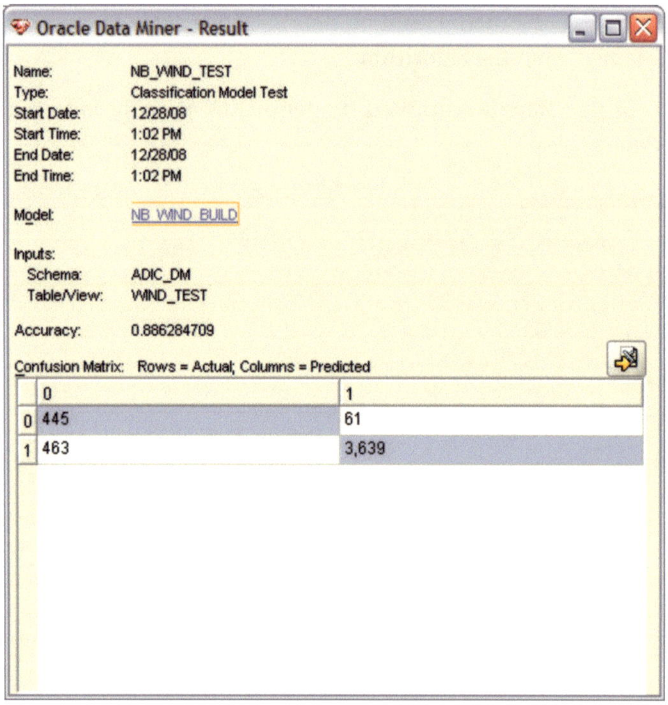

Figure 6. The results of NB algorithm on the test set

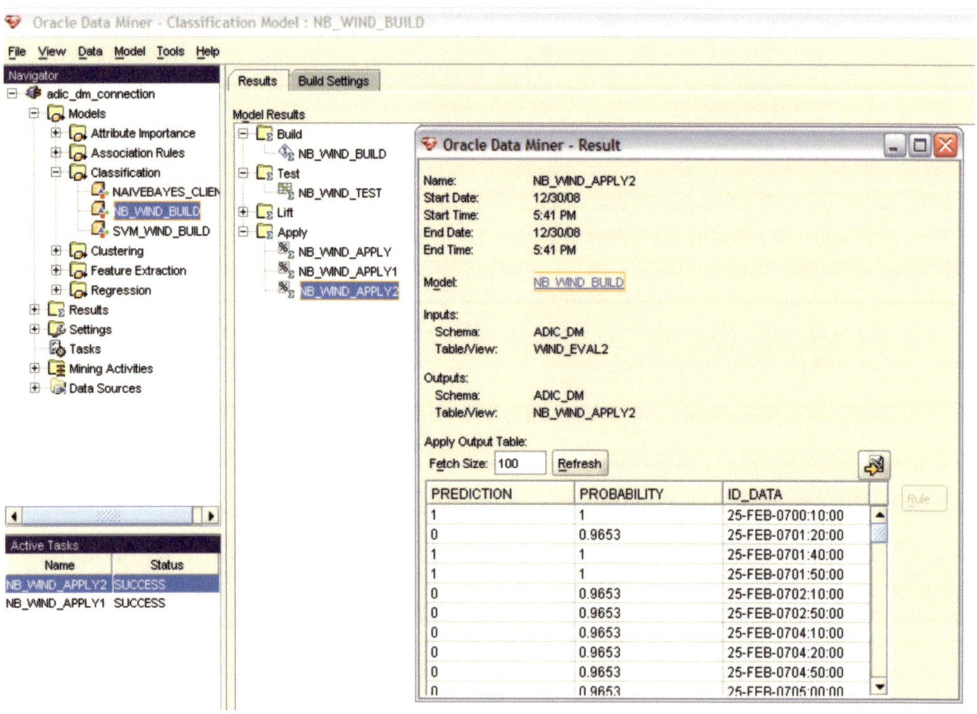

Figure 7. The results of NB algorithm

In conclusion, the error rate resulting from the application of NB algorithm is less than 8% which is considered to be satisfactory.

2.2.2. *Decision Tree results*

Another prediction algorithm applied to E_01 variable is the Decision Tree. After building and testing the model on the data sets, following the same steps presented in the previous section, we obtain an accuracy of 99.48% (Figure 8), higher than that obtained by applying the NB algorithm.

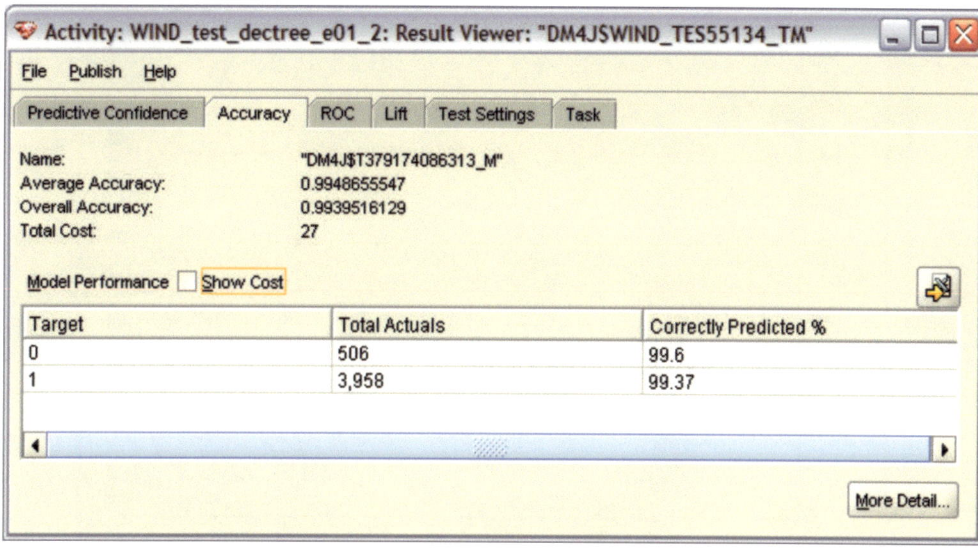

Figure 8. The results obtained by applying the decision tree algorithm

The results detailed on the three tables: the set from table wind_apply recorded an error of only 0.6%, for table wind_apply1 no errors were detected and the table wind_apply2 recorded an error of 0.7%.

In conclusion the results obtained by applying the Decision Tree algorithm are better than those obtained with the NB algorithm. But to get a real energy prediction of turbine's actual values is necessary to apply other algorithms where the target attribute has discrete values, not only values 0 or 1.

2.2.3. *The regression results*

On the initial data set we introduced column E which is the amount of power produced by wind speed (S2) measured at 50 m cubed. The values in this column will be the target attribute for the regression algorithm. We applied the regression on the data sets, following the same steps (preparation, learning, testing and applying) and the results obtained from the algorithm have an accuracy of only 57.68% (Figure 9) which gives no confidence to achieve rigorous forecasts.

We observed significant errors between actual values and the predicted values ranges from ± 250 kW (figure 9), which would mean that if the current value of the power produced is 50 kW then the algorithm will predict a value of 300 kW, the difference between them being unacceptable.

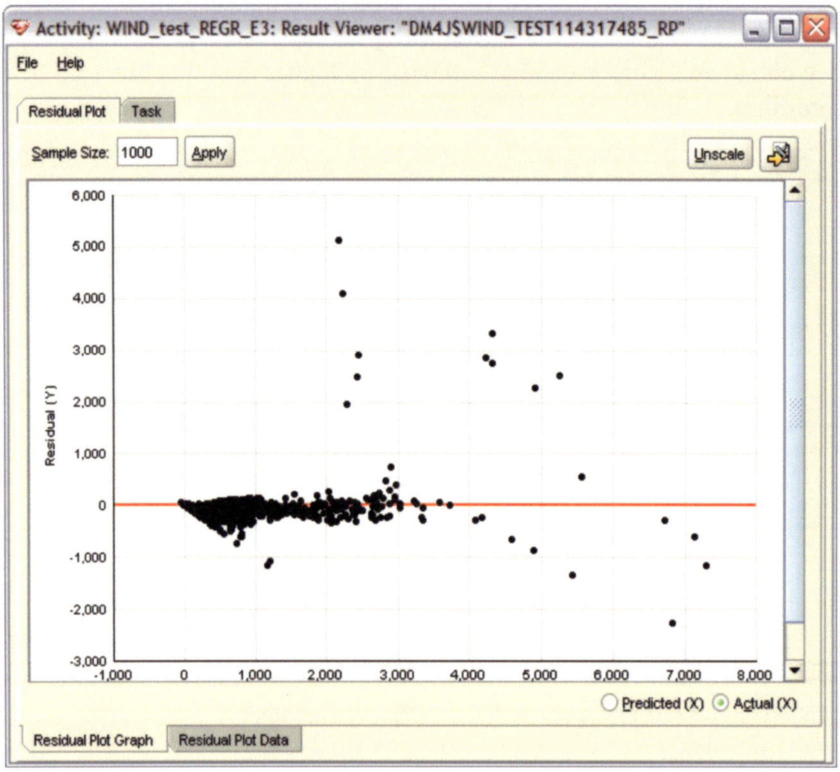

Figure 9. Deviations registered for the Regression model

Consequently, the regression model should be applied to an attribute with a low degree of scattering depending on meteorological factors. Thus, we introduced E_PRAG attribute for grouping values into intervals depending on power produced by wind velocity of 0.5 m / s. For example, we found that at wind speeds between 0 and 3.5 m / s there is 0 kW power output, at speeds ranging from 3.5 to 4 m / s power output is 43 kW, etc.. These thresholds are defined in accordance with the power characteristics of the turbines.

After building the regression model on these thresholds it shows a significant increase in prediction accuracy from 57.68% to 93.72%. Applying the model on the test set (the table wind_test) and observing the diagram in Figure 10 we found that the variation of residual value y, the deviation between the actual value and predicted value lies within ± 50 kW, which is an acceptable deviation. By placing the cursor on any point on the diagram (capture in figure 10) one can view the following information: the current value (in our case 1500 kW), the prediction (1492 kW) and the deviation Y (7.5 kW).

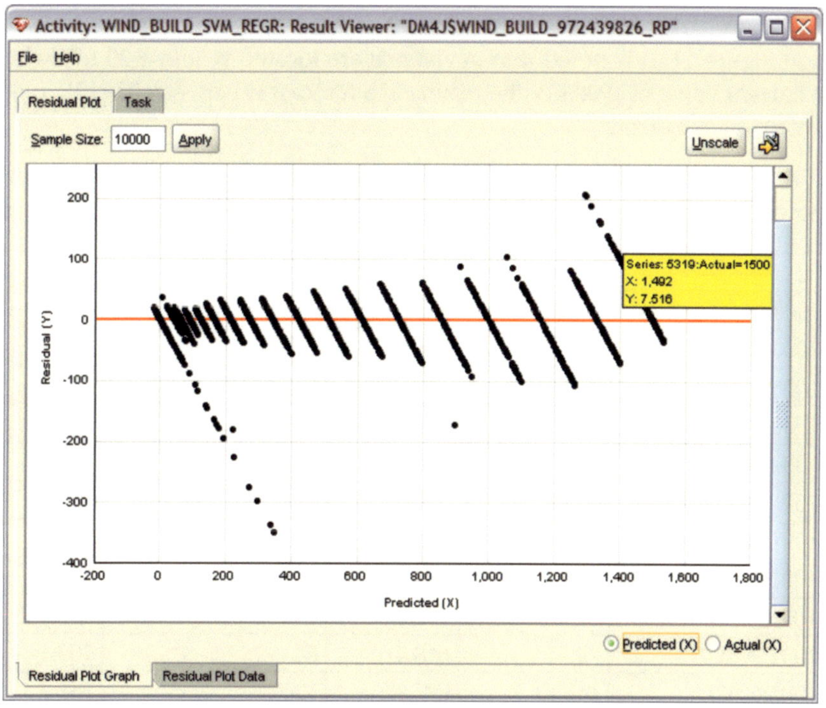

Figure 10. The regression results on E_Prag attribute with thresholds values

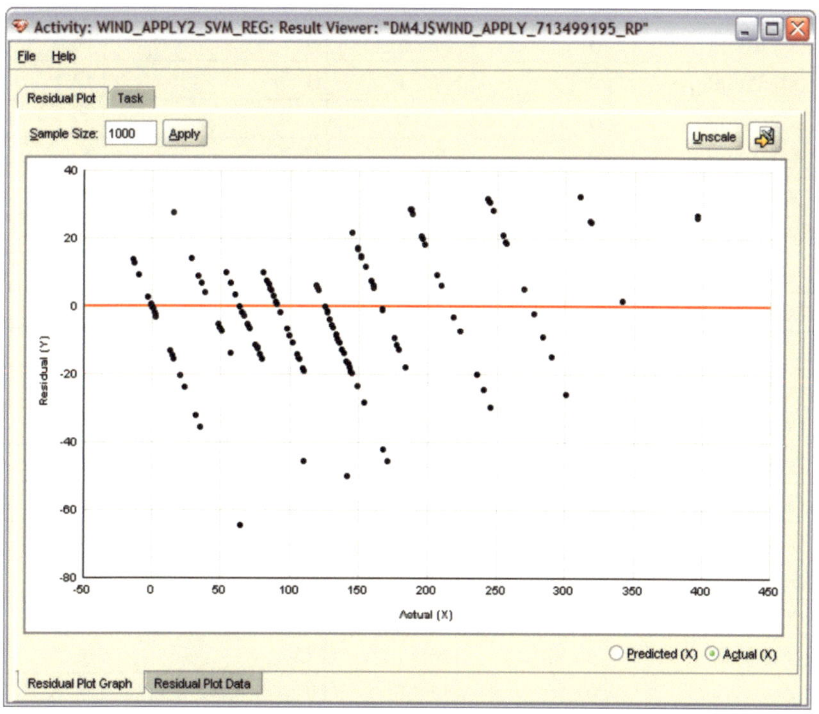

Figure 11. The deviations recorded for the E_PRAG attribute forecast for one day

At the evaluation process for the regression model for E_PRAG attribute, the results are presented in Figure 11. It is noted that deviations are located within ± 20 kW which means that at the current value of 1000 kW the results in a forecast is between 980 kW and 1020 kW, which is an acceptable error.

Summarizing the results of the evaluation phase in Table 1 (only for the schedule 0:00 to 5:00), it shows the actual and predicted values for E_PRAG attribute every 10 minutes.

Date/Time	E actual	E prog	E_prag actual	E-prag prog
25-02-201000:00:00	357.91	779.1	343	341.1
25-02-201000:10:00	250.05	694.7	216	245.7
25-02-201000:20:00	140.61	617.5	125	170.4
25-02-201000:30:00	140.61	620	125	170.7
25-02-201000:40:00	110.59	612.7	91	141.2
25-02-201000:50:00	54.87	651.1	43	56.9
25-02-201001:00:00	0	506.4	0	15.5
25-02-201001:10:00	0	695.4	0	64.5
25-02-201001:20:00	0	771.3	0	20.4
25-02-201001:30:00	79.51	618.4	64	109.5
25-02-201001:40:00	140.61	627.9	125	167.2
25-02-201001:50:00	125	622.3	125	153.3
25-02-201002:00:00	0	695.7	0	23.6
25-02-201002:10:00	0	782.9	0	14.6
25-02-201002:20:00	0	766.1	0	13.1
25-02-201002:30:00	0	798.9	0	32
25-02-201002:40:00	0	755.6	0	2.5
25-02-201002:50:00	0	739.6	0	0
25-02-201003:00:00	0	797.1	0	35.4
25-02-201003:10:00	0	682.3	0	0.8
25-02-201003:20:00	0	657.3	0	0
25-02-201003:30:00	0	733.9	0	1.6
25-02-201003:40:00	0	720.1	0	0
25-02-201003:50:00	68.92	602.6	64	66.1
25-02-201004:00:00	0	643.9	0	0.3
25-02-201004:10:00	0	506	0	0
25-02-201004:20:00	0	473.2	0	0
25-02-201004:30:00	42.88	465.8	43	15.5
25-02-201004:40:00	0	454	0	3
25-02-201004:50:00	54.87	599.1	43	38.7
25-02-201005:00:00	91.13	554.5	91	89.6

Table 1. Comparison of actual and estimated values from the regression algorithm

Applying data mining algorithms for the prediction power of WPP, notable results were achieved in particular by setting the thresholds for E_PRAG. Thus the data mining algorithm was able to learn and to establish better dependence between variables and the prognosis is much closer to actually measured values.

Finally was done the forecasting model for wind power plants produced energy, which can be applied successfully in a DSS prototype according to the architecture presented in Part I.

Author details

Adela Bâra and Ion Lungu
Academy of Economic Studies, Bucharest, Romania

Acknowledgement

This paper is a result of the research project PN II, TE Program, Code 332: "Informatics Solutions for decision making support in the uncertain and unpredictable environments in order to integrate them within a grid network", financed within the framework of People research program.

3. References

[1] Bâra A., Velicanu A., Botha I., Oprea S. V., Solutions for the Data Level's Representation in a Decision Support System in Wind PowerPlants, MAMECTICS'11 International Conference, 1-3 July 2011, Iasi, Romania, Publisher WSEAS Press, ISBN 978-1-61804-011-4

[2] Lungu I, Bara A – Executive Information Systems, ASE Publishing House, Bucharest, 2007

[3] Muntean M. – Initiation in OLAP technology: theory and practice, ASE Publishing House, Bucharest, 2004

[4] Power D.J. - Decision Support Systems: Concepts and Resources, Cedar, Falls, IA: DSSresources.com, http://dssresources.com/dssbook/

[5] Holsapple C.W, Whinston A.B - Decision Support Systems: A knowledge – Based Approach, West Publishing Company, 1996

[6] Moss L., Atre S. – Business Intelligence Roadmap – The complete project lifecycle for decision-support applications, Addison-Wesley, 2004

[7] ORACLE Corporation – Oracle Data Mining Concepts 10g, www.oracle.com, 2010

[8] www.transelectrica.ro, wind production reports, 2011

[9] Turban, E. - Decision Support Systems and Intelligent Systems, 5th ed.,Englewood Cliffs, New Jersey, Prentice Hall, 1998

[10] Watson H., R. Kelly Rainer, Chang E. Koh - Executive Information Systems: A framework for Development and a Survey of Current Practices. MIS Quarterly, Vol. 15, No. I, March, 1991.

[11] Ackerman T., Wind Power in Power Systems, Wiley, 2005

[12] Bâra A., Lungu I., Oprea S. V., Public Institutions' Investments with Data Mining Techniques, Journal WSEAS Transactions on Computers, Volume 8, 2009, ISSN: 1109-2750, http://www.worldses.org/journals/computers/computers-2009.htm

[13] Burton T., Sharpe D. - Wind Enegy Handbook, Wiley, 2001

[14] Oprea S – Renewable resources integration into the GRID. PhD Thesis, Politehnica University, Bucharest, 2009

[15] Simona Vasilica Oprea, Adela Bâra, Victor Vlăducu, Anda Velicanu - *Data Level's Integrated Model for the National Grid Company's Decision Support System*, Recent Advances in Computers, Communications, Applied Social Science and Mathematics, International Conference on Computers, Digital Communications and Computing (ICDCCC'11), Barcelona, Spain, 15-17 septembrie 2011, pp 167-172, ISBN: 978-1-61804-030-5, published by WSEAS Press, http://www.wseas.us/books/2011/Barcelona/ICICIC.pdf